Advanced FrameMaker

TIPS Technical Publishing, Inc.

Advanced FrameMaker

Kay Ethier

Robert Kern

Bradley Anderson

Bernard Aschwanden

TIPS Technical Publishing, Inc.
Carrboro, North Carolina

TIPS Technical Publishing, Inc.
108 E. Main Street, Suite 4
Carrboro, North Carolina 27510
919-933-2629
www.technicalpublishing.com

First Printing (Conference Edition): October 2003
Second Printing: June 2004

Printed in the United States of America.

Library of Congress Cataloging-in-Publication Data

Advanced framemaker / Kay Ethier ... [et al.].
p. cm.
Includes bibliographical references and index.
ISBN 1-890586-10-2
1. Adobe FrameMaker. 2. Desktop publishing. I. Ethier, Kay.
Z253.532.F7A368 2004
686.2'2544536–dc22
2004006613

Notice to the Reader

Publisher does not warrant or guarantee any of the products described herein or perform any independent analysis in connection with any of the product information contained herein. Publisher does not assume, and expressly disclaims, any obligation to obtain and include information other than what is provided to it by the manufacturer.

To Nana, who was very loved and is greatly missed.

—Kay Ethier

To my family—Terry, Claire, Benjamin, and Molly.

—Robert Kern

To my loving wife, Michelle, and to my son, Jacob, and daughter, Jessica. They are my passion in life!

—Bradley Anderson

To my co-authors, co-workers, and co-conspirators in FrameMaker and in life.

—Bernard Aschwanden

Contents

Foreword

When I was little, I spent many happy hours playing with my Lego bricks (I grew up in the 70s). I loved the endless possibilities—I could build a castle one day, a giraffe the next, and then a helicopter. My collection of bricks began modestly enough, but soon I began to build up my collection of specialist parts—wheels and axels; roof tiles and windows; motors and lights, and so on. Each set of features I added made perfect sense to me.

Ultimately I grew older, and it was time to hand down my Lego collection to my little sister. But something funny happened. Although the basic building-blocks premise was easy enough to grasp, she was overwhelmed by the wealth of options. It was clear there was a lot of potential in this newly acquired toy, but it wasn't clear how to realize that potential. Naturally, this led to a degree of frustration.

There are a number of parallels to be drawn here with FrameMaker (as you may have guessed). The tool was revolutionary when it was launched in 1986, but it had far fewer features back then than it does now. Through the late eighties and early nineties, the product evolved to include ever better features for long documents and technical publishing. The mid-nineties also saw the launch of FrameMaker+SGML, which introduced not just a new file format (SGML), but a paradigm shift in the way users could create documents—structured authoring. In 2000, recognizing the influence of the web and other new media, Adobe introduced a host of new "multichannel publishing" features and bundled WebWorks Publisher Standard Edition for the first time. The most recent seismic shift occurred with version 7, when FrameMaker and FrameMaker+SGML were combined, and a new era of XML authoring and publishing was entered.

With all this functionality added over fifteen years, it is easy for users faced with FrameMaker today to feel overwhelmed. As with my Lego bricks, it is fairly easy to get started with the basics (paragraph styles, using pre-supplied templates, and so on). But there is so much more you can do with the product, from time-saving authoring tricks (such as clever indexing and automated numbering) to elegant publishing approaches (such as automated HTML publishing and sophisticated XML production). It can be frustrating to know the possibilities, but not know how to get started.

I've felt this feeling personally. I began my journey with FrameMaker when I joined Adobe in 1998. Over the years, I've grown to learn about cross-reference styles, reference pages, text insets and structured authoring. I was fortunate enough to move to Adobe's headquarters in San Jose in 1999, and to be the product manager who introduced version 6 in 2000 and version 7 in 2002. But even today, having been with the product for more than five years, the more experienced users can still surprise me with a clever trick or two. Such is the depth of the product.

Even if I wasn't working for Adobe, I'd still be a great fan of FrameMaker. The more you know about the product, the more rewarding it is to work with. In reading this book, you'll certainly gain a much deeper appreciation of the product, and I hope that in turn your use of FrameMaker will be more productive and more enjoyable.

—Karl Matthews
Group Product Manager, FrameMaker
Adobe Systems Incorporated

Preface

This book covers a variety of advanced FrameMaker topics, as well as related technologies and applications one needs to truly be an advanced FrameMaker user. While not all of the topics are necessary for any individual, we hope that it provides you with the information you need to expand and extend your current knowledge base and increase your value. Below is a brief description of each of the chapters and appendixes.

Topical Coverage of this Book

Chapter 1: Overview of FrameMaker

This chapter outlines the changes and improvements that you will see as you explore this program and compare it to previous versions. If you are new to FrameMaker, you will get an idea of what Adobe has done to produce this product and the key features that have been added to keep on top of today's technologies and information-authoring needs.

Chapter 2: Turning FrameMaker Documents into Structured FrameMaker Documents

In this chapter, you will learn how to take your existing, unstructured FrameMaker documents and turn them into structured FrameMaker documents quickly and fairly easily.

Chapter 3: Understanding XML Round Trip

This chapter examines the FrameMaker 7.0 capabilities for using and creating XML and moving from FrameMaker to XML and back again.

Chapter 4: Developing Structured Documents

This chapter is focused on the development of the Element Definition Document (EDD) and does not directly address procedures related to the import and export of content. It is primarily designed to guide you through the development of a structured document.

Chapter 5: Automated Master Pages and Template Adjustments

This chapter introduces master pages and explores how they are used in FrameMaker, including added functionality in FrameMaker 7 that allows master pages to be automatically applied based on paragraph tags.

Chapter 6: Making the Most of Running H/F Variables

This chapter examines running header/footer variables and their interplay with other FrameMaker functions, such as paragraphs, elements, and markers. Detailed step-by-step instructions show you how to get more control over this important information-display feature.

Chapter 7: Automating Numbering in FrameMaker

FrameMaker's automatic numbering feature allows you to set up various numbering schemes. This automatic numbering capability is unmatched in the world of desktop publishing; its accuracy, stability, and reliability make it one of a kind. Due to this flexibility and power, automatic numbering is also one of the most misunderstood and misused features in FrameMaker.

Chapter 8: Tables of Contents and Other Generated Lists

This chapter explains the generated list function in relation to creating Tables of Contents and how the function can take you beyond a static or printed list.

Chapter 9: Indexes, Index Markers, and Reference Page Setup

This chapter explains the indexing function and its related concepts and how they can be used to generate useful reference materials.

Chapter 10: Creating Great Screen Captures

Creating screen captures that look good in both print and PDF can be difficult. A screen capture placed in a document for printing may look fine when printed on a laser printer; however, in the PDF version of the document, the screen capture may look terrible. This chapter will look at the reasons why and provide guidance in preparing high quality screen captures.

Chapter 11: Designing Automatic, Self-Positioning, Bleeding Thumb Tabs

This chapter introduces a comprehensive method for creating self-positioning bleeding thumb tabs. Although the process is a bit involved, you can successfully create a set of bleeding thumb tabs for your templates in less than an hour by following its instructions.

Chapter 12: Using WebWorks Publisher Standard Edition 7.0

This chapter provides an overview of the Quadralay WebWorks Publisher Standard Edition product as well as differences between the Standard and Professional editions.

Chapter 13: Prepress, Printing, and PDF

This chapter will cover all aspects of generating PDF files from FrameMaker. This includes not only generating PDF files to be viewed and navigated online, but also generating PDF files that can be used for printing—both offset and digital.

Chapter 14: An Introduction to Database Publishing with FrameMaker

This chapter is written for those individuals beginning the process of publishing information from a database. It explores different methods of retrieving data (both static and dynamic) and publishing data with FrameMaker.

Chapter 15: Filename Markers in WebWorks Publisher Professional

This chapter describes the use of Filename markers to "lock in" specific filenames.

Chapter 16: Adding PDF Support to a WebWorks Help 3.0 Project

This chapter is geared toward those using FrameMaker with WebWorks Publisher Professional Edition to create online help or Web content. Unless otherwise specified, the acronym WWP herein refers to WebWorks Publisher ***Professional*** Edition.

Chapter 17: Creating Custom Palettes

This chapter explores FrameMaker palettes and how you may create custom button sets to turn common tasks into single mouse-clicks.

Chapter 18: Extending and Adjusting FrameMaker

This chapter presents ways to adjust FrameMaker's user interface, and the use of third-party tools to extend FrameMaker's features.

Appendix A: Setting Up an ODBC Database Connection

In the examples on the following pages, you will connect to an Access database via ODBC. To make this database available, you need to make the database available to the operating system via ODBC.

Appendix B: Directory Example Using PatternStream

This appendix is a fairly complete step-by-step guide to setting up the directory example used in this chapter in PatternStream.

Appendix C: Simple Directory FrameScript Code

This appendix presents FrameScript code which will output the sample directory using an existing FrameMaker template named *SimpleDirectory.fm*. The code is well commented so you can see what each routine is doing. The logic is very similar to the PatternStream example in Appendix B.

Appendix D: Sample SQL Query that Returns MML Syntax

This appendix presents a SQL statement that demonstrates the method of "wrapping" MML markup code around data elements for importing into an existing FrameMaker template. The particular SQL statement used outputs the necessary MML markup for each firm.

Appendix E: Sample SQL Query that Returns XML Syntax

This appendix presents a SQL statement demonstrating the method of "wrapping" XML markup code around data elements for importing into an existing FrameMaker template. This particular SQL statement outputs the necessary XML markup for each firm. The SQL is executed within Access to return data wrapped in XML. Access 2002 and other more recent database applications allow for direct XML export of data.

Appendix F: Sample SQL Query that Returns MIF Syntax

The SQL statement in this appendix demonstrates the method of "wrapping" MIF markup code around data elements for importing into an existing FrameMaker template. This particular SQL statement outputs the necessary MIF markup for each firm.

Support

The files and examples referenced in this book—as well as the most current list of tips and tricks, and list of FrameMaker resources—can be downloaded from the Advanced FrameMaker book support website at

www.technicalpublishging.com/AdvFrame/

Come and explore or submit your favorite resource links or tips and tricks.

About the Authors

The authors are recognized FrameMaker experts, known worldwide for their knowledge and abilities.

Kay Ethier

Kay Ethier is an Adobe Certified Expert and a Quadralay-certified WebWorks University trainer. Her charter with Bright Path Solutions is to assist clients by providing services and software that allow them to efficiently publish to paper and electronic formats.

A FrameUser since version 4, Kay has many years of experience with project management, document creation, and technical editing. She applies this expertise to training and user support services, as well as to process evaluations and demonstrations for organizations seeking to improve current processes.

An accomplished writer, Kay co-authored *XML Weekend Crash Course* in 2001 and authored *XML and FrameMaker* this year. She contributes articles to a NC magazine, *IT: Information Technology for Professionals*, on a regular basis.

Most recently Kay has worked on a series of structured document publishing tutorials for FrameMaker 7.

Kay may be reached at Bright Path Solutions, PO Box 14265, Research Triangle Park, NC 27709-4265. Her email address is *kethier@travelthepath.com*.

Robert Kern

Robert started his publishing career in 1985 as a sales representative for college textbooks in the higher education division of Prentice Hall. After working in acquisitions, marketing, production, and technology, he moved to Chapel Hill, North Carolina to become Publisher at Ventana Communications.

In 1997, Robert Kern founded TIPS Technical Publishing, Inc. in a delightful historic building in downtown Carrboro, North Carolina. The company provides author representation, trade and corporate publishing, and book production services. It was through his work managing the composition of long technical books at TIPS that he discovered and embraced FrameMaker—which is still his tool of choice for book composition.

Robert lives with his wife, Terry, and his children, Claire Elizabeth and Benjamin, and may be reached at *bob@technicalpublishing.com*.

Bradley Anderson

Brad Anderson has been involved with the FrameMaker community since 1996 maintaining FrameUsers.com, the Framers list, and organizing an annual FrameMaker workshop that brings together worldwide experts in FrameMaker for three days of unparalleled FrameMaker training and presentations.

Brad is a dynamic trainer and public speaker who specializes in building automated publishing systems. He helps a variety of corporate and government clients set up world-class publishing systems from initial document creation to final delivery of printed and online documents. He is a veteran FrameMaker trainer and an Adobe Certified Expert. His field of expertise is the publishing process for offset printing and online document delivery. He is also the President and CEO of Beyond Print Incorporated, an Adobe Certified Training Provider that provides hands-on FrameMaker training, database publishing, document conversion, template creation, online document delivery, and printing services. Brad is responsible for several large 5-color publications that are output from FrameMaker. Visit *www.beyondprint.com* for more information.

Brad lives with his wife, Michelle, and kids, Jacob and Jessica, in Germantown, MD. Brad may be reached at *brad@beyondprint.com*.

Bernard Aschwanden

The founder and president of Front Runner, Bernard Aschwanden has a background in computers that began with the Apple II and has led to work on some of the most powerful systems in the world. He is a documentation specialist with a strong focus on the technical writing field and related technologies.

Bernard is a professional writer, trainer, courseware developer and is an expert in both Word and FrameMaker. He has an extensive background in documentation both as a writer and manager. He has been involved in the conversion of legacy documentation to both FrameMaker and FrameMaker+SGML for clients such as Boeing, Social Security, Canadian Corporate News, General Electric, and others.

Bernard is a member of the Society of Technical Communicators (STC) and actively involved in many aspects of the documentation cycle. He has been asked to present on behalf of organizations such as the Computer Trainers Network, the STC, Adobe, Microsoft, and others across Canada and throughout the United States.

The presentations that Bernard delivers are as varied as the software he uses. SGML, Digital Imaging, Website Development and Online Documentation seminars have been delivered across Canada and the USA.

He has delivered training for thousands of clients in Toronto, Boston, Atlanta, London (UK), Luxembourg, San Jose, New York, and more. Bernard has been involved in creating documentation for Nortel, Brewers Retail, various government agencies, Sun Microsystems, the Ministry of Transportation, Symantec, and other government agencies and Fortune 500 companies.

Bernard has been involved in the implementation of publishing systems for a variety of companies. Bernard may be reached at *bernard@front-runner.com*.

Production Team

This book was, of course, entirely written, edited, and composed in FrameMaker. The skills of the individuals who edited, composed, indexed, and otherwise produced the book are very greatly appreciated by the authors. Many thanks to you!

Copy Editing—Jeannine Kolbush

Jeannine Kolbush has been writing and editing professionally for fifteen years. She began her career as a technical writer in the telecommunications industry and then served as a communications manager in the database software industry. Her specialty is editing trade books, corporate policies, educational materials, and academic journals. Jeannine also has extensive experience writing newsletters, marketing brochures, and math contests. She graduated from Bucknell University, where she studied English, Mathematics, and Legal Studies.

In addition to writing and editing, Jeannine tutors math and prepares students for the PSAT/SAT. She resides in Raleigh, NC.

Development Editing and Composition—Lynanne Fowle

Lynanne is the managing editor at TIPS Technical Publishing in Carrboro, North Carolina. She designs and composes books using FrameMaker and Quark, edits manuscripts, proofreads, indexes, and provides quality control for the book production process. Her skills and personal drive have ensured TIPS books have been finished with high quality and on time.

Indexing—Richard Evans

Richard "Dick" Evans provided his professional indexing services to this book. His familiarity with FrameMaker and with computer books in general assure an index that will be helpful to you as a reader.

Dick has over thirty years experience in the computer industry. In his role as a human factors engineer, he became interested in indexing while conducting usability tests on indexes for telecommunications manuals. He retired from corporate life in 1992 and started Infodex Indexing Services, Inc. Now he specializes in indexing computer books for both corporate clients and publishing houses. He is a senior member of the Society for Technical Communication, national past-President of American Society of Indexers.

Reviewers

Special thanks also to the following reviewers for their work on this book:

- Alan Houser, Group Wellesley, *www.groupwellesley.com*
- John Skelton, FAQmasters, *www.faqmasters.com*
- Andrew VanConas & Mike Fabry, Quadralay, *www.webworks.com*
- Nancy Schroer, *www.nschroer.com*
- Dov Isaacs, Adobe Systems Inc., *www.adobe.com*
- Lin Morss, Beyond Print, *www.beyondprint.com*
- Arnis Gubins, AG Information Systems Ltd.
- Nancy McCoy, FileNET Corp, *NMcCoy@filenet.com*
- Rick Quattro, Carmen Publishing, *www.frameexpert.com*

They are all FrameMaker experts who's time and attention to this book is greatly appreciated.

Acknowledgments

Kay Ethier

Thanks to my parents for their unending support both personally and professionally. Thanks also to mom, dad, Kim, Betty, Ashlean, and Denis for their help with Riley and Nadia when I needed time for this project. To my oldest, thank you for the words of encouragement from far away.

Last but not least, thanks go to Bob Kern and Lynanne Fowle for creating and managing the production of this book.

Robert Kern

I've always thought of myself as a book person, but never as a writer. This experience reinforces that perspective. Make no mistake about it, the only reason this book was ever finished was the diligence of my friend, Kay Ethier, and the extensive editing and project management of Lynanne Fowle. That said, I am also truly thankful for the patience and love of my wife and family (and the loyalty of Molly, the office Labrador Retriever).

Bradley Anderson

Thanks to Lin Morss for providing constructive criticisms, an incredible editorial eye, and ideas for making my chapters better. Thanks to Barry Anderson and Lin for "holding down the fort" while I was consumed writing and fine tuning the book.

Part I

New and Improved Features of FrameMaker

Advanced FrameMaker

1

Overview of FrameMaker

Robert Kern and Kay Ethier

This chapter outlines the improvements you will see as you explore FrameMaker 7 or 7.1, migrating to these verions, and introduces structured authoring.

Applicable to FrameMaker versions 7.0/7.1

Assumptions and Opening Remarks

This book describes complex FrameMaker features and techniques. The authors have made some assumptions about you—that you are familiar with FrameMaker and understand basic functions like paragraph tags and most text-formatting tools, and you are interested in moving your skills to a higher level.

All the co-authors contributing to this project have included tips and techniques that have helped them in their own consulting work. Because all have used FrameMaker for a number of years and have used a variety of versions, each chapter includes information on the differences between FrameMaker 7 and previous versions. The bottom of each chapter opening page includes a reference for you that lists all versions to which the chapter is applicable.

The examples in this text will be easier for you to follow if you have worked with FrameMaker, taken a training class or two, or read the *FrameMaker User Manual* or an introductory books on FrameMaker like *The Master Series: FrameMaker 6* by Thomas Neuburger. Both are both good reference books and will help you understand FrameMaker before diving into the advanced lessons included in this book.

Many of the example files used for this book are available on the book's website—*www.technicalpublishing.com/AdvFrame*—as well as from the authors themselves. Contact information for the authors is given in "About the Authors" on page xix.

Major Feature Changes

One of the biggest changes we are sure you have found already is that FrameMaker+SGML is now no longer a separate program. FrameMaker 7 includes all the features of FrameMaker and FrameMaker+SGML in one package. When you open FrameMaker 7 for the first time, you are prompted to choose either FrameMaker or Structured FrameMaker. Once you begin using one version, you may switch to the other version by changing your selection in **File** > **Preferences** and then restarting FrameMaker.

FrameMaker 7/7.1 Features

The following list of features apply to both FrameMaker 7 and FrameMaker 7.1 releases.

- The ability to tie master page application to a paragraph format
- Improved import filters (Word, WordPerfect, etc. imports are much cleaner)
- More running H/F variables

Note: *Because of the features available in the structured version of FrameMaker, we recommend that users consider staying in Structured FrameMaker at all times. What do you lose? Well, you have to get used to several new menu items, the Element menu, and extra buttons on the right-hand edge of your documents. What do you gain? You have access to all FrameMaker 7's features and may at any point dabble in the structure features—expanding your user options and experiences. If you work in the Structured FrameMaker 7 version, and you share files with someone using the regular FrameMaker 7, they will get a message upon opening your files that indicates the presence of structure. They will get this message whether the document is "structured" or not.*

- UNIX font management
- Backward compatibility (save as FrameMaker 6.0 or MIF)
- Added graphics support (places PDF, Illustrator, SVG)
- Updated version (7.0) of WebWorks Publisher Standard Edition
- Fix to Save As PDF so that it really works
- Added Select All/Deselect All buttons in the **Import** > **Formats** menu
- An added Browse feature to place your output when printing to file
- An easier interface for printing a book to one or more output files
- Improved graphic scaling (by DPI and by percentage of original size)
- Ability to reorder custom master pages
- A revised template browser
- Revision of all older templates
- New templates, including a structured templates folder, online structured templates, and FAQ-structured templates
- File check in/check out with Workgroups (WebDAV)

Several of these items are described in more detail in the following sections.

FrameMaker 7.1 Features

The following list of features apply only to FrameMaker 7.1 releases.

- Open, edit and save XML without the need to "save as" XML
- Conditional text support for importing and exporting SGML or XML
- Support for external cross–references in structured documents (exported to or imported from XML)
- Filters to import PageMaker and QuarkXpress files
- Support for the Microsoft Intellimouse scroll wheel
- Import of Photoshop documents

Overview of Major Features in FrameMaker 7

The following features apply to both FrameMaker 7 and to FrameMaker 7.1.

XML Support

XML (a derivative of SGML) is a tagging structure that separates content from format. Because of this it is quickly becoming the *de facto* standard for many types of content—from the world of business-to-business information exchange to page composition and web-publishing. Because of FrameMaker's support of SGML, extending FrameMaker 7 into the world of XML was only natural! The release of FrameMaker 7 introduces the following XML support:

- XML round-tripping—import, edit, and export XML. Includes support for namespaces, Unicode, and CSS2.
- SVG graphics—import and export this XML-based graphics format.
- Updated applications for DocBook and xDocBook—access to "out-of-the-box" DTDs designed for technical authoring.
- XMP support—capture an expanded set of metadata about your documents for easy indexing, searching and retrieval. For more information about XMP, visit *www.adobe.com/products/xmp/main.html.*

Updated Import Filters

If you are like most of us, you have had to import Word documents into FrameMaker so that they can be made into books and published. If you have, we don't have to explain how frustrating it is to have to fix or recreate dozens of tables because FrameMaker converts all the splits and merges into separate tables.

Well, we shall be frustrated no more! Word tables—via the updated FrameMaker 7 import filter—now import very nicely. The merges and splits are reincarnated from the choppy RTF code of Word into nice, clean tables.

Note: *To even better automate the importing of tables from Word, check out the plug-in called Table Cleaner. In particular, this plug-in excels in properly reformatting tables header rows, which still come through from Word as regular table rows.*

Collaboration

In the File menu is a choice for Workgroup, which allows you to manage files. Based on WebDAV (Web Distributed Authoring and Versioning) server technology, the Workgroup feature basically gives you version control right out of the FrameMaker box!

If you have multiple authors accessing information, the Workgroup manages their access. We've only played with this a bit, but the technology is definitely promising...it also makes us wonder what will happen to the revision-tracking systems that up to now have cost nearly five figures!

Revised Features

Automated custom layout

Tired of applying master pages only to have to reapply then later in the production process when things roll due to the deletion or addition of content? Now master pages can be applied automatically according to paragraph tags that appear in your document. If you only use the standard right/left and chapter opener pages, this won't be a big deal. However, if you've ever had to build landscape pages for turning long tables and then track these pages as content rolls them, you'll really appreciate this new feature. Frame is all about automation and this feature fits squarely inside this core mission.

Authoring enhancements

- FrameMaker 7 increases the number of running headers/footers to 12. This will satisfy your design requirements for even the most complex documents
- The ability to resize an imported graphic based on its original size (not current scaled size), including resizing it back to 100% without re-importing
- The ability to rearrange customer master pages in any order
- The ability to save a document in FrameMaker 6 file format, better Save As PDF options, and new options to Select / Deselect All when importing formats from another document

Unix font management

FrameMaker for Unix now supports Open Type and True Type fonts with easy font installation.

Accessibility

FrameMaker 7 is now able to create "tagged PDF"—that is, PDF that contains extra information to allow content to be readable by screen readers, including the ability to add text descriptions to graphics.

Overview of Major Features in FrameMaker 7.1

The following features apply only to FrameMaker 7.1.

Enhanced XML Support

The release of FrameMaker 7.1 adds the following XML features:

- XML round-tripping with support for XML file naming—open, edit and save XML files without the need to "save as" and assign the XML extension to files. FrameMaker now opens an XML file and on using **File** > **Save** automatically saves in a native XML format.
- Conditional content support—by adding processing instructions to the XML document you can import and export conditional content and retain the conditional settings in both the XML document and the FrameMaker file.
- Support for external cross–references in structured documents (exported to or imported from XML)—by using specially designed attributes with cross–reference elements you can now create links between XML files (previously only internal links were supported).

Migrating Documents and Books

From Version 6 to Version 7/7.1

You will be happy to know that your FrameMaker 6 templates require no adjustments—no changes, none, nada, zip.

To migrate your existing templates or documents from FrameMaker 6 or FrameMaker+SGML 6, just do a **File** > **Open**. When the prompt appears to upgrade to the latest version, as shown in Figure 1-1, click OK.

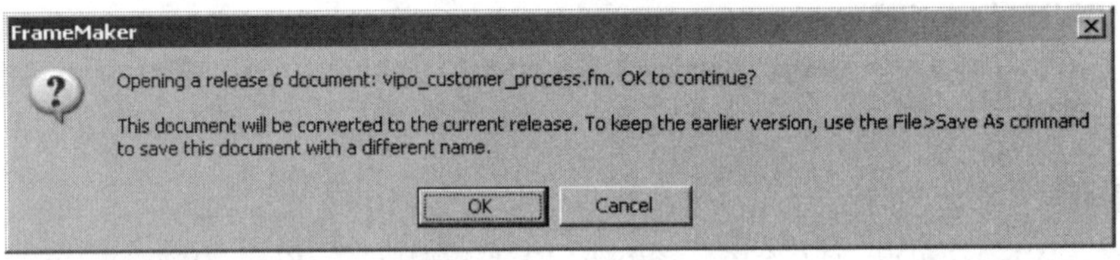

Figure 1-1 Upgrade warning dialog box.

Once you have clicked OK, the document will open and you can immediately Save. It is now a FrameMaker 7 document.

Unlike converting to version 6 from version 5.5, there are no real migration issues between FrameMaker 6 and FrameMaker 7 in regular FrameMaker documents. The numbering and book information (<ChapNum> and

Note: *If you are opening a FrameMaker+SGML 6 document that has structure, you should make sure that you are in the Structured FrameMaker interface before opening your FrameMaker+SGML document. If you are not in Structured FrameMaker, you will be prompted that you are about to lose your structure (see Figure 1-2).*

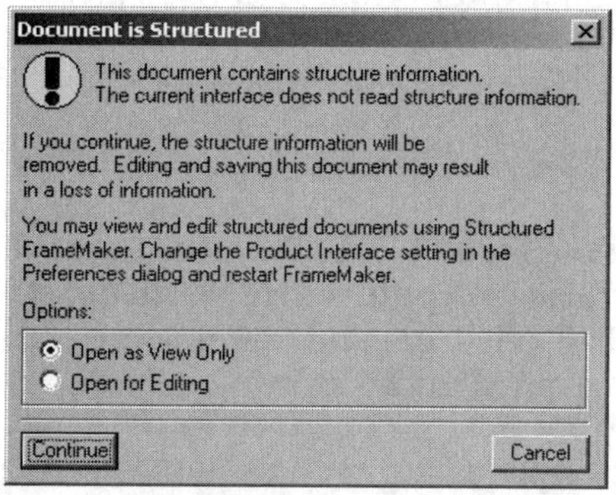

Figure 1-2 Warning dialog box when opening structured version 6 documents in unstructured version 7/7.1.

<VolNum>) are the same between these versions and are the major differences between FrameMaker 7 and 5.5. However, in structured FrameMaker+SGML 6 documents, there may be some issues within the element definitions of the structure.

Once your documents are in FrameMaker 7 format, you cannot return to earlier versions of FrameMaker or FrameMaker+SGML unless you do one of the following:

- Open the document in FrameMaker 7 and Save As MIF (Maker Interchange Format) files.
- Open the document in FrameMaker 7 and Save as FrameMaker 6.0 files.

Note: *You will get a message that saving back to FrameMaker 6 removes functionality, but there is little information lost. In fact, you can safely operate on a team where some members are using 7 and some using 6; just save the file back when a Version 6 user needs it.*

From Version 5.5.6 and Earlier to Version 7/7.1

If you are moving files from FrameMaker 5.5.6 and earlier, you will need to adjust your chapter numbering and—if you include the chapter number with your page number—the page numbering. Additionally, there may be potential TOC reference page adjustments required.

Your structured FrameMaker+SGML 5.5 documents may also have the same issues with the structure's element definitions.

Note: *If you have to save back any quantity of documents to earlier versions, instead of slugging through each document and making the adjustments time and time again, design a "save-back" template that makes the needed adjustments in Frame 7 so it will migrate backwards more easily. Then, import this template into copies of your files, SaveAs to MIF, and open in the older version of Frame to verify your work.*

Structure-Specific Adjustments

Structures and EDDs from previous versions of FrameMaker do seem to move into FrameMaker 7 without issue—usually. The exceptions may be that some EDDs need to be updated to use the new EDD structure, and you may need to rebuild your application file to access the new XML choices.

The Basics of Structured Documents

As noted earlier, structured authoring is now available for *free* in FrameMaker 7. For owners of FrameMaker+SGML there is no change—just select the **structured** option when you open FrameMaker. For those who owned unstructured FrameMaker, however, this release permits exploration of structured authoring (and valid and well-formed XML services) with no additional price tag. While moving into a new environment can be scary, take comfort in the knowledge that all you do and use in unstructured FrameMaker is still there in Structured FrameMaker. So, be brave and embrace the opportunity!

What is a Structured Document?

You already know that FrameMaker is a template-driven tool. So, each document that you start—from a new document, from an Adobe template, or from your own template—has a set of predefined formats.

These formats allow you to apply pre-set page layouts, text formatting, or object properties. But, for the formatting to be correct and consistent through all documents, you need to understand the formats and how they must be used. Each new piece of text has to have a chosen format and the user has to know which to use. This sometimes interferes with the writing (content creation) process because you get caught up in formatting.

With a structured document content is not only tagged with character and paragraph styles, it is categorized into elements. Tools within FrameMaker guide the user through document creation. Rules work in the background to manage the list of available elements that a user sees so that they can focus on the available choices and not be lost in a large list of possibilities.

If you have been working in regular FrameMaker and are getting ready to move into structured document publishing, you may have to "migrate" existing documents to structure—basically add structure to the existing documents.

To structure FrameMaker documents, all you really need are the elements, which come from Element Definition Documents (EDDs). Once you have the EDD, the elements can then be imported into your documents so that the structure is available.

Why use Structured Documents?

In a perfect situation, all content creators and editors would know how to use templates and would use them properly. They also would stay within the guidelines for the document—not making their own formats—and would follow the rules of writing procedures.

However, nothing is perfect and authors and documentation groups are no exception.

Therefore, many content creators work without an understanding of the formats in the template. Multiple writers provide sections, with no check of the document for consistency or completeness until close to deadline. This can lead to missing pieces and inaccurate formatting that has to be fixed—often within tight deadlines.

Any documentation consistency issues also need to be addressed. Within workgroups, each document author (writer) has their own preferences. Multiple authors working the same document will organize their text in different ways. Organizations may select structured document publishing as a means of enforcing document consistency, because the rules decide how sections are authored rather than the individual writers. An unstructured document can only provide formatting; therefore, a structured document may be desired since it adds rules and can prompt authors.

One of the alternatives to inconsistencies in publishing, and to missing content, is to have your template include rules for content. For instance, in a good structured template these rules can eliminate author errors like creating single item bullet or numbered lists, stacking headers, skipping levels of heads, or forgetting items like chapter introductions or summaries.

Structured documents provide this extra control on the front end of the process. There are tools within FrameMaker+SGML that clean documents up after authoring. If authors force their way outside the formatting bounds in either type of document, problems such as these may occur:

- Modified format settings
- Additional formats added and used
- Formats improperly used (i.e., a Heading3 paragraph before a Heading2)

Being able to use a structure-related tool to clean up the structure, such as validation and importing element definitions, can overcome these issues.

If you are not using structure, there is no way to enforce consistency. You are at the mercy of the authors. If you have multiple authors in your documents, you may end up with different levels of heading, different amounts of text, different ordering of content, and other consistency issues. This can be avoided by having structural 'rules' built into your document templates.

What Does Structure Look Like?

If you publish 'unstructured' or regular FrameMaker documents, you know that your documents don't describe structure and content. So, you can't use computer tools to manage the information in your documents; you just can't query the information efficiently. How can a software tool figure out what the title or author's name is if everything is text, or tagged with styles like "Heading1" or "Section"?

Structure in a document appears as markup around your content and instructs the program to treat that content in a specific way. The document can be viewed in four different ways, with the structure hidden or presented in different ways. The four views are:

- Document (WYSIWYG – "what you see is what you get")
- Structure
- Element Boundaries
- Element Boundaries as tags

Writers can choose the view that works best for them. Figure 1-3 shows the first two views.

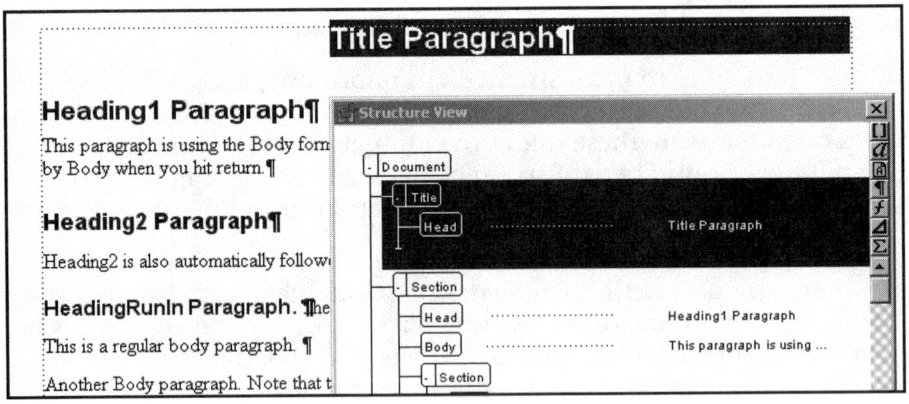

Figure 1-3 A simple document (WYSIWYG view) and its structure view.

Notice the highlighted piece. This piece of the structure has been selected so that you can see the connection between the content in the WYSIWYG view (on the left) and the structure view (on the right).

See the *element* Title and its *child element* Head? Notice that the content is the same in both views, but is treated differently by the program in the Document view.

In Figure 1-4, the same document is shown with its element boundaries turned on (**View > Element Boundaries**).

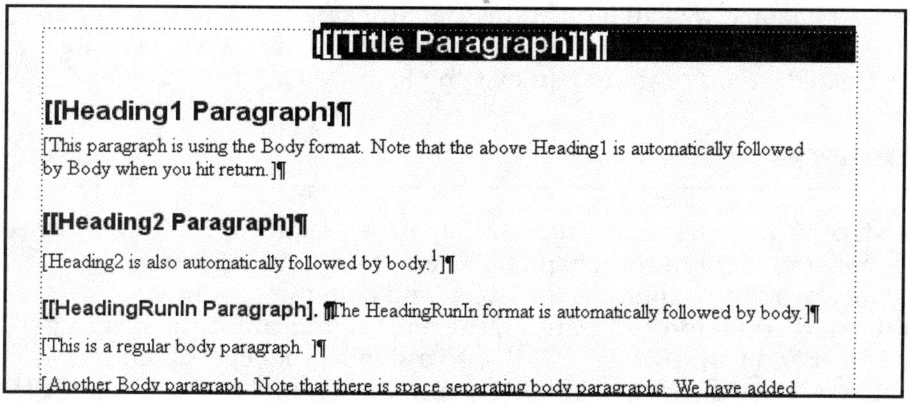

Figure 1-4 A simple document with Element Boundaries showing.

Lastly, Figure 1-5 shows this document with the Element Boundaries showing as tags, with tags referring to the names of the structure elements (**View > Element Boundaries (as Tags)**).

If you have worked in HTML or other markup languages, the view in Figure 1-5 might be the easiest for you to use.

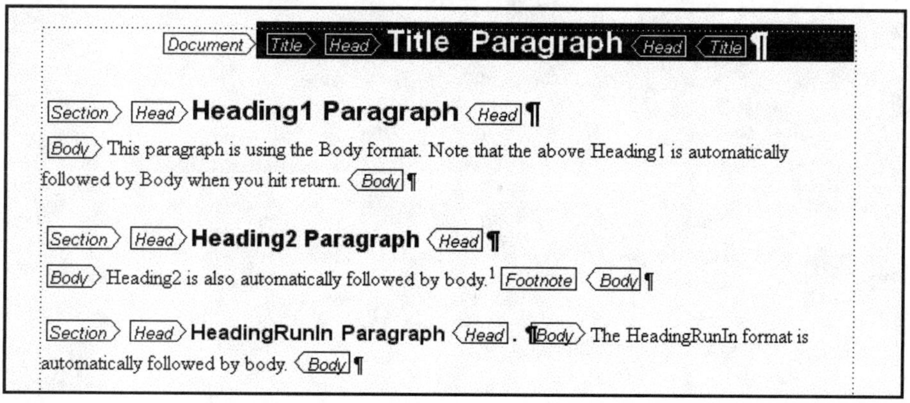

Figure 1-5 A simple document with tags showing.

Reiterating the Benefits of Structure

We have been introducing you to structure and the different ways to view a document. Before you continue, review the benefits of having structure.

- Enforces consistency
- Validates documents
- Enforces layout
- Outputs to valid XML

In the next chapter, we will look at the source of structure and begin creating it and using it in documents. Then, in Chapter 2, we use conversion tables to wrap a created structure around an existing FrameMaker document.

Summary

FrameMaker 7/7.1 offers many new and upgraded features. We have touched on a number of them in this chapter, like automated master pages, availability of additional header variables, and better import filters. However, of all the new and improved features, the most significant is the merging of FrameMaker and FrameMaker+SGML into a single product. This change opens the world of structured authoring and XML round-trip editing to all FrameMaker users. In the upcoming chapter we'll delve into structured authoring and how to take advantage of these new features.

Part II

Structured Authoring

Advanced FrameMaker

2

Turning FrameMaker Documents into Structured FrameMaker Documents

Kay Ethier

In this chapter, you learn how to take your existing, unstructured FrameMaker documents and turn them into structured FrameMaker documents quickly and fairly easily with Conversion Tables.

Applicable to FrameMaker 7.0/7.1 and FrameMaker+SGML

Introductory Comments

If you have been working in FrameMaker and are considering a move to Structured FrameMaker (or FrameMaker+SGML), you need to understand what it takes to move to structure. Especially if you have legacy documents, you will need to convert existing files at some point after moving to structure. The easiest method is by using Conversion Tables. These are created—usually along with your structure or soon after—and allow you to move legacy documents forward.

Before we explore the intricacies of conversion tables, you need to know some basic terminology. This is covered in the next section.

Important Terminology

Before launching into structured document publishing, you must understand certain structure-related terminology. These terms and their definitions are applicable to Structured FrameMaker and to XML.

Element

When working within XML, the structure of your document is created using beginning and ending tags (for example, <chapter> and </chapter>). These tags form an element in which you may enter content or other elements. In FrameMaker, these tags are displayed in the structure view as rounded rectangles, with the name of each tag inside each rectangle.

Attribute

Additional information may be attached to an element in the form of an attribute. This extra information may describe the element's content and may be used by software applications and stylesheets to adjust formatting. An attribute for a *chapter* element might be, for example, an *author* attribute. A chapter attribute provides additional data about the chapter and may even be used to select an image when the XML is displayed (but not when the FrameMaker chapter itself is displayed).

DTD

The DTD (Document Type Definition) is the list of XML elements and attributes that may be used to create XML output. The DTD also contains information on how often elements can be used, what elements must be present, and what elements can be used inside other elements. Brought into FrameMaker, a DTD becomes an EDD and may then be edited to add formatting.

EDD

The EDD (Element Definition Document) is the list of FrameMaker elements and attributes that may be used to create structured documents. The EDD contains information on how often elements can be used, what elements must be present, and what elements can be used inside other elements. It also contains formatting information for each element. This is what differentiates it from a DTD and what makes it possible for the elements to tie into FrameMaker formatting features. When exported from FrameMaker, the formatting information is dropped and the EDD becomes a DTD.

Template

A template is a file in FrameMaker that contains formatting and layout information for text, tables, graphics, and pages. When new files are created, the author often imports styles using a template to ensure that the new document matches other documents of that type. Some companies use several templates, depending upon the project.

Structured Template

A template that contains formatting information plus the element information from the EDD is referred to as a structured template.

Structured Document

In FrameMaker, a document that uses formatting plus elements is considered to be structured. These documents are usually created from structured templates. (For more information, see Chapter 4 on structured document authoring.)

Moving from Unstructured to Structured Documents

If you have created a structure and have tried to wrap your structure's elements around paragraphs, character format ranges, and objects (tables, anchored frames, etc.), then you know how tedious the process is.

Note: *As explained in Chapter 4, "Wrap" is a button on the Element Catalog. To use it, select content in the document, then select from the Element Catalog the element that you want around that content, and then click the Wrap button. The "wrap" result is that the content originally selected will have a begin tag in front of it and an end tag after it. In the structure view, it will appear as an element bubble with text snippet.*

Hand-wrapping content into elements takes time. Plus, as soon as you begin hand-wrapping any content, your formatting for the rest of the document goes away!

The easier alternative is to build a "conversion table" so that FrameMaker may do the wrapping for you. Conversion tables make the process of moving from "unstructured" to "structured" documents quick and less tedious.

Even though a conversion table requires development time (and testing), it should save you wrapping time even if you only have a few documents.

Note: *The Conversion Table feature is available only in FrameMaker 7 and FrameMaker+SGML. The menu choices in FrameMaker+SGML may differ from the choices given herein for FrameMaker 7.*

Creating and Adjusting Conversion Tables

While you may create conversion tables by hand, FrameMaker can give you a start on creating a conversion table. Using FrameMaker 7, selecting **File > Structure Tools > Generate Conversion Table** will create the beginnings of a table that you can then modify. The automatically generated conversion table bases its content upon the paragraph formats used in the file.

To ensure the most complete conversion table possible, create a sample document or sample text within the template and use each format properly. When FrameMaker generates the conversion table from the existing content, it will include all your formats. Formats that are in the paragraph and character catalogs but are not used are not placed in the conversion table. For example, if I run a conversion table on a brief document that uses only two paragraph formats and a character format, I get a simple conversion table like you see in Figure 2-1.

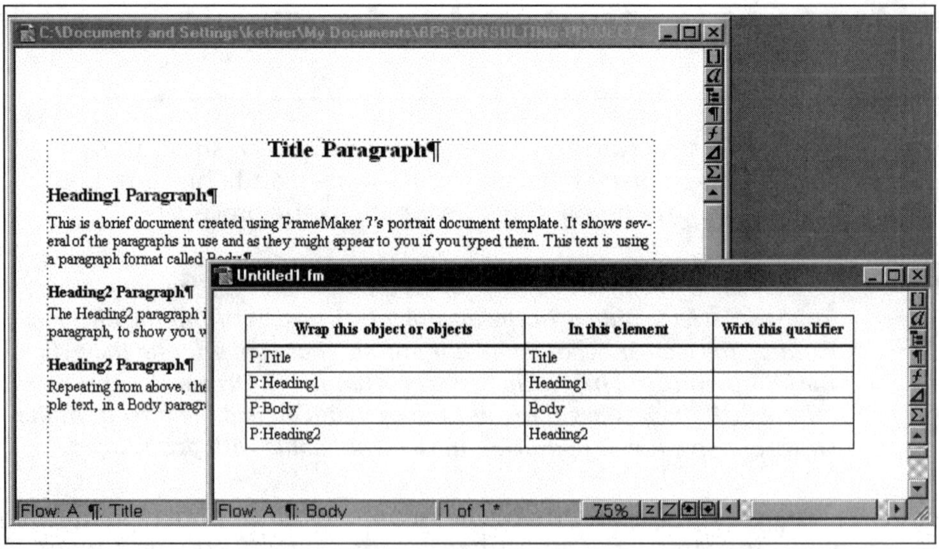

Figure 2-1 Simple document and generated conversion table.

If the document has more formats and objects, however, the result is a more complex "starter" conversion table. An example is shown in Figure 2-2.

Once you have the conversion table, you run it on your unstructured document and it becomes a structured document. You may find that you need to adjust the conversion table to fix items that are not wrapping as you would like. Close (without saving) the structured document, adjust your conversion table as needed, and then run the conversion on the *unstructured* document again until the content is wrapped (automatically structured) the way you would like it to be.

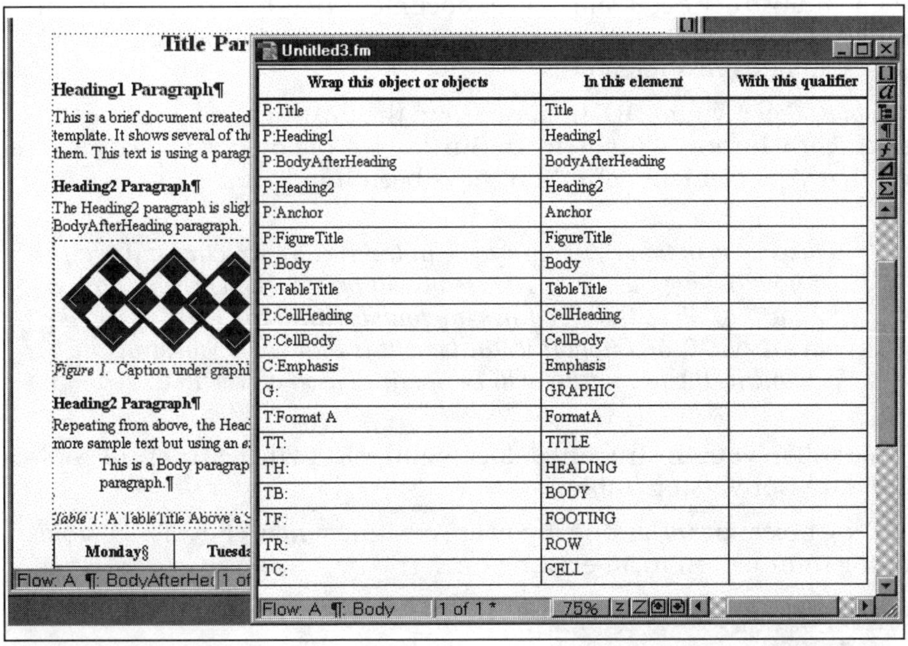

Wrap this object or objects	In this element	With this qualifier
P:Title	Title	
P:Heading1	Heading1	
P:BodyAfterHeading	BodyAfterHeading	
P:Heading2	Heading2	
P:Anchor	Anchor	
P:FigureTitle	FigureTitle	
P:Body	Body	
P:TableTitle	TableTitle	
P:CellHeading	CellHeading	
P:CellBody	CellBody	
C:Emphasis	Emphasis	
G:	GRAPHIC	
T:Format A	FormatA	
TT:	TITLE	
TH:	HEADING	
TB:	BODY	
TF:	FOOTING	
TR:	ROW	
TC:	CELL	

Figure 2-2 More complex document and generated conversion table.

Understanding the Conversion Process

If you have a FrameMaker document or template containing your paragraph formats and other formats, and if you have the structure available[1], you may run a conversion table to have FrameMaker automatically wrap structure elements around the paragraph contents.

1. This refers to the element definitions or EDD content. While you don't need the structure at this stage, at some point you will need to have the structure (elements imported from your EDD or structured template) in the document that you plan to structure. Otherwise, you will get no formatting (plain Body text). As the conversion table wraps your content in the elements, the appropriate formatting may then be applied.

Generating an Initial Conversion Table

There are two ways to create a conversion table:

- From scratch by typing
- Allowing FrameMaker to generate it from one of your unstructured documents

The process of creating a conversion table—using the FrameMaker utility—goes something like this:

1. **Open** an unstructured FrameMaker document that has in use different FrameMaker formats (such as paragraph, character) and objects (such as figures, tables, cross-references).
2. *(optional)* **Open** your EDD, then return to the unstructured document and select **File** > **Import** > **Element Definitions**. A dialog box appears telling you that your element definitions have been imported.

Note: *This step is optional because you can technically structure a document without having the EDD. The result will be a document with no text formatting, since those settings are found within the EDD. If you do have the EDD and import it, the benefit is that when you structure the document, the formatting will be applied based on the EDD settings.*

3. While still in your unstructured document, select **File** > **Structure Tools** > **Generate Conversion Table**.
4. A dialog box appears, asking if you are creating a new conversion table or adding information to an existing one.

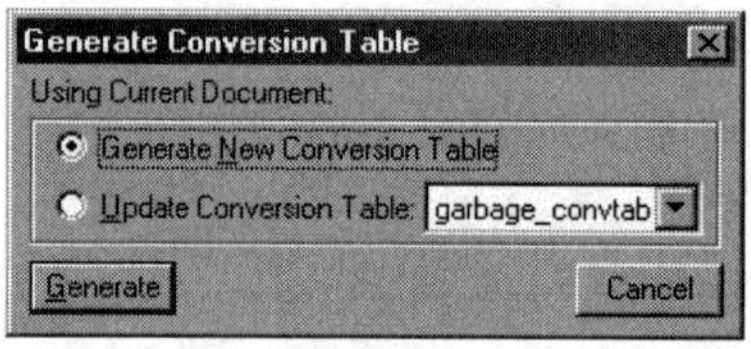

5. Select the top choice, *Generate New Conversion Table,* if it is not already selected.
6. Click **Generate**.

You now have a FrameMaker document with structure in it (because you imported the structure) and the beginnings of a conversion table (as created by FrameMaker).

Some adjustments will be needed to really make the conversion table work. The initial table is basic and normally requires adjustment. Once you have your conversion table finalized, you will run it against your document (or even a set of documents) to wrap its content. This process is discussed later in this chapter.

Understanding Your Conversion Table

Before we move forward, you need to understand the conversion table syntax. After all, you cannot be expected to edit or create a table without knowing what your options are.

Each conversion table row contains up to three columns:

- An unstructured item
- A structure element to convert to (or a conversion code)
- An additional column that may be added and used for comments. This extra column is ignored by FrameMaker and allows you to annotate the table for future reference

This information is used to wrap, in an automated fashion, some of the document content. As FrameMaker moves down through the table, wrapping may be done on all existing layers of text until the structuring is complete (see Table 2-1).

Note: *For additional information on the basic syntax of conversion tables, refer to Appendix A of Adobe's structure creator's manual that is installed with FrameMaker—Structure_Dev_Guide.pdf. This PDF may be found in your /FrameMaker7.0 install directory in a subdirectory called /OnlineManuals.*

Table 2-1 Sample Conversion Table with Multi-Level Wrapping of Content

Wrap This Object or Objects	In This Element	With This Qualifier
P:Title	Title	
P:Heading1	Section	1
P:Heading2	Section	2
P:Body	Para	
E:Para+	Section	
E:Section+	Document	

Column 1—Formats and Objects

The first cell in a conversion table contains the name of an existing item found in the unstructured document. This might be the name of a paragraph tag (for example, Title). In Table 2-1, we see "P:Title" in the first column. This refers to a paragraph format (P:) called Title. More specifically, it says that when a paragraph in your unstructured document is tagged with the format

"Title," FrameMaker should put structure around it by wrapping it in the element listed in the second column.

You may have formats or objects in the first column. As you wrap different formats and objects into elements, you will reach a point in the conversion when you need to wrap these elements into other elements, producing your complete structure hierarchy. So, in the first column you may also have element names listing the already-wrapped items.

Specific letter prefixes appear before items in the first column of the conversion table. These are listed non-alphabetically in Table 2-2.

Table 2-2 Conversion Table Codes for First Column of Table 2-1

P:	Paragraph format
C:	Character format
X:	Cross-Reference format
T:	Table format
TT:	Table Title (found above a table but attached to it)
TH:	Table Heading
TB:	Table Body
TF:	Table Footing
TR:	Table Row
TC:	Table Cell (or TC:P:paratag for cells without child elements)
Q:	Equation (E:small or E:medium or E:large)
G:	Graphic
TI:	Text Inset
F:	Footnote (F:flow) or Table Footnote (F:table)
M:	Marker
SV:	System Variable
UV:	User Variable
RG:	Rubi Group (Rubi text appears *above* Japanese or English characters and indicates pronunciation)
E:	Element (for additional wrapping once structuring begins). May include square brackets that hold the name of an attribute or qualifier in an element.

These one- and two-digit code characters are generally followed by the name of an actual format. As the table progresses (top to bottom), you may see elements wrapping within elements, such as shown in Figure 2-3.

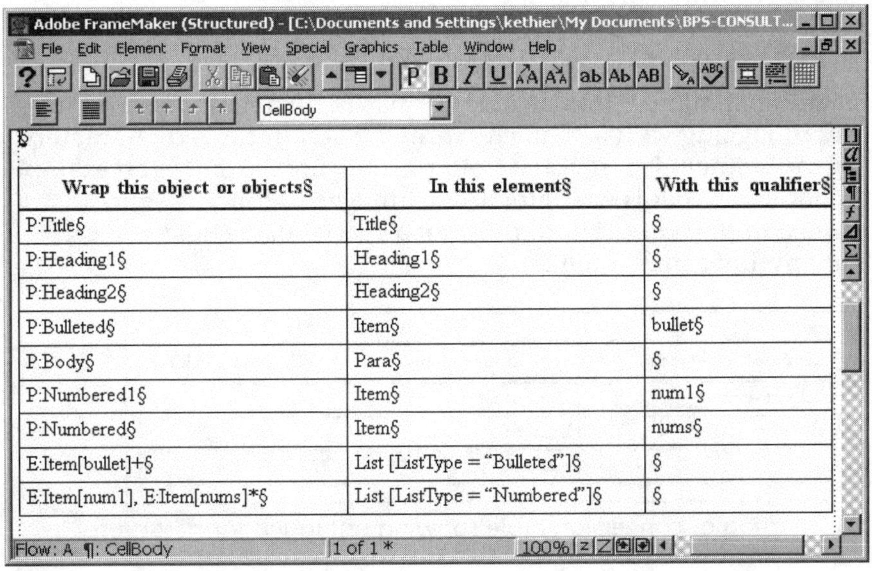

Wrap this object or objects§	In this element§	With this qualifier§
P:Title§	Title§	§
P:Heading1§	Heading1§	§
P:Heading2§	Heading2§	§
P:Bulleted§	Item§	bullet§
P:Body§	Para§	§
P:Numbered1§	Item§	num1§
P:Numbered§	Item§	nums§
E:Item[bullet]+§	List [ListType = "Bulleted"]§	§
E:Item[num1], E:Item[nums]*§	List [ListType = "Numbered"]§	§

Figure 2-3 Sample conversion table with qualifiers included.

Remember that FrameMaker is case sensitive—and space sensitive—when you type your format names (tags).

Note: *A percent symbol (%) may be used as a wildcard to match multiple tags with similar names. It matches zero or more characters, so, for example,* ***P:%Body*** *would be a match for Body paragraphs as well as CellBody.*

Column 1—Flagging Overrides

In Column 1 you may also flag paragraph or character format overrides to deal with later. To do this, you add either **flag paragraph format overrides** or **flag character format overrides** to the column. The result is shown in Figure 2-4.

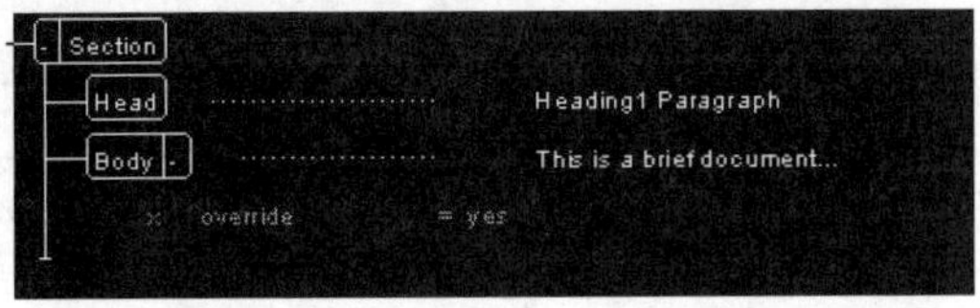

Figure 2-4 Structure view showing the added attribute.

Note: *When you use this flagging option, FrameMaker creates an attribute called Override with the value Yes as it structures your document. Attributes are extra pieces of information about an element that may be added within the structure.*

Column 1—Untagged Text Range Formatting

You may even catch manual formatting—formatting that authors have added to text without tagging with a character format. Such **untagged character formatting** can be included in visual Column 1. Figure 2-5 shows an example of a conversion table that is wrapping these untagged properties into an element named Important (Important is not a special name, and you can call the element anything that you like).

Wrap this object or objects	In this element	With this qualifier
untagged character formatting	Important	
C:Bold	Bold	
C:Emphasis	Emphasis	

Figure 2-5 Portion of conversion table showing untagged formatting set to wrap into an element.

You may also use certain symbols to wrap sequences of child elements in a parent element (for more information regarding parent-child element relationships, refer to Chapter 4). These symbols, shown in Table 2-3, mean the same thing that they mean in a general rule.

Table 2-3 Wrap Symbols

,	Child elements must occur in order given
|	Any one of child elements in group can occur
&	Child elements can occur in any order
+	This element is required and allowed to recur
*	This element is optional, and if used may recur
?	This element is optional, but if used may not recur

If these symbols look familiar, then you may recognize that they are the same symbols used within your EDD General Rules. So, if you have created an EDD and the rules for your elements, it will be easier for you to create a conversion table. The conversion table uses very similar rules, and in fact your Column 1 wrapping of elements-into-elements may match your EDD General Rule!

Column 2—Element Names

Column 2 contains the name of the element that should be wrapped around the format or previously wrapped items listed in Column 1.

Note: *Though it is optional, you may wish to type* **E:** *in front of the names in Column 2 to remind you of what these items are.*

After structuring, this element name would be what you would see in the structure. In many cases, after something is wrapped by the Column 2 item, it shows up further down Column 1 in the conversion table and is wrapped inside another element, which would then become its parent element.

Note: *If you are not familiar with structure and the parent-child relationship of elements, you may want to refer to Chapter 4 of this book or to the Adobe FrameMaker Structured Document Authoring Training Course.*

Column 2—Including Attributes

Column 2 may have more than just an element name; it may also contain attribute information that should be assigned as an item is wrapped in the element in Column 2. Be sure that the attribute value is in quotes, just as it would be in a markup language or in an EDD general rule. Figure 2-6 shows a List with its attribute value being assigned.

E:Item[Bullet]+§	List [ListType = "Bulleted"]§	§
E:Item[Num]+§	List [ListType = "Numbered"]§	§

Figure 2-6 A conversion table row showing an attribute value in Column 2 with the element name.

Column 2—Promoting Tables and Graphics

If you normally attach your tables and graphics directly to your Body paragraphs, then these anchored items will automatically become child elements of the paragraphs to which they are attached. If you prefer to have the anchored items at the same structural level as the paragraphs (be siblings to them), then you need to move the anchored items "up a level" in the structure during the conversion.

To move these items up a level when they become elements, you may need to add a promote to your conversion table. Adding a promote means that as you structure your unstructured documents, you will take—as one example—these anchored items and make them siblings to the paragraphs on which they are attached.

To move anchored objects up in the structure hierarchy in Column 2, after typing the element tag for the table or graphic, add "**(promote)**" as shown in Figure 2-7 after the object's element tag. This makes the table or graphic a sibling of the element above it, rather than its child.

Option A and Option B in Figure 2-7 show conversion table syntax for graphics (anchored frames). In Option A, the promote is not used. In Option B, the promote is used.

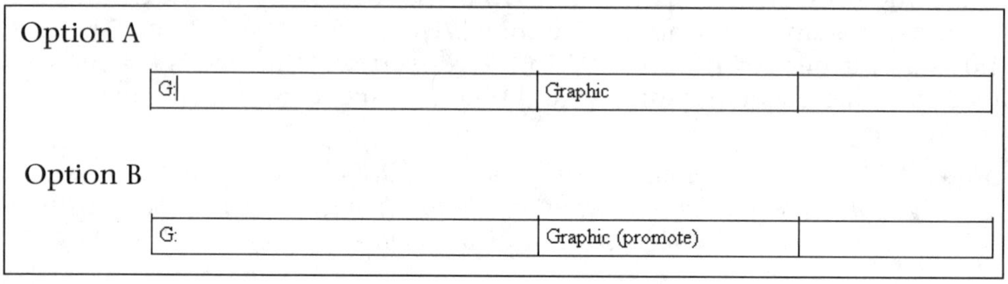

Figure 2-7 Conversion table row for each option.

The resulting structure for each option is shown in Figure 2-8. Notice that the graphic has been "promoted" up the structure from a child of Body to a sibling of Body.

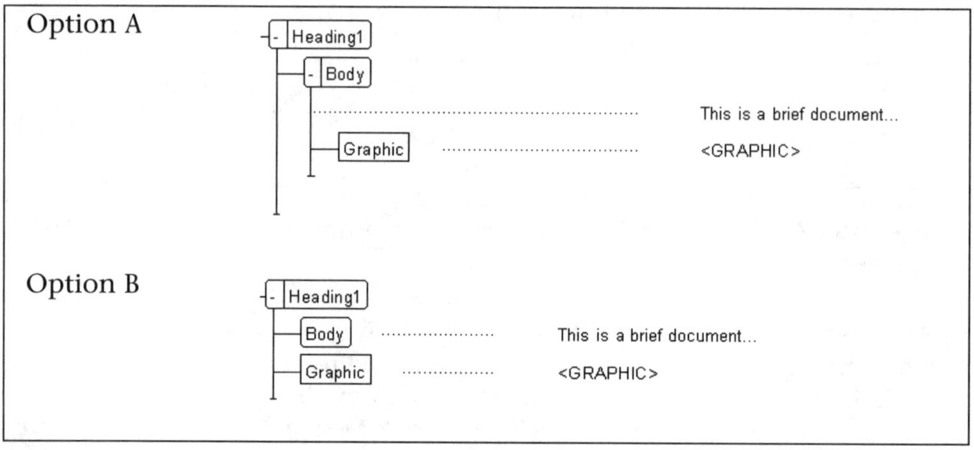

Figure 2-8 Resulting structure for each option.

One final comment on the promote option: If you have special paragraphs—perhaps called Anchor, Figure, or TableHolder, among other things—to hold your anchored objects[2], then you will be able to list these paragraphs as separate items in your conversion table. Figure 2-9 shows a sample row and its resulting structure.

2. Creating and using anchor-holder paragraphs is a good practice and recommended by the author—with or without structure.

Did you notice that "Graphic" is nested automatically inside the "Figure" element? This is because of the default behavior that makes the anchored items child elements. This was the issue resolved above by using promote. In the last case of Figure 2-9 you may not want to use promote, as the default behavior may work to your advantage—depending on your desired structure.

Conversion Rows

P:Anchor	Figure	
G:	Graphic	

Resulting Structure

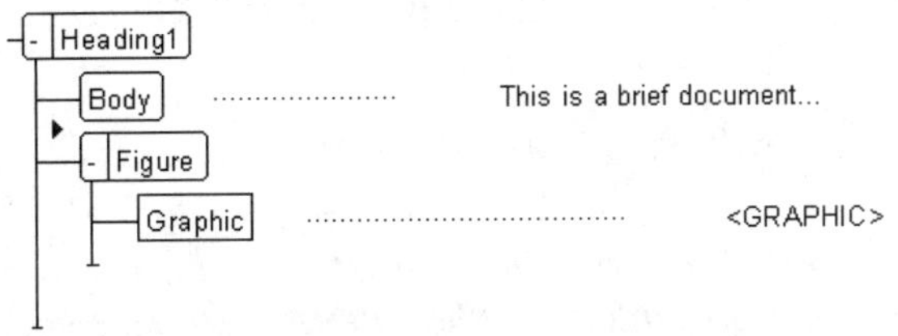

Figure 2-9 Result of an object anchored on a special paragraph.

Column 3

Column 3 is the qualifier column. This column is often empty. When populated, it contains a temporary identifier. This identifier is used whenever you wrap multiple items into the same element and need to use different parent elements.

Use of the qualifier is discussed further in "Adjusting the Initial Conversion Table" on page 33.

Running the Conversion Table

To get the conversion table to do the actual work of adding structure to your unstructured file, follow these steps:

1. **Open** the conversion table.
2. **Open** your unstructured document and make sure it is the active document.
3. Select **File** > **Utilities** > **Structure Current Document.**

   FrameMaker creates a new document by wrapping the content of your unstructured document according to your conversion table. You end up with your original unstructured document (still unstructured) and a new, untitled document (structured).
4. When you are finished, you may open the structure view and check out the untitled document's automatically created structure.

If your conversion table is set up properly, your structure will be clean and there will be no red type (structure errors). If there are red dotted lines or boxes, it is because of the way you set up the conversion table and you may need to adjust the table—or fix the errors by hand.

If you do see red type in the structure, you may have a typo in your conversion table or need to adjust the conversion table. Check your conversion table and try structuring your unstructured document again. Fixing structure errors may involve multiple iterations of conversion table adjustment, testing, and revising. The goal is a conversion that is near-100% automatic with a resulting structure that contains no errors or very few errors. The closer you can get to your ideal structure with the conversion table, the more time you will save by avoiding a lot of manual wrapping!

5. **Save** your newly structured document.

Note: *You may close the file without saving if you wish to modify the conversion table to achieve better results.*

In the next few sections we will look at specific examples of documents with different content and their conversion tables. This should help you to understand what the conversion table is doing and how you must set it up. Please note that in many cases there are several ways that a conversion table may be put together. The described set-ups are suggested ways—but not necessarily the only ways—to do each table.

Structuring a Simple Document

In the next few sections we will create and use conversion tables using the method and syntax described previously. To get you started, this section's conversion table focuses on a document that is fairly simple and that is available in all versions of FrameMaker.

Reviewing the Portrait Template

The paragraph catalog within the portrait document template is fairly simple, and its simplicity will lend itself to our starting point document. Figure 2-10 shows a sample document using paragraph formatting. It is not yet structured.

Formatted or Unformatted Documents

In FrameMaker, documents that have been created using Paragraph formats and Character formats are formatted (tagged) and may easily convert to a structure. If you do not use the formats, and instead do a lot of hand-formatting and use untagged character formatting (such as CTRL-B or CTRL-I

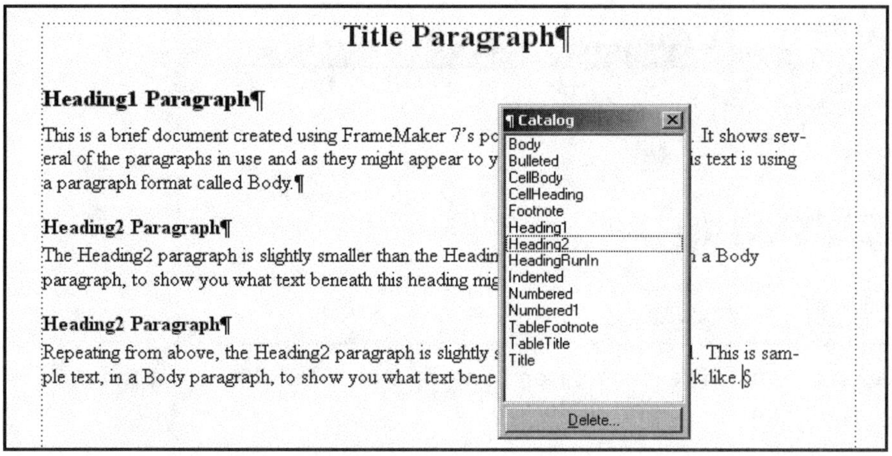

Figure 2-10 FrameMaker's portrait document template, with dummy text and the Paragraph catalog showing.

to format bold and italic), then your documents are not properly formatted and will not convert to a good structure.

To check if your document is using formats, click in the first paragraph and then hit the down arrow to move through the document. If the name of the format (shown on the status bar at the lower-left corner of your screen) continually shows "Body" or the same tag name throughout the document, then it is not properly formatted.

Options for Creating Your Structure

At this point you may run a conversion table and structure your document without having a corresponding EDD. However, if you have an EDD, you will get a formatted document as a result. Without the EDD, your document comes out structured but without formatting.

If you do have an EDD, you can import its element definitions into your sample document so that you see the formatting when the document is structured by the conversion table.

If you do not have an EDD at all, you may "trick" FrameMaker into starting one for you by creating a conversion table and structuring a sample document. Then, from the sample document, you may select **File > Structure Tools > Export Element Catalog as EDD** to produce a ready-to-edit EDD. The EDD that results from such a document is shown in Figure 2-11.

If necessary, you may work with conversion tables without worrying about having access to an EDD—although again, the formatting improves if you have one, as shown in Figure 2-12.

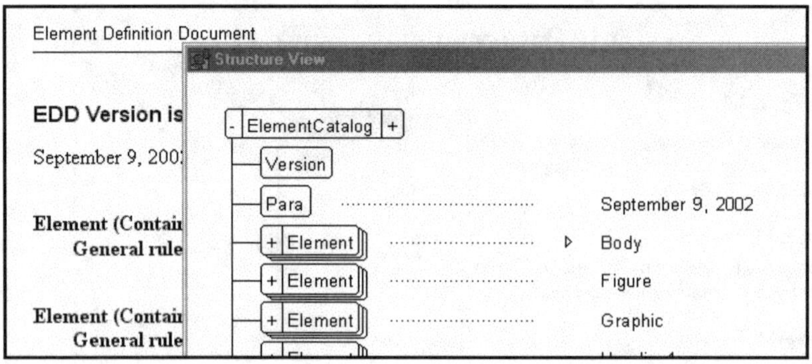

Figure 2-11 An EDD exported from a newly structured document that was structured using a conversion table.

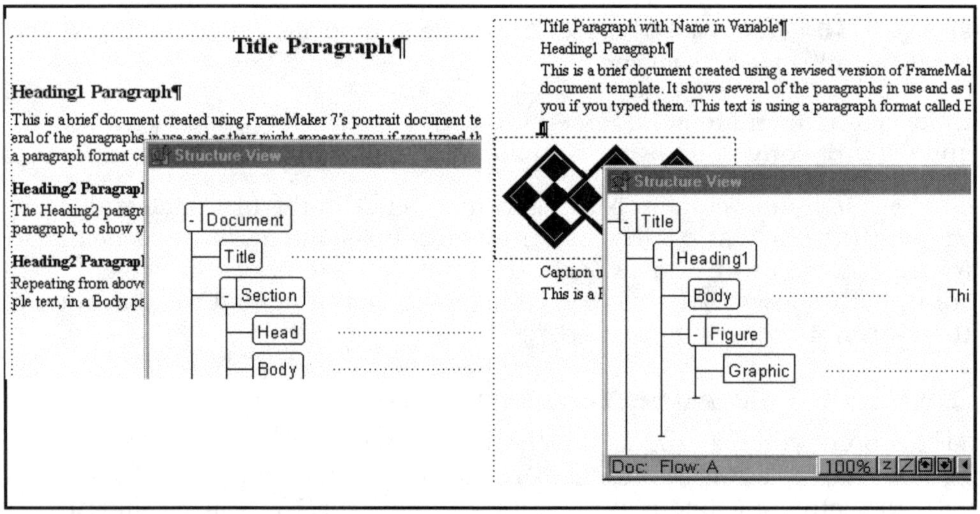

Figure 2-12 Comparison of structured document with EDD (left, formatted) and without EDD (right, plain text).

However, if you are not concerned about formatting, and are instead looking to create an EDD, then use the conversion table to create your structure and deal with the formatting later.

Creating a Conversion Table for a Simple Document

In this section you will create a final conversion table from the draft that FrameMaker creates for you. As you may recall, a draft of a conversion table was created by selecting **File > Structure Tools > Generate Conversion Table** earlier in this chapter. This table will serve as a starting point that you must now mold into the more finalized conversion table.

The conversion table shown in Table 2-4 is the start of a conversion table that might be created from the simple document shown in Figure 2-10.

Table 2-4 The Beginnings of a Conversion Table From a Simple Document

Wrap This Object or Objects	In This Element	With This Qualifier
P:Title	Title	
P:Heading1	Heading1	
P:Body	Body	
P:Heading2	Heading2	

By default, FrameMaker creates an element name in Column 2 of the conversion table that closely matches the format in Column 1. Even though there are elements with different names (and no elements with the Heading1 and Heading2 names) in the EDD, FrameMaker assigned what you see in Table 2-4 from the formats.

Adjusting the Initial Conversion Table

In our sample document, we have an EDD with structure that includes Title and Body, but not Heading1 and Heading2. These are set up in the structure as Section elements, with Head elements holding the content.

To fit with the available structure, you will need to adjust the conversion table so that it fits the structure. First, change the table so that the headings wrap into a Head element, as shown in Table 2-5. Modifying the table is done by typing directly into the cells. For example, to modify the structure so that the Heading1 and Heading2 paragraphs are wrapped in Head elements, you modify the content of Column 2 across from each of the heading paragraphs.

Table 2-5 Conversion Table Modified to Head

Wrap This Object or Objects	In This Element	With This Qualifier
P:Title	Title	
P:Heading1	Head	
P:Body	Body	
P:Heading2	Head	

Once you have the Head elements produced, you wrap them inside the Section elements using the syntax described earlier (see Table 2-6). While we are at it, we will wrap up everything into the Document element at the very top. What this refers to is the setup in the EDD that allows the Document element to be "Valid as the highest level element."

Table 2-6 Conversion Table with Section Added

Wrap This Object or Objects	In This Element	With This Qualifier
P:Title	Title	
P:Heading1	Head	
P:Body	Body	
P:Heading2	Head	
E:Head	Section	
E:Title?, Section*	Document	

While this table may appear to be complete, there is a flaw in its reasoning. It does allow wrapping of Head elements into the higher level Section element, but it does not provide any type of separation or indicator for a Heading1 versus a Heading2. This is where the Qualifier—placed in the third column—comes into play. You may use a text string to identify each of the particular headings and then note the text string as you do the wrapping. At each level, some notation will need to separate the two. This produces the more complex conversion table shown in Table 2-7.

Table 2-7 Conversion Table with Correct Heading Wraps

Wrap This Object or Objects	In This Element	With This Qualifier
P:Title	Title	
P:Heading1	Head	h1
P:Body	Body	
P:Heading2	Head	h2
E:Head[h2], Body*	Section	h2
E:Head[h1], E:Body*, E:Section[h2]*	Section	
E:Title?, Section*	Document	

There is still one more flaw in this conversion table. While it looks good and may even structure your document nicely, if you try to validate your document, an error will appear on the Title element. That is because in the EDD structure designed for this document (and in the samples available on this book's website at *www.technicalpublishing.com/AdvFrame*, the Title element is not supposed to be just Title; it should also have a Head wrapper around the text. You must adjust your table further before it is final.

Note: *If your document is the same as the sample, you will also have an error at the bottom of the document. That is because the EDD defines the document in such a way that you are required to have at least two headings at each level. Because you only have a single Heading1 in your document, you will get an error until a second is added.*

Table 2-8 Conversion Table with Title Fixed

Wrap This Object or Objects	In This Element	With This Qualifier
P:Title	Head	title
P:Heading1	Head	h1
P:Body	Body	
P:Heading2	Head	h2
E:Head[h2], Body*	Section	h2
E:Head[h1], E:Body*, E:Section[h2]*	Section	
E:Head[title]	Title	
E:Title?, Section*	Document	

Structuring Your Document

To structure your document, you would follow the procedures described in "Running the Conversion Table" on page 29. Make sure that, if you have several documents open, you run the appropriate conversion table against the appropriate document.

Figure 2-19 shows what a completed structure might look like for the sample document.

If your results have red showing, you might wish to validate your document. This procedure is described in the next section.

Validating Newly Structured Documents

When you validate a structured FrameMaker document, a FrameMaker utility found under **Element** > **Validate** walks you through your structure and points out any errors. It even finds errors when there is no red type indicator, letting you easily walk through a document and fix problems.

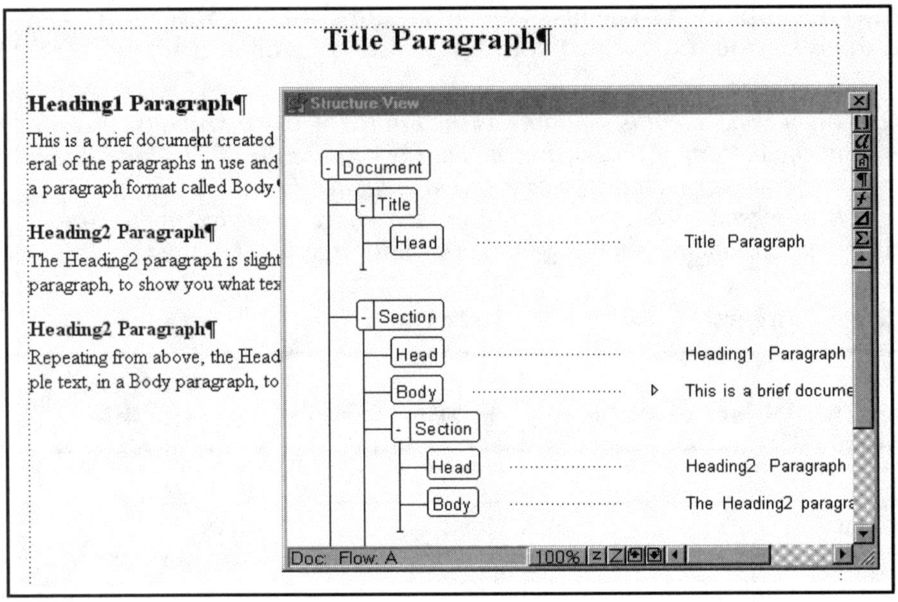

Figure 2-13 Structure created by the conversion table.

During the conversion table creation described in the previous section, an error that might occur during validation was mentioned. Specifically, the text refers to a Title element that is incorrectly wrapped and a Heading1 that is missing a sibling.

Two things will make document validation easier for you in the long run:

- Building a level of familiarity with your structure
- Using a method of writing that minimizes error creation

While the first requires you to gain an understanding of your documents over time, the second may require you to change the way that you create your content. Creating your content to minimize errors is described a little more in "The Role of Structured Writing" on page 42.

Structuring with a More Complex Conversion Table

In this section, you will work with a more complex document. This complex FrameMaker document includes a list so that you can take a closer look at multiple level element wrapping setup in a conversion table (see Figure 2-14). For lists, it is necessary to not only wrap the paragraphs containing the list items, but to take all the items and structure them inside of a list—producing a more nested, hierarchical structure.

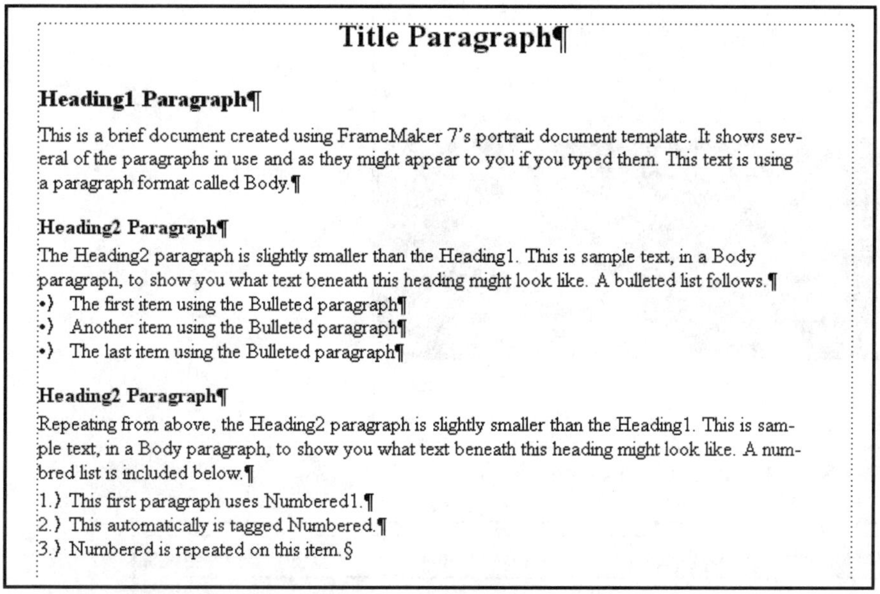

Title Paragraph¶

Heading1 Paragraph¶

This is a brief document created using FrameMaker 7's portrait document template. It shows several of the paragraphs in use and as they might appear to you if you typed them. This text is using a paragraph format called Body.¶

Heading2 Paragraph¶

The Heading2 paragraph is slightly smaller than the Heading1. This is sample text, in a Body paragraph, to show you what text beneath this heading might look like. A bulleted list follows.¶

•) The first item using the Bulleted paragraph¶
•) Another item using the Bulleted paragraph¶
•) The last item using the Bulleted paragraph¶

Heading2 Paragraph¶

Repeating from above, the Heading2 paragraph is slightly smaller than the Heading1. This is sample text, in a Body paragraph, to show you what text beneath this heading might look like. A numbred list is included below.¶

1.) This first paragraph uses Numbered1.¶
2.) This automatically is tagged Numbered.¶
3.) Numbered is repeated on this item.§

Figure 2-14 A simple document with lists added.

This document has been expanded so that it includes multiple types of lists. Remember from the beginning of this chapter that having a document with more formats or objects automatically allows FrameMaker to generate a more complex, initial conversion table.

Lists

Your original portrait document did not have any lists. To understand how to set up your conversion table, you need to understand the structure of a list.

Lists may be structured and formatted in different ways. The way described in this section is by no means the only way, but it is the author's preferred way. This preferred way is also an opportunity for you to further examine the relationship between elements and attributes.

If you refer to the EDD elements defined earlier, you will see that lists are defined to contain item elements. The result in the structure view is shown in Figure 2-15.

Adjusting the Portrait Template's Conversion Table

Because this document includes lists, the conversion table you created previously will not be enough. It must be expanded to include lists and to include references to "attributes" that tell the lists how they should be formatted (see Figure 2-16).

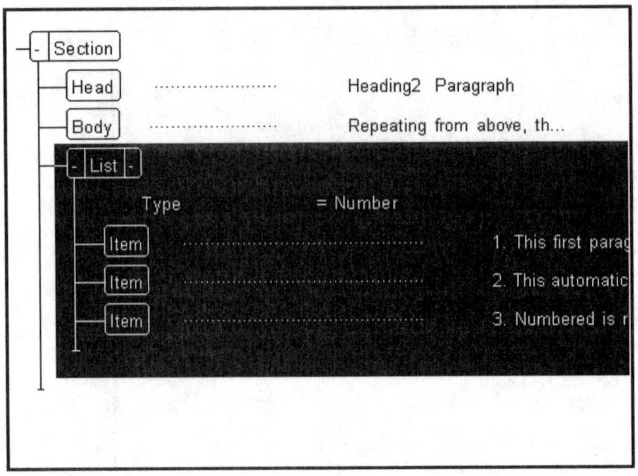

Figure 2-15 A list in the structure view.

Wrap this object or objects§	In this element§	With this qualifier§
P:Body§	Body§	§
P:Bulleted§	Item§	bullet§
P:Numbered1§	Item§	num1§
P:Numbered§	Item§	nums§
E:Item[bullet]+§	List [Type = "Bullet"]§	§
E:Item[num1], E:Item[nums]*§	List [Type = "Number"]§	§
P:Heading2§	Head§	2§
P:Heading1§	Head§	1§
E:Head[2], Body+, List*§	Section§	2§
(E:Section[2] | E:Head[1] | E:Body | E:List)+§	Section§	1§
P:Title§	Head§	title§
E:Head[title]§	Title§	§
E:Title, Section[1]+§	Document§	§

Figure 2-16 Conversion table modified to include multiple types of lists wrapped using attributes and qualifiers.

Making Better Use of Structure (Optimizing for XML)

To build on what you have done so far, this section walks you through the creation of a new structure and conversion table. This conversion table will be designed to create a document with more XML potential than the simple example previously used.

The EDD used for the previous example is rather plain. It produces a structured document and allows creation of valid XML from that document, but it does not really provide elements that describe the content. Generic element names like *Head, Body,* and *Section* do not provide any information about the text—no data about the data. In the upcoming example, we describe content more specifically by using the elements. This will make our content more extractable (reusable) from the valid XML that it produces.

If you are moving toward structure and XML output with your documents—for reuse and database storage potentials—then you might want to create/use an EDD that better describes your content.

Note: *In the real world, you want to have your template and structure defined in advance, not on the fly as we are doing here.*

So, instead of the simple EDD used earlier in this chapter, you will probably use an EDD with descriptive elements available.

Creating an XML-Ready Structure

If you plan to work with documents that will at some point be converted to XML, you need to create the EDD and create a conversion table that uses different element names and wraps according to your new structure.

The examples used in this section are of a recipe book and the individual recipes within it. The structure is designed to hold the content appropriate to a recipe. Naming conventions focus on the type of content rather than the formatting of it. Figure 2-17 shows an example of content specific to a recipe, which needs a structure that recognizes its different types of content.

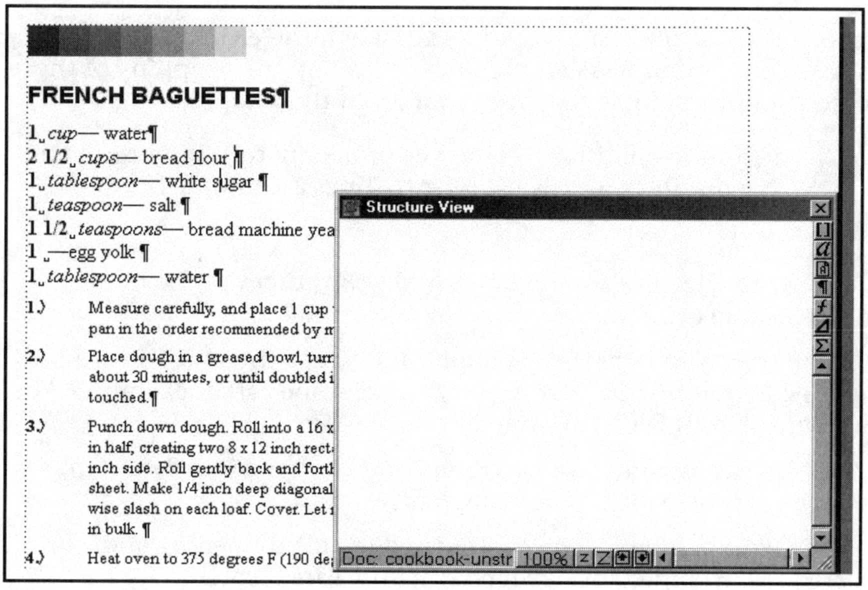

Figure 2-17 Unstructured document and empty structure view.

Creating an XML-Friendly Conversion Table

In this section you will review a conversion table that might be created for a recipe, using some of the conversion table techniques explored earlier in this chapter.

Remember that when you select **File > Structure Tools > Generate Conversion Table**, FrameMaker will create an initial conversion table. Depending on the paragraphs used in your recipe, the resulting table may look something like the one shown in Figure 2-18.

Note: *This document was created using a recipe template available in the* ***/MoreTemplates*** *directory installed with FrameMaker 7. Minor adjustments were made and new content added for this discussion.*

Wrap this object or objects	In this element	With this qualifier
P:Heading1	Heading1	
P:Ingredients	Ingredients	
P:Numbered1	Numbered1	
P:Numbered	Numbered	
P:Body	Body	
C:Bold	Bold	
C:Emphasis	Emphasis	
C:ItemName	ItemName	

Figure 2-18 Initial, auto-generated conversion table.

You will need to adjust the element names to match the elements listed in the EDD (if you have one). You will then need to set up the wrapping of those elements as seen in the simple document earlier in this chapter.

The actions in the following list are being performed by the conversion table in Figure 2-18. The numbers in this list refer to Lines 1 through 12 in Figure 2-19.

1. This line locates Heading1 paragraphs and wraps them in the more descriptive Name element.
2. This line locates Numbered1 paragraphs and wraps them in a Para element. Note that no qualifier is used, unlike some earlier examples. You will see why in your final structure.
3. Here the Numbered paragraph is located and wrapped in a Para element as was done for the Numbered1 paragraphs.
4. In this line, Para elements, recently created from Numbered1 and Numbered, are wrapped inside Step elements. Para elements are then Child elements to Step within the structure.

Wrap this object or objects	In this element	With this qualifier	
P:Heading1	Name		Line 1
P:Numbered1	Para		Line 2
P:Numbered	Para		Line 3
E:Para	Step		Line 4
E:Step+	Procedure		Line 5
P:Body	Time		Line 6
C:Bold	Quantity		Line 7
C:Emphasis	Unit		Line 8
C:ItemName	ItemName		Line 9
P:Ingredients	Item		Line 10
E:Item+	Ingredients		Line 11
E:Name, Ingredients, Procedure, Time	Recipe		Line 12

Figure 2-19 Final conversion table.

5. This line wraps multiple Step elements (using Step+, with the plus indicating there may be more than one) inside a Procedure element.
6. The only Body paragraph in the sample recipe is wrapped in a Time element.

Note: *You might refer to the sample unstructured document on this book's website (www.technicalpublishing.com/AdvFrame) to clarify this row—and the next few rows—of the conversion table.*

7. At this line, you switch to wrapping text ranges—Character Formatted text—in elements. *Bold* characters are wrapped in a Quantity element.
8. Text using the Character Format *Emphasis* is wrapped in the Unit element.
9. Text using the Character Format *ItemName* is wrapped in an ItemName element.
10. Text using the Ingredients paragraph format is wrapped in the Item element.
11. Multiple Item elements (Item+) are wrapped in an Ingredients element so that the many separate Item elements may be structurally a part of (nested inside) Ingredients.
12. In this row, the last in our table, all elements within the document are wrapped inside a top-level or "root" element called "Recipe."

Note: *If we were to continue to create a complete recipe book or a chapter of recipes, we might have Recipe wrap into additional elements that would become parents of Recipe.*

Once you have the conversion table finalized, open the recipe document that you wish to structure. Then, select **File > Utilities > Structure Current Document**. When the dialog box appears, select the conversion table name (all open documents will be listed) and click **Add Structure**.

In Figure 2-20, note the error indicated by the dotted vertical line in the structure view. This line also appears in red (not seen in this black and white book), and indicates errors in the structure. Because of some particular idiosyncrasies within the document—em dashes and reuse of paragraph tags for different components—there will be some hand cleanup needed. For instance, the em dashes within the items need to be deleted[3]. Also, at the bottom of the document, a Quantity element's removal will actually help to delete unwanted text.

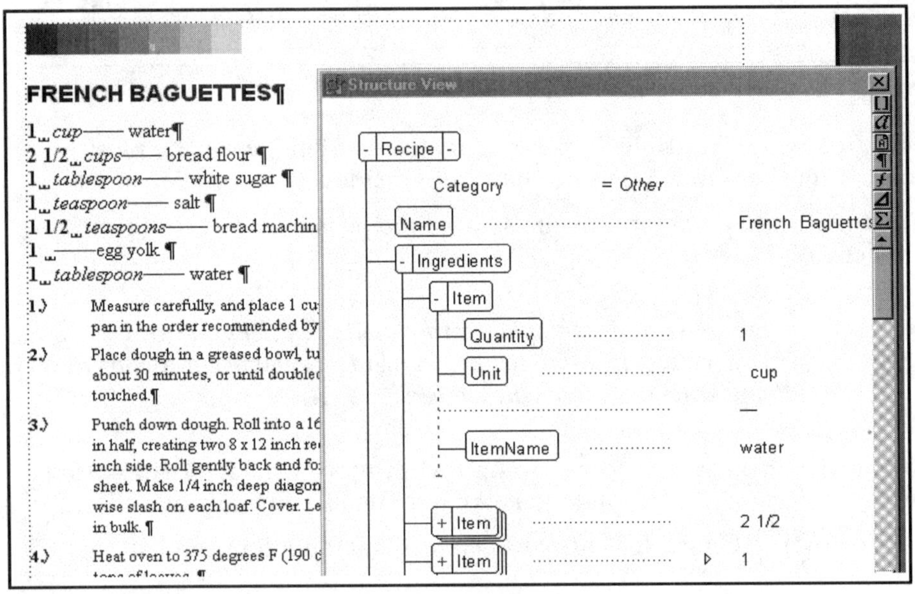

Figure 2-20 Document structured using conversion table.

The Role of Structured Writing

As you move from unstructured FrameMaker documents into structured, you may find that you need to change the way you write your content. Documents that you felt were consistently put together in the unstructured environment may show their flaws as you apply your chosen structure. Pieces may need to be removed, rewritten, and redefined to fit into the new scheme.

3. In our sample files, we actually wrote a prefix rule inside the EDD to automatically insert the em dash. So the original, which cannot easily be structured, may merely be deleted.

Starting with a new way of writing now can make your transition easier. There are many writing styles and many types of documents, each with its own unique points. It may be easier for a writer to stick to a style if there is a method behind the madness.

One such writing methodology is Information Mapping®.[4] This well-known way of creating content gives the writers certain rules to follow. A certain number of paragraphs and screenshots must be included for a document to be final.

Another such writing method is the Clustar™ method.[5] Designed with FrameMaker in mind, this method includes the setup of complex paragraph format sets (or element sets) that form patterns. These patterns or "clusters" of information not only make sense for structure, they make it easier for writers to write.

Summary

Moving from unstructured documents to structured documents does take effort. Elements and attributes must be created and structure rules defined. EDD items must be set up to call template formats into action to produce a good-looking document. And the unstructured formats must be mapped to elements in a customized conversion table.

For more information on conversion table syntax and basic information, refer to the developer's guide that is installed with FrameMaker. It is located in the FrameMaker install directory, in a subdirectory called **OnlineManuals**. The name of the guide is *Structure_Dev_Guide.pdf*; conversion tables are covered in *Appendix A*. (There are other helpful PDFs in the manual's subdirectory on XML, XHTML, and CSS.)

Other resources include the following:

- The *XML Cookbook* that is installed with FrameMaker, under the main **Install** directory, in a subdirectory called **XMLCookBook**
- The Adobe Enterprise Solutions CD, available via Adobe's website, *www.adobe.com*
- Call for technical support when you need it. There are online resources, as well as experts for hire (see the Adobe CD mentioned above), to help you make the transition to structured authoring

4. Information Mapping® is a registered trademark of Information Mapping, Inc. This is just one well-known system for writing documents with a consistent structure. Their main website is *www.infomap.com*.

5. Clustar™ is a trademark of simply written, inc. More information may be found at *www.simplywritten.com*.

3

Understanding XML Round Trip

Kay Ethier

This chapter examines the FrameMaker 7.0/7.1 capabilities for using and creating XML and moving from FrameMaker to XML and back again.

Applicable to FrameMaker 7.0/7.1

If you have heard anything about FrameMaker 7/7.1, you have heard of its ability to create XML documents from FrameMaker files and vice versa—often referred to as an XML round trip. This added functionality allows you to work within FrameMaker while providing XML to other systems and departments within your enterprise. This chapter explains the round-trip process and the issues that can arise if you do not set up a round trip specific to your needs from the very beginning of your project.

Some knowledge of XML is necessary to understand this chapter. This chapter uses structured documents; structure creation is discussed in Chapter 2.

Important Terminology

Before getting any further into structured document publishing, we would like to share some additional structure-related terminology. These terms and their definitions are applicable to Structured FrameMaker and to XML.

XML

XML is an acronym for Extensible Markup Language, which is sometimes written as eXtensible Markup Language (either is appropriate). XML is named and defined by the World Wide Web Consortium (W3C), and you may find further details on the *w3c.org* Web site.

Metadata

Metadata is sometimes referred to as "data about your data." It refers to the extra information that you include in your documents by wrapping descriptive tags around your content.

SGML

SGML is an acronym for Standard Generalized Markup Language. Though it is not specifically dealt with in this chapter, please note that it is possible to create a FrameMaker round-trip application for SGML.

Application

You may have heard the term "application" when someone is referring to a software product. FrameMaker, for example, may be called an application. This, however, is not the definition of "application" that we mean when we are working in structured document publishing.

An "Application" in the structured-documents context is a set of files that are given a name and designed to work together. You may have multiple Applications, and they may be either XML Applications or SGML Applications. The name is given by the creator of the Application. The files that work together include (but are not limited to) a structured template, read/write rules, a DTD, and stylesheet, all of which are described in this chapter's "Important Terminology" on page 46.

The Applications that are installed with FrameMaker (except the UNIX version) are DocBook, xDocBook, and XHTML. Some are written in XML and others in SGML.

Note: *A capital A will be used on Application in this chapter to help you make the distinction from general software applications. Application does not need to be capitalized, although you may note that its element name is capitalized within FrameMaker.*

Round Trip Application

A round-trip Application allows you to perform importing (XML into FrameMaker) and exporting (FrameMaker to XML) functions without loss of data, structure, or ability to format. The XML Application must be set up within FrameMaker on each machine that will work with the XML Application. You provide the name and the pointers or paths to the documents that work together (DTD, template, and so forth).

You may set up an Application to allow you to publish fully-formatted documents—formatting being one of FrameMaker's strengths—and to produce XML for use by other systems and departments within your enterprise.

Read/Write Rules

The read/write rules are an optional, separate file that may be added to a round-trip setup. The rules may be used to adjust element names (change case, shorten, lengthen), adjust the nesting of elements, or drop and add elements as XML is imported (read) into FrameMaker or exported (written) from FrameMaker. For example, because XML does not specify element types, yet FrameMaker does designate element types (containers, tables, graphics, cross-references, footnotes, and more), it may be desirable to create rules that add an element type as XML is imported. A second example is using a rule to change the FrameMaker element *Chapter Title*, which contains a space, to *ChapterTitle* to eliminate the space that XML will not allow. The same rule could even be modified to make the XML element name *chaptitle* if you so desired.

Stylesheet

A stylesheet is a document that may be used to format your XML. Although this chapter refers to stylesheets, it does not cover their use. Stylesheets are not covered in this chapter, or elsewhere in this book.

DOCTYPE

The *document type* is sometimes included in XML documents and refers to the specific DTD to be used for that document. For example, underneath your

XML declaration (*Line 1*) you might have a DOCTYPE naming your DTD by filename (*Line 2*):

```
<?xml version="1.0"?>                                   Line 1
<!DOCTYPE UserManual SYSTEM "manual.dtd">               Line 2
```

Validation

Validation merely refers to checking your document's structure against the structure defined in the DTD. In FrameMaker there is a Validate tool that moves you from error to error—if you have any—within your structured document or book.

Benefits of XML Round Trip

There are many benefits to the XML round trip process. Other portions of this book deal with structured document publishing benefits (consistency, validation, and guided writing, among others). There may be—and should be—some overlap between XML round-trip benefits and structured document publishing benefits. Publishing using XML has several benefits. Herein we describe a few:

- Multichannel publishing
- Content sharing/reusability
- Metadata
- Extensibility

Multichannel Publishing

One benefit of doing XML round trip with FrameMaker is that you can access all of FrameMaker's capabilities for multichannel publishing—publishing to many formats. Multichannel publishing is not easily accomplished with XML alone or with any other single tool. FrameMaker's ability to format documents for press, output high-quality PDF, and output to HTML and online help will allow you to do more with your XML documents.

In addition, you may combine those components into documents with completely different looks by using multiple templates. XML being what it is, there is no formatting to get in the way of adjusting the content, so it looks the way that you want it to look. You could set up multiple Applications—each using a different FrameMaker template.

Content Sharing and Reuse

XML allows you to reference XML fragments and pull them together to form complete documents. This means you can reuse pieces of XML in multiple documents by referencing them. The concept is similar to FrameMaker's text inset feature.

You may not only pull together content from multiple XML documents, you may also share your XML throughout your enterprise. The XML created by FrameMaker—any XML you create—has no formatting. You are producing data that is not in a proprietary format and is basically ASCII text. You can easily use your XML with other tools. Those using FrameMaker within your organization can certainly use your XML. Those who are using other XML-ready tools may use it as well—so you are not limiting access to your data but rather opening up access to it.

Note: *Tools such as TEXTML® by IXIASOFT (www.ixiasoft.com) allow you to store XML and other files with metadata about each file. You can then search, retrieve, and reuse the data in the XML server. This tool is mentioned specifically because it was designed for XML, yet has a software "bridge" to work with FrameMaker.*

Metadata

Instead of just storing your content (text, images, and so forth), you include data about your content—metadata—by using elements and attributes. Storing metadata along with your content makes your data more flexible and reusable. Attributes provide information about each element's content. For example, when creating a catalog, you might type your catalog data within a structure that describes the data (item, price) and has attributes with additional data (category, weight, requirements).

You may even set up database connectivity—including database connectivity for content management—if you have a database that can handle XML.

Extensibility

By definition and name, XML is "extensible." This means you can add elements and attributes as needed. This is advantageous if you wish to get a system in place and working before expanding it to suit other needs. For example, a document may be designed and rolled out for one department, then extended to add components desired by other departments to create a more complete system.

Determining Your Needs

Do you need to create an Application just for your documents? In the next few sections you will see how working with FrameMaker Applications gives you extra control over your XML and documents.

Working without an XML Round-Trip Application

It is important for you to know what FrameMaker does out of the box and then learn what additional setup you may need to do. In this section we will examine what happens to XML when no Application is selected, just to show you what FrameMaker does by default.

A round-trip Application helps you ensure that the resulting XML files are valid. This section deals with valid XML. (Therefore, this section uses structured documents, because saving a structured document as XML gives you elements with multi-level hierarchy and allows validation.

To reiterate, an XML round-trip Application allows you to export and import XML. In FrameMaker, the specific options are Save As XML (export) and Open XML (import). The next two sections describe these actions.

Exporting XML (File > Save As: type "XML")

One part of the round trip is the XML export, which is accomplished using Save As XML. Save As XML may be initiated from both regular, unstructured FrameMaker documents and from structured FrameMaker documents. The round-trip function, however, only works for structured documents.

Take a sample structured document, such as the one shown in Figure 3-1, and select **Save As XML**.

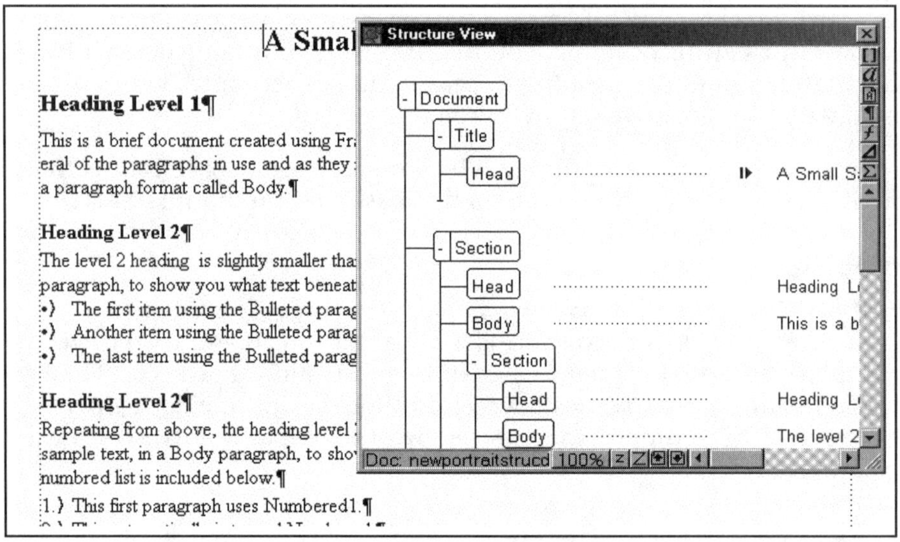

Figure 3-1 Structured FrameMaker document.

The resulting XML document has the same structure and content as the FrameMaker structured document. Notice the structure view and the elements in the structure (document, section, and so forth).

The XML document, however, has no formatting (as seen in Figure 3-2). This is normal, as XML is straight text. Notice that the structural elements (document, section, and so forth) match those of the original FrameMaker structured document.

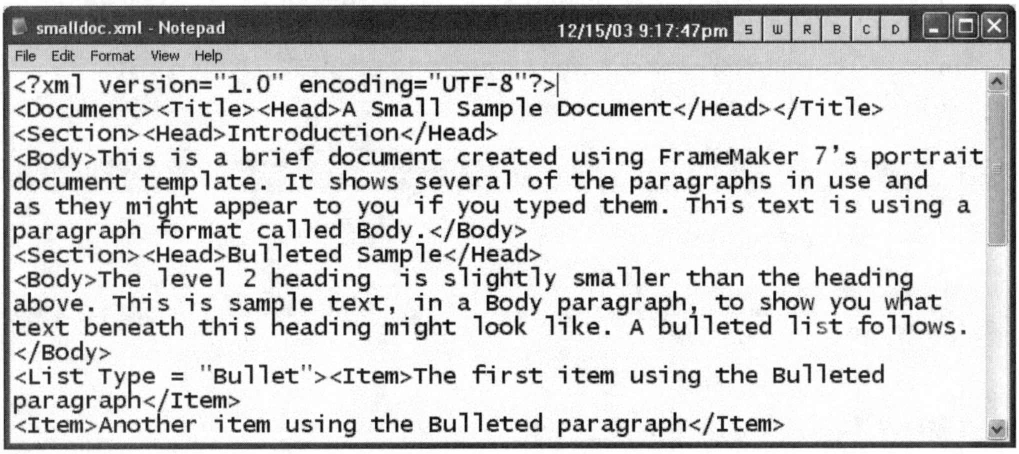

Figure 3-2 XML document created from the structured FrameMaker document.

Another way to look at this same document would be through a Web browser, such as Internet Explorer®. Viewed through Internet Explorer, we see the familiar view with colored tags and collapse/expand controls. See Figure 3-3 for an example.

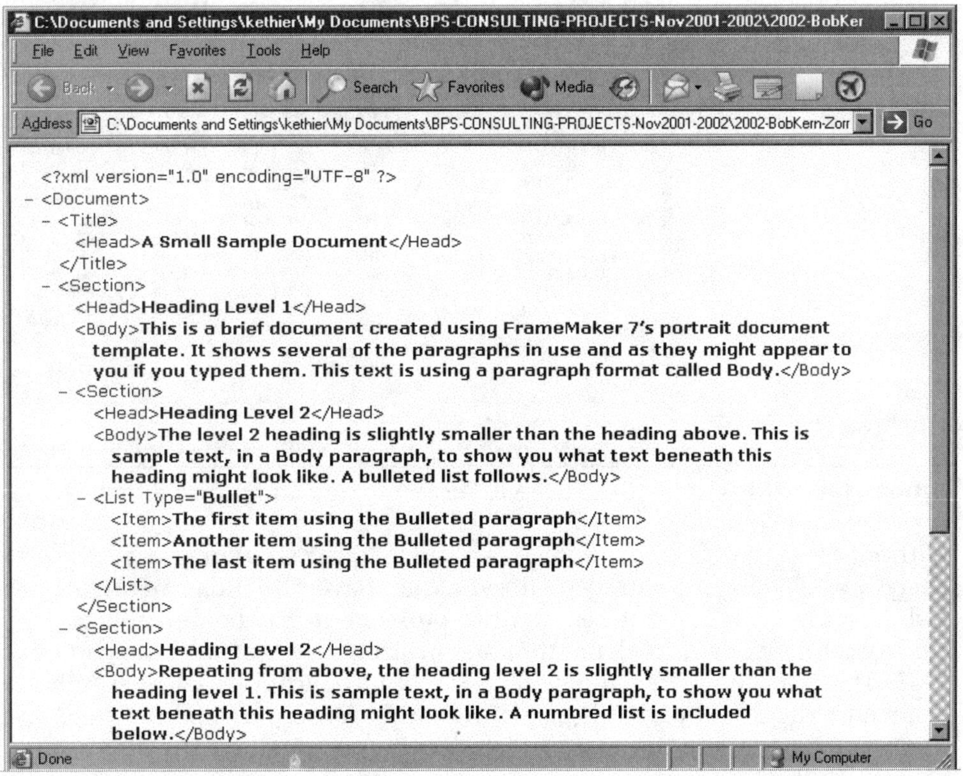

Figure 3-3 XML document viewed in browser.

This XML document has no proprietary formatting and may be easily placed in an XML database or retrieval system (see Figure 3-4). The XML document may also be shared across your enterprise and opened in Notepad, GoLive, or any other XML-capable tool.

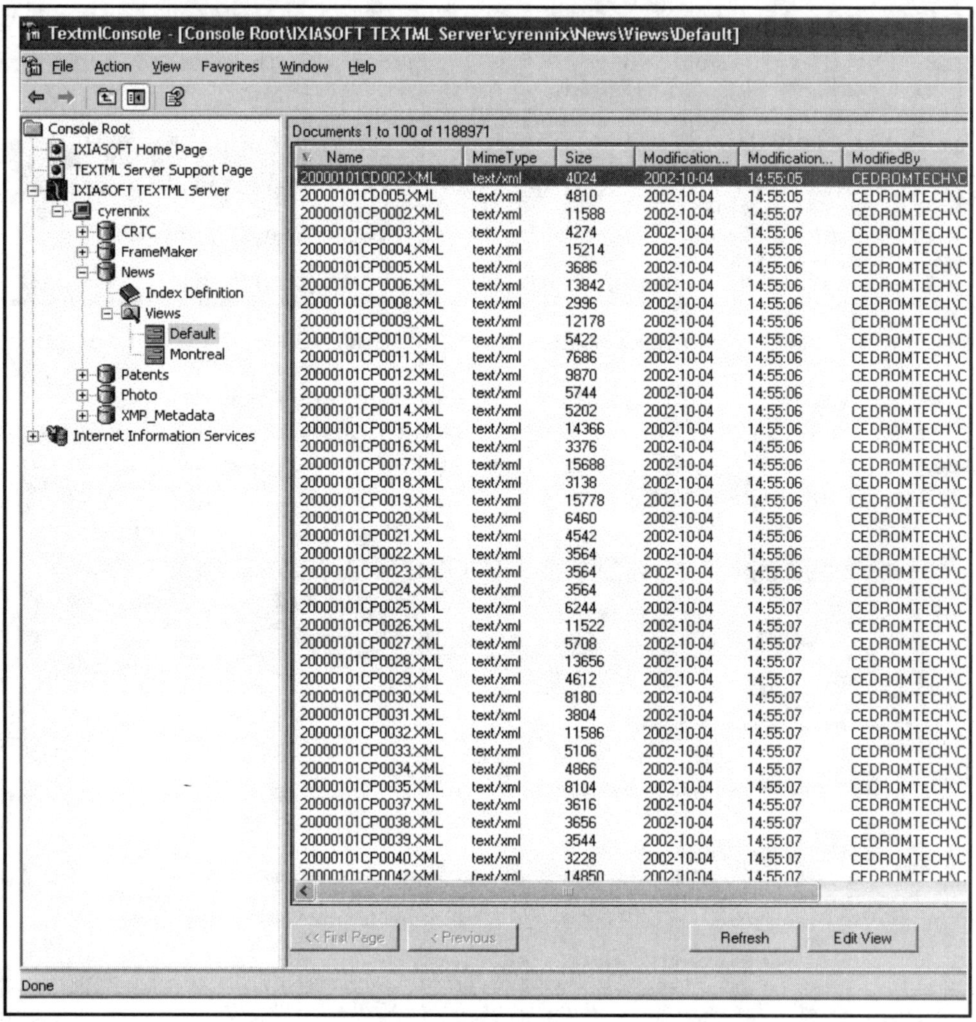

Figure 3-4 XML in the TEXTML XML Server storage and retrieval tool.

Without an Application, no changes are made to the structure upon export. Therefore, all elements with capitalized names have capitalized names in the XML document. While not necessarily a problem, it may be desirable to remove the case or adjust element names or structure when sending content to XML. This is a change that can be built into an Application—more specifically, in a read/write rules file that is part of the Application. A read/write rule to change element names is described later in this chapter after the discussion of how an Application improves the round trip process.

Importing XML (File > Open)

Part of working with XML and FrameMaker is the process of importing XML into FrameMaker. This creates a structured FrameMaker document in FrameMaker 7, with the file automatically saving with a .fm extension. In FrameMaker 7.1, the same action opens the XML in FrameMaker and shows you a structured document, but upon saving the file is automatically saved as XML.

Either way, if you do not use an Application when you bring XML into FrameMaker, the results will not be pretty. In the following example, we look at one example document.

An XML document instance may be opened by selecting **File > Open**, browsing to select the XML file, and then opening it. When the XML document opens, several dialog boxes may appear, such as

and then perhaps

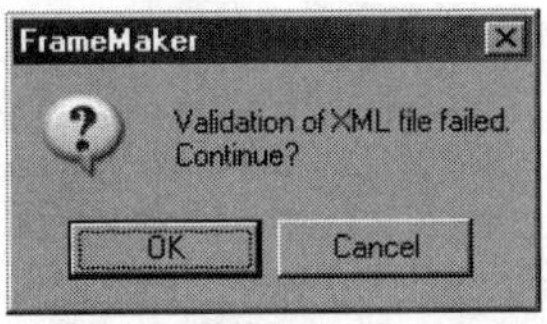

The first dialog box gives you an opportunity to select an Application. No Application is selected at this point.

The second dialog box comes up because FrameMaker cannot associate a DTD with the XML file. Since an Application is responsible for this task, selecting "No Application" means FrameMaker cannot reach the DTD.

Note: *If you create XML and include a DOCTYPE, you may get it to access the DTD without an Application. We do not deal with this scenario here, however, because the best practice is to set up an Application.*

The tags used in the XML document are used by FrameMaker. To see the resulting elements, either open the Structure View window (by clicking the button at the document window's top-right edge) or select **View > Element Boundaries (as Tags)**. The result will be pretty much the same in FrameMaker 7 and 7.1, except that in 7 the file extension will change and it will save as a FrameMaker document. Contrast that to FrameMaker 7.1, in which the file continues to have an XML file extension.

Once the XML file is opened in FrameMaker, you can move through it the same way that you would move through any structured FrameMaker document. Its structure is the same as the original structured document from which it was exported (shown in Figure 3-5). Figure 3-5 shows the unformatted FrameMaker document and corresponding structure view.

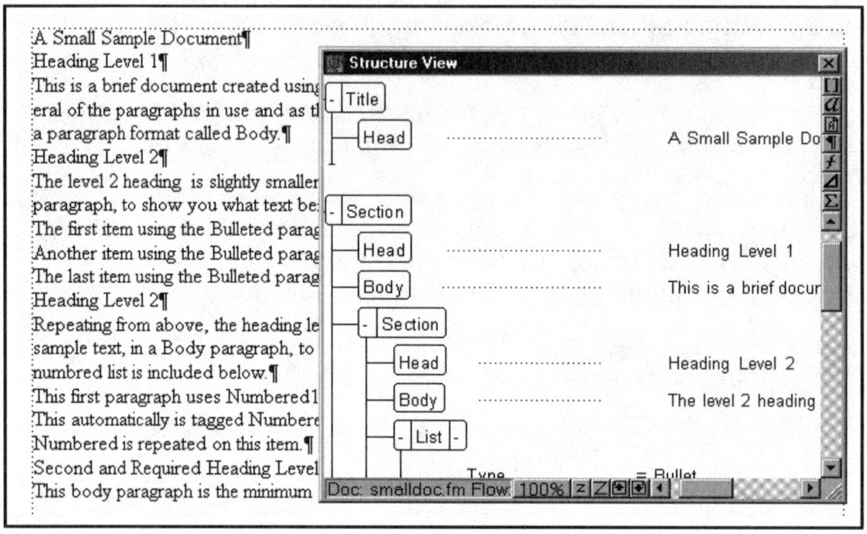

Figure 3-5 Structured FrameMaker document created from XML and containing the proper structure but no formatting.

Looking at the unformatted document, you might wonder how such a plain document might be useful. The truth is that it may not be useful without formatting. So, your round-trip Application should be set up to include a formatting component that tells FrameMaker where to locate the template. Otherwise, you will always get the plain version and have to import from the template to get files formatted—a process you will have to go through every time you open one of your XML documents in FrameMaker.

In the section that follows, you will see how an Application improves the look of your XML document by making it possible to return it to its original, fully formatted state while still containing the unformatted XML output.

Working with a Round-Trip Application

As shown in Figure 3-5, the XML with No Application came into FrameMaker unformatted. Ugly, isn't it?

To make the round trip work, you often need more than just XML and FrameMaker. You need an Application. This will save you from having to do hand-importing or perhaps accidentally distributing an unformatted document.

Exporting XML (File > Save As: type "XML")

When you use an Application to Save As XML, the XML document will be written according to the structure and any adjustments that are part of the

Application (such as the read/write rules adjustments mentioned previously). Extra information like a DOCTYPE or a stylesheet reference can also be added to the XML document. In the *simpledoc* application shown later, for example, a DTD is added to an Application, and the XML file changes to include the following:

```
<!DOCTYPE document SYSTEM "sd.dtd">
```

Importing XML (File > Open)

Importing XML into FrameMaker using an Application allows you to access the template and enjoy a formatted document right away. No formatting is lost in the transition.

Moving Forward

Hopefully you have seen some advantage to setting up an Application. In the next section you will see how an Application is created from scratch. The following are a few important things to note:

- The description of importing and exporting XML does not include a discussion of formatting the XML document. XML may be formatted using CSS, XSL, and XML-FO. When XML is generated by FrameMaker or WebWorks Publisher, either CSS or XSL files are generated. These formatting options are not covered in this chapter.
- The XML exported from unstructured documents has a simple hierarchy and allows no validation. If you don't need validated XML, you may not need structure. However, this chapter deals with using structure and producing valid XML, so validation is important for this discussion.
- Before you begin to work with XML, make sure you are in the Structured Framemaker interface, not in regular FrameMaker. Select **File > Preferences > General** and ensure that, on the Product Interface pop-up, **Structured FrameMaker** is selected.
- If you are unfamiliar with structured documents or structured document authoring, refer to Chapters 2 and 4 in this book.

Creating Your Application

In this section you will create an Application and learn how to "point" to your template and other useful files, like the DTD and read/write rules.

To adjust our import (Open) and export (Save As) options, we need to create an XML Application for our documents.

An XML Application is not as mysterious or complex as it may sound. It is a document setup that you create and name. You then insert information about where pertinent files—such as your DTD or template—are located so that FrameMaker can find them.

You can create multiple Applications for each particular document type or for all documents that use a specific template. Then, you can use your Application—when the dialog box appears—by selecting its name when importing and exporting XML.

Note: *You may also assign an Application to your files before exporting to XML. To do this, select* ***File > Set Structured Application*** *and select the appropriate Application from the pop-up list. Having this set for each file will save you the trouble of selecting it from the pop-up every time you export. (When importing, the XML document will "remember" the Application and automatically use it.)*

For a FrameMaker user, creating an Application is really no more difficult than creating a FrameMaker book! You just need to know where your files are, insert the paths to them, and then tell FrameMaker the Application exists. These steps are illustrated later in this section.

Reviewing the Installed Applications

To view the Applications installed with FrameMaker, select **File > Structure Tools > Edit Application Definitions**. The file *structapps.fm* appears, as shown in Figure 3-6. There is much to see in this file. You might want to open it in your FrameMaker "live" to get a better view than Figure 3-6 can provide.

Notice that the Application shown in Figure 3-6 is DocBook, one of the Applications that is installed with FrameMaker (except on UNIX).

Note: *DocBook is a set of elements designed for publishing software and hardware manuals in SGML or XML. Several DocBook applications are installed with FrameMaker 7, and xDocBook is the version designed with XML in mind. DocBook and xDocBook are not specific to FrameMaker, and they are maintained by organizations outside of Adobe.*

As mentioned before, the Application is a list of files and their pathnames. Notice these in Figure 3-6.

Note: *Depending on the types of documents you are publishing, and your requirements, you may be able to use one of the Applications that is installed with FrameMaker—such as DocBook. You should try to determine this before spending time creating a custom Application.*

You can create your own Applications by inserting the appropriate elements (DTD, template, stylesheet, and so on) in the Application Definition Document and then adding the path to your files. The paths may be anywhere, including on a network, although it may be easier if you drop the

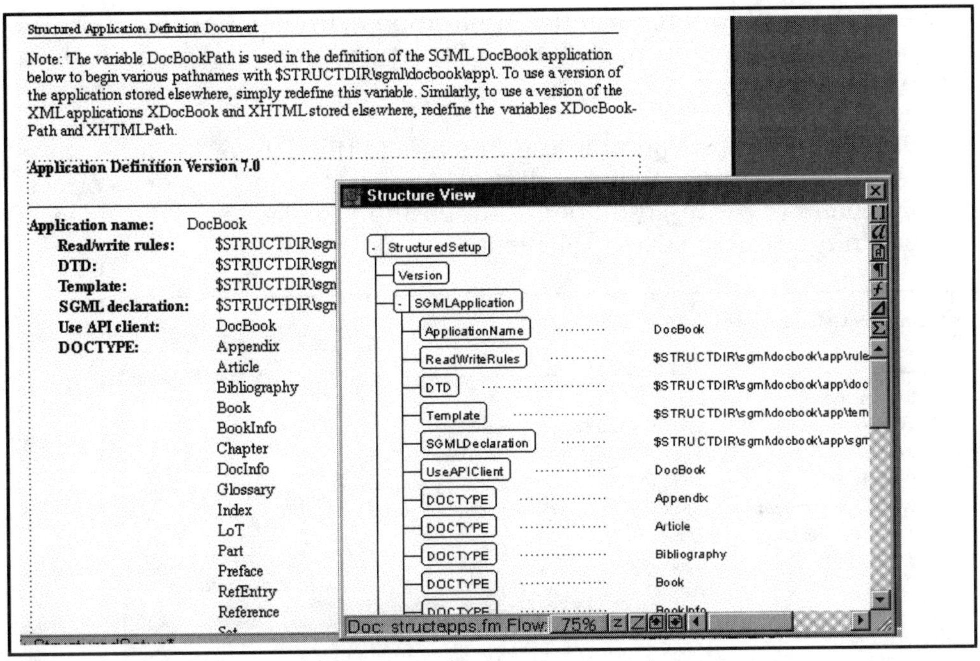

Figure 3-6 The structured Application definition document.

files into the *structure* folder within FrameMaker's install directory and then use paths similar to the DocBook paths.

The steps in the next section discuss the creation of a simple Application. While some steps include details on accessing the needed files, there are no directions in this chapter for creating the template or DTD. When creating your own Application, you need to use your own files, such as your template, sample chapters, XML samples, read/write rules, and so forth.

Note: You can find some sample files on this book's website *(www.technicalpublishing/AdvFrame/)*, or you can request some from the author (*kethier@travelthepath.com*).

Starting an Application

When you import your XML without using a template, FrameMaker displays it pretty much "as is." Since XML contains no formatting, the results in FrameMaker are also unformatted. Because FrameMaker is a layout and formatting tool, you may apply formatting by telling FrameMaker to use your templates as XML documents are opened. You do this by creating an Application pointing to your template and then selecting this Application as you import the XML.

The following steps walk you through creating an Application called *simpledoc* that points to a template file.

To create the Application, open the Application definition document. If you do not already have it open, click **File > Structure Tools > Edit Application Definitions** to open it.

1. Place your insertion point in the structure to the right of the line descending from the StructuredSetup element. Figure 3-7 shows correct placement of the insertion point—in position to place a child element within the StructuredSetup element.

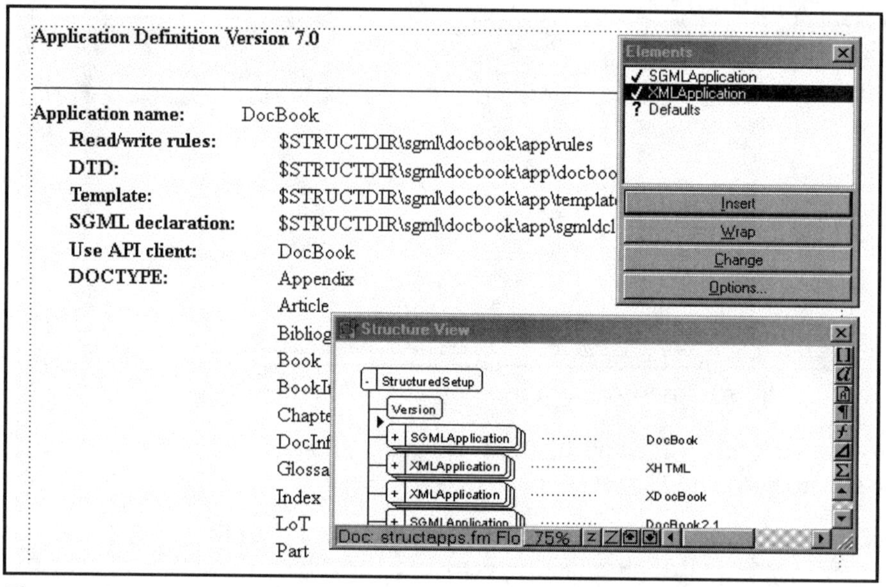

Figure 3-7 Application definition file with insertion point showing.

2. Select the **XMLApplication** element and click **Insert**. The XMLApplication element and child ApplicationName element appear.

3. Type the name *simpledoc* for your new Application, as shown in Figure 3-8.

4. Move your insertion point to just below your ApplicationName element and keep the file open.

Before continuing, make a place for the Application's files. Create a folder under the *structure* folder for your Application files for *simpledoc*. Note that placing your files in that location is easier, since you can then copy the file paths from FrameMaker's existing Applications and use them for yours.

Put your template in the folder that you create within FrameMaker's structure folder, noting the complete path. You will then include this path when you add files to your FrameMaker Application Definition file. Figure 3-9 shows the creation of a folder.

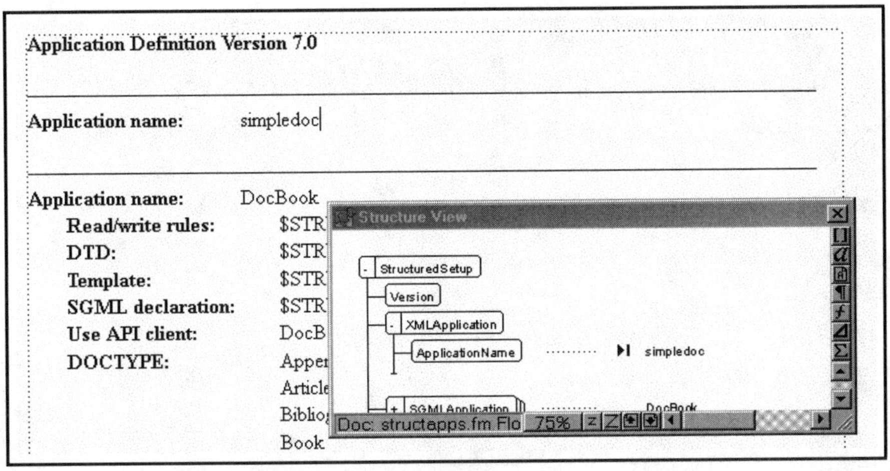

Figure 3-8 Adding the *simpledoc* Application.

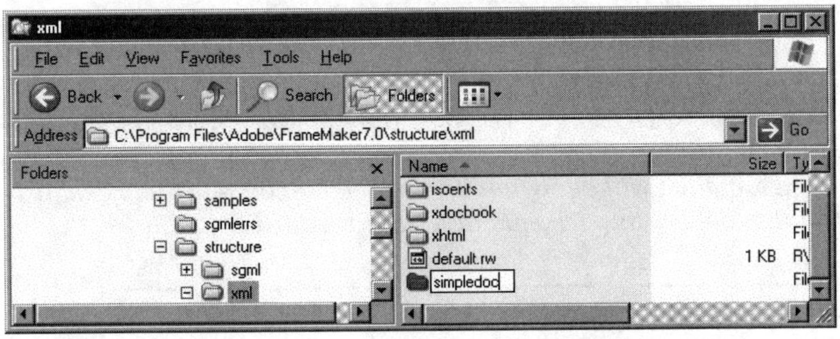

Figure 3-9 Creating the Application's folder.

Copy your template, DTD, and any other appropriate files into the new folder, and be sure to note their filenames (see Figure 3-10).

Accessing a Template

Now return to FrameMaker and, in the file *structapps.fm*, point to your template as follows:

1. With your insertion point still below ApplicationName, select the **Template** element and **Insert**.
2. Type the file path or use a variable containing the path (as used in the out-of-the-box Applications) and include the template filename. In this example, the template is *sdtemplate.fm*, as shown (circled) in Figure 3-11.
3. **Save** the file *structapps.fm*.

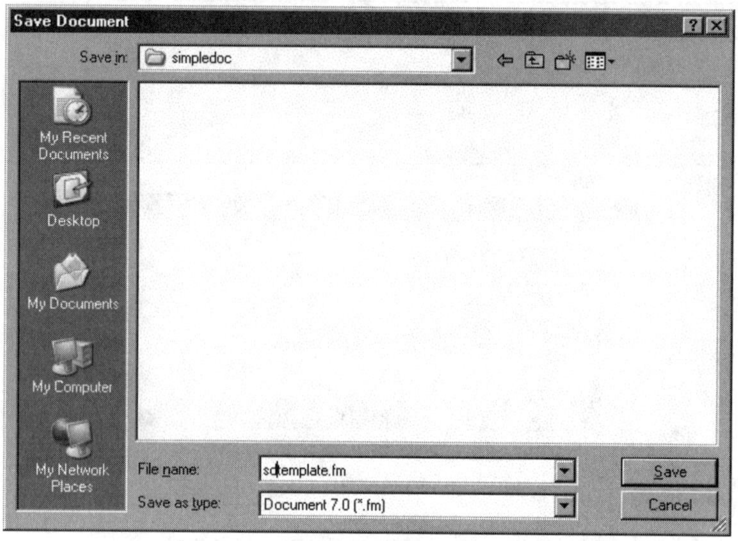

Figure 3-10 Saving the template in the Application folder.

Note: *Even though your EDD is not needed by the Application, you might also put your EDD in this folder to keep everything together. That way, the structured template will be right with the EDD if you must make adjustments and reimport the elements into the structured template.*

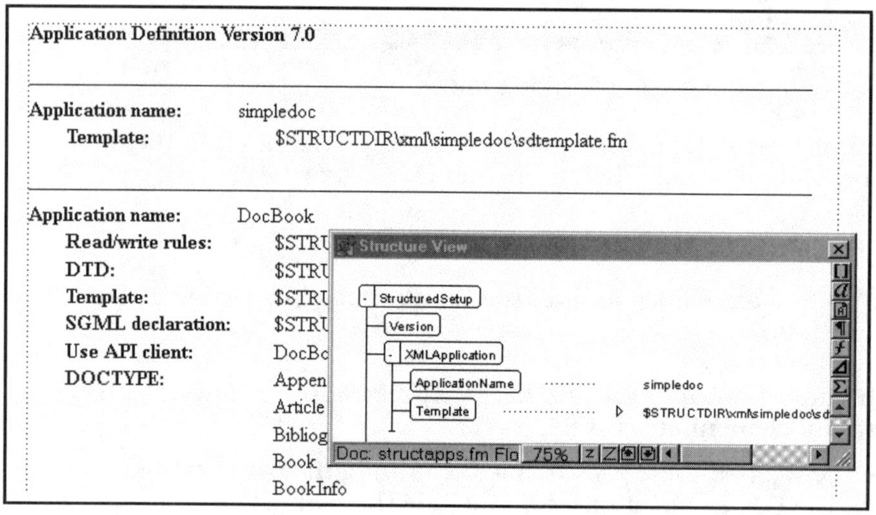

Figure 3-11 Adding template location to an Application definition.

4. Select **File** > **Structure Tools** > **Read Application Definitions.**

Note: *Any time that you adjust the Application definitions file, you must reread it so FrameMaker has a chance to review the adjustments.*

5. After FrameMaker has read (or, more precisely, reread) the Application definitions, close *structapps.fm.*

Open your XML document without an Application to review FrameMaker's out-of-the-box behavior. The results are unformatted, as shown in Figure 3-12.

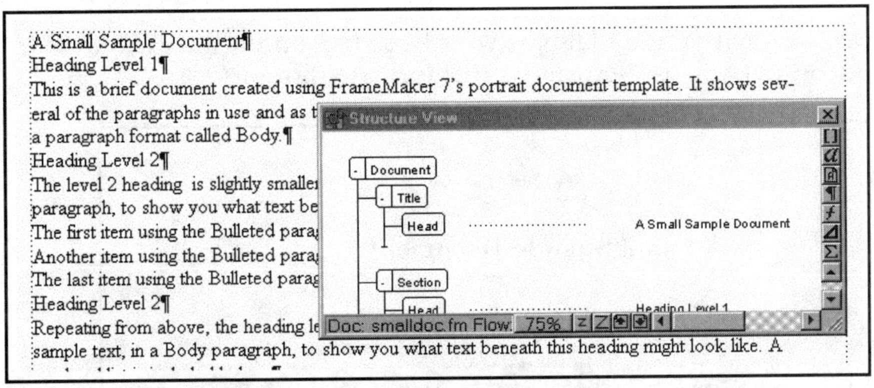

Figure 3-12 XML opened in FrameMaker without an Application.

Now follow the steps below to open your XML document and—from the Use Structured Application dialog box that appears—select the Application you just created, *simpledoc*, so that FrameMaker accesses the template *sdtemplate.fm*. FrameMaker can access this file because you put the template's file path in the structured Application file, *structapps.fm*.

1. Select **File** > **Open** and browse to get your XML document (in this case, *simpledoc.xml*).
2. When prompted, select the ***simpledoc*** Application from the list, as shown in Figure 3-13.

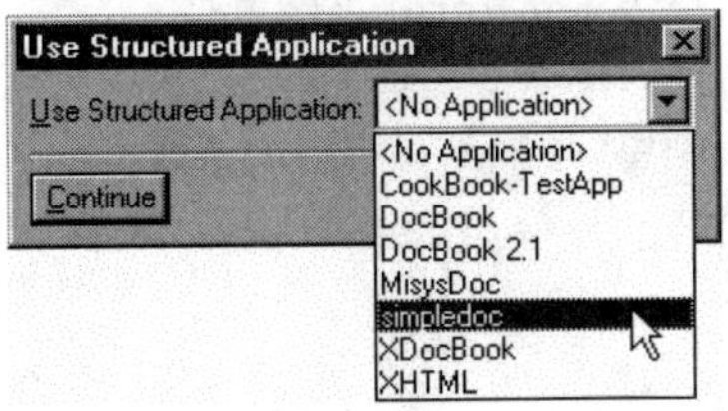

Figure 3-13 Selecting an Application.

3. Click **Continue.**

Note: *Because the Application only has the template in it right now, you will probably get an error message stating that the DTD is not available for validation. Figure 3-14 shows this error.*

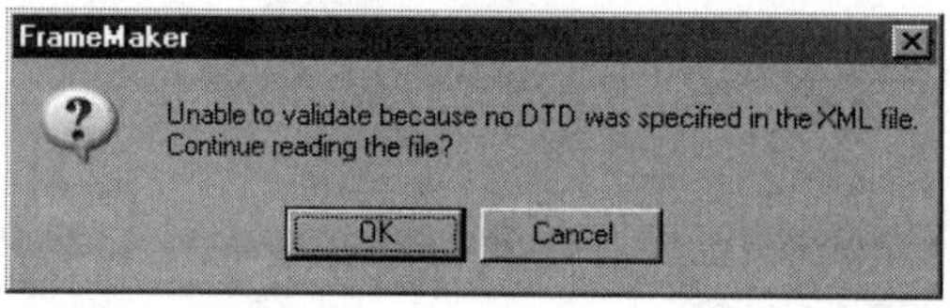

Figure 3-14 Dialog box showing error regarding DTD.

You will see a formatted file that uses your XML tags and displays your XML document content. Figure 3-15 shows this formatted result.

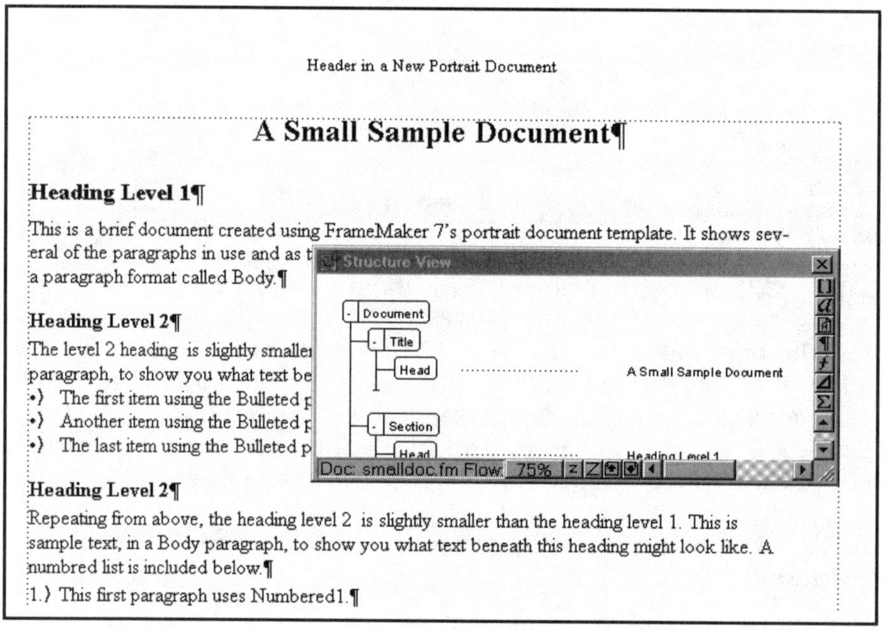

Figure 3-15 XML opened in FrameMaker using the *simpledoc* Application.

Because the Application points to the template, and the template includes page layout data, text styles, and information on which styles to use with each XML tag, the structured document is formatted just as it was originally shown in Figure 3-1. Pretty cool, don't you think?

Please note that if your template path is incorrect in the Application, you may get an error message such as the one shown in Figure 3-16. If such an error appears, check your file path and filenames.

Note: *The sample error message shown was forced to occur by editing the file structapps.fm and adding a "1" to the template's name—making it not match the template's filename. This shows a mismatch between the template filename and the structapps.fm pointer.*

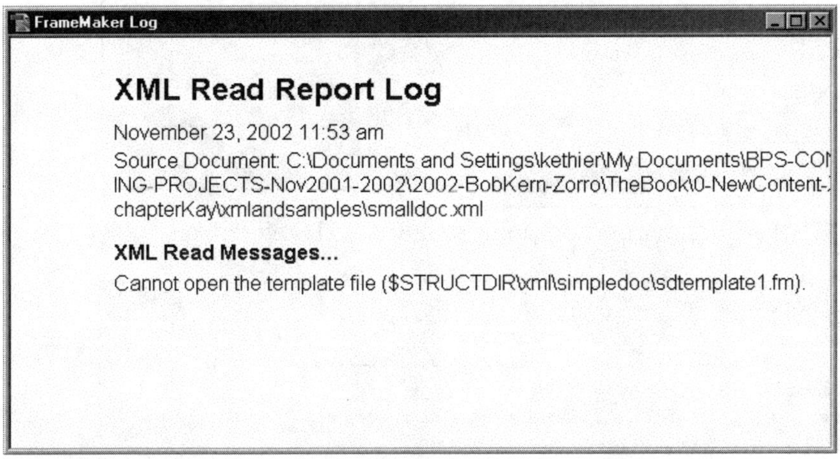

Figure 3-16 Error log caused by typo in template file path.

Accessing a DTD for Validation

The error message shown in Figure 3-14 mentions that a DTD is not available for this Application. To allow validation of your XML, make sure that you copy your DTD into the directory with your template (as discussed earlier in this chapter). You can then add the DTD pathname to your Application as follows:

1. Click in the structure of the file *structapps.fm* just below the template element. Figure 3-17 demonstrates correct insertion point placement.
2. **Insert** the DTD element from the catalog. Figure 3-18 shows the DTD element in place.
3. Type the pathname to the DTD in the directory you made—much like you did in the previous section for your template. The adjusted Application might look like that shown in Figure 3-19.
4. **Save** the file *structapps.fm*.
5. Select **File** > **Structure Tools** > **Read Application Definitions**.
6. **Close** *structapps.fm*.

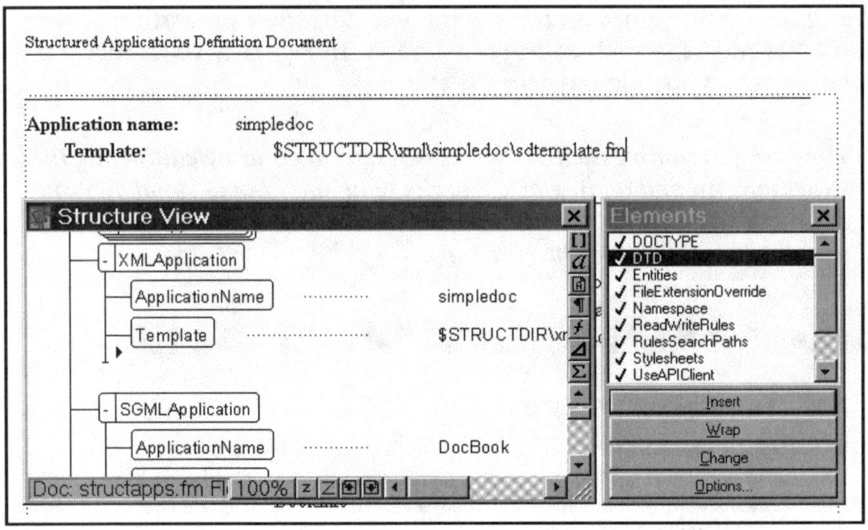

Figure 3-17 Placing an insertion point to add a DTD reference.

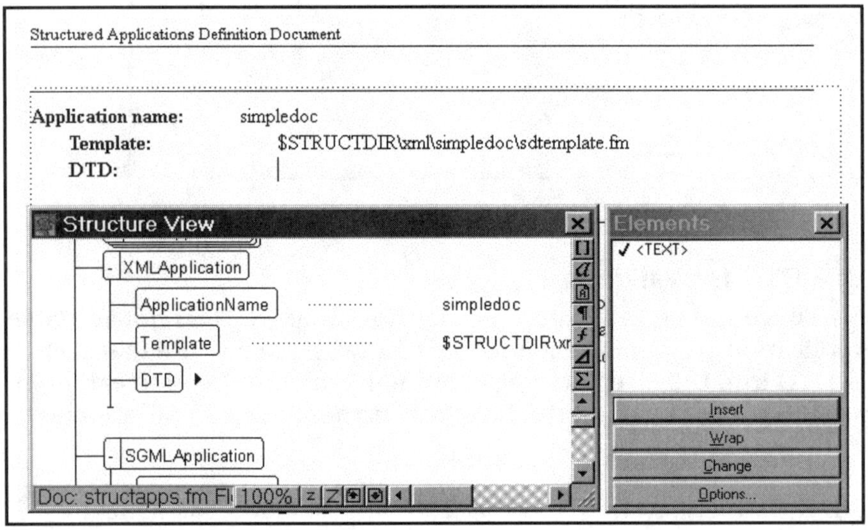

Figure 3-18 Adding the DTD element to the Application.

Now open the document again using the *simpledoc* Application; the DTD error message should not appear. If there are any validation errors, they will appear in a log file similar to the error log shown in Figure 3-16. If a log appears, check that your DTD pathname and filename are correct.)

Adding Read/Write Rules

In this section several examples are given of items that might require adjustment when XML is opened in (imported into) FrameMaker. Some common uses for read/write rules are:

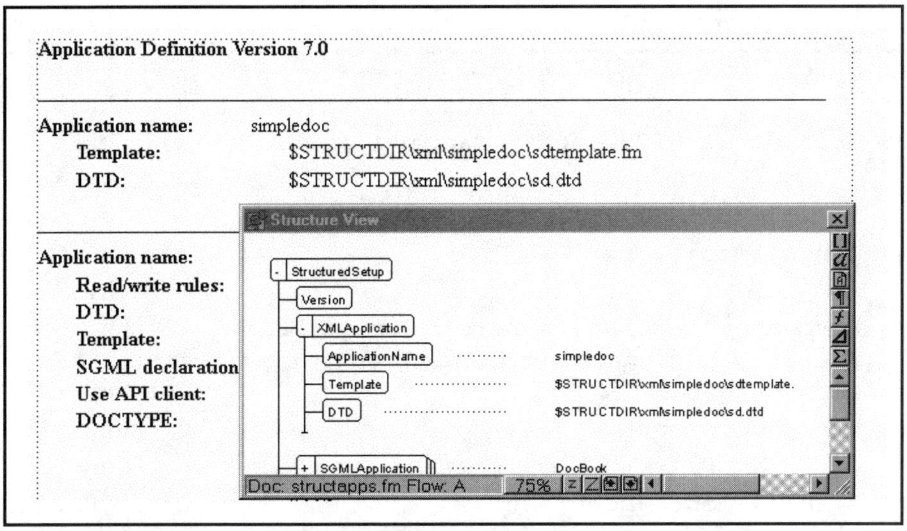

Figure 3-19 Application with DTD element and DTD file path.

- Identifying an element as a specific type of FrameMaker element (such as a TableTitle or CrossReference)

Note: *Other object types are listed in Chapter 4.*

- Adjusting an element name (such as changing chaptitle to ChapterTitle), allowing you to take advantage of FrameMaker's ability to use long element names and include spaces in names
- Mapping your XML entities to FrameMaker element types
- Dropping an element or attribute not needed or desired in FrameMaker

Read/write rules are used as XML is "read" into FrameMaker and as XML is "written" out of FrameMaker. Many rules are bidirectional—used for both exporting and importing.

Before adding the link to a read/write rules file, look at a simple rule. The read/write rules file in Table 3-1 has only one rule, which is to change an element name:

Lines 1 through 7 appear automatically when you create read/write rules. Lines 8 through 10 are a comment, which is an optional but helpful addition if you plan to have extensive rules.

The rule to change the element is shown on Lines 11 through 14. This rule says that an XML element called *document* should change its name to *Document* when the element is imported ("read") into FrameMaker. If instead

Table 3-1 Simple Rule Table

/*fm version is "7.1";	Line 1
/*	Line 2
* Include all ISO entity mapping rules.	Line 3
*/	Line 4
	Line 5
#include "isoall.rw"	Line 6
	Line 7
/* Element rules. Rules herein capitalize	Line 8
letters other than the initial one or perform	Line 9
name changes.*/	Line 10
element "document"	Line 11
{	Line 12
is fm element "Document";	Line 13
}	Line 14
/*	Line 15

you "write" by performing a Save As XML, the rule goes in reverse, and the FrameMaker element *Document* will be renamed to *document.*

> **Note:** *Element names and case need to match those in the element definitions. This means that names for the XML elements should match the DTD, and names for the fm elements should match the EDD.*

If you have a read/write rules file, make sure it is in the same directory as your template and DTD, then add the pointer to your Application:

1. Click in the structure of the file *structapps.fm* just below the DTD element, as shown in Figure 3-20.
2. **Insert** the ReadWriteRules element from the catalog. Figure 3-21 shown the Application Definition file structure after insertion of the ReadWriteRules element.
3. Type the pathname to the read/write rules in the directory you made—much like you did in the previous section for your DTD. Figure 3-22 shows a sample file path.
4. **Save** the file *structapps.fm.*
5. Select **File** > **Structure Tools** > **Read Application Definitions**.
6. **Close** *structapps.fm.*

Now that the read/write rules are added, you will see the name change if you perform a round trip. If you open the simple structured document shown in Figure 3-15 and save it as XML using the Application, you will end up with

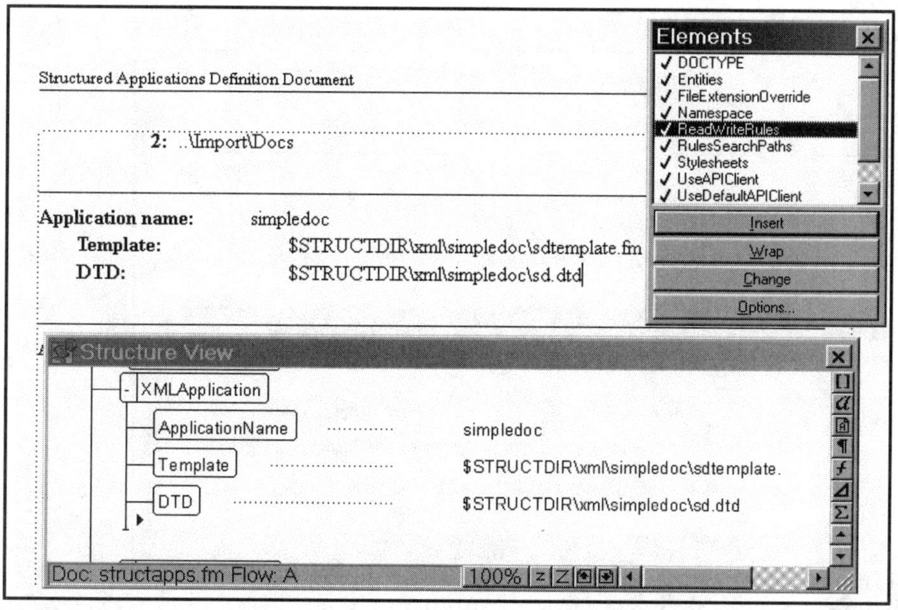

Figure 3-20 Placing an insertion point for addition of the ReadWriteRules element.

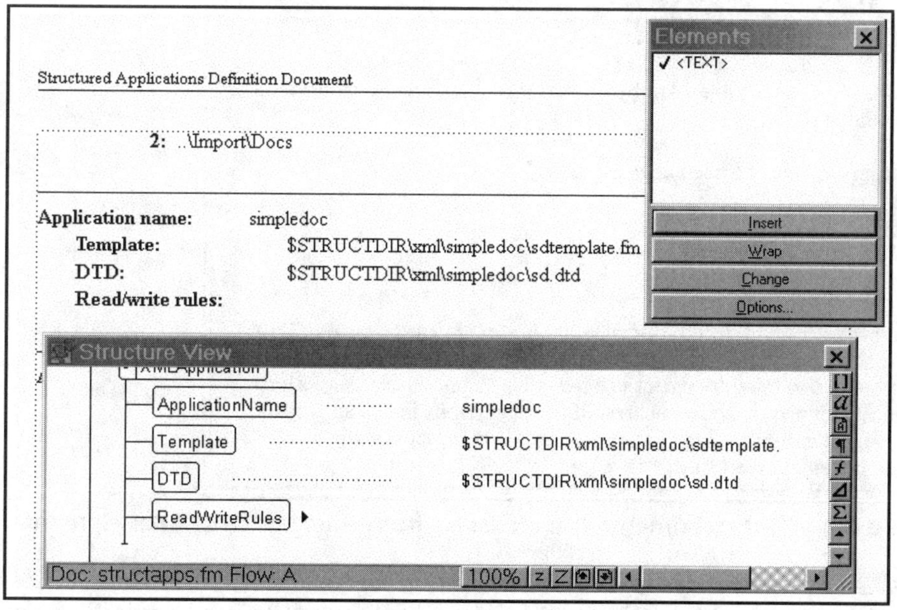

Figure 3-21 Application with ReadWriteRules element in place.

XML containing the name change (lowercase "d" in document). Figure 3-23 shows this XML document.

Please note that you may get an error log if the resulting element names do not match your DTD or EDD.

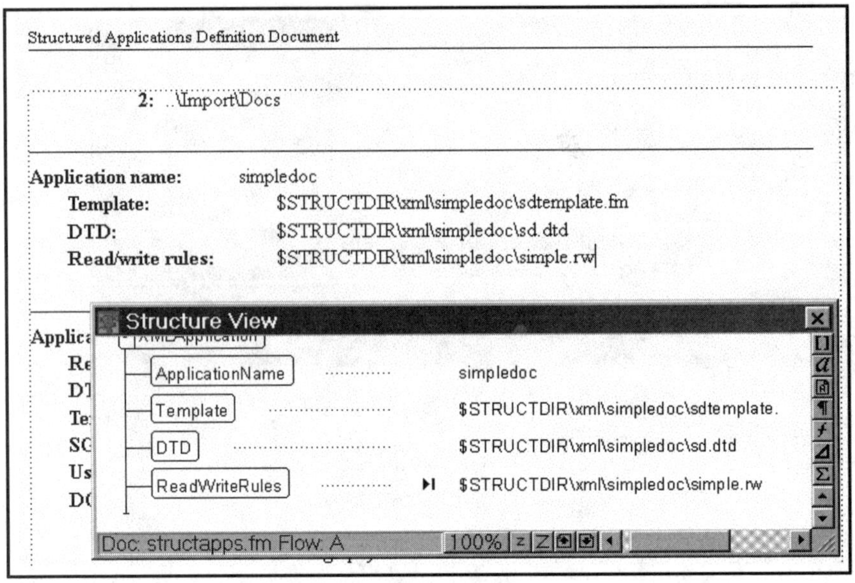

Figure 3-22 ReadWriteRules element with file path.

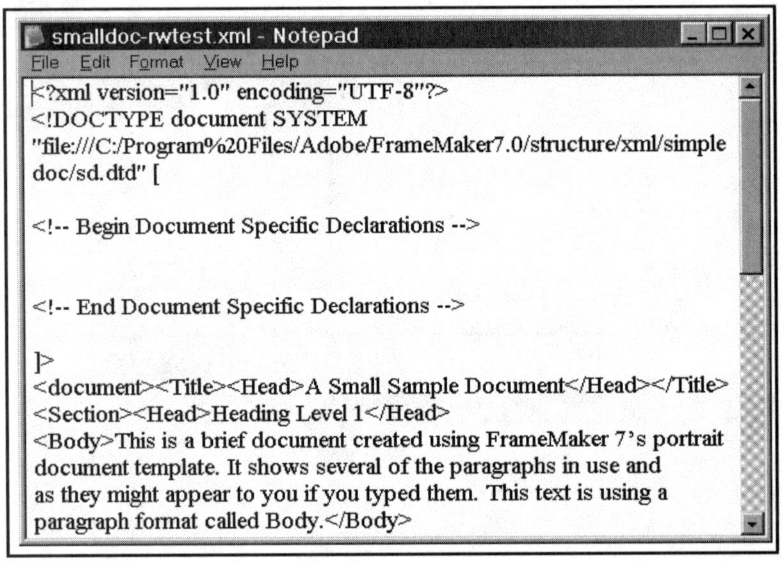

Figure 3-23 XML document with a change from the ReadWriteRules element.

Examples of read/write rules are in *The XML Cookbook*, a resource that is installed with FrameMaker 7. *The XML Cookbook* is well over a hundred pages of material that includes steps for setting up an Application, writing read/write rules, and more. It may be a good next step—for your round-trip learning—to complete *The XML Cookbook*.

You can find more examples of read/write rules in the FrameMaker folder, inside a *structure* subfolder. Details and examples are also included in the

OnlineManuals folder in a PDF called *Structure_Dev_Guide.pdf*, which serves as a reference for structure designers.

Other Application Components

In addition to your template and DTD, you may insert paths to many other files or settings such as the DocType. Figure 3-24 shows the elements available.

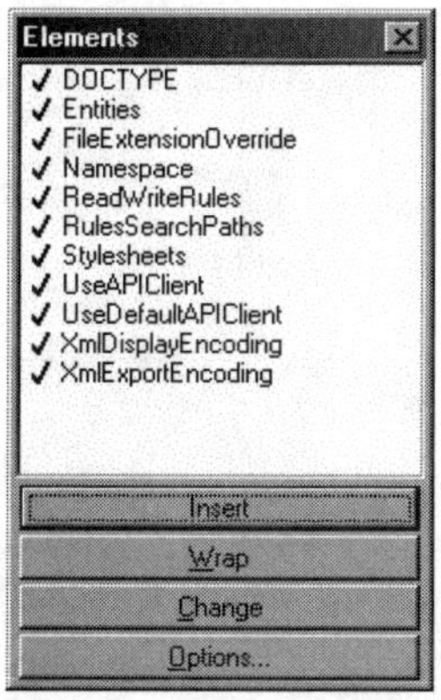

Figure 3-24 Other elements used in Applications.

This particular chapter does not deal with all of the Application components available.

Summary

FrameMaker 7 imports and exports XML. While the importing and exporting themselves are easy—and produce real, non-proprietary XML— adjustments sometimes need to be made in order to take full advantage of FrameMaker's powerful formatting capabilities. A round-trip Application may be set up to allow you to publish fully-formatted documents and still produce XML for use by others.

Once your round-trip Application has been set up, you have all of FrameMaker's strengths at your disposal and are able to work with your XML. Regardless of its source—created in Notepad, exported from another program, or drawn from a database—the XML for your document types will work within your XML Applications.

4

Developing Structured Documents

Bernard Aschwanden

This chapter takes a look at development of structure within FrameMaker. Element Definition Documents and syntax are explored.

Applicable to FrameMaker 7.0/7.1 and FrameMaker+SGML

Overview of Structured Development

Structured FrameMaker has features that allow developers to create structured templates. An author can use a structured template to create content that can be exported to and imported from SGML or XML. Structured documents provide the benefit of enabling you to write without focusing on format. A variety of documents must be developed, however, before you can take advantage of import and export features.

This chapter is focused on the development of the Element Definition Document (EDD) and does not directly address procedures related to the import and export of content. It is primarily designed to guide you through the development of a structured document. It is strongly recommended that the chapter related to authoring and using structured documents be read first (see Chapter 3).

While some of the techniques discussed in this chapter may be used for FrameMaker+SGML, please keep in mind that some of the specific code referred to in this chapter does not apply in the exact same way in all product versions. Refer to the Developers Guide (found in the FrameMaker installation folder in Online Manuals) for specific information related to developing EDD documents in versions other than FrameMaker 7.

Required Files for Structured Development

The minimum requirements for developing a structured template are the EDD and a design template.

EDD

The EDD is a structured document that contains rules related to elements, definitions of attributes, and formatting instructions. It is similar to a Document Type Definition (DTD) but includes formatting and other FrameMaker-specific instructions.

Design Template

A design template is a FrameMaker document containing formatting information for page layouts, paragraphs, characters, tables, and other data into which structure is imported from an external document—such as the EDD. Once imported and tested, the template is made available to those who are creating structured content. The structured content is validated and then can be exported to SGML or XML if supporting files are also developed.

Creating an Initial EDD

There are four primary ways to create an EDD. Depending on the circumstances in which you are developing a structured document, any one of them may be used. No one method is the "correct" way; however, it is important to consider the rationale for creating a structured document when deciding which approach to take. The following list introduces the four primary methods of creating an EDD:

- By developing a new file from a blank EDD
- By exporting the structural rules of existing structured documents

  When an EDD file does not exist, but a document based on that EDD does, that file can be exported and made into a new EDD. This allows the Element Catalog of a file to act as the basis for an EDD that can then be modified and reimported or saved for other purposes.
- By converting any valid, existing DTD to an EDD. This is often done if an EDD is to be developed to comply with a predefined DTD to ensure compliance with an industry standard. (For example, in the military, aerospace, and publishing fields document types often already exist.)
- By opening an EDD that already exists, saving it with a new name, and then modifying the file

  Reusing an existing EDD allows the structure and formatting already in place to act as a guideline for a similar document. This can reduce the development time and cost for related files. For example, DocBook is a very common DTD and EDD in the publishing field. Not all organizations benefit from all the elements, however, so customizing it can help create a new EDD from an existing standard.

Note: *An EDD that needs to be created often does not have a corresponding set of predefined rules; it may require document analysis followed by careful planning of the EDD.*

Creating a New EDD

To create a new, blank EDD, select **New EDD** from the **Structure Tools** option under the File menu. A new EDD is created with default content, as shown in Figure 4-1.

Creating an EDD from an Existing Structured File

If you are creating an EDD from an existing document, the EDD may need to be reorganized, edited, commented, and more. To create an EDD from an existing document, open the structured file to act as the basis of the EDD. Then select **File > Structure Tools > Export Element Catalog as EDD**. The structure of the document is exported and creates a new EDD file, as shown in Figure 4-2.

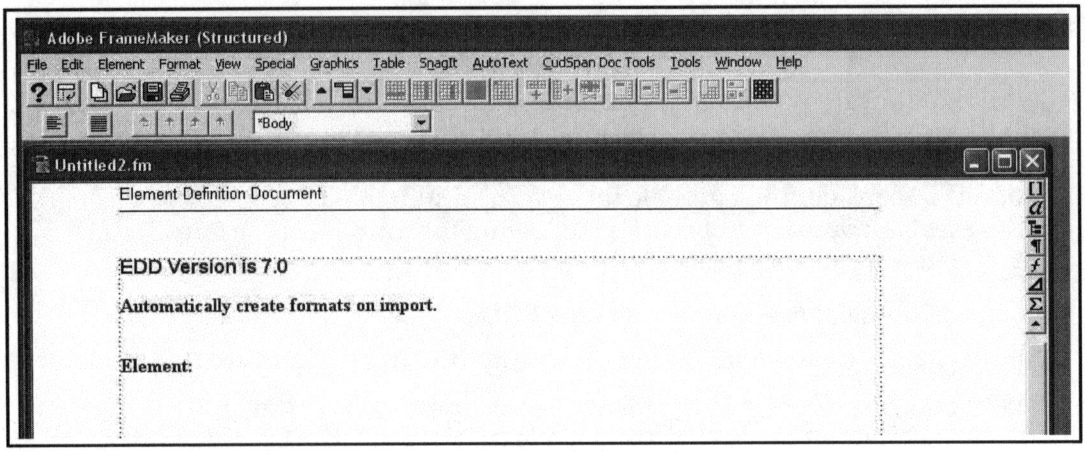

Figure 4-1 Sample blank EDD.

Creating an EDD by Importing Existing SGML or XML DTDs

Existing DTDs (either SGML- or XML-based) can be imported as a source for a new EDD. Consider the following examples in which a very simple SGML-based DTD and a very simple XML-based DTD are shown.

The SGML-based DTD and its corresponding EDD are shown here in code format and in Figure 4-3.

```
<!--DTD for Chapter. Typically invoked by
      <!DOCTYPE Chapter  SYSTEM
    "C:\sgml_chapter_dtd">
-->
<!ELEMENT Chapter     - -  (Section, Section+) >
<!ELEMENT Section     - -  (Head, Para+) >
<!ELEMENT Head        - -  (#PCDATA) >
<!ELEMENT Para        - -  (#PCDATA) >
```

The XML-based DTD and its corresponding EDD are shown here in code format and in Figure 4-4.

```
<?xml version="1.0" encoding="UTF-8"?>
<!--DTD for Chapter. Typically invoked by
      <!DOCTYPE Chapter  SYSTEM
    "C:\xml_chapter_dtd">
-->
<!ELEMENT Chapter     (Section, Section+) >
<!ELEMENT Section     (Head, Para+) >
<!ELEMENT Head        (#PCDATA) >
<!ELEMENT Para        (#PCDATA) >\
```

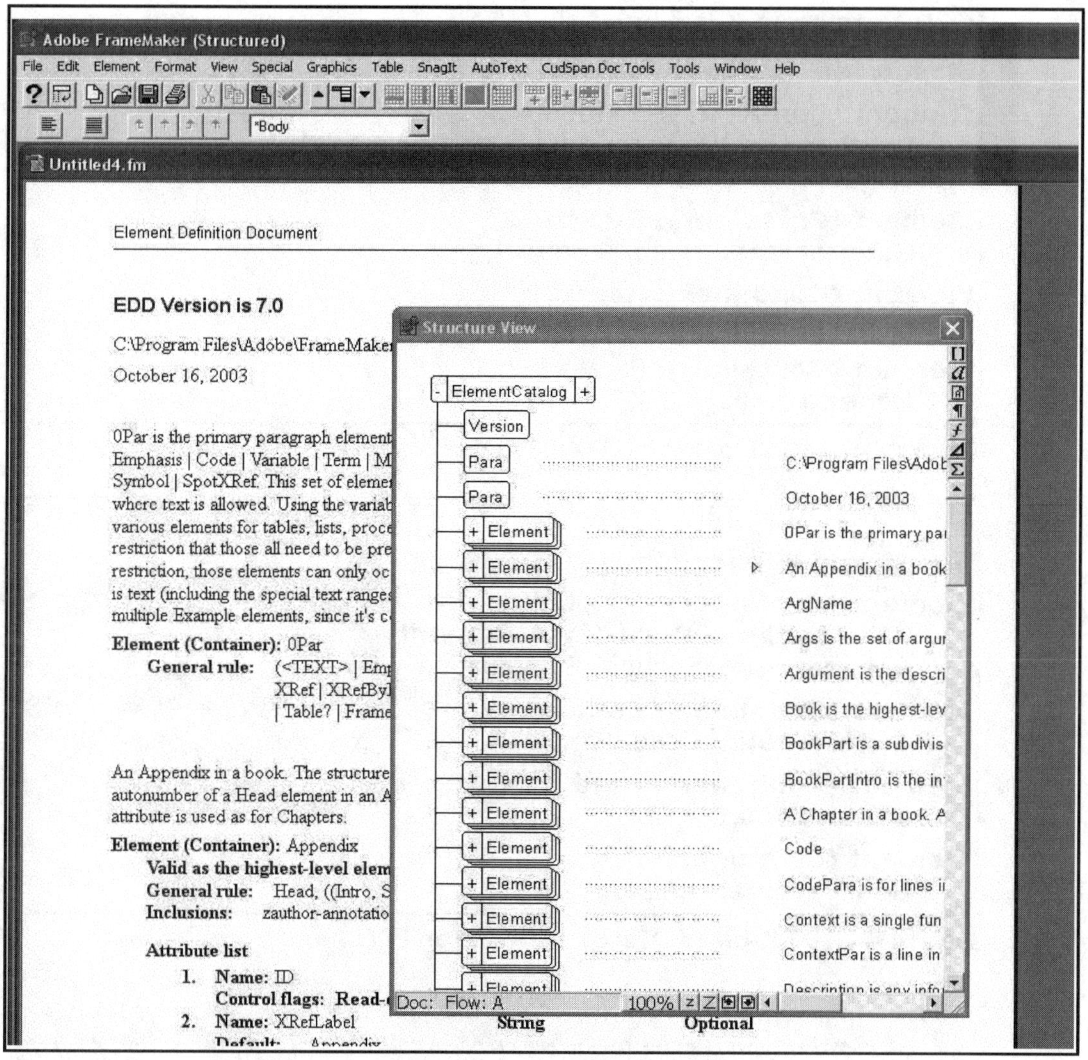

Figure 4-2 Sample EDD exported from structured file.

Either of these sample DTDs can be opened and converted to an EDD. Because they are simple documents with minimal content, they convert without any errors.

To convert a DTD to an EDD, select **File** > **Structure Tools** > **Open DTD** and select the DTD to open from the dialog box. Once you click **Open**, the Use Structured Application dialog box appears, as shown in Figure 4-5.

If there is a predefined Application that should be used, select it and click **Continue**. If there is no Application, simply click **Continue**. The likelihood of errors using this method is high, however. After selecting the Application, you are then prompted to specify whether the DTD is an SGML- or an XML-based DTD, as shown in Figure 4-6.

EDD Version is 7.0

Structured Application:

Element (Container): Chapter
    Valid as the highest-level element.
    General rule: Section, Section+

Element (Container): Section
    General rule: Head, Para+

Element (Container): Head
    General rule: <TEXT>

Element (Container): Para
    General rule: <TEXT>

Figure 4-3 SGML-based DTD converted to an EDD.

EDD Version is 7.0

Structured Application:

Element (Container): Chapter
    Valid as the highest-level element.
    General rule: Section, Section+

Element (Container): Section
    General rule: Head, Para+

Element (Container): Head
    General rule: <TEXT>

Element (Container): Para
    General rule: <TEXT>

Figure 4-4 XML-based DTD converted to an EDD.

Note: *If an error log is generated, you need to examine it and the DTD. Several methods exist to correct errors, including editing the source DTD, modifying the code that is being imported, or creating read/write rules. The most common solution is to develop read/write rules for translation from a DTD (for either SGML or XML) to an EDD. With this solution, you must develop an Application in FrameMaker that references the supporting files.*

Figure 4-5 Use Structured Application dialog box.

Note: *If no Application exists, it may be necessary to create a new Application to facilitate the import. The Application file is basically a collection of paths to the files used to support the conversion of content to or from a structured FrameMaker document. Opening a DTD for conversion does result in errors in many cases and will require read/write rules. No harm is done, however, when a DTD is opened without rules. Simply use the error log as a basis for developing the rules that are required. (The error log assists in converting files between FrameMaker and their structured formats.)*

Figure 4-6 Select Type dialog box for SGML or XML DTDs.

Select either **SGML** or **XML** and click **OK**. If an error log appears (see example in Figure 4-7), review it and develop related supporting documents or make changes to the DTD to eliminate the errors.

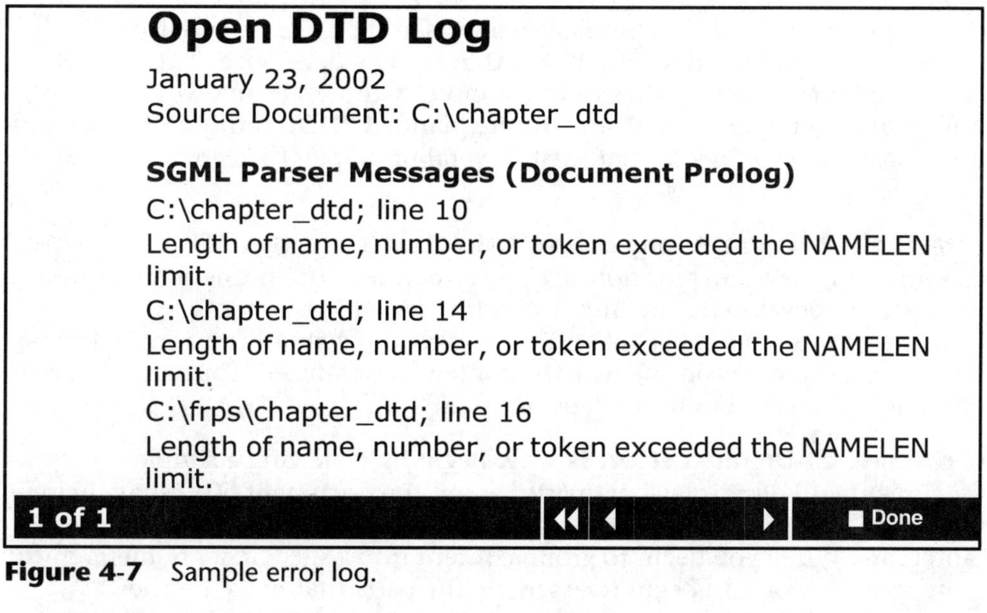

Figure 4-7 Sample error log.

Creating an EDD by Duplicating Existing EDDs

An existing EDD can be opened, saved with a new name, and modified to create a new EDD. The new document should be renamed and may require extensive editing. Open the existing EDD and select **File > Save As**. Name the EDD and edit the new document as required.

Basic EDD Development

While creating an EDD is a formidable task, the task can be broken down into several basic steps. This section addresses some of those steps and offers some background on them.

Development Workflow

When you develop an EDD (regardless of whether you create it as a new file, export it from an existing structured document, import it from a DTD, or duplicate it), you should follow several procedures:

- Add or modify elements in an EDD.
- Import and test the EDD.
- Find errors. (It happens to the best of us.)
- Repeat the process until all errors are resolved.

Once the EDD and the associated design template work correctly, the template may be delivered to the users of the file and the EDD can be exported to a DTD, if necessary.

General Document Analysis Principles

Before beginning any development work on an EDD, make sure that you really understand the document type that is to be developed. This means spending time reviewing dozens of (or more) samples. It involves reviewing files that may not even be related to the planned EDD, simply to understand the documentation needs that exist. Several principles to keep in mind are discussed below.

Principle 1: Formatting doesn't matter. The biggest hurdle to surpass is formatting. It counts for nothing in a structured environment (at least, not in regard to developing the initial structure for the document to follow). *Formatting doesn't matter.* That's all there is to know about this for the time being. Instead, focus on the way the content is organized. Formatting may offer a clue to this, but don't depend on it.

Principle 2: Organization is key. Begin by reviewing a simple document and deciding what "parts" are in the document. This may include a section, a list, a table, images and captions, a set of questions and answers, and more. When you begin to group content into a specific set of hierarchical components, you can begin to assemble the parts that make up the document. Many of these parts have their own children, and they, in turn, may have children as well. (For example, a list is a collection of multiple items, and each item may be a collection of paragraphs that in turn are a collection of text, character tags, and cross references.)

Principle 3: Frequency. Identify not only the elements, but also the frequency of them. This is the basis of an EDD document.

Principle 4: Identify what is missing. You also need to identify what is missing. Begin to look at more-complex documents to identify elements that are not in the current document, and then begin to add them to your catalog of parts. Start to identify what can be marked up as a unique structural element and what can be identified as a shared component that is unique based on an attribute setting. For example, lists may be bulleted, dashed, or numbered, but they are still lists. Therefore, a single element (in this case, the "list") may actually serve numerous purposes with the use of an attribute.

Principle 5: Analysis is group work. The analysis cannot (generally) be done by a single person. The feedback of a department or a team is usually required. Anyone who is involved in the document life cycle may need to be interviewed and have their input evaluated. People familiar with the documents need to be involved, even if there is a professional doing the document analysis. The workflow of a group (and the individuals in it) is important to the development of the EDD.

Principle 6: Content should be representational. Content that is reviewed should be, of course, representational of the entire body of work, but don't spend too much time on any one file. Instead you should share the documents and identify their content and its purpose. To best develop a functional EDD, you may need to discard some older concepts and content in favor of a more structured approach to writing.

Principle 7: Look at extra documents. It is also important to consider materials that are not a default part of the documents you deliver. These may include a corporate style guide, existing templates, or even feedback from developers, engineers, customers, managers, and more. In many cases, structural rules exist but there is no clearly defined way to validate them or enforce them. A combination of additional manual steps may also exist to ensure compliance. The review of content and procedures may also further identify structural rules that did not get clearly identified earlier.

Principle 8: Consider future needs. Consider the future needs you have for the documents as well. Is the material going to be required in other documents? Should you chunk the information into logical pieces that can then be extracted and reused? Have you explored the opportunities that may exist down the road with structured authoring?

Principle 9: Structure from the highest level down. Finally, try to structure content from the highest level down. It is often easier to identify a document and then begin to segment the parts of it than it is to try and construct a document from its parts. Develop the structure from the general to the specific until as many elements are uniquely identified as possible.

Element Types in an EDD

An EDD has its own structure, with its own main elements and other elements that are used to create the structure for your documents (the "element definitions" part of the EDD). These elements are discussed in the following sections.

Initial EDD Elements

There are a variety of elements inserted by default when a new EDD is created, as shown in Figure 4-8. This section describes these elements.

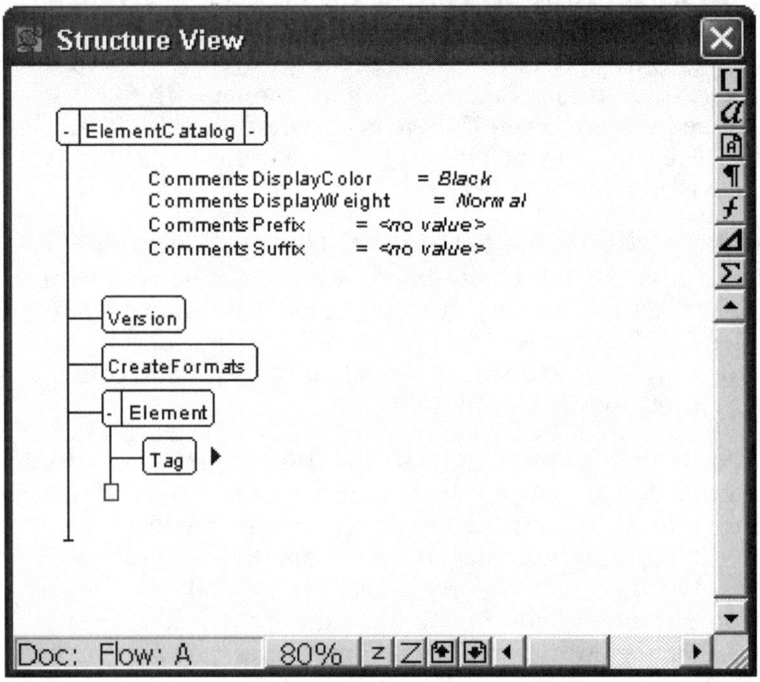

Figure 4-8 The beginning of an EDD.

Note: *If an EDD is created from existing structured documents or existing DTDs, the default element may differ from that shown in Figure 4-8.*

ElementCatalog

ElementCatalog, the highest-level element, defines the document as an EDD. This element should never be modified in any way.

There are four default attributes that define comments (which help to clearly identify data that is in the EDD). You can apply different formatting to comments in the EDD by changing the attribute values:

- *CommentsDisplayColor* changes the appearance of comment color to be blue, black (the default), or red.
- *CommentsDisplayWeight* allows comments to be displayed as normal (default) or bold.
- *CommentsPrefix* places specified characters before comments.
- *CommentsSuffix* places specified characters after comments.

Version

Version elements define the FrameMaker version used to create the EDD. This element can be replaced (but not altered) if an EDD is updated to a new version of FrameMaker.

CreateFormats and DoNotCreateFormats

Of these two elements, CreateFormats is the default. The default is to allow a template to be automatically populated by formats. The DoNotCreateFormats option requires formats to be created manually.

If, for example, an element named Head has a paragraph format assigned to it named SectionHeading, FrameMaker automatically creates this format for you when the EDD is imported to the template. You still need to define all the formatting for this paragraph, but you do not have to worry about naming conventions, because the tag is created automatically.

Elements

Elements begin the definition of the specific parts of a document. Elements are discussed further below.

Tags

Tags identify the attributes of the elements.

Element Elements

Element elements are the first part of any new element definition. They are one of the most common elements used in an EDD and are the basis of all content that a template imports from an EDD.

Note: *The nested child tag is automatically inserted if AutoInsertions is selected via **Element > New Element Options.** This is the recommended default.*

FormatChangeList Elements

FormatChangeList elements define the formatting changes that apply to content when elements are inserted in a template. They are one of many ways to apply formatting to content after it is inserted in a structured document.

The change list calls references to paragraph formats, character formats, and more. Its basic purpose is to allow the developer of an EDD to have a primary location to store formatting commands and to call them as required. The formatting of structured content may also be done inline, where an element contains a call to a paragraph, character, or other format. Formatting can be assigned by defining all aspects of the format on an element-by-element basis. These concepts are explored further in the Adobe *Structure Developer's Guide*, a PDF found in the OnlineManuals folder within many FrameMaker versions' install folder.

Para Elements

Para elements are used for "commenting" the EDD. The Para element does *not* allow a paragraph to be inserted in the finished template. It is specific to the EDD only.

Section Elements

Section elements are used for grouping components of the EDD. The Section element does *not* allow a section to be inserted in the finished template. It is specific to the EDD only.

The nested child Head element is automatically inserted with the Section element. This "autoinsertion" is designed to save you time in building your EDD and happens in other elements as well.

Highest-Level Elements

At least one element must be defined as being the highest-level element in the structure you are building. This element is the document type and acts as the ancestor to all other elements. It is also possible to have more than one highest-level element in a document.

For example, both a chapter and an appendix may be very similar in structure. The chapter, however, may allow more flexibility in the type of content it can contain. Therefore, both Chapter and Appendix elements may be stored as highest-level elements in an EDD. Each may be developed with different rules, or they may even share rules, but based on the use of a Chapter or Appendix element, the appearance of content may be different (see Figure 4-9).

If you are considering using smaller parts of a large document as highest-level elements, you can develop an EDD with numerous highest-level elements. Each of these allows writers to create documents that are actually smaller parts of a finished file set. This is especially useful for documents that are used as text insets or repeated fragments within larger structured files.

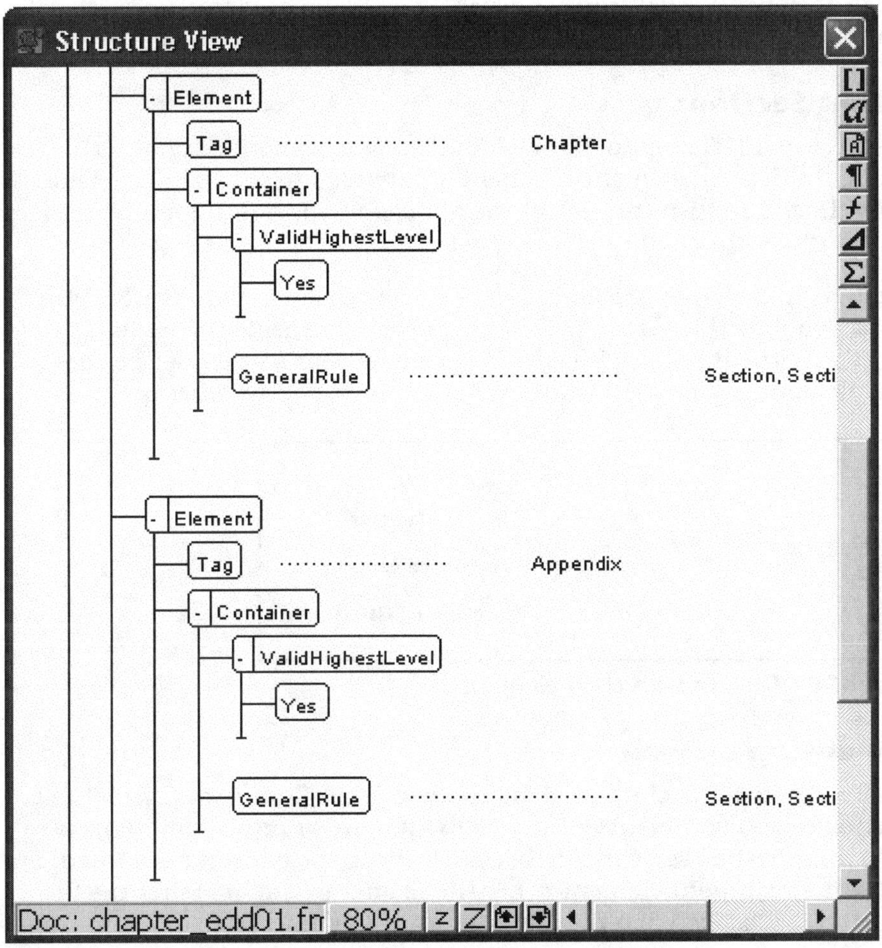

Figure 4-9 Chapter and Appendix elements in the EDD.

Organizing and Commenting an EDD

While organizing and commenting an EDD is not required, the use of structure implies that a document should follow specific rules to make it easier for the author to focus on writing. In much the same way, an organized, well-commented EDD makes it easier for a developer to focus on development rather than relearning the purpose of an EDD over and over. Logical organization and commenting make EDD documents easier to understand. A complex, well-made EDD is also easier to edit down the road. Use the Section element to begin organizing an EDD.

Any Section element should be assigned a logical name, and that name should be typed within the Head element. A Para element inserted after the Head element allows you to provide further introductory information on the Section element, if desired. Finally, a Comment element preceding an

Element element's Tag can further clarify each Element element inserted within the Section element.

Creating Sections

Inserted as a child element of the ElementCatalog element or of other Section elements, the Section element is generally intended to group other elements together. To accomplish this, select the appropriate location for a Section element and insert a Section element using the Element Catalog.

The nested child element Head is automatically inserted with the Section element. You type the name of the Section element inside the Head element. If desired, insert Para siblings to the Head element to further define the Section element. Figure 4-10 shows an example of child elements.

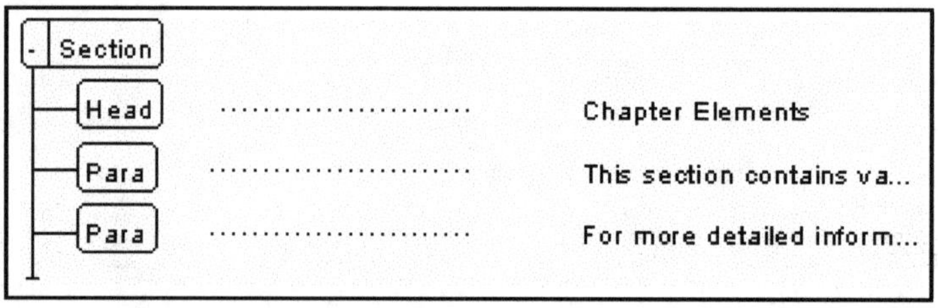

Figure 4-10 Section with child elements.

Commenting an EDD

Generally inserted as a child of Element element, a Comments element can be inserted to add comments to any element. One or more comments are inserted prior to the Tag element. Select the location to insert a comment and then insert a Ccmment element using the Element Catalog. Enter the comment to be displayed in the EDD using the Comments element, as shown in Figure 4-11.

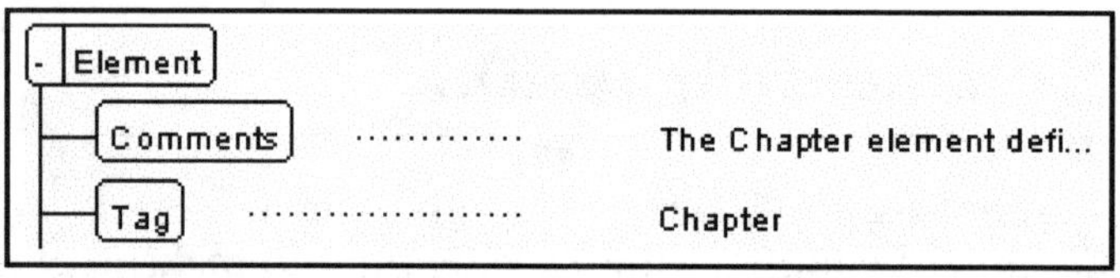

Figure 4-11 An Element element with Comment element inserted.

Since the first text snippet (in this case, the Comment rather than the Tag element is visible when an element is collapsed, it is recommended that one of the first words in the comment be the same as the name of the tag. This ensures that an Element element displays a logical name in the snippet. The benefit of this is the time saved when you try to identify the element later.

Writing Element Definitions

Once an Element element is inserted and commented, it needs to be clearly defined. While there are numerous types of Element elements, the most common are Container, CrossReference, Equation, Footnote, Graphic, Marker, Rubi, RubiGroup, SystemVariable, Table, TableBody, TableCell, TableFooting, TableHeading, TableRow, and TableTitle. Depending on the element that is inserted, other choices then become available (see Figure 4-12).

Figure 4-12 Allowable element definitions.

Containers elements, table part elements, and Footnote elements generally hold other text or elements in the template. None of the other elements do. It is necessary, therefore, to define content rules for some elements. Container elements, table part elements, and footnote elements can also be assigned format rules that drive the appearance of the element and its descendants.

Basically, only Container, Table, TableBody, TableCell, TableFooting, TableHeading, TableRow, TableTitle, and Footnotes elements are allowed to have child elements. No other element is allowed to have a child.

The name of an element in an EDD must follow strict guidelines. Many characters are restricted, so you are advised to use only alphabetical and numerical characters and the underscore (i.e., a set comprised of [a–z], [A–Z], and [0–9], as well as the "_"). Most other characters are specific to the structured development of the EDD and should be avoided.

Note: *When an EDD is developed, every element inserted likely has a child or multiple children. It is only when the elements are used in a specific template that the "childless" elements do not have any subordinate elements. To develop the element, it is necessary to insert children.*

Note: *While spaces are allowed in element names, it is strongly suggested that you not use spaces. Any spaces used will require you to create an individual read/write rule for removal of the spaces before exporting to XML or SGML.*

When creating an EDD, focus on structure before dealing with formatting to avoid distraction. Start at the highest level of the document and try to work from the start to the end of each descendant. For example, completely develop the structure for, say, a table, before beginning work on other elements, such as an image.

Before importing any EDD into a template, validate the EDD to ensure that the document has no errors that validation catches. Also ensure that at least one highest-level element exists.

Testing of the EDD is an iterative process. Define the EDD and import it into a template. Then test the EDD extensively by inserting, moving, and deleting elements, and reviewing any errors that occur until the template is exhaustively tested. Once the template acts as expected, continue to develop the EDD and repeat the import and test procedure.

GeneralRule Requirements

GeneralRule element is a required element in all Container elements, Table elements and their related elements, and Footnote elements. These are the most common elements, and they must contain a GeneralRule.

GeneralRule defines what elements are allowed in a parent. It states which children are optional or required, the order of the them, connections between the parent and the child, and the type of content an element may contain aside from other elements.

Occurrence Indicators

GeneralRule uses the following occurrence indicators to specify how often elements are allowed.

No Symbol. No symbol specifies one occurrence only. The element must therefore be inserted. The following GeneralRule forces only one Para element to be inserted for an element to be valid:

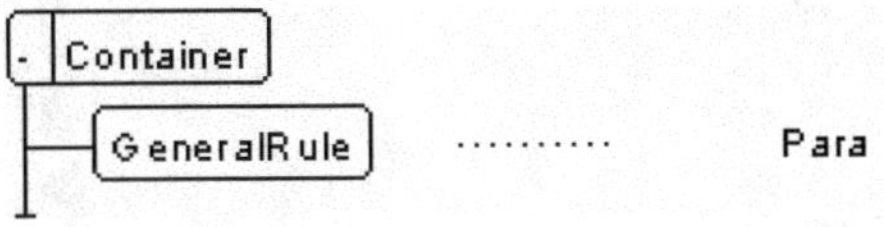

Question mark (?). A question mark specifies zero or one occurrence only. The element may therefore only be inserted once or not at all. The following GeneralRule forces zero or one Para element to be inserted for an element to be valid:

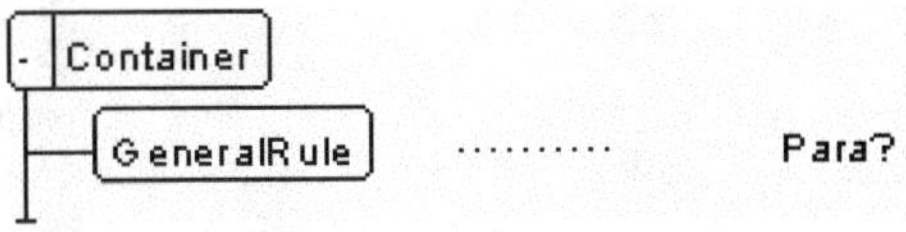

Asterisk (*). An asterisk specifies zero or more occurrences. The element does not therefore have to be inserted and has no upper limit on the number of insertions. The following GeneralRule forces zero or more Para elements to be inserted for an element to be valid:

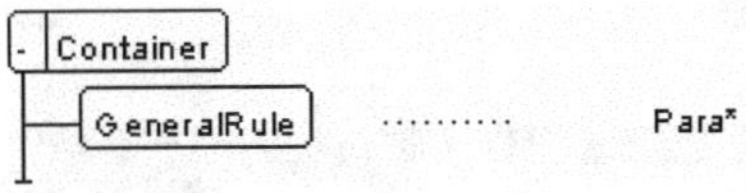

Plus sign (+). A plus sign specifies one or more occurrences. The element must therefore be inserted at least once and has no upper limit on the number of insertions. The following GeneralRule forces one or more Para elements to be inserted for an element to be valid:

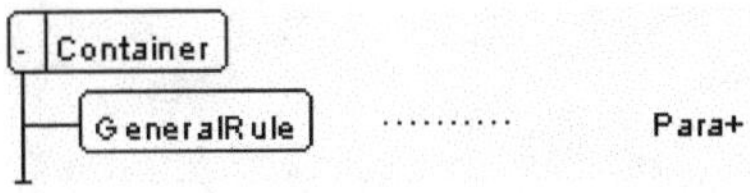

Additional Examples

Figure 4-13 and Figure 4-14 define numerous elements (based on a very simple chapter DTD). Many of them use different occurrence indicators in their GeneralRule elements.

Connectors

GeneralRule uses connectors to separate elements and specify the order in which elements are allowed.

Parentheses

Parentheses are not connectors, but they are integral to the use of connectors. They define boundaries that connectors use to avoid conflicts.

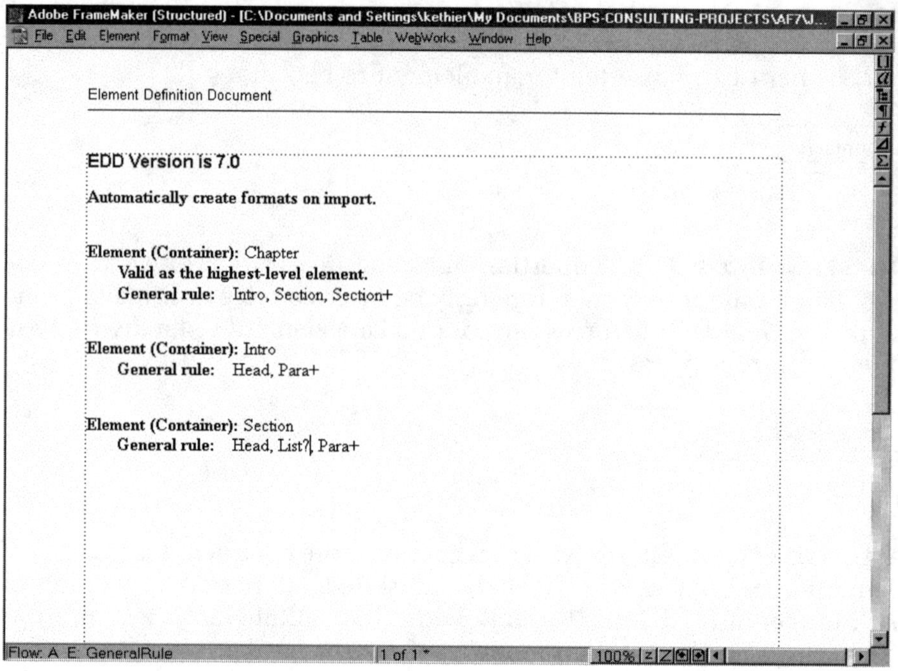

Figure 4-13 EDD sample for GeneralRule.

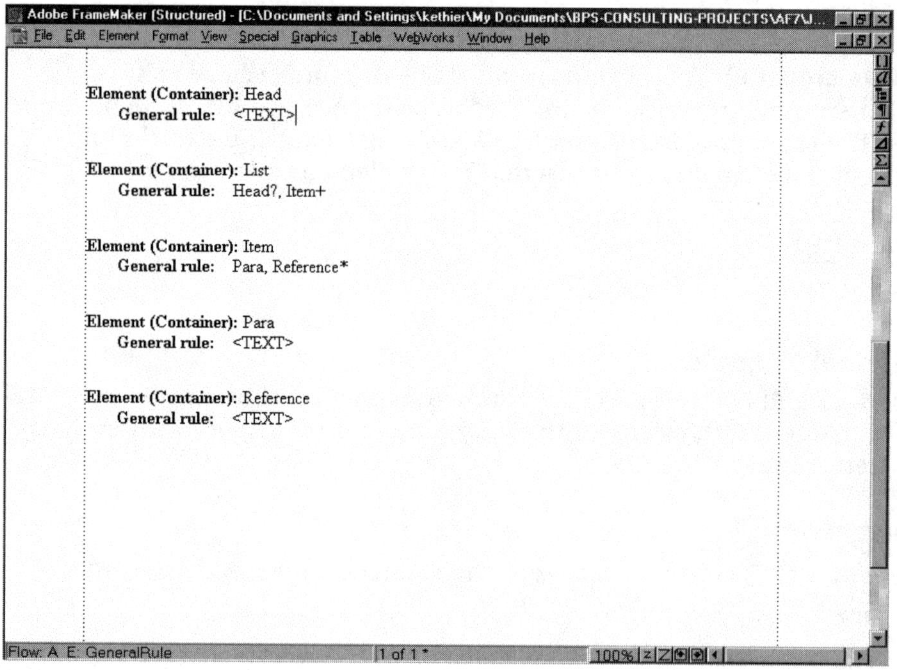

Figure 4-14 Another EDD sample for GeneralRule.

Note: *Unlike mathematics, which has an implied order of operations, structured documents follow no defaults when more than one rule exists. For example, mathematically solving the equation 2+3·4 results in a total of 14. However, this could be grouped to read either (2+3)*4 which results in 20, or it could be grouped as 2+(3*4) which is the same as the mathematically correct total of 14.*

Consider an example of an element called Section with structure written as *Head, Para | List* and where there are mixed connectors. (The comma indicates "followed by," and the pipe, or vertical bar, indicates "or" in structured development.) This structure could be interpreted in either of the following two ways:

- The Section element contains a Head element followed by a Para element as one combined unit, or it contains a single List element:

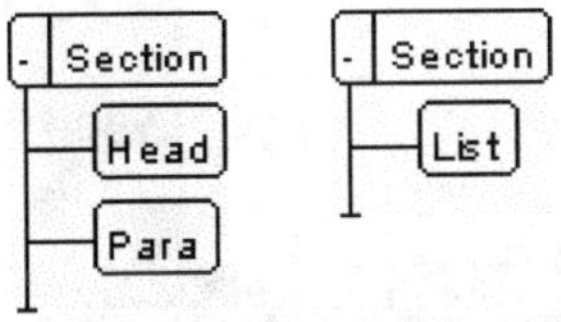

- The Section element contains a Head element as a required first element, followed by either a Para element or a List element:

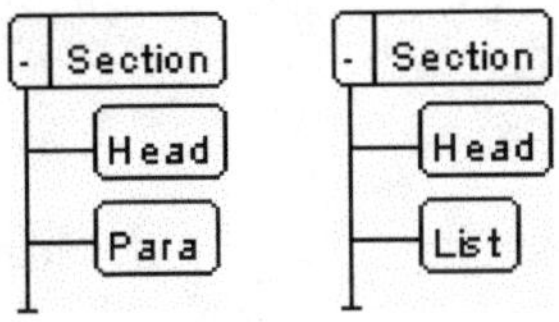

Due to the use of mixed connectors, the preceding example needs parentheses to resolve the conflict. If the GeneralRule is grouped to read *(Head, Para) | List,* then the first interpretation applies. If, however, the GeneralRule is *Head, (Para | List),* then the second interpretation applies.

When mixed connectors exist, and an EDD is imported to a template, an error log is generated, as shown in Figure 4-15. For example purposes, the GeneralRule for the Section element has been modified to produce this error.

To correct the error, edit the EDD and reimport it.

In this case, the mixed connectors error also causes a List element error, also shown in Figure 4-15.

Comma (,)

The comma is used to set a specific order for elements. For example, the following GeneralRule element indicates that a Head element is followed by a

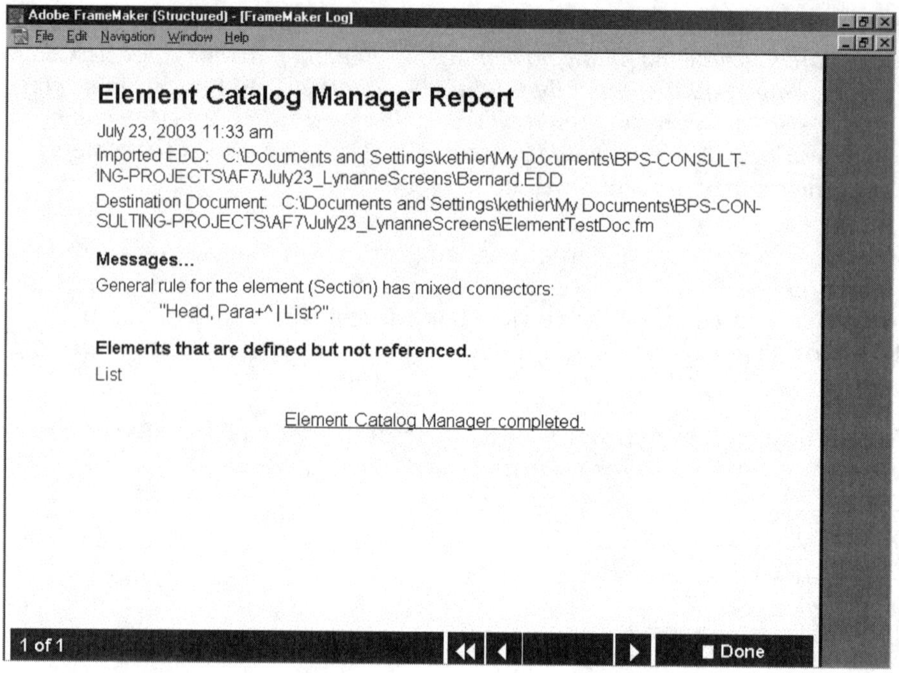

Figure 4-15 Mixed connector error sample.

Para element, which is followed by a List element. No other combinations are possible. Only one of each element is allowed in this example:

Ampersands (&)

The ampersand specifies that multiple elements may be inserted in any order. For example, the following GeneralRule indicates that Para *and* List elements are allowed in any order. Only one of each element is allowed in this example:

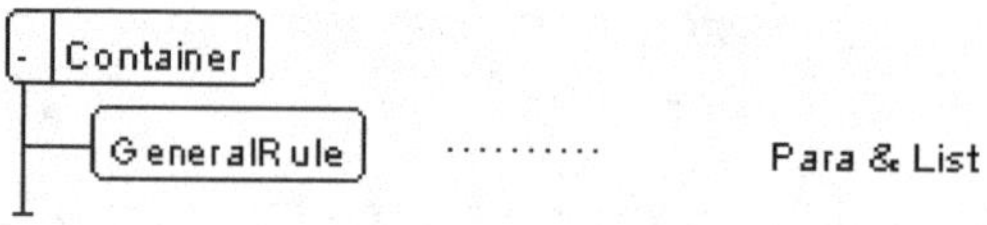

Vertical Bar or Pipe (|)

The vertical bar or pipe specifies that one element or another may be inserted. For example, the following GeneralRule indicates that *either* a Para element *or* a List element is allowed. Only one of either element is allowed in this example.

Additional Examples

Numerous elements (based on a very simple DTD) are defined in Figure 4-16. Many of them use different connectors in their GeneralRule elements.

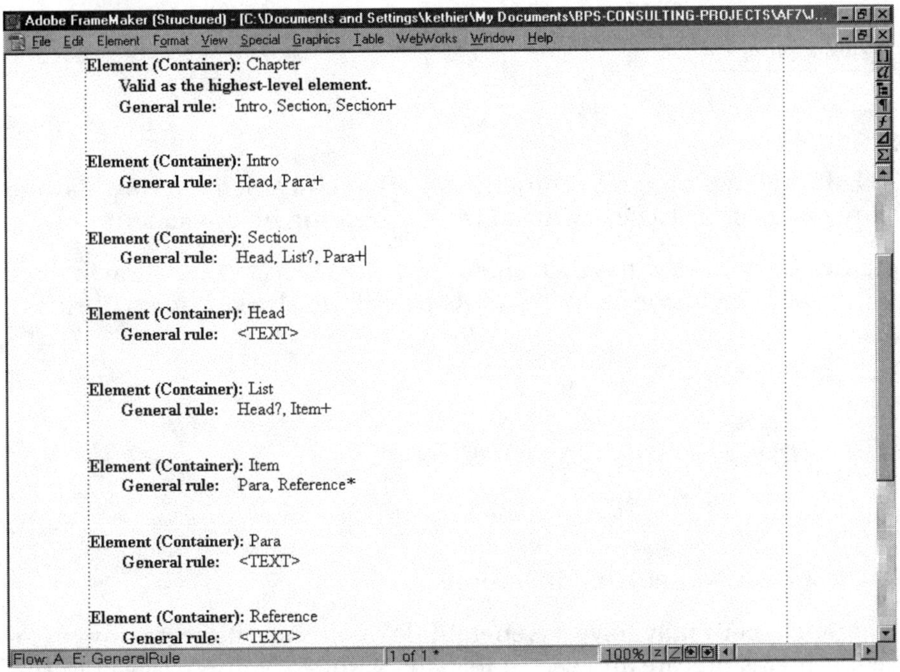

Figure 4-16 EDD sample for connectors.

Content Symbols

Some GeneralRule elements specify content other than child elements (generally text related). A default of <ANY> is used when importing from an EDD with an unspecified GeneralRule.

<TEXT>

<TEXT> allows text content and inclusions.

Note: *Regardless of the occurrence indicator used with <TEXT>, the number of occurrences of insertion of text is considered to be zero or more. Once a user is requested to add text, there is no further rule that can specify a minimum number of characters or words.*

A Container element may have a GeneralRule of <TEXT>, allowing any text to be typed. In addition, if inclusions are allowed in the parent, they are also allowed in this element.

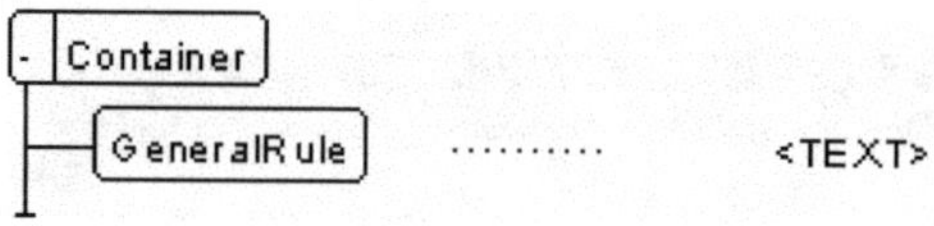

<TEXTONLY>

<TEXTONLY> allows only text content. No other child elements are allowed. This allows inclusions to be restricted from appearing in an element.

A Container element may have a GeneralRule of <TEXTONLY>, allowing only text to be typed. Inclusions allowed in its parent are also restricted in this element.

<ANY>

<ANY> allows text content and inclusions.

A Container element may have a GeneralRule of <ANY>, allowing any text to be typed. If inclusions are allowed in its parent, they are also allowed in this element.

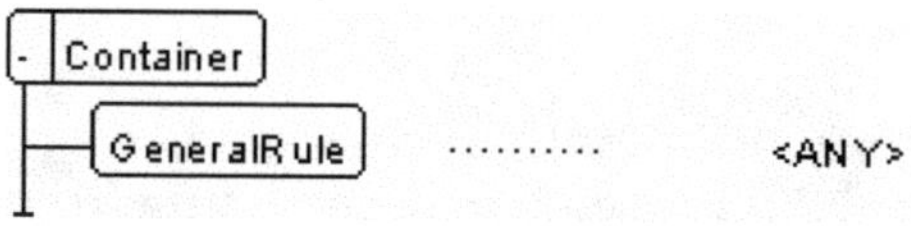

<EMPTY>

<EMPTY> indicates that the element may contain no content.

A Container element may have a GeneralRule <EMPTY>, forcing the element to be empty. This may be done to insert elements for the purpose of applying automatic markup (such as numbering) without allowing users to input any other content.

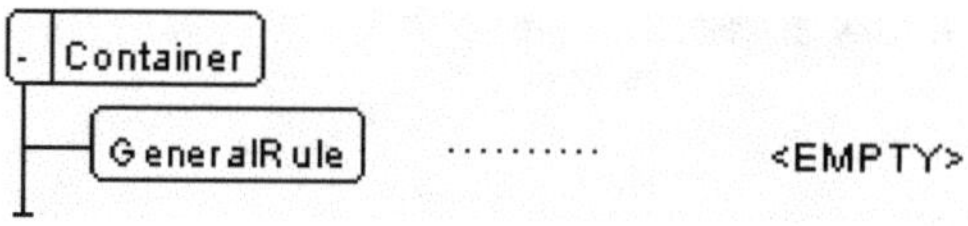

Examples of GeneralRule Elements

While the concepts of Para and List element combinations may sound simple (for example, "allow the author to insert any number of List or Para elements, but not two List elements in a row"), developing even this GeneralRule can be involved. Observe the following steps, for example:

To save your file:

a. Press **Ctrl+s**

or

b. Select **File** > **Save**

or

c. Click the **Save** icon

(Para, List?)+. This GeneralRule allows combinations of List and Para elements but restricts the author from inserting two List elements in a row. It also requires that a Para be the first element. It does not allow an author to insert a List element on its own or before the very first Para element.

(List, (Para, List?)*) | (Para, List?)+. This GeneralRule allows combinations of List and Para elements but restricts the author from inserting two List elements in a row. It allows a List or a Para on its own.

Unlike the previous example, it does allow an author to insert a List element on its own or before the very first Para element. It also restricts two List elements in a row. It therefore provides the correct setup for the "allow the author to insert any number of List or Para elements, but not two List elements in a row" rule.

Memo

The sample EDD shown in Figure 4-17 and Figure 4-18 is based on a Memo document.

In this example, Memo is the document type and the highest-level element. It contains three mandatory children—Open, followed by Body, which is followed by Close. Each child also contains elements. Open contains To and From elements (which may appear in any order) followed by a Regarding element. Body contains one or more Para elements. Close contains a single Para element. The To, From, Regarding, and Para elements all contain text that is entered by the author.

Chapter

The sample EDD in Figure 4-19 is based on a Chapter document.

In this example, Chapter is the document type and the highest-level element used. It contains three mandatory children—Intro and at least two more (both Section elements). The Intro contains a Head element and one or more Para elements. Each Section element contains various combinations of other elements.

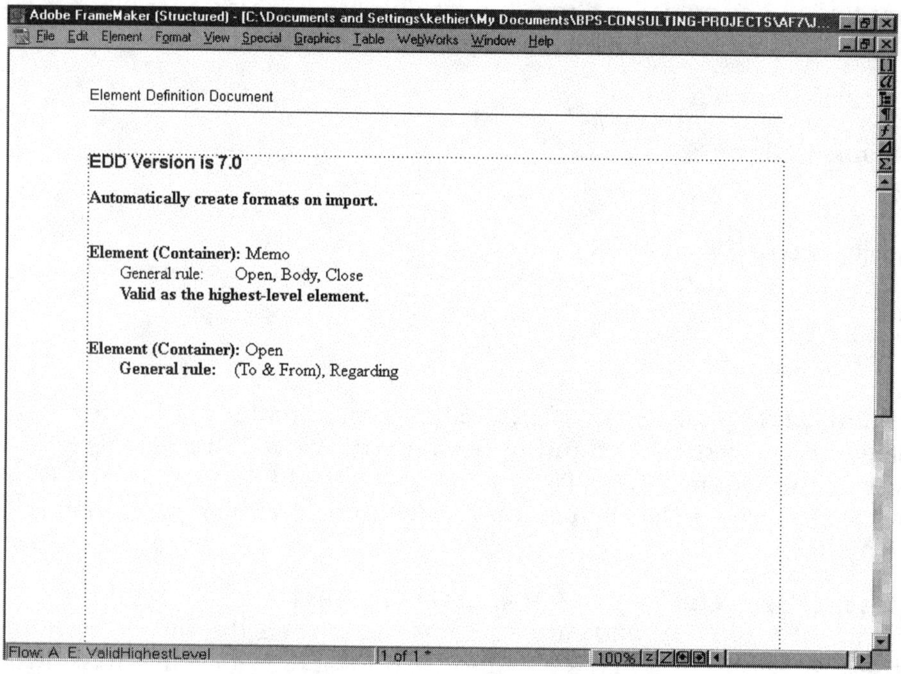

Figure 4-17 Memo EDD sample.

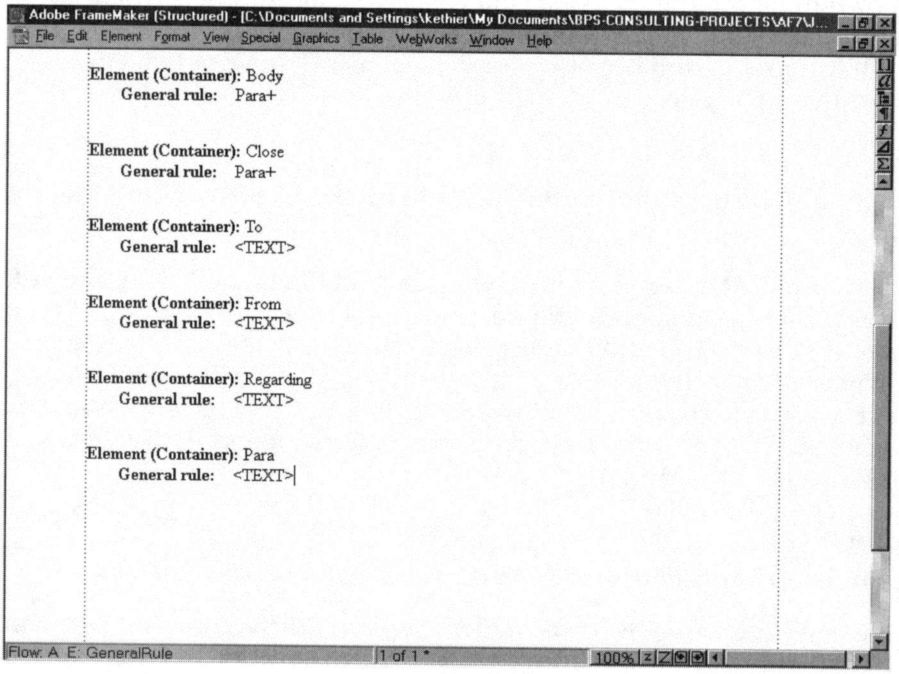

Figure 4-18 Continued memo EDD sample.

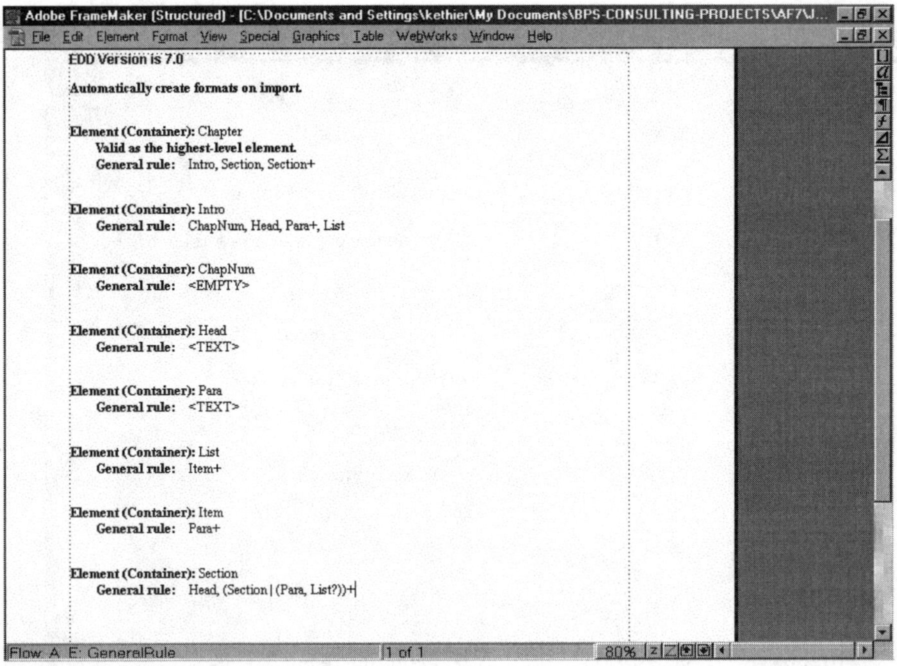

Figure 4-19 Chapter EDD sample.

The Head element must be inserted in a Section element and be followed by at least a single Section element (allowing nested Section elements to be created) or a single Para element. The Para element is followed by an optional List element (which must contain one or more Item elements, as shown in Figure 4-20). Para elements contain text that is entered by the author.

This structure allows for a flexible chapter structure with nested Section elements, combinations of Para and List elements, and a variety of content. It does not, however, allow for any content such as tables, cross-references, figures, and so on. These types of elements must still be added to the EDD and defined with GeneralRule specifications before they are allowed in the template.

The example of a structured document shown in Figure 4-21 may be created using a template that formats various elements with numerous paragraph tags, and creates structured output that can be used for various delivery formats, including print.

AutoInsertions Elements

The AutoInsertions element is an optional element in Container and TableCell elements. If either of these elements are inserted in the EDD (and generally they are the most common elements), AutoInsertions is a valid option.

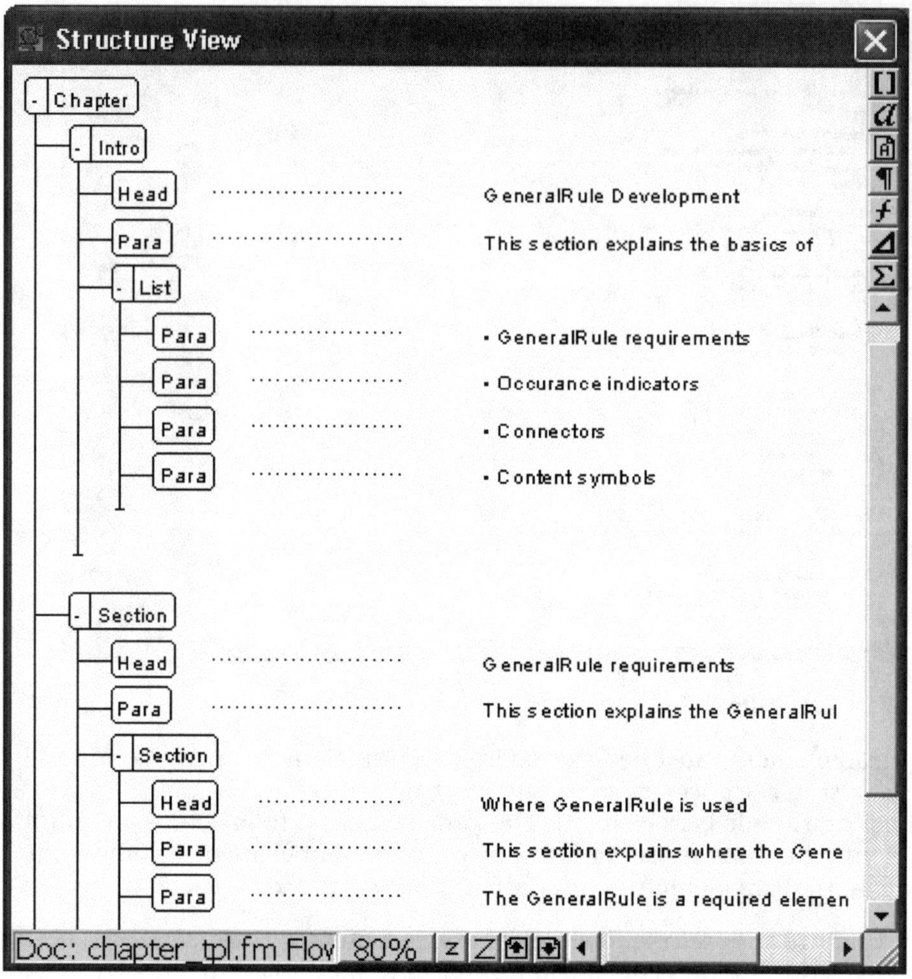

Figure 4-20 Structure sample including List and Para elements.

The Purpose of AutoInsertions

AutoInsertions elements define what elements may be automatically inserted into an element when an author inserts the parent. It also allows nested children (children of children) to be automatically inserted (see Figure 4-22). Authors can still decide, however, if automatic insertions are allowed to occur in their specific instance of FrameMaker.

AutoInsertions and InsertChild

When you add AutoInsertions elements, the cursor must be below the GeneralRule element. Inserting an AutoInsertions element automatically inserts a nested InsertChild element.

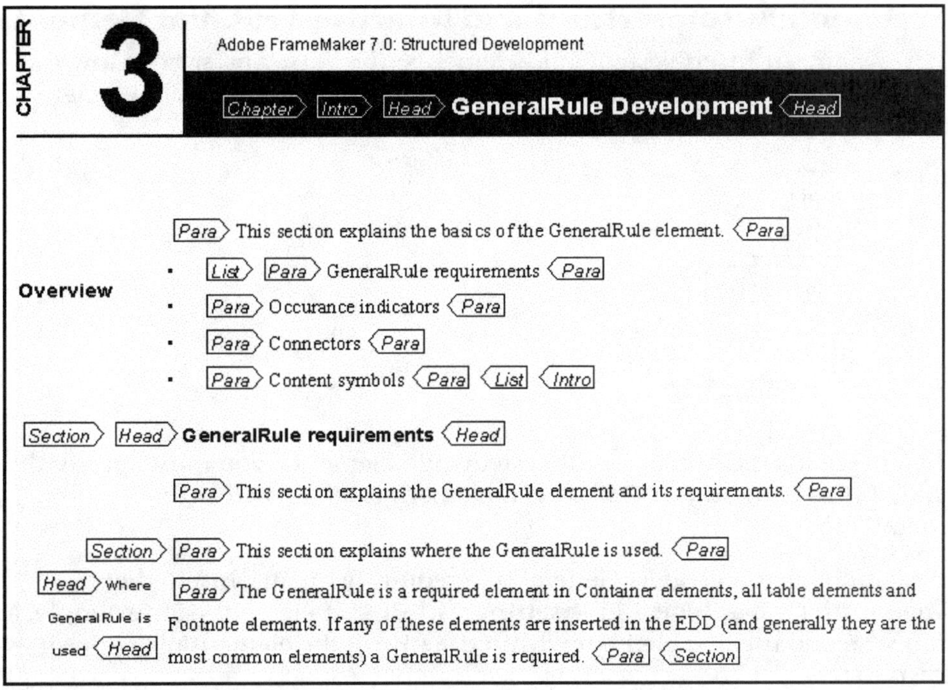

Figure 4-21 Sample structured document with Chapter element highlighted.

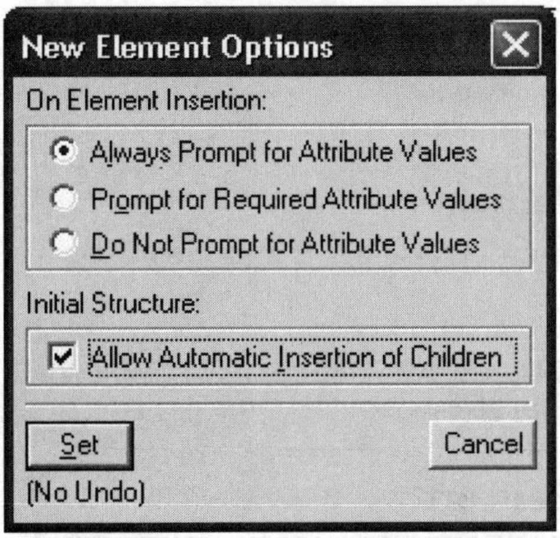

Figure 4-22 The New Element Options dialog box.

For example, if you are creating a GeneralRule that requires an autoinserted child named Head, the element may appear as seen here:

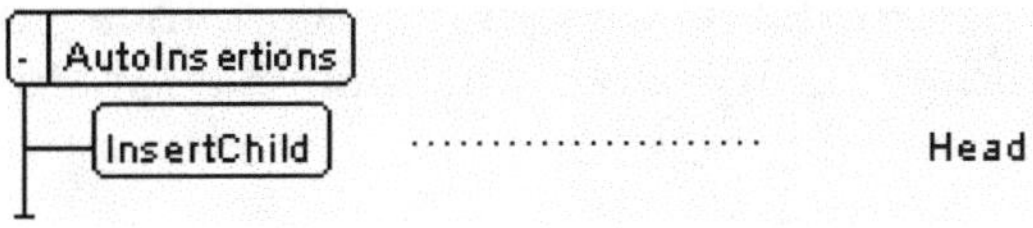

Developing AutoInsertions and InsertNestedChild Elements

When you insert InsertNestedChild elements, the cursor must be below the InsertChild element. An InsertNestedChild element places a child element automatically into an InsertChild element:

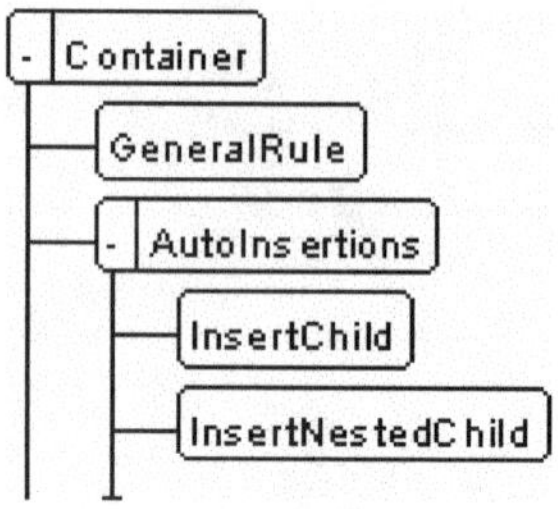

When using InsertChild or InsertNestedChild elements, you must specify the name of the element to insert as each element is added below the GeneralRule.

For example, if you create a GeneralRule requiring an autoinserted child named Intro (and a GeneralRule setting within that element—for example, a ChapNum and the first element within the Intro), the element may appear as shown here:

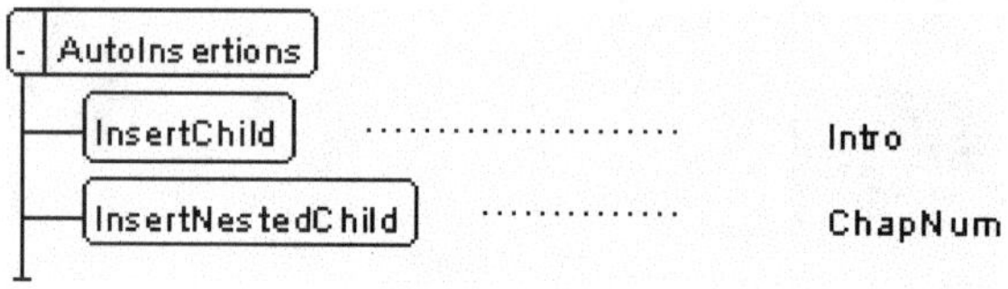

Examples of AutoInsertions Elements

This section details examples of AutoInsertions elements and their uses.

Simple Chapter Example

The example shown in Figure 4-23 and Figure 4-24 represents a simple EDD with both AutoInserting and NestedChild elements.

Inclusion and Exclusion Elements

Inclusion Elements

Inclusion is an optional element allowed in numerous other elements. If this element is inserted in the EDD, it allows a specific child to appear numerous times (by being included) in the parent that allows an inclusion. Inclusion elements are inherited by the children of the parent that allows an inclusion.

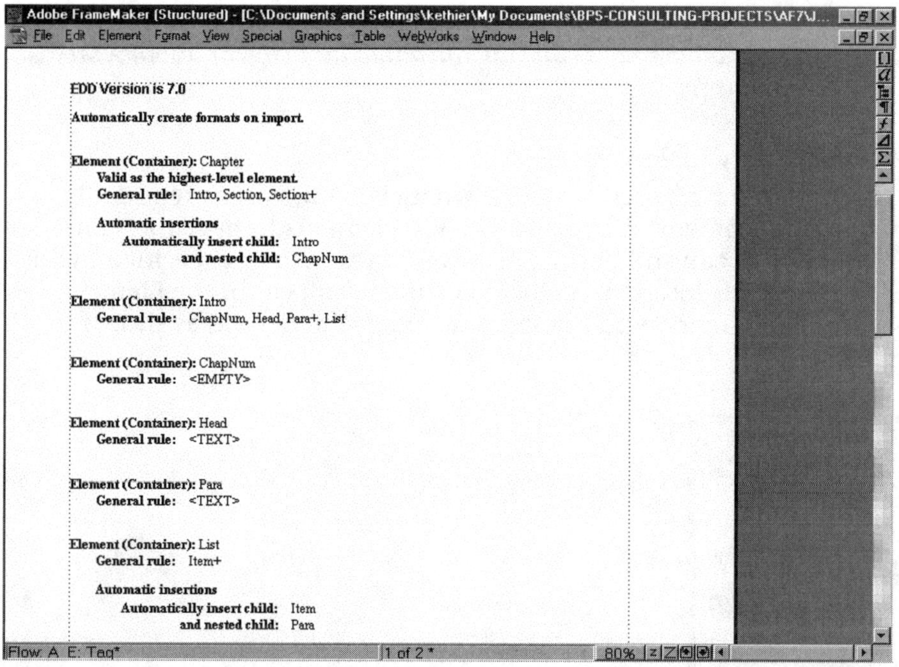

Figure 4-23 Sample chapter EDD.

Figure 4-24 Sample chapter EDD.

Note: *Inclusion and Exclusion elements are not supported in XML and therefore should not be incorporated into an EDD for use in XML environments.*

The Purpose of Inclusion

An Inclusion element is used to define what elements can be repeatedly inserted into an element. It also allows child elements to have the same inclusion. Authors can still decide, however, if the element specified by the Inclusion element is inserted. Inclusion elements appear in the Element Catalog as a check mark with a small plus sign (+) next to it, as shown in Figure 4-25.

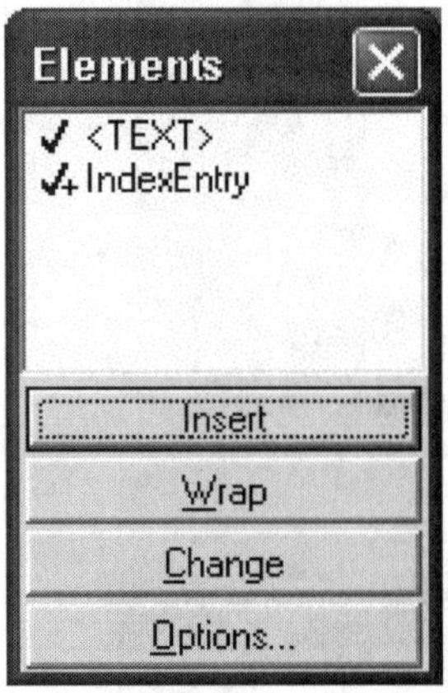

Figure 4-25 The Element Catalog with an Inclusion element showing.

Developing Inclusion Elements

When you insert Inclusion elements, the cursor must be below the GeneralRule element to achieve the following result:

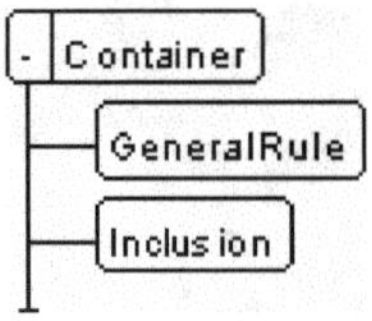

To create an Inclusion element, click beneath a GeneralRule and select **Inclusion** from the Element Catalog. Click **Insert** and name the inclusion.

For example, if you wanted to create an Inclusion element to allow an IndexEntry element, the Inclusion element would be IndexEntry:

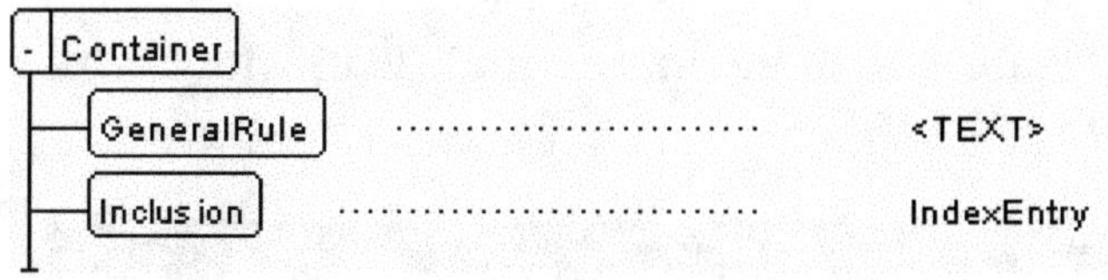

Note: *Ensure that the element being allowed as an Inclusion element is defined in the EDD.*

Exclusion Elements

An Exclusion is an optional element. It is often used as a way of preventing an Inclusion element from being used. If an Exclusion element is inserted in the EDD, it prevents a specific child from appearing in an element. An Exclusion element is inherited by the children of the parent that allows an Exclusion element.

The Purpose of Exclusion Elements

The Exclusion element is used to counter an inclusion. When authoring documents using the resulting element definitions, the Excluded elements will not be marked as valid for insertion in the Element Catalog.

Developing Exclusion Elements

When you insert Exclusion elements, the cursor must be below the GeneralRule element to achieve the following result:

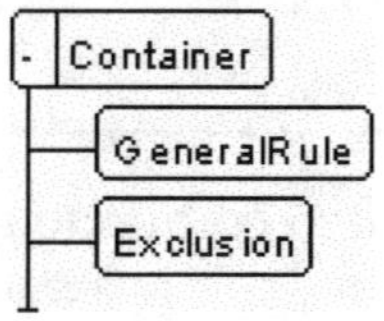

To create an Exclusion element, click beneath a GeneralRule and select **Exclusion** from the Element Catalog. Click **Insert** and name the Exclusion element.

For example, if you are creating an Exclusion element to prevent an IndexEntry element, the Exclusion element would be IndexEntry, as shown here:

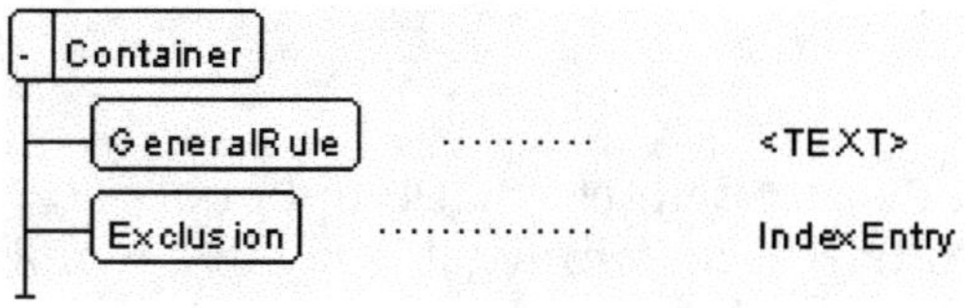

Sample Inclusion and Exclusion Elements

The example shown in Figure 4-26 represents a simple EDD with both Inclusion and Exclusion elements.

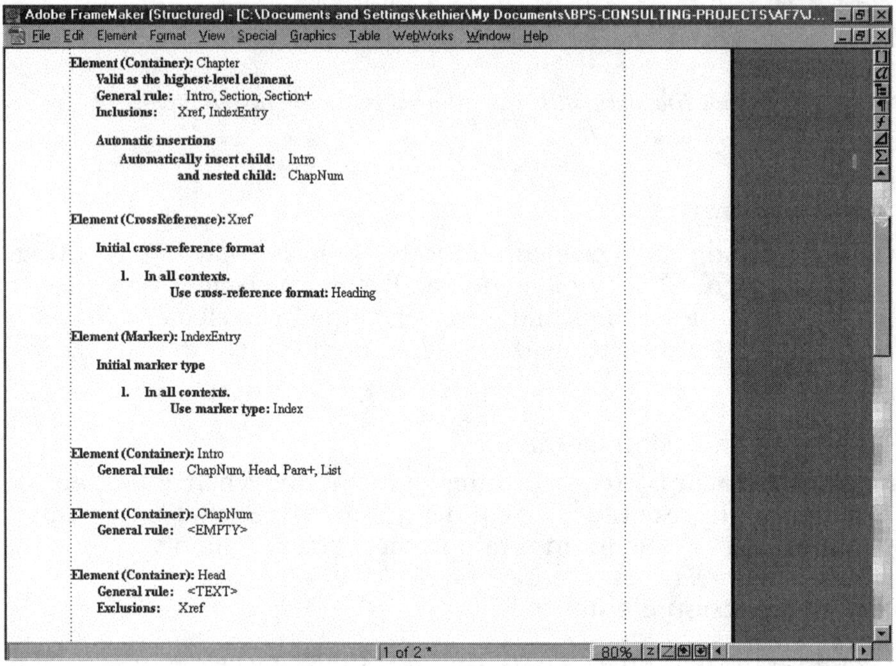

Figure 4-26 Sample EDD with Inclusions and Exclusions.

Table Components

Structured tables are comprised of several optional or required components. Tables are made up of the following four types of content:

- optional table title
- optional heading rows
- required body rows
- optional footing rows

The three types of rows (Heading, Body, and Footing) contain cells. Within the cells additional elements are inserted.

Table-Related Elements

Table elements contain a GeneralRule that defines what is optional or required in a table. This rule should have a matching table tag in a template that works with the structural rules. The rule generally allows tables to be inserted with various element types, including TableTitle, TableHeading,

TableBody, TableFooting, TableRow, and TableCell. The names of the elements do not have to match the element type names. For example, the element type is TableBody, but you might name your element TblBd (see Figure 4-27).

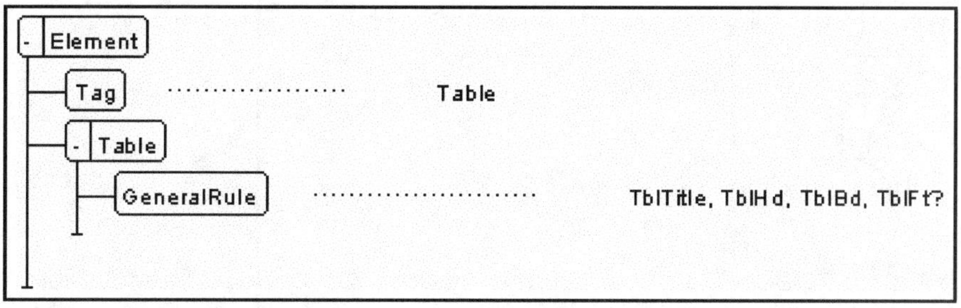

Figure 4-27 An example Table element with General Rule referencing other table parts.

Note: *Use caution when creating tables (especially the first time) to ensure that Container elements are not used to define the table.*

Consider the Figure 4-28 example of a table that contains a title, a heading, a body, and a footing. The title contains a paragraph of text, while the heading, body, and footing table parts contain rows. Each of the rows contain cells, and content is allowed within cells. No typing, therefore, is ever done in a table element. Instead, the content is inserted either within the table title or a specific cell, as shown in Figure 4-28.

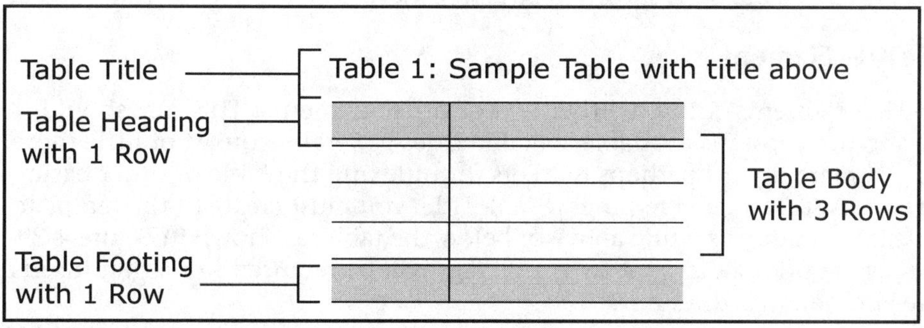

Figure 4-28 Table parts within FrameMaker tables.

Until the table is developed with structure, no content can be inserted. Also, unless the EDD explicitly states the type of content that is placed in a table, FrameMaker automatically creates the minimum required structure. This allows a table to be inserted with default names. It is strongly recommended that all elements in a table be assigned specific names to identify them based on the developer's preferences and not those of FrameMaker itself.

Figure 4-29 shows what the table shown in Figure 4-28 looks like when viewed using the Structure View.

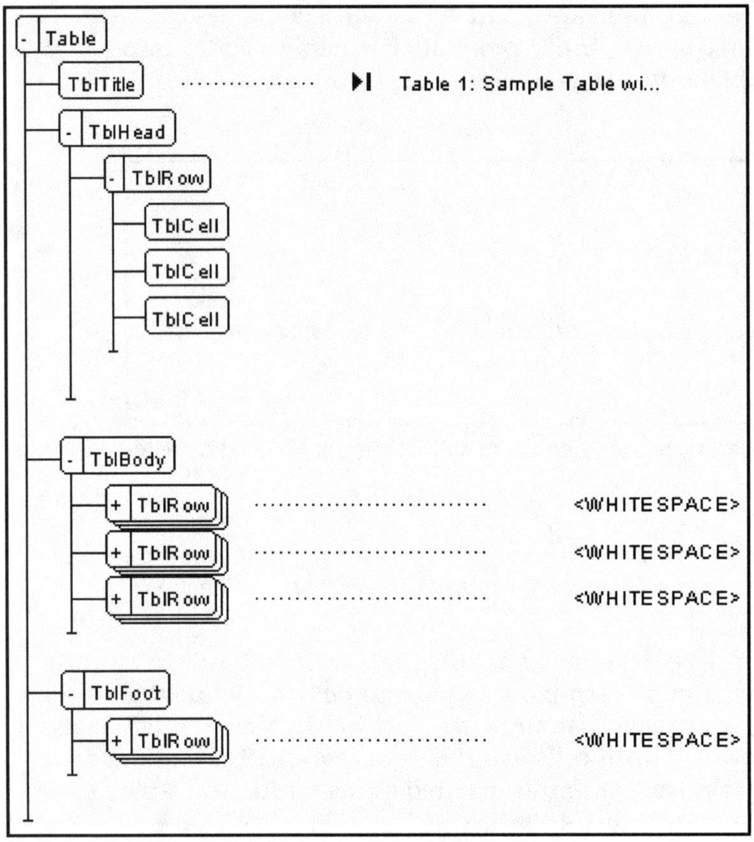

Figure 4-29 Table parts shown in Structure View.

TableTitle Element

TableTitle elements contain either text or other elements. This rule should have very few options available, as table titles generally consist of little more than a paragraph and perhaps markers for indexing the table or other basic elements. Also, if a table requires a TableTitle, you must create in the template a table tag that inserts a title above or below the table, as shown in Figure 4-29. If the tag is optional, at least two table tags will be required—one that inserts a title and one that does not.

TableHeading Element

TableHeading elements contain TableRow elements. Regardless of the name of the structured element, the type of element referenced must be a TableRow element, with a name that matches the element name referred to in the TableHeading element's general rule. This structure can be seen in Figure 4-29.

If you create a TableHeading element named, for example, TblHd with a GeneralRule of TRow+, the element TRow must be a TableRow element, as shown here:

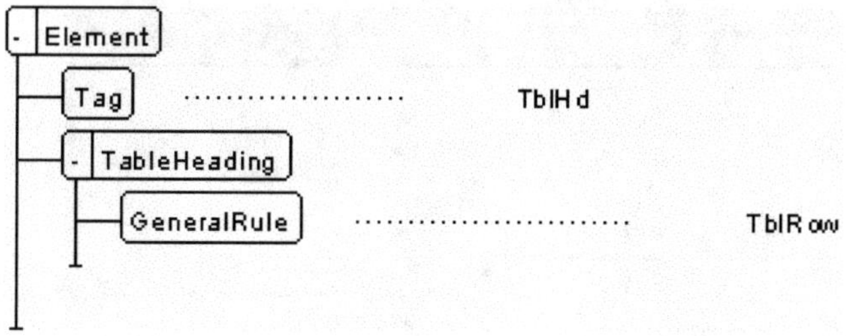

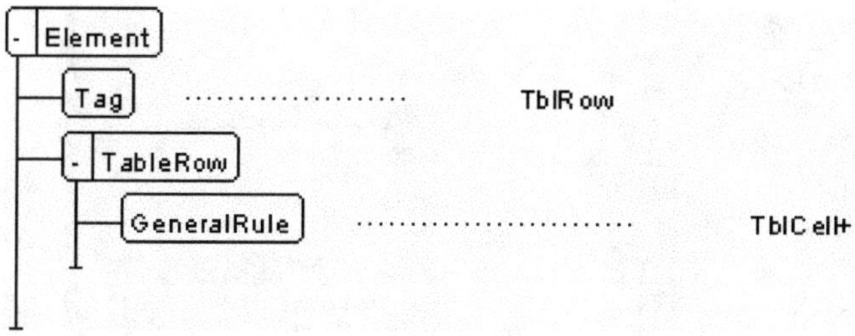

TableBody Element

TableBody elements that are the only required element in a Table element contain TableRow elements. Regardless of the name of the structured element, the type of element referenced must be a TableRow element, with a name that matches the element name used in the TableBody element. If you create a TableBody element named TblBod with a GeneralRule of TblRow+, for example, the element TblRow must be a TableRow element:

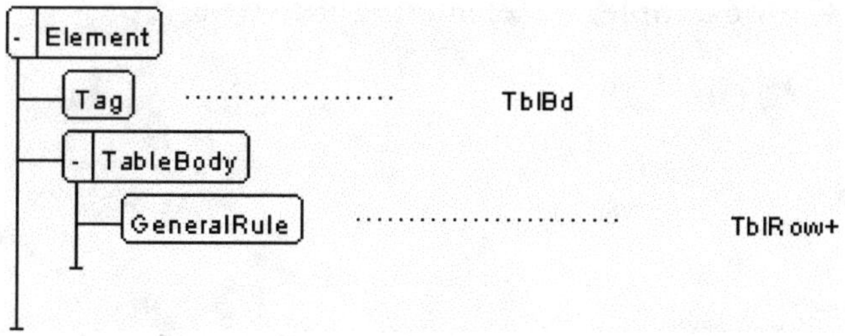

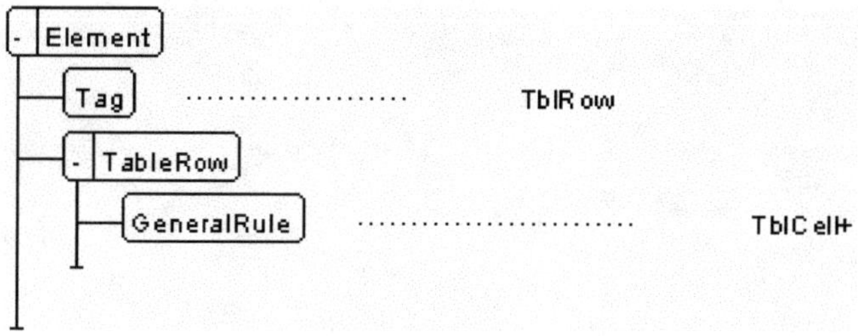

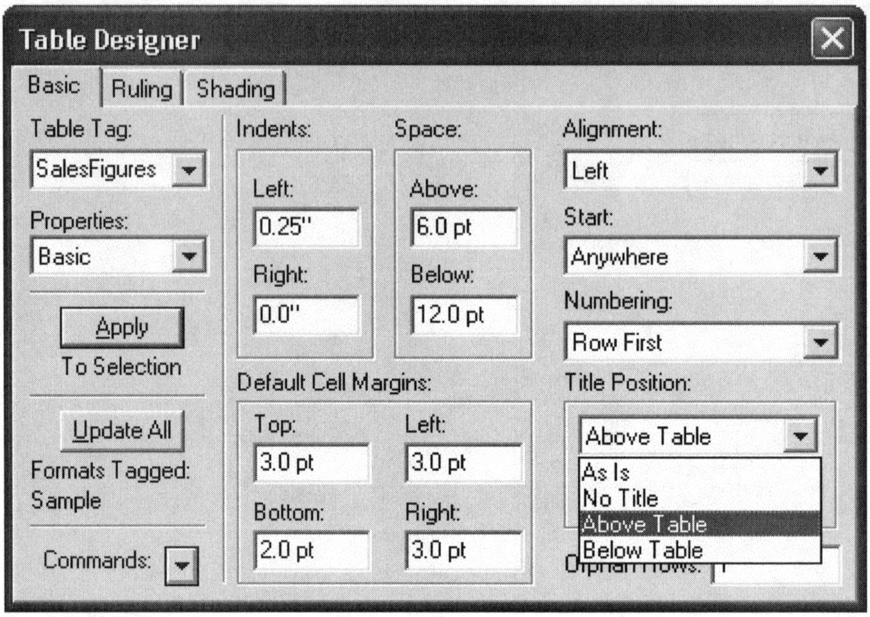

Figure 4-30 The Table Designer.

TableFooting Element

TableFooting elements contain TableRow elements. Regardless of the name of the structured element, the type of element referenced must be a TableRow with a name that matches the element name used in the TableFooting element. If you create a TableFooting element named TblFt with a GeneralRule of TblRow+, for example, the element TblRow must be a TableRow element:

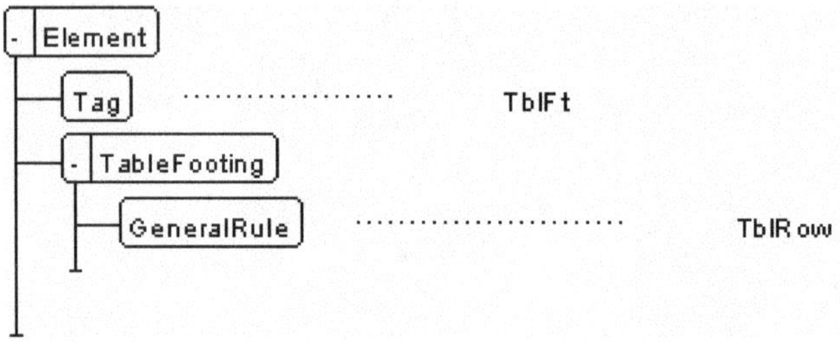

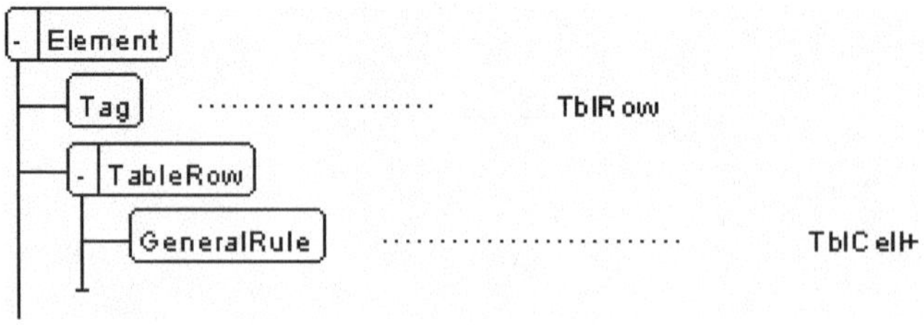

TableRow Element

TableRow elements contain TableCell elements. Regardless of the name of the structured element, the type of element referenced must be a TableCell element with a name that matches the element name used in the TableRow element. If you create a TableRow element named TblRow with a GeneralRule of TblCell+, for example, the element TblCell must be a TableCell element:

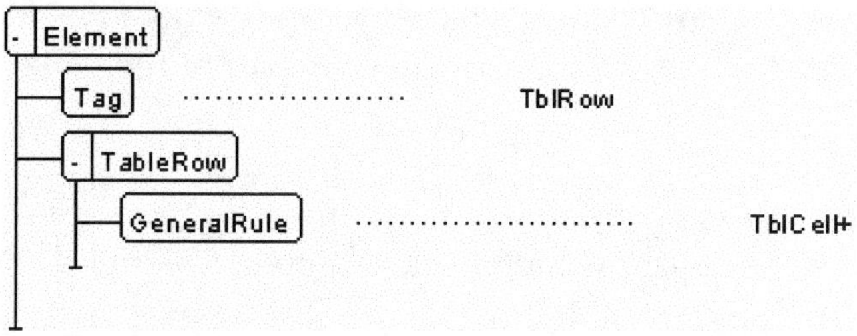

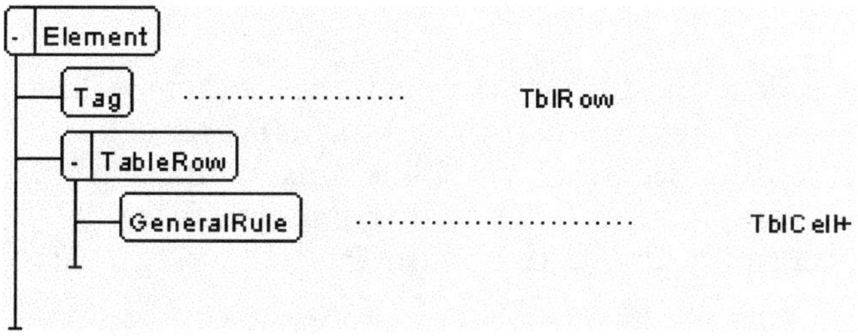

TableCell Elements

TableCell elements contain either text or other elements. If you create a TableCell element named TblCell with a GeneralRule of Para+, the element Para must be a Container element:

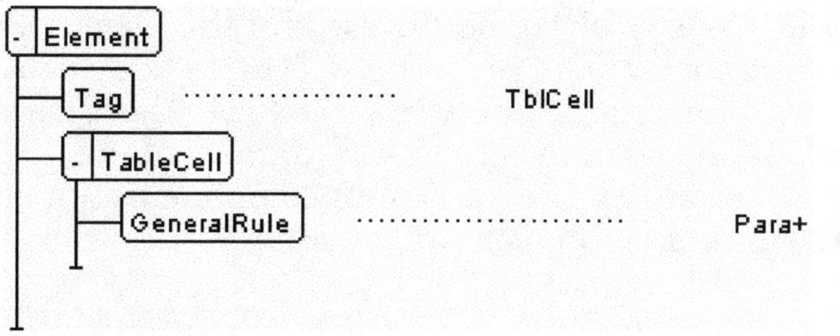

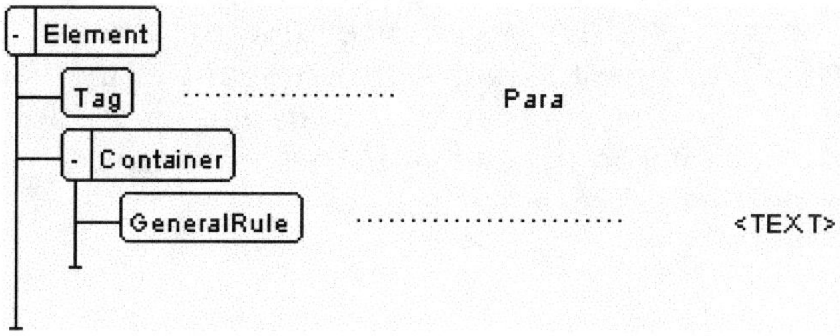

Occurrence Indicators and Tables

This section explains how occurrence indicators are used with table elements (Table, TableTitle, TableHeading, TableBody, TableFooting, TableRow, TableCell).

No Symbol

Any table element can have a "no symbol" occurrence indicator. If every element is defined with no symbol, the table consists of a title, a single heading, a single row, a single footing, a single row in each part of the table and one cell per row.

To enforce a rule that elements such as TableTitle, TableHeading, TableBody, and TableFooting each must exist only once, a table can have no symbol for each of these elements. However, tables generally allow more than one TableRow or TableCell element.

Question Mark (?)

Most table elements can include a question mark occurrence indicator. If most elements are defined with a question mark, the table consists of an optional title, heading, and footing. However, the table must contain at least a single TableBody, TableRow, and TableCell element. Therefore, these elements cannot have an occurrence indicator of a question mark.

Asterisk (*)

Very few table elements should have an asterisk occurrence indicator. Because tables generally have a single title or no title at all, the asterisk is not useful for the TableTitle element. Tables have one or none of the TableHeading and TableFooting elements, so the asterisk is not useful for these elements either.

Because tables must contain at least a TableBody element, and because the asterisk allows a zero value, the asterisk cannot be used for this element. In addition, TableRow elements are required in the head, foot, or body of a table, and TableCell elements are required only in TableRows. The asterisk cannot, therefore, be used as an occurrence indicator for most of the elements in tables. Within a row, however, numerous combinations of cells are allowed. Some of these combinations can use the asterisk.

Plus Sign (+)

Some table elements can have a plus sign occurrence indicator. If most elements are defined with a plus sign, the table consists of one or more rows and cells. The table cannot, however, contain more than one TableTitle, TableHeading, TableBody, or TableFooting element. These elements, therefore, cannot have a plus sign occurrence indicator.

Connectors and Table Elements

This section explains how connectors are used with table elements.

Parentheses

Using parentheses in tables in conjunction with other connectors allows flexibility in the types of tables that can be created.

Comma (,)

The comma is the most common connector when a table is being developed. In most cases, table-related elements are connected using the comma.

Ampersand (&)

The ampersand element may be used in tables, but its use is infrequent.

Vertical bar or Pipe (|)

The vertical bar or pipe is often used in tables to provide flexibility by allowing tables to share numerous properties.

Examples of Table Elements and Table-Related Elements

This section shows some examples of Table elements (and related elements) and their usage.

Simple Table Element Example

Figure 4-31 shows a Table element that allows basic structured content to be inserted. This may be used, for example, for tables that are very standard. For the Table element to be allowed, it must be referenced somewhere in the EDD.

PartsTable Element Example

The structure shown in Figure 4-32 allows for a table structure with a required title, header, and body, and an optional footer. The title contains a required Para element. The heading of the table contains a single row. The body is made up of one or more rows. The footer (if inserted) contains a single row. Each row contains one or more cells, and each cell contains one or more Para elements. For the PartsTable element to be allowed, it must be referenced in the general rule of another element in the EDD.

The structure shown in Figure 4-32 allows for a table structure without a title or a footer. The table contains the required PartHeading element and PartBody element. The heading of the table contains a single PartRow element. The body is made up of one or more PartRow elements. Each PartRow element contains two cells—PartName and PartNumber. These two cells contain typed text.

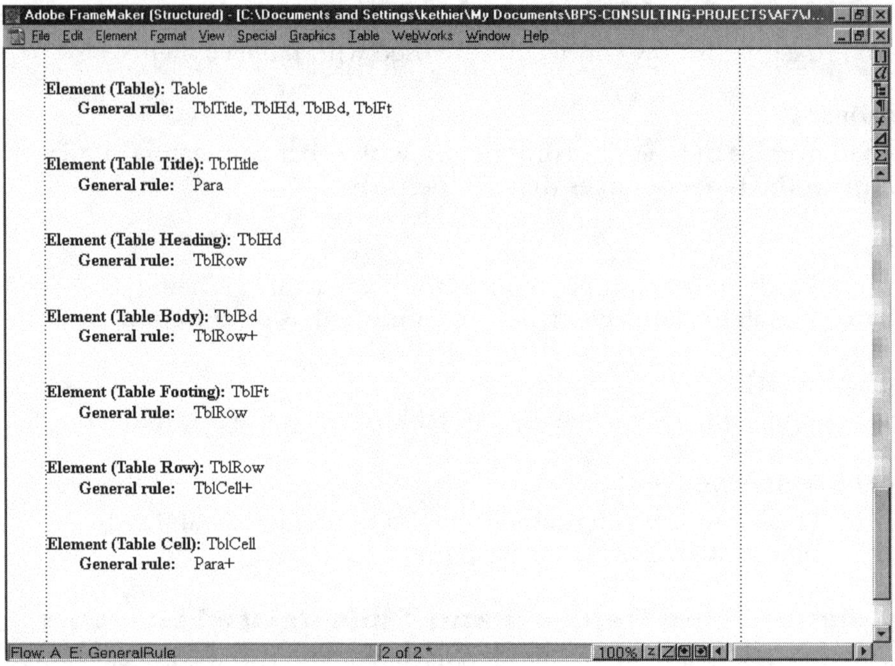

Figure 4-31 Sample structure for a simple table.

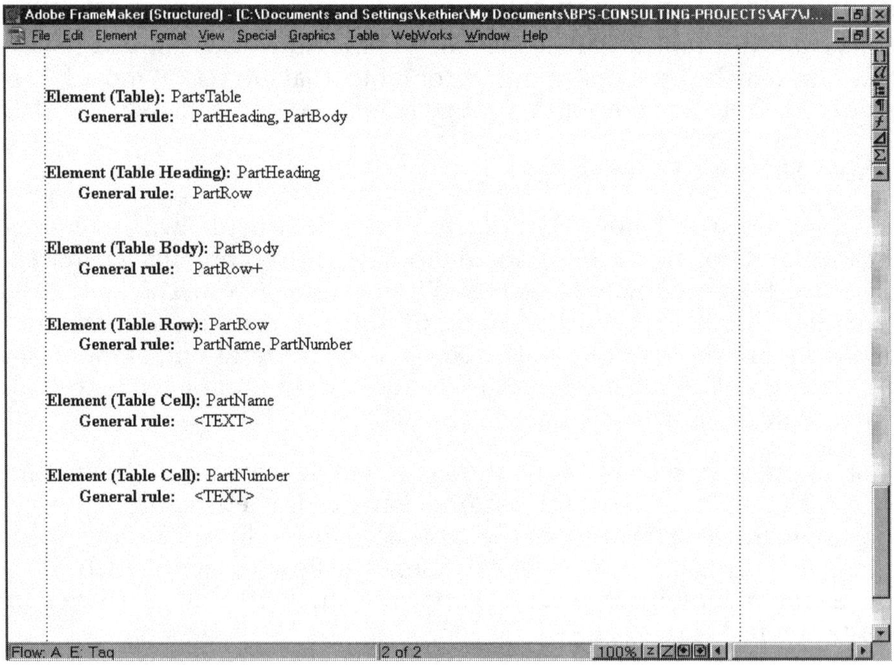

Figure 4-32 Sample structure for a PartsTable element.

ContactTable Element Example

The example shown in Figure 4-33 is extracted from an EDD based on a Chapter document. For the PartsTable element to be allowed, it must be referenced by another element in the EDD.

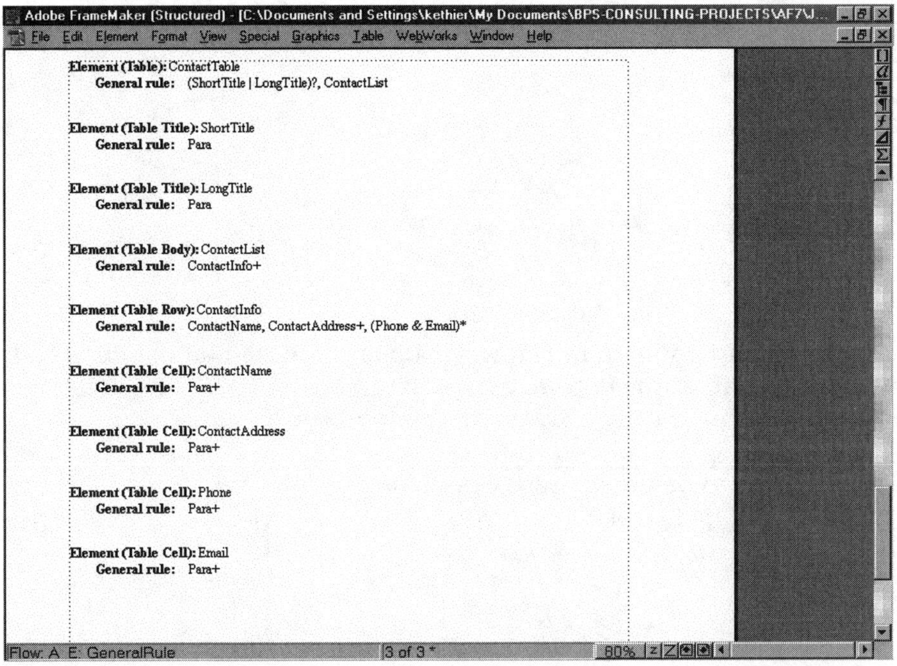

Figure 4-33 Sample structure for a ContactTable element.

This structure allows for a table structure with an optional title that could be one of two elements. The title contains a required Para element. The body is made up of one or more ContactInfo elements. Each ContactInfo element contains at least two cells—ContactName and ContactAddress. Once they are entered, the Phone and Email elements may be inserted, in either order, as often as needed. Each of these elements also contains a combination of Para elements.

Footnote Element Components

The Footnote element is a very simple element. When a Footnote element is inserted, a footnote notation appears in the document (it often appears as a number, an alphabetical character, or a symbol in superscript) and at the bottom of the page. Structurally, however, only one element is inserted.

Footnote Element

Footnote elements contain a GeneralRule that defines what is optional or required in a footnote. It is recommended that, at a minimum, <TEXT> be allowed in a footnote (otherwise the author cannot write a message in the footnote, which defeats the purpose of allowing a footnote in the first place), as shown here:

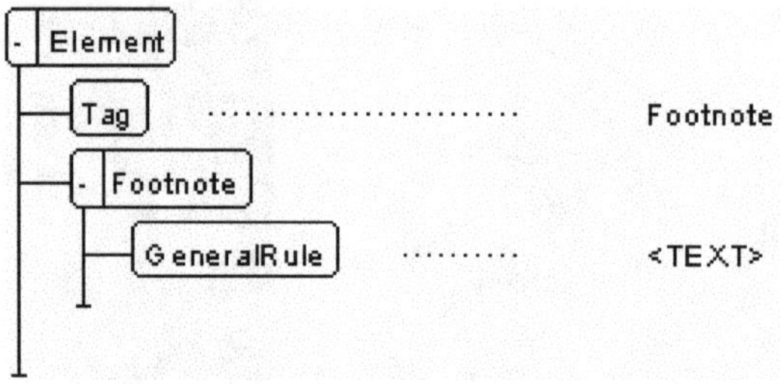

Consider the example shown in Figure 4-34 of a footnote that contains text. The footnote appears at the bottom of the text frame and contains a reference to the number automatically assigned to the footnote.

and is considered to be the definitive book on
FrameMaker 7[1] that is available.

Figure 4-34 Sample footnote.

This same structured footnote, when viewed using the Structure View, appears as follows:

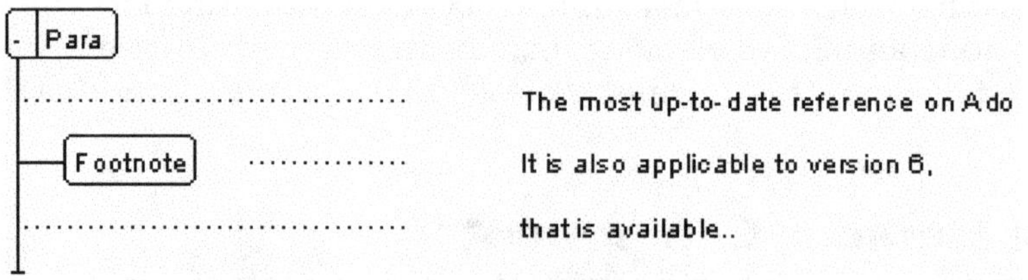

Occurrence Indicators and Footnote Elements

Because Footnote elements should allow <TEXT> at a minimum, the indicators only apply to other child elements that you want a footnote to have. Unless you are allowing child elements, there is no need for occurrence indicators to be used in a Footnote element.

Connectors and Footnote Elements

All of the standard connectors may be used in conjunction with Footnote elements. Again, unless elements other than text are allowed as child elements, there is no need to use a connector.

Developing Footnotes

To create a footnote, click beneath a GeneralRule and select **Footnote** from the Element Catalog. Click **Insert** and name the Footnote element.

Examples of a Footnote Element

Figure 4-35 shows an example of an EDD with an inserted Footnote element.

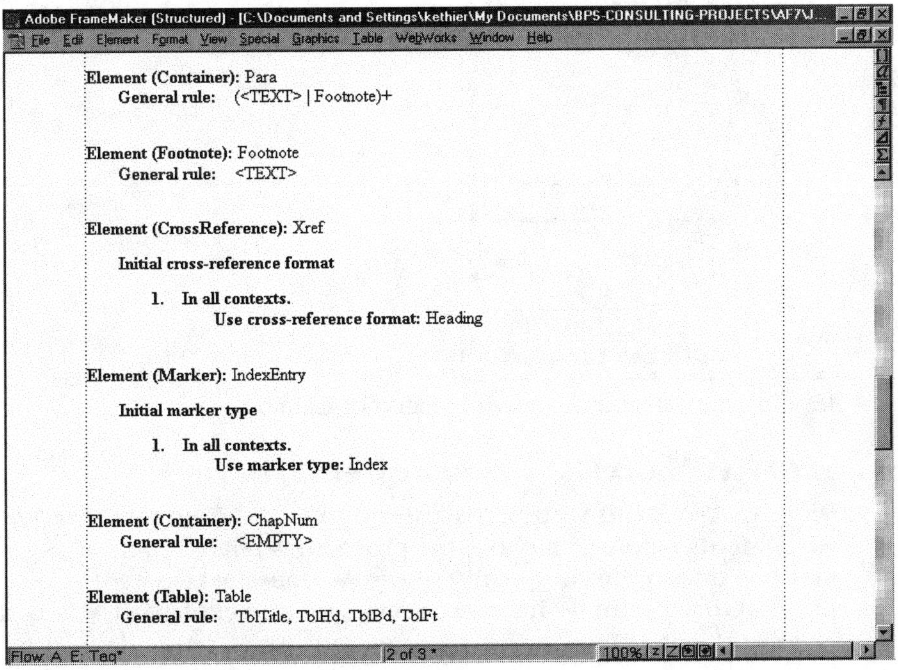

Figure 4-35 EDD sample for a footnote.

Attributes

You define attributes inserting AttributeList elements in other elements. Attributes are an optional part of elements and are often used to assign descriptive information that can be used for a variety of purposes. These may include formatting, selection of default equation types, system variables, settings for imported images, and more.

AttributeList Element

The AttributeList element does not contain a GeneralRule. Instead, the AttributeList element contains one or more Attribute child elements (see Figure 4-36). Each Attribute element contains a Name element and a definition for the type of attribute being created. The Attribute element types correspond directly to the attributes an author may select: Choice, IDReference(s), Integer(s), Real(s), String(s), and UniqueID.

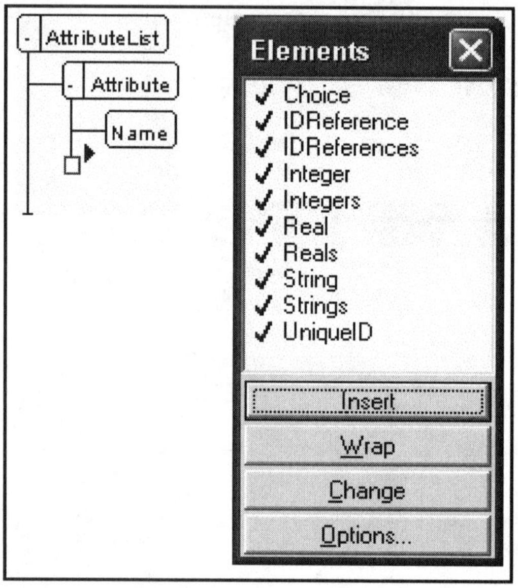

Figure 4-36 Types of attributes shown in Element Catalog.

Examples of AttributeList Element Definitions

Unlike previous sections, this section discusses numerous examples of AttributeList elements before broaching the procedures related to inserting them. This is done due to the complexity of the AttributeList element and all of its suboptions. Once examples have been reviewed and explained, you will find it easier to work with your specific requirements for attribute definitions.

Inserting an AttributeList element involves developing multiple Attribute elements. The following attributes are the types an author can work with in structured documents.

String Attributes

Consider the example shown in Figure 4-37 of a completed AttributeList element for a Section element. The AuthorName attribute is defined as a string of required text. In other words, when the author inserts any Section element in a document, he or she is prompted for a value for the AuthorName attribute prior to the element being inserted. This assumes that either Always Prompt for Attribute Values or Prompt for Required Attribute

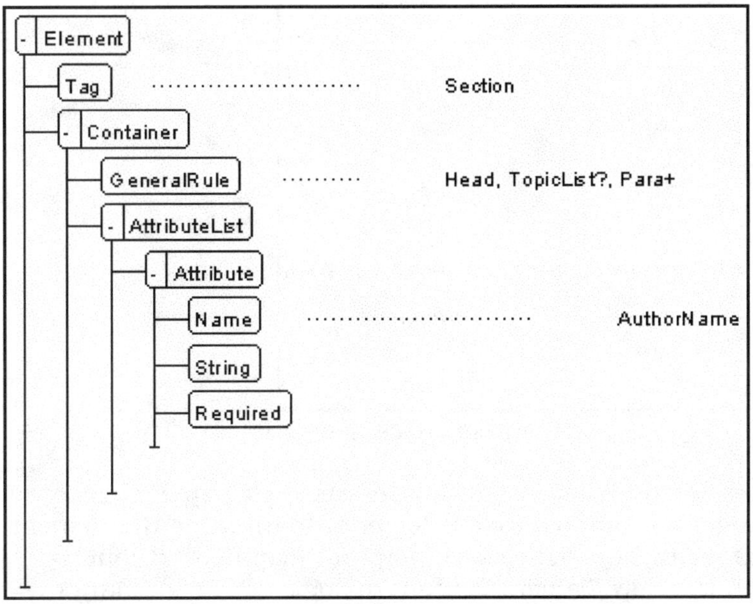

Figure 4-37 Sample String type attribute definition.

Values was selected in the New Element Options dialog box. The structured document fails validation unless a value is inserted since it is required.

Choice Attributes

Consider the example shown in Figure 4-38 of a completed AttributeList for a List element (the List element name is not showing in the screenshot). The Type attribute is defined as an optional choice (the Bullet selection is the default). In other words, when the author inserts any List element in a document, he or she is prompted for a value prior to inserting the element (if Always Prompt for Attribute Values is selected in the New Element Options dialog box). Because the attribute is optional, a default value may also be assigned in the EDD. This default is automatically selected when the attribute is inserted, but it may be modified as required.

Connectors and Attributes. This is a good time and place to mention that the rules for connectors normally state that a comma represents an implied order. The previous example, however, shows a set of three choices (Bullet, List, Dash) as options. Only one choice is applicable. The comma therefore simply acts as a divider between the choices. No "real" connector indicators are used with attributes anyway, so the comma is more of a grammatical device to identify the choices, rather than a symbol used for connection.

Integer(s) and Real(s) Attributes

Consider the example of a completed AttributeList for a Chapter element in Figure 4-39. The Version attribute is defined as an Integer type attribute that

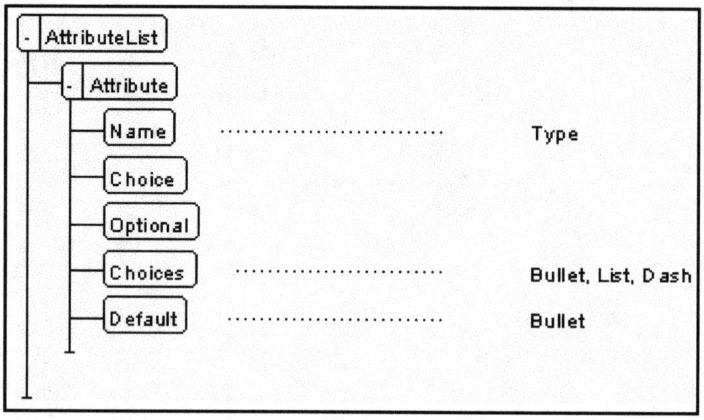

Figure 4-38 Sample Choice type attribute definition.

is Required. In other words, when the author inserts any Chapter element in a document, he or she is prompted for a value prior to inserting the element (if Always Prompt for Attribute Values or Prompt for Required Attribute Values is selected in the New Element Options dialog box). In addition, the attribute is required, and the structured document fails validation unless a value is inserted

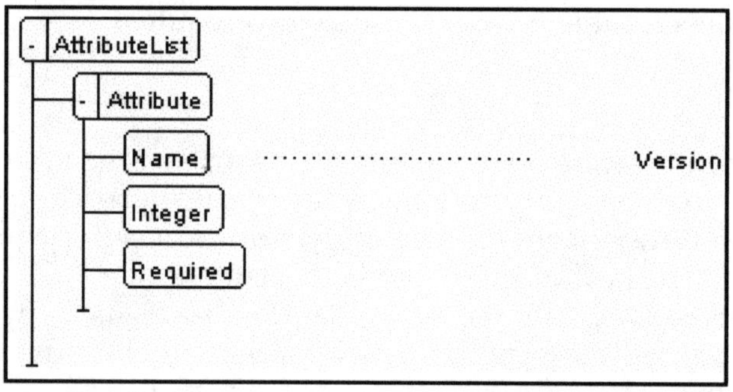

Figure 4-39 Sample Integer attribute definition.

Although it is not shown in this example, Integer(s) and Real(s) can have ranges assigned to them so that a minimum value, maximum value, or both are not exceeded by a user-defined value.

UniqueID Attributes

Consider Figure 4-40, which shows a Head element and a cross-reference

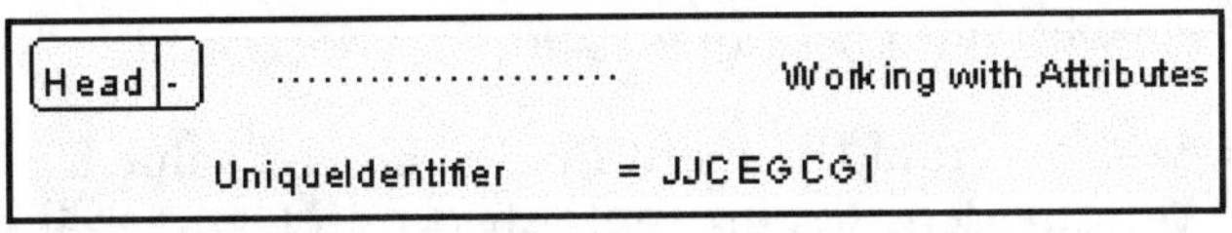

Figure 4-40 Sample UniqueID attribute with system-assigned value in a document.

element that refers to it. A UniqueID type is assigned to the Head element, and the cross-reference is linked to this identifier.

In other words, when the author inserts any cross-reference in a document, a UniqueID attribute is referenced and—in some cases—created. Users traditionally insert cross-references and expect markers to be created. The structured approach to documentation, however, is a better one for these references. It allows for edits to be made to content without concern for the inadvertent deletion of the cross-reference marker. Instead of a marker that can be selected, the value that is referenced is a part of the element's attributes.

In Figure 4-41, a UniqueID attribute is set up with the values Optional and ReadOnly. This allows an author to focus on creating content and lets FrameMaker drive both the assignment and the value of the identifier without author intervention. The benefit to this system is that the author does not have to assign values and address the possibility of conflict in UniqueID values. The values are also not editable by the author (who does not need to know the UniqueID attribute anyway). Because the assigned values are based on values driven by FrameMaker, the value does not make sense to an author viewing only the UniqueID values.

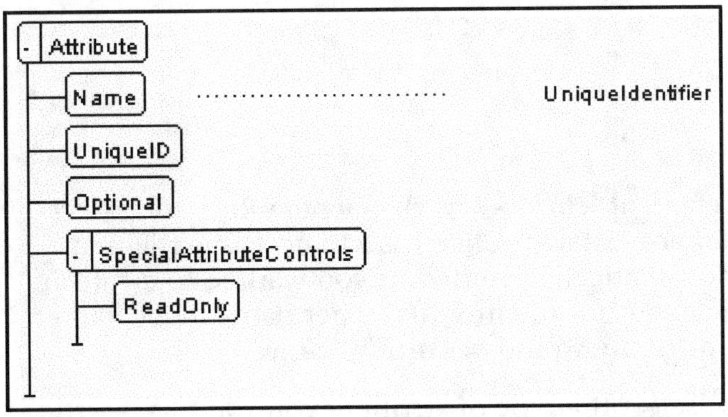

Figure 4-41 Sample UniqueID attribute definition.

When the author inserts any cross-reference in a document, a UniqueID attribute is also referenced and the cross reference notes the value of this UniqueID attribute, as shown in Figure 4-42.

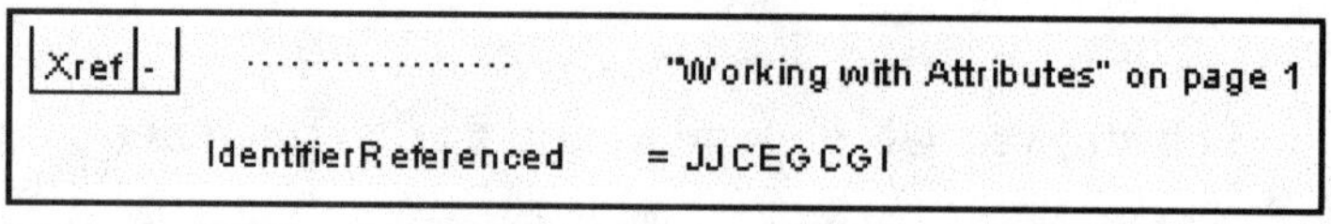

Figure 4-42 Sample UniqueID with system assigned value in a document.

Careful review of this example shows that the IdentifierReferenced value is the same as the value in the UniqueIdentifier attribute shown in Figure 4-40.

In Figure 4-43, an IdentifierReferenced value is set up with the Required value.

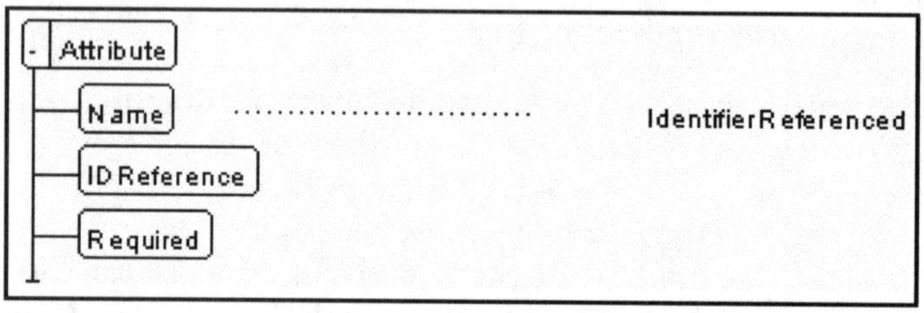

Figure 4-43 Sample IDReference attribute definition.

Developing AttributeList Elements

When you insert AttributeList elements, the cursor must be below the GeneralRule element, as shown here:

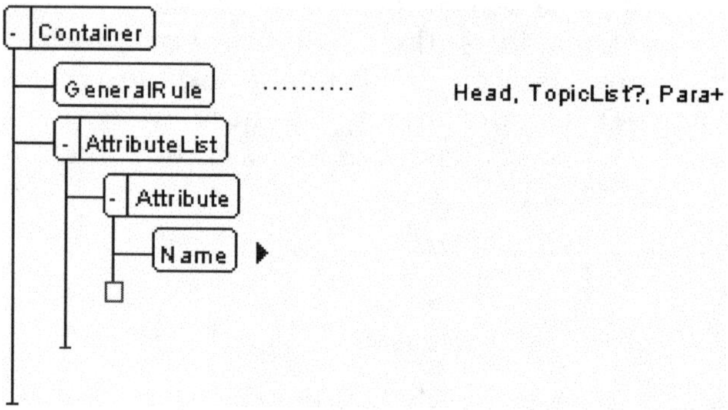

To create an AttributeList element, click below the GeneralRule and select **AttributeList** from the Element Catalog. Click **Insert** and name the first Attribute element that is automatically inserted. If you wanted to create an Attribute element to allow an author to enter his or her name in a Chapter element, for example, the attribute would be AuthorName.

After naming the attribute, select the type of attribute you want to insert. After inserting an attribute type, select whether the attribute is to be Optional or Required. (Only optional attributes may have a default value.) Finally, assign a default value, specify a range, set any special attribute controls (such as ReadOnly or Hidden) and make any other changes as required to the attribute. Once you have done this, repeat the process for each attribute that is required for a given element definition.

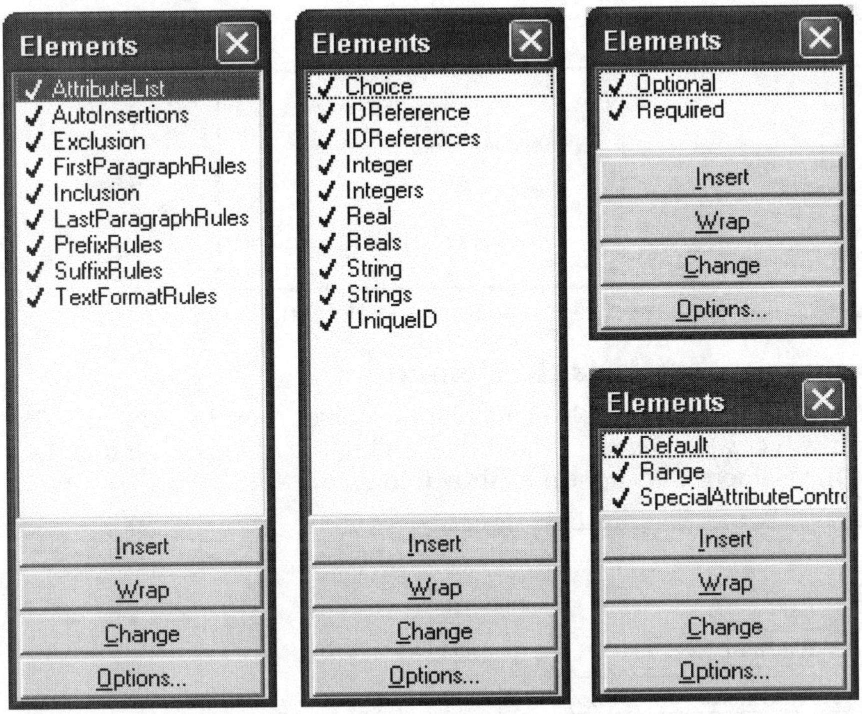

Figure 4-44 AttributeList element and related element Element Catalog choices.

SystemVariable Elements

The SystemVariable element is very simple. When it is inserted, it is inserted automatically or based on attribute values.

Parts of a SystemVariable Element

A SystemVariable element does not contain a GeneralRule. Instead, the element allows an AttributeList or SystemVariableFormat element. When you use an AttributeList element, various attributes may be defined that relate to the SystemVariable. These attributes may then be used for a variety of purposes, including formatting the variable that is inserted. Regardless of the attributes defined, the SystemVariable element must be defined and inserted.

Consider the example shown in Figure 4-45 of a system variable type element that inserts the name of the file with which you are working. The system variable (*memo.fm*) automatically appears inline with the rest of the text.

This same structured system variable element can be viewed in Figure 4-46 using the Structure View.

The name of this sample is memo.fm which is a variable and changes if the file is saved with a new name.

Figure 4-45 Sample SystemVariable.

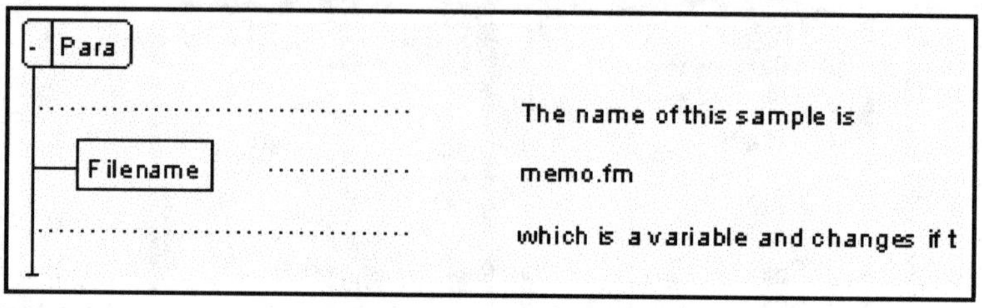

Figure 4-46 The Filename SystemVariable type element.

Developing SystemVariable Elements

When you insert SystemVariable elements, the cursor must be below the Tag element. If you create a SystemVariable specifying the name of the file, for example, the element may appear as shown in Figure 4-47.

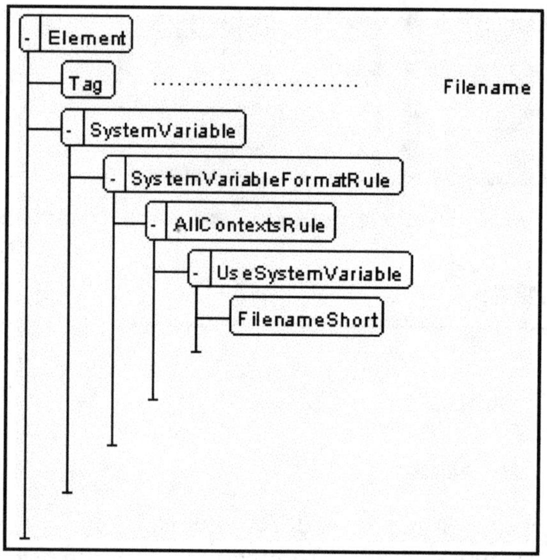

Figure 4-47 SystemVariable elements for the Filename variable.

To create a variable, click beneath a Tag and select **SystemVariable** from the Element Catalog. Click **Insert** and name the variable. If you are creating a variable to insert the filename, for example, the name assigned to the element might be Filename.

After naming the variable, insert any attributes related to the element. Then specify the SystemVariableFormatRule element using an AllContextRule, a ContextRule, or a LevelRule element. If using a ContextRule or LevelRule element, continue to develop the rule as required.

Once the rules have been set, you can specify the variable you wish to insert. This may be a system variable or a user variable. Make sure that the name of the variable matches (spelling, case, and characters such as spaces) a variable in the template into which the EDD is imported.

Example of the SystemVariable Element

Figure 4-48 shows an example of an EDD that allows a SystemVariable element to be inserted.

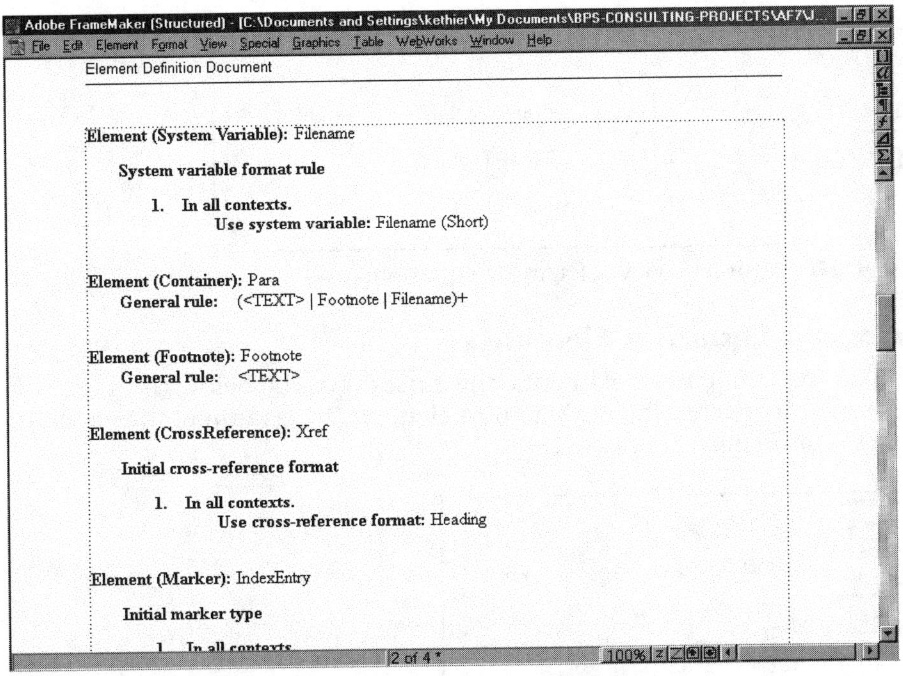

Figure 4-48 EDD sample for SystemVariable element.

Equation Elements

The Equation element is also very simple. When it is inserted, it is inserted automatically or based on attribute values.

Parts of an Equation Element

An Equation element does not contain a GeneralRule. Instead, the element allows an AttributeList or an InitialObjectFormat element. If you use an AttributeList element, various attributes may be defined that relate to the Equation element. These attributes may then be used for a variety of purposes, including formatting the equation that is inserted. Regardless of the attributes defined, the Equation element must be defined and inserted.

Consider the sample equation in Figure 4-49. The equation automatically appears inline with the rest of the text. This same structured equation is

> When calculating the weight of each widget, the formula $(a + b)c$ is used.

Figure 4-49 Sample equation.

shown in Figure 4-50 using the Structure View.

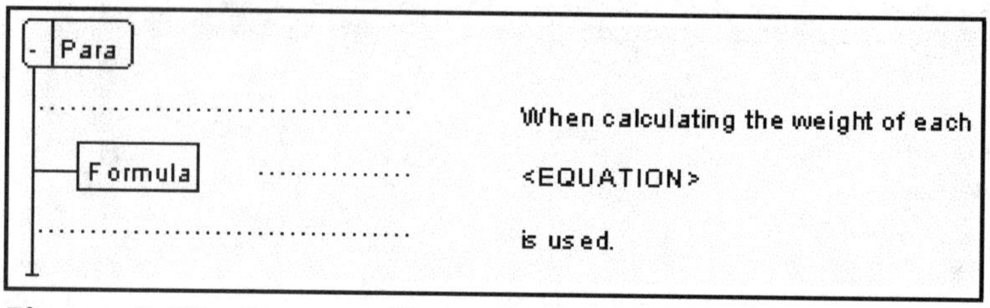

Figure 4-50 Structure View of sample equation.

Developing Equation Elements

When you insert Equation elements, the cursor must be below the Tag element. If you are creating an Equation element, for example, the element will look as shown in Figure 4-51.

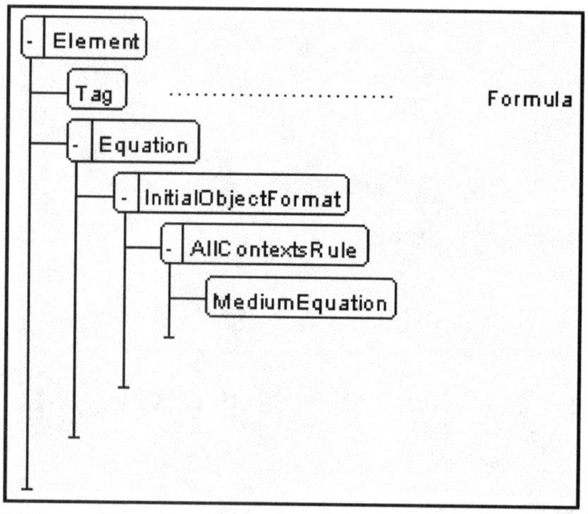

Figure 4-51 Structure View of Equation element's EDD setup.

After naming the equation, insert any attributes related to the element, and then specify the size of the element using an AllContextRule, a ContextRule, or a LevelRule element. If using a ContextRule or LevelRule element, continue to develop the rule as required.

Example of the Equation Element

Figure 4-52 shows an example of an EDD that allows an Equation element to be inserted.

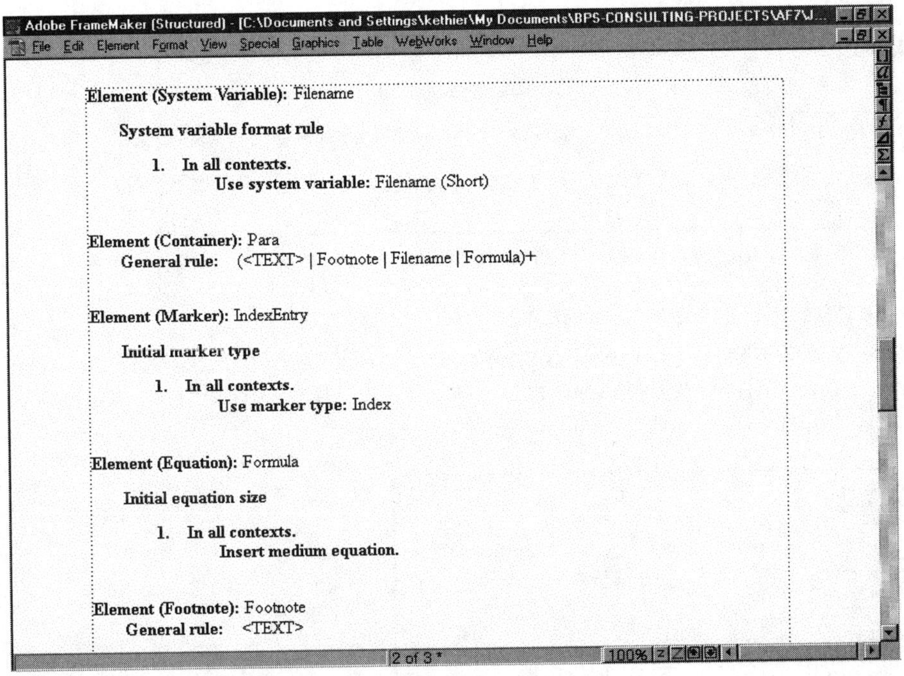

Figure 4-52 EDD sample for equation.

Marker Elements

The Marker element is also very simple. When it is inserted, it is inserted automatically or based on attribute values.

Marker Element

Marker elements do not contain a GeneralRule. Instead, the element allows an AttributeList or an InitialObjectFormat element. If you use an AttributeList element, various attributes may be defined that relate to the Marker element. These attributes may then be used for a variety of purposes, including driving the marker type that is inserted. Regardless of the attributes defined, the MarkerType element must be defined and inserted.

Consider the example of an index entry shown in Figure 4-53. The entry marker automatically appears inline with the rest of the text.

This same structured marker, when seen using the Structure View, appears as shown in Figure 4-54.

Figure 4-53 Sample index marker.

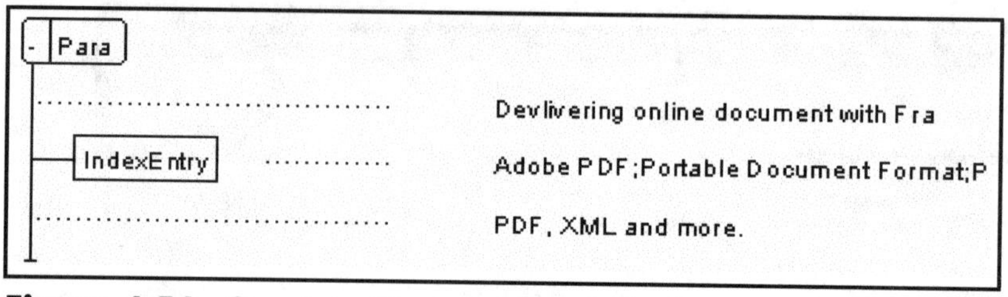

Figure 4-54 Structure View showing IndexEntry marker.

Developing Marker Elements

When you insert Marker elements, the cursor must be below the Tag element. If you are creating an Index Marker, for example, the element may appear as shown in Figure 4-55.

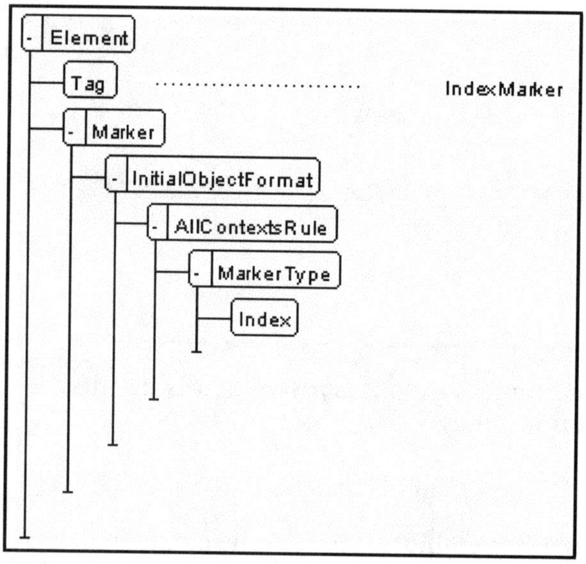

Figure 4-55 IndexMarker element setup in EDD.

After naming the marker, insert any attributes related to the element, then specify the InitialObjectFormat element using an AllContextRule, a ContextRule, or a LevelRule element. If using a ContextRule or LevelRule element, continue to develop the rule as required.

Once the rules have been set, you must specify the marker type to insert. This may be an index marker, hypertext, author marker, or any other type of marker. Make sure that the name of the marker matches the spelling, case, and characters (such as spaces) of the related marker in the template into which the EDD will be imported.

Example of Marker Element

Figure 4-56 shows an example of an EDD that allows a marker element to be inserted.

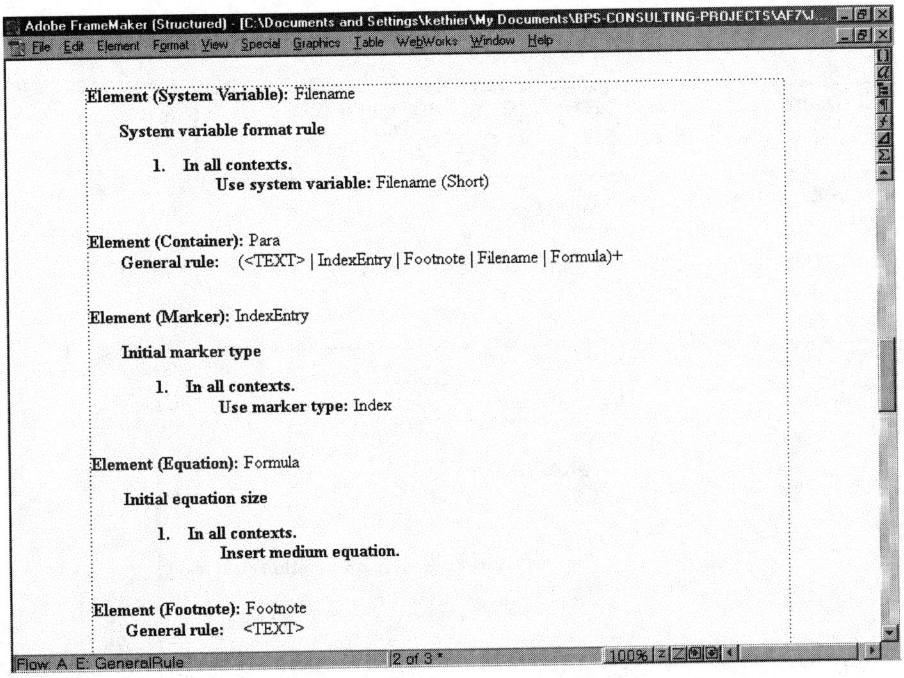

Figure 4-56 EDD sample for marker.

CrossReference Elements

The CrossReference element requires specific attributes to function correctly. When it is inserted, a cross-reference is created and you can automatically insert specific attribute values.

Cross-references generally require the use of a UniqueID type attribute to identify the location being referenced and an IDReference type attribute for the cross-reference itself, as shown in Figure 4-57. These attributes must be set up as part of the element being referenced and the cross-reference itself.

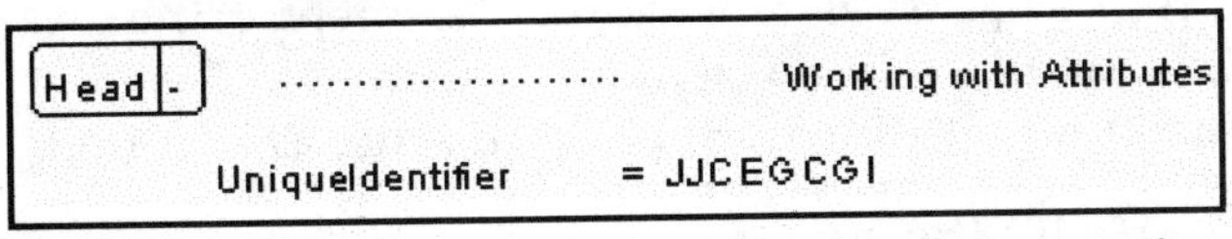

Figure 4-57 Sample UniqueID with system-assigned value in a document.

Cross-Reference Element

A Cross-reference element does not contain a GeneralRule. The element instead allows an AttributeList or an InitialObjectFormat element. If you use an AttributeList element, various attributes may be defined that relate to the cross-reference. These attributes may then be used for a variety of purposes, including formatting the inserted cross-reference. Regardless of the attributes defined, the cross-reference must be defined and inserted.

Consider the example of a heading and a cross-reference shown in Figure 4-58.

> References may be inserted, modified, or deleted as required. See "Cross references", on page 7.

Figure 4-58 Sample cross-reference.

This same structured cross-reference is shown in Figure 4-59 using the Structure View.

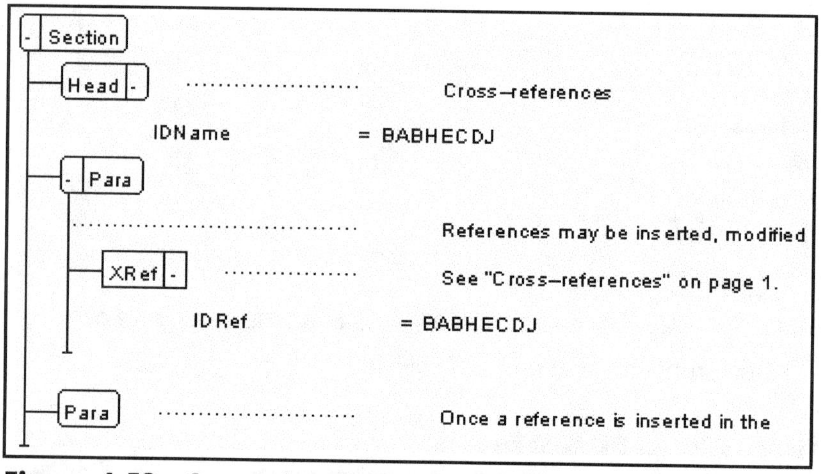

Figure 4-59 Cross-reference structure showing IDReference and related UniqueID attributes values.

Developing Cross-Reference Elements

When you insert cross-reference elements, the cursor must be below the Tag element. When you create a cross-reference, the element may appear as shown in Figure 4-60.

After naming the cross-reference, you may insert any attributes related to the element. You may then specify the CrossReferenceFormat element using an AllContextRule, a ContextRule, or a LevelRule element. If using a ContextRule or LevelRule element, continue to develop the rule as required.

Once the rules have been set, specify the cross-reference you plan to insert. Make sure that the name of the cross-reference matches the spelling, case,

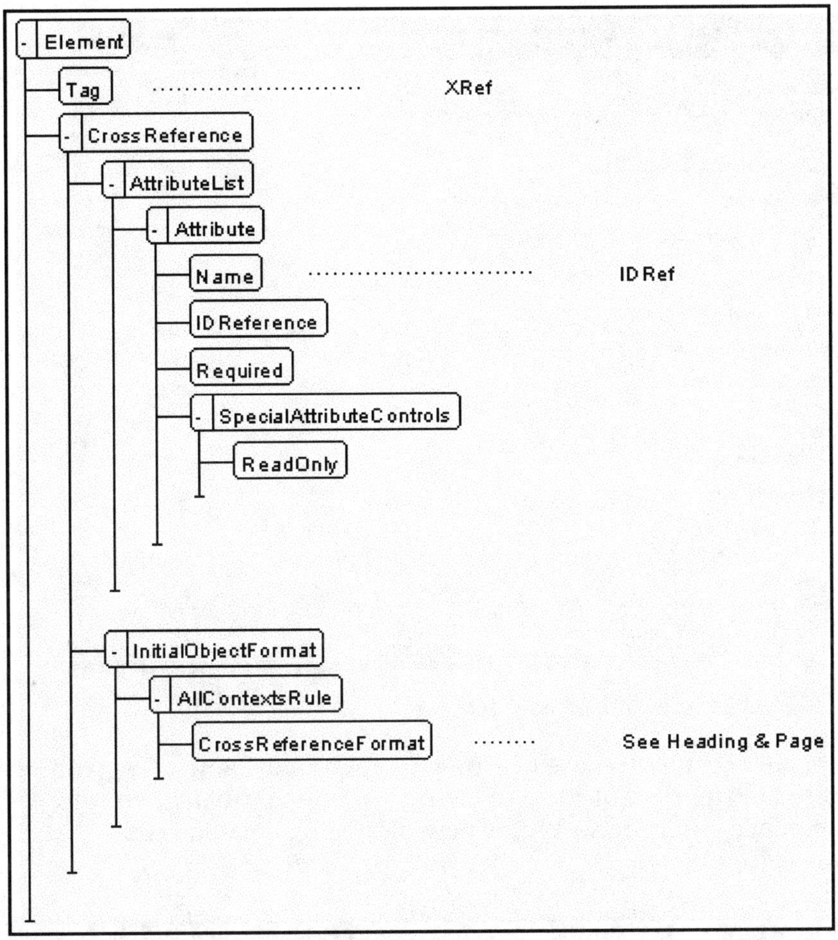

Figure 4-60 EDD setup for cross-reference.

and characters (such as spaces) of the cross-reference in the template into which the EDD is imported.

Example of Cross-Reference Elements

Figure 4-61 shows an example of an EDD that allows a cross-reference element to be inserted.

Graphic Elements

The Graphic element often requires specific attributes to function correctly. When a Graphic element is inserted, an anchored frame is created (or an image is imported), which can be automatically positioned and formatted based on specific attribute values.

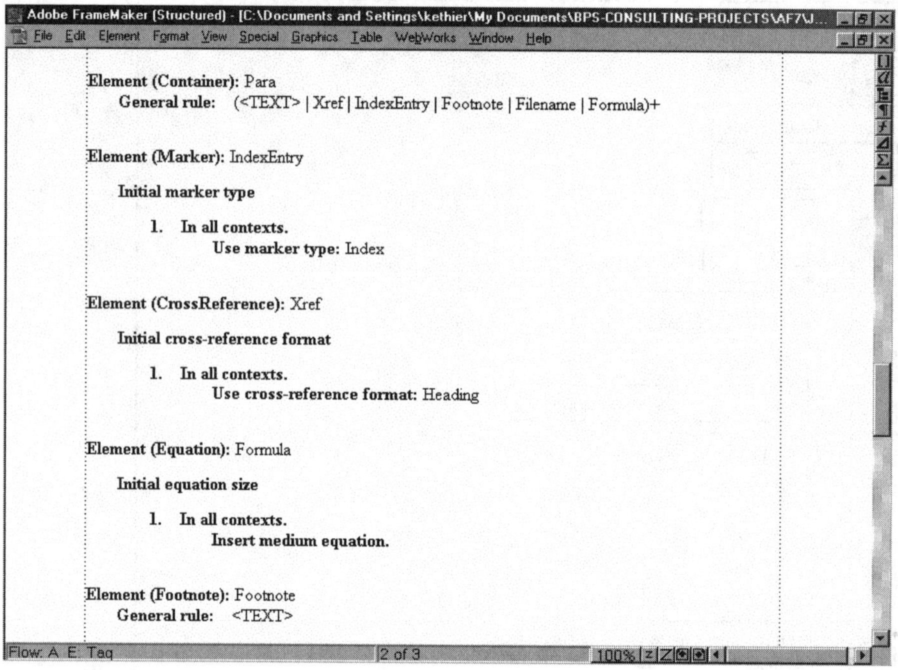

Figure 4-61 EDD sample of a cross-reference.

Graphics generally require the use of either an anchored frame or a graphic that is imported to the current file (see Figure 4-62). It is usually better to import by reference, as doing so avoids new files being created if the structured file is ever converted to either XML or SGML.

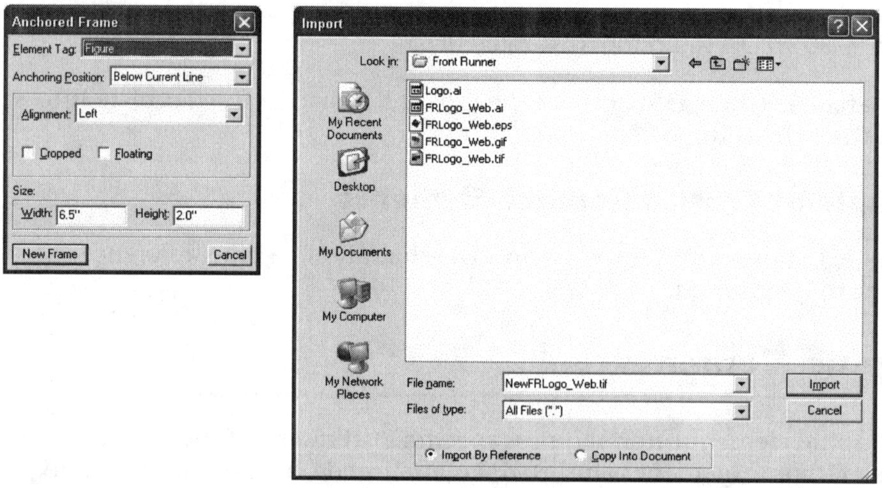

Figure 4-62 Sample graphic inserting anchored frame or imported files.

Graphic Elements

A Graphic element does not contain a GeneralRule, and the element allows an AttributeList or an InitialObjectFormat element. If you use an AttributeList element, various attributes may be defined that relate to the cross-reference. These attributes may then be used for a variety of purposes, including formatting the cross-reference that is inserted. Regardless of the attributes defined, the cross-reference must be defined and inserted.

Consider the example of a Graphic element in a paragraph shown in Figure 4-63.

To open the Tools Palette in FrameMaker, click the icon.

Figure 4-63 Sample graphic.

This same structured graphic is shown in Figure 4-64 using the Structure View.

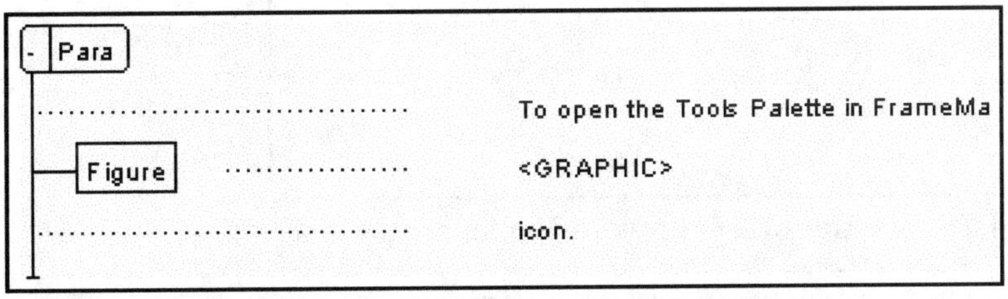

Figure 4-64 Structure View showing Figure element.

Developing Graphic Elements

When you insert Graphic elements, the cursor must be positioned below the Tag element. If you are creating a graphic, the element may appear as shown in Figure 4-65. In this example, a context rule is used. If the Figure element is inserted in a Para element that is within a Section element, then the Import dialog box appears. Otherwise, the Anchored Frame dialog box appears.

After naming the graphic, you may insert any attributes related to the element. Then specify the InitialObjectFormat elementusing an AllContextRule, a ContextRule, or a LevelRule element. If using a ContextRule or LevelRule element, continue to develop the rule as required.

Once rules have been set, specify the graphic to insert. Make sure the type of graphic is either an ImportedGraphicFile or an AnchoredFrame, and that adequate support exists in the template into which the EDD is imported.

Example of Graphic Elements

Figure 4-66 shows an example of an EDD that allows a Graphic element to be inserted.

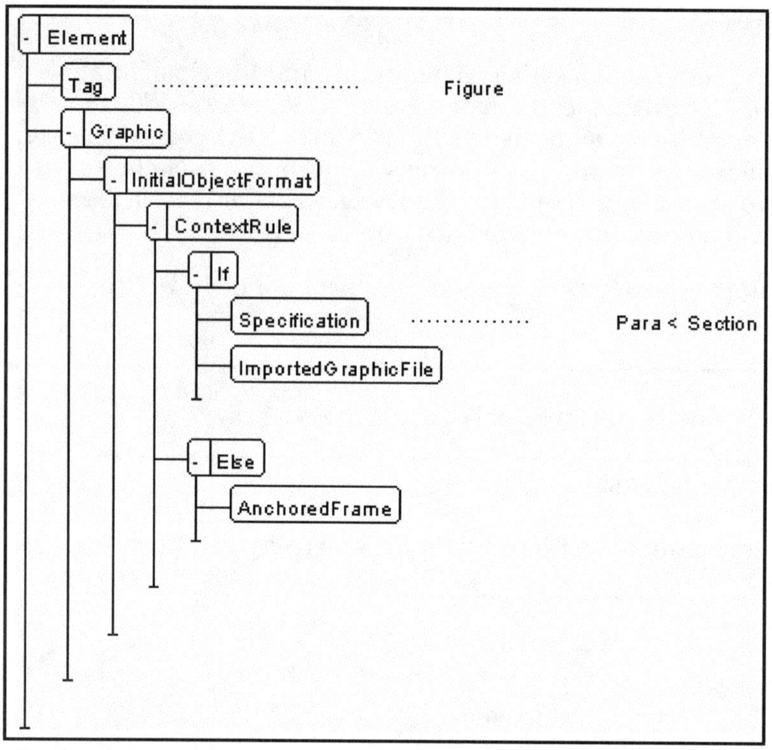

Figure 4-65 EDD structure of a Graphic type element.

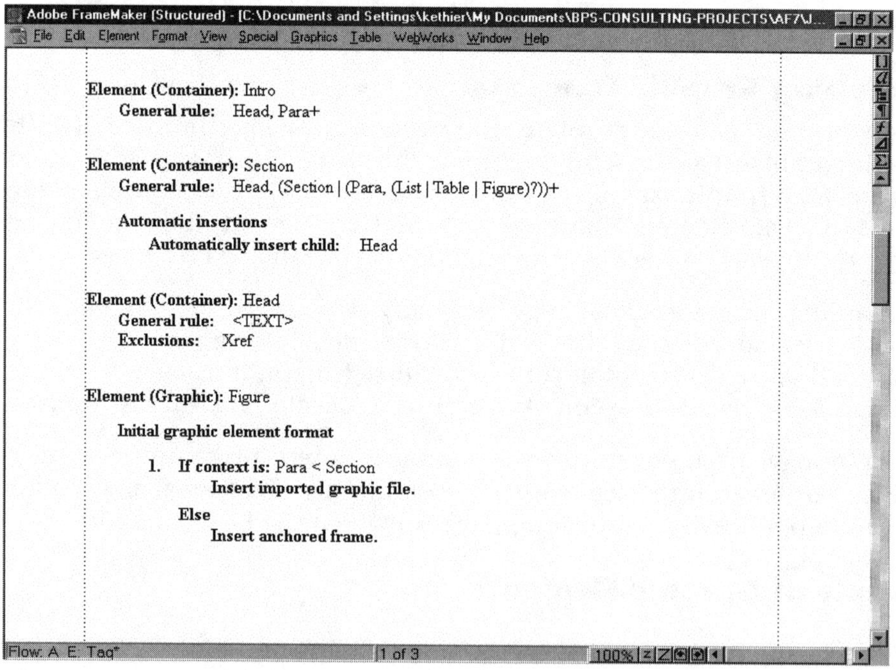

Figure 4-66 EDD sample for a graphic.

Formatting Document Templates Using an EDD

The appearance of a template that is based on the structure of an EDD can be driven in numerous ways. The primary method in unstructured documents is to format content in the template (using the various Designers; master pages; dialog boxes for variables, cross-references, and so on; reference pages; and more) and have users apply the format to the content as it is inserted in the document.

The structured document, however, uses a different approach. In structured files, the element is the master of the format. By assigning formatting to elements, the author is no longer required to remember arcane formatting instructions. As a writer, for example, you need to remember if a note in a section should be formatted using the NoteSubTopic paragraph tag, or by applying the TopicNote tag. In the same way, a list made up of many items in a procedure may need to be formatted with the ItemFirstInProcedure and ItemNextInProcedure tags. (In an installation procedure, the list would need ItemFirstInInstall and the equally bulky ItemNextInInstall.)

Aside from this being time consuming and prone to error, the author also experiences major difficulties in the application of the "correct" format when content is modified by the use of cutting and pasting or major editing of content.

The solution to this (and numerous other format questions) is to use the structured file and the elements' association with each other to drive the formatting.

Consider the humble bulleted list. If you (or, more likely, the powers that be) decide to format a bulleted list with numerous tags, a lot of manual work may be required. The first item might be a BulletFirst to reflect an extra 4 points of space before the bullet list, and the last item might be a BulletLast to accommodate the additional 8 points below. Of course, all other bullets are BulletMid. Finally, if a single bullet is required, you also need a BulletSingle to cover all possibilities.

So, recapping this scenario, we now have four tags (BulletFirst, BulletMid, BulletLast, and BulletSingle) to accommodate a bullet list of one or more items. In addition, if the writer develops a single bullet and later adds three more, then manual work will be required. If the list expands before the first item or after the last, again more manual work will be required.

In the structured document, you use formatting rules to build your design. In the example of the bulleted list, the List element may be assigned a Type attribute, which may be set to Bullet for our purposes. The Item elements are then instructed to appear in a variety of formats. This could be based on the number of elements, the order of elements, or a combination of both. The formatting rule, therefore, could read something along the lines of "if the

Item is in a List where the Type is set to Bullet then..." This would be followed by other combinations, such as "where the Type is set to Number" or "where the Type is set to Alpha," and format instructions.

Continuing with the example of Item in List with an attribute Type of Bullet, we can set subrules. If the Item is a single element with no siblings, the format may be set to use the BulletMid paragraph tag. If the Item is the first or last in the list, the BulletFirst or BulletLast tags are used. All other Item elements would use BulletMid. This automatically formats content as the author manipulates the list by adding, deleting, or rearranging the Item elements. It eliminates the need for an author to try and remember the names and reasons associated with a specific format. This reduces (or perhaps even eliminates) formatting errors and simplifies the use of content in the long term.

Part III

Advanced Design and Layout

5

Automated Master Pages and Template Adjustments

Bernard Aschwanden

This chapter introduces master pages and explores how they are used in FrameMaker. The automated master page application feature of FrameMaker 7.0/7.1 is also described.

Applicable to FrameMaker versions 5.0/5.5, 6 (except automation) and 7.0/7.1

This chapter introduces, explains, and demonstrates the use of master pages in Adobe FrameMaker 7. It also briefly explores how the master page is used in earlier releases.

In this chapter you will learn what master pages are, how they are used, and why they play an important role in the FrameMaker environment. There are detailed explanations of why master pages are required and how documents benefit from the use of master pages. You will also learn how master pages are applied to a document and the methods used to update or modify the master pages.

An Overview of Master Pages

The master page acts as a "background" for the documents that are created with FrameMaker. The master page contains layout (such as headers and footers, page numbers, and watermark images) that is generated automatically in the design of your document and is usually not accessible from the document body pages.

A single-sided document with a consistent format requires at least one master page. A document that is set up as a double-sided page requires at least two master pages.

It is not uncommon for a document to have multiple master pages. These may include a custom master page for the title page of the file, and two master pages to represent both the left and the right pages of the body of the document. In addition, custom pages may be added to support rotated pages for oversized tables or images, and so on.

Using Single (Right) Master Pages

If a document is based on a single page layout, this page will have a single header (which will eventually contain the name of the book or a section title), one primary text frame, and the page number at the bottom of the page. Each page has the exact same layout; therefore only a single master page is used.

Figure 5-1 illustrates this example in use for multiple pages. As the content of the file is added, pages are inserted and each page has the same appearance based on the default single, right-sided master page.

Using Double (Right and Left) Master Pages

If a document similar to the one used in Figure 5-1 is based on a double master page layout, all right-hand pages will look like the pages in the illustration. All left-hand pages, however, will be set up with a header that is left aligned (to oppose the header on the right master page), one primary text frame, and the page number in the bottom *left* (opposite) corner. Every other page has the exact same layout, resulting in a layout that utilizes both left

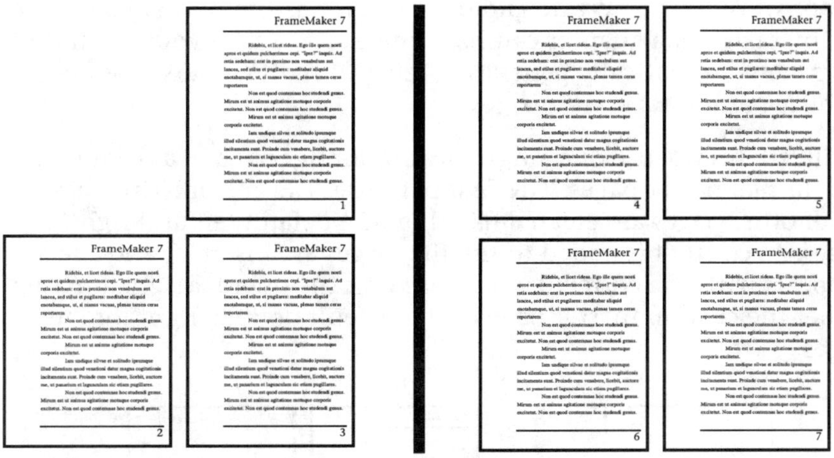

Figure 5-1 Single (right) master page example.

and right master pages in the same document. Figure 5-2 illustrates this example in use for multiple pages.

This layout format should be the default for multiple-page documents. As the content of the file is added, pages are inserted, and the content appears with the correct layout based on the use of assigned master pages.

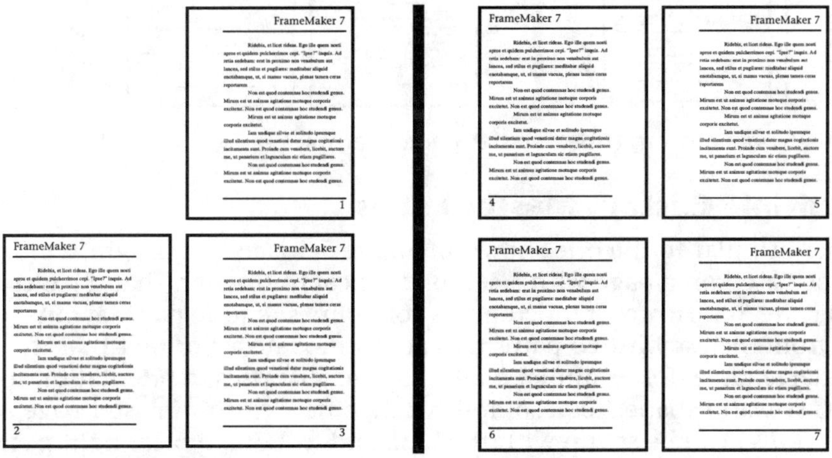

Figure 5-2 Double (right and left) master page example.

Using Single Custom Master Pages

If a document similar to the one in Figure 5-2 is used, all right- and left-hand pages will look like the ones shown in the illustration. Until they are modified, however, all *first* pages will look like any other right-hand document page. Most book chapters are set up in such a way that the first page is different from the rest of the chapter (with, for example, a text box for the chapter number and name, and another text box for the chapter's first few paragraphs). When you create and use a single custom master page called *Title*, every first page of a chapter can have the exact same layout, with the remaining pages automatically generating left and right layouts that are based on the *left* and *right* master pages.

Figure 5-3 illustrates the use of a single custom master page in a document that uses multiple master pages. The first page uses the custom Title master page, and all other pages are created based on the default left and right master pages. As content is added to the file, pages are inserted, and the content appears with the correct layout based on the use of assigned master pages—either the custom master page or the default double, right, or left master pages.

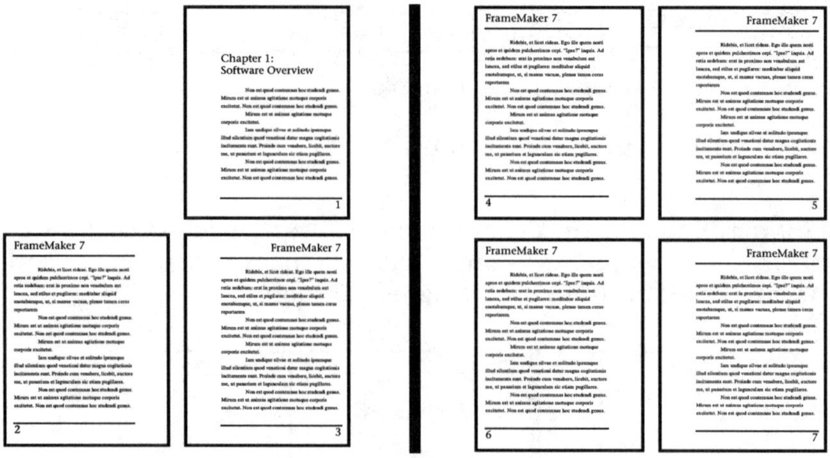

Figure 5-3 Single custom (title) master page example.

Using Multiple Custom Master Pages

If a document similar to the one shown in Figure 5-1 is used, all right-hand pages will be based on a page with a setup identical to the right-hand pages shown in Figure 5-3. However, documents sometimes require page layouts that break from the established pattern to accommodate art or text that is atypical. A large table, for example, might require a landscape orientation to allow for its size and shape. To accomplish this, a new custom master page (called *LargeTable*) can be set up with the look and feel of a typical right page but with a rotated text frame to accommodate the extended size of the table.

Figure 5-4 illustrates the use of a second custom master page in a document that uses multiple master pages. As content is added to the file, pages are inserted, and the content appears with the correct layout based on the use of assigned master pages—either the custom master pages, or the right master page.

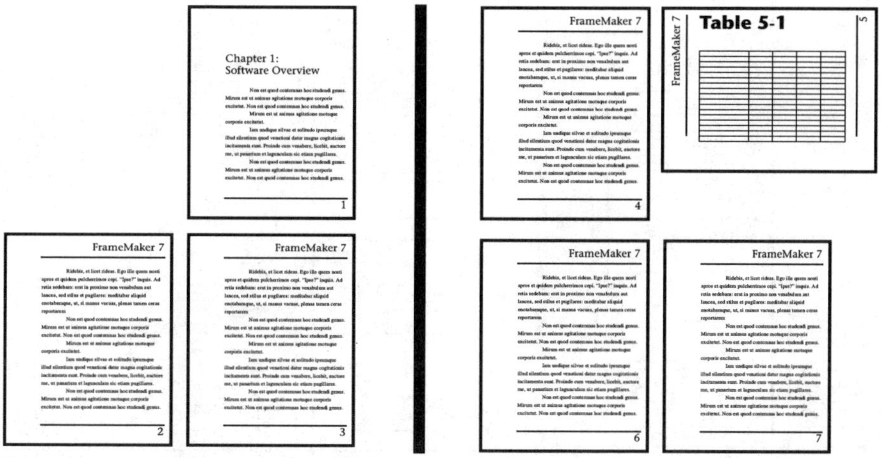

Figure 5-4 Multiple custom (Title and LargeTable) master page example.

Using Master Pages

This section addresses the way master pages are used in all FrameMaker versions.

In all versions of FrameMaker, the master page can be applied manually to pages based on instructions from the author. The application of a master page is done without any concern about whether the page appears at the beginning of a file or if it was inserted after the file was created. Inserting master pages in the middle of a document in versions of FrameMaker before 7 often results in undesired page layouts if content is later added or deleted.

Figure 5-5 illustrates a document in which most right-hand pages share an identical layout. The first page and a few body pages, however, are set up with custom master pages. The cover page is modified in appearance, and pages 5 and 6 use custom master pages with a rotated text frame to accommodate oversized tables.

As content is added to the file, pages are inserted, and the content appears with the correct layout based on the use of assigned master pages—either the custom master pages, or the right master page. If content is edited later, however, the layout of the materials change.

At this point, the document still looks as desired. If subsequent content changes do not shift the position of the table on page 5, no formatting issues will arise. As soon as content is added or removed prior to page 5, however, the table may begin to shift as shown in Figure 5-6.

If this happens, the document will require editing. The table may need to be forced to appear at the top of the page, or other document-level formatting may need to be done. If more than a few lines of text change (i.e., entire pages are added or removed), the document will likely require major changes

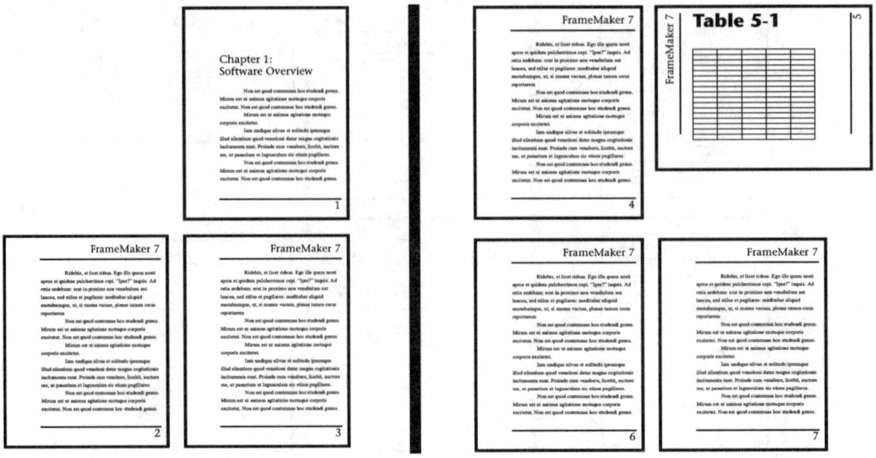

Figure 5-5 Master page applied to the default flow (no disconnected pages).

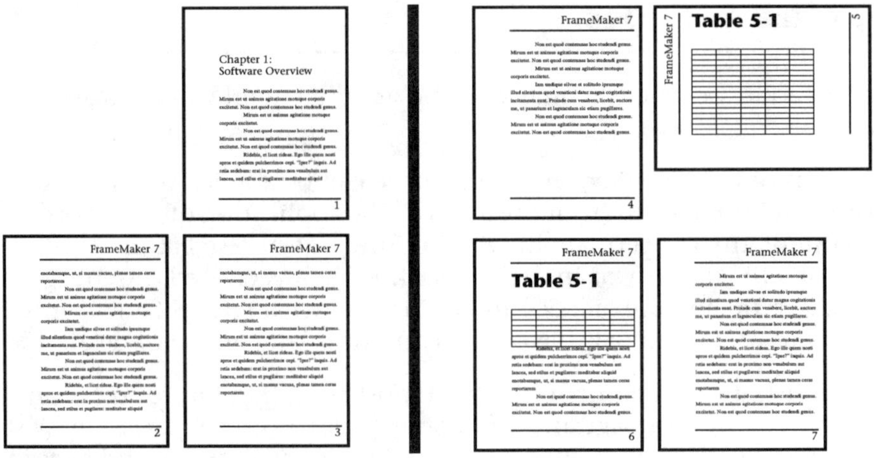

Figure 5-6 Page layout after lines of text are deleted.

to the current master page assignment and to the overall layout of the document to make it look as desired. An example is shown in Figure 5-7, with the second page of the table on a custom master page.

If the same page layout is developed using *disconnected pages*, the table remains on page 5 at all times but is no longer part of the flow of the document. In this way, the table is always on the same page regardless of any edits. This may cause confusion if, for example, a document has a text phrase such as "seen in the table on the following page" that moves from the fourth page to the second. The table remains on the fifth page, leaving the reader to wonder what table is being referenced.

Because it is not part of the document flow, the table will not be selected if you click **Edit > Select All in Flow**. You may assume that the entire chapter's

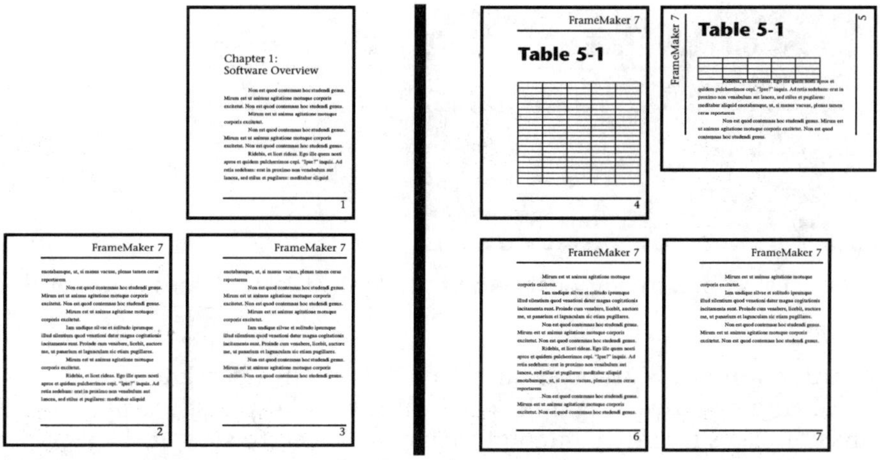

Figure 5-7 Page layout after multiple lines of text are deleted, table is shifted.

content is selected (for the purpose of copying all the content to a new document, for example), but this is not the case.

For some time users have felt there has to be a better solution to this ongoing issue of page layout and manipulation. Of course, the answer lies in the new paradigm used in FrameMaker 7—automated master page application.

Applying Master Pages

Version 6 and Earlier

In FrameMaker versions 6 and earlier, the master page is manually applied using **Format > Page Layout > Master Page Usage**. Unless a custom master page is applied at the very beginning of a file, there are limitations to be considered when planning a document.

Version 7/7.1

FrameMaker 7 and 7.1 allow master pages to be applied in multiple ways. One way is to assign the use of master pages in a document based on the use of paragraphs (or elements) within the document. Another method is to continue to manually apply master pages in the same manner as in previous versions. To do so forces you to work with the restrictions of the previous releases of the software, which is not the most desirable avenue.

FrameMaker 7 and 7.1 support the use of a command called Apply Master Pages. This command applies master pages based on instructions that are stored in the current file's reference pages. When this command is applied to a document (**Format > Page Layout > Apply Master Pages**), a dialog box appears (see Figure 5-8), prompting you to acknowledge that manually applied master pages may be overridden.

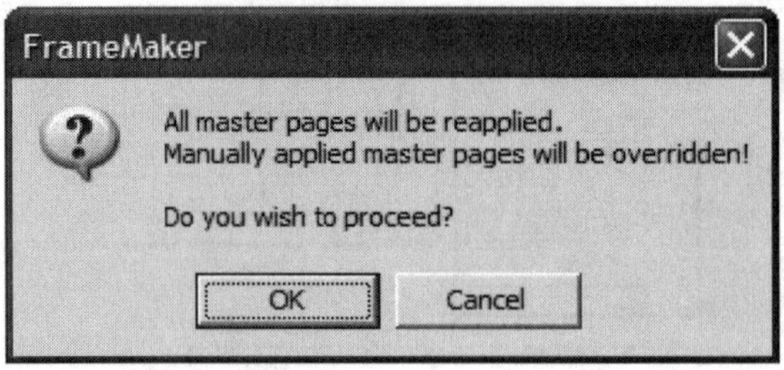

Figure 5-8 Dialog box that appears when the Apply Master Pages command is invoked.

Although this command can be applied to a document's paragraphs regardless of where those paragraphs occur, it is generally best to apply custom master pages to only paragraphs that are forced to start at the top of a page. Doing otherwise may result in sending conflicting instructions to the software. A document that has more than one paragraphs with different instructions on what master page should be used, for example, can result in an generated error log such as that shown in Figure 5-9.

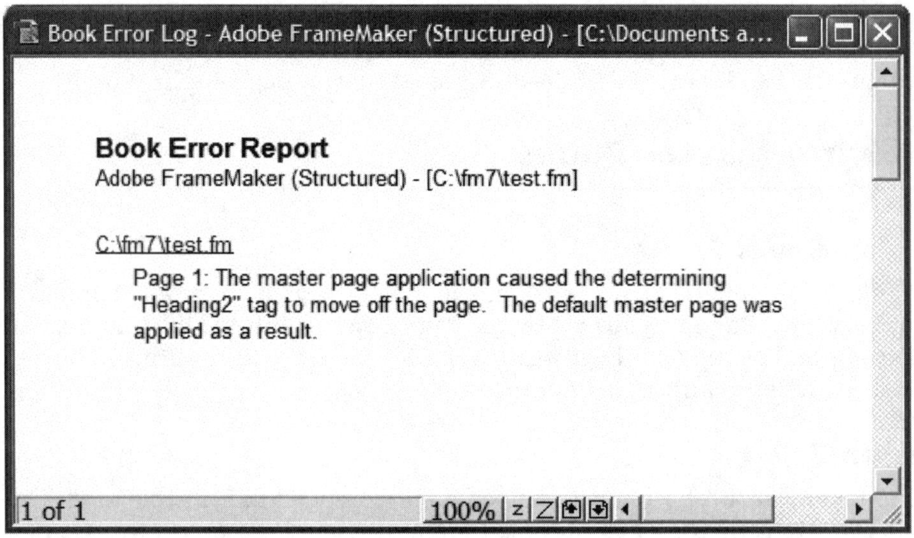

Figure 5-9 Error report on master page application conflict.

Setting Up the Apply Master Pages Command

To use the Apply Master Page command, a template must be carefully developed. Paragraph tags need to be applied consistently and correctly to the document, master pages need to be created with careful consideration of the impact of their use, and reference pages need to be set up with the appropriate code.

Paragraph Tag Considerations

In the same way that paragraph tag development is crucial to generated files, side heads, general page layout, numbering, appearance in tables, and so on, it is vital that paragraph tags be created with consideration for how they will be used with master pages. When paragraph tags are applied incorrectly or foolishly, the overall document will suffer.

Content that is expected to begin at the top of a page at all times should be formatted using the Pagination properties of the Paragraph Designer.

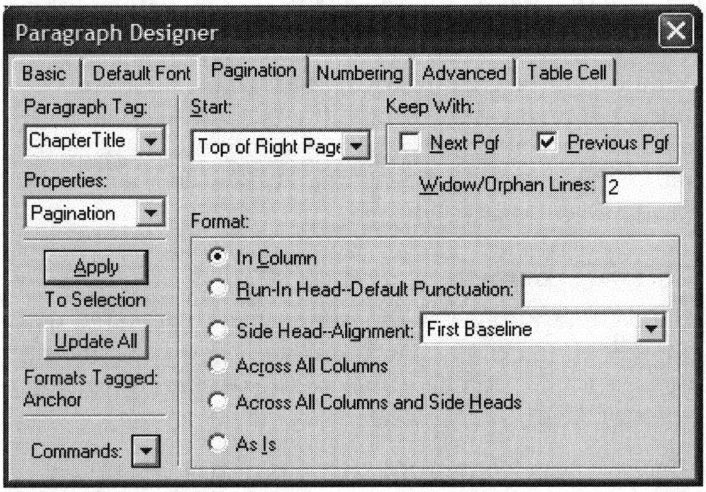

Figure 5-10 Pagination properties of the Paragraph Designer.

These pagination settings can force paragraphs to begin at the top of a given page in one of the following ways:

- Top of page
- Top of left page
- Top of right page

Once paragraphs are forced to start on the top of a page, it is much easier to consistently apply a standard master page layout throughout the document.

Master Page Considerations

When new master pages are created, the default master pages (left and right) must be taken into consideration. These formats and the layout of these pages must be set up before any other pages are created. Generally speaking, new master pages are based on existing master pages rather than on a blank page. It is therefore advisable to correctly develop the default pages and use them as the basis for subsequent pages.

Once the default pages are set up correctly with headers and footers, text frames, and any watermarks, you can begin to develop the additional custom master pages. When creating the default pages, you should consider what each master page will be used for and determine what paragraph type is most likely to appear at the start of this page.

For example, consider a document with a default left and right page and a custom page for the title of the chapter. This custom page may be named Cover, for example, and be formatted with a look that is unique to the first page of the document. In addition, a paragraph tag is created with the express purpose of being used as the first paragraph on this page. The paragraph tag can be named Title, for example, and can be formatted in a variety of ways.

In this example, a document can be created with a paragraph tag that is tied to a specific master page. In FrameMaker 7 you apply the master page by using an automated feature rather than by manually applying the page. The final result is that all pages that have the Title paragraph tag in them will adhere to the Cover master page layout.

Reference Page Considerations

Once you have created a paragraph tag and the master page associated with that paragraph tag, you need to develop code to link the page and paragraph together. After the code is created, you need to force the document to adhere to the new layout instructions.

FrameMaker 7 has a reference page containing the master page mapping table. This table contains numerous columns related to the application of the master pages based on the paragraphs in the document. Figure 5-11 shows an example of a document in which the Title paragraph tag is set to begin on a page called Cover whenever the paragraph is in use in the document.

Book Update (Yes or No): Yes

Paragraph Tag Name	Right-Handed Master Page (or Single-Sided Master Page)	Left-Handed Master Page	Range Indicator (Single, Span pages, Until changed)	Comments
Title	Cover		Single	Forces Title paragraphs to appear at the top of the Cover page.

Figure 5-11 The reference page with a master page mapping table containing automatic application settings.

There is a separate row for each paragraph tag that needs to be mapped to a master page, and each column of the table in Figure 5-11 contains data relating to the following items:

Paragraph Tags. The first column is used to identify the paragraph tag that is used in the document to mark where a new page should be assigned. Therefore, each paragraph tag that is set up to start at the top of a custom page requires its own row in this table.

Page Format. The second and third columns determine the page that is assigned if the paragraph tag appears, by default, on a right-hand page (for double-sided documents) or on any single-sided page of a document that is set up with a single default master page.

Range. The third column is only referenced when a document is double-sided and there is content that appears by default on a left-hand page.

Comments. The final column is used to include comments related to the row to assist anyone reviewing the materials at a later date or time.

Note: *The reference page required for automating the application of master pages is new to FrameMaker 7 and therefore does not exist in documents created using earlier versions of the software. It also does not appear by default in many of the templates included with FrameMaker 7. You can add the required page by selecting* ***Format > Page Layout > Apply Master Pages****. A dialog box related to the application of the master pages appears. If you click* ***OK*** *and there is not a master page mapping table in the reference pages, a dialog box like the one shown in Figure 5-12 appears to inform you that a page will be created to hold the master page mapping table.*

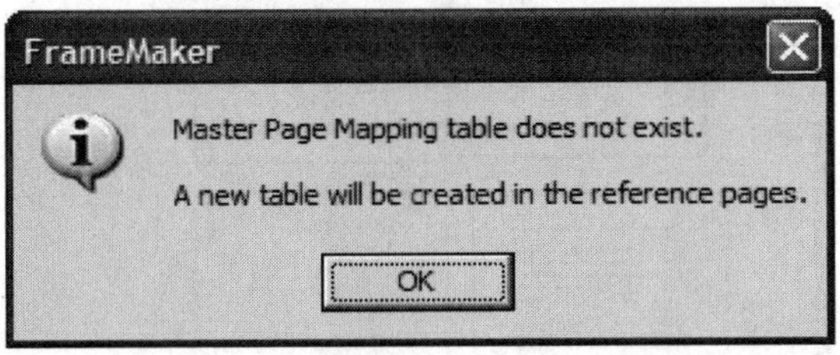

Figure 5-12 Dialog box confirming that a mapping table has been created within a template that did not have one.

Using the Infrastructure Development Function

To use automated application of master pages, you will need paragraphs, master pages, and reference pages that work together.

To create paragraph tags, use the Paragraph Designer. Ensure that the paragraph is formatted to appear at the top of a page (any page, left, or right). Once the paragraph tag is created, apply it to the document. Make sure that there is also a master page set up to accommodate the required page layout. Then develop the reference page by setting up the master page mapping table.

Developing Custom Master Pages Associated with a Paragraph Tag

The following instructions show how to create a new format for paragraphs that are to be used as identifiers for content that will be associated with a custom master page. The following assumptions are made about the document shown in Figure 5-13:

- The document already contains an assortment of text.
- The pages are all based on one master page—the default right-hand master page.
- There is a paragraph at the very beginning of the file that is tagged "Title."
- The Title tag is only used to identify the name of the chapter.

The document in Figure 5-13 is a very basic file. You need to assign a custom master page to the very first page of the document so that each time a new chapter is inserted in a document, the title page has a format that makes it distinctive.

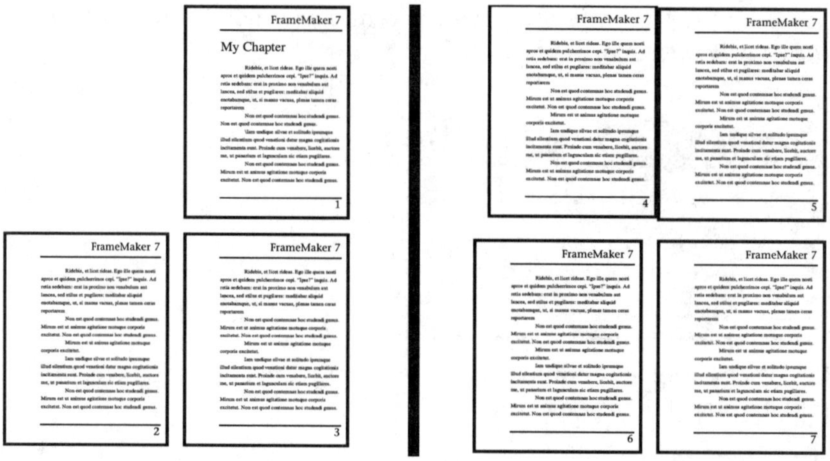

Figure 5-13 Single (right) master page example before custom master page application.

Based on the above assumptions, you must take the following steps:

1. Identify the name of the paragraph tag used on the first page, including the case and any spaces that are used in the naming convention. In this case, the paragraph tag will be Title. The name is case and space sensitive. This tag will be required later when the reference page is developed.
2. Create a new master page to be used for the first page of the document. Display the document's master pages (**View > Master Page**) and create the new page as required (**Special > Add Master Page**). As with the paragraph tags, the page name is both case and space sensitive. In this case, the new page will be named ChapterCover.
3. Display the reference pages (**View > Reference Pages**) and find the page containing the master page mapping table (see Figure 5-14). This page is often the very last reference page in the document. It is named MasterPageMaps. If this page does not exist, you need to follow the procedures in the note under "Reference Page Considerations" on page 144 in this section.
4. In the first column, enter the name of the paragraph tag that will be associated with the new custom master page. In this example, you should type Title.
5. In the second column, enter the name of the custom master page to be used. In this example, you should type ChapterCover.
6. Because this example is based on a default right-hand page layout for all pages, no entry is required in the third column.
7. In the fourth column, type the word Single. This informs FrameMaker that the custom master page applies to one page only.
8. Type any comments into the fifth column. In this example, no comments are required.

UnstructMasterPageMaps

Book Update (Yes or No): Yes

Paragraph Tag Name	Right-Handed Master Page (or Single-Sided Master Page)	Left-Handed Master Page	Range Indicator (Single, Span pages, Until changed)	Comments
Title	ChapterCover		Single	

Figure 5-14 An example of a master page mapping table.

Applying Custom Master Pages

Once the paragraph tags have been assigned in the body of the document, the master pages have been created, and the reference pages have been configured with a master page mapping table, you can easily apply page layout changes within the document. Use the following steps to apply custom master pages:

1. View the body pages of the document.
2. Select **Format > Page Layout > Apply Master Pages.**

   The dialog box shown in Figure 5-15 will pop up to indicate that the manually applied master pages in the document will be overridden if you proceed.

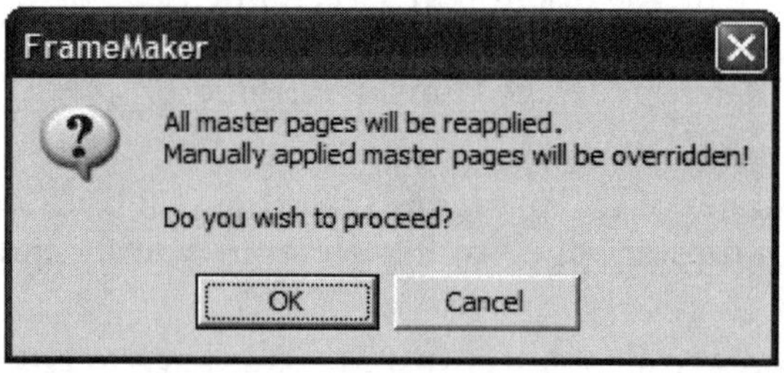

Figure 5-15 Dialog box to confirm update of master page application.

3. Click **OK** to proceed.

   Depending on the speed of your system and the complexity of your document, the new master page layout is applied.

Adjusting Your Settings

Should you need to override the default pages that are applied using the automated master page application function, you can do so by using the Master Page Usage command as you did in earlier versions. Please note that this override is removed if you use the Apply Master Pages command again. Therefore, manually adjusting the settings applied by the Master Page Usage should be done with caution if there are master pages already in use. Figure 5-16 shows the manual master page application dialog box.

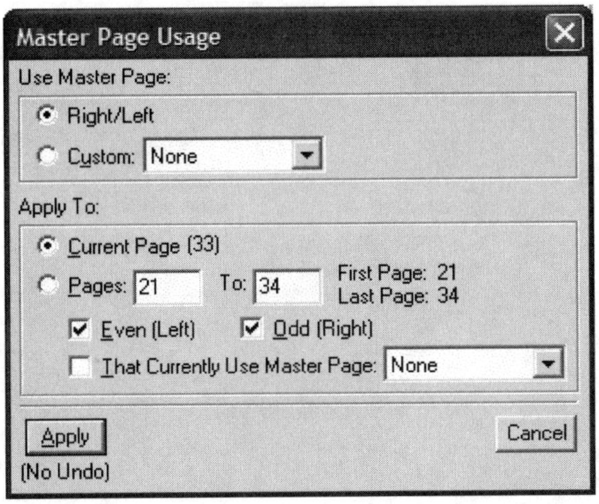

Figure 5-16 Manual master page application dialog box.

Summary

FrameMaker provides powerful page layout capabilities with its master pages. You have many options, from all pages looking alike to a variety of page layouts. In this chapter, we have explored the basics of layout and pagination (including right/left alternating pages), as well as more complex options like the automated master pages application.

If you have an existing template that you have used for prior FrameMaker versions, now may be the time to update your template and add this automation feature. Moving forward, hopefully, some of the things discussed in this chapter will give you ideas on making additional changes as well.

6

Making the Most of Running H/F Variables

Kay Ethier

This chapter examines running header/footer variables and their interplay with other FrameMaker functions, such as paragraphs, elements, and markers.

Applicable to FrameMaker versions 5.0/5.5, 6, and 7.0/7.1

Using Running H/F Variables

Have you ever seen a document with header text that changes as you move through the document? A FrameMaker running header/footer variable—or running H/F—allows you to automatically display header, footer, or background information. These variables pull pieces of your content and display them as automated background text.

The Scenario

In a document that uses running header/footer variables, the text showing up at the top of each page changes as the content of the page changes, depending on how you define your variable. When you look through a section about bolts, you see that it displays "Bolts" at the top of the page (the header). Then, when you get into the section about nails, you see "Nails" at the top of the page instead of "Bolts." This type of "instant change" is the "running" part of these variables. The variables are basically set up to pay attention to what you are typing and then to display text along the edges of the page so readers can easily locate information.

Viewing Running H/F Variables

Running H/F variables may only be created or modified on master pages. You place them on the master pages as part of your layout. They may be inserted in any background frame. Once positioned, they pull content from your documents as you type, using paragraph formats or marker types as their source.

If you haven't designed a FrameMaker template before, you may not recognize the term "*background frame.*" To elaborate, a master page is made up of three things: graphics, templates for body page text frames, and background frames. When you create a text frame on the master page (using the text frame tool on the graphics palette), you are asked to select whether you want the frame to be a template for a body page, or a background frame. Figure 6-1 shows the Add New Text Frame dialog box used to add a new text frame.

Let's take a look at a fairly simple example. You will use Running H/F 1 (defined as the default) to produce header text.

Note: *FrameMaker and FrameMaker+SGML 6 and earlier versions have only four running H/F variables. FrameMaker 7 has 12 of these variables.*

Modifying Running H/F Variables

Before you begin you will need to open a sample document that has an existing header. Then continue as follows:

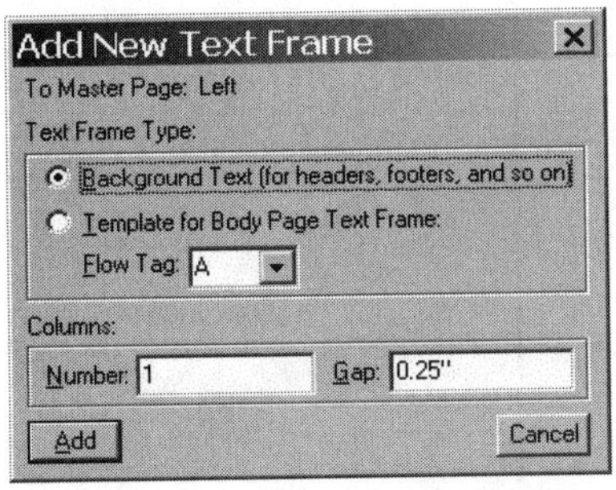

Figure 6-1 The dialog box used to select background or template text frames.

1. Click **File** > **New** > **Document.**
2. On the New dialog box, click the **Explore Standard Templates** button located along the bottom.
3. Once the Template Browser appears, select **Report, Numeric** from the left column.
4. Click **Show Sample.**

Note: *Show Sample opens a complete, filled-in document from the FrameMaker Samples folder. The document that opens has all the necessary formatting plus dummy text. If you click Create instead, you will get an empty document with all the necessary formatting.*

The sample document that appears should be similar to the one shown in Figure 6-2. If you'd like to continue working with this file, save it in a folder somewhere on your hard drive as ***numreport.fm***.

If you scroll down to the top of page 2 in the *numreport.fm* document, you will see the header information. Examining the document (see Figure 6-3), you see that there is a paragraph containing the text "2.0 Surrender is Complete." If you place your insertion point in this paragraph, you will see that it is tagged as a Heading1 paragraph. This paragraph's text—"Surrender is Complete"—is showing in the page header. This redisplay of the Heading1 text is created by a Running H/F variable.

Testing the Variable

You need to see the variable in action to understand more clearly what it is doing:

1. Go to the Heading1 paragraph numbered 2.0 that includes the text "Surrender is Complete."
2. Delete the text and replace it by typing the new text "Resistance is Futile."

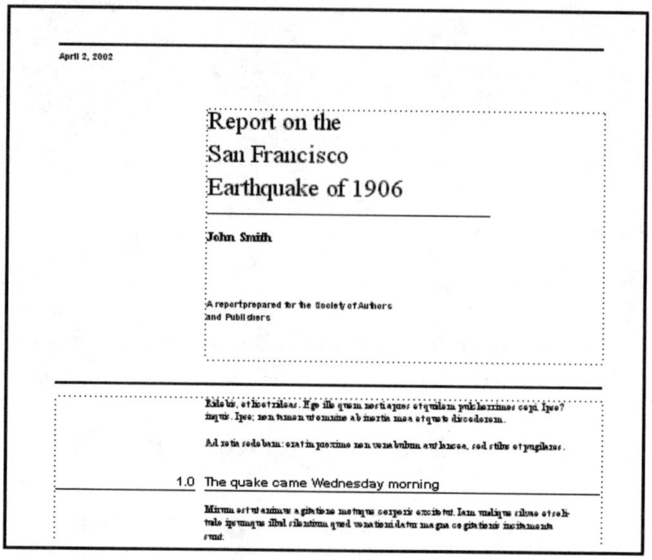

Figure 6-2 The Report, Numeric sample document.

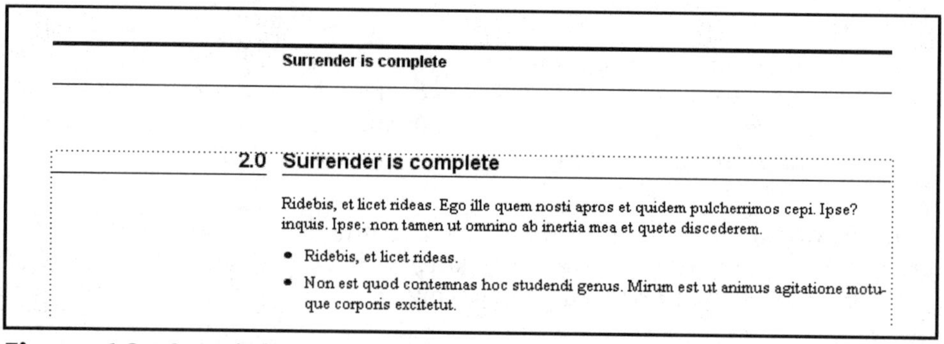

Figure 6-3 Sample document with header showing.

Note: *If you try to select header text in your document, you will not be able to because it is background text. It displays here due to headers placed on the master pages of your document.*

3. Scroll to another page and then come back. You will see that the page's header now says "Resistance is Futile," typed as you typed it, with the capital letters matching.
4. If you wish, try adjusting your text by retyping one of the words in all caps. Scroll away and come back, and you will see the display in the header change again.

FrameMaker watches what is typed on the page and "fetches" the new text as necessary. This means that you can write your documents as you like and not even have to think about the header text—it manages itself quite nicely.

Note: *If you get tired of scrolling away and coming back, use your FrameMaker shortcut for a screen redraw. In Windows, this shortcut is CTRL-L.*

Editing the Variable

Now you will make a change to the document. Instead of picking up text from the Heading1 paragraph for left-hand pages (such as shown in Figure 6-3), you will insert a variable that draws its text from the ReportTitle paragraph. The ReportTitle on page 1 of the document reads, "Report on the San Francisco Earthquake of 1906." This is the content you will pick up.

To make the change, you must go to the master pages. No changes can be made to the background text or layout unless you are viewing the master pages.

1. Go to the master pages and make sure you are on the master page called "Left."

Note: *If you switch to master page view while on a specific document page, FrameMaker will automatically choose the master page for the page you are viewing. In this case, it automatically chose "Left" because page 2 uses the left master page.*

2. Double-click the Running H/F 2 variable to bring up the Variable dialog box, as shown in Figure 6-4.

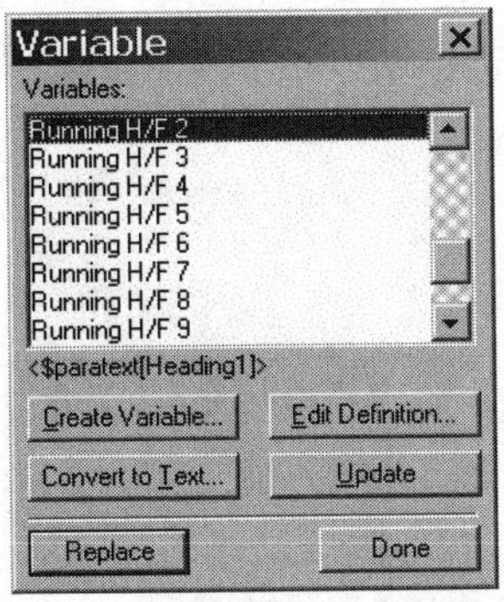

Figure 6-4 The Variable dialog box.

Notice that the definition shown for this variable is <$paratext[Heading1]>, which explains why it was displaying "Surrender is Complete" in Figure 6-3, and then "Resistence is Futile" from the Heading1 paragraph.

3. Click the **Edit Definition** button to edit this system variable. The Edit System Variable dialog box is displayed, as shown in Figure 6-5.

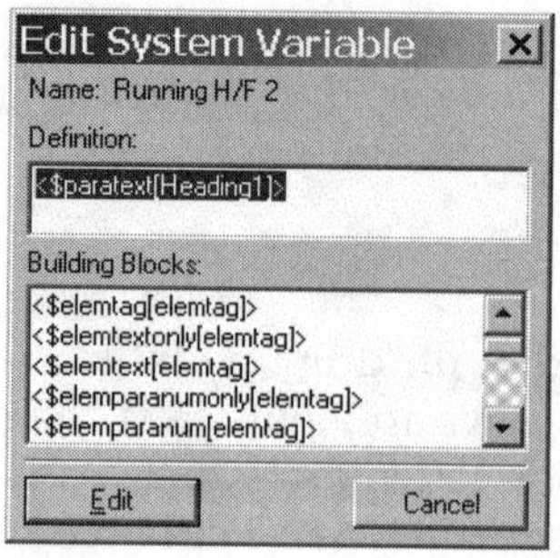

Figure 6-5 The Edit System Variable dialog box.

4. To pull content from the ReportTitle paragraph instead of Heading1, you need to change the paragraph tag inside the square brackets, as shown in Figure 6-6.

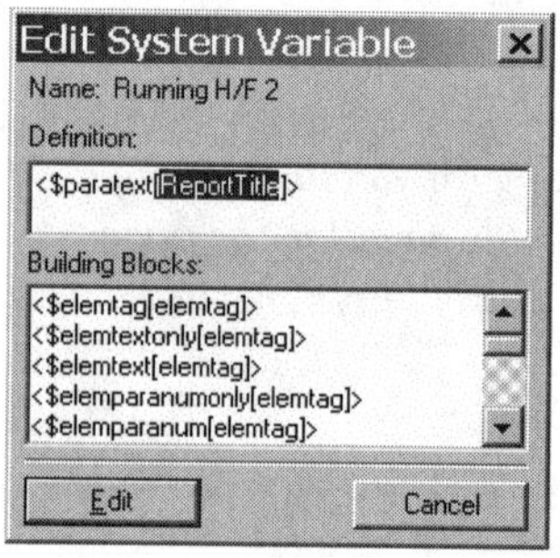

Figure 6-6 Adjusting the variable definition.

5. Click **Edit** to go back to the Variable dialog box and save your changes.
6. Click **Done**.

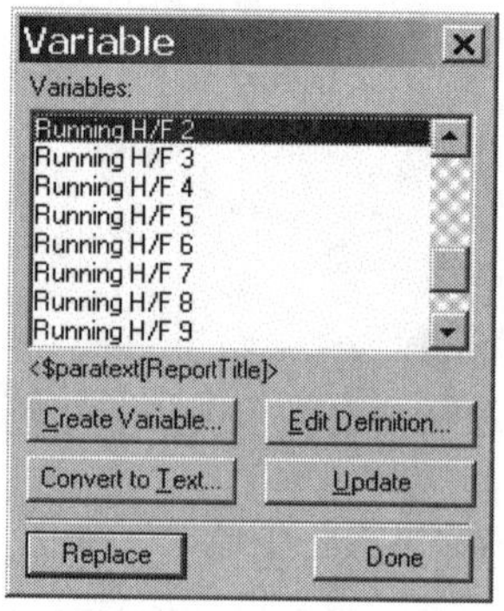

Figure 6-7 The variable with its new definition.

All occurrences of the Running H/F 2 variable are now adjusted throughout this document.

Note: *If you are using variables throughout a book, you will need to import the revised variable definitions into all the applicable files in the book, or else the changes will only take place in the file in which you were working.*

7. Go to the body pages of the document and scroll through them to see the change in the header text. On pages using the left master page, it will now say "Report on the San Francisco Earthquake of 1906" where it previously said "Resistance is Futile."

You may use Running H/F variables as they are—with their default definition—or you may edit them, as you have done just now. In many cases, you will be adjusting them.

Tagging Paragraphs to Invoke a Variable

Now you will adjust the variable so that it pulls from a Heading2 paragraph instead of a Heading1 paragraph. How? By editing the variable, similar to the way that you just did.

You may remember from a few pages ago that the definition of the H/F variable was originally *<$paratext[Heading1]>*. You can change the variable's definition back to *<$paratext[Heading1]>* by going to the master pages and editing the definition via the Variables dialog box (**Special** > **Variable**). Once you have reverted the variable's definition to *<$paratext[Heading1]>*, notice that the text "Resistance is Futile" is in the header again.

You will now change the variable so that the header shows the text "The First Day." This time, change the "1" in Heading2 to a "2" so that you have *<$paratext[Heading2]>*. Then, to see the result of your new variable definition, you need to use a Heading2 paragraph somewhere on the page:

1. In your document, go to the end of the "2.0 Resistance is Futile" paragraph and hit **Return**.
2. Type **The Final Day.**
3. Tag the paragraph as a Heading2.
4. Hit your redraw keystrokes shortcut (**CTRL-L**) or scroll away and come back. Your header text should now read "The First Day," drawing the text from your new Heading2 paragraph.

That should be enough practice for now. By this point you should be very clear on what Running H/F variables can do for you. In the upcoming sections you will take a closer look at the building blocks of variables and some advanced punctuation for making the variables work harder.

Setting Variable Definitions

When modifying Running H/F variables, you are often changing from the default definition—that assigned by Adobe—to your own definition. Editing may mean adjusting the paragraph format as you did above, or it may mean adjusting the building block that is used within the variable itself.

To ensure that you know what you need to know to adjust your own variables—as opposed to knowing enough to change your variable from the above example—you need to take a closer look at the building blocks.

Variable Building Blocks

With FrameMaker 7/7.1, you have 12 Running H/F Variables, with variables 5 through 12 defined as *<$paratext[paratag]>*. The first four variables have more specific definitions given to them by Adobe. Table 6-1 shows the default definitions of these first four Running H/F variables.

Table 6-1 Default Definitions of Running H/F 1 through 4

Variable	Default Definition
Running H/F 1	<$paratext[Title]>
Running H/F 2	<$paratext[Heading1]>
Running H/F 3	<$marker1>
Running H/F 4	<$marker2>

Note: *FrameMaker versions 6 and earlier had only the first four Running H/F variables. That is why these variables have unique definitions, while the others—new for FrameMaker 7—all have the same "generic" definition of <$paratext[paratag]>.*

Any of these definitions may be adjusted; variables 5 through 12 must be adjusted because their default is just a placeholder and produces no display. When modifying the variable definitions, you must check a few things:

- That the paragraph format being referenced is the one that you really want (Heading1 versus Title, for example)
- That you have spelled the paragraph format tag correctly, including necessary spaces (Heading 1 versus Heading1)
- That you have matched your paragraph tag capitalization precisely (ChapterTitle versus Chaptertitle)
- That you select the appropriate building block(s) to get the display you desire

Let me elaborate a bit on that last bulleted item. Using the correct building block, or building blocks, means choosing the term that gives you the information you want from the paragraph.

Note: *Some building blocks are designed to pull content, such as the text or numbering, from paragraph formats. In structured documents you also have building blocks that can pull this data from elements. There are also miscellaneous other building blocks that allow the grabbing and display of content. These are dealt with in the next section.*

Available Building Blocks

The main building blocks within an unstructured document pull content from paragraph tags. A list of the most-often used building blocks follows. For example purposes, refer to this heading:

Chapter 4: Mechanical Analysis

Assume this heading is tagged with a paragraph format called ChapterTitle.

<$paratext[ChapterTitle]>. This building block pulls the text from your paragraph, so the resulting content pulled into your header/footer is '**Mechanical Analysis.**"

<$paranum[ChapterTitle]>. The first of two building blocks that pulls numbering, this one displays the entire autonumber sequence, including words and punctuation; therefore, "**Chapter 4**" is displayed.

<$paranumonly[ChapterTitle]>. The second of two building blocks that pull numbering, this one displays the autonumber without any words or punctuation; therefore, "**4**" is displayed.

Note: *The <$paranumonly> building block is used in previous versions of FrameMaker to display the chapter number in front of the page number, as in "4-1." Starting with, FrameMaker 6, there is an additional building block, <$chapnum>, that accomplishes this.*

<$paratag[ChapterTitle]>. A less-used building block, this prints the paragraph tag instead of content; thus "**ChapterTitle**" is displayed.

If you are doing structured document publishing, then you have additional pieces of your document that you can pull content from: elements. The building blocks associated with elements follow with descriptions. For example purposes, assume that the element name is **Chapter**.

<$elemtext[Chapter]>. This building block displays all text (up to the end of paragraph, without the autonumbering, but including any prefix and suffix specified in the element definition document (EDD).

<$elemtextonly[Chapter]>. This building block displays all text (up to the end of paragraph, without the autonumbering and prefix/suffix.

<$elemparanum[Chapter]>. This building block gets the autonumbering of the element's first paragraph, including any words and punctuation.

<$elemparanumonly[Chapter]>. This building block gets the autonumbering of the element's first paragraph, without any words and punctuation.

<$elemtag[Chapter]>. This less-used building block prints the element tag instead of content.

Additional available building blocks include the following, which pull attributes from elements in structured documents. For example purposes, assume an attribute name of Author.

<$attribute[Author]>. This building block gets the attribute's value. (If no value is specified, it will display the default value for the attribute.)

<$highchoice[Author]>. This building block selects the named attribute's highest value and displays it.

<$lowchoice[Author]>. This building block selects the named attribute's lowest value and displays it.

Running H/F variables may also pull information from conditions applied to text:

<$condtag[hitag,...,lotag,nomatch]>. This building block pulls content from the condition, moving through the tags in the order that you specify (high to low) and displaying from the first conditional text that it finds on the page. *Nomatch* is what is displayed if there are no conditions.

Finally, the Running H/F variable definitions may include date- and time-related information using the date/time building blocks. These are not elaborated on here, as their names are fairly descriptive (such as <$second> and <$second00>).

Moving forward through this chapter, you will see that the building blocks are just the beginning of your Running H/F variable definitions. You can also add character formats, adjust which variable on the page is selected, and use multiple building blocks for more complex displays.

Syntax for Dictionary-Style Headings

What is "dictionary style"? It means that you have information that appears in the header or footer—usually the header—that lets the user know the *first* information that appears on the left-hand page and the last information that appears on the right-hand page. Dictionary style is used in dictionaries and sometimes in indexes, glossaries, and other lists of terms.

Figure 6-8 shows a sample document that uses two Running H/F variables to create the dictionary-style header. The first variable is used on the left-hand page and pulls from the first "Term" paragraph on the page. In this case, the content pulled is "Antelope." The second variable is used on the right-hand page and pulls from the last "Term" paragraph on the page. In this case, the content pulled is "Zebra." (This entire sample document is available from this book's Web site (*www.technicalpublishing.com/AdvFrame*) for you to review.)

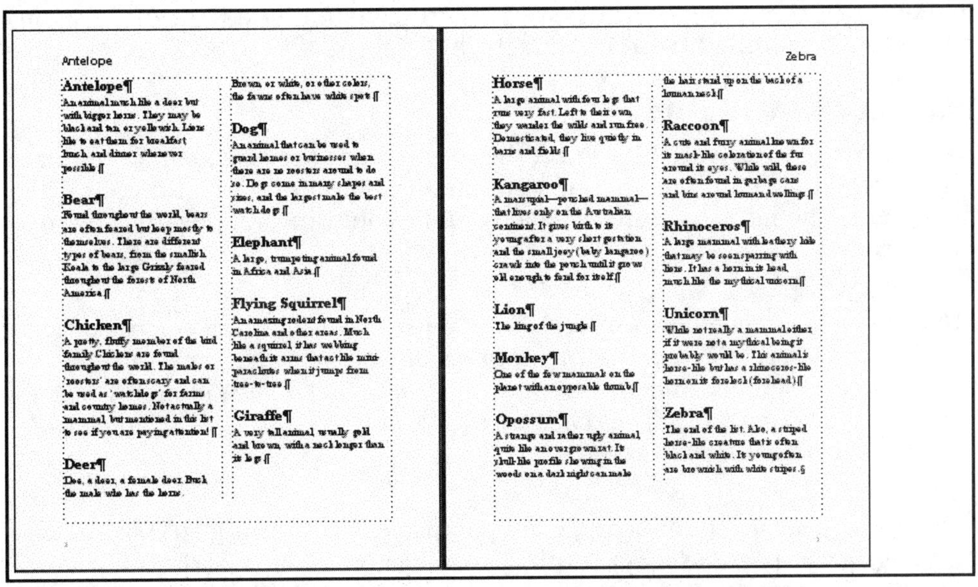

Figure 6-8 A sample document with dictionary-style headings.

This document uses the Running H/F 1 variable defined as <$paratext[Term]> on the left-hand page. The right-hand page uses Running H/F 2 defined as <$paratext[+,Term]>, with the plus indicating that FrameMaker should skip to the last paragraph tagged as Term on that page and use its content.

Note: *You may use any of the Running H/F # variables and do not have to use the first and second as you have been doing here. Note, too, that you should substitute your own paragraph's tag for "Term" if you use this technique.*

Using Headers/Footers with Markers

In addition to having variables pulling content from paragraphs, you can have variables pull content from markers: specifically, the Header/Footer $1 and Header/Footer $2 markers.

To pull content from markers, you need to define your variables differently. In fact, you can use two variables that are already set up for this purpose:

- Running H/F 3 is defined by default to use <$marker1>. You can use this definition to pull information from Header/Footer $1 markers.
- Running H/F 4 is defined by default to use <$marker2>. As you might have guessed, this definition can be used to pull information from Header/Footer $2 markers.

While you can define any of the other Running H/F variables to use the marker definitions, you might as well use the two that you have (unless you have already modified them for something else).

Placing the Variables

Drop either of these variables in on the master page (in a header, footer, or other background frame). Then insert markers as appropriate into your document. The markers contain exactly what you want to appear at the top of the page.

Note: *Header/footer markers are often used to display text that otherwise does not appear in a document, or to modify the content. For example, if in the previous example you wanted to show "Zebra (end of list)" instead of "Zebra," then you could have used a marker and put "Zebra (end of list)" in the marker.*

For the purpose of the following example, place the Running H/F 3 variable on your master pages as an example. If you like, you may use the *numreport.fm* document, which you saved earlier in this chapter.

1. With the document open, go to the master pages (**View > Master Pages**) and make sure you are on the "Left" master page.
2. Select the Running H/F variable already in the header frame and delete it.
3. With your insertion point still in the header frame, bring up the variables menu (**Special > Variable**).
4. Select **Running H/F 3** from the list.

   Note that its definition is <$marker1>. It will therefore pull content from Header/Footer $1 markers.
5. Click **Insert.**

Once you have the variable in the header, you may return to the body pages (**View > Body Pages**) so that you can insert markers.

You may also adjust the right master page so it uses the same variable, or so it uses the Running H/F 4 variable that by default is defined as <$marker2> and draws from Header/Footer $2 marker content.

Placing the Markers

Once you have the master pages using the variables that draw content from markers, you need to place some markers. Continue using the same document for this example:

1. With the *numreport.fm* document still open, make sure you are on the body pages.
2. Open the marker dialog box (**Special** > **Marker**) so that you can place one—or many—markers in your document.

Note: *The upper left corner of page 2 is blank right now.*

3. Put your insertion point on page 2, near the upper right corner. You will modify page 2 because it is using the left master page, and you modified the left master page in the previous section.

Note: *You want your insertion point to be in the upper right corner but not too close to the top. Markers must be placed on the page that you want, and in a location so that they cannot easily slip to another page. Plus, and most importantly, they must be as close to the content that applies to them as possible.*

4. With your insertion point, say, in the term "Bear," drop in a marker that is of the type **Header/Footer $1** (select from the pop-up menu of marker types if this is not showing) and that contains the simple content "**Bear, Grizzly**."

Note: *While capitalization is as you prefer, note that FrameMaker will display it as you type it. Punctuation is allowed.*

5. Refresh your view and note that the upper right corner of the page now says exactly what you typed: **Bear, Grizzly**.
6. Continue placing markers in the document and watch what happens on each page.

Multiple markers on a page are ignored, but they will "kick in" when needed and if they rise to the top of a new page. So, you may safely drop these markers in at key junctures of your document, and they will come up when appropriate. You may adjust them later, if needed.

If you added the Running H/F 4 marker in the previous exercise, you might also place some markers of type Header/Footer $2 in your document.

Note: *You can use character formats in the marker dialog box by typing the character format tag in angle brackets: for example, <Emphasis>. Capitalization does count, and you would use <Default Para Font> when you want the special formatting to stop.*

You may also use special options, such as \t for tab and \r for return (enter).

Marker Placement Tips

While you have some freedom in placing Header/Footer markers—and really any markers (even index markers)—there are several things you need to consider:

- **Do not place markers at the very beginning of a paragraph.** This is where FrameMaker places cross-reference markers, and you may end up with markers on top of markers. These become difficult to edit, although they should cause no problems with output or links. (Some problems may be evident in FrameMaker 5.5.x documents when you output to online formats like HTML and XML.)
- **Place markers as close as possible to the information pertinent to them.** Otherwise they may become separated from their relevant data and refer your readers to the wrong page.
- **Try to separate markers by placing them between words and not placing them next to each other.**
- **Never ever place a marker in the middle of a word.** If you output to HTML or XML, the marker will turn into a space and break the word. This will not only make your document look funny, but it will keep it from being fully searchable (due to breaks in words that cannot be anticipated by searchers).
- **If using conditional text, make sure when you grab text that you grab the appropriate markers; make sure your text symbols are visible to simplify this.**

Creating Complex Displays with Multiple Building Blocks

You can create even more complex header/footer displays by setting up Running H/F variables to pull content from multiple paragraphs—even a combination of paragraphs and markers. Examples of different scenarios follow.

<$paranum[ChapterTitle]>:<$paratext[ChapterTitle]>. In an earlier example, you pulled text from a ChapterTitle paragraph to produce the display of "Mechanical Analysis." You could adjust the variable definition to show not only the text but the numbering as well:

<$paranum[ChapterTitle]>:<$paratext[ChapterTitle]>. This would give us a display of "Chapter 4: Mechanical Analysis" instead. You may combine building blocks like this to create more complex displays.

Because previous versions of FrameMaker only had four Running H/F variables, doubling up within a variable like this allowed you to "stretch" your available variables.

<$paratext[ChapterTitle,AppendixTitle,GenFileTitle]>. Sometimes your template is more complex, and files require several different paragraph tags to maintain your numbering. This is especially true with templates created before FrameMaker 6 (before the <$volnum> and <$chapnum> building blocks were available).

Perhaps you have a chapter template that you intend to use. This template is numbered and has the name "ChapterTitle" for the top-level paragraph tag. You may also have an appendix template for building appendices, and it has alphabetical numbering. This numbering may be produced by a paragraph tag at the beginning of the file with a name like AppendixTitle. Finally, you may have a template for beginning front matter, and the top level heading would have no numbering. This might be called TitleNoNum (or, as in the example here, GenFileTitle). In this scenario—with multiple top-level paragraph tags—you can define a Running H/F variable to check which heading is being used at the top of the file and display content accordingly.

Note: *If you want the numbering to be displayed also, you can expand this example to fit better with the previous example; thus:*

<$paranum[ChapterTitle,AppendixTitle,GenFileTitle]>:
<$paratext[ChapterTitle,AppendixTitle,GenFileTitle]>

FrameMaker uses the information inside the square brackets from left to right. Therefore, it will first check for a ChapterTitle. If it finds one, it displays it and stops looking. If it does not find one, it checks for an AppendixTitle. If it finds one, it displays it and stops looking, and so on. You don't have to worry about FrameMaker displaying two pieces of information—it stops looking when it finds something.

<$paratext[Heading1]><$marker1>. Similar to the previous item, this variable allows you to pull content from different pieces of the document depending on what you have on the page.

As it did for the previous variable, the program would first check for a Heading1. If it does not find one, then it looks for a marker.

Note: *If FrameMaker does find a Heading1, it will display it and then look for a marker with content. If it also finds a marker, it will display both. If you are mixing markers and paragraphs (or elements), however, there is no way to "nest" the <$marker#> choice inside the list. For example, the following string is not valid because the marker cannot be inside the square bracket with the paragraphs:*

<$paratext[ChapterTitle,AppendixTitle,GenFileTitle,<$marker1>]>

Use caution in this mixed scenario. If using markers and paragraphs, you should create different variables for each and use different master pages. There are many options; make sure you set your document up with the right formatting for your need.

<$paratext[Heading1]>\r\t<$paratext[Heading2]>. If you want a very complex header with multiple lines, you can certainly accomplish this using multiple variables and multiple paragraphs.

You can also get clever and make one variable and one paragraph do a lot of work. Use the animal example of Figure 6-8 butexpand it to display more or insert things like soft returns (\r) or tabs (\t). Create a heading with more information to display, but do not take the time to build separate paragraphs and separate variables (which creates more to modify and maintain).

In this variable definition, notice that there are two building blocks used: <$paratext[Term]> and <$marker1>. You may substitute other building blocks to suit your needs, or expand it yet another level by adding more building blocks.

The \t tag is also being used (see above) to force FrameMaker to insert a tab (allowing us to artificially indent and emulate multiple paragraphs), and the \r tag to insert a soft return and allow the single variable to act as two variables.

You can add additional \r (soft returns) to other building blocks and \t (tabs) to go to a third level of information or even additional levels. Just be sure to set up the paragraph with tabs at even intervals along the ruler, and you can go to as many levels as you can stand!

<$elemparanum[Chapter]>:<$attribute[Author]>. Similar to the concept of combining building blocks for paragraphs, you may combine building blocks that pull content from structure data such as elements and attributes.

You may also combine information being pulled from paragraphs and elements to produce a mixed display. For example, you might display a chapter title using either the paragraph or element, then list the first heading paragraph after it.

Troubleshooting

If your headers/footers do not appear as expected—or there are no displays—then you need to check a couple of things:

- Did you use the appropriate paragraph tag in both the variable and in the document?
- When typing the paragraph tag in the variable definition, did you add any extra spaces or remember to leave in spaces that are a part of the paragraph tag? If you use spaces in the paragraph tag, the space is considered part of the name and must be replicated in the variable definition.
- Does your case (upper/lower) in the variable definition match that of the paragraph tag? FrameMaker is case sensitive and case must match exactly.

Cautions

If you are using Running H/F variables to grab several levels of text, you need to be aware that a change in one variable is not necessarily reflected in the others. This is easier to understand with an example.

Say that you have a document that has text on a page, as shown in Figure 6-9.

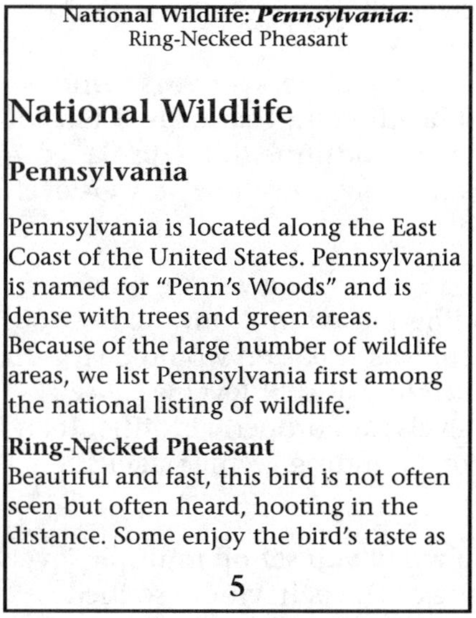

National Wildlife: ***Pennsylvania***:
Ring-Necked Pheasant

National Wildlife

Pennsylvania

Pennsylvania is located along the East Coast of the United States. Pennsylvania is named for "Penn's Woods" and is dense with trees and green areas. Because of the large number of wildlife areas, we list Pennsylvania first among the national listing of wildlife.

Ring-Necked Pheasant
Beautiful and fast, this bird is not often seen but often heard, hooting in the distance. Some enjoy the bird's taste as

5

Figure 6-9 Sample document with multiple levels of headings.

Right now, the header at the top of the page is showing the first, second, and third levels of text. The heading "National Wildlife" is picked up, along with the state and then the first animal listed (third level of content) on the page.

Because of the way Running H/F variables work, this text will adjust as it moves to subsequent pages, listing the first, second, and third levels automatically. If it encounters a new third level, it should pick it up as easily as it did the first animal. On the next page, shown in Figure 6-10, you can see that the header is working and has appropriately changed the animal while holding on to the already-determined level one and two headings.

National Wildlife: ***Pennsylvania***:
Red-Tailed Hawk

Red-Tailed Hawk

These birds are found throughout the woodlands and mountain ranges. Often, you will catch a glimpse of one flying not alone, but with some poor prey clenched in its powerful talons.

White-Tailed Deer

This deer is widespread across the state of Pennsylvania. It is light to dark brown with a tail markedly white underneath. The tail is lifted in danger.

Barn Swallow

Often mistaken for bats, these birds build their nests in the rafters of barns

6

Figure 6-10 Sample document with multiple heading levels in page header.

Now, the caution: If you move to the next page and cross a new second-level heading, but do not have a third-level heading on that page, then the third-level content from the previous page may continue to be displayed—erroneously. For example, Figure 6-11 shows the "Barn Swallow" lower-level heading displaying beneath an "Ohio" heading.

In Figure 6-11, you have crossed into information for a new state; however, FrameMaker leaves the "Barn Swallow" heading picked up from the previous page and from the previous state! The ideal for this situation would be for the "Barn Swallow" display to be blank until a heading at that level was used within the "Ohio" section. Resetting lower-levels tags properly is difficult and may require a FrameScript (a separate tool for extending FrameMaker's capabilities) to do a thorough cleanup.

So, make sure you know what you are doing when you set up multiple levels of Running H/F variable information. Because of the behavior described herein, you should also do a quality check and ensure that your readers are seeing the appropriate content.

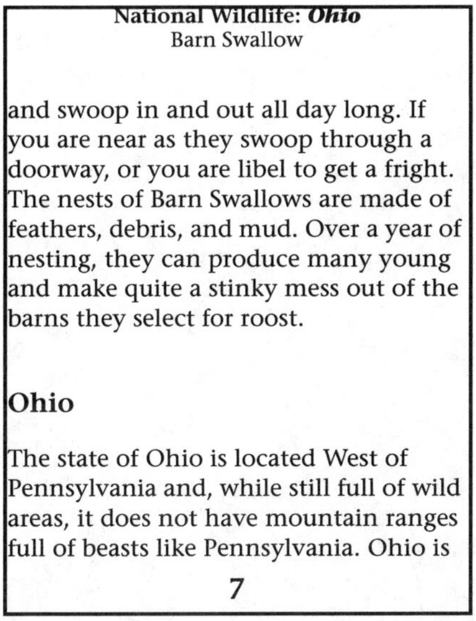
National Wildlife: ***Ohio***
Barn Swallow

and swoop in and out all day long. If you are near as they swoop through a doorway, or you are libel to get a fright. The nests of Barn Swallows are made of feathers, debris, and mud. Over a year of nesting, they can produce many young and make quite a stinky mess out of the barns they select for roost.

Ohio

The state of Ohio is located West of Pennsylvania and, while still full of wild areas, it does not have mountain ranges full of beasts like Pennsylvania. Ohio is

7

Figure 6-11 Lower-level headings displayed incorrectly.

Variables at the Book Level

Running H/F variables do have some limitations. They cannot pull content from other files within a FrameMaker book.

To manage variables at the book level, you may need to do extra or special adjustments. You also may need to use markers quite often and perhaps copy/ paste them between files.

Summary

While the default definitions of the Running H/F variables are fairly straight forward, they have the potential to do complex displays for you. The many examples throughout this chapter demonstrate the range of options. You can define them to display information that appears in your paragraphs, elements, or both. When content is not in the document to draw from, you can define these variables to use marker content. Or, you can use a combination of these along with special items like tabs and soft returns.

Whether you need to pull information for display from multiple paragraphs, different types of content, or produce a multiline display, the variety available within these special variables should give you the flexibility that you need.

7

Automating Numbering in FrameMaker

Bradley Anderson

This chapter explores how FrameMaker autonumbering works, including setup of paragraph styles.

Applicable to FrameMaker versions 5.0/5.5, 6, and 7.0/7.1

Introduction to Numbering

If set up properly, FrameMaker will handle all of the numbering in your document automatically. FrameMaker's automatic numbering feature allows you to set up various numbering schemes. This automatic numbering capability is unmatched in the world of desktop publishing; its accuracy, stability, and reliability make it one of a kind. Due to this flexibility and power, automatic numbering is also one of the most misunderstood and misused features in FrameMaker.

Paragraph Numbering Examples

Paragraph numbering can include the numbers in chapter or appendix titles, step numbers, list numbers, and table and figure numbers:

- Chapter 1, 2, 3...
- Appendix I, II, III...
- Step 1, 2, 3...
- Table 1, 2, 3...
- Figure 1, 2, 3...
- 1, 2, 3, ...; a, b, c, ...; A, B, C...; i, ii, iii...; I, II, III...

These numbers can be used together to form more complex numbering schemes such as figure and table numbers that contain chapter or appendix numbers, or heading levels that contain the number of previous superior heading levels, such as those used in legal and government documents:

- Figure 1-1, 1-2, 1-3...
- Table 1-1, 1-2, 1-3...
- 1.1..., 1.1.1..., 1.1.1.1..., 1.1.1.1.1..., 1.1.1.1.1.1...

Page Numbering Examples

The method for creating complex page numbers changed with the release of FrameMaker 6. In FrameMaker 5.5 and earlier, prefixes and suffixes on page numbers were inserted manually from the book window for each chapter. FrameMaker 6, however, introduced two new system variables to control volume and chapter numbering. These make creating complex page numbers easier but limit you to a maximum of three numbers that can automatically increase:

- Page 1, 2, 3...
- Page 1-1, 1-2, 1-3...
- Page 1-1-1, 1-1-2, 1-1-3...

Note: *You are restricted to only three numbers that can automatically increase for page numbering schemes in automatically generated lists, such as the list of tables, list of figures, or table of contents. You can add numbers manually by using the text format of the chapter and volume numbers.*

Footnote Numbering Examples

Document footnotes or table footnotes can use any of the numbering schemes below. The number can be set to increase straight through a book, restart for each document, or restart on each page.

- 1, 2, 3, ... (numbers)
- a, b, c, ... (lowercase letters, referred to as "lowercase alphabetic" characters)
- A, B, C... (uppercase letters, referred to as "uppercase alphabetic" characters)
- i, ii, iii... (lowercase roman numerals)
- I, II, III... (uppercase roman numerals)
- *,†,‡... (custom definable characters)

Paragraph Numbering Building Blocks

FrameMaker uses several building blocks to create numbering schemes. FrameMaker 6 changed the behavior of numbering for page and chapters by adding two new building blocks. Table 7-1 lists the numbering building blocks.

Building Block Definitions

Using these building blocks you can structure your numbering properties to automatically number your paragraphs. Correctly setting up your autonumbering in FrameMaker benefits you in three major ways:

- Works always and automatically
- Limits the number of paragraph tags needed in your template
- Helps to force/maintain the logical structure of your document

You should never have to set up more than one paragraph tag for each type of paragraph that contains numbering. Many FrameMaker templates (in fact, most that I've seen) implement autonumbering by requiring two paragraph tags for each numbered list. One tag is used to "reset" the numbered list to 1, and the other tag is used to increase the list numbering.

Table 7-1 Numbering Building Blocks

Building Block	Description
•	Simple disc bullet character that can be used for bulleted lists
\t	FrameMaker code for a tab character
<n>	Placeholder for a number. The number is remembered and displayed
<n+>	Increases a numeric counter by one
<n=1>	Resets a numeric counter to one
<a>	Placeholder for a lowercase alphabetic character. The letter is remembered and displayed
<a+>	Increases a lowercase alphabetic character by one letter
<a=1>	Resets a lowercase alphabetic character counter to the letter "a"
<A>	Placeholder for an uppercase alphabetic character. The letter is remembered and displayed
<A+>	Increases an uppercase alphabetic character by one letter
<A=1>	Resets an uppercase alphabetic character counter to the letter "A"
<r>	Placeholder for a lowercase roman numeral. The number is remembered and displayed
<r+>	Increases a lowercase roman numeral by one number
<r=1>	Resets a lowercase roman numeral counter to the number "i"
<R>	Placeholder for an uppercase roman numeral. The number is remembered and displayed
<R+>	Increases an uppercase roman numeral by one number
<R=1>	Resets an uppercase roman numeral counter to the number "I"
<$volnum>	Controls a number at the book level—commonly used for volume, chapter, or appendix numbering
<$chapnum>	Controls a number at the book level—commonly used for volume, chapter, or appendix numbering
< >	Placeholder for a number that remembers the number of the counter, but does not display it
< =0>	Resets a counter to zero

Introduction to the Counter Matrix

The Counter Matrix is simply a table that lists all the paragraph tags that will contain autonumbers, and all the paragraph tags that will reset the numbering. This is the easiest way to describe and understand how autonumbering works in FrameMaker.

Figure 7-1 shows an overview of the Counter Matrix. Note the different types of information you need to organize autonumbering in your document. Before you set up your Counter Matrix, you need to define what you want your numbering scheme to look like. The next few pages will provide several different examples.

	Paragraph Tag Name	**Desired Output**	**Series Label**	**One Column for Each Paragraph Counter**					
Paragraph Tags Displaying the Numbering		Example of the Desired Numbering Output	Series Label Used in the Autonumbering Sequence	Paragraph tag 1 Counter	Paragraph tag 2 Counter	Paragraph tag 3 Counter	Paragraph tag 4 Counter	Paragraph tag 5 Counter	Paragraph tag 6 Counter
Paragraph Tags that Reset the Numbering but Do Not Display the Numbers	*Paragraphs that Reset Counters*								

Figure 7-1 Overview of the Counter Matrix.

Note: *You should only have to set up one paragraph tag for each autonumber sequence in your template. You do not need another special paragraph format to "reset" the numbering.*

The only exception to this rule is when you have a numbered list in a table that continues in more than one column, and you want the numbers to "restart" at the top of each column. For this, you will need another paragraph tag to restart the numbering, if there are no heading or body cells without numbering that can be used to reset the counters.

Simple Outline Example

Let's suppose that you need to set up a FrameMaker template to build a five-level outline. In this example, there are five heading levels:

- 1Heading will use capital roman numerals
- 2Heading will use capital letters
- 3Heading will use numbers
- 4Heading will use lowercase letters
- 5Heading will use lowercase roman numerals

Figure 7-2 shows an example of what the five heading levels with their associated numbering will look like.

```
I.  1Heading
II.
    A.  2Heading
    B.
        1.  3Heading
        2.
            a.  4Heading
            b.
                i.  5Heading
                ii.
    C.
    D.
III.
    A.
    B.
        1.
        2.
            a.
            b.
                i.
                ii.
IV.
```

Figure 7-2 Simple outline numbering sample.

Setting Up the Counter Matrix

Now that you have defined what counters each paragraph tag will use, create a Counter Matrix:

1. Print out the counter matrix of Figure 7-3. You will use five rows and eight columns of the table.
2. In the first column, list the paragraph tags (one per row) in the order of their hierarchy in the document structure—the highest level in the first row to the lowest (most subordinate) level in the last row.
3. In the heading columns 4–8, repeat the paragraph tag names again in order of their hierarchy from left to right, from the highest level in column 4 to the lowest level in column 8 (as in Figure 7-3). These columns represent the counter for each paragraph.

(1)	(2)	(3)	(4)	(5)	(6)	(7)	(8)
Tag Name	**Desired Output**	**Series Label**	**1Heading Counter**	**2Heading Counter**	**3Heading Counter**	**4Heading Counter**	**5Heading Counter**
1Heading							
2Heading							
3Heading							
4Heading							
5Heading							

Figure 7-3 Heading Counter worksheet.

4. Now describe the desired display for content for each paragraph tag. Under the "Desired Output" column, simply write what number you want the counter to display (as in Figure 7-4)

Tag Name	Desired Output	Series Label	1Heading Counter	2Heading Counter	3Heading Counter	4Heading Counter	5Heading Counter
1Heading	I.						
2Heading	A.						
3Heading	1.						
4Heading	a.						
5Heading	i.						

Figure 7-4 Desired output added to worksheet.

5. Next, give the Counter Matrix a series label. The series label is just a way to tell FrameMaker what matrix a paragraph belongs to. Think of the series label as the "name" that you are giving the Counter Matrix table. You can use any single letter for the series label. The series label is always followed by a colon (:). I use the series label "N:" for my main numbering matrix (see Figure 7-5).

Tag Name	Desired Output	Series Label	1Heading Counter	2Heading Counter	3Heading Counter	4Heading Counter	5Heading Counter
1Heading	I.	N:					
2Heading	A.	N:					
3Heading	1.	N:					
4Heading	a.	N:					
5Heading	i.	N:					

Figure 7-5 Series label added to worksheet.

Use the numbering building blocks in Table 7-1 to figure out which building block is necessary for each counter. Because we want the number to increase, we will use the building blocks that contain the "+". Because the 1Heading paragraph tag needs a capital roman number, the "<R+>" building block needs to be used. The other paragraph tags will use building blocks as follows:

- 2Heading will use <A+>
- 3Heading will use <n+>
- 4Heading will use <a+>
- 5Heading will use <r+>

6. Place the corresponding counter type (<n+>, <R+>, etc.) for each paragraph tag in its counter column and row. After inserting the building blocks, you should end up with a table like the one in Figure 7-6.

Tag Name	Desired Output	Series Label	1Heading Counter	2Heading Counter	3Heading Counter	4Heading Counter	5Heading Counter
1Heading	I.	N:	<R+>				
2Heading	A.	N:		<A+>			
3Heading	1.	N:			<n+>		
4Heading	a.	N:				<a+>	
5Heading	i.	N:					<r+>

Figure 7-6 Counters added to worksheet.

Notice that the counter for each paragraph tag is in its own column. Every counter must be in its own column, and each paragraph tag that contains an autonumber must be in its own counter. By placing the dominant paragraph of the document structure in the first row and the most subordinate paragraph in the last row, you end up with counters in a diagonal pattern (see Figure 7-7).

Tag Name	Desired Output	Series Label	1Heading Counter	2Heading Counter	3Heading Counter	4Heading Counter	5Heading Counter
1Heading	I.	N:	<R+>				
2Heading	A.	N:		<A+>			
3Heading	1.	N:			<n+>		
4Heading	a.	N:				<a+>	
5Heading	i.	N:					<r+>

Figure 7-7 Counter pattern on worksheet.

Filling in the Counter Matrix

Every cell in the table must be filled in. The remaining cells in the Counter Matrix define how each paragraph tag will affect each counter. Each of the paragraph tags in the matrix will affect the counter of every paragraph in the matrix. For each counter in the series, you must decide if the paragraph tag will reset the counter, and remember the counter value or just reset.

Remembering the Value of the Counter

Let's use the 2Heading row under the 1Heading Counter column as an example. What do you want a 2Heading paragraph to do to the 1Heading counter? What happens to the 1Heading number when it follows a 2Heading paragraph in the document? Refer to the counters and determine:

- Does the counter get reset to "0" (< =0>) so the paragraph number starts over at 1?
- Does the counter value get remembered, or "passed through" (< >) and not displayed?
- Does the counter value get displayed (<R>)?

In the case of this simple outline, we would want the 1Heading to continue numbering after a 2Heading, so we would choose < > (brackets with a space) to place in that cell (see Figure 7-8).

Tag Name	Desired Output	Series Label	1Heading Counter	2Heading Counter	3Heading Counter	4Heading Counter	5Heading Counter
1Heading	I.	N:	<R+>				
2Heading	A.	N:	< >	<A+>			
3Heading	1.	N:			<n+>		
4Heading	a.	N:				<a+>	
5Heading	i.	N:					<r+>

Figure 7-8 Using placeholders.

Resetting the Counter to Zero

In the 1Heading row under the 2Heading Counter column, we would want the 2Heading to restart at 1 after a 1Heading, so we would choose < =0> ("'space' equals zero") to place in that cell (see Figure 7-9).

Tag Name	Desired Output	Series Label	1Heading Counter	2Heading Counter	3Heading Counter	4Heading Counter	5Heading Counter
1Heading	I.	N:	<R+>	< =0>			
2Heading	A.	N:	< >	<A+>			
3Heading	1.	N:			<n+>		
4Heading	a.	N:				<a+>	
5Heading	i.	N:					<r+>

Figure 7-9 Adding counters for restarting.

Filling in the Rest

Using the same logic, fill in the rest of the values of the Counter Matrix. The next table shows the correct values for the simple outline Counter Matrix (see Figure 7-10).

Tag Name	Desired Output	Series Label	1Heading Counter	2Heading Counter	3Heading Counter	4Heading Counter	5Heading Counter
1Heading	I.	N:	<R+>	< =0>	< =0>	< =0>	< =0>
2Heading	A.	N:	< >	<A+>	< =0>	< =0>	< =0>
3Heading	1.	N:	< >	< >	<n+>	< =0>	< =0>
4Heading	a.	N:	< >	< >	< >	<a+>	< =0>
5Heading	i.	N:	< >	< >	< >	< >	<r+>

Figure 7-10 Placeholders and restarts in place.

After you have completed the Counter Matrix, you can format your paragraph tags. Copy the information in the shaded columns for each paragraph tag (paragraph row in matrix) to the autonumber format string in the Paragraph Designer. Each paragraph tag should contain the same number of building blocks. For example, the 1Heading paragraph tag's autonumber format string would initially look like this:

```
N:<R+>< =0>< =0>< =0>< =0>
```

Now the punctuation or text that follows the autonumber has to be entered.

Note: *Do not add any extra spaces to the autonumber string unless you want a space to be output.*

Punctuation other than that needed between numbers (e.g. 2.1.3.2) should always be placed outside the building blocks—just to the right of the colon from the series label or to the right of the final building block. This will keep your cross-references that use the <$paranumonly> cross-reference building block from picking up the punctuation contained in the autonumber string. If ".\t" was placed between "<R+>" and "< >", the cross-reference would pick up the number plus ".\t".

The only punctuation needed in this example are a period (.) and a tab (\t) to appear after the number:

```
N:<R+>< =0>< =0>< =0>< =0>.\t
```

The following three sections provide more numbering examples with the counter matrices.

Government/Legal Outline Example

Figure 7-11 and Figure 7-12 show an government/legal example and its associated counter matrix.

```
1. 1Heading
2.
   2.1. 2Heading
   2.2.
      2.2.1. 3Heading
      2.2.2.
         2.2.2.1. 4Heading
         2.2.2.2.
            2.2.2.2.1. 5Heading
            2.2.2.2.2.
   2.3.
   2.4.
3.
   3.1.
      3.1.1.
         3.1.1.1.
            3.1.1.1.1.
4.
```

Figure 7-11 Government/legal outline numbering example.

Complex Chapter Numbering Example

Figure 7-13 and Figure 7-14 show a complex chapter numbering example and its associated counter matrix.

Tag Name	Desired Output	Series Label	1Heading Counter	2Heading Counter	3Heading Counter	4Heading Counter	5Heading Counter
1Heading	I.	N:	<n+>	< =0>	< =0>	< =0>	< =0>
2Heading	1.1	N:	<n>	<n+>	< =0>	< =0>	< =0>
3Heading	1.1.1	N:	<n>	<n>	<n+>	< =0>	< =0>
4Heading	1.1.1.1	N:	<n>	<n>	<n>	<n+>	< =0>
5Heading	1.1.1.1.1	N:	<n>	<n>	<n>	<n>	<n+>

Figure 7-12 Alternate numbering scheme for headings.

Chapter 1
Figure 1-1
Figure 1-2
Table 1-1
Table 1-2
1.
2.
a.
b.
i.
ii.
Figure 1-3
Table 1-3
Chapter 2
Figure 2-1
Table 2-1
Figure 2-2
Table 2-2
Chapter 3
Chapter 4
Chapter 5
Chapter 6

Figure 7-13 Complex chapter numbering sample.

Complex Book Numbering Example

Figure 7-15 and Table 7-16 show a complex book numbering example and its associated counter matrix.

Autonumbering Counter Matrix Worksheet

Figure 7-15 is an example of an autonumbering counter matrix worksheet.

Document Numbering Properties

FrameMaker allows you to control various aspects of the numbering properties either on a document-by-document basis, or by setting up the numbering properties of multiple files from within the book file.

Tag Name	Desired Output	Series Label	Title Counter	Figure Title Counter	Table Title Counter	L1 NumList 1 Counter	L2 NumList 2 Counter	L3 NumList 3 Counter
Title	Chapter 1	N:	<n>	< >	< >	< =0>	< =0>	< =0>
Figure Title	Figure 1	N:	< >	<n+>	< >	< >	< >	< >
Table Title	Table 1	N:	< >	< >	<n+>	< >	< >	< >
L1 NumList 1	1.	N:	< >	< >	< >	<n+>	< =0>	< =0>
L2 NumList 2	a.	N:	< >	< >	< >	< >	<a+>	< =0>
L3 NumList 3	i.	N:	< >	< >	< >	< >	< >	<r+>
Paragraphs Resetting Counters[a]								
1Heading		N:	< >	< >	< >	< =0>	< =0>	< =0>
2Heading		N:	< >	< >	< >	< =0>	< =0>	< =0>
3Heading		N:	< >	< >	< >	< =0>	< =0>	< =0>
Body		N:	< >	< >	< >	< =0>	< =0>	< =0>

Figure 7-14 Complex chapter numbering.

a. Paragraph tags used to reset counter(s) can be used instead of separate paragraph tags used to restarting numbering. In this example, the 1Heading, 2Heading, 3Heading, and Body tags reset the list counters but do not display a number.

Volume I
- Chapter 1
  - Figure 1-1
  - Figure 1-2
  - Table 1-1
  - Table 1-2
    - 1.
    - 2.
      - a.
      - b.
        - i.
        - ii.
- Chapter 2
  - Figure 2-1
  - Table 2-1

Volume II
- Chapter 1
  - Figure 1-1
  - Table 1-1
  - Figure 1-2
  - Table 1-2
- Chapter 2
- Chapter 3
- Chapter 4
- Chapter 5

Figure 7-15 Complex book numbering sample.

Tag Name	Desired Output	Series Label	Volume Counter	Chapter Title Counter	Figure Title Counter	Table Title Counter	L1 NumList 1 Counter	L2 NumList 2 Counter	L3 NumList 3 Counter
Volume	Volume I	N:	<$volnum>	< =0>	< =0>	< =0>	< =0>	< =0>	< =0>
Chapter Title	Chapter 1	N:	< >	<$chapnum>	< =0>	< =0>	< =0>	< =0>	< =0>
Figure Title	Figure 1-1	N:	< >	<n>	<n+>	< >	< >	< >	< >
Table Title	Table 1-1	N:	< >	<n>	< >	<n+>	< >	< >	< >
L1 NumList 1	1.	N:	< >	< >	< >	< >	<n+>	< =0>	< =0>
L2 NumList 2	a.	N:	< >	< >	< >	< >	< >	<a+>	< =0>
L3 NumList 3	i.	N:	< >	< >	< >	< >	< >	< >	<r+>
Paragraphs Resetting Counters									
1Heading		N:	< >	< >	< >	< >	< =0>	< =0>	< =0>
2Heading		N:	< >	< >	< >	< >	< =0>	< =0>	< =0>
3Heading		N:	< >	< >	< >	< >	< =0>	< =0>	< =0>
Body		N:	< >	< >	< >	< >	< =0>	< =0>	< =0>

Figure 7-16 Complex book numbering.

beyond print

http://www.BeyondPrint.com

Paragraph Tag	Desired Output	Series Label									
Paragraphs Resetting Counters											

Figure 7-17 Blank numbering worksheet.

Setting an Individual Document's Numbering Properties

1. Select **Format > Document > Numbering** (see Figure 7-18).

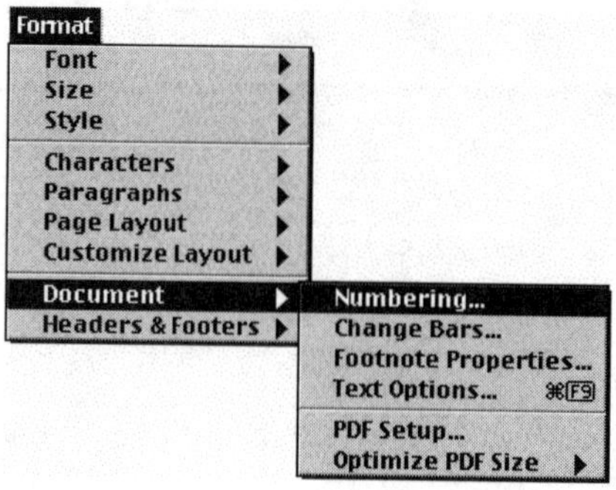

Figure 7-18 Document numbering properties menu.

2. Set the various options you wish to change.
3. Click **Set**.

Setting Properties from the Book File

1. Select the files for which you wish to change the numbering setup.
2. **Right-click** (in Windows) or **control-click** (on a Mac) and select **Numbering**.
3. Set the various options you wish to change.
4. Click **Set**.

Note: *If you receive inconsistent numbering property errors while generating/ updating a book, the numbering properties of each file in the book are not consistent. Double-check the numbering properties for each file and regenerate the book.*

Setting the <$volnum> System Variable

The $volnum system variable was introduced in FrameMaker 6 to make it easier to set volume and chapter numbering within a file—especially with page numbers. The $volnum variable can be set at the document or book level. The volume number can be set to be a specific number or text, to continue from the previous file in the book, or to use the same number as the previous file in the book. To set the $volnum value, do the following:

1. From the numbering properties, choose the **Volume** tab or choose **Volume** from the pop-up menu.
2. Set the numeric or textual value for $volnum next to Volume #: and select the number format from the pop-up menu. The available numbering formats include numeric, lowercase roman, uppercase roman, lowercase alphabetic, uppercase alphabetic, or text.
3. You can also set the $volnum to continue from the previous file in the book or to use the same number as the previous file in the book by choosing the appropriate option.

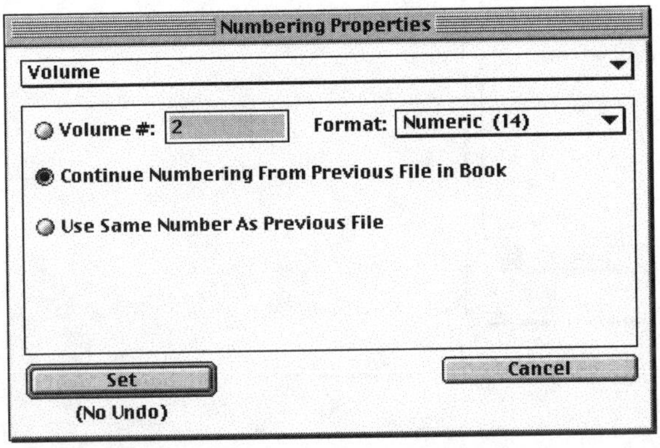

Figure 7-19 Volume numbering (<$volnum>) properties.

Setting the <$chapnum> System Variable

The $chapnum system variable was also introduced in FrameMaker 6. It works identically to the $volnum system variable. The $chapnum can be set at the document or book level. The chapter number can be set to be a specific number or text, be set to increase from the previous file in the book, or be set to use the same number as the previous file in the book. To set the $chapnum value, do the following:

1. From the numbering properties, choose the **Chapter** tab or **Chapter** from the pop-up menu.
2. Set the numeric or textual value for $chapnum next to Chapter #: and select the number format from the pop-up menu. The available numbering formats include numeric, lowercase roman, uppercase roman, lowercase alphabetic, uppercase alphabetic, or text.
3. You can also set $chapnum to continue from the previous file in the book or to use the same number as the previous file in the book by choosing the appropriate option (see Figure 7-20).

Note: *If you are using the $volnum or $chapnum system variables in your page numbering scheme, you will also have to use these as building blocks for your generated lists. For example, if your page numbers include both a volume and chapter number so that your page numbers look like "2-1-34," the entry on the reference pages of your generated files will include <$volnum>-<$chapnum>-<$pagenum>.*

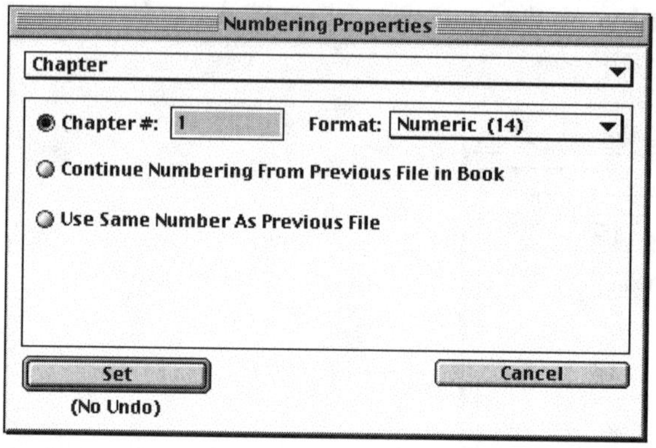

Figure 7-20 Chapter numbering (<$chapnum>) properties.

Setting the Page Numbers

The page number of a single document or set of documents in a book is controlled in the page numbering properties. To set the starting page number of your document along with the format for the page number, follow these steps:

1. Select the **Page** tab or **Page** pop-up menu. The numbering formats available include numeric, lowercase roman, uppercase roman, lowercase alphabetic, or uppercase alphabetic.
2. Set the starting page number of the document along with the desired format for the numbers, or tell FrameMaker to continue the page numbering from the previous file in the book to make multiple files into a "single" document (see Figure 7-21).

Paragraph Numbering Properties

Paragraphs that use an autonumber can be controlled at the document level as well. Paragraph numbering can be set to restart with the beginning of the document or to continue numbering from the previous file in the book. Paragraph numbering is controlled in the paragraph numbering properties menu (see Figure 7-22).

Footnote Numbering Properties

Footnote numbering can be controlled in one of three ways:

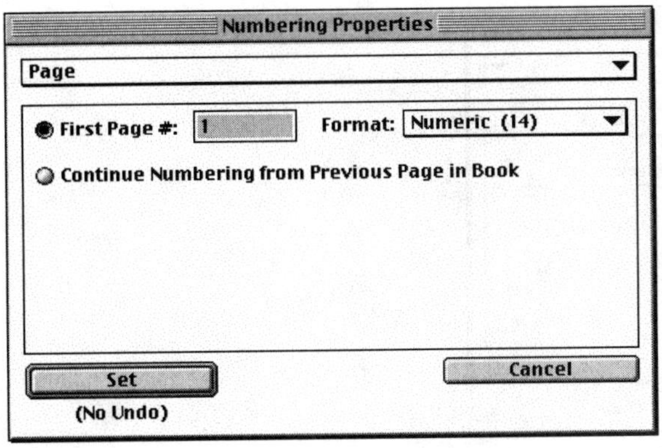

Figure 7-21 Page number settings.

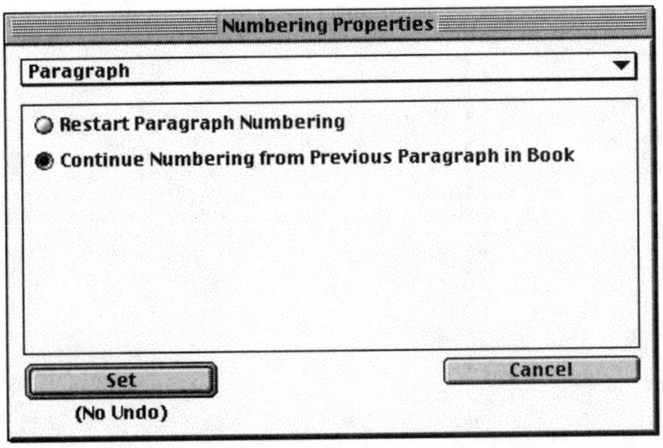

Figure 7-22 Paragraph numbering properties.

- Restart the numbering in each file
- Restart the numbering on each page
- Continue footnote numbering through multiple files in a book

The format of the footnote number can also be controlled in the footnote numbering properties. The numbering formats available include numeric, lowercase roman, uppercase roman, lowercase alphabetic, uppercase alphabetic, and custom characters (see Figure 7-21).

Table Footnote Numbering Properties

Table footnotes restart in each table. The only property that can be changed in the table footnote numbering properties is the format of the number to be used. The numbering formats available include numeric, lowercase roman, uppercase roman, lowercase alphabetic, uppercase alphabetic, and custom characters (see Figure 7-22).

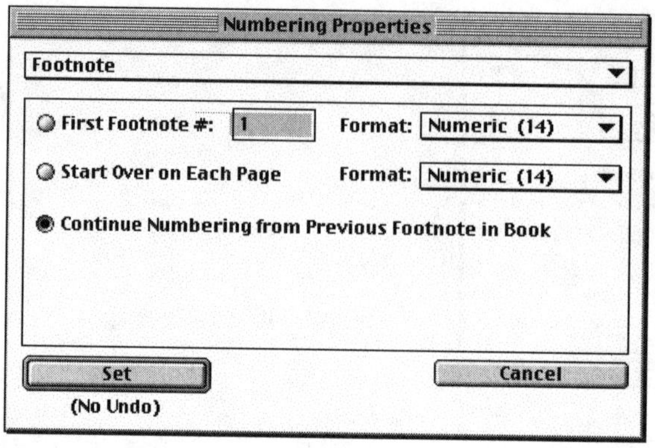

Figure 7-23 Footnote numbering properties.

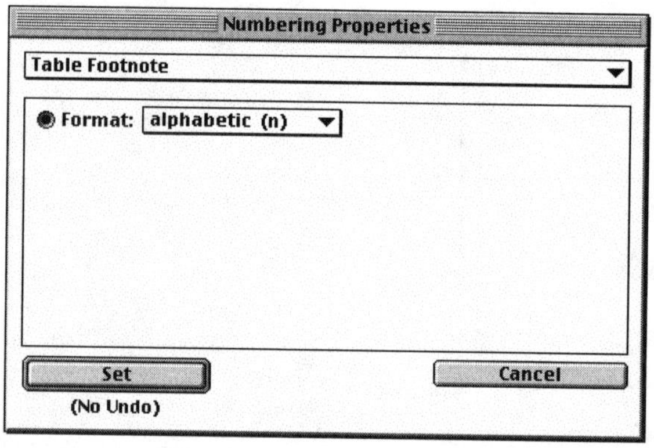

Figure 7-24 Table footnote numbering properties.

Summary

FrameMaker's numbering capabilities are phenomenal. It can be difficult to set up an initial FrameMaker template in which the numbering works as desired. However, once the document is set up properly, the numbering will work correctly every time. To help set up your numbering sequence(s), make sure you use "Complex Chapter Numbering Example" on page 182 to help map out each numbering sequence needed in your document.

8

Tables of Contents and Other Generated Lists

Bernard Aschwanden

This chapter explains the generated list function in relation to creating Tables of Contents and how the function can take you beyond a static or printed list.

Applicable to FrameMaker versions 5.5, 6, and 7.0/7.1

Note: *Because FrameMaker 6 and later include the <$chapnum> and <$volnum> building blocks for numbering generated materials (such as a Table of Contents), the software can incorporate the numbering system detailed in this chapter. The use of chapter and volume numbering allows for the creation of a much more robust generated document but requires that you have the more current versions of the software. If you do not have 6 or later and need to make extensive use of both chapter and volume numbers, consider upgrading. You can also work within the restrictions of the earlier versions using standard numbering and related building blocks. If you do, disregard the sections of this chapter that relate to the <$chapnum> and <$volnum> building blocks.*

How a Generated List Works

A generated list is made up of content that is extracted from FrameMaker documents. Files based on a standard template contain paragraphs that are tagged using style tags in the Paragraph Catalog. This content is then selected and extracted to generate a document based on the tags. The extracted content is formatted based on instructions that are stored in a template. When required, the generated file can be recreated, replacing textual content that was extracted previously with the newer, updated content.

This type of generated content may be used to create and maintain a Table of Contents, a List of Figures, a List of Tables, or several other generated list types.

Prior to developing any list, you must mark paragraphs or text in a source document. These "tags" are used by FrameMaker to pull the needed list information from the document files. This process requires that care be taken when creating a document template, as the placement of tags can affect the final look and feel of a generated list. Often when text in a file is extracted to a generated list, the page number is added. Other content, such as paragraph numbering, may also be extracted to the generated list.

When tagging paragraph content for use by a generated list, you should implement a standard system (a template, for example). Content in a generated file is primarily text. In some cases, numeric values or symbols are added to a generated file as well. Reference pages are then coded in the template for the generated list document with the commands required to build the document set. If this is done correctly, FrameMaker automatically organizes the content according to very specific coded instructions. This code is stored in the document's reference pages and may be modified as required.

The process for developing a generated list (after paragraphs have been correctly tagged) is based on code in reference pages, page layout as set by master pages, and a combination of paragraph and character formats in the body pages. Content is automatically created based on the content of the paragraphs used within the FrameMaker file.

When FrameMaker creates a generated list, content may be extracted based on a variety of paragraph tags, and all content is sorted by the page order in which the content appears. All content of a given type is extracted from the first page, then from the second, and so on. The generated list, therefore, is based on the sequential content of a FrameMaker document.

Due to the use of tagged paragraphs within documents, a generated list is a dynamic document. As the source documents are modified (by adding, changing, or deleting content), the document automatically adjusts the order of text within the pages.

Once a document is tagged, the generated list is automatically maintained as a generated file. Therefore, when files or their contents are modified and the generated file is regenerated, FrameMaker automatically modifies the content to display the new entries and page numbers. A book document or a standalone file that has a generated file associated with it may be updated at any time.

All page references in a generated list may be set up as hypertext links. When the generated list is converted to PDF, HTML, or online help systems using WebWorks Publisher, these links will remain active hypertext. Each page reference within the FrameMaker-generated list is a link to the paragraph that was used to create the entry and may be accessed using standard hypertext linking options. If necessary, the hypertext links can be disabled in a generated file.

Tables of Contents

The most common generated list that is created from documents in FrameMaker is the Table of Contents (TOC). The TOC usually contains a variety of paragraph tags such as Title, Heading1, Subject, ChapterName, and so on. This content is dependent on the names in the book template used by the documents that are referenced by the TOC. For the remainder of this chapter, we will use a TOC as our primary example as we prepare for and create a generated list.

Adjusting Reference Page Data

Generated lists are created based on paragraph and character formats, master page layouts, and sample code in the reference pages. To view the reference pages, select **View > Reference Pages**.

Sample Reference Page Code for Generated Lists

The code in the references pages for a TOC, List of Figures (LOF), List of Tables (LOT), or another standard default generated list may appear as follows:

```
openObjectId <$relfilename>:<$ObjectType>
  <$ObjectId>
<$paratext> <$pagenum>
<$paratext> <$pagenum>
<$paratext> <$pagenum>
```

Notice that the last few lines look the same. You will have one of these lines created automatically for each paragraph format that you add to the table of contents initially. Each numbered line of code is described as follows:

1. Commands used to build hypertext links between generated entries and their appropriate locations within FrameMaker documents. This specifies the form of hypertext links used by the generated files.
2. Code used to develop paragraph formats into content on the body pages of the generated file.
3. Code used to develop paragraph formats into content on the body pages of the generated file.
4. Code used to develop paragraph formats into content on the body pages of the generated file.

Each entry may be customized to create a unique generated list. The list is based on much of the same code that you use when you work with cross–references or variables (see Table 8-1).

Custom Codes for Generated List

Using the default values that are assigned to a generated list, the following samples show various methods of configuring the appearance of the content. Most generated content is formatted using a combination of master pages and the various style designers (Table, Paragraph, Character, etc.), but code on the reference pages may be used to configure how a generated list is developed. Any time code is modified on the reference pages of a generated list, the list must be generated from the source document to reapply the new formatting.

Table 8-1 FrameMaker Building Blocks

Building Block	Purpose of Building Block
<$pagenum>	Displays the page number of the paragraph extracted by the generated file
<$paratext>	Displays the text of the paragraph extracted by the generated file
<$paranum>	Displays the entire number of the paragraph extracted by the generated file
<$paranumonly>	Displays only the numbering (from the first building block to the last building block of numbering code) of the paragraph extracted by the generated file
<$volnum>	Displays the volume number of the paragraph extracted by the generated file
<$chapnum>	Displays the chapter number of the paragraph extracted by the generated file
<Default ¶ Font>	Resets the font of the paragraph to the default as defined for the generated file
<Emphasis>	Adds the character format of the Emphasis character tag

Default Code

The default code used by unformatted generated lists usually appears as follows:

```
openObjectId <$relfilename>:<$ObjectType>
  <$ObjectId>
<$paratext> <$pagenum>
<$paratext> <$pagenum>
<$paratext> <$pagenum>
```

A generated file such as a TOC, therefore, may appear as follows:

```
Introduction 1
Adobe FrameMaker Conceptual Model 1
Word Processing Capabilities 1
Desktop Publishing Features 2
High-End Publishing Features 2
```

The following sections use this example and apply modifications to the source code in the reference pages and to the resulting output.

Paragraph Numbering

By modifying the code on reference pages that is used by unformatted generated lists to extract the <$paranum> tag, you can extract the paragraph numbering of a source document. This is dependent upon the content that uses the Paragraph Designer and correct numbering properties. The source code in the generated list's reference pages is modified to appear as follows:

```
openObjectId <$relfilename>:<$ObjectType>
  <$ObjectId>
<$paranum>-<$paratext> <$pagenum>
<$paranum>-<$paratext> <$pagenum>
<$paranum>-<$paratext> <$pagenum>
```

A generated file based on this code may then appear as follows:

```
Chapter 1:–Introduction 1
Section 1.A:–Adobe FrameMaker 7.1 Conceptual Model 1
1.A.i)–Word Processing Capabilities 1
1.A.ii)–Desktop Publishing Features 2
1.A.iii)–High-End Publishing Features 2
```

The numbered content is correctly extracted from the source file. All characters and text used by the numbering in the source document are also extracted (in this case, adding full colons and parentheses) into the generated list.

Paragraph Numbering Only

By modifying the code on the reference page to use the <$paranumonly> tag, you can extract just the paragraph numbering (without punctuation) of a source document. This is dependent upon the content that uses the Paragraph Designer and correct numbering properties. The source code in the generated list reference pages is modified to appear as follows:

```
openObjectId <$relfilename>:<$ObjectType>
  <$ObjectId>
<$paranumonly>-<$paratext> <$pagenum>
<$paranumonly>-<$paratext> <$pagenum>
<$paranumonly>-<$paratext> <$pagenum>
```

A generated file based on this code may then appear as follows:

```
1–Introduction 1
1.A–Adobe FrameMaker 7.1 Conceptual Model 1
1.A.i–Word Processing Capabilities 1
1.A.ii–Desktop Publishing Features 2
1.A.iii–High-End Publishing Features 2
```

The numbered content is correctly extracted from the source file set. However, all characters and text used by the numbering in the source document are not extracted. (In this case, they do not add colons or parentheses.)

Paragraph Numbering with Added Text

By modifying the code on the unformatted generated list's reference pages to extract the <$paranumonly> tag and then adding text, you can extract the paragraph numbering (without punctuation) of a source document plus some added text, such as "Chapter." This allows the generated list to display correctly formatted content in its body pages. The source code in the generated list's reference pages is modified to appear as follows:

```
openObjectId <$relfilename>:<$ObjectType>
  <$ObjectId>
Chapter <$paranumonly>-<$paratext> <$pagenum>
Section <$paranumonly>-<$paratext> <$pagenum>
<$paranumonly>-<$paratext> <$pagenum>
```

A generated file based on this code may then appear as follows:

Chapter 1–Introduction 1
Section 1.A–Adobe FrameMaker 7.1 Conceptual Model 1
1.A.i–Word Processing Capabilities 1
1.A.ii–Desktop Publishing Features 2
1.A.iii–High-End Publishing Features 2

The numbered content is correctly extracted from the source file with additional text that the designer feels is necessary in the finished generated list. Not all characters and text used by the numbering in the source document are extracted into the generated list (no colons or parentheses), but the list reads "Chapter 1" instead of just the chapter number.

Paragraph Numbering and Text with Delimiters

By modifying the code on reference pages used by unformatted generated lists to extract the <$paranumonly> tag and then adding delimited text, you can extract just the paragraph numbering (without punctuation) of a source document and add appropriate tabs to position content on the page. To accomplish this, source code in the generated list's reference pages is modified to appear as follows:

```
openObjectId <$relfilename>:<$ObjectType>
  <$ObjectId>
Chapter <$paranumonly>-<$paratext> <$pagenum>
Section <$paranumonly>-<$paratext> <$pagenum>
<$paranumonly>-<$paratext> <$pagenum>
```

A generated file based on this code may then appear as follows:

Chapter 1–Introduction 1
Section 1.A–Adobe FrameMaker 7.1 Conceptual Model . . 1
1.A.i–Word Processing Capabilities 1
1.A.ii–Desktop Publishing Features 2
1.A.iii–High-End Publishing Features. 2

In this example, not all characters and text used by the numbering in the source document are extracted, "Chapter" or "Section" is added as appropriate (automatically based on the reference page code), the automatic tab is inserted, and the page number is displayed.

Volume and Chapter Numbers

By modifying the code on the unformatted generated list's reference pages to extract the <$volnum> or <$chapnum> tags, you can extract just the volume or chapter numbering of a source document. The code can also add appropriate text to display correctly formatted content on the generated body pages. The source code in the generated list's reference pages can be modified to appear as follows:

```
openObjectId <$relfilename>:<$ObjectType>
  <$ObjectId>
Chapter <$chapnum>-<$paratext> <$pagenum>
<$paratext> <$pagenum>
<$paratext> <$pagenum>
```

A generated file based on this code would then appear as follows:

Chapter 1–Introduction 1
Adobe FrameMaker 7.1 Conceptual Model 1
Word Processing Capabilities 1
Desktop Publishing Features 2
High-End Publishing Features 2

The numbered content is correctly extracted from the source file, but not all text used by the numbering in the source document is extracted. "Chapter" is added automatically based on the reference page code, and the text of the paragraph is inserted with an automatic tab and a page number.

Character Formatting

By modifying the code on the reference pages to add the <$CharacterTagName> tag, you can format generated content to be displayed with unique character formats applied. The source code on the reference pages can be modified to appear as follows:

```
openObjectId <$relfilename>:<$ObjectType>
  <$ObjectId>
<$paratext> <Emphasis><$pagenum>
<$paratext> <Emphasis><$pagenum>
<$paratext> <Emphasis><$pagenum>
```

A generated file based on this code then appears as follows:

Introduction *1*
Adobe FrameMaker 7 Conceptual Model *1*
Word Processing Capabilities *1*
Desktop Publishing Features *2*
High–End Publishing Features *2*

The numbered content is extracted from the source file with the page numbers formatted with Emphasis tag, thus impacting the finished look of the generated list by adding italic to the resulting page numbers.

The Book and File Update Process (Rebuilding Your Data)

Books may be updated to reflect the most current content of files within the book. The update is done to modify various settings; however, only those settings that are specified are updated. To update your book or files, follow these steps:

1. Select **Edit > Update Book**, or click . The Update Book dialog box appears.
2. Select the types of content to update.
3. Move generated file names to the appropriate scroll list using the arrow buttons.
4. Click **Update.**

Once these steps are taken, the book document is updated. If there are issues that cannot be automatically resolved by FrameMaker, an error log may be generated. A message will also appear, as shown in Figure 8-1, indicating any errors that have occurred.

Adding Generated Files to Book Documents

Any generated documents may be used as standalone files or added to book documents. Naming conventions for generated materials in books are the same as for individual files. For example, when generated files are added to a book, the generated files are named *BooknameEXT.fm*, where EXT is the

Book Error Report

F:\Using FrameMaker.book

November 3, 2001 11:55:30 am

F:\Page layout.fm

Couldn't open Page layout.fm, because it is locked or in use by another user.

F:\Color.fm

Print setting for color Black is inconsistent.
Print setting for color Cyan is inconsistent.
Print setting for color Magenta is inconsistent.
Print setting for color Yellow is inconsistent.
Print setting for color DarkBlue is inconsistent.

F:\Indexing.fm

Couldn't open Indexing.fm, because it uses unavailable fonts.

FrameMaker did not update the generated files because of errors such as: Couldn't open Indexing.fm

Figure 8-1 Sample book error report.

Note: *Any errors that occur must be resolved individually or collectively as required. In some instances, the errors cannot be resolved without modifications to the source documents.*

extension used by the generated file. (For example, *BooknameTOC.fm* would be the book file generated for a TOC).

The generated file also needs to be set up to use a template, to import a template, or to be able to configure the content, reference pages, and so on. To add a generated file to a book document, follow these steps:

1. Select **Add > Table of Contents** or **Add > List Of....**
2. Set up the file as required and click **Add** in the setup window.
3. In the Update Book dialog box, make sure **Generate Table of Contents, Lists, and Indexes** is checked.
4. Click **Update** to generate the new TOC or list.

Using a Finished TOC as a Template

When FrameMaker builds a generated list that does not have a template associated with it, the default format is based on the appearance of the source document. To simplify the creation process, a template may be used when a generated list is created.

Consider an example in which a new TOC is created from a file named *Configuration.fm*. We know the TOC is named *ConfigurationTOC.fm* by default. By opening a template and then saving it with the correct name and path (in this example, the location is the folder containing *Configuration.fm* and the file name is *ConfigurationTOC.fm*), you create a file with the correct name required by the source file. This occurs regardless of the fact that the TOC has not yet been generated.

Once the file has been placed in an appropriate location with the correct name, the actual TOC can be generated. FrameMaker recognizes the TOC file and populates it with the generated content from the source files. All formatting and layout is correctly applied without the need to import formatting or to recreate a file. To generate the TOC, follow these steps:

1. Open the template to use as the basis for the new TOC and choose **File > Save As**.
2. Select the correct location to save the template to and name the file correctly (*bookfileTOC.fm*).
3. Save and close the new TOC file.
4. Generate the TOC from the source document or book file.

Creating a Book with Multiple TOCs (Brief and Expanded)

Some documents are, by their nature, so lengthy or complex that a full TOC is unwieldy. At the same time, a complete reference of generated front matter would be of benefit to the reader. In a situation such as this, the introduction of a Brief TOC, List of Figures, or List of Tables is often beneficial to your document set.

The Brief TOC may contain only the primary headings and document titles in it. The second, expanded TOC may contain the same information, as well as third- or fourth-level (or more) headings from the source document.

To create multiple TOCs, create each of the source documents as if they were standalone files. Reference only the first level of headings in the first document, and reference much more content in the second document. This allows a reader to quickly identify the contents of each chapter but also to refer to the second TOC for more information if necessary.

To create a second TOC, follow the procedures for creating the first generated document but use a modified file suffix (as shown in Figure 8-2). Also remember to update the document correctly and add it to the book document if necessary.

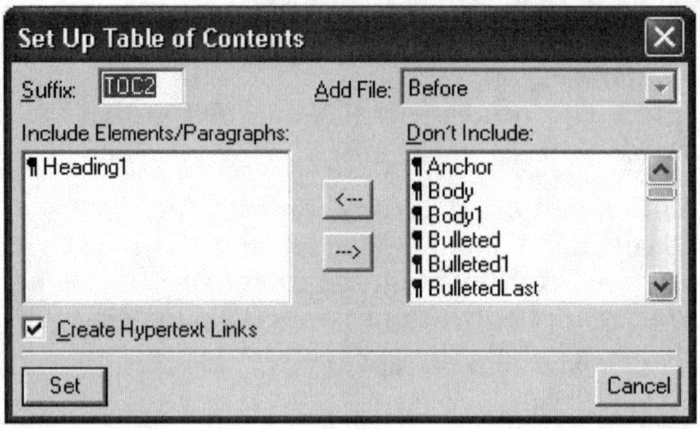

Figure 8-2 TOC setup dialog box with second suffix chosen.

Other Generated Lists

A variety of generated lists may be created, and the file extensions that are added usually relate to the file type, as shown in Table 8-2.

Table 8-2 Other Types of Generated Lists

Default Extension	File Type
TOC	Table of Contents
LOF	List of Figures
LOT	List of Tables
LOP	List of Paragraphs
APL	Alphabetical Paragraph List
LOM	List of Markers
AML	Alphabetical Marker List
LOR	List of References

The paragraph tags that are used to create a generated list are identified as ParatagExtension paragraphs. The term "Paratag" is the name of the paragraph followed by the extension of the file type. Each paragraph type should be used only for the generated lists, and not within the documents from which the generated list is created. This ensures that the paragraphs are unique to the generated list. Table 8-3 shows some examples of the paragraph names that may be seen in generated files.

Table 8-3 Sample Paratag Names

File Type	Sample Paragraph Names
TOC	TitleTOC, Heading1TOC, Heading2TOC, SubTopicTOC
TOC2	TitleTOC2, Heading1TOC2
LOF	FigureTitleLOF, FigureNameLOF, FigureNumberLOF
LOT	TableTitleLOT, TableNameLOT, TableNumberLOT

Moving Your TOC into PDF (Hypertext Links)

When you create your TOC, you can select an option that will make all of the entries hypertext links. These links will be active in both FrameMaker and in any PDF documents that you create.

To make your TOC entries hypertext links, make sure that Create Hypertext Links is selected in the Set Up Table of Contents dialog box, as shown in Figure 8-3.

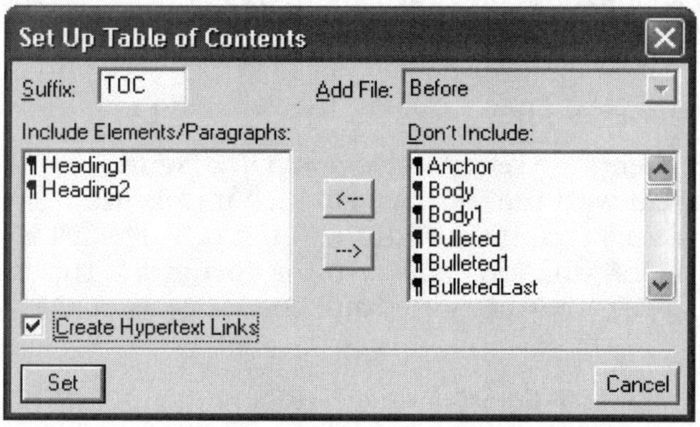

Figure 8-3 Create Hypertext Links box checked in TOC setup.

To test your hypertext links in FrameMaker, press and hold **Ctrl+Alt** and single-click on a TOC entry. FrameMaker displays the entry source file, with the TOC cross-reference marker selected. In a PDF, you simply single-click on an entry to view its source.

Cool Generated Lists Stuff

In addition to a TOC, you can generate a variety of cool lists from a FrameMaker document or book. Some of these lesser-known generated lists are described in detail in this section. To generate these other lists, select **Add > List Of...** from a book file, as shown in Figure 8-4 . From a document, select **Special > List Of**.

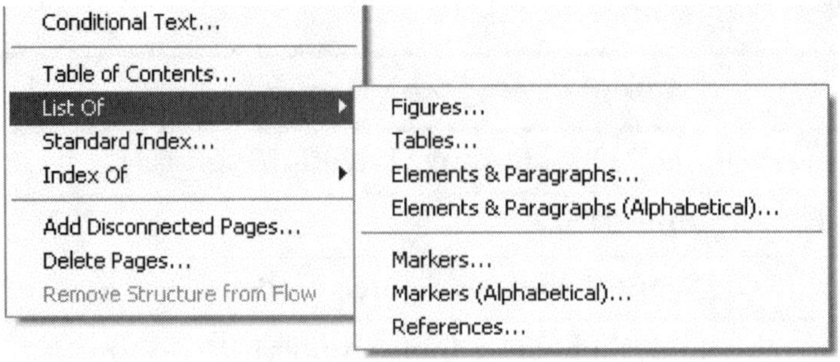

Figure 8-4 Drop-down menu for adding a generated list.

Lists of Graphics and Graphics-Related Information

You can create a generated list of graphics, images, or figure captions, as well as a list of file names and paths for referenced graphics. This latter function is especially useful for managing graphics that are shared between different files and books.

To create a list of graphic captions, you must already have the information in your documents, and it must be assigned a unique paragraph tag. For example, you could set up a paragraph tag called Graphic into which you place anchored frames with a paragraph tag called GraphicCaption underneath. You might want to set up GraphicCaption with numbering in the Paragraph Designer, and set Graphic with Next Pgf Tag GraphicCaption in the Basic tab, and Keep With Next Pgf checked in the Pagination tab.

Once your FrameMaker documents are set up, select **List Of > Figures**. FrameMaker creates a document with the suffix LOF, which means the generated content inside has a paragraph tag with the suffix LOF. The list is created chronologically as the information appears in the document. This is true of most generated lists, unless they are sorted alphabetically, as in generated indexes.

To create a list of all of your referenced graphics, with their path and file names, select **List Of > References**. You then select the types of items you wish to reference, such as Imported Graphics or Fonts. FrameMaker then creates a separate document listing all occurrences of those items.

List of Tables

To create a list of tables, select **List Of > Tables** and include the appropriate paragraph tag—usually the one used for your table title. If you have different table title paragraph tags for different tables, you can include multiple paragraph tags in this list. In a default portrait document, the paragraph tag to include is TableTitle.

List of Elements and Paragraphs

The Elements and Paragraphs options allow you to make a list of any paragraph tags' text, or if you are working with structured documents, elements. You can choose to make this list either chronological or alphabetical. A neat application of this list option is that you can make a very basic but very quick index by including your heading paragraph tags in the list. To make this basic index, select **List Of > Elements and Paragraphs (Alphabetical)** and include all the paragraph tags you use for your various heading levels. Here's another tip: If you are editing your index by changing capitalized heading entries to lowercase, select the phrase to be changed to lowercase, and then press **Ctrl+Alt+l** (Ctrl+Alt+lowercase L).

Marker Lists

Marker lists can also be either chronological or alphabetical. Some marker lists that may be useful to you include lists of cross-reference markers, conditional text markers, hypertext markers, and TopicAlias markers. To create a chronological list of markers, select **List Of > Markers**. To create an alphabetical list of markers, select **List Of > Markers (Alphabetical)**.

List of References

The options shown in Figure 8-5 are made available via **List Of > References**.

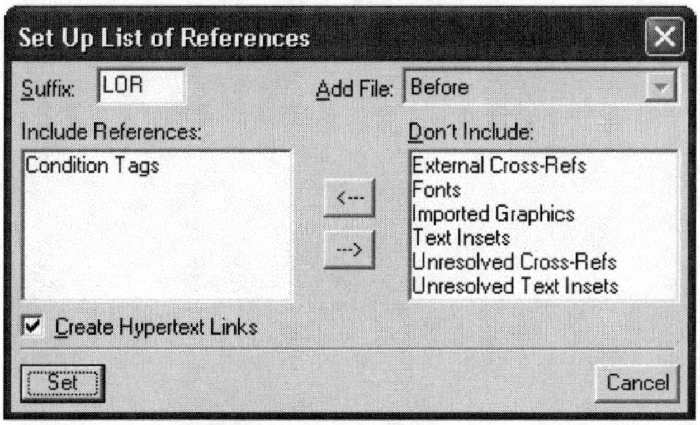

Figure 8-5 Reference list options.

Lists of references do not give you a list of what is available. Instead, they give you a list of what is in use, in order of its appearance in the document. Therefore, choosing to create a list of imported graphics generates a list that identifies the path name of each image referenced in a file or book. In the same way, text insets create a list of referenced locations for text insets.

Summary

FrameMaker produces generated lists and keeps them updated. This functionality provides you with quality, hypertext-linked lists of document contents. With a quick, one-time setup, you can produce the lists that you need and have them formatted as desired.

9

Indexes, Index Markers, and Reference Page Setup

Bernard Aschwanden

This chapter explains the indexing function, its related concepts, and how they can be used to generate useful reference materials.

Applicable to FrameMaker versions 5.5, 6, and 7.0/7.1

How an Index Works

There are numerous types of indices that can be created using FrameMaker. The most common is a "traditional" or "standard" index—similar to the one at the end of this book—in which numeric entries, symbols, and alphabetic content extracted from markers are sorted. However, FrameMaker also allows you to create documents that are alphabetical listings of content such as font types, images, authors, and so on.

Standard Index

A standard index is made up of content that is extracted from index markers in FrameMaker documents. Files based on a standard template contain content that is tagged using the Marker dialog box, as shown in Figure 9-1. The marker type is selected and extracted to a generated document based on the content in the marker. The extracted content is formatted based on instructions stored in a template. When required, the generated file can be re-created, replacing textual content that was extracted previously with the newer, updated content.

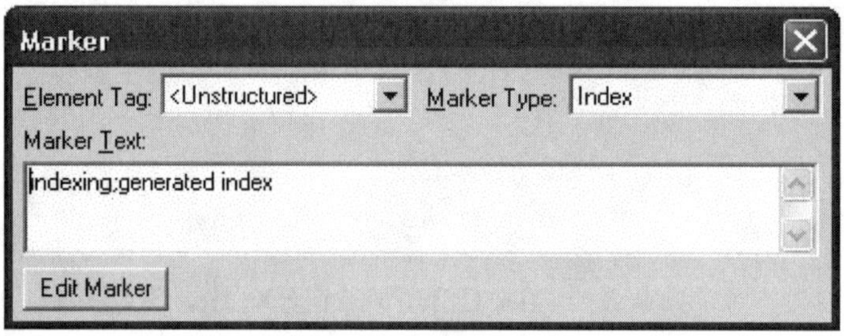

Figure 9-1 Marker dialog box with sample code.

Most of this chapter addresses the creation of a standard index. Other types of index files are detailed at the end of this chapter.

Setting Up Files for Use with Markers

Before you develop any index, content in a source document must be "marked" with index tags, or "text markers." When generating an index, FrameMaker pulls the information it needs from the index tags scattered throughout the book and then automatically alphabetizes it. It is critical, therefore, that you take care when creating a document template before any generated indices are added to the file set.

When tagging content for use by an index, you should implement a standard system. Content that is added to a generated index is generally text. In some cases, numeric values or symbols are added to a generated index as well. (Page numbers are generally added when the content in a file is extracted to the generated index.)

Reference pages are coded in the template for the generated index document, along with the commands required to build the document set. If this is done correctly, FrameMaker automatically organizes the content according to very specific coded instructions. This code is stored in the document's reference pages (as shown in the top left corner of Figure 9-2) and may be modified if required.

```
Level2IX
1, 2–3

Symbols[\ ];Numer-
ics[0];A;B;C;D;E;F;G;H;I;J;K;L;M;N;O;P;Q;R;S;T;U;V;W;X;Y;Z

<$symbols><$numerics><$alphabetics>
--——
Level1IX
openObjectId <$relfilename>:<$ObjectType> <$ObjectId>
<$pagenum>
```

Figure 9-2 Sample reference page code for indexing.

The system that is used to develop a generated index (after content has been correctly marked) is based on code in reference pages, the page layout set by master pages, and a combination of paragraph and character formats in the body pages. Content is automatically created based on the content of the markers used within the FrameMaker file.

When FrameMaker generates an index, content is extracted based on the content in the markers. All content is sorted by the alphanumeric order in which the content appears. All content of a given type is extracted from the first page, then from the second, and so on. The content is then sorted and the list is built.

Using markers within documents creates a generated index that is a dynamic document. As the source documents are modified (by adding, changing, or deleting content), the flow of the document automatically adjusts the order of text in the chapter or section units.

Once a document is marked with index tags, the generated index is automatically maintained as a generated file. Therefore, when files or their contents are modified, when the index is regenerated, it automatically modifies content to display changes to entries and page numbers. A book document or a standalone file that has an index associated with it may be updated at any time.

All page references in a generated index may be set up to act as hypertext links. When the generated index is converted to PDF, HTML, or online help systems using WebWorks Publisher, these links remain active hypertext. Each page reference within the FrameMaker generated index is a link to the marker used to create the entry and may be accessed using standard hypertext linking options. If required, the hypertext links may be disabled in a generated file (see Figure 9-3).

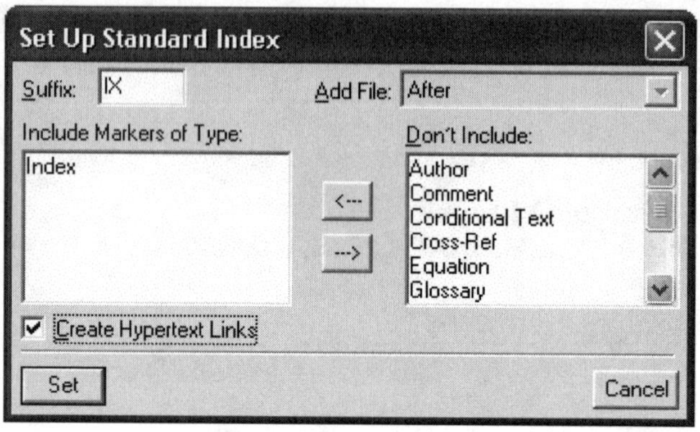

Figure 9-3 Automatic creation of hypertext links.

Note: *If your documents will be distributed electronically, you may need to reconsider marker placement practices to fit your media. For example, in HTML created from FrameMaker, the markers often are used as the endpoint for hyperlinks. When a link is clicked, the HTML page is displayed with the marker location moved to the top in the browser. You may want to place markers for improved online viewing; use caution, though, to avoid in your printed documents incorrect page numbers that can result from poorly placed markers.*

Inserting Markers

The successful creation of an index is dependent upon the markers that are inserted into a document. These markers are inserted into the flow of the document at the location to which the index marker will point. It is good practice to have the marker as close to the word or element to which the index entry will point so that any page reflows do not separate your markers from the text or element to which they are referring. Therefore, markers should be placed in the following locations:

- At the beginning of the word or phrase to be indexed
- In the word
- At the end of the word

Once the location of the marker is decided, select that location. While numerous shortcuts exist to insert index markers, you must use caution when using them. The most common shortcut is to select the phrase to be indexed and then automatically populate the marker window with the selected phrase. The inherent danger of using this shortcut is that any markers that are already placed in the phrase will be picked up by the new marker and incorrectly displayed in the generated index entry.

The next step is to display the marker window by selecting **Special** > **Marker**. Before you insert a new index marker, the Marker dialog box must appear with an Index marker type (see the Marker Type field in Figure 9-4).

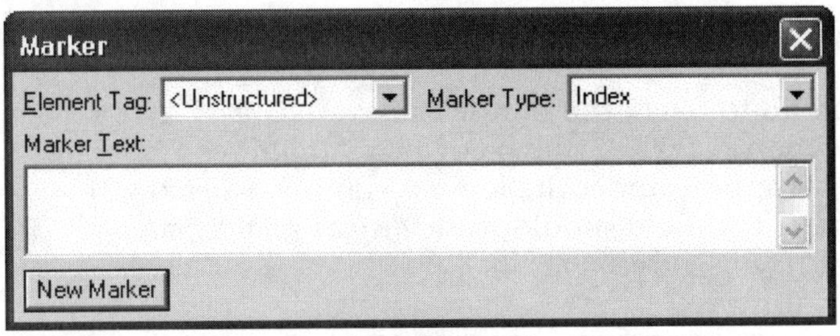

Figure 9-4 Marker dialog box.

As we introduce the different types of index entries and how to create markers for them, we will use the following sentence as our sample text:

> *Adjust the display adapter by using the on-screen settings.*

Index Entries and Case or Content

When you create index entries, make sure that the case in the marker text is the case that is desired in the index. If the phrase *"display adapter"* is to appear as *"Display adapter,"* it must be entered in that case in the Marker dialog box shown in Figure 9-4.

If the text *"Adjust"* should appear as *"adjustment,"* both the case and the phrase need to be correctly set in the dialog box.

Single Index Entry

To create a single index entry, populate the Marker text field in the Marker dialog box with the text that is to appear in the index entry.

For example, if you intend to index the phrase *"display adapter"* so it appears under the letter D, the marker text in the dialog box should read *"display adapter."* As a shortcut, you can double-click on the text to make it appear automatically in the dialog box (see Figure 9-5).

Multiple Index Entries

To create multiple index entries, populate the Marker text field in the Marker dialog box with the text that is to appear in each index entry, separated by a semi–colon. The order of the content is not relevant.

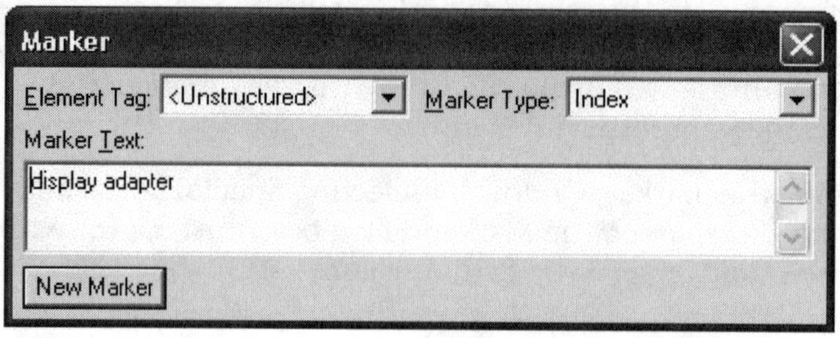

Figure 9-5 Display of simple index entry.

For example, if you intend to index the phrase *"display adapter"* so it appears under the letter D, the marker text in the dialog box should read *"display adapter."* If it should also appear under the letter A—as in *"adapter"*—the marker text in the Marker text field should read *"display adapter;adapter"* or *"adapter;display adapter"* (see Figure 9-6).

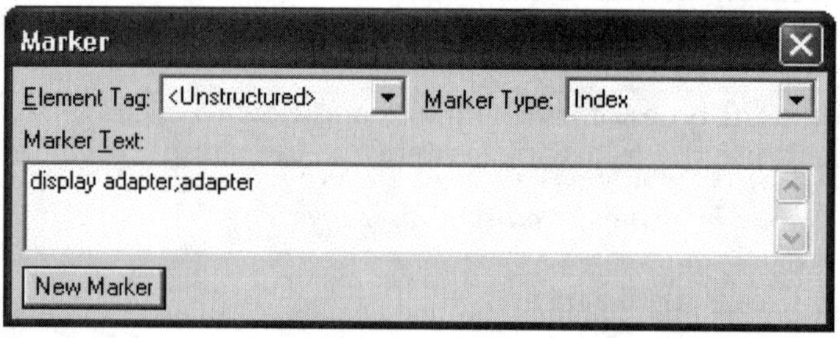

Figure 9-6 Display of multiple index entries.

If the phrase should appear in three locations, the content of the dialog box may read something like *"video display;adapters;display adapter."* This would place three entries in the index: one under A, one under D, and the last one under V.

Subordinate Index Entries

To create subordinate index entries, populate the Marker text field in the Marker dialog box with the text that is to appear at the highest level, followed by a colon and the text that is to appear at the next level. Repeat this as required. The order of the content in the generated index is completely dependent upon the hierarchy you use to build the index marker in the text.

For example, if you intend to index the phrase *"display adapter"* so it appears under the letter A as a subtopic of "adapters," the text in the Marker text field might read *"adapter:display adapter,"* as shown in Figure 9-7.

If you intend to index the phrase *"on-screen settings"* to appear under the letter S as a subtopic of settings, the marker text in the dialog box might read *"settings:on-screen."*

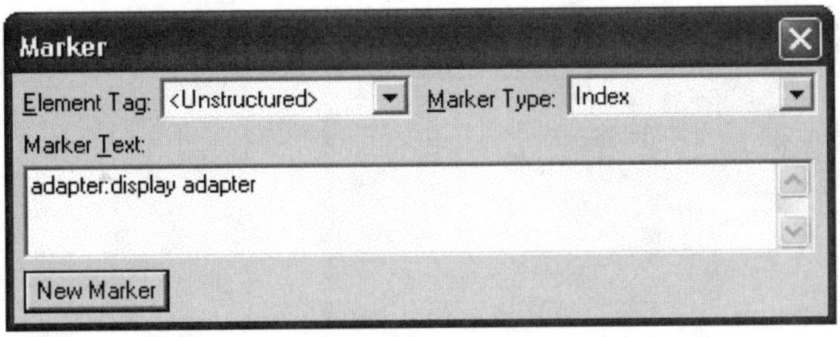

Figure 9-7 Display of subordinate index entries.

Note: *Combining multiple entries with subordinate entries allows you to create complex entries. For example, "adapter:display adapter;display adapter" creates two entries. The first is "display adapter" as a subordinate entry to "adapters" under the letter A. The second is the full phrase "display adapter" under the letter D, as shown in Figure 9-8.*

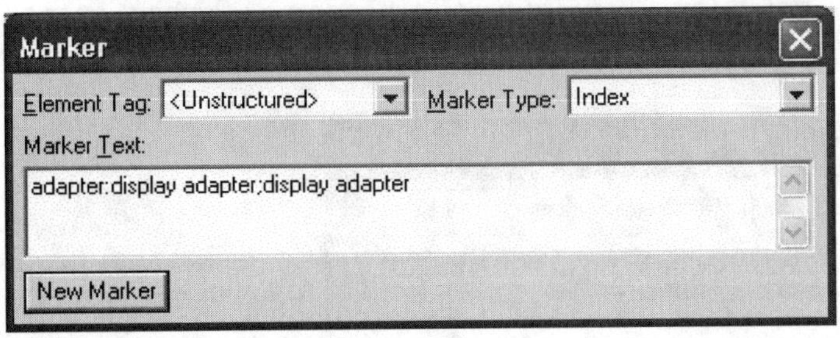

Figure 9-8 Combined multiple and subordinate index entries.

Pageless Index Entries

To create pageless index entries, populate the Marker text field in the Marker dialog box with the text that is to appear in the index entry, preceded by *<$nopage>*, as shown in Figure 9-9. Use caution when inserting any pageless entries to ensure that the topic they point to has a valid entry as well.

For example, if you intend to index the phrase *"display adapter"* so it appears under the letter D but references the entry *"monitors,"* the marker text in the Marker dialog box might read *"<$nopage>display adapters. See monitors,"* which creates an entry that does not reference a page. It is crucial, however, that the entry *"monitors"* exists in the index; otherwise users get frustrated with the index and can potentially refuse to use the index (and maybe even the product).

A great solution to the issue of pageless entries and their matching values is to combine the use of the semi-colon for multiple entries with the pageless entry. This means that the Marker text field could be populated with the phrase *"monitors;<$nopage>display adapters, See monitors"* so both entries are generated from a single marker, as shown in Figure 9-10. This ensures that

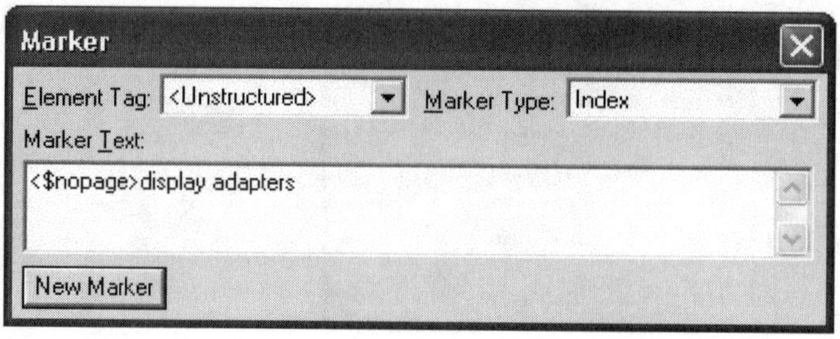

Figure 9-9 Display of pageless index entries.

Note: *It is important to ensure that entries that should be indexed with page references are placed prior to the appearance of the <$nopage> tag. All content (regardless of the use of the colon or semi-colon) after the <$nopage> tag will appear in the index without a page reference.*

"*monitors*" is added to the index under the letter *M*. If you are combining entries in this fashion, you should remember to add the page-driven entry before using the *<$nopage>* tag.

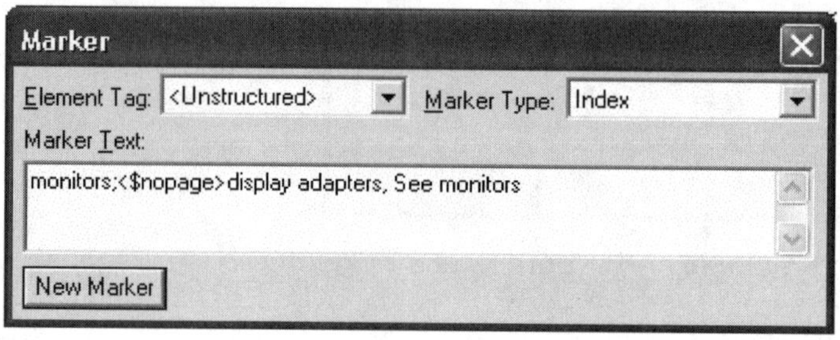

Figure 9-10 Multiple index entry with <$nopage> tag.

Note: *If it is necessary to continue the page numbering for index entries after the <$nopage> tag, the phrase tag <$singlepage> can be used to restart the page numbering within the same marker (see Figure 9-11).*

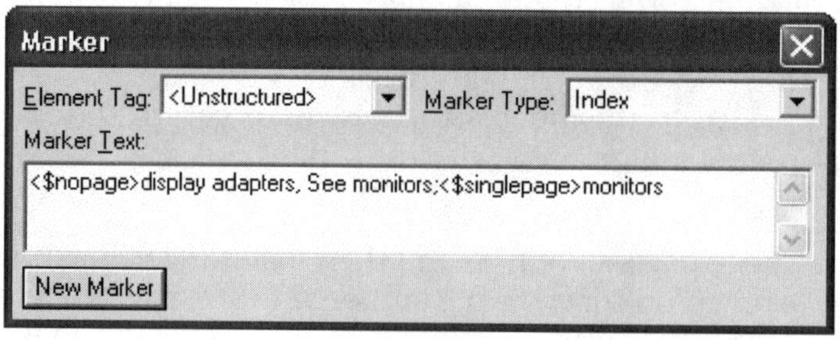

Figure 9-11 Display of <$nopage> and <$singlepage> index marker tags.

Page Range Index Entries

To create page range index entries, populate the Marker text field in the Marker dialog box with the text that is to appear in each index entry, preceded by either the *<$startrange>* or *<$endrange>* tag. The order of the content is relevant to the way that these entries will look in the generated index. The *<$startrange>* tag must appear prior to the *<$startrange>* tag. Use caution when inserting any entries using page ranges to ensure that the tags do not end up in reverse order (due to cutting and pasting content or rearranging files in a book document).

For example, if you intend to index the phrase *"display adapter"* to appear under the letter D beginning on page 7, for example, the text in the Marker text field for the marker on page 7 should read *"<$startrange>display adapter."* To complete the range, you index the phrase *"display adapter"* to end on page 12, for example, and the text in the Marker text field for the marker on page 12 should read *"<$endrange>display adapter."*

The warning related to using index entries with page ranges is a major one. Most users expect FrameMaker to create index entries correctly, so they never look at the generated content. (The joy of working with FrameMaker is that it DOES correctly create generated files based on what is contained in the source files!) We therefore don't often consider a review of the generated files to be too necessary, and that's where the first mistake lies.

If a *<$startrange>* or an *<$endrange>* tag exists without its corresponding partner tag, generated index entries appear incorrectly. The appearance of a set of entries that span pages 7 through 12 should normally appear as "7–12." If the *<$startrange>* or *<$endrange>* entry is missing, however, the entry may appear instead as either "??–12" or "7–??." You must correct this by either removing the reference to a *<$startrange>* or an *<$endrange>* or by adding the required matching tag to the correct marker in the source document.

Note: *An automated approach to this type of range entry is to modify the reference pages of the generated index. To do this, you must modify the IndexIX paragraph tag. (For more detail on this and other tags, refer to "Adjusting the Reference Page Data" on page 217.) To create a range automatically, <$autorange> may be placed as the very first building block in IndexIX. This causes FrameMaker to find entries based on the exact same Marker dialog box content on consecutive pages and creates a range for you. If there is a range that should span three pages, but the required markers are only on the first and last pages, the use of the <$autorange> tag is prevented. Only consecutive pages with the same marker are flagged. This means that you have to mark every page with the index markers. Finally, even if this is done, future content edits may result in markers shifting off a page (or being deleted), thereby negating the usefulness of <$autorange>.*

Index Entries and Character Formats

If you are creating index entries and content is to be formatted using character formats, there are two methods you may use. The first (and undesirable) method is to manually apply character formats to the index after it is generated. This creates the immediate problem, however, of having to manually repeat this process each time the index is generated.

The second approach—and, in the opinion of this author, the only correct one—is to incorporate the character formats directly into the index marker content. Character tags that are incorporated into markers must also exist in the template used to create the index file. For example, if you are using a tag such as *Emphasis* in a marker, make sure that *Emphasis* is also used in the template.

To add a character format into a marker, place the name of the tag between greater-than and less-than tags. For example, to incorporate the *Emphasis* character tag, "*<Emphasis>*" needs to appear in the marker text. The default paragraph format can also be applied at any time using the *<Default Para Font>* tag, as shown in Figure 9-12.

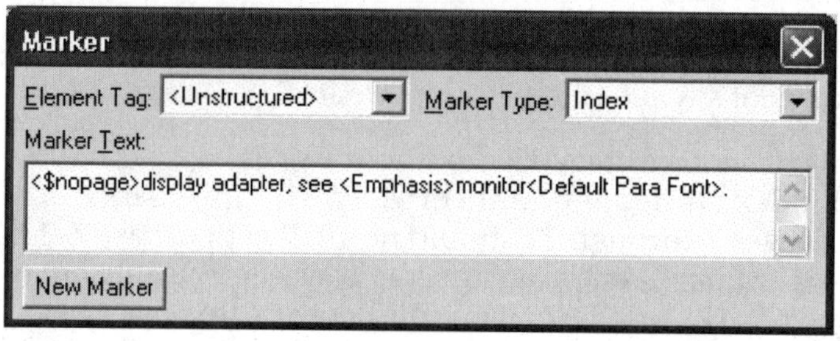

Figure 9-12 Character formats and index entries.

The example shown in Figure 9-12 would display the phrase "display adapter, see *monitor*" under the letter D without a page reference.

Sorting Index Entries

The default sort order of index entries can be modified on a case-by-case basis, allowing content to be sorted in customized ways. For example, an entry that is numeric may need to be sorted alphabetically rather than numerically. To create a custom sort of an entry, populate the Marker text field in the Marker dialog box with the text that is to appear in the index entry, followed by the sort order in brackets (using "[" and "]" to mark the sort order).

For example, if you want to index the phrase "*2000 Compliant*" so it appears under the letter T (*for "two thousand compliant"*), the marker text in the Marker dialog box should read "*2000 Compliant[two thousand compliant],*" as shown in Figure 9-13.

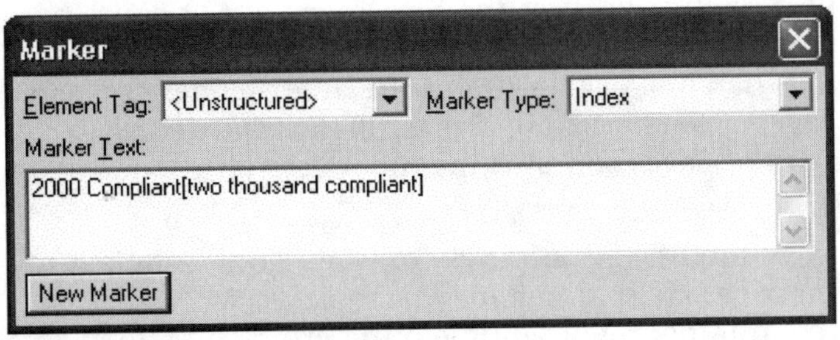

Figure 9-13 Display of marker text used to sort index entries.

Of course, if the entry is to appear under both the numeric entry and the textual entry, the text in the Marker text field should be set up with two entries separated by a semi-colon. For the example in Figure 9-13, the marker entry would be *"2000 Compliant[two thousand compliant];2000 Compliant."*

Index Entries and Special Characters

If you need to insert special characters (for example, en dashes, less-than or greater-than symbols, backslashes, and other reserved characters) into an index, they must be preceded by a backslash. Therefore, the en dash would appear as \=, the less-than or greater-than as \< or \>, and the backslash as \\ in the Marker text field of the Marker dialog box.

Adjusting the Reference Page Data

The generated index is created based on paragraph and character formats, the master page layout, and sample code in the reference pages. To view the reference pages, select **View > Reference Pages**.

Sample Reference Page Code for Generated Lists

The code in the reference page of a standard generated index may appear as shown in Figure 9-14. Each line is described as follows:

```
 1, 2-3
Level2IX
Symbols[\
  ];Numerics[0];A;B;C;D;E;F;G;H;I;J;K;L;M;N;O;P;Q;R;
  S;T;U;V;W;X;Y;Z
<$symbols><$numerics><$alphabetics>
----
Level1IX
openObjectId <$relfilename>:<$ObjectType>
  <$ObjectId>
<$pagenum>
```

Figure 9-14 Default index entry code.

1. The SeparatorsIX paragraph appears as the first line above. It contains dividers used between page numbers or ranges. The comma is the default character when more than one page contains the index reference (such as a topic that is on pages 7, 53, and 207). The hyphen is the default character when a span of pages contains the index reference (such as a topic that is on pages 7–12).

   This paragraph may be modified in a variety of ways. For example, the character used when pages are spanned may be replaced with a phrase. If you are using chapter numbering or volume numbering and referencing them in the index, entries may appear in a format that is not conducive to the use of the hyphen.

   If, for example, an entry is on the third page of Chapter Seven (page 7–3) and spans until the twelfth page (page 7–12), the default appearance in the index may appear as *7–3-7–12*. Obviously this format is confusing to a reader. Therefore, replacing the hyphen between the numbers 2 and 3 in the SeparatorsIX paragraph in with a different symbol (or even text) can resolve this. This means that the page range in the index could be displayed as *7–3 to 7–12* instead.

Note: *The paragraph format of SeparatorsIX and IndexIX should generally be the same as the default font. This ensures that the page numbering (set by the IndexIX) and the dividers between pages in a range (set by the SeparatorsIX) appear in the same font when generated.*

2. Level2IX is used for second-level (or subordinate) index entries. This paragraph may be modified in a variety of ways. For example, the paragraph may be configured to use pagination features such as *Keep With Previous Pgf,* or change text alignment.
3. GroupTitlesIX organizes grouping and titles. Above each "section" of an index, a title for that section appears. For example, the word Symbols, the word Numerics, or characters (A, B, C,...) appear as "groupings" in the index.

   The GroupTitlesIX paragraph may be modified in a variety of ways. For example, if the letters W, X, Y and Z should be grouped together (to appear as W–Z and have all index entries associated with these letters sorted under the combined entry), the phrase *"V;W;X;Y;Z"* should be replaced with *"V;W–Z."* In the same way, if the phrase "Symbols" should be replaced with "Special Symbols," the content in the reference page will need to be modified.
4. SortOrderIX specifies the system used to sort the content. In this example, any symbols appear prior to numeric entries. Once these are inserted, the remainder of the alphabetical content is inserted.

   This paragraph may be modified in a variety of ways. For example, the default order may be modified to allow numeric entries to appear first, then alphabetical content, and finally symbols by rearranging the content of the paragraph to read "<$numerics><$alphabetics><$symbols>."

5. IgnoreCharsIX specifies characters to ignore when sorting index entries. By default, this is set to hyphens, en dashes, and em dashes.

   This paragraph may be modified in a variety of ways. For example, if characters such as parentheses, brackets, and braces are to be ignored, you should add those characters (which are keyed in as *(,), [,], {,* and *}* in the paragraph) to this paragraph's contents. For example, the revised entry may be entered as "()[]{}."
   In the same way, if characters for quotations, less-than signs, or greater-than signs are the only characters to ignore when sorting, the revised entry may be entered as "<>"".".

6. Level1IX is used for first-level (or primary) index entries.

   This paragraph may be modified in a variety of ways. For example, the paragraph may be configured to use a font that differs from other entries, or the default alignment may be changed.

7. ActiveIX contains commands used to build hypertext commands between generated entries and their appropriate locations within FrameMaker documents. This specifies the form of the hypertext commands used by the generated files.

   This paragraph should never be modified, as it may create errors in generated materials when links are automatically inserted.

8. IndexIX contains commands that determine what page information is extracted for numbering. Only the page number is active as a link in the index file. Therefore, if you are using hypertext to link entries to their markers, you must click the page number, not the actual text of the entry.

   This paragraph may be modified in a variety of ways. For example, if you are using chapter numbering or volume numbering and referencing those variables in the index, entries may be modified.
   If, for example, an entry is on the third page of Chapter Seven (page 7–3), the default entry in the index may appear as *"3."* Obviously this format is confusing to a reader because the specific chapter is not referenced. Therefore, changing the default entry to *"<$chapnum>–<$pagenum>"* creates an entry in the index that is displayed as *"7–3"* instead.

Note: *The paragraph format of SeparatorsIX and IndexIX should generally be the same as the default font. This ensures that the page numbering (set by the IndexIX) and the dividers between pages in a range (set by the SeparatorsIX) appear in the same font when generated.*

When indexing, content may be sorted in several ways. Entries are sorted by special symbols, followed by numeric values, and then alphabetical content. Therefore, an index may appear as shown in Table 9-1.

Table 9-1 Sample Index Content

Symbols	Compact Disc 32	IPO, *See Initial Public*
@ERROR 14	Computer 34	
@TERMINATE 12		**M**
#DISCONNECT 15	**E**	Market Information
	Electronic Devices	Estimated Sales 5 to 8
Numerics	Compact Disc 32	IPO, *See Initial Public*
133 Router 24	Computer 34	Music Players 32, 42
1998 Incorporation 3	Stereo System 39	
2000 Compliance 6	Television 36	**S**
	Estimated Sales 5 to 8	Sales Estimates 5 to 8
A		Stereo Systems 42
Accept carrier code 42	**I**	Systems, Computer 34
Autoconnect 23	Initial Public Offering 2	
Autodial 23	Internet Enabled Devices	**T**
	Cellular Phone 32	Television. *See Electronic*
C	PDA 39	2000 Compliance 6
Cellular Phone 32	Investor Relations 2	TX Exchange System 14

In Table 9-1, information is sorted first by symbols, then by numbers, and finally by letters. Within the Symbols section, sorting is done first by symbol, then by text. Numbers are sorted by ascending value. Letters are sorted by primary alphabetical character. If the initial character matches (as it does in many of the samples), the second letter is used to continue the sort, then the third, and so on, until each entry is uniquely sorted. Each entry needs to be correctly coded in the source document.

This example contains second-level entries (under Electronic Devices, Internet Enabled Devices, and Market Information) that are sorted alphabetically as subtopics. In this example, the subtopics are also sorted using the same symbols, numbers, and alphabetic values. Secondary sorting ensures that content is correctly placed and simple to reference. Each subentry needs to be correctly coded in the source document.

Several entries exist two or more times under different headings. "Compact Disc" links exist under *C* (*Compact Disc*), under *E* (*Electronic Devices* with a subtopic of *Compact Disc*), and under *M* (*Music Players*). "Cellular Phone" appears under *C* (*Cellular Phone*) as well as under *I* (*Internet Enabled Devices,* with a subtopic of *Cellular Phone*). This is achieved by specifying additional code when the marker is developed.

The numeric entry for "2000 Compliance" is sorted twice. It appears in the numeric section—correctly placed at the end of the numeric list—and also under T, correctly placed at the location where "two thousand" would appear if it had been entered as text. This is done by specifying additional code when the marker is developed, as shown in Figure 9-15.

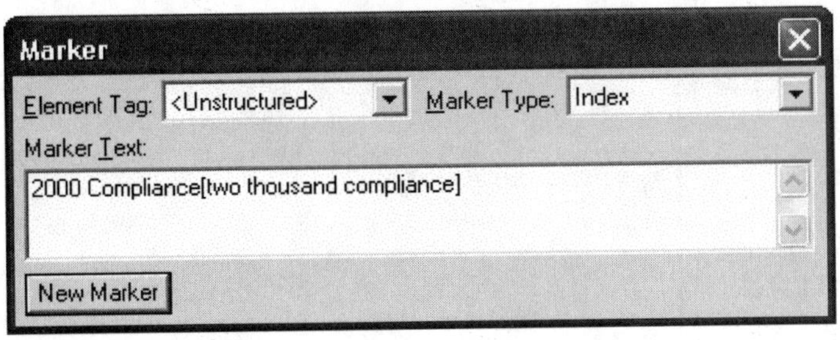

Figure 9-15 Numeric entry sorted textually.

Some of the index entries have multiple page ranges assigned to them. This occurs in two situations. The first is under E ("Estimated Sales 5 to 8") and the second occurs under M ("Music Players 32, 42"). The first instance is a page range defined with a start range (on page 5) and an end range (on page 8). The second example occurs because the phrase "Music Players" is indexed as two separate entries, one on page 32 and the other on page 42.

Including Character Formatting

By modifying marker code used by FrameMaker documents by adding <CharacterTagName>, you can format generated content to be displayed with character formats applied, as shown in Figure 9-16.

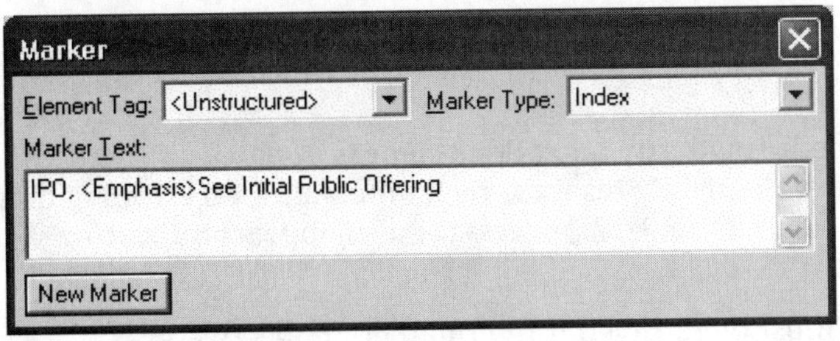

Figure 9-16 Character-formatted index entry.

A generated file—for example, an index—based on this concept of character formatting may then appear as shown in Table 9-2.

Entries for *"See Initial Public Offering"* and *"IPO, See Initial Public Offering"* appear formatted in italics per the Emphasis tag in the generated index.

Table 9-2 Sample Index with Character Formats

I

Initial Public Offering 2

IPO, *See Initial Public Offering*

M

Market Information

  Estimated Sales 5 to 8

  IPO, *See Initial Public Offering*

  Television 36

The Book and File Update Process (Rebuilding Your Data)

Books may be updated to reflect the most current content of files within the book. The update is done to modify various settings; however, only those specified are updated. To update a book, follow these steps:

1. Select **Edit > Update Book**, or click ; the Update Book dialog box appears.
2. Select the types of content to update.
3. Move generated file names to the appropriate scroll list using the arrow buttons.
4. Click **Update**.

Once these steps are performed, the book document is updated. If there are issues that cannot be automatically resolved by FrameMaker, an error log may be generated, as shown in Figure 9-17. A message also appears indicating errors have occurred.

Any errors that occur must be resolved individually or collectively, as required. In some instances, the errors cannot be resolved without modifications to the source documents.

Adding Generated Files to Book Documents

Any generated documents may be added to book documents or used as standalone files. Naming conventions for generated materials in books are the same as for individual files. For example, when generated files are added to a book, the generated files are named *BooknameEXT.fm*, where EXT is the extension used by the generated file.

Book Error Report
F:\Using FrameMaker.book

January 23, 2002 1:23:00 pm

F:\Page layout.fm
Couldn't open Page layout.fm, because it is locked or in use by another user.

F:\Color.fm
Print setting for color Black is inconsistent.
Print setting for color Cyan is inconsistent.
Print setting for color Magenta is inconsistent.
Print setting for color Yellow is inconsistent.
Print setting for color DarkBlue is inconsistent.

F:\Indexing.fm
Couldn't open Indexing.fm, because it uses unavailable fonts.

FrameMaker did not update the generated files because of errors such as: Couldn't open Indexing.fm

Figure 9-17 Book error log sample.

The generated file also needs to be set up to use a template, to import a template, or to configure the content, reference pages, and so on. To generate a file, follow these instructions:

1. Select **Add > Standard Index** or **Index Of**, as appropriate.
2. Set up the file as required, and click **OK** in the setup window.
3. Generate the book as required.

Using a Finished Index As a Template

When FrameMaker builds a generated index that does not have a template associated with it, the default format is based on the appearance of the source document. To simplify the creation process, you can use a template to give the new index a particular "look."

For example, a new index is created from a file named *Configuration.fm*. The index is named *ConfigurationIX.fm* by default. When you open a template and save it with the correct name and path (in this example, the location is the folder containing *Configuration.fm*, and the filename is *ConfigurationIX.fm*), a file is created with the correct name, as required by the source file. This is done regardless of the fact that the index has not yet been generated.

Once the file has been placed in an appropriate location with the correct name, the index can be generated. FrameMaker recognizes the index and populates it from the markers in the source. All formatting and layout is correctly applied without the need to import formatting or re-create a file.

1. Open the template you want to use as the basis for the new index and then choose **File > Save As**.
2. Select the correct location to save the template to and name the file correctly.
3. **Save** and **Close** the index file.
4. Generate the index from the source document or book file.

Other Types of Generated Indices

Other indices (alphabetical lists) can be generated based on content in your FrameMaker documents. This includes generated files such as an index of fonts, an index of figures, and so on. These documents contain information extracted from FrameMaker and sorted alphabetically.

As with a standard index, the extracted content is formatted based on instructions stored in a template. When required, the generated file can be re-created, replacing textual content that was extracted previously with the newer, updated content.

The file extensions that are added to the various other index types usually relate to the file type, as shown in Table 9-3.

Table 9-3 Types of Generated Indices

Default Extension	File Type
IX	General Index
AIX	Index of Authors
SIX	Index of Subjects
IOM	Index of Markers
IOR	Index of References

Note: *For each file type, a reference page with the extension as its name is created, using the extension name as its flow tag.*

The contents that are extracted to create a generated index are identified as a specific marker type. Each marker type should be used only for content specific to the generated index. This ensures that the contents are unique to the generated index. Some examples of the marker types that may be used include those listed in Table 9-4.

Table 9-4 Marker Types and Usage

Marker Type	Common Usage
Index	Standard index, alphabetical list of topics
Author	List of authors, alphabetical reference
Subject	List of subjects, alphabetical reference

To insert a specific marker type, select it from the Marker Type drop-down menu in the Marker dialog box (see Figure 9-18). Populate the marker as required using the codes described earlier in this chapter, and then insert the new marker.

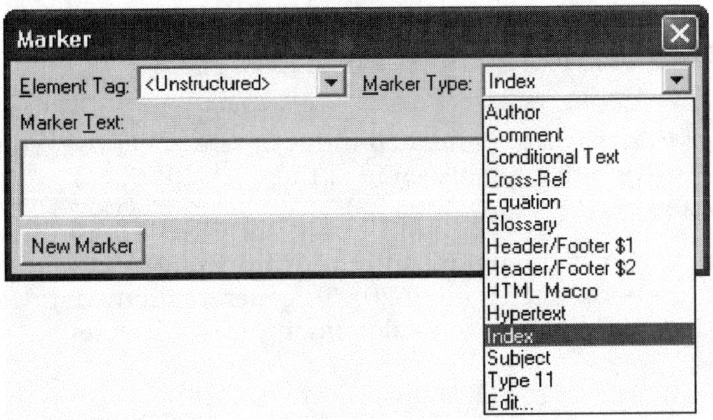

Figure 9-18 Marker dialog box with pop-up expanded.

Moving Your Index into PDF

When you create your indices, you can select an option that will make all of the entries hypertext links. These links will be active in both FrameMaker and in the subsequent PDF documents that you create.

To choose the option that makes your index entries hypertext links, select the Create Hypertext Links checkbox in the Set Up Standard Index dialog box shown in Figure 9-19.

To test your hypertext links in FrameMaker, press and hold **Ctrl+Alt** and single-click on an index page number. FrameMaker displays the entry source file with the index marker selected. In a PDF, simply single-click on an entry to view its source.

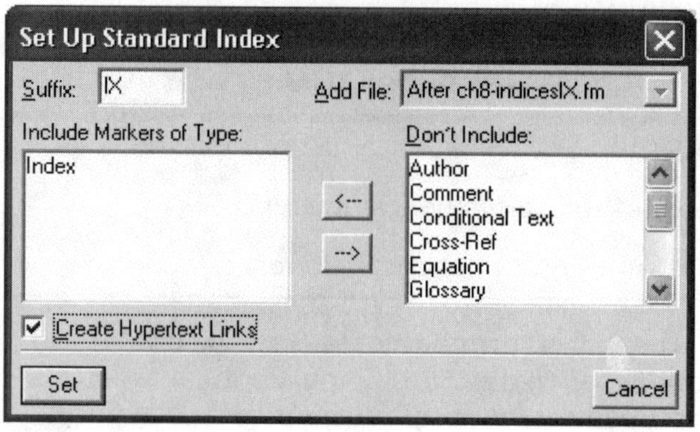

Figure 9-19 Set Up Standard Index dialog box with Create Hypertext Links selected.

Cool Stuff To Do with Generated Indices

You can do a lot of cool things with a generated index of references that you may not be aware of. This section explains some of these lesser-known generated index applications.

Besides a standard index, you can generate an index of references from a FrameMaker document or book (see Figure 9-20). To generate such an index from a book, select **Add** > **Index Of**. From a document, select **Special** > **Index Of**.

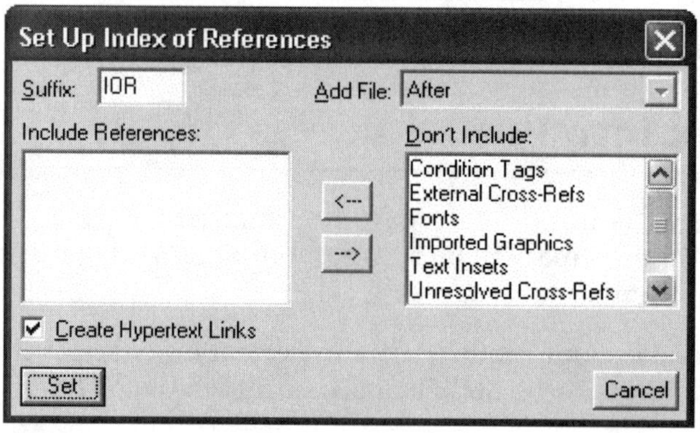

Figure 9-20 Set Up Index of References dialog box.

Condition Tags

You can create a generated index of conditions used in a document or book. This function is especially useful for managing documents with a variety of conditions that span numerous pages and have nested levels of complexity. You should note that the list shows only the types of conditions in use and the pages on which they are used, not the content of the condition.

To create an index of condition tags, you must already have conditional content in your documents.

Once your FrameMaker documents are set up, select **Add** > **Index Of** in a book (or **Index Of** > **References** for a standalone list) and include Condition Tags by moving them to the left column in the dialog box that appears. FrameMaker creates a document with the suffix IOR, with the generated content inside containing a list of all conditions in use listed alphabetically by pathname.

External Cross-References

You can create a generated index of cross-references used in a document or book. This function is especially useful for managing documents with a variety of external cross-references that span numerous documents and need to be managed. Note that the list shows only the content of the cross-references in use and the pages on which they are used.

To create an index of cross-references, you must already have external cross-references in your documents.

Once your FrameMaker documents are set up, select **Add** > **Index Of** in a book (or **Index Of** > **References** for a standalone list), and include External Cross-Refs (move left in the dialog box as above). FrameMaker creates a document with the suffix IOR, with the generated content inside containing a list of all external cross- references listed alphabetically.

Fonts

You can create a generated index of the fonts used in a document or book. This function is especially useful for managing documents with a variety of fonts that may be required by others. The list shows fonts in use, the size of each font, and the pages on which the fonts are used.

Once your FrameMaker documents are set up, select **Index Of** > **References** and include Fonts (move left in the dialog box as above). FrameMaker creates a document with the suffix IOR, with the generated content inside containing a list of all fonts in use listed alphabetically by font name.

Imported Graphics

You can create a generated index of graphic file names and paths for referenced graphics. This function is especially useful for managing graphics that are shared between different files and books. To create an index of graphics, you must already have graphics in your documents, and they must be imported by reference.

Once your FrameMaker documents are set up, select **Add** > **Index Of** in a book (or **Index Of** > **References** for a standalone list), and include Imported Graphics (move left in the dialog box as above). FrameMaker creates a document with the suffix IOR, with the generated content inside containing a list of all referenced images listed alphabetically by pathname.

Text Insets

You can create a generated index of text insets, and paths for the text insets. This function is especially useful for managing text insets that are shared between different files and books.

To create an index of text insets, you must already have text insets in your documents, and they must be imported by reference. (Since any other type of text inset becomes a piece of editable text in the source document, the only way imported text can be an inset is for it to be referenced.)

Once your FrameMaker documents are set up, select **Add** > **Index Of** in a book (or **Index Of** > **References** for a standalone list), and include Text Insets (move left in the dialog box as above). FrameMaker creates a document with the suffix IOR, with the generated content inside containing a list of all referenced text insets listed alphabetically by pathname.

Unresolved Cross-References and Text Insets

You can create a generated index of unresolved cross-references, as well as text insets and their paths. This function is especially useful for managing unresolved references and insets from a single location, rather than opening each document and searching its contents.

To create an index of unresolved content, you must already have cross-references or text insets in your documents, and they must be unresolved. (Otherwise the generated document is blank.)

Once your FrameMaker documents are set up, select **Add** > **Index Of** in a book (or **Index Of** > **References** for a standalone list), and include either Unresolved Cross-Refs or Unresolved Text Insets. FrameMaker creates a document with the suffix IOR, with the generated content inside containing a list of all unresolved content listed alphabetically by pathname.

Example of Custom Indices

Imagine a book that is a collection of historical data. A custom index may be created based on ranges that are driven primarily by the year (or a range of years) rather than based on traditional text entries.

The default grouping in an index is determined based on the content of the paragraph GroupTitlesIX (using headings such as Symbols, Numerics, and the various letters of the alphabet). When you change these entries, however, a custom index can be created.

For example, to set a range of years, the revised GroupTitlesIX may instead appear as the following:

Symbols[\ ];Before 1500[0-1499];1500 to 1900[1500-1900];
Twentieth Century[1901-2000];2000 and Beyond[2000-99999];
A;B;C;D;E;F;G;H;I;J;K;L;M;N;O;P;Q;R;S;T;U;V;W;X;Y;Z

Summary

FrameMaker has powerful capabilities for generating and updating indexes. With some advance setup and careful insertion of markers, you can produce a quality index. The indexing feature can work well for paper documents, allowing easy reference to page numbers. The same index can be used to create interactive, easily navigable online documents as well. This FrameMaker feature, used properly, can move you further into the world of single sourcing or "multichannel publishing" of your information.

10

Creating Great Screen Captures

Bradley Anderson

If you captures screens for placement in your FrameMaker documents, this tutorial will show you techniques for optimizing captures for print or online.

Applicable to all versions of FrameMaker

A Short Introduction to Graphics Terminology

Creating screen captures that look good in both print and PDF can be difficult. A screen capture placed in a document for printing may look fine when printed on a laser printer; however, in the PDF version of the document, the screen capture may look terrible. Before we look at the reasons this may happen, we must first understand a little about image formats and resolution

Vector Images

A vector image is an image that was drawn in a program such as Adobe Illustrator, Corel Draw, Macromedia Freehand, or Deneba Canvas. These programs allow you to draw images with mathematical curves, or vectors. Because the image is mathematically based, you can scale the images larger or smaller without a loss in resolution. These images should be saved as EPS or PDF files. Figure 10-1 shows a vector image.

Raster Images

Raster images are often called bitmapped images. A bitmap is just one type of raster image. A raster image is composed of a bunch of pixels. Raster images include screen captures, scanned images, and digital photos. You can scale raster images smaller without affecting their quality, but increasing the size of the image past its current resolution will result in a pixelated image Figure 10-1 shows a raster image.

Screen Resolution and DPI

Resolution is measured in dpi, which stands for dots per inch. The dpi of an image on-screen or in print is made up of a certain number of dots per inch. Screen resolution is the number of pixels (dots) that make up the image on your computer screen.

The discussion in this chapter assumes that 300 dpi is the desired resolution for printed images. (The desired dpi of your project may vary, since the dpi of images needs to be twice (2x) the line screen (lpi) used in the printing process.) The discussion also assumes that on-screen images are 72 dpi on the Mac and 96 dpi on the PC—the defaults for these platforms.

Stretching and Shrinking (Scaling) Graphics

Stretching and shrinking graphics should be avoided. Even stretching or shrinking a graphic proportionally may still adversely affect the image. This is especially true with screen captures. Notice in Figure 10-2 the moire pattern on the Image Capture button. This pattern is not displayed in the actual software window; it appears only in the screen capture.

Figure 10-1 The top image is a raster (bitmap) image. Notice the pixelation when the graphic is enlarged. The bottom image is a vector image. This image can be enlarged without the loss of resolution.

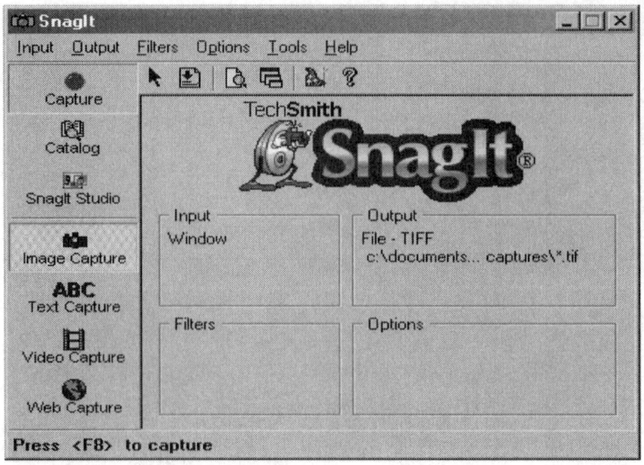

Figure 10-2 Hand-shrunk screen capture.

Resampling/Downsampling an Image

Resampling (or, more specifically, downsampling) an image means changing its resolution. Resampling can be done by hand in a program such as Photoshop, or automatically in Acrobat Distiller. Often, it is the resampling setting in Acrobat Distiller that makes images look "fuzzy" in PDF files.

If you import a screen capture into a document at a higher resolution (150 or 300 dpi) and then distill the file with the resampling in Acrobat Distiller set to 72 dpi, the screen captures will be illegible in the PDF (see Figure 10-3).

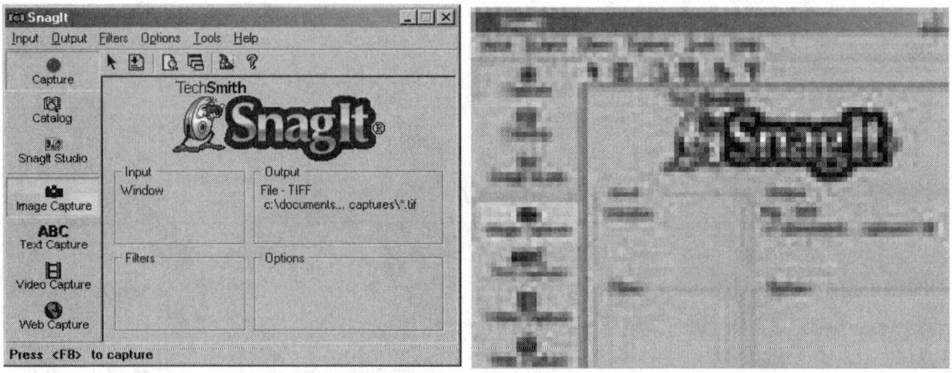

Figure 10-3 The left image has a resolution of 300 dpi. The right image is the same image downsampled to 72 dpi.

Screen Capture Utilities

A screen capture utility should be the 3rd most important tool when on a documentation project that requires screen captures—the first being a outstanding documentation specialist/technical writer and the second being a capable tool for composing the documents (i.e., FrameMaker). A screen capture utility pays for itself very quickly—usually by the time the first project is completed.

Use a Screen Capture Utility

Always use a screen capture utility to capture your screens. The tools have become more robust over the years and are *very* affordable. Many of the good screen capture utilities allow you to capture screens in multiple formats and multiple files, annotate on the capture itself, and capture the portion of the screen that you need (e.g., a particular button, menu, window, etc.).

Refusing to purchase and use a screen capture utility is being penny-wise and pound foolish. Even though you can capture screens natively in Windows or the Mac, the file format is not optimal for printing purposes. If you factor in the amount of time it takes to capture a screen to the clipboard or hard drive, put the image in an application such as Photoshop, and save the image as a TIF or EPS file, it doesn't take long before the $40 cost of a good screen capture utility is easily covered just in time savings alone.

Recommended Screen Capture Utilities

Table lists four recommended screen-capture utilities. Although there are other capable screen-capture utilities on the market, these four utilities offer the greatest number of features at a very reasonable price.

Table 10-1 Recommended Screen Capture Utilities

Recommended Windows Utilities	Recommended Mac Utilities
FullShot 7 *http://www.fullshot.com/* $50, $80, & $150	Snapz Pro 2 (Mac OS 8-9.x) *http://www.AmbrosiaSW.com/* $40
SnagIt! 6.3 *http://www.snagit.com/* $40[a]	Snapz Pro X (Mac OS X) *http://www.AmbrosiaSW.com/* $40

a. SnagIt! has released a new FrameMaker with a plug-in. This plug-in installs a "SnagIt" menu option on FrameMaker's main menu and permits the user to directly setup the capture parameters, select the type of capture, and executre a capture—without ever having to leave the FrameMaker interface!

Graphic Formats To Use in Screen Captures

A question frequently asked by FrameMaker users is what graphic format to use for screen captures. Two recommendations are TIF and EPS. If you use one of these formats, your chance of printing problems decreases dramatically. Many people use file formats that use lossy compression schemes (a compression method that drops information from an image like JPG) or are limited to the number of colors it supports (like GIF's 256-color limit). Because of the low-resolution nature of the screen captures, using file formats other than TIF and EPS can degrade your captures in print and PDF.

TIF

TIFF or TIF (the Tagged Image File Format) is used for raster graphics. A raster graphic is made up of a bunch of pixels and is resolution dependent. This means that if you insert a graphic on a printed page and make it bigger than its resolution allows, you will start to see the pixels (dots) that make up the image. Figure 10-4 shows an example of this phenomenon.

Logo at print resolution of 300 dpi.

Logo at screen resolution of 72 dpi.

Figure 10-4 Beyond Print logo as a TIF image at different resolutions. Notice that the screen resolution of the bottom logo is not sufficient for printing and that pixelation occurs.

Make sure that when you save your TIF file, you set the image compression to NONE or LZW. (Do not use JPG.) Also, make sure that the file is saved in PC format rather than Macintosh. FrameMaker on the Mac will handle the PC files just fine and display the images. FrameMaker on the PC will display a gray box for the image if the TIF is in Mac format. Each utility or image-editing program's interface for setting these options will differ. Photoshop's "saved as TIF" options look like those shown in Figure 10-5.

EPS

The EPS (Encapsulated PostScript) file format is commonly used for vector graphics—images drawn in a program such as Illustrator, Freehand, or Corel Draw. These graphics are *resolution independent*—the shapes and colors used in

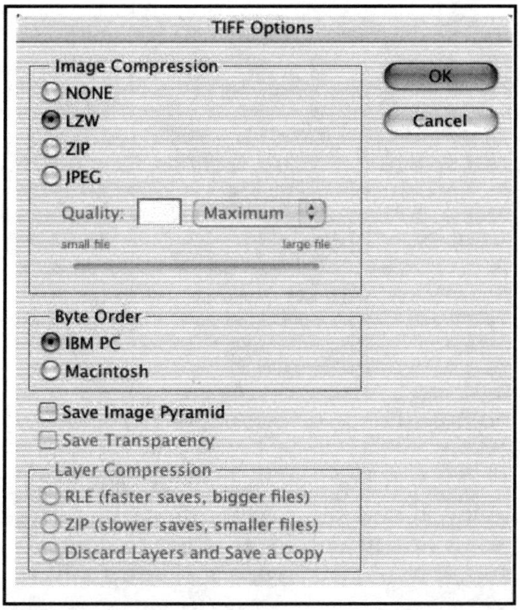

Figure 10-5 Suggested TIF setting in Photoshop.

the images are mathematical definitions, and it doesn't matter if the graphic is the size of a postage stamp or the size of a billboard.

EPS files can also contain raster images—but a raster image saved as an EPS file is still *resolution dependent*. Simply saving a raster image as an EPS file does not convert it to a vector image. *Screen captures are raster images and will be resolution dependent.*

There are only two reasons to save your screen captures as EPS files:

1. You are working in Windows, printing your screen captures in color, and producing the color separations from FrameMaker.
2. You want to enable image interpolation at the file level so that your screen captures will look good online in the PDF file.

If neither of these reasons apply to you, then save your screen captures as LZW-compressed TIF files. Your file sizes will be much smaller and you will save hard drive space.

When saving your screen captures as an EPS file from Photoshop, make sure you set the preview to TIFF (8 bits/pixel), the encoding to Binary, and that Image Interpolation is enabled (see Figure 10-6). The 8-bit preview will give you the highest quality preview for placing the image in FrameMaker, although the image will still look grainy. Encoding as binary will make the file size smaller. Enabling image interpolation will help the screen capture look good at all zoom levels in a PDF file.

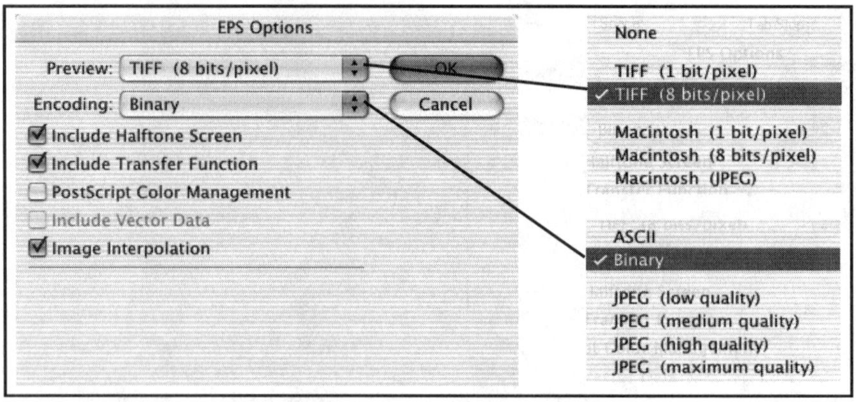

Figure 10-6 Suggested EPS settings in Photoshop.

When you import an EPS file into FrameMaker, FrameMaker places the EPS file into the document and uses its preview image on-screen. Most EPS files will not look really good on-screen in your document—you're looking at a 1- or 8-bit preview—but they will print perfectly to any PostScript-compatible laser printer and distill perfectly to PDF.

Conserving Disk Space with Small File Sizes

Many individuals choose to save screen captures in formats other than TIF or EPS to save disk space and make their files smaller in size. Many choose GIF or JPG. Neither of these formats is a good choice for screen captures—JPG files use a lossy compression method so data is lost from the screen capture each time it is saved, and the GIF format supports only 256 colors.

You'll achieve good compression results by using the TIF format with LZW compression. Saving a file in EPS format will consume large amounts of disk space. The list in Figure 10-7 shows the file sizes necessary for a screen capture of FrameMaker's Paragraph Designer saved in TIF with no compression), EPS, and TIF with LZW compression. Notice that the LZW-compressed TIF is very small.

xp_blue_no_lzw.tif	Today, 11:41 PM	372 KB
xp_blue.eps	Today, 11:40 PM	584 KB
xp_blue.tif	Today, 11:39 PM	48 KB

Figure 10-7 Differences in file sizes for TIF with no compression, EPS, and TIF with LZW compression.

Another option in many image-editing programs is the ability to save previews with the image. To conserve disk space, disable this option. Figure 10-8 shows Photoshop's dialog box for image previews. In the File Handling area of the main preferences, set the Image Previews to Never Save (). This can save you 100 KB or more per image!

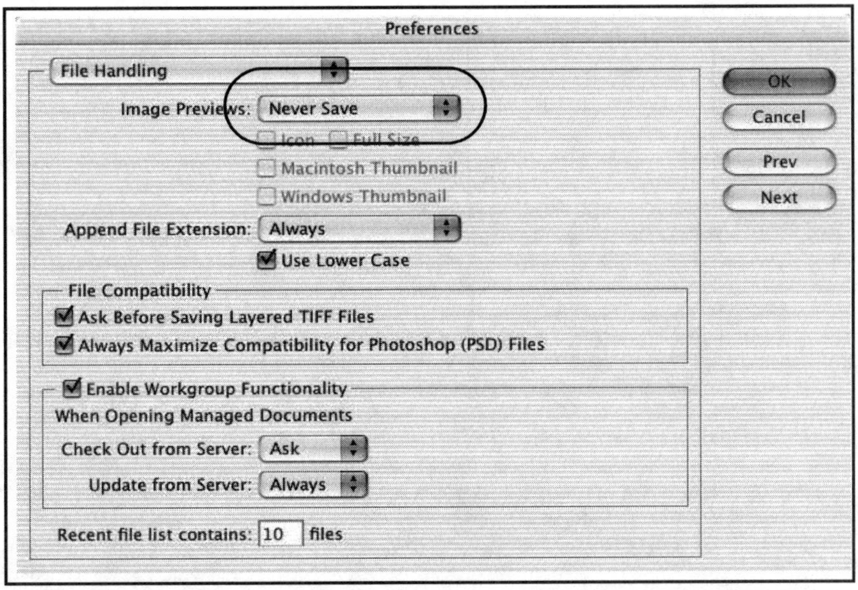

Figure 10-8 Set Photoshop to never save image previews.

Color Themes and Schemes

The color theme can affect the way icons and other parts of your screen appear. The color scheme of your computer can affect the way your screen captures look. The following discussion shows you how to alter the look of your screens and helps you to choose which color theme or scheme will work best.

The most import thing to remember when picking a color scheme is to be consistent through a single document. Don't collect a variety of screen captures from machines that use different settings. Keep your screen color consistent through a document.

Setting a Theme on the Mac

Although the Mac allows you to customize the look of the user interface, the dialog boxes all appear the same, with the exception of the font used. The examples shown here show both the OS9 platinum look and the aqua look in OSX. To set a theme on the Mac, do the following:

1. From the Apple menu, select **Control Panels** > **Appearance** (see Figure 10-9). The Appearance dialog box appears.
2. Click on the **Appearance** tab (see Figure 10-10).
3. Select **Apple Platinum** from the Appearance pop-up.
4. Close the Appearance dialog box.

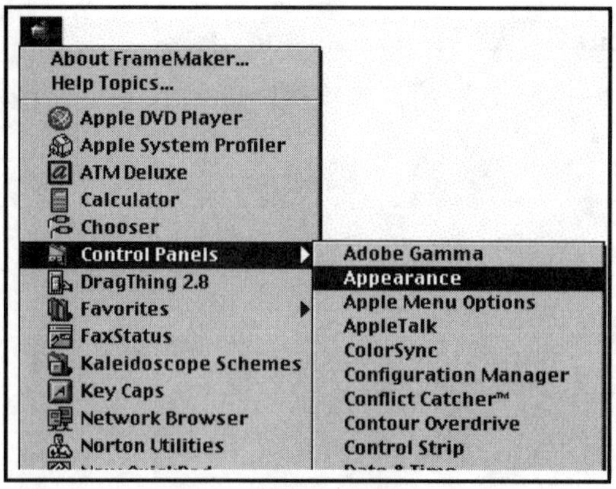

Figure 10-9 Opening the Appearance control panel.

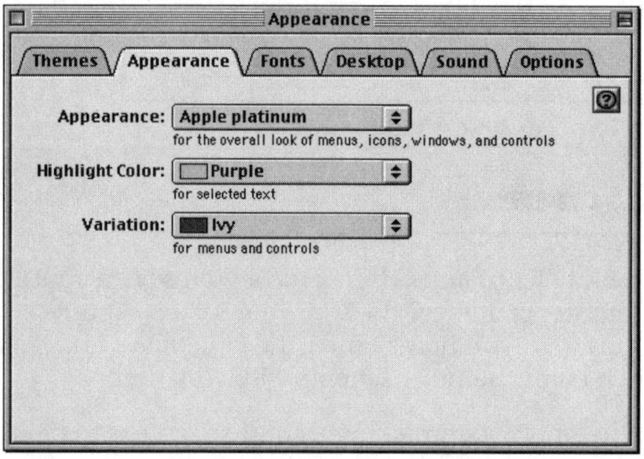

Figure 10-10 Macintosh Appearance dialog box.

Sample Macintosh Color Schemes

The screen captures shown in Figure 10-11 and Figure 10-12 show what a screen will look like in print in OS 9 and OS X.

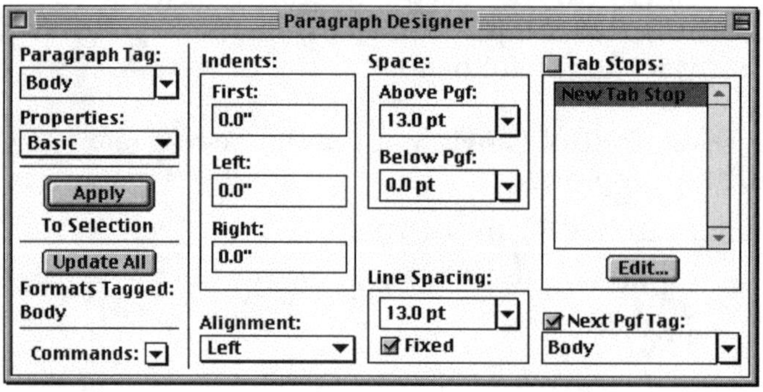

Figure 10-11 Platinum theme.

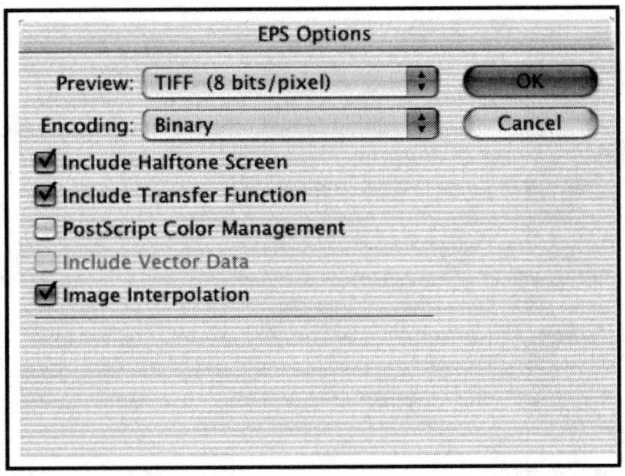

Figure 10-12 Mac OS X screen capture.

Setting the Color Scheme in Windows

Windows allows you to customize the appearance of the user interface. Here are a quick explanation of how to set the color scheme in Windows and examples of screen captures using the different color schemes. To set the color scheme in Windows, do the following:

1. Right-click on a blank portion of the desktop. A menu will appear as shown in Figure 10-14.
2. Select **Properties.** A dialog box will appear as shown in Figure 10-13.
3. Click on the **Appearance** tab.

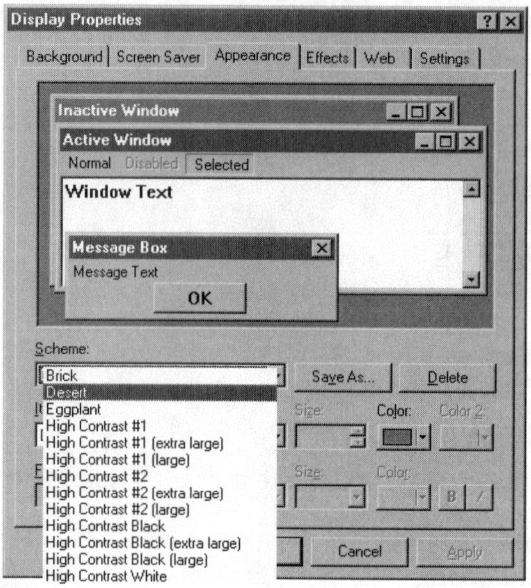

Figure 10-13 Setting the color scheme in Windows.

4. In the Scheme pop-up, select the desired color scheme. Just make sure you use the same setup on each machine grabbing screens so that you have consistent screen-capture colors in your documents.
5. Click **Apply**.
6. Click **OK**.

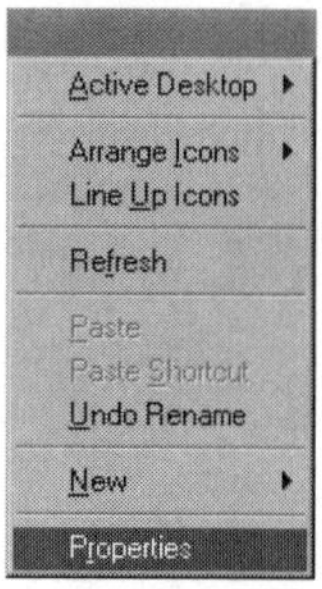

Figure 10-14 Pop-up menu displayed in Windows.

Sample Windows Color Schemes

The screen captures of the Paragraph Designer in FrameMaker, shown in Figure 10-16 and Figure 10-17, show what the screens will look like in print using the various color schemes in Windows. (While you cannot see the colors in the printed version of this book, you can still observe differences.)

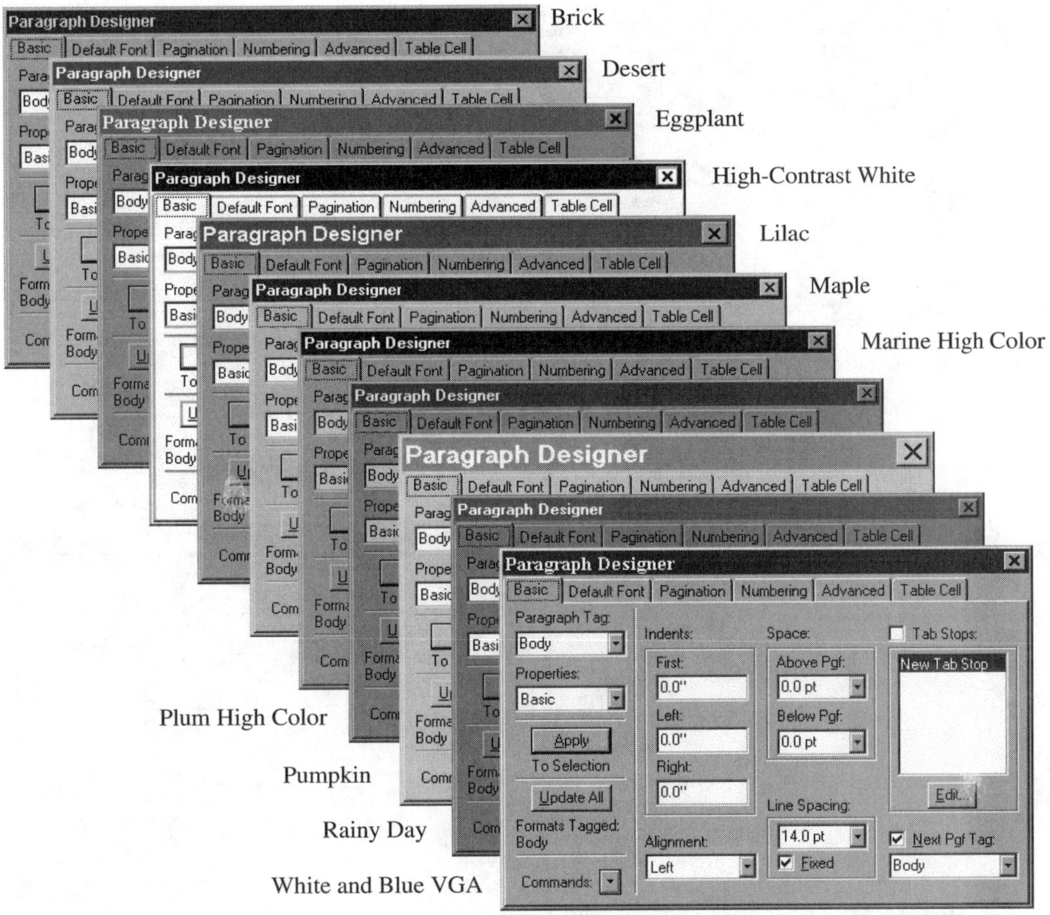

Figure 10-15 Sample Windows color schemes.

Capturing Screens

This section explains the process of using SnagIt! to capture your screens. Each of the recommended utilities differs slightly in configuration, but the same principles apply. The Macintosh screen-capture utilities are much easier to configure and use, but their feature set is half as big as that of their Windows counterparts. Because configuration is more difficult on the PC, this section will go into detail demonstrating what a correctly configured screen capture utility can do for you.

Dos and Don'ts of Screen Captures

When you capture screens, DO the following:

- Capture the images with the greatest number of colors that your video card supports. Having a maximum number of colors and color depth

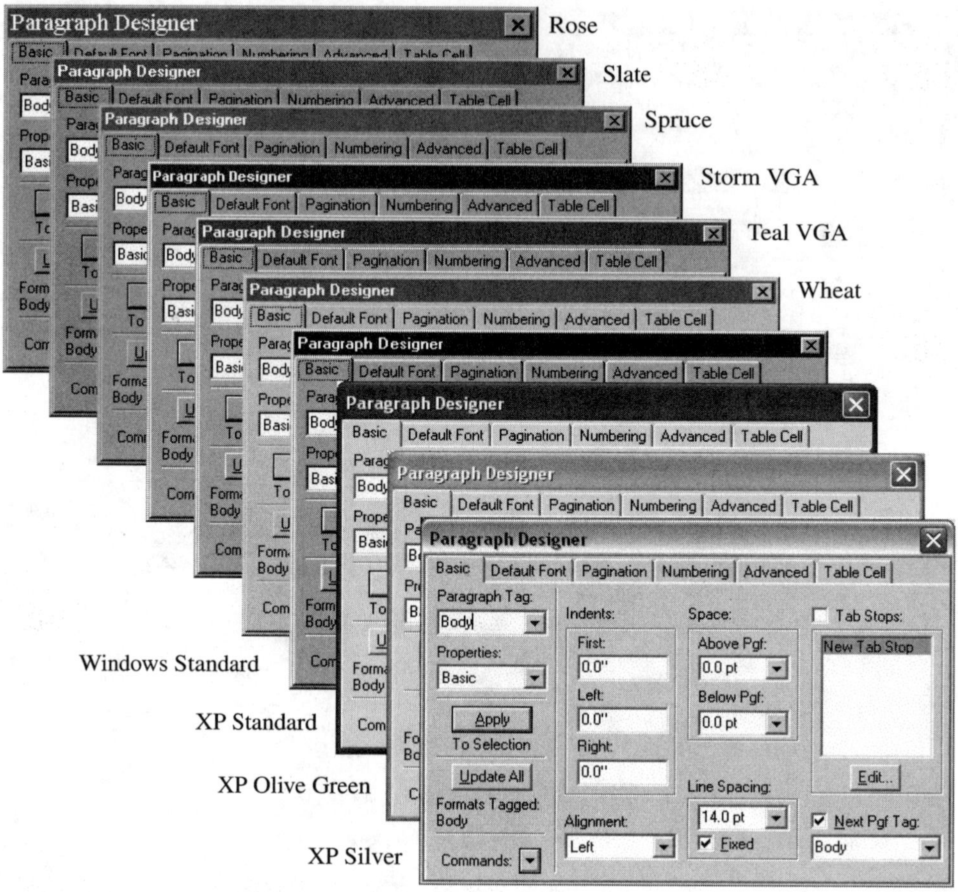

Figure 10-16 More sample Windows color schemes.

allows the capture to be reproduced well under the maximum number of printing conditions

- Capture the images directly to a TIF file on your hard drive, which captures the image directly in the format dictated by the capture utility.

DO NOT do the following:

- Enlarge/shrink/scale your images upon capture. Doing so could add artifacts to the screen or make text on the screen illegible.
- Change the color of your image upon capture (unless you are simply converting them to CMYK). Doing so could reduce the number of colors used in the screen.
- Resize your screen captures by hand. Doing so could add artifacts to the screen or make text on the screen illegible.

- Capture your screen to the clipboard and paste it into your documents. Doing so would embed the screen in your document. Always import your screen captures by reference from a file on the hard drive.

Preparing to Capture Screens

The following is the configuration process used to set up SnagIt! to successfully capture great menus and windows—the two most commonly captured screen elements.

Setting a Hotkey

1. Open SnagIt!.
2. Select **Options** > **Program Preferences** (see Figure 10-18).

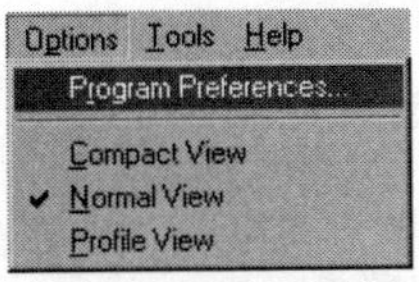

Figure 10-17 Options menu.

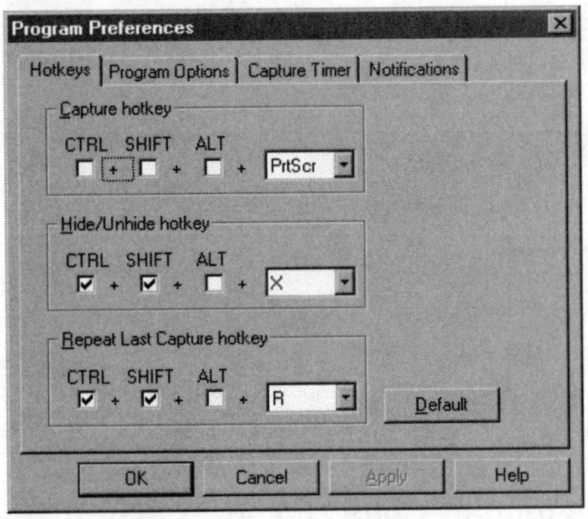

Figure 10-18 Capture hotkeys.

3. Click on the **Hotkeys** tab (see Figure 10-19).
4. Uncheck the **CTRL**, **SHIFT**, and **ALT** checkboxes.
5. Select **PrtScr** from the pop-up.
6. Click **Apply**.
7. Click **OK**.

Setting Input Properties

1. Select **Input** > **Properties....**
2. Click on the **Menu** tab (see Figure 10-20).
3. Check the "**Include menu bar**" and "**Capture cascaded menu**" options.
4. Click the **Set Background Color...** button. Set the background color to white.
5. Click **OK**.
6. Click **Apply**.
7. Click **OK**.

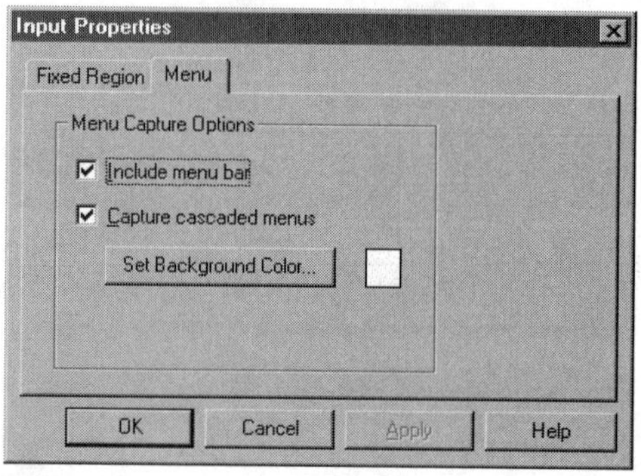

Figure 10-19 Menu capture options.

Setting Output Properties

1. Select **Output** > **Properties....**
2. Click on the **Image File** tab (see Figure 10-20).
3. Select **TIF–Tagged Image File** for the **file format**.
4. Click the **Options...** button.
5. Select **Automatic (optimal color)** from the **Colors** pop-up.
6. Select **LZW RGB** (for online) or **LZW CMYK** (for print) from the **Subfile Type** pop-up.
7. Select **Ask for File Name**.
8. Click on the ... button after the **Output Folder** pop-up.
9. Choose the folder that you would like to save your screen captures in.

Note: *I usually set up a screen capture folder on one of my root drives to initially store the screen captures that I take*

Note: *Pre-OS X Macintosh users can capture screens in TIF format using Snapz Pro. You will have to post-process all of the captures, however, because Snapz Pro adds an alpha channel to the graphic. Because of the alpha channel, the TIF will appear as a gray box if you import it into FrameMaker. Snapz Pro X does not capture TIF files with an alpha channel.*

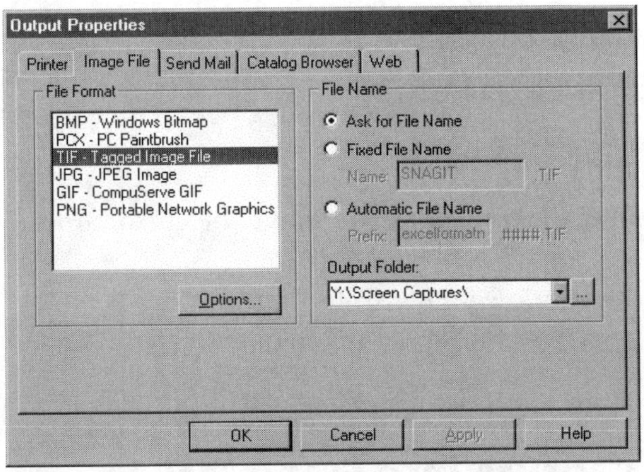

Figure 10-20 Output image format options.

Capturing a Menu

To capture a menu or submenu, do the following:

1. Open SnagIt!.
2. Select **Input** > **Menu** (see Figure 10-21).

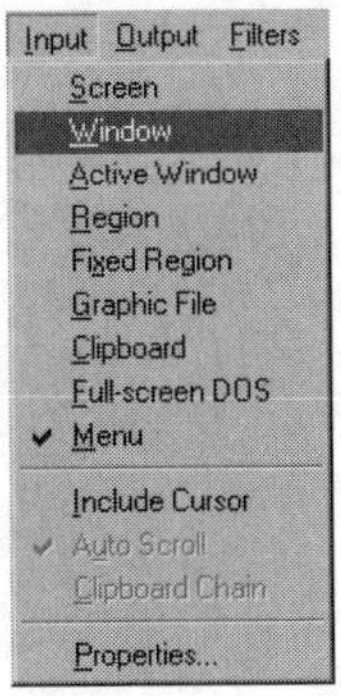

Figure 10-21 Input menu.

3. Minimize SnagIt!
4. Select the menu that you wish to capture.

5. Press the **Print Screen** button.
6. Name your file.
7. Click **Save**.

Capturing a Window

To capture an entire window, do the following:

1. Open SnagIt!.
2. Select **Input** > **Window**.
3. Minimize SnagIt!.
4. Press the **Print Screen** button.

   A red square will surround each window as you move the cursor around the screen.
5. Click on the title bar of the window you wish to capture.
6. Name your file.
7. Click **Save**.

Inserting a Screen Capture into FrameMaker

When you're ready to import a screen capture into your FrameMaker document, do the following:

1. Select **File** > **Import** > **File**.
2. Select the file you wish to import (see Figure 10-23).
3. Make sure **Import by Reference** is selected.

Note: *It is always a good idea to import your images by reference. This keeps the FrameMaker file size to a minimum, makes updating the image easy (just replace the original with the update), and ensures that you have a reusable copy of the image (in case the FrameMaker file is lost or corrupted).*

4. Click **Import**.
5. A dialog box will open, asking how you want FrameMaker to scale the image (see Figure 10-23). If you select only the options given in this dialog box (or if you set the custom dpi in increments of 25), you will not have trouble with poor screen captures when you go to press. Selecting 150 dpi or 300 dpi usually works the best. The smaller the dpi, the larger the image—the larger the dpi, the smaller the image. Keep the dpi to increments of 25. For example, if 150 or 300 doesn't work because the

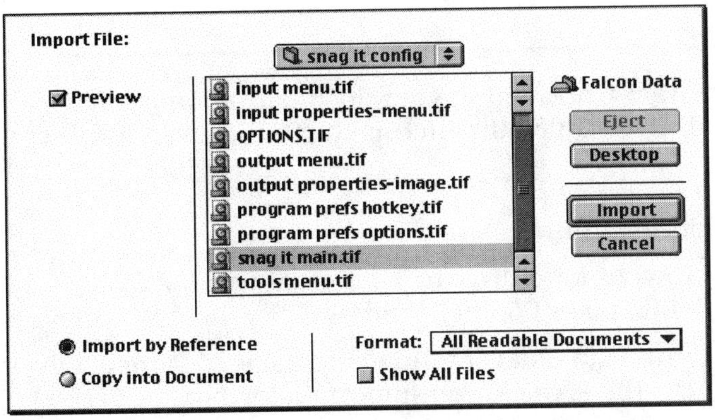

Figure 10-22 FrameMaker's File Import dialog box.

image is too small or too big, add or subtract 25 from the dpi and put that number in the custom dpi setting.

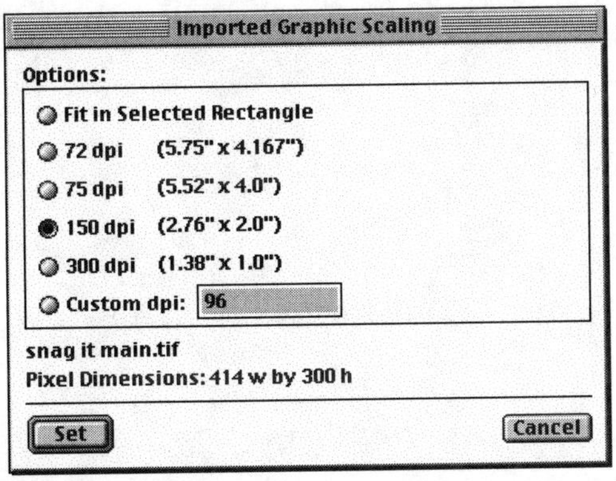

Figure 10-23 FrameMaker's Graphic Scaling dialog box.

6. Click **Set**.

Note: *Do not resize the image by hand once it is imported into FrameMaker.*

Your document now contains a beautiful screen capture.

Note: *Snag-It! has created a plug-in for FrameMaker. This plug-in has three options that are immediately accessible from the main menu in FrameMaker once the plug-in is installed. They are (1) perform a capture, (2) setup a capture, and (3) select input type. If you have multiple captures to create, this tool is worth investigating!*

Summary

Creating screen captures that work well in your documentation is a fairly simple process if you follow the guidelines in this chapter. These guidelines in a snapshot are as follows:

- Use a good screen capture utility.
- Capture the screens to your hard drive in TIF format with LZW compression at 72 dpi (Mac) or 96 dpi (Windows).
- Import by reference into FrameMaker in increments of 25—preferably at 150 or 300 dpi through the FrameMaker Import dialog box.
- Don't downsample/resample the images in Acrobat Distiller.

Advanced FrameMaker

11

Designing Automatic, Self-Positioning, Bleeding Thumb Tabs

Bradley Anderson

Thumb tabs may be designed to move down the page as you move from chapter-to-chapter within your book. This tutorial explains this concept and how to make it work in FrameMaker.

Also applicable to FrameMaker versions

Introduction

The following method of creating self-positioning bleeding thumb tabs is a comprehensive solution for accomplishing this task. Although the process is a bit involved, you can successfully create a set of bleeding thumb tabs for your templates in less than an hour by following these instructions. This method of creating automatic bleeding thumb tabs allows you the flexibility of having a single sequence of tabs running from top to bottom of the document, or restarting the tabs every certain number of chapters (see Figure 11-1). This method also allows you to use the tabs within a single FrameMaker file or within separate FrameMaker files in a book.

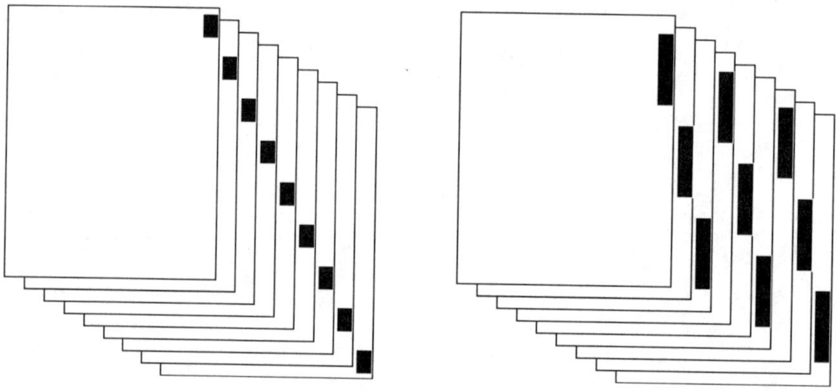

Figure 11-1 Distribute tabs automatically or restart as necessary.

These are some of the benefits of using this method to create tabs:

- Uses the same master page layout for all of your documents
- Positions the thumb tabs automatically on both the left and right pages of a document
- Automatically positions the tabs vertically within a document or between documents
- Restarts the tabs at the top of the page when needed
- Changes the spacing of the tabs automatically
- Uses a solid color or graphic as the tab—tabs can be any size and can be set to bleed off the page
- Places text on the thumb tabs automatically
- Automatically centers the text—both horizontally and vertically—on the thumb tab

A Quick Overview

For this tutorial you will use a document size of 8.5" x 11". The thumb tabs will be set up on the right page of a double-sided document on the outside edge. The tabs will start at the top of the page and move to the bottom of the page.

Creating the Thumb Tabs

Creating Paragraph Tags

We will create two paragraph tags to use for the bleeding thumb tabs. One paragraph tag will be used to position the thumb tab, and the other will be used to format the actual text on the tab. The instructions list only the important settings to use for these paragraph tags.

Creating the "Positioning" Paragraph Tag

1. Create a new paragraph tag and name it **zTabPlaceholder**. (Place the "z" in front of the paragraph tag so that it is listed at the bottom of the Paragraph Catalog window).
2. Make the font 4 points in size.
3. Make the font color white.
4. Make sure to make the line spacing fixed by checking the option in the basic paragraph properties.

Note: *Make sure that you make the line spacing fixed. The check box under the line spacing options of the basic paragraph tag properties should be checked. If this option is unchecked, you will be unable to position the anchored frame needed for the thumb tab.*

Creating the Tab Text Paragraph Tag

1. Create a new paragraph tag and name it **zTabText**.
2. Make the font size 7 points.
3. Make the font color white.
4. Set the cell's vertical alignment to *middle*.

Creating a Text Flow

You need to create a text flow on the master page to hold the thumb tab and to allow the tab to move "up and down" the outside edge of the document:

1. Go to your right master page.
2. Draw a short, wide text box across the middle of the page (see Figure 11-2).

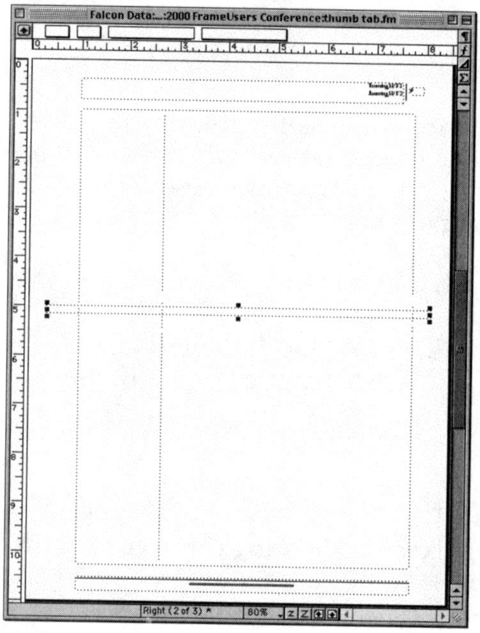

Figure 11-2 Text box on the right master page.

3. Right-click on the text box and choose **Object Properties....**
4. Set the width of the text box to **11**" and the height to **0.13**" (see Figure 11-3).

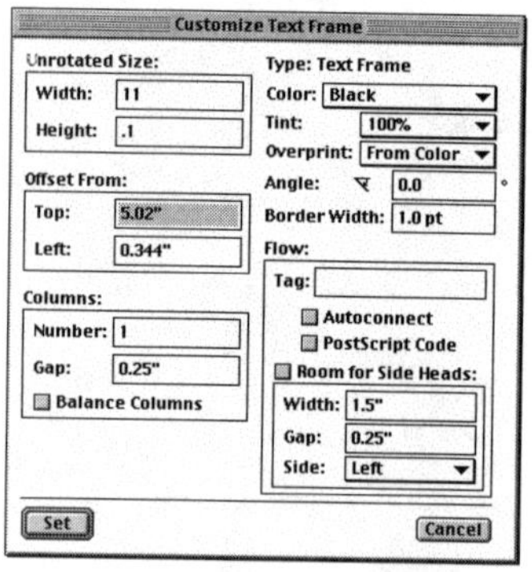

Figure 11-3 Height and width settings.

5. Click **Set**.
6. Make sure the paragraph in the new text flow is set to **zTabPlaceholder**.

Creating an Anchored Frame

Now create an anchored frame that will become the bleeding thumb tab. The anchored frame could contain a graphic or be filled with a solid color. The width of the anchored frame will be the width of the tab. The height of the anchored frame will be the "depth" of the tab plus 0.25" for the bleed.

1. Place your cursor in the text frame that you created.
2. Select **Special** > **Anchored Frame** (see Figure 11-4).
3. Set **Anchoring Position** to **"At Insertion Point."**
4. Set **Distance above Baseline** to **0.0**.
5. Set **Width** to **1.5**.
6. Set **Height** to **0.75**.
7. Click **New Frame**.

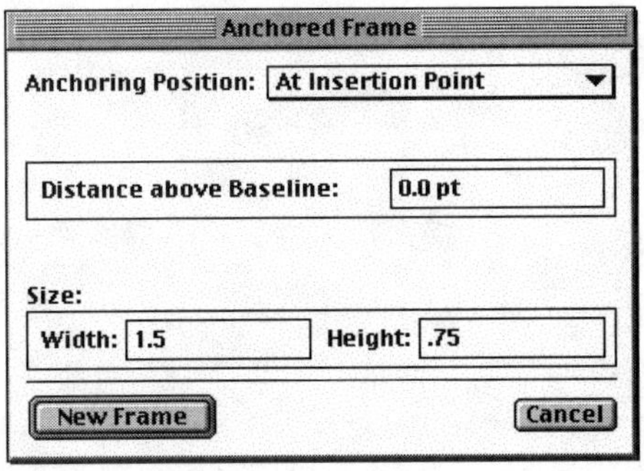

Figure 11-4 Defining an anchored frame.

Coloring the Anchored Frame

1. Select the anchored frame you just created.
2. Open the tool palette in FrameMaker (see Figure 11-5).
3. Set the fill to **solid**.
4. Set the color to **black**.

Drawing a Text Box in the Anchored Frame

Now you will draw a text box in the anchored frame you've just created. The text box will be used to hold a table and text for the thumb tabs.

1. Draw a text box in the anchored frame.
2. Select **Graphics** > **Object Properties...** (see Figure 11-6).
3. Set **Width** to **1.5**.
4. Set **Height** to **0.5**.
5. Set **Top** to **0.25**.
6. Set **Left** to **0.0**.

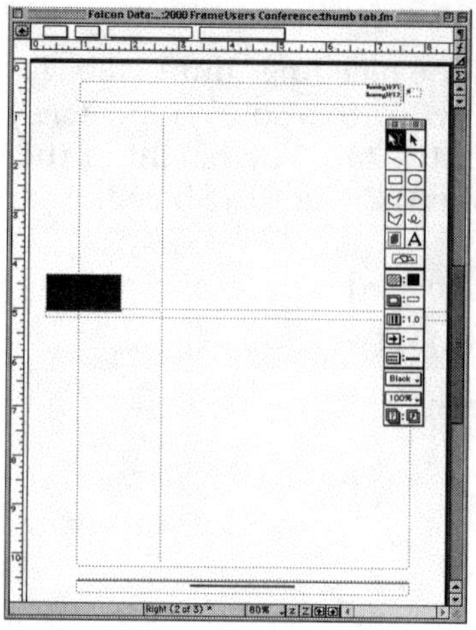

Figure 11-5 Coloring the anchored frame.

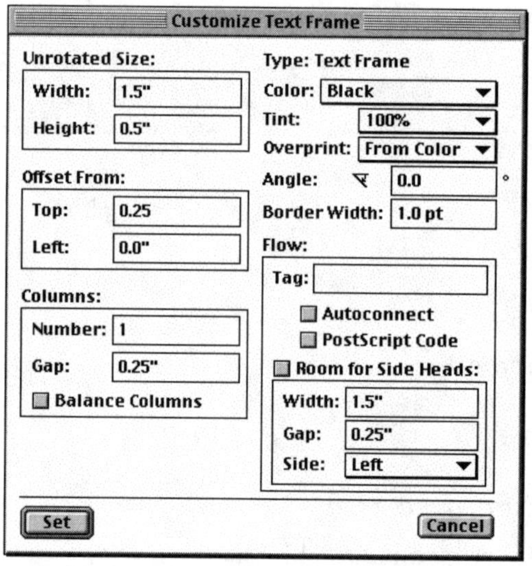

Figure 11-6 Setting the text frame.

Inserting a Table

You will now use the following instructions to insert a single-celled table in the text box you just created. This will allow you to have the text automatically center vertically on the thumb tab.

1. Tag the paragraph in the new text box with your placeholder or the anchor paragraph tag that you use in your regular document to anchor tables. This paragraph must allow the table to have no space above it.
2. Select **Table > Insert Table....**
3. Select any table format.

4. Set **Columns** to **1.**
5. Set **Body Rows** to **1.**
6. Set **Heading Rows** to **0.**
7. Set **Footing Rows** to **0.**
8. Click **Insert.**

Formatting the Table

1. Place your cursor in the new table.
2. Select **Table > Table Designer** (see Figure 11-7).
3. Set Space **Above** to **-2.0.**
4. Set Space **Below** to **0.0.**
5. Set the Top and Bottom margins to **0.0.**
6. Set **Alignment** to "**Center.**"
7. Set **Title Position** to "**No Title.**"
8. Remove all cell ruling (see Figure 11-8).
9. Remove all cell shading.
10. Create a new format and call it **ThumbTab.**

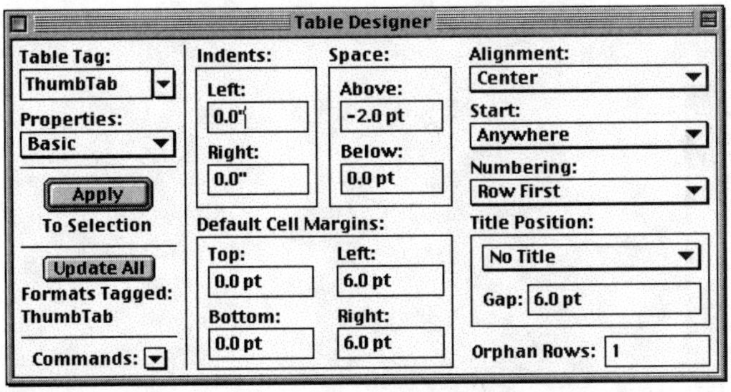

Figure 11-7 Table Designer basic properties.

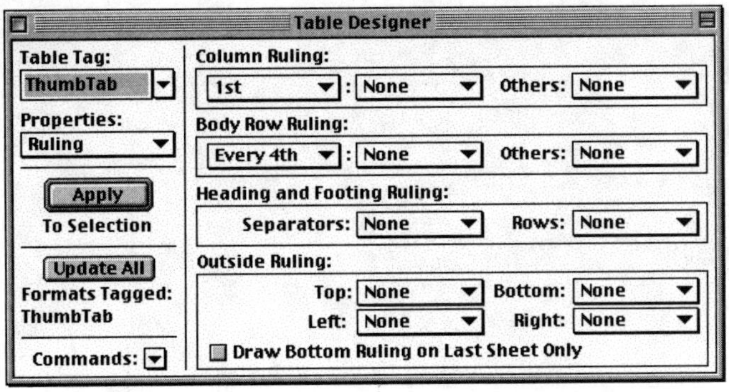

Figure 11-8 Table Designer ruling properties.

Resizing Table Cells and Setting Row Format

1. With your cursor still in the table cell, select **Table > Resize Columns....**
2. Select **By Scaling to Widths Totalling: 1.5** (see Figure 11-9).
3. Click **Resize.**
4. Select **Table > Row Format....**
5. Set the **Minimum** and **Maximum Height Limits** to **0.5** (see Figure 11-10).
6. Set the paragraph tag in the table cell to **zTabText.**
7. Your thumb tab should now look like Figure 11-11.

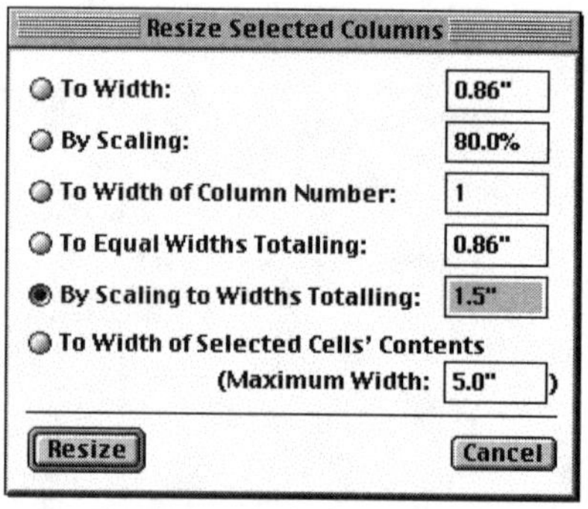

Figure 11-9 Resizing columns.

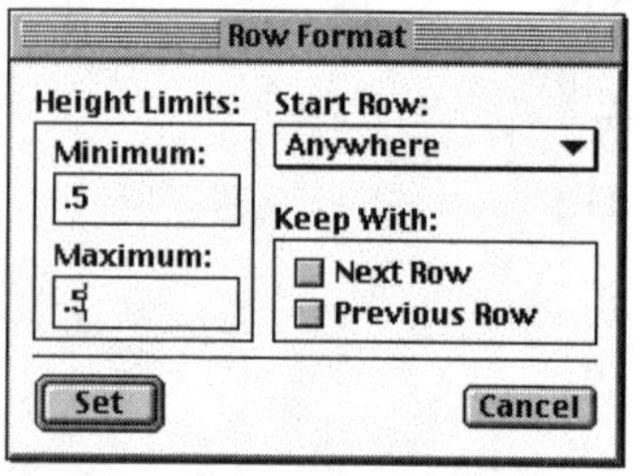

Figure 11-10 Row format.

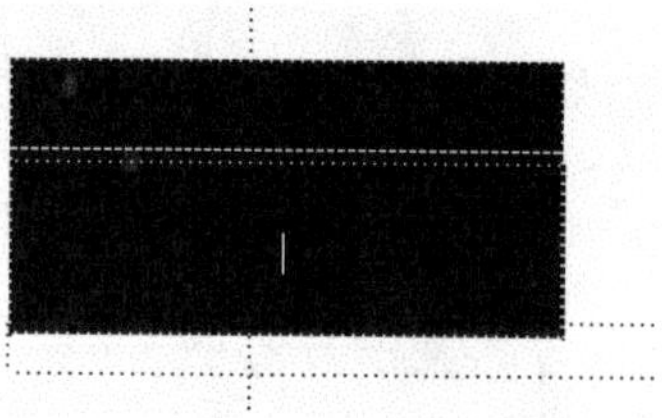

Figure 11-11 The thumb tab.

Inserting Running H/F Variables

The most difficult part of setting up the thumb tabs is now complete. The only remaining tasks are to insert two running header/footer variables to place the desired text on the tab and position the tab down the margin of the page:

1. Place your cursor in the table on the thumb tab.
2. Select **Special** > **Variable....**
3. Select the **Running H/F** variable that you want to use. In this particular case, the **Running H/F 3** variable is set up to pick up the text of the title paragraph and the text of the author paragraph. You'll need to set the Running H/F variable to your particular paragraph(s).
4. Click **Insert** (see Figure 11-12).
5. Place your cursor in the long narrow text box that you first created.
6. Make sure that your cursor is at the very left-hand side of the text box and in front of the anchor for the anchored frame.
7. Select **Special** > **Variable....**
8. Select the **Running H/F** variable that you want to use. In this particular case, the **Running H/F 4** variable needs to be set to <$marker2>, which picks up the text in a special marker that is inserted on the body page. You can choose to use a Running H/F variable other than Running H/F 4, but it has to be set to <$marker2>. This is what will be used to move the tabs.
9. Click **Insert** (see Figure 11-13).
10. Your thumb tab should now look something like Figure 11-14.

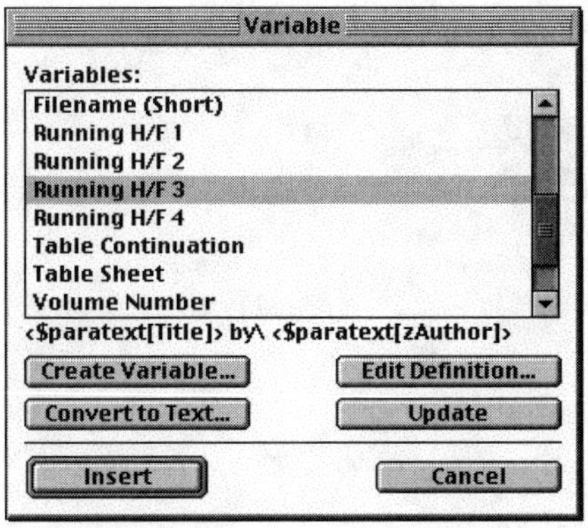

Figure 11-12 Inserting the Running H/F 3 variable.

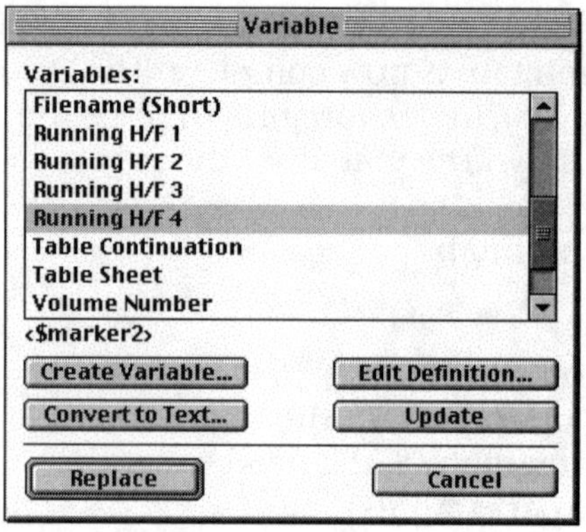

Figure 11-13 Inserting the Running H/F 4 variable.

Figure 11-14 The thumb tab with the variable.

Positioning the Long Text Frame

You must now rotate and position the long text frame to get the tab into the correct position.

Rotating the Text Frame

1. Select the long text frame.
2. Select **Graphics > Rotate....**
3. Rotate the text frame **90° clockwise**.
4. Click **Rotate**.

Aligning the Text Frame

1. Select the text frame.
2. Select **Graphics > Align...** (see Figure 11-15).
3. Select **T/B Centers and Right Sides**.

Finalizing the Text Frame's Position

1. Select the text frame.
2. Select **Graphics > Object Properties**.

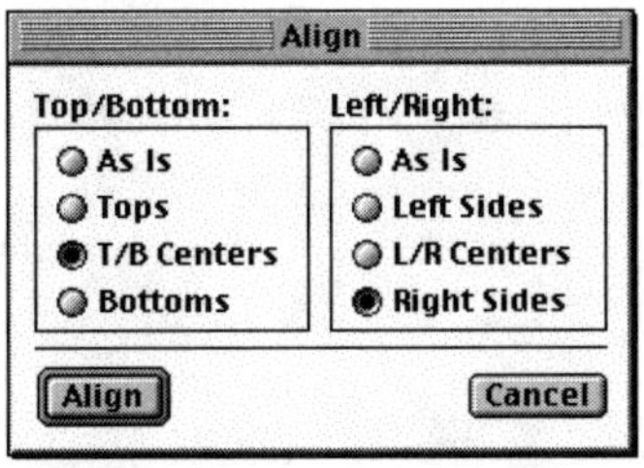

Figure 11-15 Aligning the text frame.

3. **Reduce** the **Offset From Left** by **0.5**. In this particular example, you would set it to **7.87** (see Figure 11-16).
4. Click **Set**.

The thumb tab and text frame should now be positioned as shown in Figure 11-17.

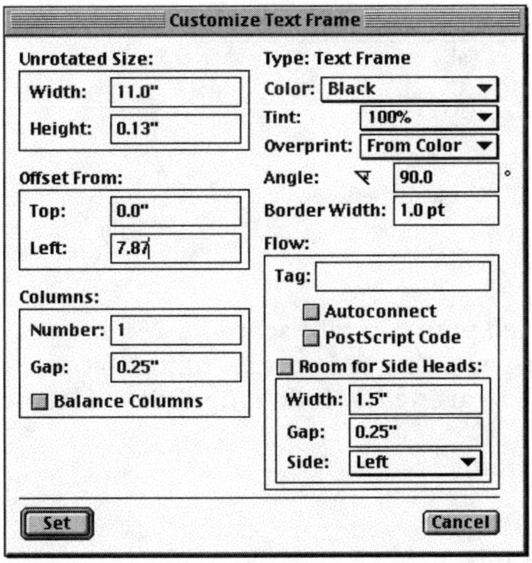

Figure 11-16 Text frame settings.

Setting the Tabs for the Thumb Tabs

You have now successfully created your first automatic bleeding thumb tab. You now need to set tab stops in your zTabPlaceholder paragraph tag to position the tabs and insert the marker to move the tab in the body of the document. You'll need to figure out where you need the tab stops in the paragraph.

Figure 11-18 shows you how to figure out what tab stops are needed.

For discussion purposes, let's say that you have ten tabs that you want running down the page (see Figure 11-19).

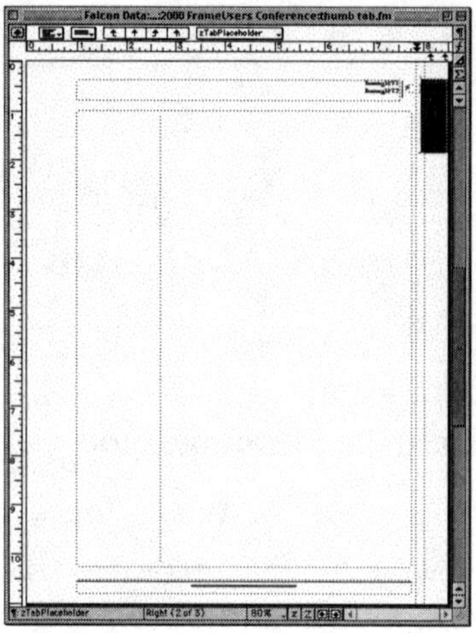

Figure 11-17 Positioned text frame.

$$\frac{\text{Paper Height} - (\text{Top Margin} + \text{Bottom Margin} + \text{Tab Width})}{\text{Number of Tabs}}$$

Figure 11-18 Determining needed tab stops.

$$\frac{11 - (1 + 0.75 + 1.5)}{10 \text{ tabs}} = 0.775 \text{ inches between tabs}$$

Figure 11-19 Positioning for ten tabs.

Figure 11-20 indicates that you will need your ten tabs spaced 0.775 inches apart to feather them evenly down the page. You can now set up the tab stops in your zTabPlaceholder paragraph tag by using the following series of steps:

1. Place your cursor in the long text frame.
2. Open the Paragraph Designer.
3. Under the tab stops, click the **Edit** button.
4. Click the **Delete All** button.
5. Click the **Edit** button again.
6. Set **New Position** to **1** (see Figure 11-20).
7. Set **Repeat Every to 0.775** and make sure the checkbox is checked.
8. Click **Continue**.
9. Click the **Update All** button in the Paragraph Designer (see Figure 11-21).

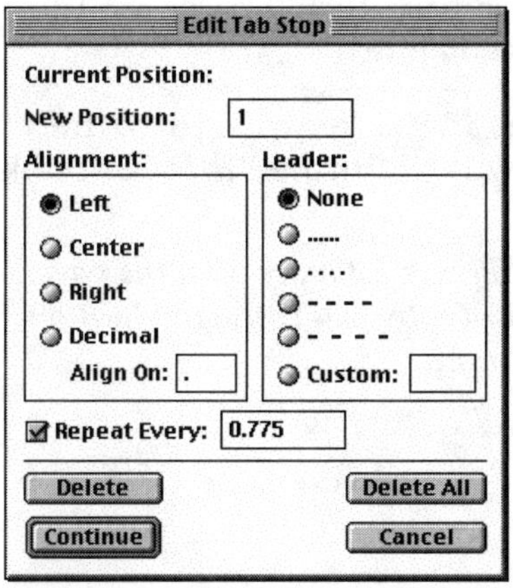

Figure 11-20 Adjusting the tab stop.

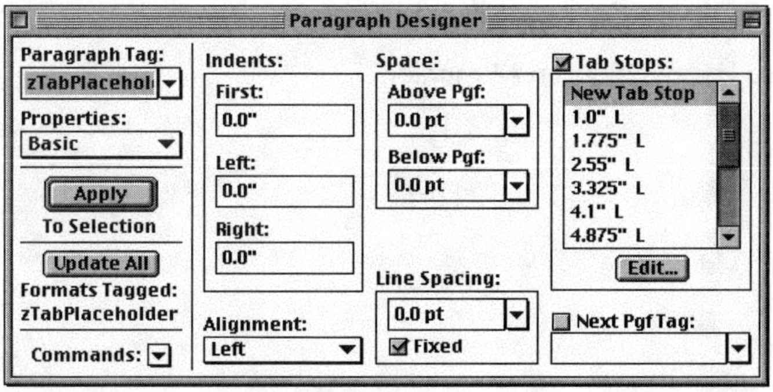

Figure 11-21 Updating the paragraph format.

Making the Tabs Move

You will now insert the "code" on the body pages to make the tabs move:

1. Return to the body pages.
2. Make sure you are on the first page of the document.
3. Place your cursor at the beginning of the title paragraph tag.
4. Select **Special** > **Marker....**
5. Select **Header/Footer $2** from the **Marker Type** pop-up.
6. Insert the number of "tabs" needed for this particular chapter. For example, if this were chapter 5, we would insert five "tabs." The code for a tab in FrameMaker is "\t" (see Figure 11-22).
7. Click **New Marker.**

The thumb tab should now move into position automatically based on the tabs inserted in the Header/Footer $2 marker (see Figure 11-23).

All you have to do now is insert a Header/Footer $2 marker with the correct number of tabs for each chapter, and your tabs will be finished for your book.

Note: *Make sure you only have a single Header/Footer $2 marker on the page. A second marker with a different number of tabs will cause the tabs on subsequent pages to be at a different location.*

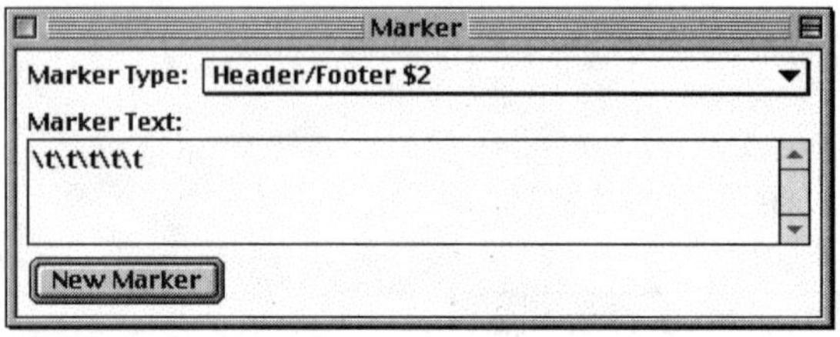

Figure 11-22 Inserting a Header/Footer $2 marker.

Figure 11-23 Positioned thumb tab.

Other Tricks/Examples

You may make several modifications to the thumb tabs you created. Here are a few quick ideas:

- Create another thumb tab on the left-hand page. By rotating the anchored frame and positioning the text frame so inserting a tab moves the thumb tab down the page, you will get thumb tabs that move on both the left and right pages synchronously. (Don't put a tab on the left page if you're printing on a DocuTech printer/copier. The tab does not print well.)

- Instead of using a system running header variable that uses text from a paragraph tag, insert a variable that picks up text from the other H/F marker. This enables you to place text on the tab related to the content of the chapter, but does not rely on the text in the document itself.
- Instead of filling the anchored frame with a color for the tab, try placing a graphic in the anchored frame for the tab.

FrameScript Automation of Tabs

If you have FrameScript, a utility that allows you to write scripts for FrameMaker (available at *http://www.FrameScript.com*), you can further automate the bleeding thumb tabs. You will need a licensed copy of FrameScript to be able to use this script.

This FrameScript script allows you to automate the insertion of the "\t" in the markers used to move the thumb tabs. You must follow the directions for setting up the bleeding thumb tabs as described in this chapter. Here's how it works:

1. Simply place a blank **Header/Footer $2** marker in each chapter that will affect the thumb tab placement. You must place this marker in every file in which you want the tab to move.
2. From the book file, run this FrameScript script. This script will search through every file in the book and insert the proper number of "\t"s in each Header/Footer $2 marker that it finds. All other files will be skipped. This may be seen in the script below.

```
//-----------------------------------------------------
// FrameScript to automate Brad's Bleeding Thumb
// Tabs. Script written by Frank Elmore.
// Copyright 2000, Beyond Print Incorporated
// All rights reserved. Script may be copied
// in its entirety and used as long as it is
// copied along with this copyright notice.
//-----------------------------------------------------

//-----------------------------------------------------
// Modify the 2 values below to set the current
// tab count (usually 0) and the tab threshold.
// The tab threshold is the maximum number of tabs
// that you want down the side of the page. If you
// have more than this number of tabs, the script
// will start the tabs over at the top of the
// document once this number is reached.
//-----------------------------------------------------

SET currTabCount = 0;
SET TabThreshold = 12;
```

```
//------------------------------------------------------
// Do not modify anything below this line
//------------------------------------------------------

IF fslVersionMajor < 1
   MSGBOX 'Requires FrameScript Version 1 or greater';
   LEAVESUB;
ENDIF

IF ActiveBook = 0
   MSGBOX 'No Active Book'
   LEAVESUB;
ENDIF

SET BookObj = ActiveBook;

LOOP ForEach(BookComponent) In(BookObj)
  LoopVar(bookcomp)
   RUN isDocOpenAlready filename(bookcomp.Name)
  returns DocObj(dobj);
   IF dobj = 0
      SET errorcode = 0;
      OPEN Document File(bookcomp.Name)
  FileIsOldVersion FontNotFoundInDoc NewVar(dobj);
      IF errorcode not 0
         MSGBOX 'Error opening component-
  '+bookcomp.Name+'  Msg-'+ErrorMsg;
      ENDIF
   ENDIF
   IF dobj not = 0
      RUN SetMarkerInDoc DocObject (dobj);
   ENDIF
ENDLOOP

MSGBOX 'Done';

SUB SetMarkerInDoc DocObject

   Get Object Type(MarkerType) Name('Header/Footer
  $2') NewVar(mrkTypeVar);

   LOOP ForEach(Marker) In(DocObject) LoopVar(mrkVar)
      IF mrkVar.MarkerTypeId = mrkTypeVar
         SET mCount = mCount + 1;
         SET foundType = mrkVar;
      ENDIF
   ENDLOOP
```

```
    IF mCount > 1
       SET mrkVar = DocObject.FirstMarkerInDoc;
       LOOP While(mrkVar)
          SET nextMrkVar = mrkVar.NextMarkerInDoc;
         IF mrkVar.MarkerTypeId = mrkTypeVar and mrkVar
   not= foundType
             DELETE Object(mrkVar);
          ENDIF
          SET mrkVar = nextMrkVar;
       ENDLOOP
       SET mCount = 1;
    ENDIF

    IF mCount = 1
       SET tabText = '\t';
       SET currTabCount = currTabCount + 1;
       LOOP LoopVar(idx) InitVal(1) Incr(1)
  While(idx<=currTabCount)
//        SET tabText = tabText + CHARTAB;
          SET tabText = tabText + '\t';
       ENDIF
       SET foundType.MarkerText = tabText;
    ENDIF

ENDSUB
//------------------------------------------------------
//   This subroutine checks the list of open documents
  to see if the
//   specified document is already open.
//
//   Format:
//        Run IsDocAlreadyOpen Filename(testfilename)
  returns DocObj(retdocvar)
//
//    If it is open, it returns the document object
//    and returns zero if it is not open.
//------------------------------------------------------
SUB isDocOpenAlready using filename DocObj

   GET String FromString (filename) Uppercase
  NewVar(tfilename);  // Upper case the string
   SET DocObj = 0;
   LOOP ForEach(Doc) In(Session) LoopVar(testdocobj)
     GET String FromString (testdocobj.Name) Uppercase
  NewVar(tname); // Upper case the string
       IF tname = tfilename
          SET DocObj = testdocobj;
```

```
            LEAVELOOP;
        ENDIF
    ENDLOOP
ENDSUB
//--------------------------------------------------------
```

Summary

Thumb tab positioning can be tedious if handled manually. The positioning may be automated using the techniques described in this chapter. With careful planning and setup, positioning can become easy to manage.

Part IV

PDF, HTML, XML, and Database Publishing

12

Using WebWorks Publisher Standard Edition 7.0

Bernard Aschwanden

This chapter provides an overview of the Quadralay WebWorks Publisher Standard Edition product as well as differences between the Standard and Professional editions.

Applicable to FrameMaker versions 6.0 and 7.0/7.1

In this chapter, you will investigate publishing options when you use Quadralay WebWorks Publisher Standard Edition 7.0[1] to create HTML, eBooks, and XML content from a single source. Unless otherwise specified, the term WebWorks Publisher SE will mean the Standard Edition that is shipped with Adobe FrameMaker 7 (rather than any previous version), or WebWorks Publisher Professional Edition 7.0, or WebWorks Publisher for FrameMaker 2003, which are sold as separate applications.

WebWorks Publisher SE is a tool that allows you to publish FrameMaker files in a wide variety of electronic formats. This is accomplished by mapping FrameMaker content based on a variety of styles and then converting the content to output that is specific to the template used. Supported content includes cross–references, graphics, tables, paragraph tags, character tags, and more.

Overview

Adobe FrameMaker ships with WebWorks Publisher SE. WebWorks Publisher SE is a tool used in the conversion of well-structured FrameMaker documents (written either in a structured template or based on specific guidelines) to a variety of online formats.

For this conversion to be successful, the original content must be well structured. The term "well structured" refers to the way the content is written and formatted, not the use of FrameMaker as structured content or the use of a specific template. Well-structured documents are the following:

- Documents that, for lack of a better phrase, are created "correctly"
- Documents with content that is formatted using tags (paragraphs, characters, and tables) rather than manual overrides
- Documents that do not use hard returns to add spacing between text
- Documents with numbering that is driven by the correct use of the Paragraph Designer, not by the manual insertion of hard-coded numbering
- Documents that make use of cross-references and anchored frames
- Documents that have a flow to them that can be completely reformatted in seconds
- Documents that follow templates with the same dedication that some people follow sports, gameshows, daily news, or the ongoing "lives" of characters in a television show

---

1. Earlier versions of FrameMaker may include other versions with different product names (such as Standard Edition, Lite and so on).

When a document is created correctly, the content is based on tags, and the use of the tags drives the appearance of the content. Content is created based on its purpose, not the whim of the author. Essentially, a file that is well developed and thought out uses a robust template that is designed—by a writer who understands and utilizes the strengths (and limitations) of the software—with the needs of the publishing community in mind.

Most of the content that you see when WebWorks Publisher SE converts FrameMaker files is formatted based on specific templates, specified mappings, and referenced support files. A variety of templates are included with WebWorks Publisher SE, and new ones can always be added to your template library. Mapping is project-specific and determines the conversion of content such as tables, images, and text. Support files usually have extensions such as *.asp and can be edited using applications such as Notepad, DreamWeaver, FrontPage, and GoLive.

Note: *The extension *.asp is used to associate the file with specific applications (for easier opening by users) and is not indicative of an active server page. The WebWorks use of the *.asp is completely different from the traditional interpretation of this extension in most other environments.*

Hopefully, the documents we have just described are the types of files you create. If so, this chapter teaches you how to best use WebWorks Publisher SE to convert your documents to a variety of online output formats.

Technical Overview of WebWorks Publisher SE

WebWorks Publisher SE works by converting FrameMaker files to temporary MIF (Maker Interchange Format) documents. Once this is done, the MIF file is parsed by WebWorks Publisher SE, and information found in the file is extracted, manipulated, and written as output. This output is based on the template used by WebWorks Publisher SE.

Note: *The MIF creation happens in the background during certain WebWorks Publisher SE operations and requires no additional action by the user.*

The documents used by FrameMaker and WebWorks Publisher SE share the same source, but WebWorks Publisher SE creates its own temporary MIF file in the process of converting FrameMaker files into electronic documents. The user creates content in FrameMaker, and the document is accessed by FrameMaker when it needs to be opened. There is an ongoing relationship between the FrameMaker document and the software used to create the document, as illustrated in Figure 12-1.

Once WebWorks Publisher SE accesses FrameMaker to open the document, the temporary MIF file that is created is stored in a temporary folder used by WebWorks Publisher SE.

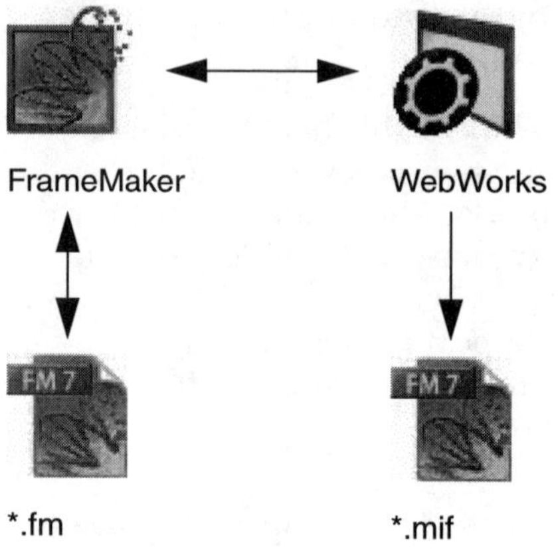

Figure 12-1 FrameMaker and WebWorks Publisher SE workflow.

Once WebWorks Publisher SE has created the MIF file, the content in the MIF can be parsed. WebWorks Publisher SE scans the MIF document and compares the date and time of the MIF to that of the FrameMaker document. If the MIF is newer than the FrameMaker source document, the MIF document is not recreated. If the MIF document is older than the FrameMaker file, however, the MIF document is recreated to ensure that the most current version of the file is used.

Depending on instructions in the WebWorks Publisher SE template, output is generated based on the MIF document. This content may include XML, HTML, CSS, XSL, GIF, JPG, or other documents, depending on the WebWorks Publisher SE template in use, as shown in Figure 12-2.

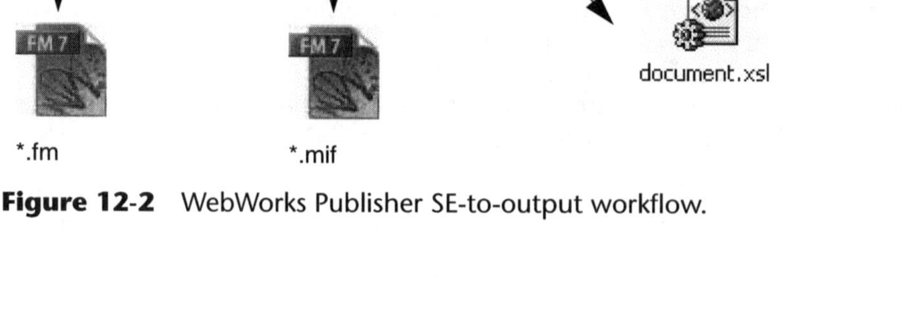

Figure 12-2 WebWorks Publisher SE-to-output workflow.

Types of Output

WebWorks Publisher SE supports six different templates for converting content from your FrameMaker source files. These templates have been redeveloped for use with WebWorks Publisher SE, or are completely new. The templates, which are detailed in this section, are generally as follows:

- Basic HTML that formats content without the use of a cascading stylesheet (CSS)
- Dynamic HTML that formats content with the use of a CSS
- Microsoft Reader eBook format
- Palm Reader eBook formats
- Extensible markup language (XML) content with support for CSS
- XML content with support for extensible stylesheet language (XSL) formatting

Portable HTML

The Portable HTML Standard Edition template allows you to create basic HTML content that can be viewed in most browsers. Content is compliant with the HTML version 3.2 specification. Therefore, the output can be viewed in most major browsers (including Internet Explorer 3.0 and Netscape Navigator 2.0).

Dynamic HTML

The Dynamic HTML Standard Edition template allows you to create basic HTML content that can be viewed in most browsers. Formatting instructions are included in a CSS file. Content is compliant with the HTML version 4.0 specification. Therefore, the output can be viewed in most major browsers (including Internet Explorer 4.0 and later and Netscape Navigator 4.0 and later).

eBook for the Microsoft Reader

The eBook for the Microsoft Reader template allows you to create content that can be viewed using the Microsoft Reader. (This document has the .lit extension associated with it.) Formatting instructions are included in a CSS file.

eBook for the Palm Reader

The eBook for the Palm Reader template allows you to create content that can be viewed using the Palm Reader with the Palm OS or a Pocket PC device. (This document has the .pdb extension associated with it.) Formatting instructions are included in the file *preface.txt*.

XML Using CSS

The XML+CSS Standard Edition template allows you to create XML content that can be viewed in browsers supporting XML and CSS. Formatting instructions are included in a CSS file. Displaying content using a CSS is not ideal, but it is useful if your audience does not use a browser that fully supports the XSL standard.

XML Using XSL

The XML+XSL Standard Edition template allows you to create XML content that can be viewed in browsers supporting XML and XSL. Formatting instructions are included in an XSL file. Content created is more clearly defined as content and is independent of the visual display medium. Therefore it is easier to re-purpose the same content for delivery through different devices (for example, a browser or a wireless device).

XSL-based content gives you greater control over the content and the method in which it is displayed. It consists of three parts:

- XSL Transformations (XSLT)—a language for taking XML documents and transforming them. This allows you to display structured information in a variety of ways by filtering or even reordering information.
- XML Path Language (XPath)—allows you to use XSLT to access or reference elements within an XML document. XPath also provides a basic approach towards the manipulation of strings, numbers, and booleans.
- XSL Formatting Objects—used to specify formatting instructions. It provides a way to produce print or display output from XML content. It can be considered to be similar to a stylesheet or a document template into which content is placed for delivery in a variety of formats—print (paper), online (a browser), or even a combination of both (PDF).

Working Directly from FrameMaker (Save As)

You can save FrameMaker documents as HTML or XML by using the dialog box that appears when a file is first saved, or by selecting **File > Save As** and then choosing HTML or XML from the drop-down menu in the Save Document dialog box. Depending on how the file is saved, you will wind up with HTML or XML with a range of qualities and settings.

Documents created with Structured FrameMaker, using a structured template, can be saved as HTML, as XML, or as XML using a specific application. Saving files using an application allows you to convert each document to XML based on the read/write rules stored with that application.

Documents created in either the Structure Framemaker interface without a structured template or using the FrameMaker unstructured product interface can also be converted to HTML or XML using the Save Document dialog box. Setup of the conversion is driven by the HTML or XML Mapping Table in the reference pages. This type of conversion, which is done by manually opening each FrameMaker document and selecting to save it as an HTML or XML document, can become very cumbersome and time-consuming. It also requires the use of the reference pages to manipulate content that is to be converted to HTML or XML.

An alternative to this conversion method is to install and use WebWorks Publisher SE.

WebWorks Publisher SE Interface

The WebWorks Publisher SE Interface shown in Figure 12-3 is based on a set of FrameMaker files. These documents contain text that has been formatted using the Paragraph or Character catalogs, tables, markers, cross-references, and more. The files are set up to generate output based on mappings in WebWorks Publisher SE. Some FrameMaker files generate multiple pages, some generate images, and some generate both. Regardless, the generated materials are dynamically built based on the FrameMaker source materials, and they require little if any manual intervention. Files shown in the project interface of Figure 12-3 include the following, which are numbered for easy reference:

❶ FrameMaker documents listed based on the order of output. Therefore, the TOC is the first page a user will see, the Introduction the next, and so on.

❷ Pages generated by File *editing.fm* during conversion. These pages are named based on defaults used by WebWorks Publisher SE.

❸ Images generated by File *editing.fm* during conversion. These images are named based on defaults used by WebWorks Publisher SE.

❹ Support files used by WebWorks Publisher SE.

❺ Images used by WebWorks Publisher SE.

Launching and Setting Up WebWorks Publisher SE

Once WebWorks Publisher SE has been installed on your computer, you can launch it in a variety of ways. One standard method is to simply double-click any existing project that is on your system. If your system is configured to recognize the project as a WebWorks Publisher SE file, the software is launched and your project is opened. You can also launch WebWorks Publisher SE as a traditional application in much the same way you launch FrameMaker. Finally, FrameMaker has a **WebWorks Publisher Standard**

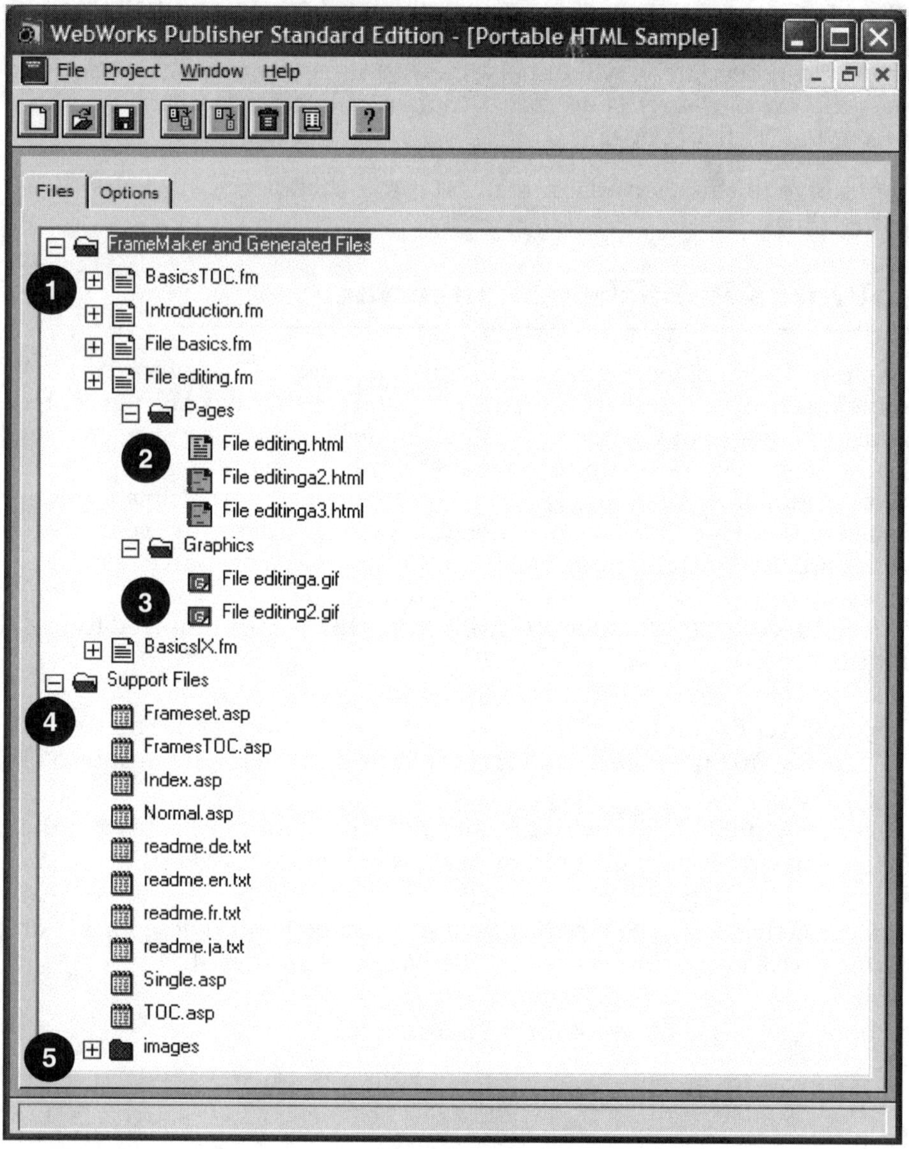

Figure 12-3 WebWorks Publisher SE components.

Edition option in the **File** menu that allows you to launch WebWorks Publisher SE directly from within your FrameMaker session.

Launching for the First Time

When WebWorks Publisher SE is first launched, it also launches an HTML site that connects to the *www.webworks.com* site to register. While registration is optional, you may want to do it because registration gives you access to the WebWorks FAQ, Knowledge Base, and other tools and support services from Quadralay.

WebWorks Publisher SE is launched behind the scenes, and the Project Launcher window appears by default, although you can configure this setting in the Preferences Dialog window (see Figure 12-4). The Project Launcher is the single location from which you can quickly open a recently used file (whose name is stored in the bottom portion of the dialog box) or create a new project by choosing a template (located in the upper portion of the dialog box). Clicking **Cancel** displays the WebWorks Publisher SE interface.

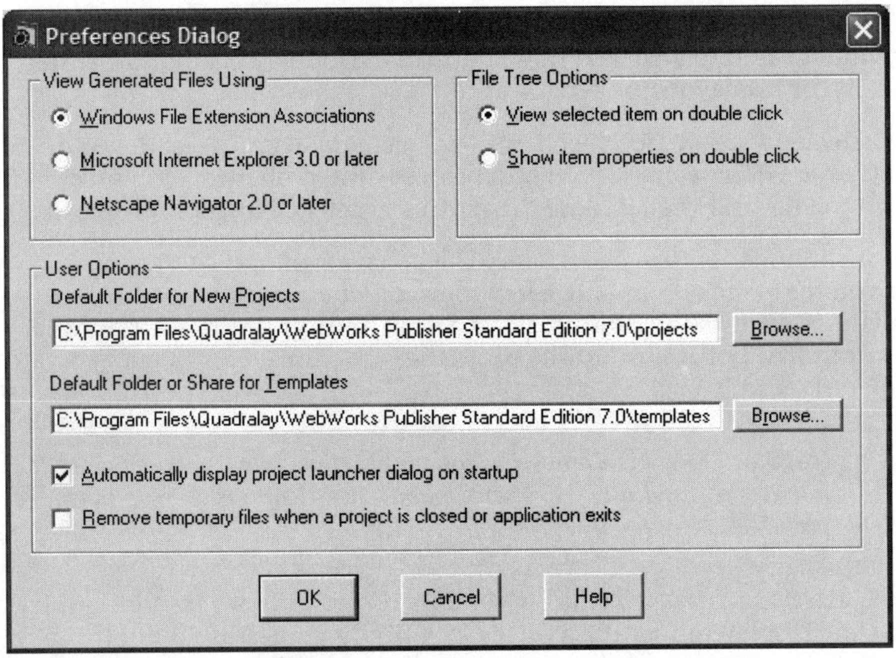

Figure 12-4 Preferences dialog box.

Setting Preferences

Preferences apply to the entire WebWorks Publisher SE environment and only need to be set once. There are times, however, when you may need to modify the preferences based on the specific projects on which you are working.

To display the Preferences Dialog window, select **File > Preferences.** (As with FrameMaker itself, preferences apply to the entire application, from the point of accepting changes onward). Once the Preferences Dialog window appears, you may select the various options and apply them to the application. The options are described as follows.

View Generated Files Using. The Preferences Dialog window allows you to specify the preferred method for viewing content created by WebWorks Publisher SE. I generally suggest using the default setting (Windows File Extension Associations is the default shown in Figure 12-4), as this uses the same application that is set as your default tool for viewing online content. Because the majority of the content you create is likely to be viewed using either Internet Explorer or Netscape Navigator, however, those two options are also available.

Selecting either Internet Explorer or Netscape Navigator forces WebWorks Publisher SE to associate all files that are opened with a specific browser. The browser must be installed on your computer in order for it to be used. Therefore, regardless of your selection, you should make sure that you have the appropriate browser or that your default browser is used.

File Tree Options. The File Tree Options preference allows you to determine how double-clicked files are treated. Double-clicking can either open a file or display its properties.

"View selected item on double click" is the default. This forces files to open when they are double-clicked. In order to view the properties, you must right-click on the file and then choose **Properties** or select **Project > Properties**.

If you wish, however, you can modify the behavior of files so they open only when you right-click them and select View, or when you choose **Project > View File**. If you wish to do this, select **Show item properties on double click**. From that point onward file properties are displayed when a generated document is double-clicked.

Note: *If set to "Show item properties on double click," the support files will not display anything when you double-click them, as they do not have properties associated with them.*

Because most operating systems are set up to open a file when it is double-clicked and display properties only by specifically requesting them (from a menu in most cases), you should choose to use the "View selected item on double click" default setting.

User Options. User Options allows you to set the default folders for specific files, decide how temporary files are handled, and decide if the Project Launcher should appear.

The Default Folder for New Projects field allows you to designate where all new projects are stored by default. You can overwrite this default on a file-by-file basis to store a project in any location you prefer. The default is to store projects in the same location as the application itself. Depending on how your FrameMaker files are set up, you may want to configure this location to be on a server, in a local folder, or on a different hard drive.

The Default Folder or Share for Templates field allows you to designate where all templates used by WebWorks Publisher SE are stored. The default is to store templates in the same location as the application itself. This location can be modified as required. In addition, you can browse for a template when creating a new project, therefore this location is the ideal path in which the majority of the templates you use on a regular basis are stored.

If selected, the "Automatically display project launcher dialog on startup" option displays the Project Launcher each time WebWorks Publisher SE is started.

Note: *You can also display the Project Launcher at any time by selecting **File > New**.*

WebWorks Publisher SE creates a set of temporary documents for each FrameMaker file that is being converted to some form of output. These files are stored in a folder and can be removed when a project is closed or when WebWorks Publisher SE is closed. Temporary files need to exist in order for a project to be updated, but they require hard drive space. Therefore, a trade-off exists between storing temporary files and quickly opening or updating projects, versus deleting temporary files between iterations and saving file space. Even if you decide to keep temporary files as a part of your project, it is recommended that you delete them once a project is completed. To remove temporary files automatically, set the Preference to "Remove temporary files when a project is closed or application exits." The temporary files can always be re-created later if required.

Creating New Projects

The true power of WebWorks Publisher SE is in the *creation* of projects. This section addresses how to develop a new project in WebWorks Publisher SE and may require that you have files in FrameMaker that you can develop into a project. Make sure you have content set up correctly, as discussed earlier in this chapter and in the next section.

Things to Consider Before Creating a Project

Before creating a project, you should do the following in FrameMaker:

- Set up conditional content correctly.

  Conditional content should be shown or hidden depending on the type of online content to be created. If you have conditions that are showing, the content appears in the output generated by WebWorks Publisher SE. If the conditions are hidden, the content does not appear.

- Review any unresolved cross-references.

  Since WebWorks Publisher SE converts content to online formats, you must update cross-references so they do not get converted as incorrect links.

- Review graphics.

  All images in anchored frames are converted by WebWorks Publisher SE. It is therefore important that graphics required in the online format are in anchored frames. You also need to make sure that all images imported by reference can be located by FrameMaker.

- Save all open files.

  WebWorks Publisher SE uses the most current saved file. Therefore, a file that is open and part of a project may not convert with the most current content unless it is saved first.

- Make sure that you have a TOC and an index if you are creating help or multiple pages of output.

  WebWorks Publisher SE uses TOCs and indexes as the first and last documents in a project. It is crucial, therefore, that these files exist (and are set up as the first and last document in the WebWorks Publisher SE project), contain content with hypertext links, and are updated and saved. If the files do not exist, make sure that the project is set up with correct information in the *.asp files; otherwise the navigation system will not work as expected.

- Specify that hypertext links are to be generated in any generated materials to be used by WebWorks Publisher SE.

  If you have content such as a TOC or an index in FrameMaker and it is to be used in your project, make sure that you have hypertext links within the file. Failure to do so results in a file that has text content but no links from the content to the specific files. Therefore, the generated materials cannot act as a navigation system in the finished output files.

- Update any generated materials to be used by WebWorks Publisher SE.

  If you are working with content that is part of a book document, update the book file first. This should generally be done at least once after all the previous precautions have been taken. In addition, if there are any errors that result when the book is updated, correct them and update the book again.

Creating a New Project

Once all the content in your FrameMaker files has been set up correctly for use with WebWorks Publisher SE,you need to create a project. The project stores paths to all the files used by WebWorks Publisher SE. It also stores settings that apply to all the files being converted to an online output.

You create new projects are by selecting **File** > **New Project**. This displays the Project Launcher. The Project Launcher displays a list of all templates in the default template directory. You can also select templates by clicking the **Browse** button and finding a specific template in a location other than the default location set in the WebWorks Publisher SE preferences. Instructions from a Readme file appear to further describe a template that is selected. Once you select a template and click **OK**, WebWorks Publisher SE launches a wizard that walks you through the initial setup of the project.

The wizard is made up of the four screens shown in Figure 12-5, which guide

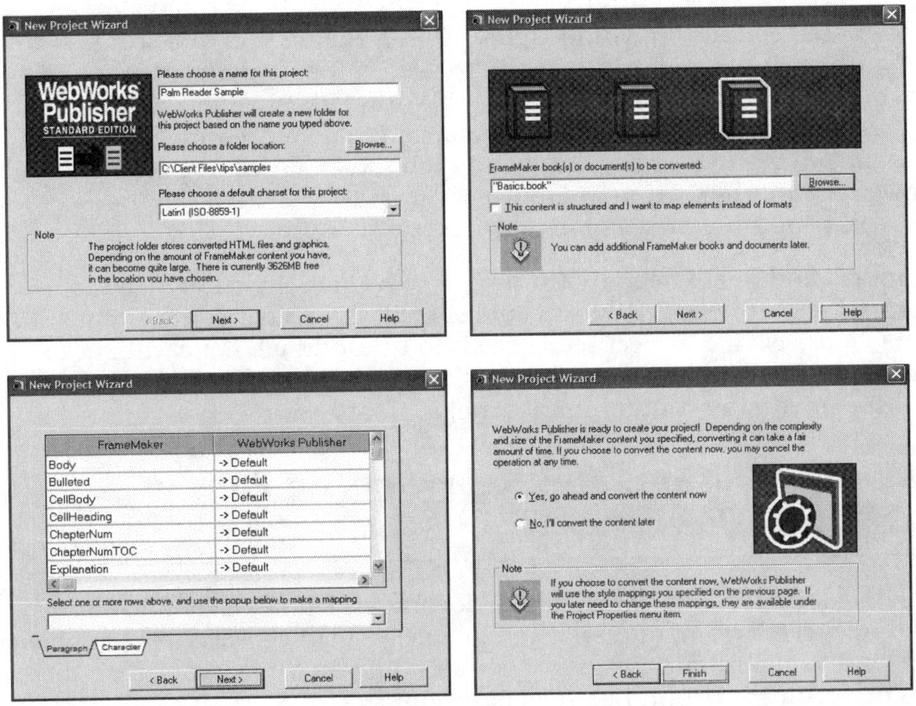

Figure 12-5 New Project Wizard.

you through the setup of the FrameMaker files that will be used by WebWorks Publisher SE. Any settings specified in the wizard may also be overwritten later, if desired.

Through the new project wizard, you continue and enter the name of the project, the folder in which to store the project, and the character set to be used in the first screen. The name of the project should be a descriptive name that can be used to clearly identify it in the future. In some projects, the output file is chosen based on the project name. The folder where the project is to be stored has the same name you assign to the project in this dialog box.

The character set allows you to choose the way that the output is generated. This may be based on the language of the output, output requirements, or the type of device.

The second screen (top right of Figure 12-5) allows you to specify the FrameMaker file or book document to use for the conversion. Selecting a book document automatically selects all the files in that book document. You can also select a single file to convert and then specify whether that file is a structured document or a standard document. Once a document or book is selected and you click **Next**, WebWorks Publisher SE begins to convert all the FrameMaker files into MIF files to scan. During the scan of the files, all the content in FrameMaker is recognized, and the setup begins for the next screen.

The third screen (bottom left of Figure 12-5) is the most complex screen to work with in the wizard. It allows you to specify the mapping of FrameMaker paragraph tags and character tags in WebWorks Publisher SE. Each FrameMaker paragraph tag should be mapped to a WebWorks Publisher tag. There are numerous tags available, and each serves a specific purpose in WebWorks Publisher. For more information on the tags, refer to the WebWorks Publisher SE documentation.

The fourth and final screen (bottom right of Figure 12-5) allows you to specify whether or not WebWorks Publisher SE should convert content at this time. Choose No if a project setup needs to be modified; if any files need to be added, deleted, or rearranged; or if you want to convert content at a later time. To convert the content immediately, choose Yes.

Adding, Deleting, and Rearranging Files in WebWorks Publisher SE

Much like files in a FrameMaker book document, FrameMaker files can be added to, deleted from, or rearranged in a project. Since WebWorks Publisher SE also uses support documents for conversion, you can add or delete these types of documents from the project as well.

FrameMaker files and support files are treated differently, however. If a FrameMaker file is deleted from a project, only the path to the document and its reference in the project are deleted. If a support file is deleted, however, it is removed from the folder on the hard drive as well. Therefore, you must use extreme caution when deleting files from a project.

Selecting the **Project** menu allows you to then select **Add**, **Delete**, or **Rearrange**. Selecting any one of these displays a dialog box related to the selection.

Note: *The files in a project do not need to match the files in the source book document. You can remove documents (such as the cover, or the preface) from the online version of your materials if they are not required, yet still keep them in your FrameMaker book.*

Since files can be rearranged or deleted independently of the content in FrameMaker, WebWorks Publisher SE does not automatically update its files from the book. This also means that new files added to your FrameMaker book are not added to the project. You will need to manually add files to the project if they are added to the book after the WebWorks Publisher SE project is developed and you want their content in your output.

Adding Files

The Add File to Project dialog box (shown in Figure 12-6) allows you to select files to add to the current project. These files can be either support files or FrameMaker documents.

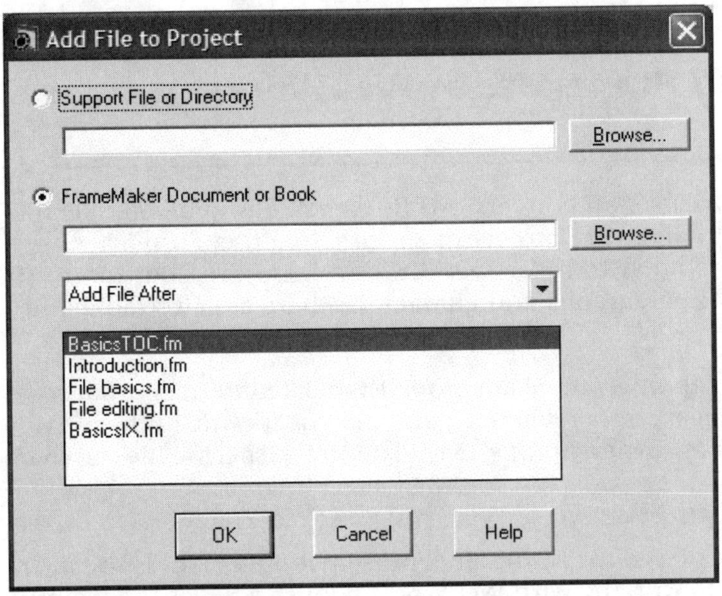

Figure 12-6 Add File to Project dialog box.

Rearranging Files

Much like FrameMaker, WebWorks Publisher SE allows you to rearrange files. Again, much like as in FrameMaker, the same dialog box used to rearrange files allows you to delete files, as shown in Figure 12-7.

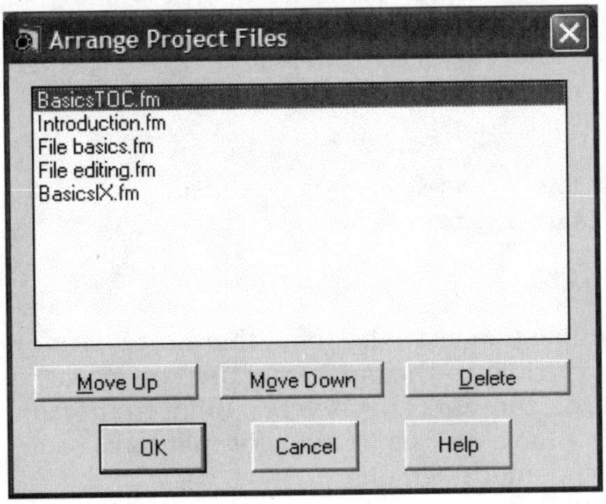

Figure 12-7 Arrange Project Files dialog box.

Deleting Files

When you attempt to delete files, you are prompted to confirm the deletion of the file from the project. If the file is a support document, it is deleted from the support folder used by WebWorks Publisher SE. If the file is a FrameMaker file, it is deleted from the project but not from the folder in which the document resides.

Working with Properties in WebWorks Publisher SE

Properties are the basis of all conversions in WebWorks Publisher SE and are either general to an entire project or specific to a file. Properties include mappings (similar to those seen in the wizard). In addition to the default mappings of paragraphs and characters, there are also table and font mappings.

In addition to the mappings, there are properties related to the output of both HTML and images, cross-references, and macros specific to the conversion of the files. General properties relate to the specific file selected.

Properties for All Files

Properties can be displayed for all files in a project at once. This is the most common approach to working with WebWorks Publisher SE, as the majority of content should follow the same guidelines for converting to online content. This is very similar to the idea of having multiple documents in FrameMaker that use the same layout—the same style of headers, footers, page numbers, table format, document layout, and so on.

To display the properties for an entire set of files in WebWorks Publisher SE, right-click the FrameMaker files and generated files to display a context menu that allows you to choose Properties to display the File Properties dialog box. You can also open this dialog box by first clicking on the FrameMaker files and generated files and then selecting **Project > Properties.** Doing so displays the properties for the current set of FrameMaker documents as shown in Figure 12-8.

Any of the tabs or subtabs in the File Properties dialog box display information related to all the files in the current project.

Properties for a Single File

Properties can be displayed for single files as well. This is the most common approach to creating single-file overrides to the guidelines used by all documents for converting to online content. This is very similar to the idea of having files in FrameMaker that have unique formats, or that have been formatted with overrides to the document defaults.

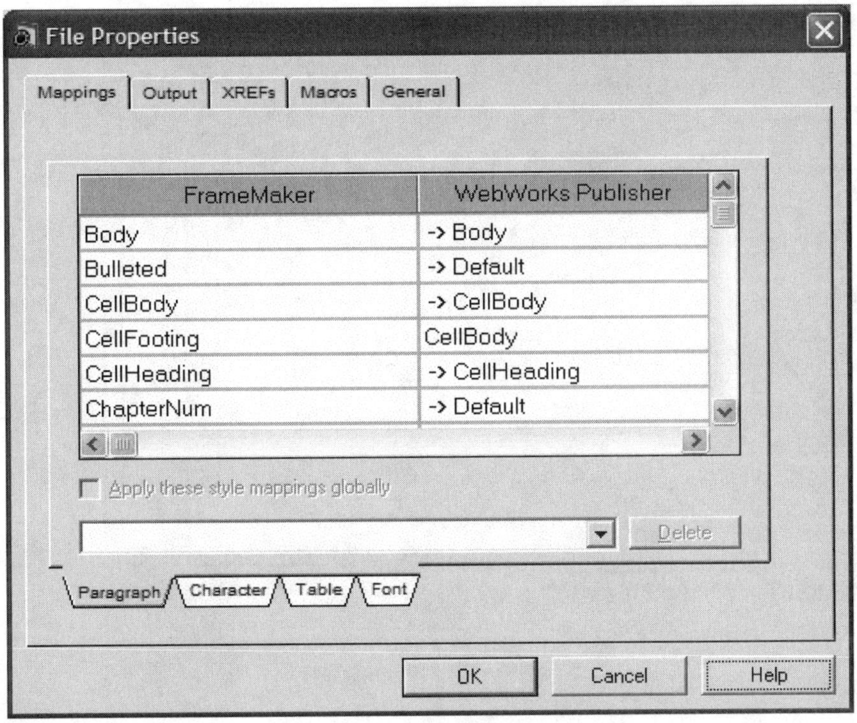

Figure 12-8 File Properties dialog box for all files.

To display the properties of a single file in WebWorks Publisher SE, use the mouse and right-click over the document (not the FrameMaker files and generated files) to display a context menu that allows you to choose Properties. Alternatively, you can access the properties by first clicking on the single file and then selecting **Project > Properties**. Doing so displays the properties for the current FrameMaker document (see Figure 12-9).

Any of the tabs or subtabs in the Properties dialog box display information related to just the current file in the current project.

Mapping Content in WebWorks Publisher SE

The true power of WebWorks Publisher SE lies in the mappings. Mappings attach code that is stored with the template and associated with content created in FrameMaker. Much like a FrameMaker document that has a variety of content formatted with paragraph tags, character tags, table tags, and so on, WebWorks Publisher SE is dependent on the mapping instructions to drive the appearance of the output.

You need to regenerate content in WebWorks Publisher SE after making changes, the same way FrameMaker content is regenerated when you work with a book document. You must do this each time mappings change; otherwise, only the output based on the previous mappings is displayed.

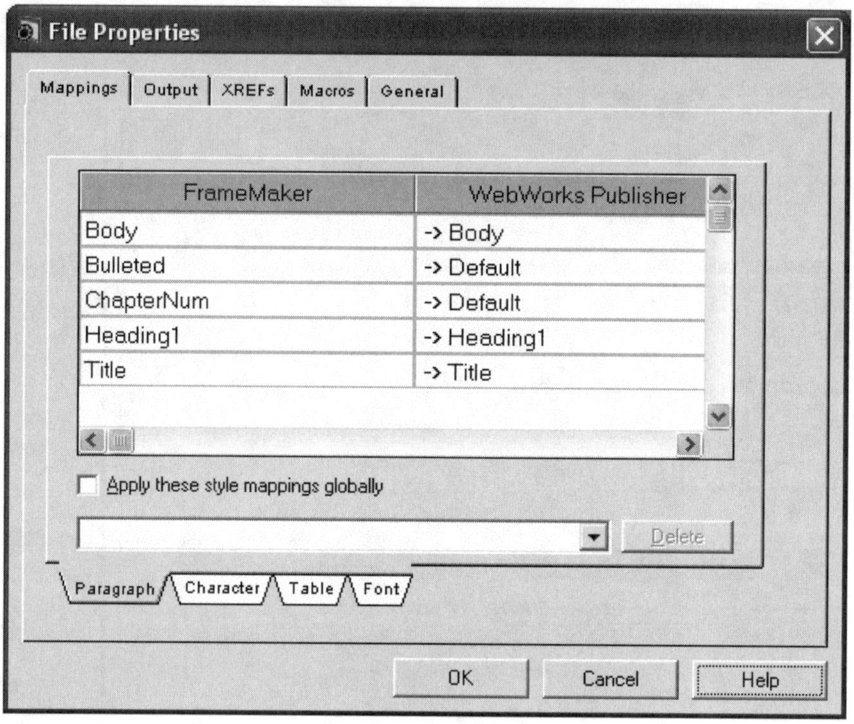

Figure 12-9 File Properties dialog box for a single file.

Mapping Paragraph Formats from FrameMaker

During the conversion to MIF, each FrameMaker paragraph is reviewed by WebWorks Publisher SE. Depending on the relationship between the content in FrameMaker and the template in WebWorks Publisher SE, different defaults may occur. Depending on your preferences, these can be kept or modified as required.

Default mappings. WebWorks Publisher SE automatically maps some content from FrameMaker when paragraphs are converted. If the name of the FrameMaker paragraph tag exactly matches the name (including the case) of a tag in WebWorks Publisher SE, the mapping is automatic. Should the default mapping need to be changed, however, or if the FrameMaker tag is not recognized, you need to manually map the FrameMaker content.

If at any time the default mapping that is used is overwritten and needs to be reset, you should reset the mapping by selecting **Unmap** from the style pull-down menu. Setting the format to Default forces WebWorks Publisher SE to use the standard default settings even if a matching tag name is used in the template.

Custom mappings. In some templates a developer has already created custom mappings. Custom mappings arise when the template developer recognizes that some formats in FrameMaker should use WebWorks formats other than their defaults when converted to online content. A developer may also decide that the default mapping needs to be modified to conform to a common appearance in the output.

Consider, for example, a FrameMaker document in which two formats are used for the general body of text. BodyFirst is used for the first paragraph of content after a Heading1 or a Heading2 format, and Body is used in all other cases. Both formats are used extensively in the document. The online versions of these formats, however, should look identical. In this example, the WebWorks Publisher SE template developer may decide to allow the default mapping (which appears as ->**Body** in the File Properties dialog box) to remain for the FrameMaker tag named Body. But in this case, the developer changes the default for the BodyFirst paragraph (which appears as -> **Default** in the File Properties dialog box) to Body as well. In this example, the newly mapped information no longer has the symbols -> in front of the name, since it is no longer mapped to its default. Instead, we see that the format of the BodyFirst is mapped to Body.

To map content manually, you first need to make sure that the correct tabs are displayed in the File Properties dialog box. Check that the Mappings tab is selected from the top of the dialog box and that Paragraph is selected from the subtabs. Once this is done, simply select the FrameMaker tag that you want to map to a different tag, and then select a new value from the applicable pull-down menu.

Mapping Guidelines for Paragraphs

Since paragraphs make up the majority of content that is passed from FrameMaker to WebWorks Publisher SE, it is important to follow a few simple guidelines to make the conversion easier. Unless a template is developed for your specific needs and instructions are included with the new template, you should follow these guidelines:

- Lists in FrameMaker (including numbered content and bulleted or dashed lists) should be mapped to a SmartList format that automatically detects the numbering used in the source and correctly maps it to an unordered or ordered list as required.

  As a general rule, the mapping should be to a SmartList of the same level as the list in FrameMaker. Therefore, a numbered list (made up of, for example, NumberBegin and NumberContinue tags) should be mapped to SmartList1. If the numbered list has a sublist within it (for example, a set of bullets based on a tag named NumberSubBullet), the sublist should be formatted to follow SmartList2 (see Figure 12-10).

- Tables of contents in FrameMaker should be set up to map content to either NoOutput or TOC formats (see Figure 12-10).

  As a general rule, the various titles, headings, and so on that are added to a TOC in FrameMaker should be mapped to TOC1, TOC2, and so on. Any content that exists as text, rather than as generated content, should also

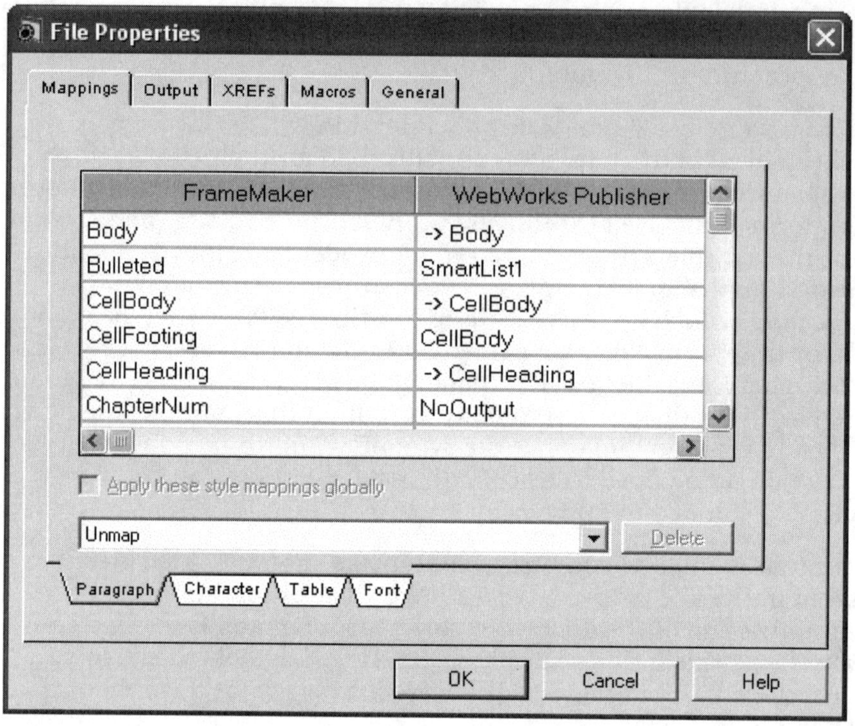

Figure 12-10 File Properties dialog box after mapping.

be mapped to NoOutput. For example, if your TOC file has the phrase "Table of Contents" at the top of the first body page, and it is formatted as ContentTitle, you should map it to NoOutput in the project. If you have content such as TitleTOC, Heading1TOC, and Heading2TOC, you should map each of them to TOC1, TOC2, and TOC3 in your project. Failure to do so results in content that is not formatted correctly or is not displayed at all.

- Content within a FrameMaker document that should create a new page should be mapped to NewHTMLPage or an equivalent setting.

  If your documents are quite long, a logical break may be, for example, at each Heading1 and Heading2. If you name your tags TitleChapter, TitleSection, and TitleSubSection, you may want to map these to NewHTMLPage. This creates a new page (dividing large files into smaller parts) that can be faster to download or easier for users to manage.

Mapping Character Formats from FrameMaker

Character formats are reviewed by WebWorks Publisher SE in the same way that each FrameMaker paragraph is reviewed. Depending on the relationship between the content in FrameMaker and the template in WebWorks Publisher SE, different defaults may occur. Depending on your preferences, these can be maintained or modified as required.

Default mappings. In the same way that WebWorks Publisher SE automatically maps some content from FrameMaker paragraph tags, it also automatically maps character tags. As with paragraph tags, you may keep the default mapping or manually map the FrameMaker content.

Custom mappings. As it is with paragraph tags, the custom mappings are also available for character tags.

For example, consider a FrameMaker document in which two formats are used for marking up characters within paragraphs. Emphasis is used for specific words that are, in this example, italic. In the same fashion the character tag KeyWord is used to format specific words to appear as, for example, bold. Both formats are used extensively in the document.

The WebWorks Publisher SE template developer may decide to allow the default mapping to remain for the FrameMaker tag named Emphasis. However, the developer decides that the default for the KeyWord characters should be changed and forced to appear as BoldPhrase, a style that the developer has created.

In this example the newly mapped information no longer has the content –> **Default** at its beginning. Instead we see that the format of the KeyWord is mapped to BoldPhrase.

To map content manually, you first need to make sure that the correct tabs are displayed in the File Properties dialog box. Make sure that the Mappings tab is selected from the top of the dialog box and that Characters is selected from the subtabs. Once this is done, simply select the FrameMaker tag to map and select a new value from the pull-down menu.

Mapping Table Formats from FrameMaker

During the conversion to MIF, each FrameMaker table is reviewed by WebWorks Publisher SE. Depending on the relationship between the content in FrameMaker and the template in WebWorks Publisher SE, different defaults may occur. Depending on your preferences, these can be kept or modified as required.

Default mappings. WebWorks Publisher SE automatically maps some content from FrameMaker when tables are converted. In the same way that the paragraph tags and character tags can be mapped by their name, tables can be mapped.

Custom mappings. In some templates used with WebWorks Publisher SE a developer has already created custom mappings. For tables, these may include a custom look for the table.

Consider, for example, a FrameMaker document in which two formats are used for tables. A tag named Shaded is used for tables with an alternating shaded pattern. Another tag—in this example, Ruled—is used for tables that have lines between cells, rows, and columns. Both formats are used extensively in the document.

In this example, the WebWorks Publisher SE template developer may decide to allow the default mapping to remain for the FrameMaker tag named Ruled but decide that the Shaded FrameMaker table tag should be changed and forced to appear as the AlternateShading style in WebWorks.

To map content manually, you first need to make sure that the correct tabs are displayed in the File Properties dialog box. Make sure that the Mappings tab is selected from the top of the dialog box and that Table is selected from the subtabs. Once this is done, simply select the FrameMaker tag to map and select a new value from the pull-down menu.

Mapping Specific Fonts from FrameMaker

Font mapping usually only needs to be done in situations where multiple languages or character sets are used in the FrameMaker source file.

Default mappings. WebWorks Publisher SE automatically maps some content from FrameMaker when files are converted. The tagging that WebWorks Publisher SE uses is generally correct. However, there are times when the defaults need to be modified.

In some templates used with WebWorks Publisher SE, a developer has already created custom mappings. Custom mappings arise when the template developer recognizes that some formats in FrameMaker should use different WebWorks formats when converted to online content. A developer may also decide that the default mapping needs to be modified to conform to a common appearance in the output.

To map content manually, you first need to make sure that the correct tabs are displayed in the File Properties dialog box. Make sure that the Mappings tab is selected from the top of the dialog box and that Font is selected from the subtabs. Once this is done, select the FrameMaker tag to map and select a new value from the pull-down menu.

Specifying Output Mappings for Pages and Images

WebWorks Publisher SE automatically manages the templates used to convert content for output to online formats. The names of output files for pages and images are also managed automatically. The default mappings and file names generally work well for projects that need to be delivered online. If the mapping or the output name of a file needs to be modified, however, it can be done using the File Properties dialog box.

You must make sure that either a single file or all files display their properties. Once the Properties dialog box is open, select the **Output** tab at the top and

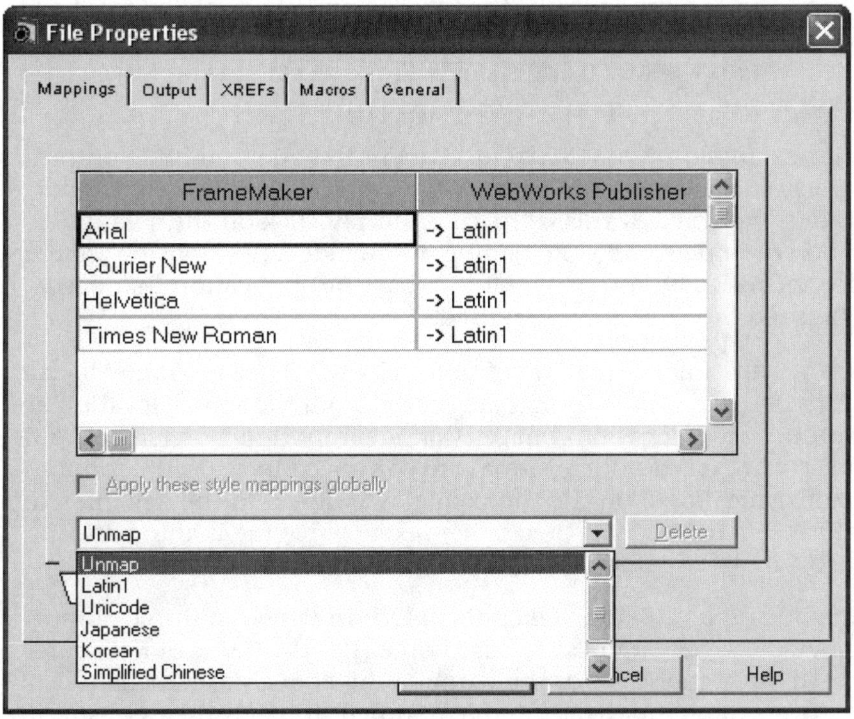

Figure 12-11 File Properties dialog box for font mapping.

either the **Pages** or **Graphics** subtab at the bottom. Doing so displays all the names of output files in the current document and their mappings. Properties mappings are further discussed in the following sections.

General mapping issues. WebWorks Publisher SE automatically maps FrameMaker files when documents are converted. There is automatic naming assigned to files based on their FrameMaker file name and the setup of the WebWorks Publisher SE template. Should the default mapping need to be changed, however, you need to manually map the FrameMaker content. If the file name needs to be changed, you need to specify the change within the project mappings.

If at any time the default mapping is overwritten and needs to be reset, you should reset the mapping selecting **Unmap** from the style drop-down menu. Setting the format to Default forces WebWorks Publisher SE to use the standard default settings. Should a different style be required for any content, select the file and choose a new mapping from the Style drop-down menu.

If your project is based on a template that supports frames, the TOC should be mapped to the FramesTOC style. This creates an additional set of files that are located at the very bottom of the project window in a location named Frameset File. The name assigned to the output is the same as that of the current project. This is the file that will be opened if you want to review the output.

Page mapping. As a general rule, the first document should be mapped to the TOC format, and the last to the Index format. If required, rearrange files in the project window before using the File Properties dialog box to change the output style.

Consider, for example, a FrameMaker document in which multiple output files are generated. The names of these files are automatically assigned but may need to be modified. If this is the case, simply click on the default filename and type a new name. Remember to include any extensions that are required for the file to be correctly identified by the application that needs to open the finished file.

Image mapping. Images that are imported by reference in FrameMaker and have a recognized online format are copied from the source location and placed into the output location. Images that are imported by reference and do not have a recognized online format are converted to a specific format, and a default name, based on the source file, is assigned to the new file. Any image that is not referenced in the FrameMaker source file is automatically converted to a new format and assigned a default name.

Consider, for example, a FrameMaker document in which multiple output files are generated. These names are based on either the name of the source file referenced by FrameMaker or the name of the FrameMaker source document. These names may need to be modified. If this is the case, simply click on the default filename and type a new name. Remember to include any extensions that are required for the file to be correctly identified by the application that needs to open the finished file.

Converting Cross-References

The conversion of cross-references to online formats is done using the exact same code that FrameMaker uses; therefore, anyone familiar with the standard building blocks used by FrameMaker can understand and use the cross-reference features of WebWorks Publisher SE.

To change any cross-reference formats, you first need to make sure that the correct tab is displayed in the File Properties dialog box (see Figure 12-12). Select the XREFs tab from the top of the dialog box. Then simply select the FrameMaker cross-reference code and enter new values. You should drop page references and, in some cases, section or chapter numbering.

User Macros and Overrides

User macros drive much of the code that is used by WebWorks Publisher SE to create output. There are also a variety of building blocks that are only available with the Professional Edition.

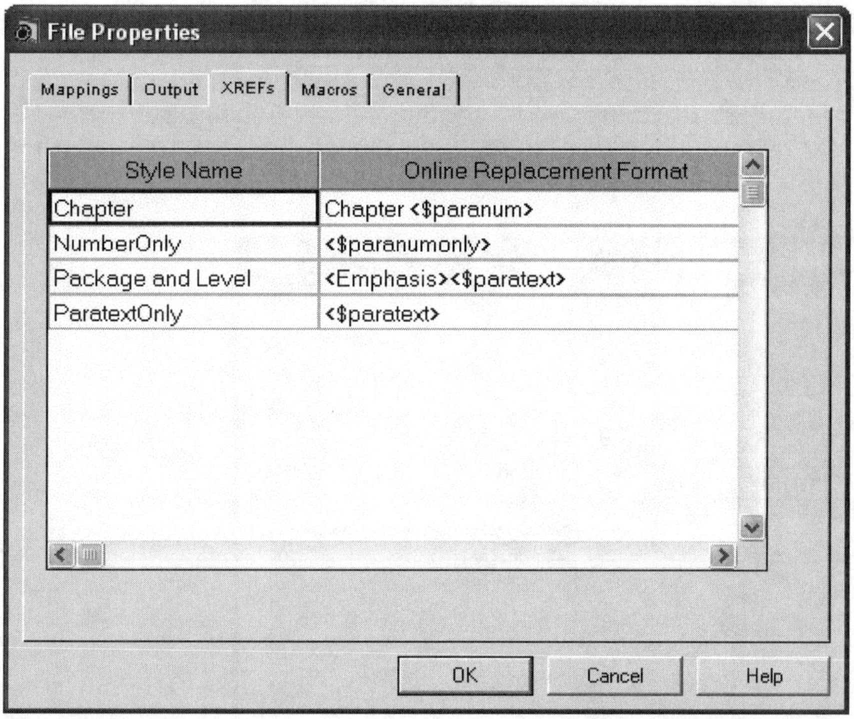

Figure 12-12 File Properties dialog box for cross-references.

While most user macros should apply to all documents in the same way, there are times when individual overrides are required. Depending on the values of the user macros, some output documents may have content or display settings that can be configured. There are numerous user macros available, and each serves a specific purpose in WebWorks Publisher SE. For more information on the user macros, refer to the WebWorks Publisher SE documentation.

To create an override of any user macros, select the **Macros** tab in the File Properties dialog box. Then select the macro you want to override and select "Let me override the value for this macro when converting this file." You can now enter new values to be used in any document that accesses this macro.

Working with Options

Each WebWorks Publisher SE project has a set of options. These options are used to determine directory locations, file generation management, default character encoding, structured FrameMaker information, and details about the template used to develop the current project.

Directories Used by WebWorks Publisher SE

Four directories are used with WebWorks Publisher SE. They relate to the output directory, images in relation to the output, support files, and temporary files. Each directory can be configured individually, but the output, images, and support files are in folders located relative to each other and should be located in similar locations, as shown in Figure 12-13.

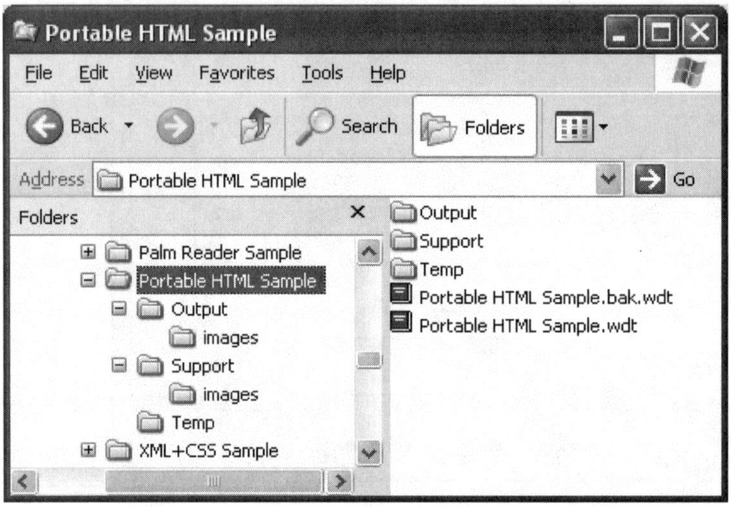

Figure 12-13 WebWorks Publisher SE sample directory structure.

The output directory is the location in which the finished content created by WebWorks Publisher SE is stored. All files required for the deliverable should be located in this directory. To change the directory, click **Browse** and select the new location.

The images related to a project should generally be located in the same folder as the rest of the output, or as a sibling to the output folder. This path, however, can be specified as any location relative to the output. You can change this folder by manually entering a new path for the images.

The directory containing the support files used by WebWorks Publisher SE in the conversion process is generally a sibling to the output folder, although you can also modify this by manually changing the path. Files located in the support directory can be copied by WebWorks Publisher SE automatically to the output directory. This ensures that content such as navigation buttons in the support folder are available in the output folder.

Temporary files that are kept or cleared when the project or application is closed are the MIF files that WebWorks Publisher SE scans to create content that is then placed in the output location. Because temporary files may end up being very large, you may need to specify a path that points to a different drive if you are low on hard drive space. To set the temporary folder location, click Browse and select the new location.

WebWorks Publisher SE also allows you to specify whether files should be kept on a relative path if the project is moved. Again, this is generally a good idea, as it ensures that files and paths are not disrupted if the project files are moved to a new location.

File Generation Settings

File generation in WebWorks Publisher SE includes a choice of options:

File naming. Generated content has filenames assigned automatically in most cases. The name length is based on either an open naming convention or a restricted naming convention. Files can be truncated to use DOS-based naming conventions. This restricts names to a maximum of eight characters with a three-character extension. If this is option is chosen, you should review the names of any files that are being manually referenced to accommodate the restricted naming convention. Content such as a corporate logo or custom files must also adhere to the chosen naming conventions.

Automatic page or image generation. Pages or images generated by WebWorks Publisher SE can be set to be automatically generated during a conversion. If only images or only pages are needed, select or deselect these options as required.

Line endings. Line endings can be based on DOS, Macintosh, or Unix conventions. Depending on the platform on which you are working, select the specific setting as required.

Character Encoding

The character encoding used by the current project should be a default setting based on the language of the source and output. This value can be overwritten for specific fonts if required.

Structured FrameMaker and WebWorks Publisher SE

If the content to be converted is structured, and elements should be used for the mapping (rather than a combination of table, character, and paragraph formats), select this option checkbox.

Additional Template Information

The additional template information is used primarily for troubleshooting purposes. This data is automatically managed by WebWorks Publisher SE.

Working with Support Files for HTML Content

Projects based on either Portable HTML or Dynamic HTML use very similar support files. The primary difference between the two projects is the inclusion of a CSS file in Dynamic HTML.

While the files in the support folder end in either *.txt or *.asp (and, in Dynamic HTML, *.css), the documents are not restricted by their extension. The extensions actually exist to classify the files for editing.

The files that end with the *.txt extension are by default used to include instructions to users. The characters "de," "en," "fr," and "ja" are used in filenames to signify content in German (Deutsch), English, French, or Japanese.

The files that end with *.asp are not traditional *.asp files. They are not active server pages—they are templates that drive the appearance of output files. Generally speaking, these documents contain instructions that drive the appearance of output that appears at the top and bottom of pages. Output pages may have navigation buttons at the top of the page, content from FrameMaker in the body of the page, and contact information at the bottom of the page. This appearance is generally created based on instructions in the *.asp files. These documents may be edited using any tool you prefer that supports either text-only or Web page content, including—but not limited to—tools such as Notepad, DreamWeaver, FrontPage, and GoLive.

If you are working with the support files, you should never change the code related to the FrameMaker content. This code can be easily identified, as it is wrapped inside <!— (BeginHiddenExpansion) and —> (EndHiddenExpansion) in the file.

Many of the support files contain tables and information related to the navigation system used by WebWorks Publisher SE. If the navigation images are modified in size, the tables and information need to be updated to reflect the physical size of the image.

Figure 12-14 shows the difference between support files in the Portable and Dynamic HTML templates.

Frameset.asp and FramesTOC.asp Files

The files *Frameset.asp* and *FramesTOC.asp* are both directly related to the use of a frameset in the output. In order for you to use these files, the TOC from your FrameMaker document must be mapped to the FramesTOC style.

The file *Frameset.asp* is the actual frameset (a special type of HTML file that may be used to display portions of a Web site in different, predetermined areas). It determines the size of the frames and the default initial content. It rarely needs to be modified unless you need to change the size of the frameset or make other changes that most users will not see. These changes may include changing meta tags or the instructions related to handling content if no frame support is detected.

FramesTOC.asp drives the appearance of the TOC when a frameset is used. Again, this file is generally not modified unless changes need to be made to the appearance of the TOC. Any text within the TOC is generally a hypertext link and is formatted based on the instructions passed on from the

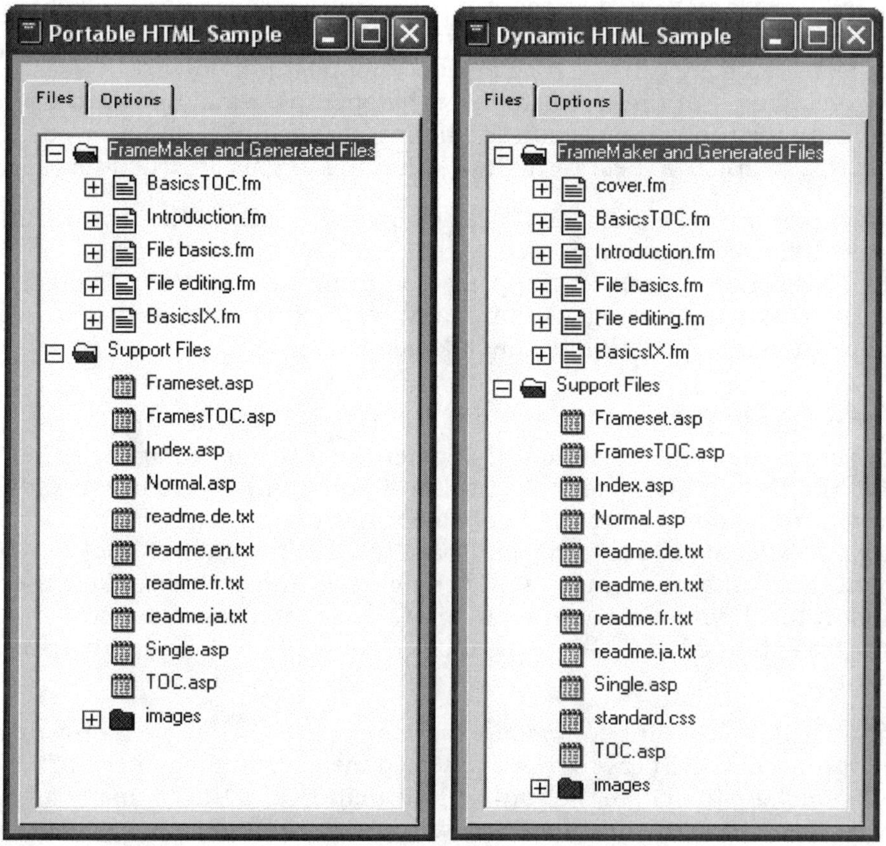

Figure 12-14 HTML support files.

WebWorks Publisher SE template through mappings. Additionally, formatting of the text is based on the browser's interpretation of the link elements.

Index.asp File

The file *Index.asp* is directly related to the use of an index in the output. In order for you to use this file, the index from your FrameMaker document must be the last document in your project (which is automatically mapped to the index). If you do not have an index in your FrameMaker file set, this document needs to be modified or ignored. If you want a different appearance to your last page (for example, no navigation button marked Next, or no alphabetical list at the top of your page for index entries), you need to modify this document.

It may be easier to create an index in FrameMaker and simply populate it with a title that reads something along the lines of "No Index Included." While this is a quick solution, it is likely that a strong index will be used repeatedly in an online document.

The file *Index.asp* is also the document that determines the appearance of the last page of a project. If you need to change the file often (for example, if each project you create is based on a default template that you update), consider changing it in the template folder by opening it and updating the content using the tool of your choice. This ensures that all future projects based on this template appear formatted according to your instructions.

Index.asp drives the appearance of the index as well. Much of the text within an index is followed by a numeric value that is a hypertext link and is formatted based on the instructions passed on from the WebWorks Publisher SE template through mappings. Additionally, formatting of the text is based on the browser's interpretation of the link elements.

Normal.asp File

The file *Normal.asp* is the document that determines the appearance of all pages but the first and last pages of a project. In order for you to use this file, the content from your FrameMaker document must be converted as numerous documents in your project. Basically, any FrameMaker book document that contains at least a TOC, a single file, and an index likely uses this support file. If you want a different appearance for any of your content (with the exception of the TOC or the index), you will need to modify this document.

The only exception to using *Normal.asp* is a project in which there is only one page of output, in which case *Single.asp* is used instead. You may need to modify *Normal.asp* to update the contact information and the company logo. If you need to change the file often (for example, if each project you create is based on a default template that you update), consider changing it in the template folder by opening it and updating the content using the tool of your choice. This ensures that all future projects based on this template appear formatted according to your instructions.

Much of the body of your document is generally text, tables, and images, which are formatted based on the instructions passed on from the WebWorks Publisher SE template through mappings. Formatting of the text is also based on the browser's interpretation of the content.

Readme Files

The Readme files simply contain information about the template in a variety of languages. If you have updated the template or require instructions that appear when the Project Wizard is first launched, you should modify these documents.

Note: *You may safely delete these files without harming your project. Alternatively, you may want to edit their content to reflect the purpose and use of your template more accurately.*

Single.asp File

The file *Single.asp* is the document that determines the appearance of a lone output page of a project. As soon as more than one page is created (even from a single FrameMaker file), other support files apply. In order for you to use the file *Single.asp*, the content from your FrameMaker document must be converted as a single document in your project. Basically, any single FrameMaker document that has no content mapped to a NewHTMLPage likely uses this support file. If you want a different appearance for this single output file, you need to modify this document.

You may need to modify *Single.asp* occasionally to update the contact information and the company logo. If you need to change the file often (for example, if the project is created based on a default template that you update), consider changing it in the template folder by opening it and updating the content using a tool of your choice. This ensures that all future projects based on this template appear formatted according to your instructions.

TOC.asp File

The file *TOC.asp* is directly related to the TOC in the output unless a frameset is used. In order for you to use this file, the TOC from your FrameMaker document must be the first document in your project (which is automatically mapped to the TOC). If you do not have a TOC in your FrameMaker file set, this document needs to be modified or ignored. If you want a different appearance to your first page (for example, a splash page with your company logo), you will need to modify this document.

It may be easier to create a TOC in FrameMaker and simply populate it with a title that reads something along the lines of "No Table of Contents Included." While this is a quick solution, it is likely that a TOC will be used repeatedly in an online document.

The file *TOC.asp* is also the document that determines the appearance of the first page of a project. You may need to modify it to update the contact information and the company logo. If you need to change the file often (for example, if each project you create is based on a default template that you update), consider changing it in the template folder by opening it and updating the content using the tool of your choice. This ensures that all future projects based on this template appear formatted according to your instructions.

TOC.asp drives the appearance of the TOC unless a frameset is used. Any text within the TOC is generally a hypertext link and is formatted based on the instructions passed on from the WebWorks Publisher SE template through mappings. Formatting of the text is also based on the browser's interpretation of the link elements.

Standard.css File

The CSS document is used to drive the appearance of the content in Dynamic HTML. When you edit the content of the file, the output can be configured to produce a variety of formats.

The file *Standard.css* is the document that determines the appearance of the majority of the content of a Dynamic HTML project. You may need to modify *Standard.css* to configure content based on your specific needs. If you need to change the file often (for example, if each project you create is based on a default template that you update), consider changing it in the template folder by opening it and updating the content using the tool of your choice. This ensures that all future projects based on this template appear formatted according to your instructions.

Images Folder

The images folder stores images used by WebWorks Publisher SE in all files it creates. These generally include the navigation buttons and the corporate logo. Additional shared images (aside from those already in the FrameMaker documents that are converted by WebWorks Publisher SE based on their position and type in the FrameMaker source) should be placed into this folder.

Working with Support Files for XML Content

Most of the files for XML content are the same (conceptually) as the files used by HTML-based projects. Key differences include the use of XML rules related to well-formed or valid content. In addition, the stylesheet information differs in some files, depending on whether an XSL or a CSS document is used.

Readme Files

The Readme files simply contain information about the template in a variety of languages. If you have updated the template or require instructions that appear when the Project Wizard is first launched, you should modify these documents.

Document.css and Document.xsl Files

The CSS document or the XSL document is used to drive the appearance of the content in XML. When you edit the content of the file, the output can be configured to produce a variety of formats.

The stylesheet file is the document that determines the appearance of most of the content in an XML project. It often needs to be modified to configure content based on your specific needs. If you need to change the file often (for example, if each project you create is based on a default template that you update), consider changing it in the template folder by opening it and updating the content using the tool of your choice. This ensures that all future projects based on this template appear formatted according to your instructions.

Working with Support Files for Palm Reader

Most of the support files for Palm Reader content are the same (conceptually) as the files used by HTML-based projects. The Palm Reader template only has one additional support file. To use the Palm Reader, however, you need to first download and install the Palm DropBook utility from *http://www.peanutpress.com/makebook/index.cgi.*

Once this file has been downloaded and unzipped, place the DropBook.exe file into the same bin folder where WebWorks Publisher SE is installed.

Preface.txt File

The only support file that needs any modification is *Preface.txt.* You can configure this document to determine the name of the finished file, the splashscreen, the copyright information, and the contact information. Because it is a text-based file, it can be opened by any tool used to edit text.

The file *Preface.txt* is the actual document that determines the appearance of the majority of the content of a Palm Reader project. You may need to modify *Preface.txt* to configure content based on your specific needs. If you need to change the file often (for example, if each project you create is based on a default template that you update), consider changing it in the template folder by opening it and updating the content using a tool of your choice. This ensures that all future projects based on this template appear formatted according to your instructions.

Readme Files

Readme files simply contain information about the template in a variety of languages. If you have updated the template or require instructions that appear when the Project Wizard is first launched, you should modify these documents.

Working with Support Files for Microsoft Reader

Most of the support files for Microsoft Reader content are the same (conceptually) as the files used by HTML-based projects. The Microsoft template, however, has four additional support files: the Readme file, *Document.css*, *Chapter.asp*, and *Package.asp*.

Readme Files

Readme files simply contain information about the template in a variety of languages. If you have updated the template, or require instructions that appear when the Project Wizard is first launched, you should modify these documents.

Document.css File

The CSS document is used to drive the appearance of the content in the Microsoft Reader. When you edit the content of the file, the output appearance can be configured to have a variety of formats.

The file *Document.css* is the document that determines the appearance of the majority of the content of a Microsoft Reader project. You may need to modify *Document.css* to configure content based on your specific needs. If you need to change the file often (for example, if each project you create is based on a default template that you update), you should consider changing it in the template folder by opening it and updating the content using the tool of your choice. This ensures that all future projects based on this template appear formatted according to your instructions.

Chapter.asp File

The file *Chapter.asp* is directly related to the use of all files in the output document.

The file *Chapter.asp* is the actual document that determines the appearance of the output of a project. You may need to modify *Chapter.asp* to add contact information or a company logo. If you need to change the file often (for example, if each project you create is based on a default template that you update), consider changing it in the template folder by opening it and updating the content using the tool of your choice. This ensures that all future projects based on this template appear formatted according to your instructions.

Much of the body is text, tables, and images, which are formatted based on the instructions passed on from the WebWorks Publisher SE template through mappings. Formatting of the text is also based on the browser's interpretation of the content.

Package.asp File

The file *Package.asp* is directly related to the use of the finished *.lit file.

Package.asp is used to drive the appearance and output of the finished fileset. It differs from the file *Chapter.asp* in many ways. *Chapter.asp* drives the content of the finished document, while *Package.asp* drives the finished *.lit file.

You may need to modify *Package.asp* to change images used for the cover, title, or thumbnails. If you need to change the file often, consider changing it in the template folder by opening it and updating the content using the tool of your choice. This ensures that all future projects based on this template appear formatted according to your instructions. Changing images and generating content are discussed more fully below.

Changing images used by Package.asp. The images used for the cover, title, and thumbnails can be customized. You can either change the default appearance of the files located in the images folder for the project, or you can use your own custom images with different names.

If the images that already exist need modification, open the files *coverbvt.jpg, titlebvt.jpg,* or *thumbbvt.jpg* and edit the images directly. Another approach is to completely replace the three default images with your images and use the same names. This allows you to replace images quickly without having to update any support files (such as the *Package.asp* document). Finally, if you need to replace any or all of the default images with files that have different names, you must update the file *Package.asp* and the support folder. *Package.asp* needs to have up to three lines modified (for the cover, title, and thumbnail) in two locations. You must ensure that they are all correctly modified.

Each of these lines need to be modified with the name of the image to be used. Once the new name has been specified, the documents need to be generated to reflect the new images.

Controlling the output filename. The name of the finished *.lit file can always be overwritten. By default, it is the same name as the project. Because this is driven by a user macro, however, you can overwrite it. Display the File Properties for all documents in the Microsoft Reader and display the Macros tab. Once you do this, you can modify the UMLitFileName macro with the new name you wish to use.

Generating and Viewing Output

Once all FrameMaker content has been developed and a project has been set up in WebWorks Publisher SE, all output needs to be generated. You may want to review materials and see how they appear during the development process. Once the project has been set up correctly, all files in FrameMaker have been added and rearranged as required, content has been mapped, files have been named appropriately and so on, you need to create the finished files.

WebWorks Publisher SE allows you to convert and review your content at any time. In some cases, however, your previously generated files must be manually deleted or your systems cache must be purged to display the newest content. This is necessary in many cases with older browsers or with some eBook formats.

Generating Content

Once all setup has been completed, the content needs to be converted from FrameMaker to your online format. In much the same way that a generated document in FrameMaker is set up in advance of the generation, you need to set up your files in WebWorks Publisher SE prior to generating output. The generation may take some time, depending on the complexity of the content.

If you want to generate only one file first, select it and then choose **Generate Selected** from the Project menu. You can also click the **Regenerate the selected file only** icon on the toolbar.

To generate the entire project, choose **Generate All** from the Project menu.

When to Consider WebWorks Publisher Professional Edition

If at any time you need to modify a template beyond what this chapter has outlined, create your own templates, or develop help content, you should consider using WebWorks Publisher Professional Edition. The Professional Edition allows you to create custom templates and modify all aspects of existing templates. It also allows you to create help content, such as JavaHelp or content specific to Microsoft WinHelp or HTML Help, for delivery via the Internet. Finally, you can use the Professional Edition to develop content beyond the confines of the Standard Edition and create entire publishing systems that conform to all of your specific needs (see Table 12-1).

Table 12-1 Comparison between WebWorks Standard and Professional Editions

FUNCTIONALITY	Standard Edition 7.0	Professional Edition
HTML/XML output	Supported	Supported
Graphics conversion	Limited	Full control of placement, float, and format
Style designer	Limited to changes in the CSS or XSL files.	Complete point-and-click customization capabilities
Template reusability	Limited to six predefined templates	Complete creation, customization, and re-purposing capabilities
Mapping reusability	Requires you to set mappings on every project	Save and reuse mappings between projects/templates

Table 12-1 Comparison between WebWorks Standard and Professional Editions (Continued)

FUNCTIONALITY	Standard Edition 7.0	Professional Edition
Online help templates	Not available	Supports HTML Help, JavaHelp, WinHelp, and WebWorks Help
Palm Reader and Microsoft Reader	Included	Not included, but can be copied from the Standard Edition template folder
Conditional text settings	Not available	Set Show/Hide conditions on all output
Marker mapping	Not available	Control how markers are processed
Accessibility template	Not available	Conforms to W3C guidelines and provides reporting
Style preview	Not available	One-click style definitions views
Scripts functionality	Not available	Customizable and event-triggered during generation process
Migration Wizard	Not available	Automates cross-version migration
Log files	Limited	Integrated and available for troubleshooting

Summary

WebWorks Publisher Standard Edition is included with several versions of FrameMaker. It allows you to easily output your FrameMaker documents or books to multiple online formats. Once you understand the mappings and properties as discussed herein, you are well on your way to single sourcing your content.

13

Prepress, Printing, and PDF

Bradley Anderson

This chapter discusses options for outputting your documents to print and PDF. It includes detailed descriptions of print settings.

Applicable to all version of FrameMaker

Introduction and Organization

This chapter will cover all aspects of generating PDF files from FrameMaker. This includes not only generating PDF files to be viewed and navigated online, but also generating PDF files that can be used for printing—both offset and digital.

This chapter is organized into three sections: terminology, configuration, and creation. Creating a PDF file from FrameMaker might seem relatively straightforward. However, creating a PDF file correctly is not without its difficulties. Most of the confusion over creating a PDF file for online distribution or for offset printing comes from not understanding the terminology or the printing process. Configuration of both the printer driver and Acrobat Distiller are vital. This chapter will take you step by step through installation and configuration to ensure that your PDFs will be created correctly. Once you understand the terminology and your machine is configured, you'll learn how to create a PDF file for online distribution, digital black and white printing, and offset full-color printing.

Which Sections Should You Read?

Creating PDFs with Acrobat 4

You should read the following sections if you are using Acrobat 4 to create PDF files that will be viewed online. These sections will walk you through the process of setting up your PostScript printer driver; configuring distiller to give the smallest PDF files and to maintain reasonable resolution on images; and what settings should be used in FrameMaker to make the PDF.

- "Printing and PDF Terminology" on page 311
- "Downloading Adobe's PostScript Printer Driver" on page 314
- "Installing a PostScript Printer for Acrobat 4" on page 316
- "Acrobat Distiller Printer Settings" on page 327
- "Setting Up Custom PDF Job Options" on page 339
- "FrameMaker Page/Print Setup" on page 347
- "Description of PDF Options for FrameMaker" on page 351
- "Creating a PDF from FrameMaker" on page 355

Creating PDFs with Acrobat 5

You should read the following sections if you are using Acrobat 5 to create PDF files that will be viewed online. These sections will walk you through the process of setting up your PostScript printer driver; configuring distiller to give the smallest PDF files and to maintain reasonable resolution on images; and what settings should be used in FrameMaker to make the PDF.

Creating PDFs with Acrobat 6

Acrobat 6 was released after this book was written. The instructions for Acrobat 5 can be used with Acrobat 6, though you may see minor differences in the settings.

Printing and PDF Terminology

PostScript and PDF

When you prepare files for offset printing or for conversion to Acrobat PDF, the required language is PostScript. PostScript is a mathematical language that describes the page and the locations of objects on the page. Adobe created this language in 1984 with PostScript Level 1 and has continued to develop it; it is now at Level 3. PDF is an outgrowth of PostScript.

Prepress

Prepress is the process by which files are prepared for printing. Preparing files for prepress means saving your documents and/or graphics so that a print house can output printed text and/or images from them. Output can be to a simple laser printer or a color laser printer, to film, or to a plate for off-set printing.

Most prepress output devices now support Level 2 and/or Level 3 PostScript. Files can be delivered in PostScript or PDF formats. These instructions will guide you in configuring the printer drivers on your workstations and preparing PDF files in Acrobat 4 or 5 that will output successfully.

Adobe PostScript Printer Drivers

The PostScript printer driver creates a PostScript file from FrameMaker and other desktop publishing programs. The objects, text, and graphics on each FrameMaker page are converted to PostScript through the printer driver. It is very important that Adobe's PostScript printer driver is used. Otherwise, your PostScript or PDF may not meet the specifications in the PostScript language, and your PDF may not look or print correctly.

PostScript Printer Description Files (PPDs)

When you install a printer instance on your computer with Adobe's PostScript printer driver (never use the Add Printer wizard in Windows), the installer will ask what PostScript printer description (PPD) file to use. A PPD file contains specific information regarding the device that you use to print. Every PostScript-compatible device has an associated PPD.

A PPD file contains information such as what page sizes the device supports, supported output resolution, paper trays, and font substitutions.

Use the Linotronic 330 PPD or Acrobat 5 PPD with Acrobat 4, and the Acrobat 5 PPD with Acrobat 5. The Linotronic 330 and Acrobat 5 PPD files are preferred (over the Acrobat 4 PPD) with Acrobat 4 because they support custom page sizes while the Acrobat 4 PPD does not. (You may choose to use the Acrobat 4 PPD if you are not printing any custom page sizes.) When you use Acrobat 5, the Acrobat 5 PPD file supports custom page sizes. If you work with a single vendor to output your files, you might want to ask the prepress department to supply you with the PPD file specific to their output device(s).

Registration Marks

When a document is printed with more than one color on an offset press, the printer needs special markings on the page. These markings are referred to as printer's marks, crop marks, or registration marks (see Figure 13-1). In a typical four-color job, the paper is fed through the press four times—once for each of the colors cyan, magenta, yellow, and black. These colors then mix where they overlap and create the colors you see. In order to make sure that everything is printed in the correct place on the page, the printer has to have some method of lining up the paper so that it goes through the press at exactly the same spot it did before. Registration marks provide the method for lining up the pages. Trim marks are provided to show the printer where to trim the pages to the final page size when printing is completed.

Note: *It is good practice to print using registration marks unless a printer or publisher requests otherwise.*

Bleeds

Any image or object that extends beyond the physical boundary of the page is said to "bleed" off the page (see Figure 13-2). Probably the most common use for a bleed is for a thumb tab that helps a reader find a particular chapter in a book. (See Chapter 10, "Creating Great Screen Captures" on page 231 for more information about bleeding thumb tabs.) If your documents contain any bleeding object(s), you must make sure you prepare your final PostScript or PDF files so that the bleed prints correctly.

The final PDF with bleeds and registration marks will look as shown in Figure 13-3.

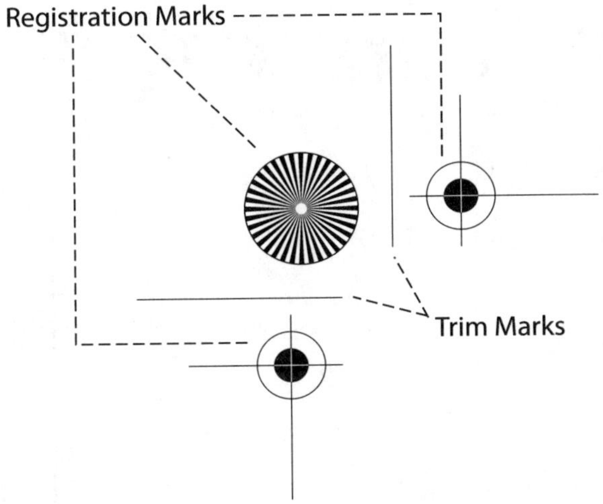

Figure 13-1 Example of a FrameMaker registration mark.

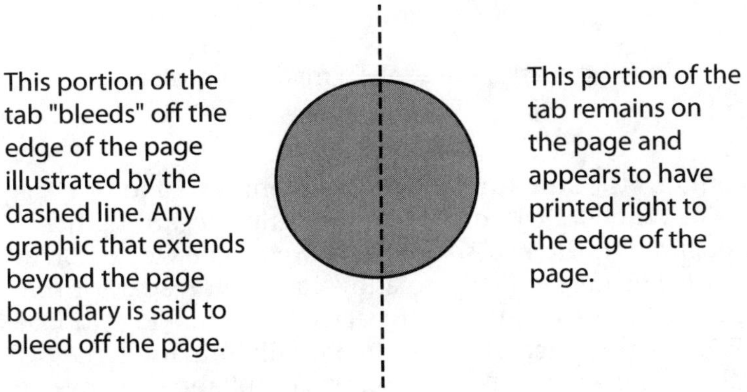

Figure 13-2 Example of a bleed.

Bookmarks

PDF bookmarks provide a method of navigation and a visual representation of the hierarchy of the structure of the document. FrameMaker paragraph tags (or elements in a structured document) can be "mapped" to bookmarks in a PDF file (see Figure 13-4).

Thumbnails

PDF thumbnails provide another method of navigation. Thumbnails can be generated automatically at the time of distillation or manually within the PDF file. A thumbnail is simply a small representation of each page of the PDF (see Figure 13-5).

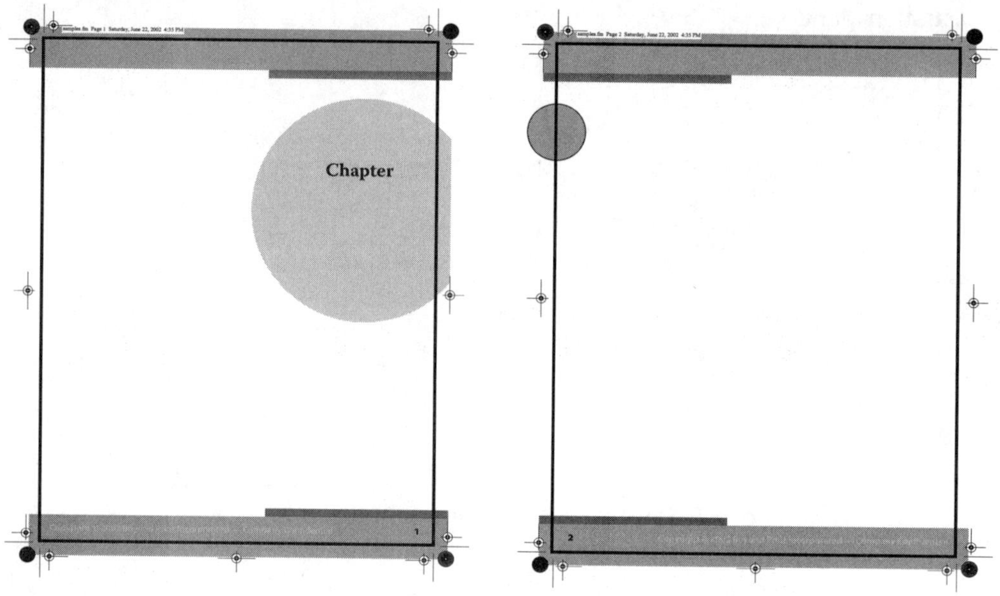

Figure 13-3 Page output with crop marks, registration marks, and bleeds.

Tagged PDF

A PDF file that contains the structure of the document is said to be a "tagged" or "structured" PDF. When a PDF contains information regarding the structure of the document, the PDF may be reflowed to be viewed on a PDA such as a Palm Pilot. The tagged PDF also allows a screen reader for the visually impaired to read the document correctly—in fact, a tagged PDF is necessary for a PDF file to be accessible to the visually impaired. In government circles this is known as Section 508 compliance—a government standard for making online information accessible to those with visual impairments.

PDF Mark

A PDF mark is a special command or code put into the PostScript output that gets converted to a special Acrobat function. For example, you can place in your FrameMaker documents PDF marks that will set the view size, set page transitions, and/or fill in the document information fields in the final PDF.

Downloading Adobe's PostScript Printer Driver

You will need to download the latest PostScript printer driver from Adobe's Web site. Due to the ever-changing nature of the Web, the exact steps required to download the printer driver may differ from the steps listed

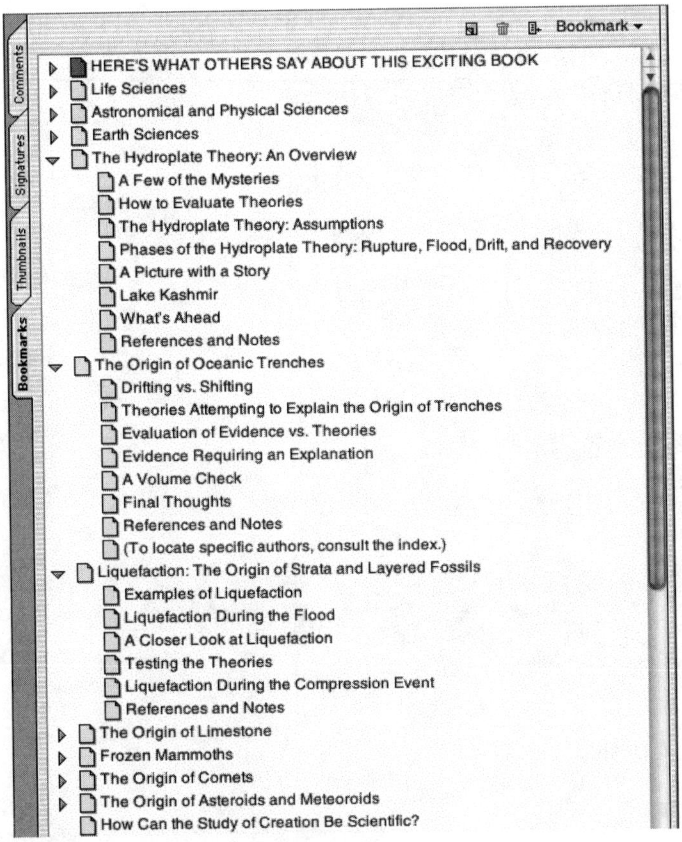

Figure 13-4 Example of bookmarks in a PDF file.

below. If the steps do differ, just find the **Downloads** section of the Web site, find the printer driver section, and then download the appropriate driver for your operating system.

Windows Universal Installer

1. From Adobe's Web site (*http://www.adobe.com*), click on the **Downloads** link under the **Support** category at the top of the page.
2. Scroll down to the **Printer Drivers** section and click on the Windows link.
3. Click on the link for the **English** version of the **1.0.6 printer driver** (or the most recent version).
4. Click the red **Download** button on the left side of the page.
5. Choose to save the **Winsteng.exe** file on your **desktop**.

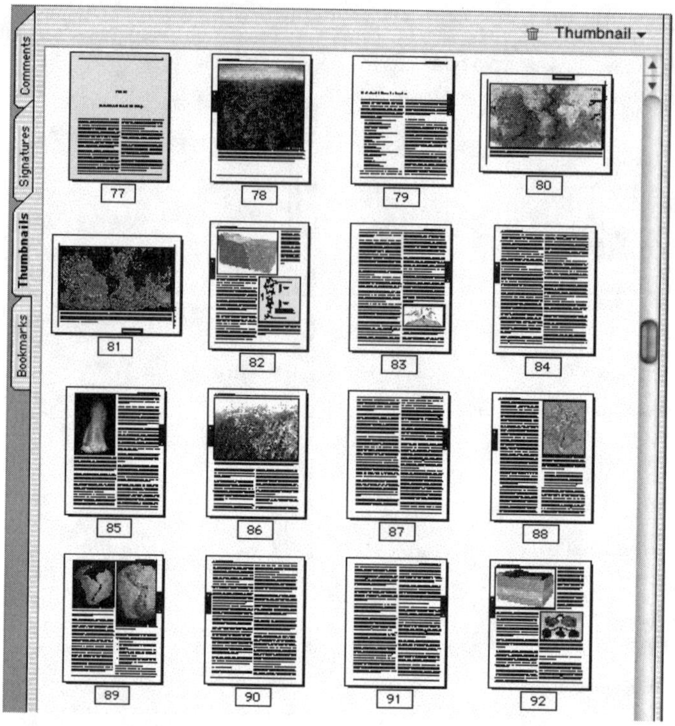

Figure 13-5 Example of page thumbnails in a PDF file.

Macintosh Installer

1. From Adobe's Web site (*http://www.adobe.com*), click on the **Downloads** link under the **Support** category at the top of the page.
2. Scroll down to the **Printer Drivers** section and click on the **Macintosh** link.
3. Click on the link for the **English** version of the **8.8 printer driver** (or the most recent version).
4. Click the red **Download** button on the left side of the page.
5. If asked, choose to save the *US.sea.hqx* file to your **desktop**.

Installing a PostScript Printer for Acrobat 4

The installation of the PostScript printer driver for Acrobat 4 requires one of three possible PPD files. The standard Acrobat Distiller PPD that comes with Acrobat 4/Frame 6 does not support custom page sizes—only the standard page sizes. It is recommended that you use the Linotronic 330 PPD or Acrobat 5 PPD with Acrobat 4. Doing so will enable you to set a custom page size, which is very important if you are going to print registration marks or create an odd-sized/screen-sized page. The following steps walk you through installation of an Acrobat 4 Distiller print driver with the Linotronic PPD.

Substitute the Acrobat Distiller PPD if you will only be printing standard page sizes without a bleed or if you don't need registration marks.

Windows Installation

1. Double-click on the **Winsteng.exe** file that you downloaded to your desktop. The Adobe PostScript Driver Installer will open.

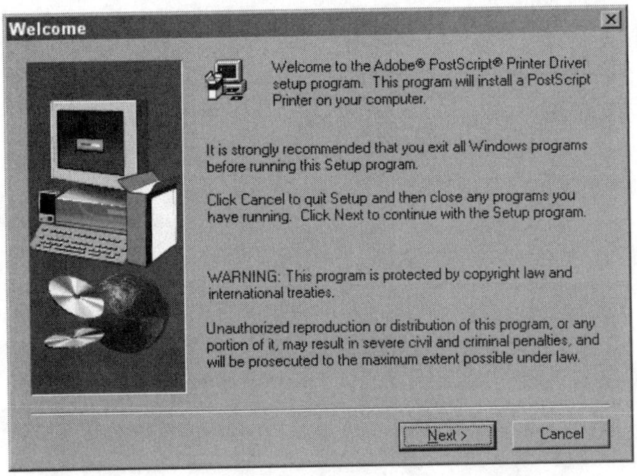

2. Click **Next**.

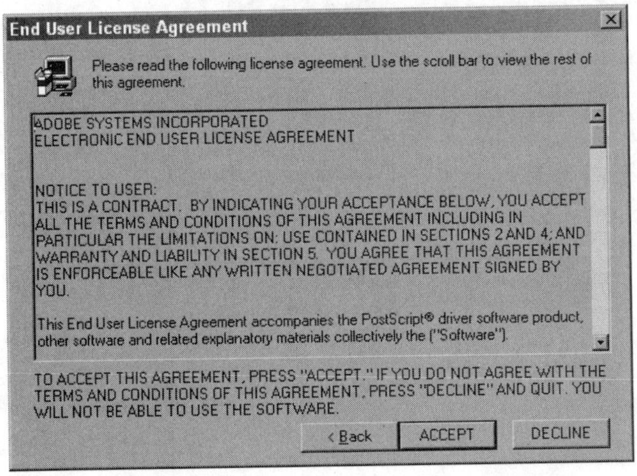

3. Click **Accept**.

4. Choose **Install a new PostScript printer.**

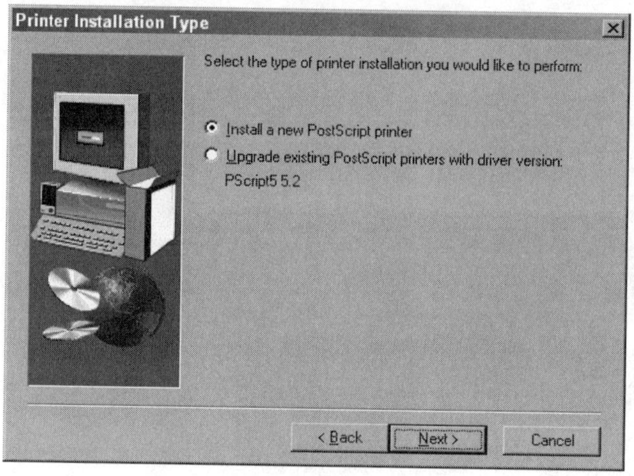

5. Click **Next.**
6. Choose **Local Printer.**

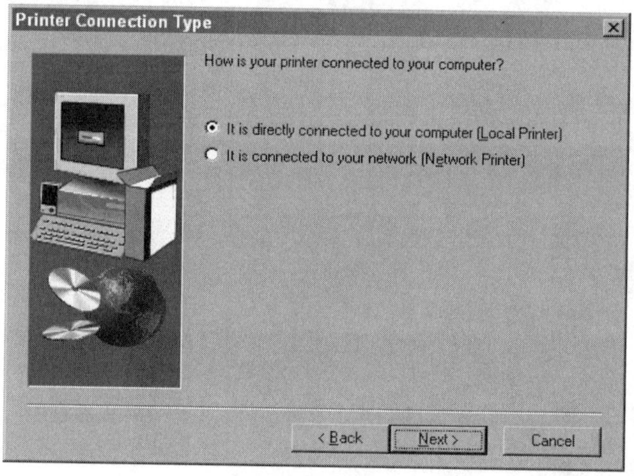

7. Click **Next.**

8. Choose **FILE: Local Port**.

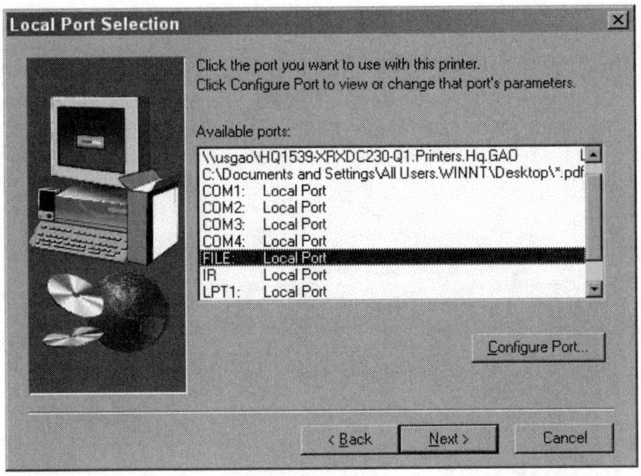

9. Click **Next**.
10. In the **Select Printer Model** dialog box, click **Browse...**.

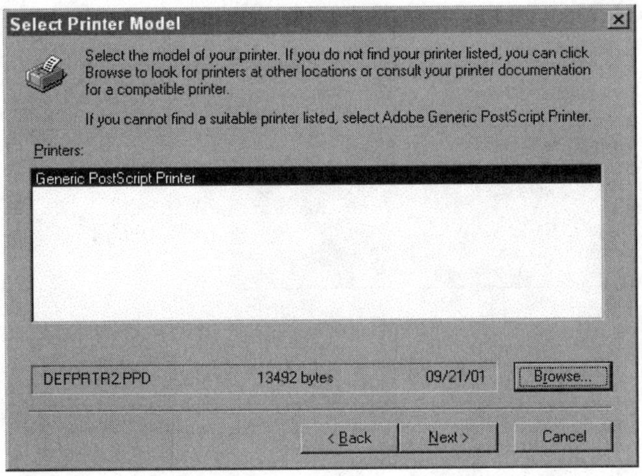

11. Navigate to the location of the Linotronic 330 or Acrobat PPD and choose **Linotronic 330 or Acrobat Distiller** under the **Printers** list.

Note: *The Linotronic 330 PPD will need to be downloaded from Adobe's Web site (http://www.adobe.com) or from the support Web site for this book. The Acrobat Distiller PPD can be found in the Acrobat installation directory in the Distiller > Xtras folder.*

12. Click **OK**.

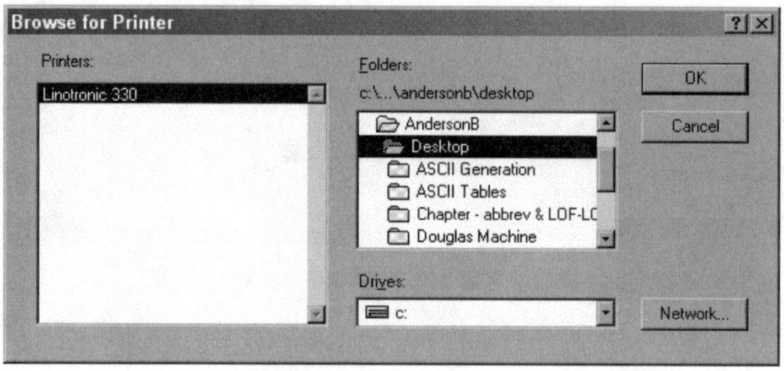

13. Select **Linotronic 330**.

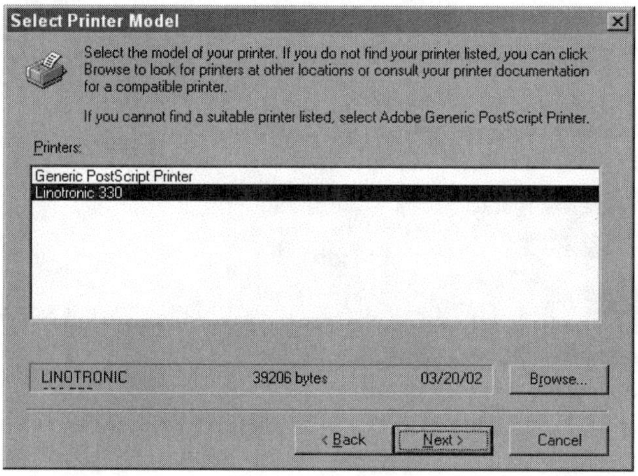

14. Click **Next**.

15. Select **Not shared**.

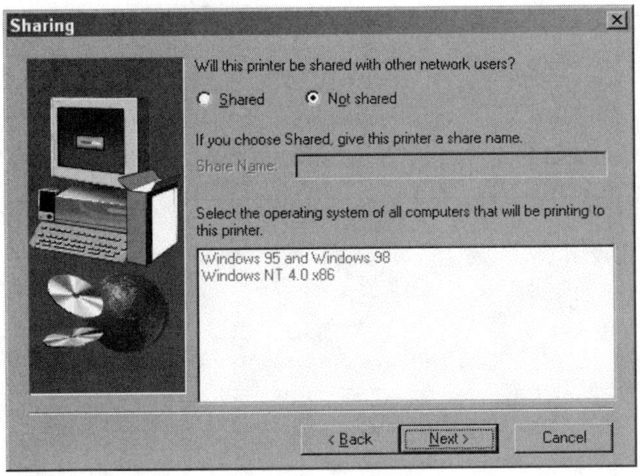

16. Click **Next**.
17. Name the printer **Prepress - Linotronic 330**.

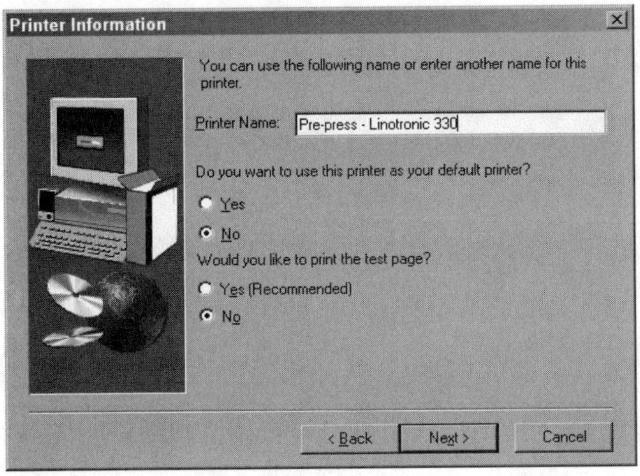

18. Select **No** to the questions about the default printer and test page.

19. Click **Next.**

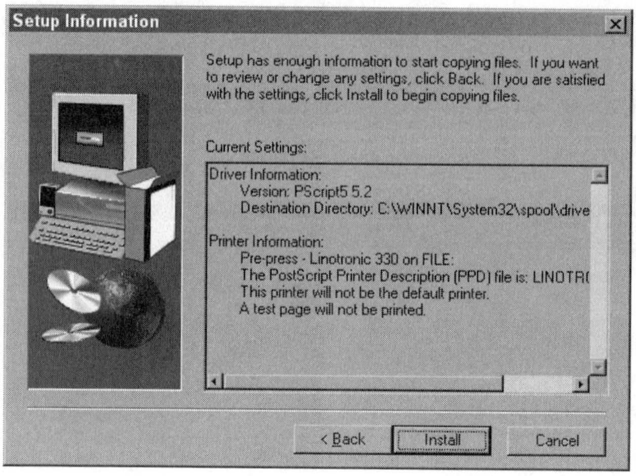

20. Click **Install.**
21. Answer **Yes** to configure your printer.

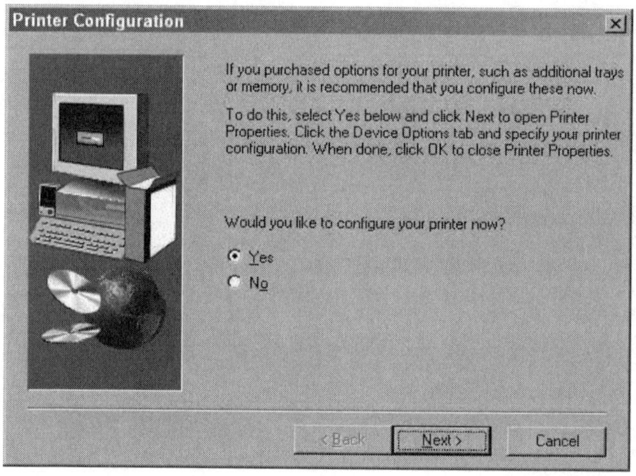

22. Click **Next.**
23. Set **Output Protocol to Binary**. This will make your PostScript file smaller.
24. Set Convert Gray Text to PostScript Gray to **Yes.**
25. Set Convert Gray Text to PostScript Gray to **Yes.**
26. Set Add Euro Currency Symbol to PostScript Fonts to **No.** Use the actual Euro currency symbol fonts from Adobe's Web site (*http://www.adobe.com*) if needed. This is only a hack.

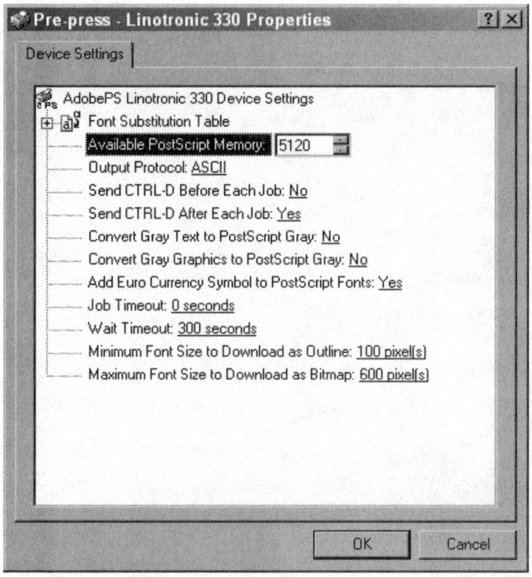

27. Click **OK**.
28. Uncheck the **Yes, I want to view the ReadMe file** option.
29. Click **Finish**.

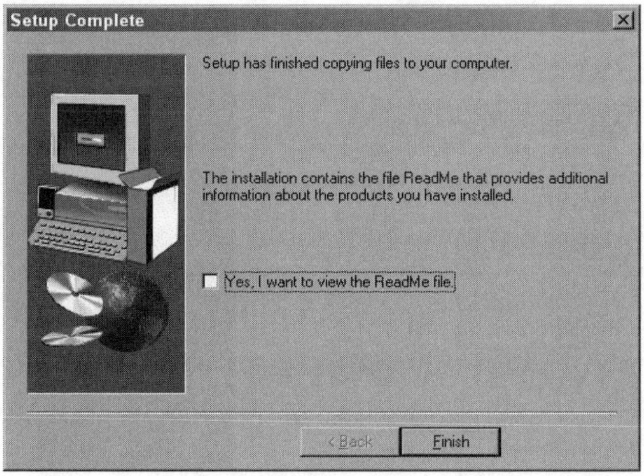

30. Select **Yes, I want to restart my computer now** to restart your computer.

31. Click **Finish**.

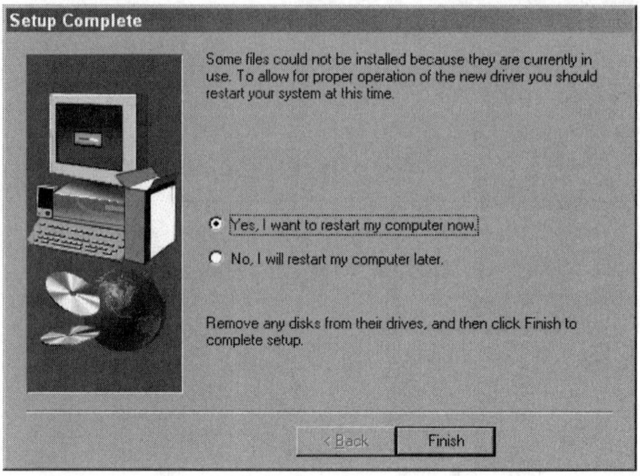

32. Your computer will reboot.

Macintosh Installation/Upgrade

Installing or upgrading Adobe's PostScript printer driver on the Mac is a very easy process. After you have downloaded (see "Downloading Adobe's PostScript Printer Driver" on page 314 for instructions) and unstuffed the installer, do the following:

1. Open the **AdobePS** folder.
2. Double-click on the **AdobePS Installer**.

3. Adobe's PostScript printer driver installer will open. Click **Continue.**

4. Accept the license agreement by clicking **Accept**.

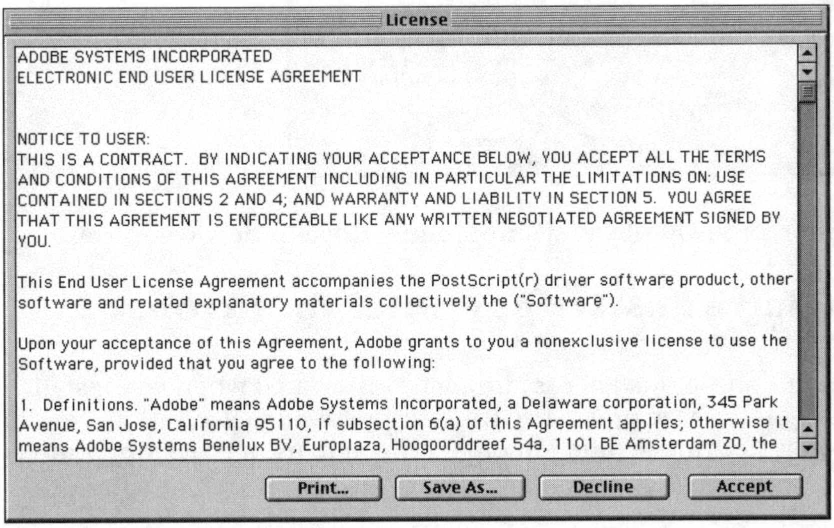

5. Select the hard drive that contains your OS 8 or 9 system folder from the Install Location options. (OS X users, select the drive that contains your classic system.)

6. Click **Install.**

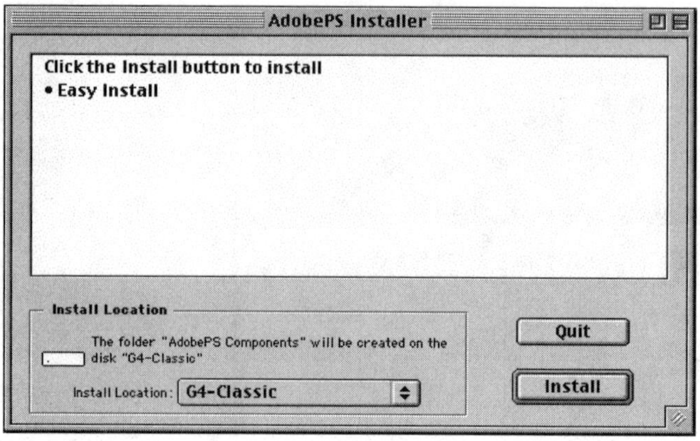

7. After installing the printer driver, you will need to restart your computer. Click **Restart**.

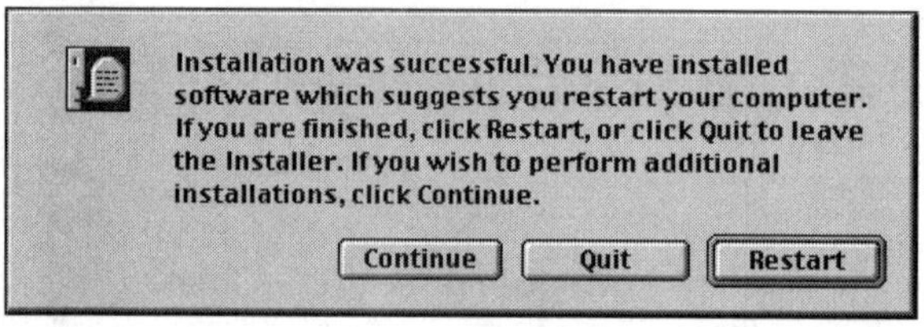

Installation of the Adobe PostScript printer driver is now complete.

Installing a PostScript Printer for Acrobat 5

A PostScript printer instance is automatically created when you install Acrobat 5 on the Mac or PC. Use this printer for all PDF creation. No other installation steps are required in order for you to use a PostScript printer with Acrobat 5.

Upgrading to the Latest PostScript Driver

The process of upgrading the PostScript printer driver is simple:

1. Download the latest PostScript printer driver from Adobe's Web site (*www.adobe.com*). See "Downloading Adobe's PostScript Printer Driver" on page 314 for instructions.
2. For PC Users:

   Run the installer and choose to update the existing printers.All desktop printers will then use this new driver.

For Mac Users:

Run the installer and install the new version of the driver. See "Macintosh Installation/Upgrade" on page 324 for instructions. All desktop printers will then use this new driver.

Acrobat Distiller Printer Settings

After you install the PostScript printer drivers, you must configure the driver for optimal output.

Printer Configuration in Windows

1. Select **Start** > **Settings** > **Printers.** A folder containing the printers on your machine will open.
2. Right-click on the Acrobat Distiller printer and select **Properties....**
3. Click on the **Device Settings** tab.
4. Set Output Protocol to **Binary.** This will create the smallest PostScript file possible.
5. Set Convert Gray Text to PostScript Gray to **Yes.**
6. Set Convert Gray Graphics to PostScript Gray to **Yes.**
7. Set Add Euro Currency Symbol in PostScript Fonts to **No.** This is a hack and is prone to creating problems. Use Adobe's free Euro PostScript fonts if the Euro symbol is needed.

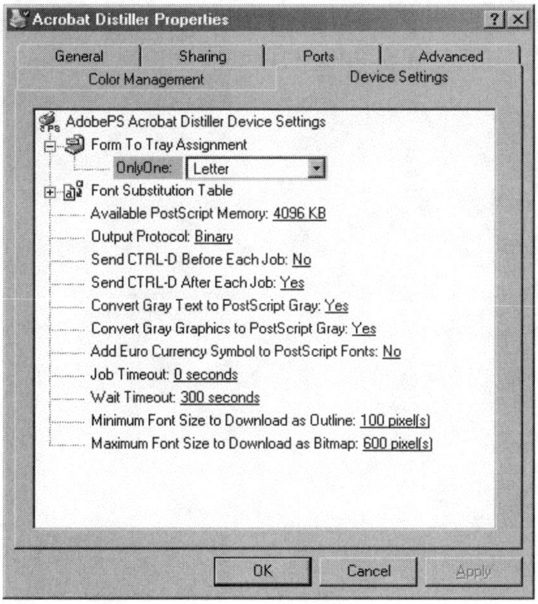

8. Click on the **Ports** tab and verify that it is using the **PDF Port** if you are using Acrobat 5, or the **Print to File** port if you are using Acrobat 4. If the PDF port is not available and you are using Acrobat 5, reinstall Acrobat 5. (See "Installing a PostScript Printer for Acrobat 5" on page 326 for instructions.)

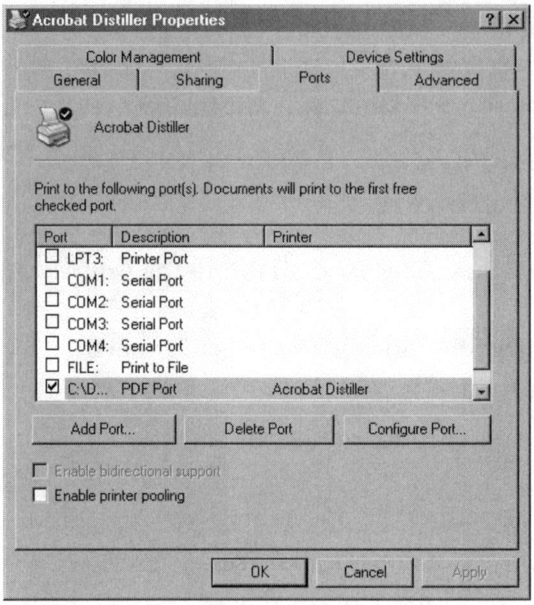

9. Click on the **Advanced** tab.
10. Select **Spool print documents so program finishes printing faster**.
11. Select **Start printing immediately. This option and the previous option** allow Windows to spool the print job so that printing occurs in the background.

12. Make sure **Enable advanced printing features** is checked.

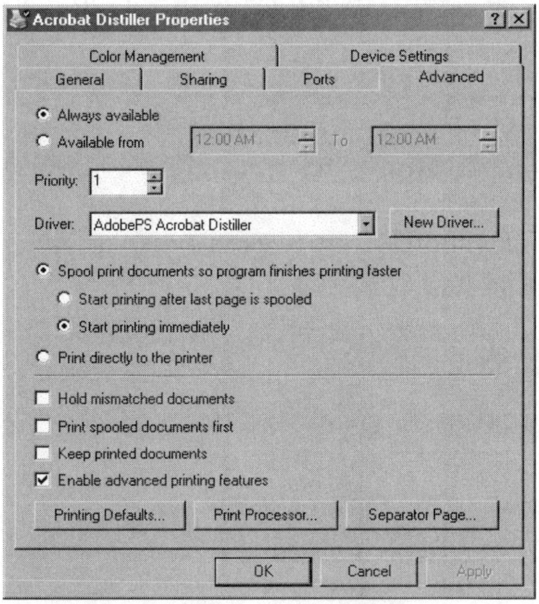

13. Click on the **Printing Defaults...** button in the lower-left corner of the Advanced tab.
14. Click on the **Advanced...** button in the lower right-hand corner of the Layout tab.

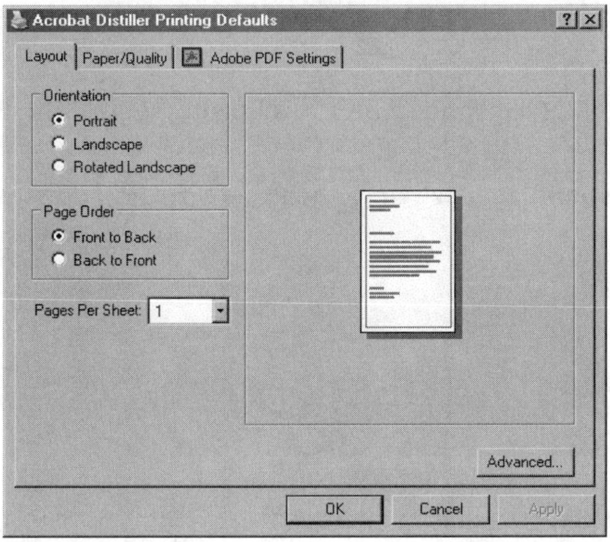

15. Set Print Quality to **600 dpi.** Doing so gets around a bug in the printer driver on the PC platform that incorrectly prints high-resolution/large EPS graphics.
16. Set TrueType Font to **Download as Softfont**.
17. Expand the **PostScript Options** if they are not expanded.
18. Set PostScript Output Option to **Optimize for Speed.** Doing so will create the smallest PostScript file possible.
19. Set TrueType Font Download Option to **Native True Type**.
20. Set PostScript Language Level to **3**.

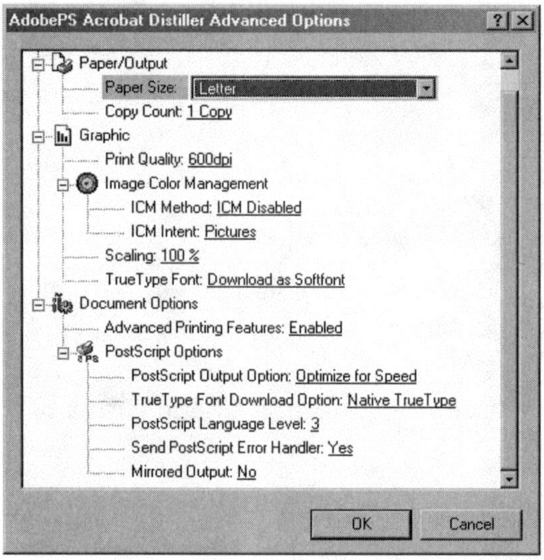

If you need a custom page size, continue with the following steps. Otherwise, skip to step 25.

21. Select **PostScript Custom Page Size** from the Paper Size drop-down list.

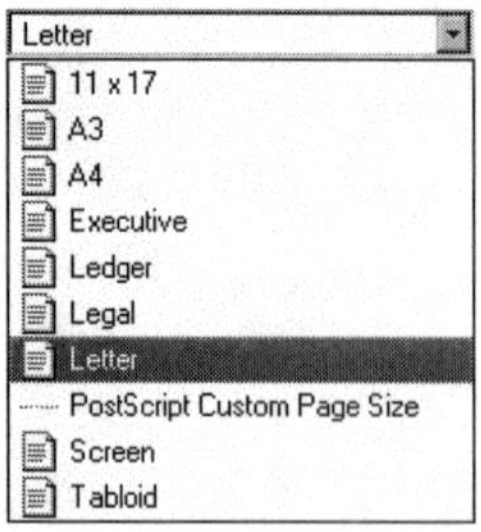

22. Set the paper size by defining the custom **width** and **height**.

23. Click **OK**.

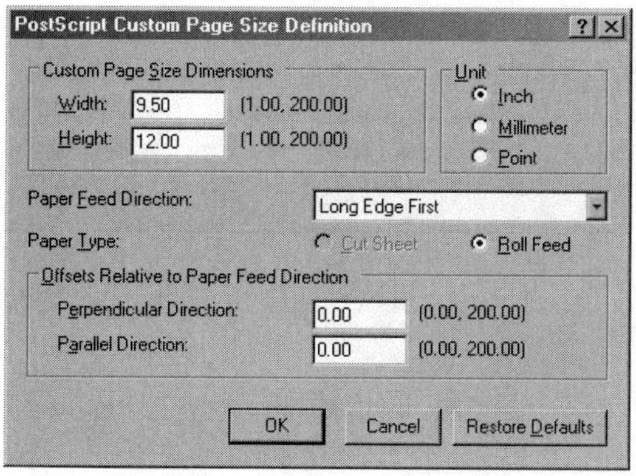

24. The Paper Size will now have changed to PostScript Custom Page Size. Click **OK**.

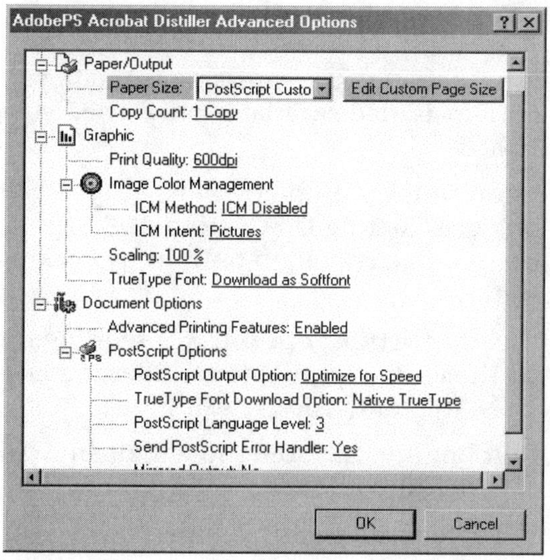

25. Click the **Paper/Quality** tab.

26. Make sure the Color option is set to **Color**.

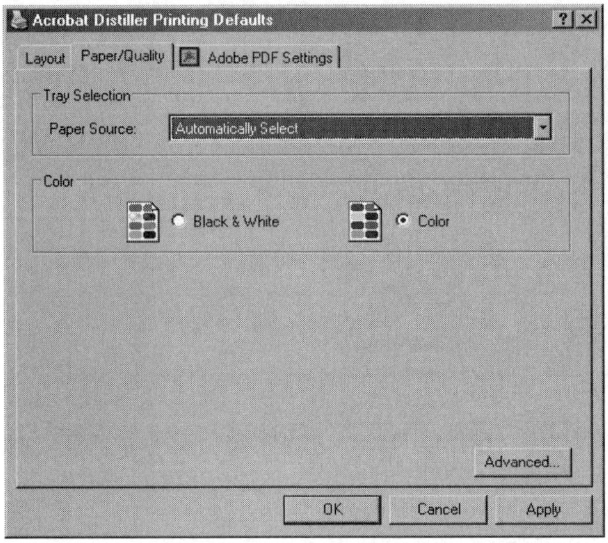

27. Click on the **Adobe PDF Settings** tab. If you are missing this tab, you will need to reinstall Acrobat 5. This tab is made available only when you do a complete installation of Acrobat 5.
28. Select **Press** from the Conversion Settings drop-down list. (If you want to set up custom PDF Job Options, see "Setting Up Custom PDF Job Options" on page 339. You can set up custom job options by clicking the **Edit Conversion Settings...** button.)
29. Uncheck the **Do not send fonts to Distiller option.** Not sending the fonts (embedding the fonts in the PostScript file) to Distiller requires Distiller to know where to access the fonts you are using.
30. Check the **View Results in Acrobat** option. Doing so will open Acrobat after the PDF is created so that you can view the completed PDF.
31. Check the **Prompt for the PDF Filename option.** Doing so will give you the opportunity to name your PDF.
32. Check the **Delete log files for successful jobs option.** Doing so will keep unnecessary log files from accumulating on your hard drive.
33. Check the **Ask to Replace existing PDF file option.** Doing so will give you a warning if you name the PDF file you are about to create with the same name as a PDF file that already exists.

34. Click **OK**.

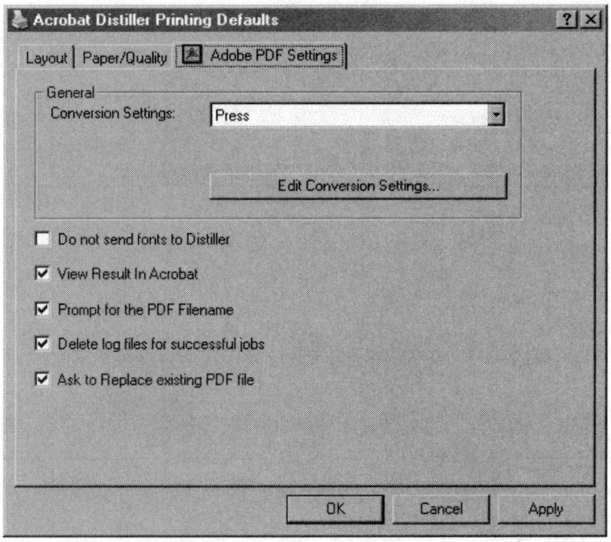

Macintosh Printer Configuration

Printer configuration on the Macintosh may be done through the Page Setup menu in FrameMaker. You can also set up desktop printers using Adobe's Desktop Printer Utility.

A desktop printer named Create Adobe PDF is installed with Acrobat 5. A desktop printer named FrameMakerPDFWriter is installed with FrameMaker 7. These printer instances and the use of the Virtual Printer can all be access through the Page Setup menu in FrameMaker.

Selecting a Printer

1. Select **File** > **Print....**
2. Make sure the **Virtual Printer** is selected for **Printer**. Make sure **File** is selected for **Destination**.

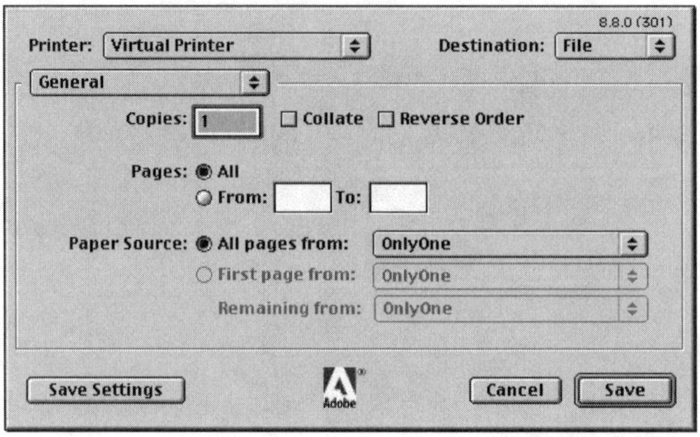

3. Select **FrameMaker** 5.x/6.x/7.x from the second pop-up. Make sure that **Odd-Numbered Pages** and **Even-Numbered Pages** are checked and that **Skip Blank Pages** is unchecked.

Including Registration Marks

1. If you wish to include registration marks, select **Western** or **Tombo** from the **Registration Marks** drop-down list—use the more common **Western** crop marks if you are unsure which one to use.
2. Make sure **Generate Acrobat Data** is unchecked. If it is checked, Acrobat Distiller will crop the PDF to the actual FrameMaker page size and you will not have the registration marks in the final PDF.

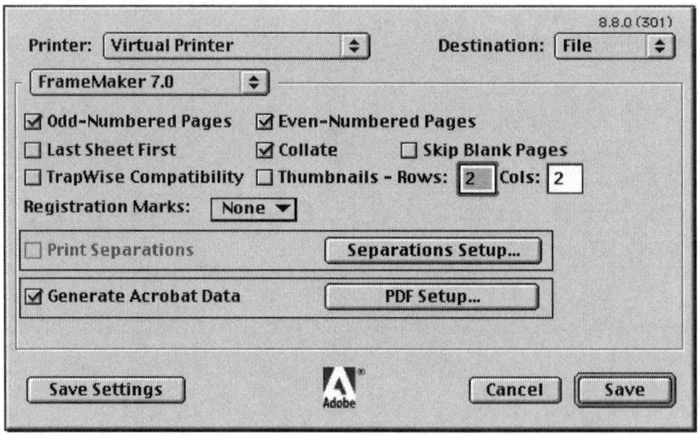

Creating Separations Settings

1. If you need to create color separations, click the **Separations Setup...** button. Otherwise, skip to “FrameMaker Page/Print Setup” on page 347. If you are using advanced features in drawing programs such as Illustrator, Freehand, or Corel Draw, it is not advisable to create color separations

from FrameMaker. Instead, create a composite PDF and let the prepress house create the separations from Acrobat.

2. After clicking the **Separations Setup...** button, you may receive a warning about the PPD not supporting CMYK separations. Click **Cancel** and see "Macintosh Configuration" on page 347 to correctly set up your virtual printer with the correct PPD.

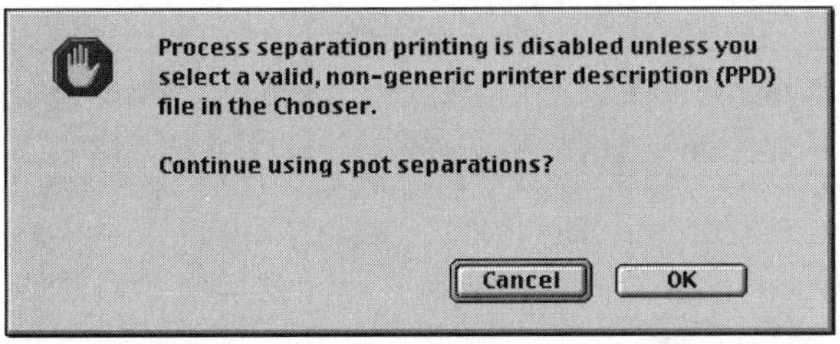

3. Make sure that **cyan**, **magenta**, **yellow**, **black**, **red**, **green**, and **blue** are in the Print As Process column. Make sure that **white** is in the Don't Print column. If your document contains any special spot colors (colors that will be printed from five or more inks), they must be listed in the **Print As Spot** column. Any color listed in the **Print As Spot** column will create a separate plate when you output. If you are unsure in which column the color should be listed, place it in the **Print As Process** column by default and then check with your printer to make sure.

Setting Halftone Screens Options

1. Select **Halftone Screens Resolution** from the drop-down list that your printer recommends you use. The options will vary depending on the PPD in use. If the default options are not satisfactory, choose **Custom** from the bottom of the list.

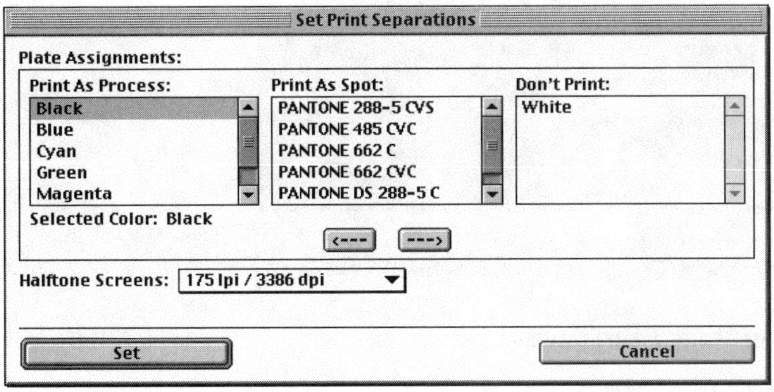

2. If you chose custom halftone screens, enter for each color the desired values for **Frequency** and for Print Angle. Set Dot Shape to **Round** unless otherwise recommended by your printer. Click **Set**.

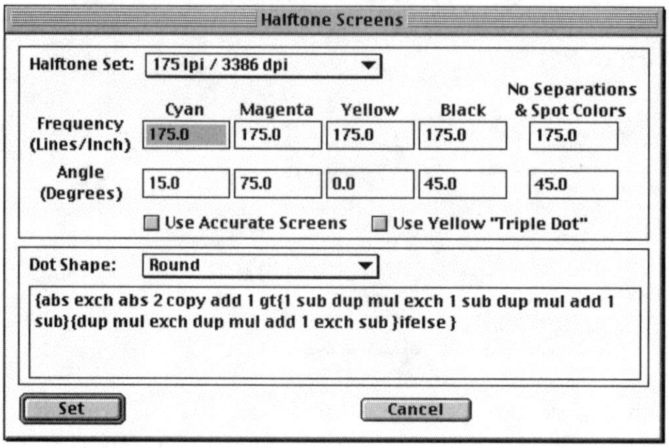

Setting Background Printing Options

1. Select **Background Printing** from the second pop-up.
2. Select **Print in Background**.
3. Select **Print Time Normal**.

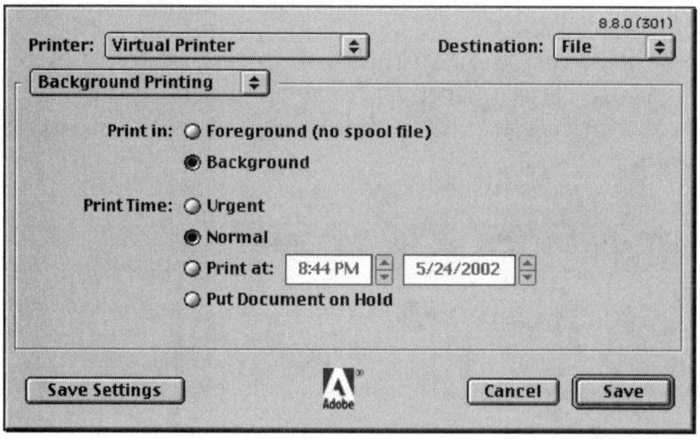

Setting Cover Page Options

1. Select **Cover Page** from the second pop-up.
2. Set Print Cover Page to **None**.

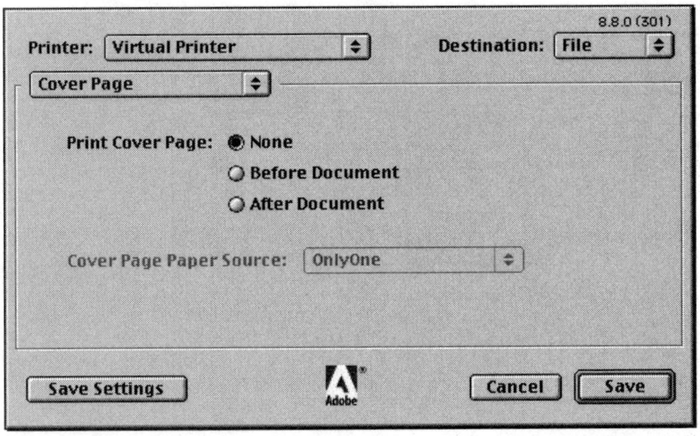

Setting Color Matching Options

1. Select **Color Matching** from the second pop-up.
2. Set Print Color to **Color/Grayscale**.

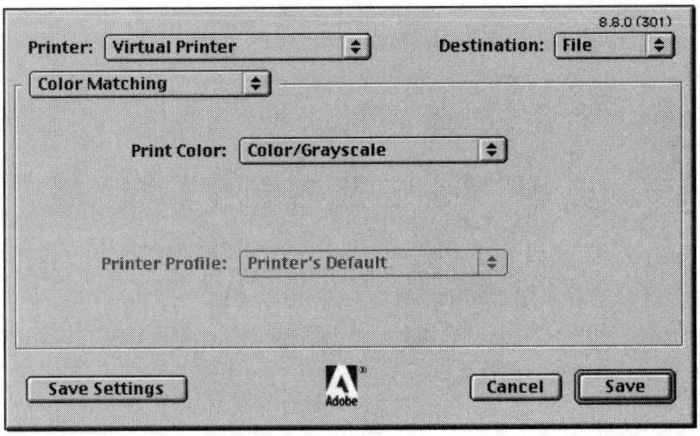

Setting Layout Options

1. Select **Layout** from the second pop-up.
2. Set "Pages per sheet" to **1**.
3. Set "Layout direction" to **1|2**.
4. Set Border to **none**.
5. Uncheck the **Print on Both Sides** option.

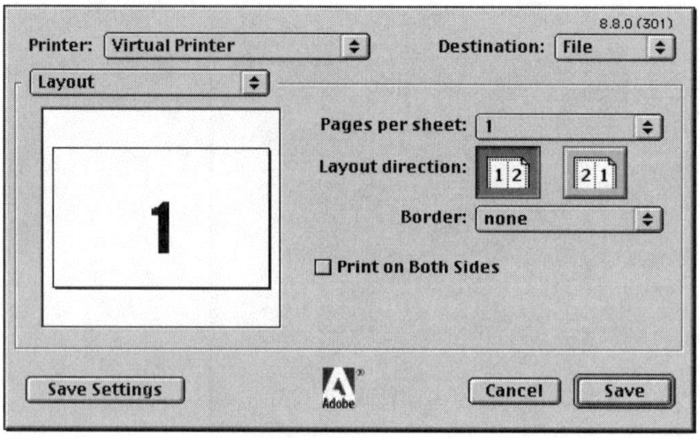

Setting Error Handling Options

1. Select **Error Handling** from the second pop-up menu.
2. Make sure **No special reporting** is selected.

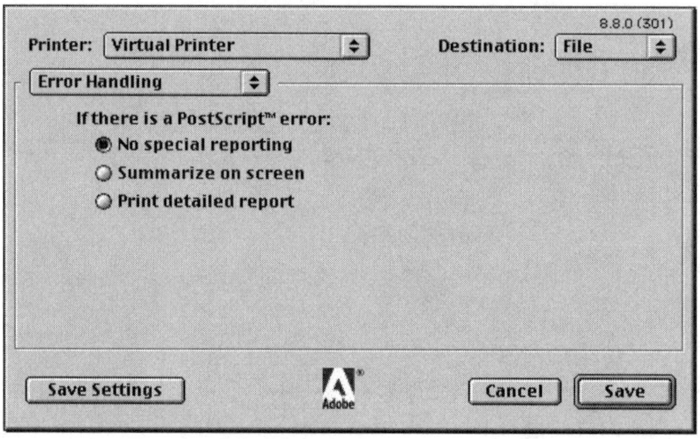

Setting PostScript Options

1. Select **PostScript Settings** from the second pop-up.
2. Set Format to **PostScript Job**.
3. Set PostScript Level to **Level 3 Only**.
4. Set Data Format to **Binary**.
5. Set Font Inclusion to **All**.

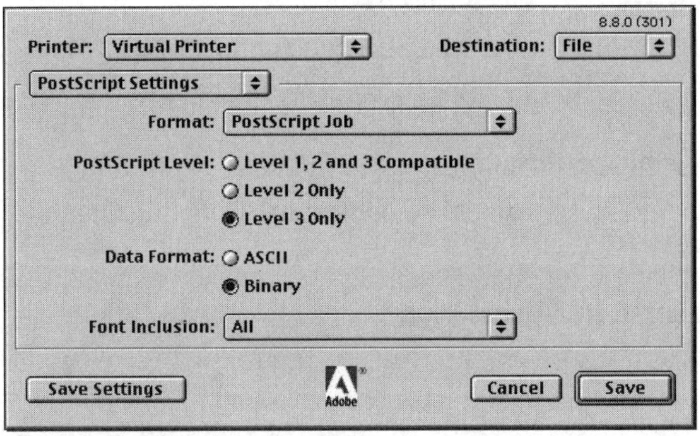

Setting Printer-Specific Options

1. Select **Printer Specific Options** from the second pop-up.
2. Set Resolution to **1200 dpi**.

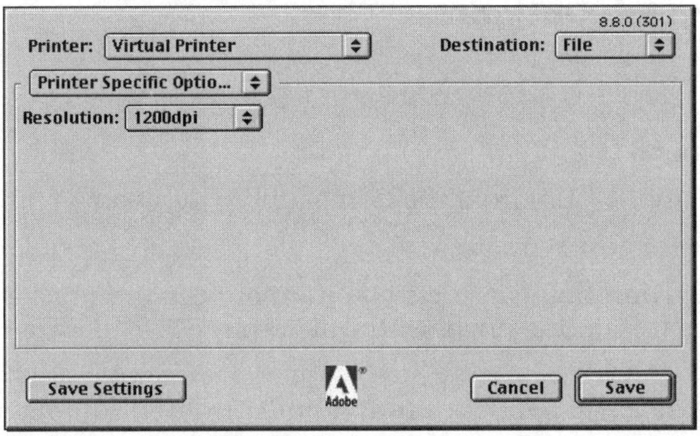

3. Click **Save Settings** in the lower-left corner of the dialog box to save your print settings.

Setting Up Custom PDF Job Options

Setting up custom job options for Acrobat Distiller allows you to vary the size of the PDF, the resolution of the images, the fonts that are embedded, and the color optimization that you'd like to use. You can access these settings from two places on the PC and from one on the Mac. The job options are then used in conjunction with the Acrobat Distiller printer on the PC, or with FrameMaker 7's "Save as PDF" functionality.

Finding Job Options on the Macintosh

To define custom job options on the Mac, first do the following:

1. Open Acrobat Distiller.
2. Select **Settings** > **Job Options....**
3. Make changes to the job options as suggested in "Defining Custom Job Options" on page 340.

Finding Job Options in Windows

To set up custom job options on the PC, first do the following:

1. In the Adobe PDF Settings tab of the Acrobat Distiller printer properties, click on the **Edit Conversion Settings...** button, or
2. Open Acrobat Distiller.
3. Select **Settings** > **Job Options....**
4. Make changes to the job options as suggested in the following section.

Defining Custom Job Options

General Settings

1. Click on the **General** tab.
2. Select **Acrobat 5.0 (PDF 1.4)** from the Compatibility drop-down list.
3. Check **Optimize for Fast Web View.**
4. Uncheck **Embed Thumbnails.** Unless you want or need thumbnails in your PDF, leaving this option unchecked will keep the PDF file size smaller.
5. Check **Auto-Rotate Pages** and select **Individually** from the drop-down list—this allows Acrobat to rotate a landscape page automatically so that it is horizontal on-screen.
6. Set Page Range to **All**.
7. Set Binding to **Left**—unless, of course, your binding is on a different edge of the document.
8. Set Resolution to **2400** dpi.
9. Unless you are regularly printing to a page size other than US Letter (8.5 x 11 inches), leave the height and width set to 612 x 782 points (8.5 x 11 inches).

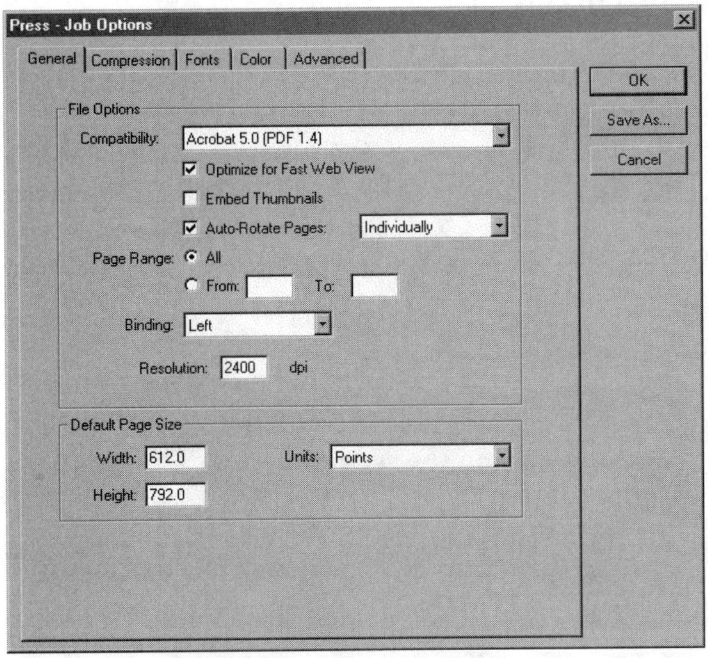

Compression Settings for Prepress

When you prepare a PDF for offset printing, it is necessary to maintain high resolution in all of your images. If you have enough disk space, I would recommend turning off (unchecking) all of the compression options except for **Compress Text and Line Art**. If you want to make your PDF smaller and still maintain good resolution, do the following:

1. Click on the **Compression** tab.
2. Check both compression settings under Color Images.
3. Set the downsampling to **Bicubic Downsampling to 300 dpi for images above 300 dpi**. (This is assuming you are printing at 150 line-screen. If you are not sure, check with your printer and then multiply the line-screen by 2 and substitute that number for the 300 dpi above.)
4. Set Compression to **Automatic** and Quality to **Maximum**.
5. Check both compression settings under Grayscale Images.
6. Set the downsampling to **Bicubic Downsampling to 300 dpi for images above 300 dpi**. (Again, assume printing at 150 line-screen.)
7. Set Compression to **Automatic** and Quality to **Maximum**.
8. Check both compression settings under Monochrome Images.
9. Set the downsampling to **Bicubic Downsampling to 1200 dpi for images above 1800 dpi**.
10. Set Compression to **CCITT Group 4**.

11. Uncheck **Anti-Alias to gray.**
12. Check **Compress Text and Line Art.**

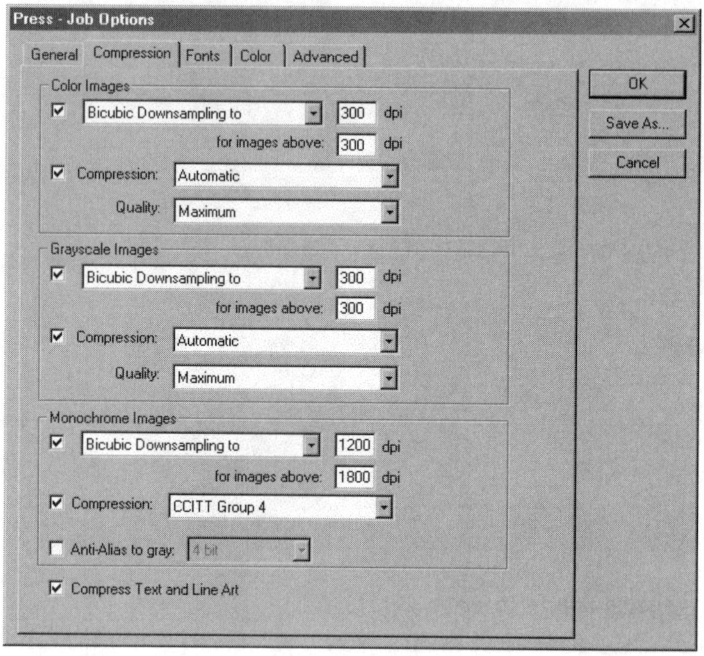

Compression Settings for On-Screen Viewing or Laser Printing

When preparing a PDF for on-screen viewing or for printing on a laser printer, it is not necessary to maintain the highest-resolution images. It is more important to make the PDF smaller so that it can be downloaded faster and viewed more quickly on-screen.

1. Click on the **Compression** tab.
2. Check both compression settings under Color Images.
3. Under Color Images, set the downsampling to **Bicubic Downsampling to 225 dpi for images above 225 dpi**. (If you want to make an even smaller PDF file, you can set the downsampling to 72 dpi—Acrobat's default setting for displaying on-screen at 100%. If you do set the downsampling to this level, you images will only look good on-screen at 100% or less. If you zoom in or print to a laser printer, your images will look "fuzzy.")
4. Set Compression to **JPEG** and Quality to **High**.
5. Check both compression settings under Grayscale Images.
6. Under Grayscale Images, set the downsampling to **Bicubic Downsampling to 225 dpi for images above 225 dpi**.
7. Set Compression to **JPEG** and Quality to **High**.

8. Check both compression settings under Monochrome Images.
9. Under Monochrome Images, set the downsampling to **Bicubic Downsampling to 1200 dpi for images above 1800 dpi**.
10. Set Compression to **CCITT Group 4**.
11. Uncheck **Anti-Alias to gray**.
12. Check **Compress Text and Line Art**.

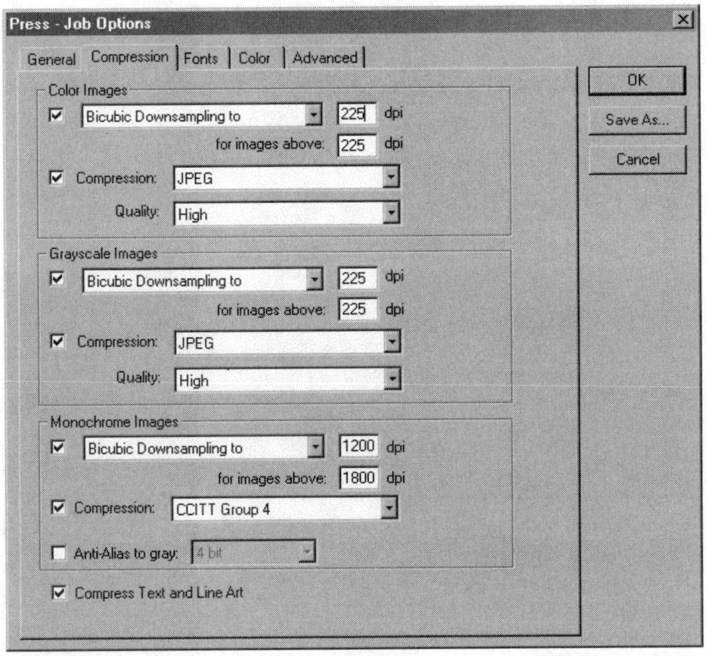

Setting Font Options

1. Click on the **Fonts** tab.
2. Check **Embed All Fonts**.
3. Check **Subset embedded fonts when percent of characters used is less than 100%**.
4. Select **Warn and Continue** from the **When Embedding Fails** drop-down list. Make sure that you check the log after creating the PDF, and make sure that any fonts that "could not be embedded" are not really used in the file. If a font cannot be embedded and it is printed, another font will be substituted for the characters that use that font—usually Courier.
5. Make sure that no fonts are listed under **Always Embed**. You don't want to embed fonts that are not used; doing so will only add to the PDF file size.

6. Make sure that no fonts are listed under **Never Embed**—you always want to embed the fonts that are used in a document so that the document will print successfully.

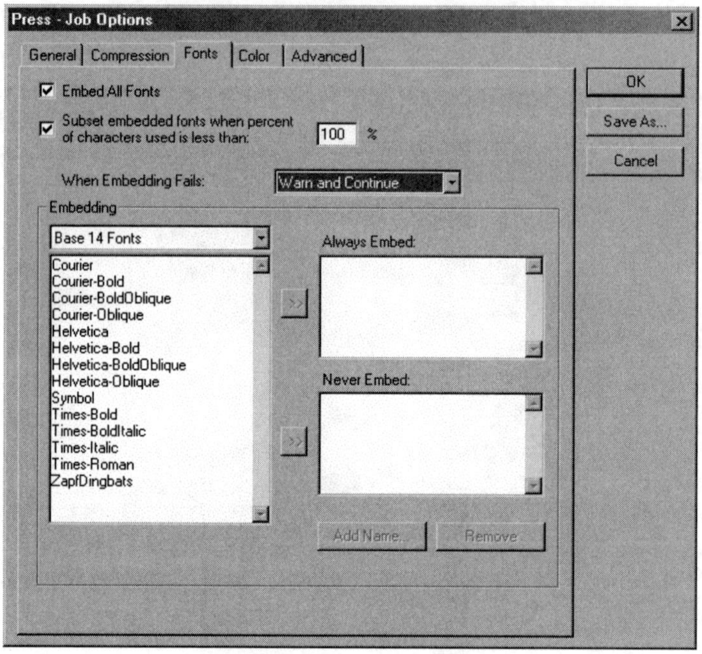

Color Settings

1. Select the Color tab.
2. Unless you are working with a printing company that has set up a successful PDF workflow and has provided color profiles, select **Color Management Off** from the Settings File drop-down list under Adobe Color Settings.
3. Check **Preserve Overprint Settings**.
4. Check **Preserve Under Color Removal and Black Generation Settings**.
5. Select **Preserve** from the Transfer Functions drop-down list.
6. Uncheck **Preserver Halftone Information**.

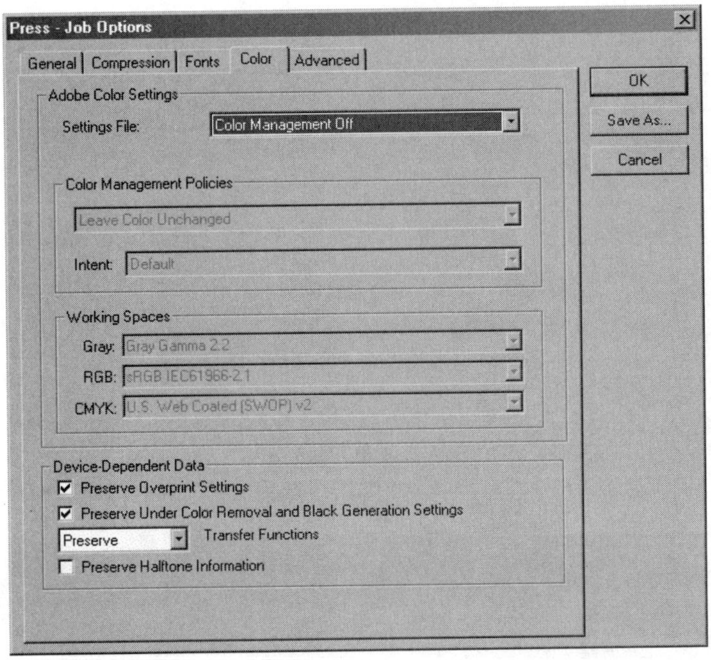

Advanced Settings

1. Uncheck **Use Prologue.ps and Epilogue.ps.**
2. Check **Allow PostScript file to Override Job Options.**
3. Check **Preserve Level 2 copypage Semantics.**
4. Check **Save Portable Job Ticket inside PDF file.**
5. Check **Illustrator Overprint Mode.**
6. Check **Convert gradients to smooth shades.**
7. Uncheck **ASCII Format.**
8. Check **Process DSC Comments.**
9. Uncheck **Log DSC Warnings.**
10. Check **Resize Page and Center Artwork for EPS Files.**
11. Check **Preserve EPS Information from DSC.**
12. Check **Preserve OPI Comments.**
13. Check **Preserve Document Information from DSC.**

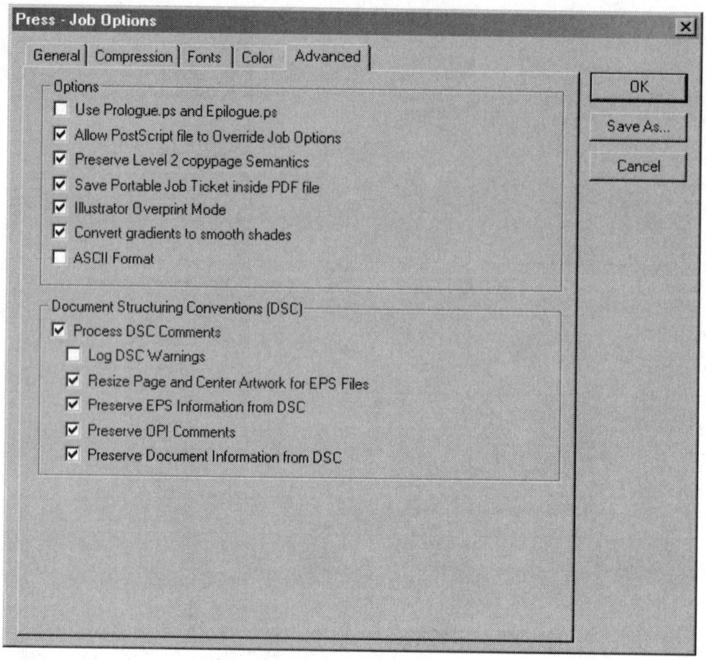

Saving Custom Settings

1. Click the **Save As...** button.
2. Name the job options "Prepress" (if you used the high-resolution compression settings) or "Online" (if you used the low-resolution compression settings).
3. Click **Save**.

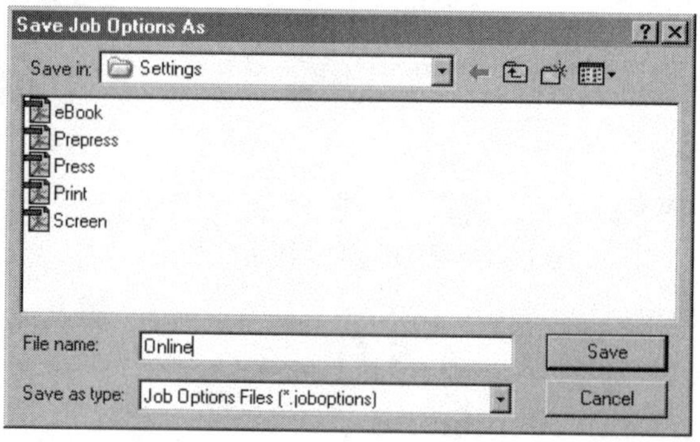

4. You'll now notice that the custom job option will be available in Acrobat Distiller, the Acrobat Distiller printer PDF settings on Windows, and in the Save As PDF option in FrameMaker 7.

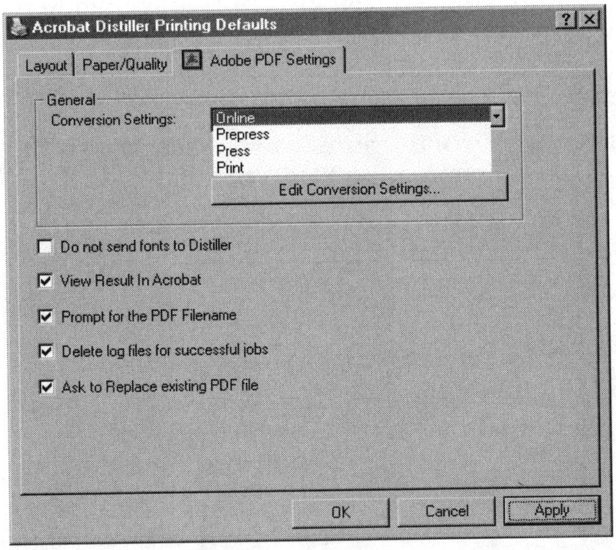

FrameMaker Page/Print Setup

Windows Configuration

Most of the printer settings can be made the default settings for the Acrobat Distiller printer in the printer properties. These same options can be temporarily changed in the Print Setup menu. To make a temporary change to the Acrobat Distiller printer, follow these steps:

1. Select **File** > **Print Setup....**
2. Make sure **Acrobat Distiller** is your chosen printer.
3. Click the **Properties...** button.
4. Follow the instructions for "Acrobat Distiller Printer Settings" on page 327 and make the necessary adjustment for job options and page size.

Macintosh Configuration

The configuration options for printers described here apply to FrameMaker 6 or 7 in either OS 9 or OS X. The Create Adobe PDF and FrameMakerPDFWriter are similar desktop printers. The Create Adobe PDF is created by Acrobat 5 upon installation. The FrameMakerPDFWriter is created when you install FrameMaker 7. Both of these printers will actually invoke Acrobat Distiller so that a PDF is created directly from FrameMaker. Using the Virtual Printer will allow you to create a PostScript file that will manually have to distill to PDF. Although I have gotten the Create Adobe PDF and FrameMakerPDFWriter to work in OS X, I recommend using the Virtual Printer to ensure that the PostScript file is created, and then distilling the file to PDF with Acrobat Distiller. Use the Create Adobe PDF from FrameMaker 6, and FrameMakerPDFWriter from FrameMaker 7 in OS 9. To configure these printers, do the following:

1. Select **File > Page Setup....**
2. In OS X Classic Mode, select **Virtual Printer as your printer. In OS 9 select Create Adobe PDF** or **FrameMakerPDFWriter.**
3. Select **Watermark** from the second pop-up and make sure that it is set to **None**—this will keep a Watermark from appearing on every page of the PDF.

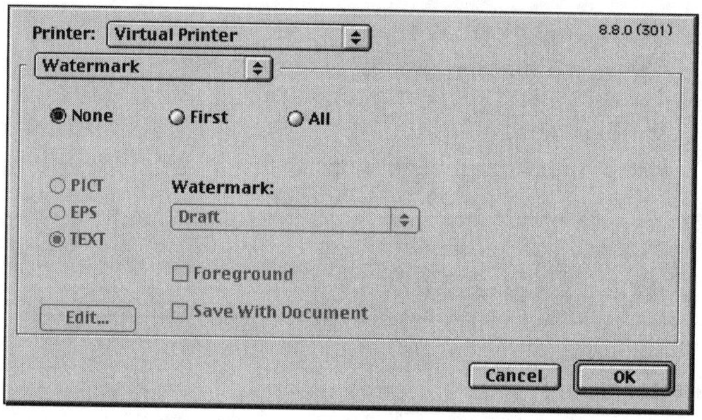

4. Select **PostScript Options** from the second pop-up and make sure that all checkboxes are unchecked—allow Acrobat to smooth text and graphics as well as take care of font substitution.

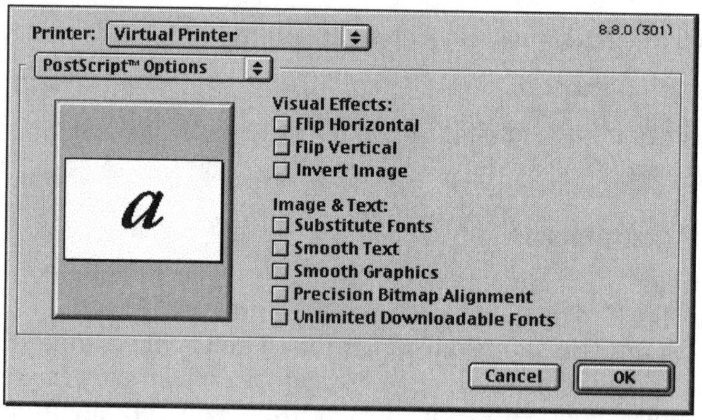

5. If you are using the Create Adobe PDF or FrameMakerPDFWriter printers, go to step 11. Otherwise, continue setting up the **Virtual Printer.**
6. From the second pop-up, select **Virtual Printer.**

7. If the current PPD is **NOT** Acrobat Distiller (or Linotronic 330 if you're using Acrobat 4), click the **Select PPD...** button.

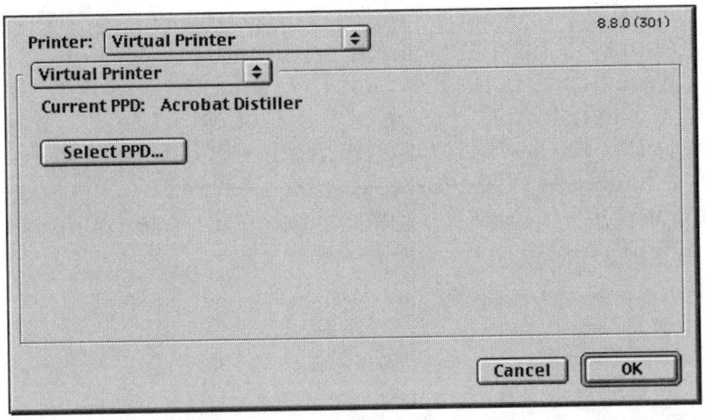

8. Select the **Acrobat Distiller** PPD (or Linotronic 330 if using Acrobat 4).
9. Click **Select**.

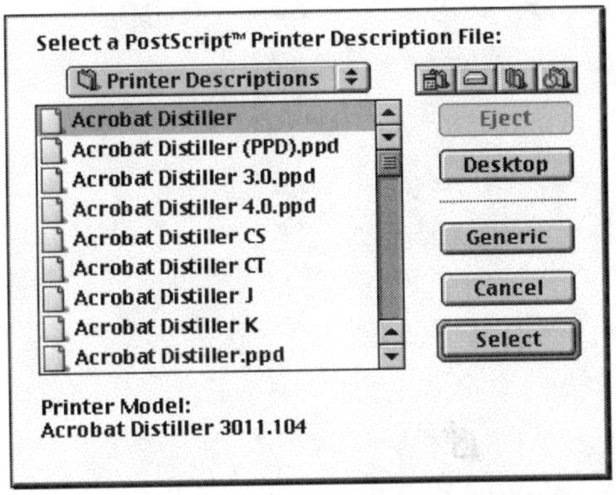

10. You may get the following warning after changing PPDs. Click **OK**.

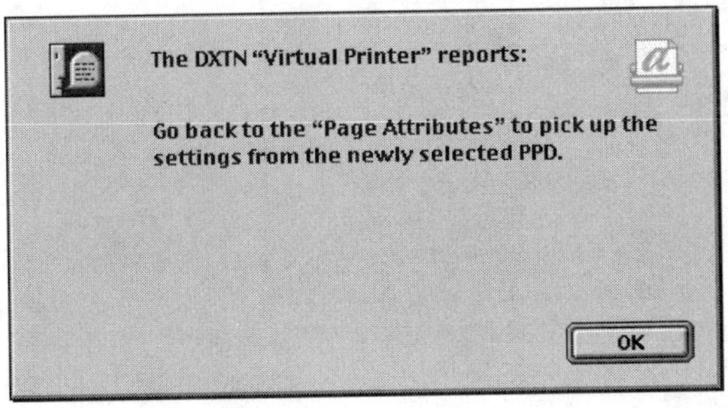

11. Select **Page Attributes** from the second pop-up.

12. From the **Paper** drop-down list, select a page size that matches your document size. If you are printing a PDF for printing and need registration marks, make sure the paper size is set at least one inch larger than the actual page size—this allows enough room for the crop marks. For example, if you have a 7-inch x 9-inch document, select Letter as the paper size. If you were printing an 8.5-inch × 11-inch document, you would have to set up a custom page size of 9.5-inches × 12-inches—sometimes called Letter Extra. If you are printing a PDF for printing with registration marks, make sure **Generate Acrobat Data** is unchecked in the FrameMaker options—otherwise, Acrobat will crop the final PDF to the actual page size in Frame.
13. If you need to set up a custom page size, continue with steps 14–19. Otherwise, click **OK**.

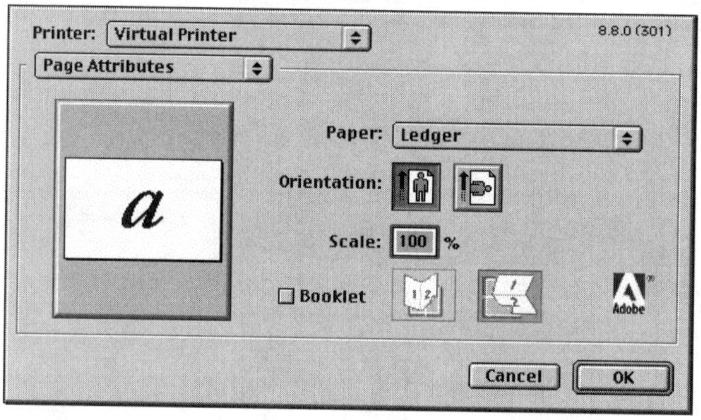

14. Select **Custom Page Default** from the second pop-up.

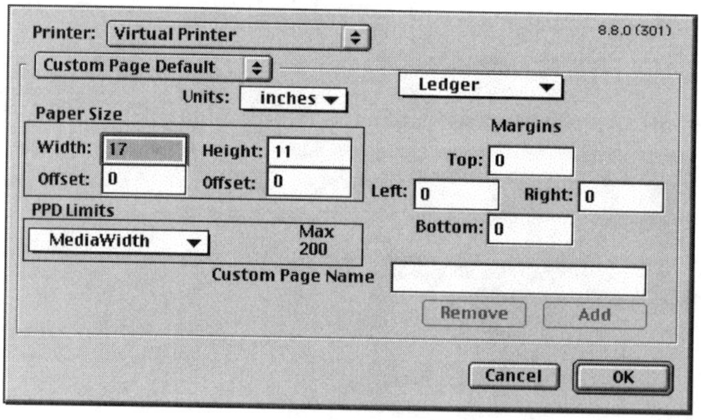

15. So you can include registration marks, define a page size that is one inch wider and taller than your page size.
16. Type a name for the new custom page size in the **Custom Page Name** input dialog.

17. Click **Add.**
18. Select **Page Attributes** from the second pop-up menu.
19. Verify that the **Paper** is set to your newly-created custom page size.
20. Click **OK.**

Windows

1. Select **File > Print Setup....**
2. Make sure that **Acrobat Distiller** is selected as the printer.
3. Click the **Properties** button.

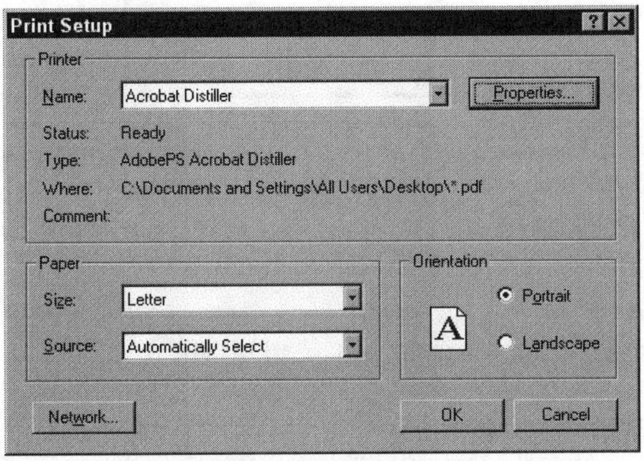

4. Select the **Adobe PDF Settings** tab—this tab will only be available with the printer that is installed with Acrobat 5. If you installed the Acrobat Distiller printer yourself or with Acrobat 4, this option will not be available.
5. Select from the **Conversion Settings** drop-down list those Acrobat job options you wish to use. If your conversion settings are not available, click **Edit Conversion Settings...** and see "Setting Up Custom PDF Job Options" on page 339 for instructions on setting up job options.

Description of PDF Options for FrameMaker

PDF Settings

The PDF settings option is new to FrameMaker 7. These options allow you to control certain elements of the PDF setup when using FrameMaker's "Save as PDF" functionality.

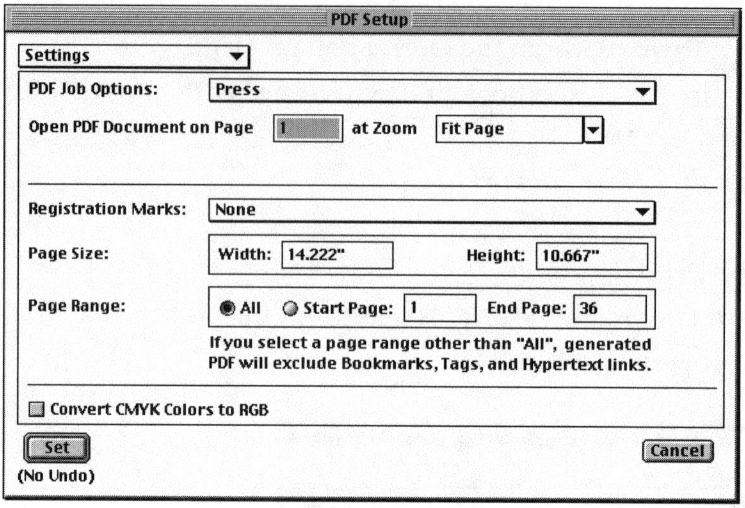

- The **PDF Job Options** drop-down list lists the job options available to Acrobat Distiller. These options contain settings such as image resolution, font embedding, color management, etc. Once you define job options within Acrobat Distiller, they will then be listed here.
- The **Open PDF Document on Page x at Zoom x** setting allows you to control which page and at what zoom level the PDF will display when opened.
- **Registration Marks** allows you to include registration marks for the printer in the PDF.
- The **Page Size** options allow you to choose the final page size of the PDF—this size can be larger or smaller than the FrameMaker page size. Setting a larger page size would allow for crop marks in the final PDF.
- The **Page Range** option allows you to specify a range of pages if you only want to output a certain number of consecutive pages.
- The **Convert CMYK Colors to RGB** option will convert all colors to the RGB color space. Only use this option for PDFs that will be viewed on-screen—do not enable this feature for a PDF that will be used to print.

Bookmarks

FrameMaker allows you to map your paragraph styles or elements to Acrobat bookmarks (see Figure 13-6).

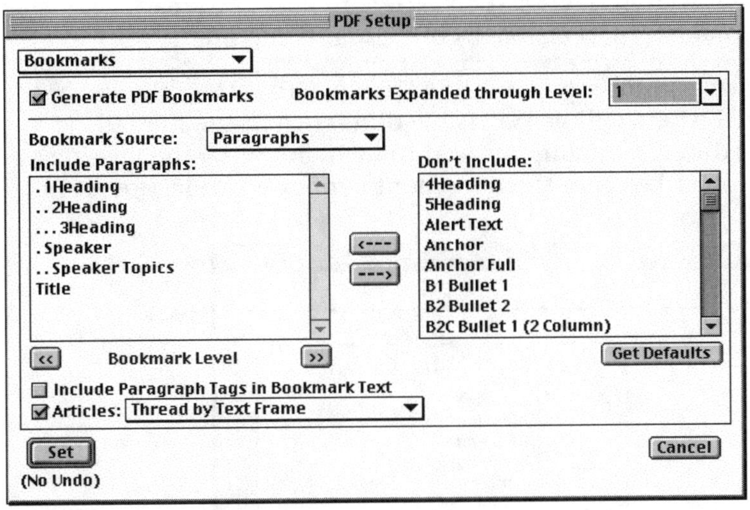

Figure 13-6 Bookmark settings.

To do so, follow these steps:

1. Enable the **Generate PDF Bookmarks** option to generate bookmarks.
2. Set **Bookmarks Expanded through Level** to the level you want.
3. Set **Bookmark Source** to either **Paragraphs** (in a regular FrameMaker file) or **Elements** (in a structured FrameMaker file).
4. Move the paragraph tags or elements you wish to show as bookmarks from the right-hand **Don't Include** window to the left-hand **Include Paragraphs/Elements** window. You can move paragraph tag names by either double-clicking on them in either window or by selecting the name and clicking the arrow buttons in the middle of the dialog box.
5. Position the paragraphs/elements by adjusting their **Bookmark Level** using the two arrow buttons at the bottom of the Include Paragraphs window. The paragraphs/elements listed furthest to the left will be the highest-level bookmarks. Dots in front of the paragraph/element name indicate the sublevel of the bookmark.
6. **Include Paragraph Tags in Bookmark Text** includes the paragraph tag name (i.e., 1Heading) in each bookmark, which may be helpful in proofreading a document but may not look good in the final PDF.
7. **The Articles options**, Thread by Text Frame or Thread by Column, help to dictate the flow of text in the PDF. For most purposes, the **Thread by Text Frame** option is the best selection.

Tagged PDF

By creating a tagged or structured PDF, you are including the overall structure of the document in your PDF file. A new functionality of Acrobat 5 allows a document to be reflowed in devices such as a Palm Pilot. By creating a tagged PDF, you are also making it accessible to the visually impaired.

The "tagged" information is stored in the PDF file. Other than the larger file size of the final PDF, there will be no visible difference in the file. All paragraph tags used in the document need to be included in the tagging at the paragraphs' correct levels in the document structure (see Figure 13-7).

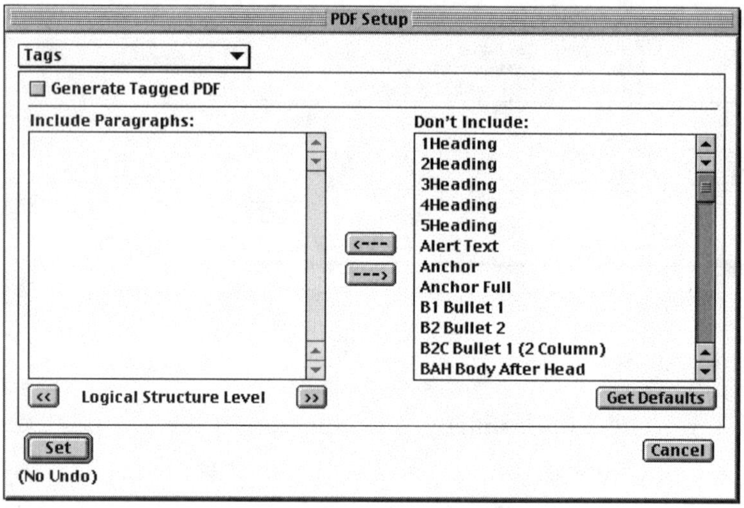

Figure 13-7 Tags settings.

The following steps descripe the setup for creating a tagged PDF:

1. Enable the **Generate Tagged PDF** option to include document structure information in the final PDF.
2. Move the paragraph tags you wish to include in the structure from the right-hand **Don't Include** window to the left-hand **Include Paragraphs** window. You can move paragraph tag names by either double-clicking on them in either window or by selecting the name and clicking the right or left arrow buttons in the middle of the dialog box.
3. Position the paragraphs by adjusting their **Logical Structure Level**. The paragraphs listed furthest to the left will be the highest level in the structure. Dots in front of the paragraph name indicate their subordination to paragraphs with a higher priority.

Links

Every object in FrameMaker has a unique code. These codes can be included for all elements and/or paragraph tags. When you include all of these codes, separate links from other Web pages/PDFs can be created to a particular point in your PDF. When you activate this option, your PDF files will be significantly larger. Only activate this option if you are creating separate PDF files for each chapter/file in your book or if you are creating a bunch of interlinked PDFs. If your final delivery is a single, self-contained PDF, do not activate this option.

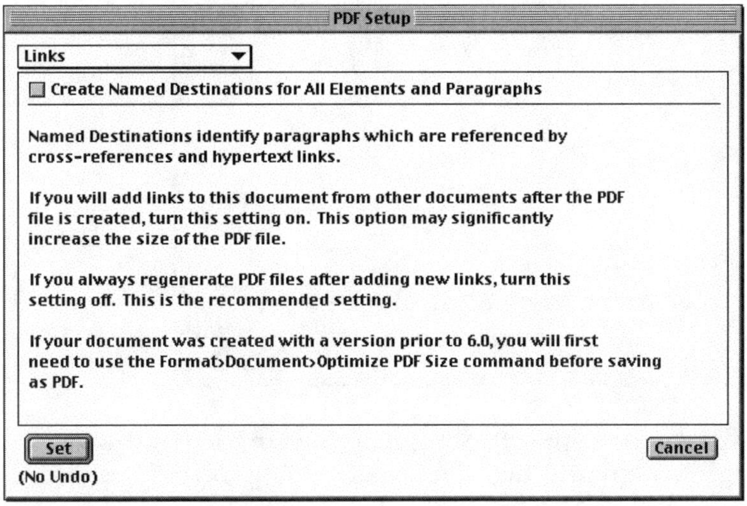

Figure 13-8 Links settings.

Creating a PDF from FrameMaker

Saving a PDF from FrameMaker 7

FrameMaker 7 has finally resolved the problems associated with the Save As PDF function in FrameMaker 5.5 and 6—now it really works (except in OS X on the Macintosh). If you are using FrameMaker 7, create PDF files by saving your file or book as PDF:

1. Select **File** > **Save As...**.
2. Navigate to the location in which you wish the PDF to be saved.
3. Name the PDF file. (Include the .pdf extension.)
4. Select **PDF...(*.pdf)** from the Save as type drop-down list.

5. Click **Save**.

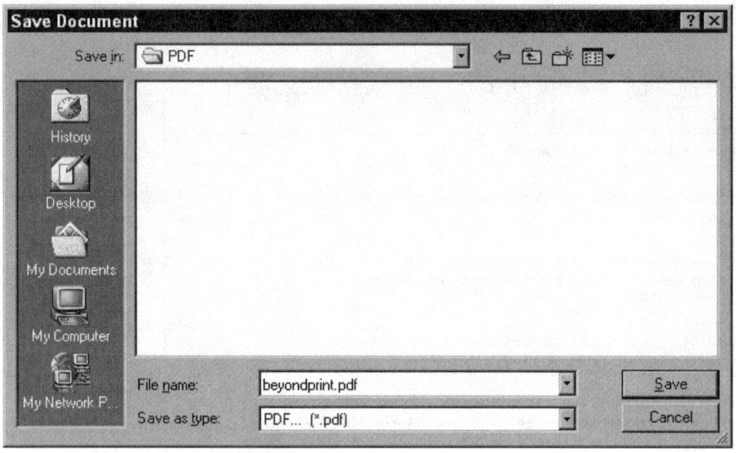

6. The PDF Setup dialog box appears. Set the options in each of the four folders—Settings, Bookmarks, Tags, Links—according to your desired settings. See "Description of PDF Options for FrameMaker" on page 351 for a description of each option available.
7. Click **Set**.

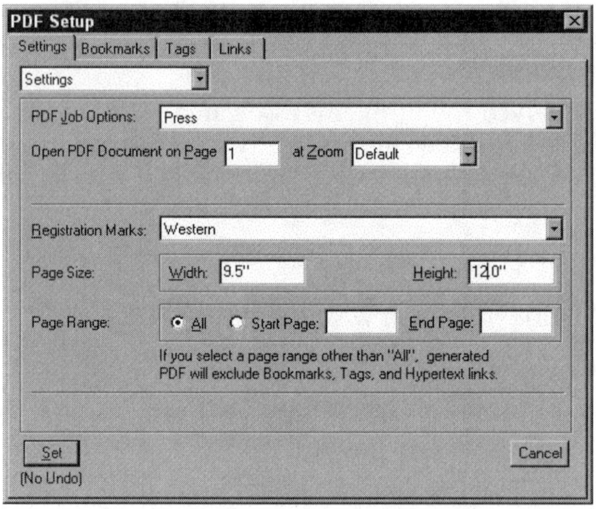

8. FrameMaker will now generate a PDF file in the location you specified, and Acrobat (Acrobat Reader) will then open the PDF file once it is created.

Creating a PDF from Acrobat 4

1. Set **Acrobat Distiller** as your default printer on the PC, or as **Virtual Printer** on the Mac.
2. With your single FrameMaker file or book file open and selected, print the file by selecting **File** > **Print**.
3. After you click **Print**, you will be asked where you want to save the file and what you want to name the file. Name the file with a **.ps** extension—if you are using Windows 95 or 98, windows may substitute the .ps extension with .prn.
4. Navigate to the location that you specified and find the **PS** file.
5. Open **Acrobat Distiller**.
6. Drag the **PS** file onto the Acrobat Distiller interface.
7. Acrobat Distiller will now ask where you want to save the PDF. Save the **PDF** file to your desktop.
8. Open the PDF file and verify that it looks correct.

Creating a PDF from Acrobat 5

1. Set **Acrobat Distiller** as your default printer on the PC, or **as Create Adobe PDF** on the Mac.
2. With your single FrameMaker file or book file open and selected, print the file by selecting **File** > **Print**.
3. After you click **Print**, you will be asked where you want to save the file and what you want to name the file. Name the file with a **.pdf** extension.
4. The PDF file will open automatically in Acrobat after the printing is finished. Verify that it looks correct.

Note: *Acrobat 6 is available and has been released in Professional and Standard versions. When you install Adobe Acrobat 6.0 (Standard or Professional edition), an Adobe PDF printer installs. This printer may be used with FrameMaker. Select this printer and follow the PDF Setup procedures, which are similar to the PDF Setup for the Acrobat 5.0 printer drivers. If you are using Acrobat 6.0 and FrameMaker 7/7.1, you should be able to safely use the "Save As PDF" (in addition to the Print to Postscript method that works for all versions of FrameMaker). Caution—the Save As PDF does not work properly in all versions of FrameMaker. See the Adobe website for more information.*

Summary

Creating a PDF for printing or for online distribution is a very simple and fast process using FrameMaker. It is important that the printer driver has the correct settings and that Acrobat Distiller has properly configured job options. If both the printer driver and Acrobat Distiller have been configured correctly, creating a PDF from FrameMaker 7 is a one-step process.

14

An Introduction to Database Publishing with FrameMaker

Bradley Anderson

This chapter explores options for database publishing using FrameMaker.

Applicable to all versions of FrameMaker

An Introduction to Database Publishing

Database publishing is the process by which information is automatically taken from one or more data sources—including any number of databases, flat files, and images—and assembled into a complete document. Examples of publications produced by database publishing include directories, catalogs, price lists, invoices, financial statements, and reports. This chapter is written for those individuals beginning the process of publishing information from a database. It explores different methods of retrieving data (both static and dynamic) and publishing data with FrameMaker.

Note: *With the release of FrameMaker 7, the desktop version of FrameMaker is not licensed for entirely-automated, server based publishing. FrameMaker Server 7 has the same technology as the desktop version of FrameMaker but has a license for use in server-based solutions. See Adobe's website for more information about FrameMaker Server 7 and download their white paper on database publishing.*

Automated Tagged Publishing vs. Data-Driven Publishing

Database publishing can be segregated into two broad categories—automated tagged publishing and data-driven, dynamic publishing. What's the difference? Automated tagged publishing is the process by which a flat file (basically a big text file with special markups or tags in it) is parsed and published with FrameMaker. Data-driven publishing is the process by which data is retrieved (in real time) from the database and published (in real time) into FrameMaker—there is no need for an intermediary markup language or text file. Although automated tagged publishing solutions are partially data-driven (e.g., they decide what to publish based on values in the tagged file they are parsing), the entire process is not data-driven.

There are many applications on the market that claim to be data-driven publishing solutions when, in fact, they are nothing more than sophisticated flat-file parsers. Many database publishing applications do not communicate directly with a database when they publish. Many use an intermediary markup language that the application parses when they publish. In other words, a markup file such as MML, XML, or MIF needs to be created from the database. Then the database publishing application parses the markup file and "publishes" the information. Automated publishing with FrameMaker can be done with MML, MIF, XML, Miramo, Unimerge, or DL Formatter.

Database Publishing Applications

There are many applications on the market for database publishing. The following database publishing applications work (at some level) with FrameMaker.

Data-Driven Publishing Applications

- BookDB from Sabern—*www.sabern.nl/bookdb.html*
- CatBase from CatBase Software Ltd.—*www.catbase.com*
- Catalogger from Guidance—*www.guidance.nl/products/catalogger.php*
- Expert Publisher from Shared Content Solutions—*www.databasepub.com/expert_publisher.htm*
- FrameScript® from Finite Matters Ltd.—*www.framescript.com*
- PatternStream® from Finite Matters Ltd.—*www.patternstream.com*

Automated Tagged Publishing Applications

- Miramo from Datazone Ltd.—*www.miramo.com*
- Unimerge from Refined Reports—No Web site available
- DL Formatter from Datalogics—*www.datalogics.com/formatter.asp*

Variable Printing Applications

- DL Pager from Datalogics—*www.datalogics.com/pager.asp*

Author's Choice

The author has been involved with database publishing for many years. After evaluating the tools on the market, he chose PatternStream as his preferred database publishing solution. In addition to PatternStream, he also uses FrameScript for very simple database publishing projects (like the example used in this chapter).

The examples in this chapter will give you a representative idea of what is involved in database publishing. Even though a couple of examples refer to specific database publishing applications, this chapter is not meant to endorse any particular database publishing application or solution. There is not enough room to lay out a step-by-step example for each product.

The Cost of Setting Up the Initial Database Publishing System

The costs involved in a database publishing project can be hard to quantify. Many (if not most) companies fail to understand or are unable to quantify the costs involved. Many software vendors selling database publishing solutions are not clear on what additional costs are involved other than the software they are selling. The costs involved in database publishing encompass more than just the software, and will be the highest up front. Once the system is in place, the savings resulting from the now-automated process should pay for the initial setup costs very quickly (see Table 14-1).

Table 14-1 High-Level Project Steps and Time Requirements

High-Level Project Steps	Percentage of Time
Setting up the database	30%–60%
Getting information from the database to publish	10%–30%
Setting up the publishing application	10%–40%
On-going Support	0%–20%

Setting Up the Database

The first cost in database publishing is the cost of the database itself. This step is the most important to consider as it will affect the ease of publishing and the actual content of your final product. Setting up and populating the database will comprise 40%–60% of the time necessary to set up a database publishing solution. This could be the most costly part of the project as well—usually involving a database administrator. Setting up the database can be the most important step in any project. The structure of the database will determine the flexibility with which the data is retrieved or output.

Before you can set up the database, you need to answer some questions:

- Who will set up the database structure and populate the data?
- Will you use an off-the-shelf solution (such as CatBase) or will you set up a custom database solution with a database such as Access, FileMaker Pro, SQL Server, MySQL, SyBase, or Oracle, along with possible flat files such as Excel spreadsheets and ASCII?
- How many people will be involved in setting up the database and populating it?
- How much time will this take?

Getting Information from the Database to Publish

Getting the data from the database and putting it in the desired order and format is the next big budget hurdle in a database publishing project. Before you start, you'll need to answer some more questions:

- How will you get the data to FrameMaker for publishing?
- Will you "dump" the data from the database in a markup language such as MML, XML, MIF, or some other markup language that then needs to be run through another database publishing application that understands the markup and then output in Frame?
- Will the database be queried directly and the data pushed into FrameMaker on the fly?

If the data is "dumped" into a markup file, the initial cost involved is usually more because a database administrator is usually required. If the data is directly queried from the database, the costs are usually lower because the database administrator is only needed to answer occasional questions from the publishing staff person performing the queries during the initial setup. After the initial setup using either technique, the only further cost will be for executing the queries. The time requirement for getting the initial data (writing the SQL queries and/or reports) will be 10%–30% of the project.

Setting Up the Publishing Application

The next step in database publishing is setting up the publishing application. This step includes designing the final FrameMaker templates, getting the data (whether directly from the database or from static markup files), and putting the data into the template. This step will comprise 10%–30% of the time required to complete the project.

Here are some questions you'll need to answer before you set up the publishing application:

- Are you using a solution that will need to parse markup files generated from the database?
- Are you using a solution that will query the data directly from the database?
- Will you design the FrameMaker templates yourself?

Ongoing Support

The final cost to consider when starting a database publishing project is the cost of ongoing support. In order to choose your method of ongoing support, you need to answer these questions:

- What will future editions of your project cost?
- How often will you need to upgrade the software/hardware involved?
- Will you need further support from a database administrator to build custom queries?
- Will you need to maintain a support contract on the software or process you are using?
- What is the cost of keeping your employee(s) current in the software used versus outsourcing the publishing?

When considering the cost of implementing a database publishing project, make sure to consider all of these costs and not just a single cost (such as the price of software). The cost of the software may only be a small portion of the total cost of the project.

Publishing a Simple Directory from a Database

Figure 14-1 is a sample page from a large directory published from a relational database. In this example you will see the decisions that need to be made when you embark on a database publishing project. Although most database publishing projects are much more complex than this and include items such as images and tables, this examples gives a basic idea of what is involved in database publishing and the approach you should use for your project.

Determining the Output of a Directory Listing

Now take a closer look at one of the directory entries from this sample. At first glance, the entry looks fairly easy and straight-forward. We are outputting a company's FML number, name, trade name, address, city, state, zip+5, zip+4, phone number, list of executives and his/her titles, SIC number(s), and SIC description(s). Each of these items has a particular paragraph style associated with it (see Figure 14-2).

Now take a closer look at the decisions that need to be made for each entry:

- Does the company have a trade name? If so, output it. If not, don't output the default text "Trade Name" or the paragraph allocated for it.
- Does the company have a zip+4 code? If so, output the zip+5 and the zip+4 with an en dash in between them. If not, output only the zip+5 without the en dash.
- Does the company have a phone number? If so, format the phone number as (###) ###-#### and output it. If not, don't output the paragraph allocated for it.
- Does the company have any executives listed? If so, output each of them in a separate paragraph. If not, don't output the paragraph(s) allocated for them.
- If the company has executives, does the executive have a title? If so, output the executive's name along with a tab and the executive's title. If not, output only the executive name without the tab (so you're not left with a leader and no text following it).
- Does the company have any SIC codes? If so, how many? If one, output the SIC code (with a character format applied to make it red) followed by a colon. If more than one, output each SIC code (with a character format applied to make it red) with a comma in between each SIC code. The last SIC code should be followed by a colon.
- If the company has one or more SIC codes, how many SIC descriptions does the company have? If one, output the description followed by a period. If more than one, output each SIC description followed by a semicolon, except for the last description, which should be followed by a period.

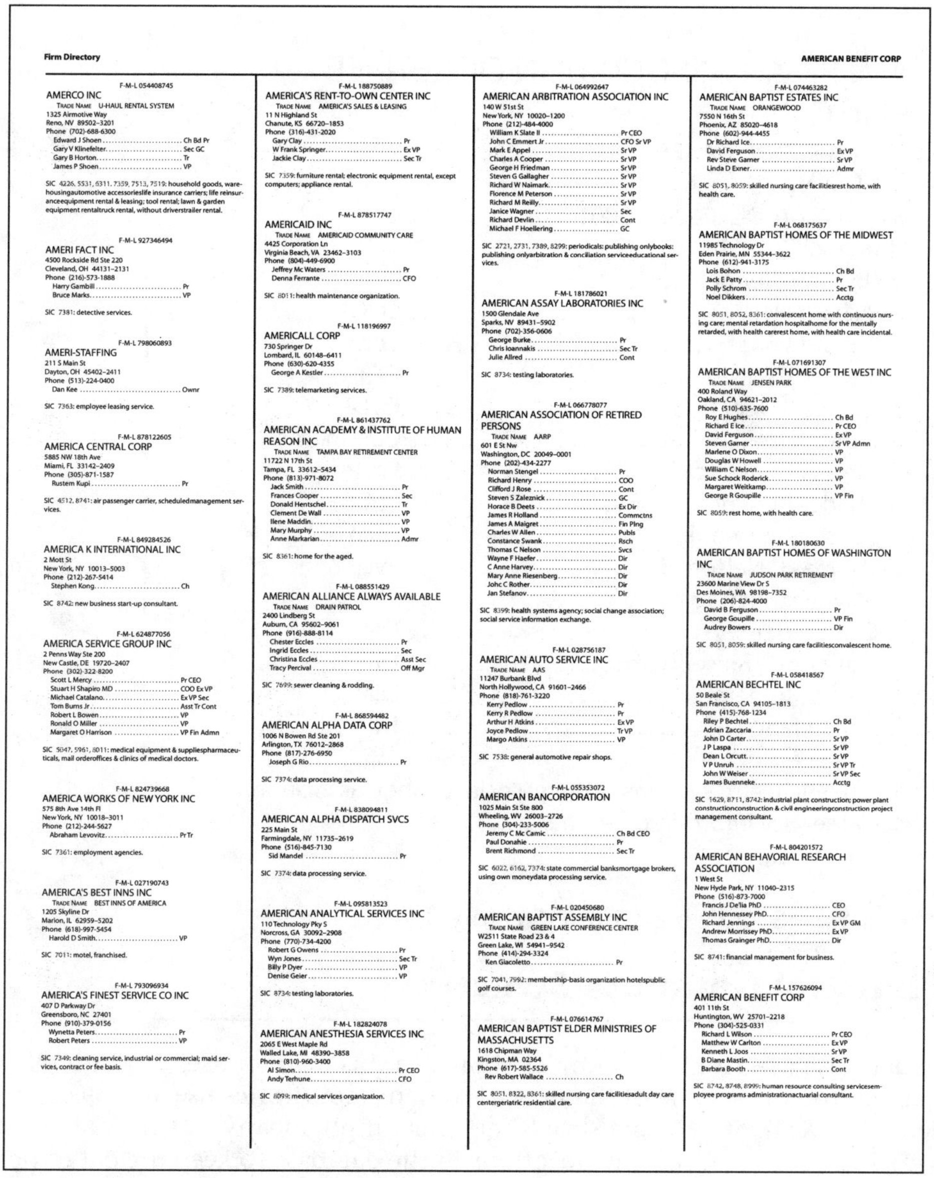

Firm Directory **AMERICAN BENEFIT CORP**

F-M-L 054408745
AMERCO INC
TRADE NAME U-HAUL RENTAL SYSTEM
1325 Airmotive Way
Reno, NV 89502–3201
Phone (702)-688-6300
Edward J Shoen .... Ch Bd Pr
Gary V Klinefelter .... Sec GC
Gary B Horton .... Tr
James P Shoen .... VP

SIC 4226, 5531, 6311, 7359, 7513, 7519: household goods, warehousingautomotive accessorieslife insurance carriers; life reinsuranceequipment rental & leasing; tool rental; lawn & garden equipment rentaltruck rental, without driverstrailer rental.

F-M-L 927346494
AMERI FACT INC
4500 Rockside Rd Ste 220
Cleveland, OH 44131–2131
Phone (216)-573-1888
Harry Gambill .... Pr
Bruce Marks .... VP

SIC 7381: detective services.

F-M-L 798060893
AMERI-STAFFING
211 S Main St
Dayton, OH 45402–2411
Phone (513)-224-0400
Dan Kee .... Ownr

SIC 7363: employee leasing service.

F-M-L 878122605
AMERICA CENTRAL CORP
5885 NW 18th Ave
Miami, FL 33142–2409
Phone (305)-871-1587
Rustem Kupi .... Pr

SIC 4512, 8741: air passenger carrier, scheduledmanagement services.

F-M-L 849284526
AMERICA K INTERNATIONAL INC
2 Mott St
New York, NY 10013–5003
Phone (212)-267-5414
Stephen Kong .... Ch

SIC 8742: new business start-up consultant.

F-M-L 624877056
AMERICA SERVICE GROUP INC
2 Penns Way Ste 200
New Castle, DE 19720–2407
Phone (302)-322-8200
Scott L Mercy .... Pr CEO
Stuart H Shapiro MD .... COO Ex VP
Michael Catalano .... Ex VP Sec
Tom Burns Jr .... Asst Tr Cont
Robert L Bowen .... VP
Ronald O Miller .... VP
Margaret O Harrison .... VP Fin Admn

SIC 5047, 5961, 8011: medical equipment & suppliespharmaceuticals, mail orderoffices & clinics of medical doctors.

F-M-L 824739668
AMERICA WORKS OF NEW YORK INC
575 8th Ave 14th Fl
New York, NY 10018–3011
Phone (212)-244-5627
Abraham Levovitz .... Pr Tr

SIC 7361: employment agencies.

F-M-L 027190743
AMERICA'S BEST INNS INC
TRADE NAME BEST INNS OF AMERICA
1205 Skyline Dr
Marion, IL 62959–5202
Phone (618)-997-5454
Harold D Smith .... VP

SIC 7011: motel, franchised.

F-M-L 793096934
AMERICA'S FINEST SERVICE CO INC
407 D Parkway Dr
Greensboro, NC 27401
Phone (910)-379-0156
Wynetta Peters .... Pr
Robert Peters .... VP

SIC 7349: cleaning service, industrial or commercial; maid services, contract or fee basis.

F-M-L 188750889
AMERICA'S RENT-TO-OWN CENTER INC
TRADE NAME AMERICA'S SALES & LEASING
11 N Highland St
Chanute, KS 66720–1853
Phone (316)-431-2020
Gary Clay .... Pr
W Frank Springer .... Ex VP
Jackie Clay .... Sec Tr

SIC 7359: furniture rental; electronic equipment rental, except computers; appliance rental.

F-M-L 878517747
AMERICAID INC
TRADE NAME AMERICAID COMMUNITY CARE
4425 Corporation Ln
Virginia Beach, VA 23462–3103
Phone (804)-449-6900
Jeffrey Mc Waters .... Pr
Denna Ferrante .... CFO

SIC 8011: health maintenance organization.

F-M-L 118196997
AMERICALL CORP
730 Springer Dr
Lombard, IL 60148–6411
Phone (630)-620-4355
George A Kestler .... Pr

SIC 7389: telemarketing services.

F-M-L 861437762
AMERICAN ACADEMY & INSTITUTE OF HUMAN REASON INC
TRADE NAME TAMPA BAY RETIREMENT CENTER
11722 N 17th St
Tampa, FL 33612–5434
Phone (813)-971-8072
Jack Smith .... Pr
Frances Cooper .... Sec
Donald Hentschel .... Tr
Clement De Wall .... VP
Ilene Maddin .... VP
Mary Murphy .... VP
Anne Markarian .... Admr

SIC 8361: home for the aged.

F-M-L 088551429
AMERICAN ALLIANCE ALWAYS AVAILABLE
TRADE NAME DRAIN PATROL
2400 Lindberg St
Auburn, CA 95602–9061
Phone (916)-888-8114
Chester Eccles .... Pr
Ingrid Eccles .... Sec
Christina Eccles .... Asst Sec
Tracy Percival .... Off Mgr

SIC 7699: sewer cleaning & rodding.

F-M-L 868594482
AMERICAN ALPHA DATA CORP
1006 N Bowen Rd Ste 201
Arlington, TX 76012–2868
Phone (817)-276-6950
Joseph G Rio .... Pr

SIC 7374: data processing service.

F-M-L 838094811
AMERICAN ALPHA DISPATCH SVCS
225 Main St
Farmingdale, NY 11735–2619
Phone (516)-845-7130
Sid Mandel .... Pr

SIC 7374: data processing service.

F-M-L 095813523
AMERICAN ANALYTICAL SERVICES INC
110 Technology Pky S
Norcross, GA 30092–2908
Phone (770)-734-4200
Robert G Owens .... Pr
Wyn Jones .... Sec Tr
Billy P Dyer .... VP
Denise Geier .... VP

SIC 8734: testing laboratories.

F-M-L 182824078
AMERICAN ANESTHESIA SERVICES INC
2065 E West Maple Rd
Walled Lake, MI 48390–3858
Phone (810)-960-3400
Al Simon .... Pr CEO
Andy Terhune .... CFO

SIC 8099: medical services organization.

F-M-L 064992647
AMERICAN ARBITRATION ASSOCIATION INC
140 W 51st St
New York, NY 10020–1200
Phone (212)-484-4000
William K Slate II .... Pr CEO
John C Emmert Jr .... CFO Sr VP
Mark E Appel .... Sr VP
Charles A Cooper .... Sr VP
George H Friedman .... Sr VP
Steven G Gallagher .... Sr VP
Richard W Naimark .... Sr VP
Florence M Peterson .... Sr VP
Richard M Reilly .... Sr VP
Janice Wagner .... Sec
Richard Devlin .... Cont
Michael F Hoellering .... GC

SIC 2721, 2731, 7389, 8299: periodicals: publishing onlybooks: publishing onlyarbitration & conciliation serviceeducational services.

F-M-L 181786021
AMERICAN ASSAY LABORATORIES INC
1500 Glendale Ave
Sparks, NV 89431–5902
Phone (702)-356-0606
George Burke .... Pr
Chris Ioannakis .... Sec Tr
Julie Allred .... Cont

SIC 8734: testing laboratories.

F-M-L 066778077
AMERICAN ASSOCIATION OF RETIRED PERSONS
TRADE NAME AARP
601 E St Nw
Washington, DC 20049–0001
Phone (202)-434-2277
Norman Stengel .... Pr
Richard Henry .... COO
Clifford J Rose .... Cont
Steven S Zaleznick .... GC
Horace B Deets .... Ex Dir
James R Holland .... Commctns
James A Maigret .... Fin Plng
Charles W Allen .... Publs
Constance Swank .... Rsch
Thomas C Nelson .... Svcs
Wayne F Haefer .... Dir
C Anne Harvey .... Dir
Mary Anne Riesenberg .... Dir
Johc C Rother .... Dir
Jan Stefanov .... Dir

SIC 8399: health systems agency; social change association; social service information exchange.

F-M-L 028756187
AMERICAN AUTO SERVICE INC
TRADE NAME AAS
11247 Burbank Blvd
North Hollywood, CA 91601–2466
Phone (818)-761-3220
Kerry Pedlow .... Pr
Kerry R Pedlow .... Pr
Arthur H Atkins .... Ex VP
Joyce Pedlow .... Tr VP
Margo Atkins .... VP

SIC 7538: general automotive repair shops.

F-M-L 055353072
AMERICAN BANCORPORATION
1025 Main St Ste 800
Wheeling, WV 26003–2726
Phone (304)-233-5006
Jeremy C Mc Camic .... Ch Bd CEO
Paul Donahie .... Pr
Brent Richmond .... Sec Tr

SIC 6022, 6162, 7374: state commercial banksmortgage brokers, using own moneydata processing service.

F-M-L 020450680
AMERICAN BAPTIST ASSEMBLY INC
TRADE NAME GREEN LAKE CONFERENCE CENTER
W2511 State Road 23 & 4
Green Lake, WI 54941–9542
Phone (414)-294-3324
Ken Giacoletto .... Pr

SIC 7041, 7992: membership-basis organization hotelspublic golf courses.

F-M-L 076614767
AMERICAN BAPTIST ELDER MINISTRIES OF MASSACHUSETTS
1618 Chipman Way
Kingston, MA 02364
Phone (617)-585-5526
Rev Robert Wallace .... Ch

SIC 8051, 8322, 8361: skilled nursing care facilitiesadult day care centergeriatric residential care.

F-M-L 074463282
AMERICAN BAPTIST ESTATES INC
TRADE NAME ORANGEWOOD
7550 N 16th St
Phoenix, AZ 85020–4618
Phone (602)-944-4455
Dr Richard Ice .... Pr
David Ferguson .... Ex VP
Rev Steve Garner .... Sr VP
Linda D Exner .... Admr

SIC 8051, 8059: skilled nursing care facilitiesrest home, with health care.

F-M-L 068175637
AMERICAN BAPTIST HOMES OF THE MIDWEST
11985 Technology Dr
Eden Prairie, MN 55344–3622
Phone (612)-941-3175
Lois Bohon .... Ch Bd
Jack E Patty .... Pr
Polly Schrom .... Sec Tr
Noel Dikkers .... Acctg

SIC 8051, 8052, 8361: convalescent home with continuous nursing care; mental retardation hospitalhome for the mentally retarded, with health carerest home, with health care incidental.

F-M-L 071691307
AMERICAN BAPTIST HOMES OF THE WEST INC
TRADE NAME JENSEN PARK
400 Roland Way
Oakland, CA 94621–2012
Phone (510)-635-7600
Roy E Hughes .... Ch Bd
Richard E Ice .... Pr CEO
David Ferguson .... Ex VP
Steven Garner .... Sr VP Admn
Marlene O Dixon .... VP
Douglas W Howell .... VP
William C Nelson .... VP
Sue Schock Roderick .... VP
Margaret Weitkamp .... VP
George R Goupille .... VP Fin

SIC 8059: rest home, with health care.

F-M-L 180180630
AMERICAN BAPTIST HOMES OF WASHINGTON INC
TRADE NAME JUDSON PARK RETIREMENT
23600 Marine View Dr S
Des Moines, WA 98198–7352
Phone (206)-824-4000
David B Ferguson .... Pr
George Goupille .... VP Fin
Audrey Bowers .... Dir

SIC 8051, 8059: skilled nursing care facilitiesconvalescent home.

F-M-L 058418567
AMERICAN BECHTEL INC
50 Beale St
San Francisco, CA 94105–1813
Phone (415)-768-1234
Riley P Bechtel .... Ch Bd
Adrian Zaccaria .... Pr
John D Carter .... Sr VP
J P Laspa .... Sr VP
Dean L Orcutt .... Sr VP
V P Unruh .... Sr VP Tr
John W Weiser .... Sr VP Sec
James Buenneke .... Acctg

SIC 1629, 8711, 8742: industrial plant construction; power plant constructionconstruction & civil engineeringconstruction project management consultant.

F-M-L 804201572
AMERICAN BEHAVORIAL RESEARCH ASSOCIATION
1 West St
New Hyde Park, NY 11040–2315
Phone (516)-873-7000
Francis J De'lia PhD .... CEO
John Hennessey PhD .... CFO
Richard Jennings .... Ex VP GM
Andrew Morrissey PhD .... Ex VP
Thomas Grainger PhD .... Dir

SIC 8741: financial management for business.

F-M-L 157626094
AMERICAN BENEFIT CORP
401 11th St
Huntington, WV 25701–2218
Phone (304)-525-0331
Richard L Wilson .... Pr CEO
Matthew W Carlton .... Ex VP
Kenneth L Joos .... Sr VP
B Diane Mastin .... Sec Tr
Barbara Booth .... Cont

SIC 8742, 8748, 8999: human resource consulting servicesemployee programs administrationactuarial consultant.

Figure 14-1 Directory page sample.

- One item that is not visible to the naked eye is the index marker for the company name that gets outputted with the company name.
- In what order do the entries appear? Alphabetically or in a special sequence?

Now that you've looked at output and the desired layout and data, you need to look at the actual database structure to see how the data is organized and how to access it. We will now look at the database structure and introduce the structured query language (SQL) that will be used to request the data from the database.

AMERICAN ASSOCIATION OF RETIRED PERSONS

TRADE NAME AARP

601 E St Nw
Washington, DC 20049–0001
Phone (202) 434-2277

Norman Stengel	Pr
Richard Henry	COO
Clifford J Rose	Cont
Steven S Zaleznick	GC
Horace B Deets	Ex Dir
James R Holland	Commctns
James A Maigret	Fin Plng
Charles W Allen	Publs
Constance Swank	Rsch
Thomas C Nelson	Svcs
Wayne F Haefer	Dir
C Anne Harvey	Dir
Mary Anne Riesenberg	Dir
Johc C Rother	Dir
Jan Stefanov	Dir

SIC 8399: health systems agency; social change association; social service information exchange.

Figure 14-2 Sample entry from directory.

Relational Database Structure

The database used for the examples shown in this chapter uses a relational database structure (some of the new document repositories use an object-oriented or XML/SGML data structure). This simply means that the data is divided and stored in separate locations in the database to keep the data from being repeated. For example, if you had a database of customers and kept track of each order that was placed by each customer, you could store the data in two manners. You could reenter the customers' contact information (address, phone number, etc.) along with each order. Or you could keep the customers' contact information in one location, the orders in another, and use a customer number to "relate" the contact information to the order information.

Database Tables

In this example, the database used to generate the directory is a simple Access database. It contains three tables—Firms, Executives, and SIC_numbers. These three tables are related to each other by the ID field called FML_Number. In other words, each record in each table will have an FML_Number—this allows the executives and SIC information to be associated with the appropriate firm.

Firms Table

The Firms table contains company information such as the company name, trade name, street address, city, state, zip5, zip4, and phone number. Notice the FML number 066778077 for the highlighted AARP entry (see Figure 14-3). This is the number used to related the entries in the next two figures.

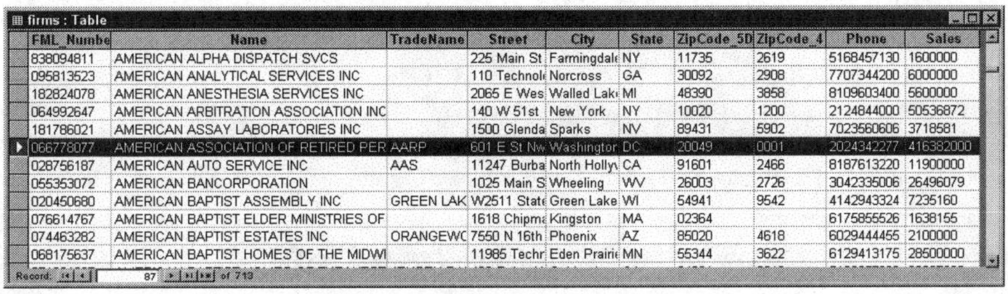

firms : Table

FML_Numbe	Name	TradeName	Street	City	State	ZipCode_5D	ZipCode_4	Phone	Sales
838094811	AMERICAN ALPHA DISPATCH SVCS		225 Main St	Farmingdal	NY	11735	2619	5168457130	1600000
095813523	AMERICAN ANALYTICAL SERVICES INC		110 Technol	Norcross	GA	30092	2908	7707344200	6000000
182824078	AMERICAN ANESTHESIA SERVICES INC		2065 E Wes	Walled Lak	MI	48390	3858	8109603400	5600000
064992647	AMERICAN ARBITRATION ASSOCIATION INC		140 W 51st	New York	NY	10020	1200	2124844000	50536872
181786021	AMERICAN ASSAY LABORATORIES INC		1500 Glenda	Sparks	NV	89431	5902	7023560606	3718581
066778077	AMERICAN ASSOCIATION OF RETIRED PER	AARP	601 E St Nw	Washingtor	DC	20049	0001	2024342277	416382000
028756187	AMERICAN AUTO SERVICE INC	AAS	11247 Burba	North Hollyv	CA	91601	2466	8187613220	11900000
055353072	AMERICAN BANCORPORATION		1025 Main S	Wheeling	WV	26003	2726	3042335006	26496079
020450680	AMERICAN BAPTIST ASSEMBLY INC	GREEN LAK	W2511 State	Green Lake	WI	54941	9542	4142943324	7235160
076614767	AMERICAN BAPTIST ELDER MINISTRIES OF		1618 Chipma	Kingston	MA	02364		6175855526	1638155
074463282	AMERICAN BAPTIST ESTATES INC	ORANGEWC	7550 N 16th	Phoenix	AZ	85020	4618	6029444455	2100000
068175637	AMERICAN BAPTIST HOMES OF THE MIDWI		11985 Techr	Eden Prairi	MN	55344	3622	6129413175	28500000

Record: 87 of 713

Figure 14-3 Firms table in Access.

Executives Table

The Executives table contains the executive names and titles, and the sequence in which the names should appear. Notice that the highlighted executives all have the FML number 066778077 to associate these names with AARP (see Figure 14-4).

SIC_numbers Table

The final table contains the SIC numbers and descriptions for each firm (see Figure 14-5). The FML number 066778077 associates the SIC number and descriptions to the AARP entry.

Writing SQL Queries

Introduction to SQL

To communicate with a database, the most commonly used method is the structured query language (SQL). SQL (pronounced "sequel") statements are issued to the database to return the desired data. A general SQL statement looks like the following:

```
SELECT <<field(s)>> FROM <<table(s)>>
```

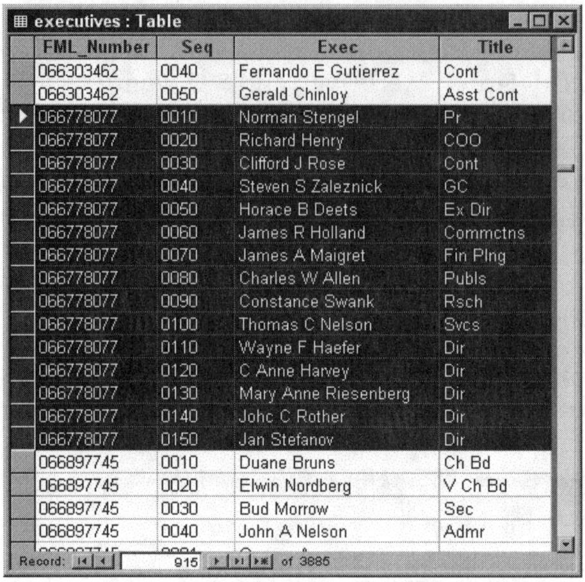

executives : Table

FML_Number	Seq	Exec	Title
066303462	0040	Fernando E Gutierrez	Cont
066303462	0050	Gerald Chinloy	Asst Cont
066778077	0010	Norman Stengel	Pr
066778077	0020	Richard Henry	COO
066778077	0030	Clifford J Rose	Cont
066778077	0040	Steven S Zaleznick	GC
066778077	0050	Horace B Deets	Ex Dir
066778077	0060	James R Holland	Commctns
066778077	0070	James A Maigret	Fin Plng
066778077	0080	Charles W Allen	Publs
066778077	0090	Constance Swank	Rsch
066778077	0100	Thomas C Nelson	Svcs
066778077	0110	Wayne F Haefer	Dir
066778077	0120	C Anne Harvey	Dir
066778077	0130	Mary Anne Riesenberg	Dir
066778077	0140	Johc C Rother	Dir
066778077	0150	Jan Stefanov	Dir
066897745	0010	Duane Bruns	Ch Bd
066897745	0020	Elwin Nordberg	V Ch Bd
066897745	0030	Bud Morrow	Sec
066897745	0040	John A Nelson	Admr

Record: 915 of 3885

Figure 14-4 Executives table in Access.

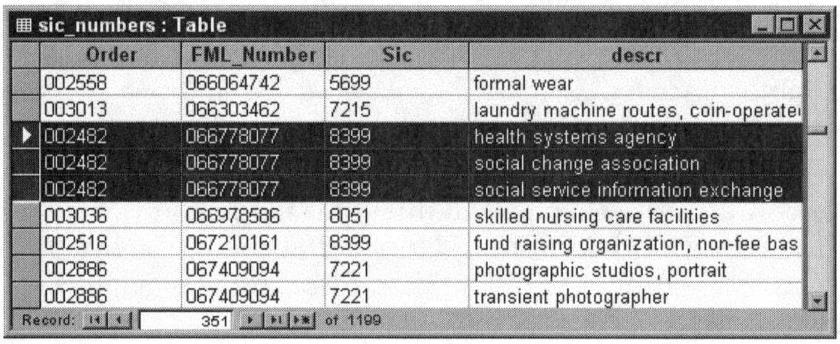

sic_numbers : Table

Order	FML_Number	Sic	descr
002558	066064742	5699	formal wear
003013	066303462	7215	laundry machine routes, coin-operate
002482	066778077	8399	health systems agency
002482	066778077	8399	social change association
002482	066778077	8399	social service information exchange
003036	066978586	8051	skilled nursing care facilities
002518	067210161	8399	fund raising organization, non-fee bas
002886	067409094	7221	photographic studios, portrait
002886	067409094	7221	transient photographer

Record: 351 of 1199

Figure 14-5 SIC_numbers table in Access.

This statement simply tells the database to select one or more fields from a particular table in the database. For example, if the following SQL statement is issued:

```
SELECT Name FROM firms
```

the database will return a list of all company names in the database. A complex SQL statement looks like this:

```
SELECT <<DISTINCT>> <<field(s)>> FROM <<table(s)>>
WHERE (<<some value>> <<(= <> > <)>> <<some value>>)
ORDERBY <<field(s)>>
GROUPBY <<field(s)>>
```

The added options in the SQL statement allow you to further limit, order, and group the returned data.

Nested Queries

When you use a data-driven publishing application, queries can be "nested." This means that a second query can be run "inside" the first query to return information based on the first query. The example shown here uses a total of four queries to produce the final directory. The first query returns the company information. The second and third queries are run as subqueries to the first—they are nested in the first query. The second query returns the executive information for the company. The third query returns the SIC numbers for the company. The fourth query is a sub-subquery that is nested under the third query. The fourth query returns the SIC descriptions for each SIC number for each company.

Queries Used in the Example

Firm Query

The Firm query returns one record for each company in the Firms table, along with the company name, phone number, street address, FML number, trade name, 5-digit zip code, 4-digit PO box number, state, and city:

```
SELECT Name, Phone, Street, FML_Number, TradeName,
  ZipCode_5Digit, ZipCode_4Digit, State, City
FROM firms
```

This query returns a data value for each field named after the select statement from the table named Firms in the database. It will return each of the values for every company in the Firms table.

Executive Query

The Executive query is run as a subquery to the Firm query. It returns every executive with his/her title from the Executives table. The executives are limited to the previously selected company in the Firm query by the FML number from the firm query. The records are ordered by the values in the seq column.

```
SELECT exec, title
FROM executives
WHERE FML_Number = :FML Number
ORDER BY seq
```

This query returns an executive name and his/her title from the table named Executives for the particular company (matching the FML_Number) returned in the Firm query.

SIC Query

The SIC query is run as a subquery to the Firm query. It returns every SIC number limited to the previously selected company in the Firm query based on the FML number from the Firm query:

```
SELECT DISTINCT sic
FROM sic_numbers
WHERE FML_Number = :FML Number
```

This query returns all SIC numbers from the table named SIC_numbers for the particular company (matching the FML_Number) returned in the Firm query.

SIC Description Query

The SIC Description query is run as a subquery to the SIC query. It returns every SIC description for each SIC number. It is limited by the FML number returned in the Firm query and the SIC number returned in the SIC query.

```
SELECT descr
FROM sic_numbers
WHERE (FML_Number = :FML Number and SIC = :SIC Number)
```

This query returns the SIC description from the table named SIC_numbers for each SIC number returned in the SIC query.

Now that you've constructed the queries needed to retrieve the desired data, you need to execute the queries to output the data.

Retrieving the Data from the Database

Retrieving the data from the database can be done in two different manners. The SQL queries can be executed from within the database application and the data can be "dumped" into an ASCII (text) file, or the queries can be executed from an external program via open database connectivity (ODBC).

Dumping the Data from the Database

Executing the SQL queries from within the database will result in the data and any markup being written to a file on the hard drive. This file is then post-processed during publishing. This data dump becomes a "snapshot" of the database at the time the queries were executed.

Connecting to the Database via ODBC

ODBC is a commonly used protocol for connecting to a database. When you use ODBC, a database is made available to the operating system. Any ODBC-compliant application can then retrieve information from the database. FrameMaker is not natively ODBC compliant—in other words, it does not have a mechanism to connect to and communicate via ODBC. A third-party product is necessary to query information from a database into FrameMaker, or the data must be generated by the database for importing into FrameMaker. Most database publishing applications on the Mac and in Windows support ODBC database connectivity and can be used with FrameMaker for database publishing. To set up an ODBC connection, see Appendix A, "Setting Up an ODBC Database Connection."

The external application can then communicate with the database and execute the SQL queries to retrieve the data. The data can then be outputted to a file on the hard drive or sent directly into FrameMaker for publishing.

Examples of Database Publishing with FrameMaker

The examples in this section of database publishing project will explore five different methods of database publishing with FrameMaker. First you will look at database publishing with PatternStream—a tool that allows you to set up the entire publishing system with a graphical user interface. Next, you will set up the same project using FrameScript. The last three examples show how database publishing is done with markup languages; you'll see how to publish using MML, XML, and MIF.

Data-Driven Publishing with PatternStream™

PatternStream is a plug-in to FrameMaker that communicates directly with one or more databases (either natively or via an ODBC connection) and/or flat files (such as Excel, HTML, Word, or FrameMaker documents) to retrieve data, insert the data into a FrameMaker document, and format the data on the fly. No intermediary markup files are necessary for publishing. Prototyping is a very rapid process because changes can be made and samples can be run interactively as the data is outputted directly to FrameMaker.

PatternStream's graphical user interface (GUI) allows even a newcomer to database publishing to develop with ease. PatternStream is a great tool for rapid prototyping and development for any database publishing project. The instructions provided in this book highlight the ease of setting up a database publishing project from a GUI. To see the process of setting up a PatternStream project, see Appendix B, "Directory Example Using PatternStream."

Data-Driven Publishing with FrameScript

FrameScript is a scripting language for FrameMaker. It has support for ODBC data connections and can be used for simple database publishing projects. Very simple database publishing/mail merge applications can be done effectively with FrameScript. FrameScript also communicates directly with any ODBC-compliant database and passes the data received directly into FrameMaker, where it is formatted on the fly. Although any size of project can theoretically be done with FrameScript, the cost in development time or contracting time would soon make a large project cost prohibitive, and a solution like PatternStream would become a better option. To view the FrameScript code necessary for this project, see Appendix C, "Simple Directory FrameScript Code."

Automated Publishing with MML

MML is short for Maker Markup Language. MML is a very simple "tagging" structure that allows text files to be mapped to the formats of a FrameMaker template. This method of automated publishing is best used for a very simple layout. MML can only contain paragraph and character formats. If tables are necessary in the output, MML will not suffice.

As with any markup language, time and support will need to come from the IT department (or whoever maintains the database). The markup will need to be added as the data is exported from the database and written out to the MML text file. Below is a sample MML file for the directory sample used in this discussion. The MML assumes that an existing FrameMaker template exists, with the formats defined. To view the process of setting up a query or a set of queries to output MML from a database, see Appendix D, "Sample SQL Query that Returns MML Syntax."

After the query is run to add the MML markup to the data, the data can be saved as a text file from Access (or you can add further code to export it automatically). The resulting MML file can then be imported into your FrameMaker template. The MML tags "map" to the paragraph and character formats in your template. MML supports only paragraph and character formats, so it is only a valid option for database publishing the simplest projects.

FrameMaker is shipped with a complete MML reference guide in PDF format. This guide is located in the FrameMaker install directory in a subdirectory called OnlineManuals:

```
Adobe FrameMaker7.0\OnlineManuals\MML_Reference.pdf
```

FrameMaker is also shipped with a complete set of sample MML files. They are located in the FrameMaker install directory in a directory called Samples:

```
Adobe FrameMaker7.0\Samples\MML\
```

Automated Publishing with XML

XML stands for eXtensible Markup Language. This markup is more complex than MML and requires opening and closing tags. This section will only deal with XML as it relates to database publishing. For further information on XML syntax and importing/exporting XML into FrameMaker, see Chapter 3. To view the process of setting up a query or a set of queries to output XML from a database, see Appendix E, "Sample XQL Query that Returns XML Syntax."

XML is becoming the standard for data exchange. Using a markup language such as XML can be a reasonable method of database publishing. Keep in mind that the XML generated by the database will need to be valid XML. A structured FrameMaker template and application will then need to be created in order for FrameMaker to be able to import the XML and format it.

FrameMaker 7 is shipped with a complete XML cookbook in PDF format. The PDF file is located in the FrameMaker install directory in a directory called **XMLCookbook**. This cookbook and sample files demonstrate how to import and export valid XML in FrameMaker:

```
Adobe FrameMaker7.0\XMLCookbook\UserGuide.pdf
```

Automated Publishing with MIF

Maker Interchange Format (MIF) is the ASCII version of a FrameMaker file. When saving a FrameMaker document, FrameMaker usually saves the file in a proprietary binary format that only FrameMaker can understand. When saving a FrameMaker document as a MIF file, FrameMaker encodes the document in markup and saves it in ASCII format. The markup is very complex and can support any feature/function of FrameMaker. This markup can be used by other programs to create FrameMaker files.

When you do database publishing with MIF, the MIF syntax is wrapped around the data elements. A very large text (ASCII) file is then generated from the database and then is subsequently opened or imported into the final FrameMaker template. MIF files are very verbose and can be difficult to read and troubleshoot. MIF can be combined with MML to make the files easier to read and understand. To view the process of setting up a query or set of queries to output MIF from a database, see see Appendix E, "Sample XQL Query that Returns XML Syntax."

By using MIF in database publishing, you can create a document almost as complex as if you had taken a data-driven approach, with a few exceptions. Because any feature in FrameMaker has an equivalent in MIF, the entire document (including the template) can be generated automatically from the database. The biggest drawback to this solution is the time required (almost all of it on the database end) to create the SQL to generate the initial MIF syntax. Refering to Appendix F, notice the amount of syntax required just for a simple entry in the directory.

FrameMaker is shipped with a complete MIF reference guide in PDF format. The PDF file is located in the FrameMaker install directory in a directory called OnlineManuals:

```
Adobe FrameMaker7.0\OnlineManuals\MIF_Reference.pdf
```

FrameMaker is also shipped with a complete set of sample MIF files. They are located in the FrameMaker install directory in a directory called Samples:

```
Adobe FrameMaker7.0\Samples\MIF\
```

Summary

Database publishing is an emerging marketplace. Many applications can be used to publish information from one or more databases and static files with FrameMaker. The example given in this chapter was very simple in order to better explain the different methods and applications that can be used. Obviously, much more complex publications can be generated by some of these tools.

The reason the author tends to favor a more data-driven approach like PatternStream or FrameScript is because the formatting is done at the same time. As I acquire data from the database, I can literally watch the data get formatted on the screen. When using a markup language, I must first export the data as valid XML and then set up a structured FrameMaker template and application to read the XML in and format it. The time spent creating the valid XML and structured FrameMaker template is generally more than is required in the data-driven approach. Changing the design is also much faster in the data-driven approach.

Visit the websites listed in the section "Database Publishing Applications" on page 360 to request a demo version of these applications to see which product might best suit your specific needs. The author would also be happy to answer any questions you may have regarding getting started in database publishing. Drop Brad Anderson an email message with your questions at brad@BeyondPrint.com.

Advanced FrameMaker

15

Filename Markers in WebWorks Publisher Professional

Kay Ethier

This chapter describes the use of filename markers to "lock in" specific filenames for your WebWorks Publisher Professional Edition output files.

Applicable to FrameMaker versions 6.0 and 7.0/7.1

Using WebWorks Publisher Professional Edition opens up many possibilities for output. Due to its power, WebWorks Publisher Professional Edition—much like FrameMaker—may become difficult to use. In this chapter you will optimize file naming using a special type of marker.

This chapter is geared toward those using FrameMaker with WebWorks Publisher Professional Edition to create online help or Web content. Unless otherwise specified, the acronym WWP herein refers to WebWorks Publisher Professional Edition. In this example, the WWP template used is the HTML template, but you may use Filename markers in other types of WWP projects.

Utilizing Filename Markers for Context Sensitivity

The following sections walk you through the use of Filename markers to mark up documents in a manner that allows you to control output file naming. By controlling the filenames of your WWP output, you may have more consistent output, which makes context sensitivity easier to implement.

Note: *WebWorks Publisher Standard Edition does not support Filename markers or other custom marker types.*

Some comments on the project described herein are as follows:

- Because of limitations in clients' systems, you may sometimes want a context-sensitive help system that is plain HTML.
- For simplicity, Filename markers allow developers to request names of HTML files that they may link to, and to have assurances that the filenames will not change or shift.
- This how-to was developed using WWP 7 and FrameMaker versions 6 and 7 books (no structure). Results may vary slightly using other versions.

Note: *Several generic Adobe demonstration files (book, chapters, and generated files) have been used for this presentation. You may substitute your own files but you must adjust the paragraph tags as necessary to match your content's tags.*

Filename Marker Definition

A Filename marker is a FrameMaker marker type. It is also a marker type in WWP and is used by WWP to specify a filename for a page (chunk) of output *or* a name for a generated graphic.

The Problem (Default Behavior)

When you generate output from a WWP project, WWP automatically names the output file. It names:

- graphics not imported by reference (since there is no referenced filename to use)
- split files (one file turned into many)

WWP uses default naming, which uses the FrameMaker filename. As more split files are created, sometimes letters or numbers are appended to the output filenames. Graphics files, HTML files, and other outputs end up with these default names, which may change as the project is adjusted.

Figure 15-1 shows a WWP Professional project that uses the default naming.

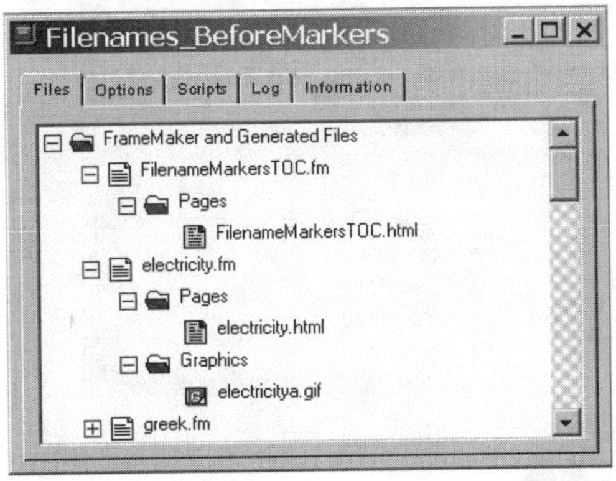

Figure 15-1 Default naming within a WWP project.

Figure 15-2 shows the same project using the default naming with split files (more files to name).

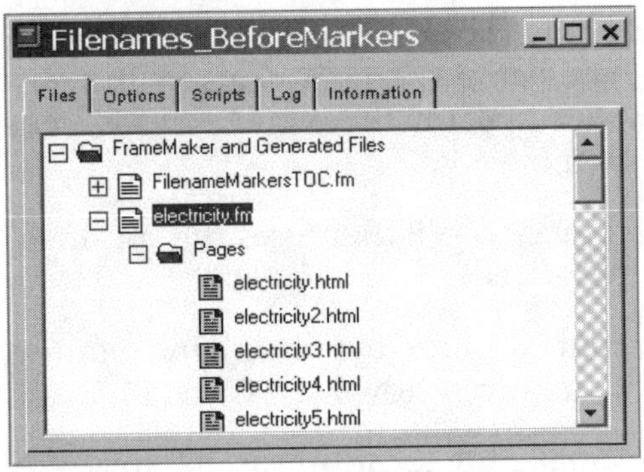

Figure 15-2 Default naming of split files.

Note: *Figures 15-1 and 15-2 show a DHTML project, but Filename markers work in all types of WWP Professional projects.*

In the split-file example, the output pages from the file *electricity.fm* file are named *electricity.html*, *electricity2.html*, and so on. Some graphics in the output may be called *electricitya.gif* or some similar default name. Then, as the *electricity.fm* file is edited and content is added and deleted, the names may change. This means that the topic that used to be in *electricity3.html* may now be in *electricity4.html*—not an ideal situation for setting up context- sensitive help.

So, basically these default filenames are too generic (as shown in Figure 15-3), may shift, and can make selecting files difficult.

Figure 15-3 Generic naming makes finding files and content difficult.

The Fix (or Improvement)

To avoid problems with vague and constantly changing filenames, you may instead pick the filenames. You do this by placing Filename markers in your FrameMaker document wherever you want a specific filename to be given to that part of the document as it is outputted by WWP.

Once you have the Filename markers in place, WWP then uses the specified names each time the WWP output is regenerated.

Using Filename markers changes the output from the default, vague naming shown in Figure 15-4 to the more-specific naming shown in Figure 15-5.

Having output with these specific names make file location easier. Link checking also becomes easier, since in the output—in this case HTML—you may hover over a link in the browser, see the link on the status bar, and immediately know if it is correct.

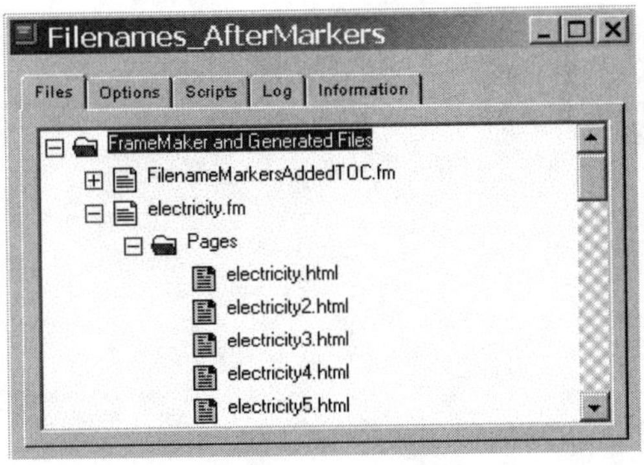

Figure 15-4 Vague filenames.

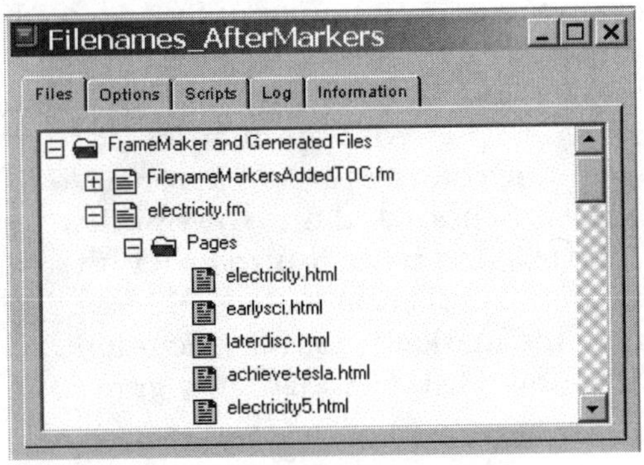

Figure 15-5 Specific filenames.

Note: *If you have any two files with the same name, WWP adds letters and numbers to the end of each one to distinguish them.*

Creating Filename Markers

In order to use Filename markers, you need to first add the Filename marker type to your FrameMaker documents and templates.

Note: *You name this marker type Filename because this is the name of the related marker in WWP's templates. When you use the exact same name in FrameMaker and WWP, WWP automatically does the mapping for you when you begin using the markers.*

If you are just starting out with FrameMaker and creating a template, then you may easily add this marker type, and all files created from the template will have the marker. Within the Marker window, select Edit to bring up the dialog box to create your custom marker (see Figure 15-6).

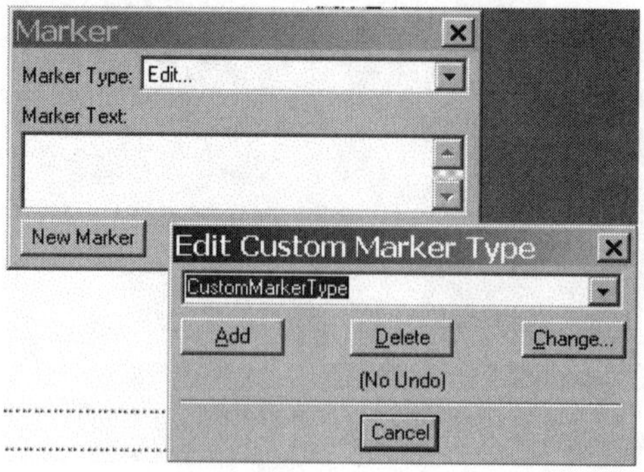

Figure 15-6 Creation of a custom marker type.

If, however, you already have many files created, then you may find yourself adding the markers to each document individually. This is because marker types are imported (**File > Import > Formats**) as part of Document Properties. Because importing Document Properties may upset your numbering schemes (among other things), it may be a problem for you to import them. So, you can either add the marker type to each document or add one to your first document, place the marker on the clipboard, and paste it into other files. (FrameMaker will automatically add Filename markers as an available type in a FrameMaker file when you paste a Filename marker into that document.) It will then appear in the Marker Type drop-down list, as shown in Figure 15-7.

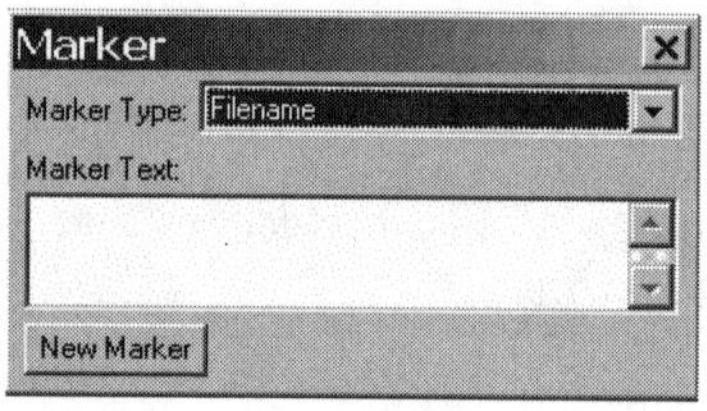

Figure 15-7 The Marker window with the Filename marker type available.

Once you have the Filename marker listed as an available marker type, you may then place the markers throughout your content.

Note: *Because WWP reviews your FrameMaker documents each time they change, it does not matter if you place the Filename markers when you first author the document or if you wait until you are working on the output to add the markers.*

Comments on Marker Placement

Place markers within the text (headings or body paragraphs) that goes with each split file. A good practice is to insert markers at or near the end of the paragraph rather than at the beginning, where it may overlap a cross-reference marker.

In this example, paragraphs named Section were used and mapped to a style in WWP that created a new HTML (split) file each time it encountered a Section paragraph in a FrameMaker file.

The markers were placed either in the paragraph tagged Section or in the paragraphs beneath it. Markers placed in the paragraphs under Section must come before the next Section paragraph.

If there are multiple markers for any reason, WWP grabs the first.

Using Filename Markers to Adjust Graphics Filenames

You may also rename graphics using Filename markers. As mentioned earlier, you may have *electricity.html* and end up with *electricitya.gif*. WWP ignores the extension on the filename and then refuses to allow any two files to have the same name.

To select a name for your graphic, place the Filename marker inside a text frame that is inside the graphic's anchored frame. For instance, in Figure 15-8 a graphic that has been assigned a default name (by WWP) is going to be renamed *microphone*.

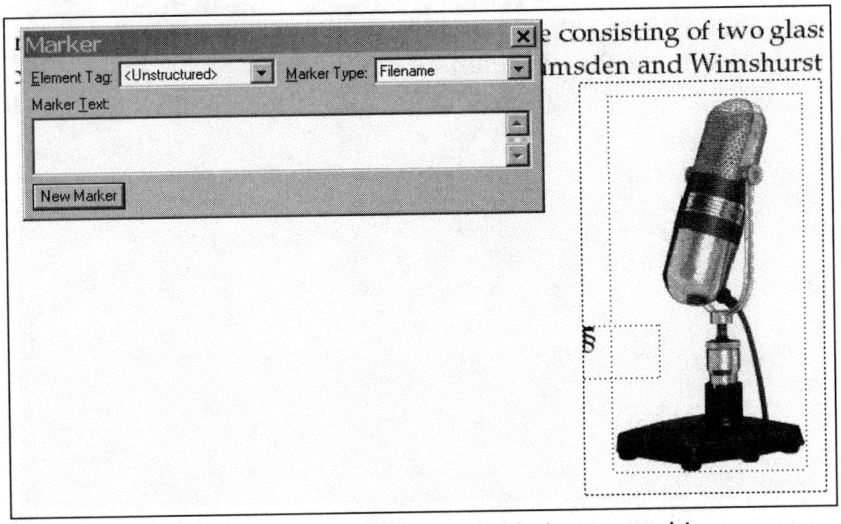

Figure 15-8 Filename marker being added to a graphic.

Once you place the Filename markers for your graphics, you will see the changes in your output—similar to what you saw for your HTML files. Figure 15-9 shows an example of "before" and "after" the placement of Filename markers.

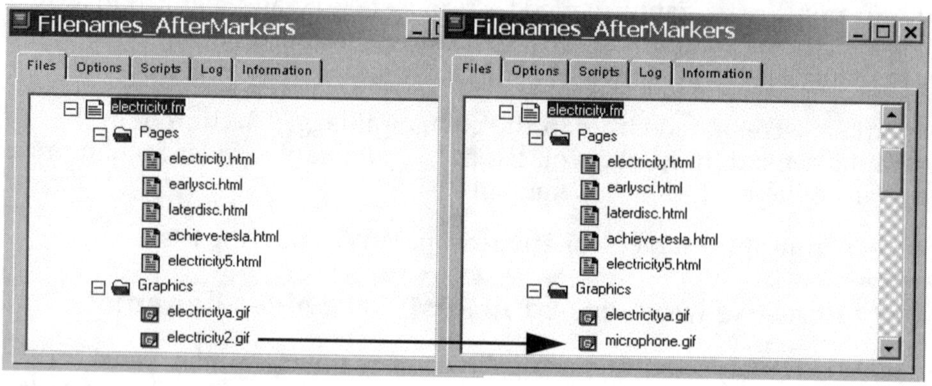

Figure 15-9 Graphic filename before and after marker placement.

Summary

WWP automatically assigns filenames unless you tell it otherwise. Setting up custom filenames can be accomplished using Filename markers.

Filename markers can be used for text or graphics. Place the markers throughout your documents, and from that point forward your WWP regenerated projects will use the new filenames.

Advanced FrameMaker

16

Adding PDF Support to a WebWorks Help 3.0 Project

Kay Ethier

WebWorks Publisher Professional Edition provides functionality for adding context-sensitive links to PDFs from your online help.

Applicable to FrameMaker versions 6.0 and 7.0/7.1

Using WebWorks Publisher Professional Edition opens up many possibilities for electronic outputs. One of these output options is the cross-browser, cross-platform WebWorks Help format. In this chapter you will learn how to implement PDF support within this type of help project.

This chapter is geared toward those using FrameMaker with WebWorks Publisher Professional Edition to create online help or Web content. Unless otherwise specified, the acronym WWP herein refers to WebWorks Publisher Professional Edition.

Adding PDF Links

In this section you will modify the WWP WebWorks Help 3.0 online help template to include PDF support.

This added PDF support allows you to click buttons within the help interface and open different PDFs depending on your position. For example, if you are in the browser viewing Chapter 3 and you click the PDF button, then a PDF for Chapter 3 is opened. If you are in Chapter 1, then the Chapter 1 PDF is opened. You can also add buttons that can be clicked from any point to open a PDF for your entire book.

In this chapter's implementation, the WebWorks Help 3.0 template is used to create online help with added buttons for viewing the current chapter in PDF or viewing the entire book in PDF. This may sound like an easy thing to do, but it is not as simple to implement as it sounds.

Code must be added to allow WWP to "sense" what chapter you are currently in and to ensure that the link goes to the corresponding PDF. Plus, adjustments must be made to ensure that the PDFs are located. The steps herein walk you through the implementation of PDF support, showing each of the items that must be adjusted. The project was done using WebWorks Publisher 7 and FrameMaker 7 (no structure). Some variance may occur in other versions.

Note: *Make sure that you back up your files before beginning the adjustments described here. Because of the extensive changes required, extra care must be taken in implementation.*

Also, WebWorks Publisher Standard *Edition does not support WebWorks Help 3.0, so it cannot be used.*

Starting the Project

You will start with the creation of a WebWorks Help 3.0 project.

Note: *From this point forward, that type of project will be referred to as WWH3.*

The following steps are specific to WWH3 and may not work the same way with other versions. Also, since this is a fairly advanced topic, and some assumptions have been made about you as a reader, some of the more basic steps are skipped.

1. Start a WWH3 project, as shown in Figure 16-1, and give it a name.

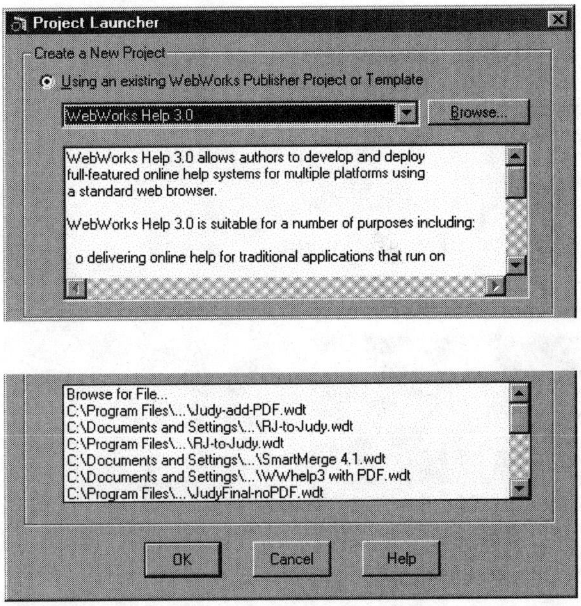

Figure 16-1 Starting a WWH3 project.

These instructions refer to a project called **PDF1, so that project is shown in** the screenshots and directory references. Be sure to adjust to whatever you call your own projects.

2. Next, do some of the project Mappings so that headings are mapped to headings, lists to SmartLists, TOC items to TOC styles, and so on.

   The examples in this chapter use a Section paragraph (mapped to WWP Heading1) and a Title (mapped to WWP Title) at the start of each chapter in the sample book. Also, the TOC paragraphs have been mapped to the WWP TOC styles to ensure that the Help Contents are not empty.

3. Generate the output right away so that—especially if you haven't worked in WWH3 before—you can view the default WWH3 layout and navigation.

   The view in Figure 16-2 shows how WWH3 projects look when you use the default project layout.

In contrast, the view in Figure 16-3 shows the project with added PDF support.

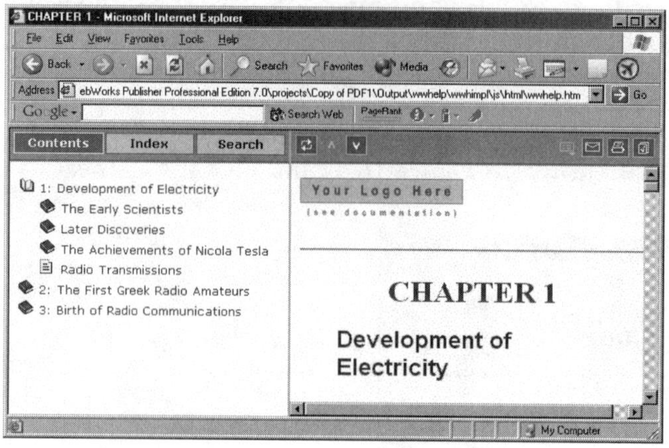

Figure 16-2 Out-of-the-box WebWorks Help 3.0 layout.

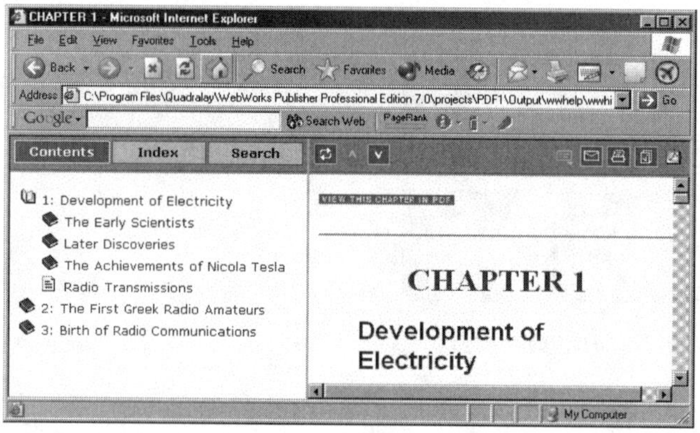

Figure 16-3 A WWH3 project modified with PDF support.

The sections that follows walk you through adding a button linked to the chapter PDF at the top of the page (and an optional button for the book PDF), then adding an icon for the book PDF next to the other icons on the navigation bar.

Changing Project Options

If you plan to add buttons to open PDF files, then one of the changes that you need to make is in your project options. The default for the option "Copy the following files from SUPPORTDIR to OUTPUTDIR" does not include PDF. As shown in Figure 16-4, you must add ***.pdf** to the list of file types so that your PDFs are copied to the **Output** directory. (Also, make sure that this option is checkmarked.)

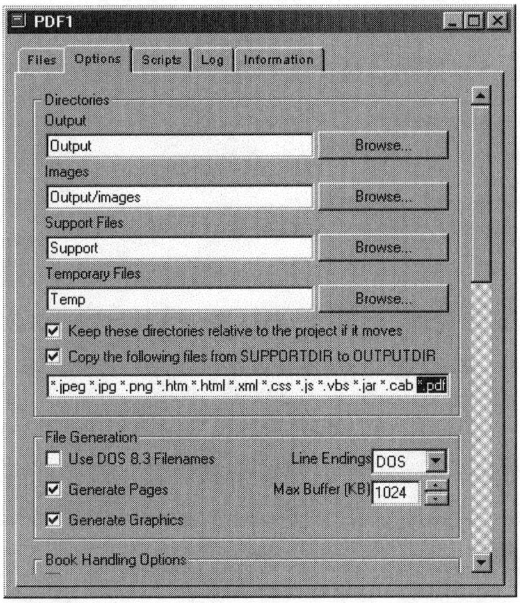

Figure 16-4 The project options.

Additionally, you need to add a **PDF** directory under **Support** in your project. Of course, the next step is to put your PDF files into the **Support/pdf** directory so that they are available for WWP to copy into **Output/pdf**.

Adding a Chapter PDF Button to the Page (*Normal.asp*)

To add the chapter PDF button to the top of the pages, modify the file *Normal.asp* so it includes a button and a link. The code in the ASP file, which is XHTML (HTML following the stricter rules of XML), begins as shown in Figure 16-5.

The area that you modify is very small—the start of the body contains an onLoad, and then follows a paragraph with an image in it and a horizontal rule.

You need to add some additional code after the body element, as shown in Figure 16-6.

Adding a Chapter PDF Macro

The code shown in Figure 16-6 is one way of making a link to the PDF. (In WWP, there is often more than one way to perform a task.) This code references a user macro called *UMPDFLink*, which must be part of your project. If it does not exist, add it and insert the code as shown in Figure 16-7.

Note that the code shown previously includes references to a graphic named *pdfchapter.gif*. When you reference a graphic—no matter what you name it—

```
<!DOCTYPE html PUBLIC "-//W3C//DTD XHTML 1.0 Transitional//EN" "http://www.w3.org/TR/
   xhtml1/DTD/xhtml1-transitional.dtd">

<html xmlns="http://www.w3.org/1999/xhtml" xml:lang="en" lang="en">
 <head>
  <meta http-equiv="Content-Type" content="text/html; charset=$CHARSET;" />
  <meta http-equiv="Content-Style-Type" content="text/css" />
  <meta name="GENERATOR" content="$VERSION;" />
  <meta name="TEMPLATEBASE" content="$TEMPLATENAME;" />
  <meta name="LASTUPDATED" content="$DATE(c);" />
<!--BeginHiddenExpansion
$BP70WWHPageASP_Keywords;
EndHiddenExpansion-->
  <title>$GET_ATTR($PAGE;, title);</title>
  <link rel="StyleSheet" href="document.css" type="text/css" />
  <link rel="StyleSheet" href="catalog.css" type="text/css" />
<!--BeginHiddenExpansion
$BP70WWHPageASP_Header;
EndHiddenExpansion-->
 </head>

 <body onLoad="WWHUpdate();">

    <p>
      <img src="images/logo.gif" width="174" height="46" alt="Put your logo here!" />
    </p>
    <hr align="left" />

 <blockquote>
<!--BeginHiddenExpansion
$DATA;
$NOTES;
EndHiddenExpansion-->
<!--BeginHiddenExpansion
$BP70WWHPageASP_RelatedTopics_Inline;
EndHiddenExpansion-->
 </blockquote>

 <hr />

 <table align="right" border="0" cellspacing="0" cellpadding="0">
  <tr>
        <td align="right">
          <span style="font-size: 16px ; font-weight: bold">
            Your Company<br />
          </span>
          <span style="font-size: 10px">
            <a href="Your Company's URL">Your Company's Web Site</a><br />
            Voice: (555) 555-1234<br />
            Fax: (555) 555-5678<br />
            <a href="mailto:Your Company">Your Company's E-mail Address</a><br />
          </span>
    </td>
   </tr>
  </table>

<!--BeginHiddenExpansion
$BP70WWHPageASP_Footer;
EndHiddenExpansion-->

 </body>
</html>
```

Figure 16-5 Content of the file *Normal.asp.*

```
<body onLoad="WWHUpdate();">
<a href="$UMPDFLink;"><img src="images/pdfchapter.gif" alt="Open current
   chapter PDF" border="0" /></a>

<p>
</p>
<hr align="left" />
```

Figure 16-6 Modified Normal.asp code—added PDF link and graphic.

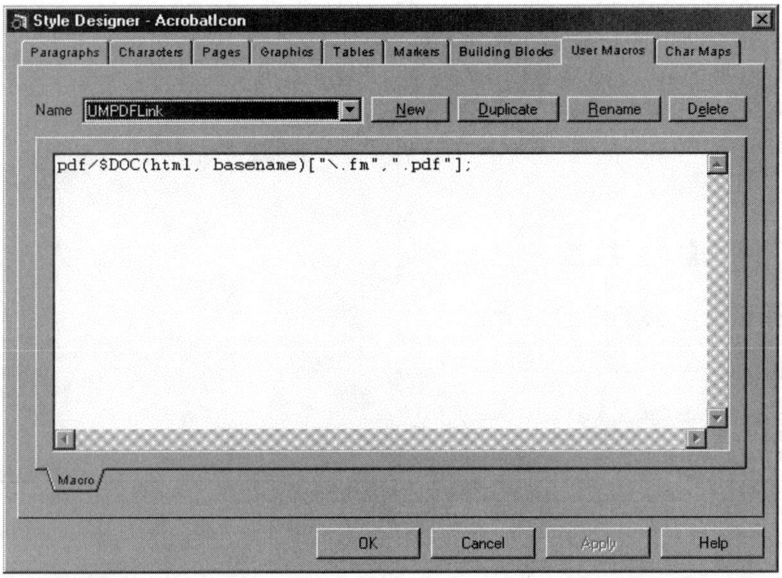

Figure 16-7 The UMPDFLink macro definition in the Style Designer.

you must make sure that you put that graphic into the directory for the project. Specifically, if you are in the default projects directory, then the graphic goes in as follows:

...\WebWorks Publisher Professional Edition
7.0\projects***YourProjectName***\Support\images

YourProjectName refers to the directory created when you named your project. Be sure to keep that in mind when seeking these files. The name of the project referred to in this chapter is PDF1. The result is that the page layout adjusts to include the button (see Figure 16-8), and when the button is clicked, the PDF will appear in the browser.

Note: *You must have Acrobat or Acrobat Reader on your system to view PDFs.*

If you forgot to put the graphic in the directory, you will see an "x" in your browser, as shown in Figure 16-9.

Do you see the x indicating a missing graphic? Alongside the x is the ***alt*** text typed in our code ("Open current chapter PDF"). Once you have your graphic in the appropriate directory and showing in the browser, click it to ensure that it opens the PDF in the browser.

If you change the *Normal.asp* code above, then place the graphic in the appropriate directory and have the PDFs in place, you may regenerate the view of the layout.

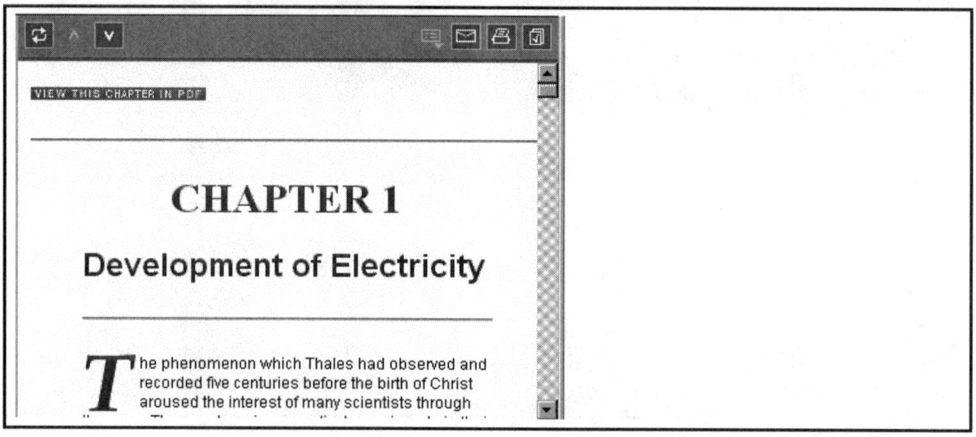

Figure 16-8 Button added to page.

Figure 16-9 Missing graphic at the start of the page.

Adding Book PDF Macro and Optional Button

If you wished to also place a graphic and link to the book PDF next to the link above, you could add to *Normal.asp* code such as the following:

```
<a href="$UMPDFBookLink;"><img
src="images/pdfbook.gif" alt="Open this book PDF"
border="0" /></a>
```

The corresponding code inside the macro *UMPDFBookLink*, which you must create since it is referenced in the code just mentioned, would be as follows:

```
pdf/$DOCFIRST(html, basename)["TOC[.]fm", ".pdf"];
```

This macro code, combined with the link the the *Normal.asp*, creates a button (the GIF) with a link to the entire book PDF, automatically filling in the book filename.

Summary

Once your project is working and looks the way that you want it to look, you may want to select **Save As Template** from within WWP so that this PDF-support template may be reused.

Be sure to stress to all those who use the template that an integral part of the process is creating the PDF directory and putting the PDFs in place. If there are no PDFs, then testing becomes frustrating. Ensure that the PDFs are in place from the start of the project, and that they are updated if the FrameMaker book is adjusted or chapters are added and deleted.

17

Creating Custom Palettes

Kay Ethier

This chapter explores FrameMaker palettes and how you may create custom button sets to turn common tasks into single mouse-clicks.

Applicable to FrameMaker versions 5.0/5.5, 6.0, and 7.0/7.1

Introducing FrameMaker Palettes

A palette is a set of menu options (or buttons) that may be kept open for easy access. One example is the FrameMaker Tools palette (accessed via **Graphics > Tools**).

FrameMaker's interface is the same for every (US English language) user, but not all users work the same way or create similar documents. You may want certain buttons available that are not in the default FrameMaker interface so you can use them to access functions you often use.

You can also create custom palettes to drop in special characters that you use frequently, such as a copyright, yen symbol, or em dash.

You can even create buttons on your palette that take you to Web sites, such as your home site, so you may easily check information. The commands behind these buttons may be adjusted to allow you to do such things as start an email while still in FrameMaker.

Shortcut keys are provided for many, many FrameMaker functions, however, not everyone likes to use shortcut keys. It is fairly easy to mix them up or forget them. But, if you have a palette of buttons at your fingertips, their images will clue you in to what they do.

Getting Started

Follow the instructions in this chapter to build a series of practice palettes. Once you have some experience pulling the elements together, you can create your own using the FrameMaker codes—or "fcodes"—that are available.[1]

You create a palette by first creating a regular FrameMaker document, then adjusting it to make it a special "palette" document. The palette document will then perform functions when you click its buttons while you work within any FrameMaker document.

Before you begin creating your palette, use FrameMaker as you normally would and watch for functions that you use frequently. Each time you wish for an easier way to get at a menu selection, write it down. (Or, make a generic palette now and add to it as you want additional options.) The steps required to create your palette are as follows:

1. List which functions you want on your palette.
2. Sketch your palette using the graphics you would like to have on the palette. Select intuitive graphics that will mean something to you (and others) using your palette.

1. The list of fcodes is in a *menu.cfg* file and is described later in this chapter.

3. Create a new FrameMaker document with a small (palette-sized) page size.
4. Set up the palette layout and functions using the methods described in this chapter.
5. **Save** your document as a **.fm* file (to allow easy future editing).
6. Select **Save As** to save your document as a **.mif* file (as explained later).
7. Lock your document to make it into a palette (which is reversible, but not easily so).
8. Open your palette document (**.mif*) and use the functions in other open FrameMaker documents.

The sections that follow will walk you through the creation of several sample palettes. These should give you enough information about the creation process and the available fcode actions to create palettes to suit your needs.

Available Actions (fcodes)

There are many fcodes, along with special character codes, available for your palette actions. Table 17-1 is a partial listing of these codes. A more complete listing is available in your FrameMaker install, in the file *cmds.cfg*.

Table 17-1 A Few of the Available fcodes from the File cmds.cfg

Structure-Related Command	fcode
Help	302
New Book	308
Import File	314
Document Compare Report	31F
Paste Special	D10
Create Table of Contents	2B0
View Rulers On	3F3
View Borders On	3F1

Inside the file *cmds.cfg*, the codes are included along with other data, so that in addition to the name of the action and the code, there is often also a label, a key sequence, and the mode information.

In the action item shown in Figure 17-1, the action is *Wrap Element* and the fcode is **F49**.

In the sections that follow, you will see how the fcodes fit into the palette creation process.

```
<Command WrapElement
   <Label Wrap Element>
   <KeySequence \!Ew>
   <Definition \xF49>
   <Mode All>>
```

Figure 17-1 A menu item as it appears within the file *cmds.cfg.*

Producing a Palette to Change Pages

In this section you will create a palette with three buttons. The buttons will allow you to click to change from body pages to reference pages to master pages.

Creating the Initial Palette to Change Pages

The steps below walk you through the creation of a palette with a large area (big and ugly). This first project uses a large area so that you may become accustomed to working with the palette components before you work in a more constricted area.

1. Create a new FrameMaker document with a small page size (palette-sized).
   a. Select **File** > **New** > **Document**.
   b. In the New dialog box that appears, select **Custom**.
   c. In the Custom Blank Paper dialog box, make a page size using the following properties so that when it is a palette you may set it aside in your FrameMaker application work space:
      Width: 3.5"
      Height: 2.0"
      Single-Sided
      Margins: 0.3" for Top, Bottom, Left, and Right[2]
      Your settings should look like those shown in Figure 17-2 (menus may vary slightly between FrameMaker versions).
   d. Click the **Create** button. Your new, small document should appear.
2. Press **CTRL-click** to highlight the text frame, then click **Delete** to remove the text frame from the newly created document, leaving a blank palette area.
3. Optionally, you may delete the text frame from the Master Pages.
4. Save your palette file as *pages.fm*.

---

2. The smallest margin setting may be around 0.3" and may need to be adjusted depending on your selected printer driver. Try 0.3" first, but increase that number if error messages pop up when you click **Create**. The size is not important, as the resulting frame is deleted immediately. However, you must adjust the margin setting to a size that allows you to get around the margin-related error messages and to create the document.

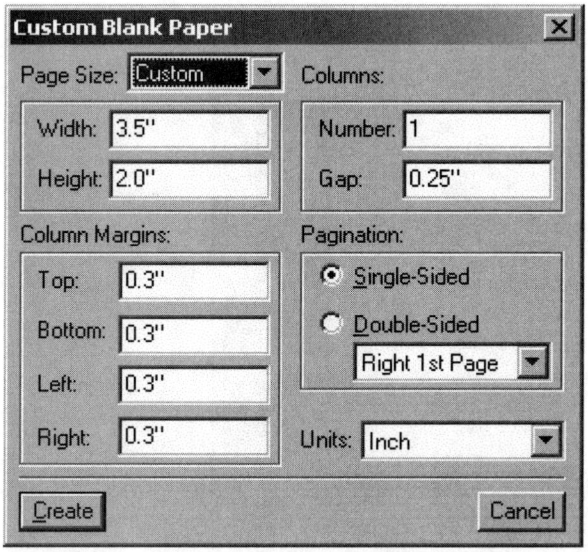

Figure 17-2 Setting the page size for the palette document.

Adding a Button for Master Pages

You need to create each button on your palette and give it a graphic, a text frame, and a marker containing the action information. In this section you will create the first button for your palette.

1. Select **Graphics** > **Tools** to open the Graphics toolbar.
2. From the Graphics toolbar, use the Text Frame tool ( ) to draw a small text frame (see Figure 17-3).
3. In the dialog box that pops up, leave the number of columns at 1 and click **Set**.

   Now that you have a text frame, you can drop in a marker that turns this frame into an active area.
4. Select **Special** > **Hypertext** to open the Hypertext dialog box.
5. Place the insertion point inside the text frame and type the following: **fcodes 343** (see Figure 17-4).

   The term "fcodes" is specific to FrameMaker and tells FrameMaker to perform an action. The action is designated by a code, which may be numbers or letters. In this case, the number 343 refers to the action "Go To Master Pages."[3]
6. Click the **New Hypertext Marker** button to place the marker in your text frame.

---

3. More fcodes are listed in the file *cmds.cfg* in FrameMaker's install directory under */fminit/configui*.

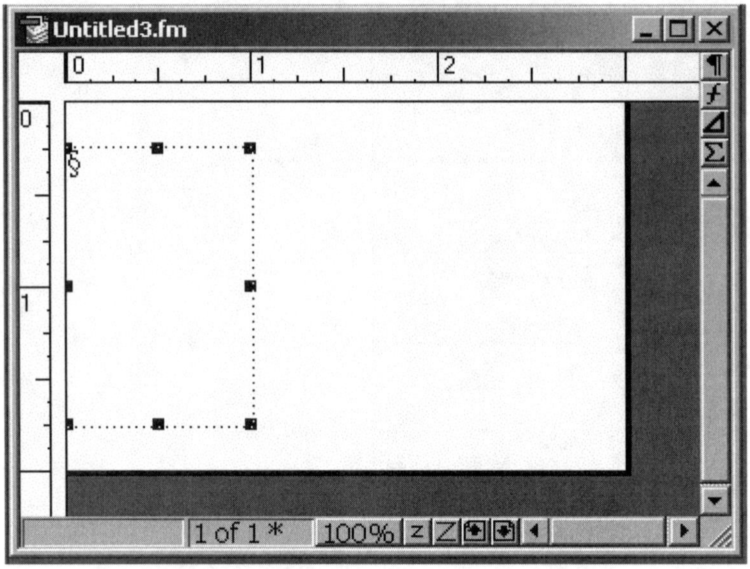

Figure 17-3 Text frame drawn on the palette-sized document.

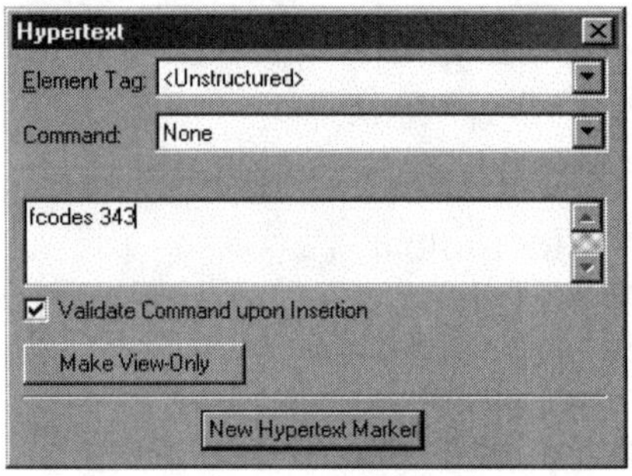

Figure 17-4 The Hypertext marker window.

You now have your first action area. Since your text symbols are (probably) on, you will see a marker (T) appear at your insertion point.

7. Place an appropriate graphic (in this case, a picture designating a jump to the master pages) over the active area. Import this graphic into your palette document.[4]

   a. **Click** outside your text frame so that you do not have an insertion point.

   b. Import by selecting **File** > **Import** > **File** and selecting an appropriate graphic.

   c. Select *either* **Import By Reference** or **Copy Into Document** and then click the **Import** button.

---

4. While the descriptions in this chapter refer to imported graphics, alternatively you may use the FrameMaker drawing tools to create graphics. Just remember to set all graphics to back, behind the text frame containing the action marker.

Note: *For palettes that will be used by multiple users, using Copy Into Document is recommended. Doing so will ensure that the palette will look the same on different users' machines.*

d. In the Dpi dialog box, type **100** for the dpi as a starting point. (You may then need to adjust the graphic to make it approximately the same size as your text frame.) The master page graphic should appear in your document and should still be selected.

e. From the **Graphics** menu, select **Send to Back**.

f. Set the **Graphics** > **Runaround Properties** to **Don't Run Around**.

g. To align the master page graphic with your text frame, **CTRL-click** on the text frame (while the graphic is still selected) and choose **Graphics** > **Align** > **T/B Centers** and **L/R Centers**.

h. To avoid any errors in moving later, select **Graphics** > **Group** to group the text frame and graphic.

Adding Another Button to the Palette

You now have one active area with a related graphic. Create another active area for the body pages:

1. Continue by again using the Text Frame tool (▤) to draw a small text frame.

   In the dialog box that pops up, click **Set**.

Note: *To save time, you can copy the existing text frame and modify the hypertext marker fcode to match the code shown in Step 3.*

2. Select **Special** > **Hypertext** to open the Hypertext dialog box.
3. Place your insertion point inside your text frame and then type the following inside the Hypertext box: **fcodes 342** (a code that means "Go To Body Pages").
4. Click the **New Hypertext Marker** button to place the marker in your text frame.

   You now have your action area.
5. Place over the active area a graphic that is appropriate to the action. Import this graphic into your palette document using the instructions provided in the previous section.
6. While the graphic is selected, select **Graphics** > **Send to Back** to so that your text area and marker are on top. This ensures that the active area is not obscured by the graphic (which would limit clickable area).
7. **Save** your palette file.

Adding a Third Button to the Palette

You now have two active areas. Create a third and final active area for the reference pages:

1. Again use the Text Frame tool (▤) to draw a small text frame.

   In the dialog box that pops up, click **Set**.

Note: *To save time, you can copy the existing text frame and modify the hypertext marker fcode to the code shown in Step 3.*

2. Select **Special** > **Hypertext** to open the Hypertext dialog box.
3. Place your insertion point inside your text frame and type the following inside the Hypertext box: **fcodes 344** (a code that means "Go To Reference Pages").
4. Click the **New Hypertext Marker** button to place the marker in your text frame. You now have your action area.
5. Place over the active area a graphic that is appropriate to the action. Import this graphic into your document and remember to select **Send to Back** per the previous instructions.
6. **Save** your file.

   You now have a document with actions that may be set up as a palette similar to the palette shown in Figure 17-5.

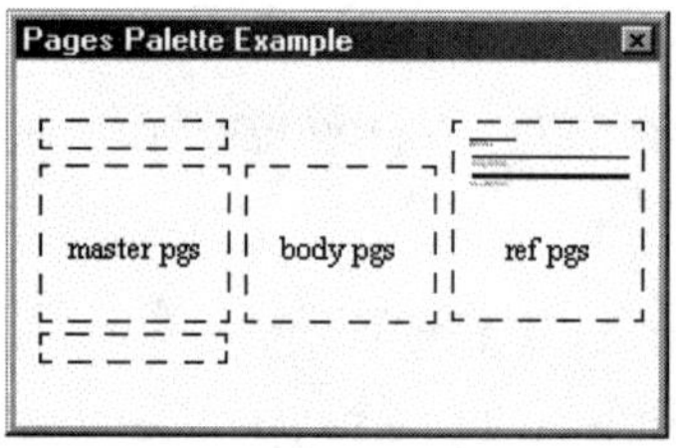

Figure 17-5 Your three-button palette.

Finishing As a Palette Using MIF

Once you have your file saved, you need to save it again as a Maker Interchange Format (MIF) file. This type of file is editable using text editors and can be manipulated into opening as a palette.

1. From the **View** menu, turn off **Borders** and **Text Symbols**.
2. With your file *pages.fm* saved, select **File** > **Save As** and then select **MIF** from the File Type drop-down list.

   Be sure to change the filename to *pages.mif*.

3. Click **Save**.
4. Close your FrameMaker document *pages.mif*. If FrameMaker asks you to save, you can close without saving (as you already have saved the FM file).
5. Open the MIF file so that you can edit it. You may use Notepad or another text editor. If you like, you can open it in FrameMaker by following these steps:
   a. Select **File** > **Open**.
   b. Select the MIF file that you just created.
   c. Hold down your **Shift** key, then click the **Open** button. You may then release the **Shift** key.

Note: *The Shift key tells FrameMaker that you want to open your file as a text file. If you do not hold Shift, then FrameMaker will "interpret" the MIF and open it as an FM document.*

   d. In the *Reading Text File* dialog box that pops up, accept the selected choices and click **Read**.

      The MIF file opens as a text file, with the start of its contents looking something like the contents shown in Figure 17-6.
6. Now you can edit your MIF file. Several items need to be adjusted so that your file changes from a regular document into a palette.
   a. Do a **Find** for the term "viewonly."
   b. When Find takes you to it, review the lines of text relating to palette views (see Figure 17-7).
   c. For **DViewOnly**, change **No** to **Yes**. This ensures that your MIF opens as a locked, view-only FrameMaker document.
   d. For **DViewOnlyWinBorders**, change **Yes** to **No**. This removes the outer window edging from your document.
   e. For **DViewOnlyWinMenuBar**, change **Yes** to **No**. This line removes your menus from the MIF.
   f. For **DViewOnlyWinPalette**, change **No** to **Yes**. The most important step, this turns your document into a FrameMaker palette.
   g. Select **Save As** and save the file as a **Text Only...** text file, changing the filename to ***Pages Palette*** (with no extension).

      When the Save As Text dialog box appears, accept the selected items and click **Save**.
   h. Close the file ***pages.mif*** and any other open files.

Note: *If your computer adds an extension to the filename, go to Windows Explorer and remove the extension.*

7. Open the file ***Pages Palette***.

   Note that the filename appears as the palette title. This is why you wanted the filename to have no extension.

```
<MIFFile 7.00> # Generated by FrameMaker 7.0p578
# Options:
#     Paragraph Text
#     Paragraph Tags
#     Paragraph Formats
#     Font Information
#     Markers
#     Anchored Frames
#     Tables
```

Figure 17-6 The first few lines of an MIF file.

```
<DViewOnly No>
<DViewOnlyXRef GotoBehavior>
<DViewOnlySelect UserOnly>
<DViewOnlyWinBorders Yes>
<DViewOnlyWinMenubar Yes>
<DViewOnlyWinPopup Yes>
<DViewOnlyWinPalette No>
```

Figure 17-7 ViewOnly section of the MIF file.

8. Open a new document by selecting **File** > **New** > **Document** and then selecting **Portrait**.
9. Test each of your palette buttons by clicking them. You should see the view of your new document change from master pages to body pages to reference pages as you click through your buttons.

Viewing a More Complex Palette

In this section you will view a more complex palette. This palette is available from this book's website and from the author.

This palette has buttons for fcodes functions, plus some functions for hypertext jumps and alerts. Figure 17-8 shows a screenshot of what the palette might look like. This palette is created to illustrate possibilities, and some options may not be practical in the real world.

Figure 17-8 A view of a complex palette (with graphics, text, markers).

Creating a More Complex Palette

Now that you have created a simple palette and viewed a more complex palette, you may want to create a complex palette for yourself. Note that the biggest hurdle to overcome is selecting the items you want to include and performing minor adjustments in the cramped space of a palette.

You may choose to draw a palette in another program and import it into FrameMaker as a single unit. You can then draw text boxes over the areas and insert markers.

Note: *Change your View to 200% or higher to be able to view your palette better as you create it.*

In this palette you will combine what you have seen of fcodes with different types of Hypertext markers. The palette you create will include links to start email messages and to go to Web sites.

The steps in this section produce the palette shown in Figure 17-9.

1. Create a new document of a small size:
   a. Select **File > New > Document**.
   b. In the New window that appears, select **Custom**.
   c. Set the size using the following properties:
      Width: 2.0"
      Height: 4.0"
      Single-Sided
      Margins: 0.3" for top, bottom, left, and right
   d. Click the **Create** button. Your new, small document should appear.
2. **Delete** the text frame from the newly created document, leaving a clean palette area.

Optionally, you may delete the frames from the master pages.

3. Draw the palette as you would like it to appear. Use small graphics and graphic lines to make it look good.
4. Use the text frame tool to create a small rectangle.
5. Over the text frame tool, add graphics or text that depict the actions you are going to add to the palette. Make sure you select all of these, and then select **Graphics** > **Send to Back** to ensure that your text frame stays on top and is easy to select.[5] Your first button may look like the button shown in Figure 17-10.
6. **Save** your palette document as *special.fm*.
7. Place your insertion point in the text frame (by the end-of-flow mark) and insert a Hypertext marker for the action "Paste Special."
   a. Select **Special** > **Hypertext** to open the Hypertext dialog box.
   b. In the Hypertext box, type the following fcode for Paste Special: **fcodes D10**
   c. Click the **New Hypertext Marker** button to place the marker in your text frame. You now have your action.

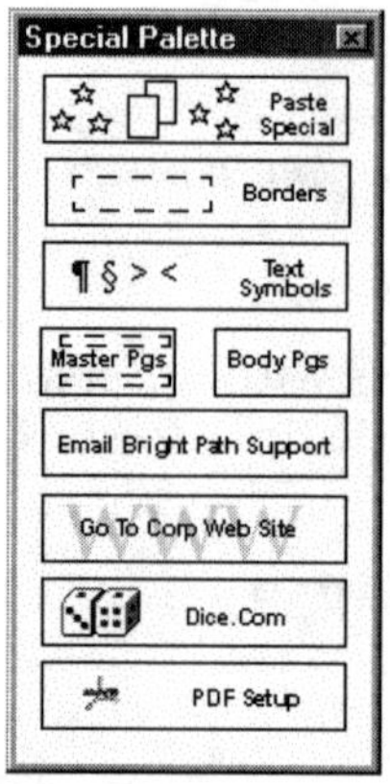

Figure 17-9 A palette with many types of actions.

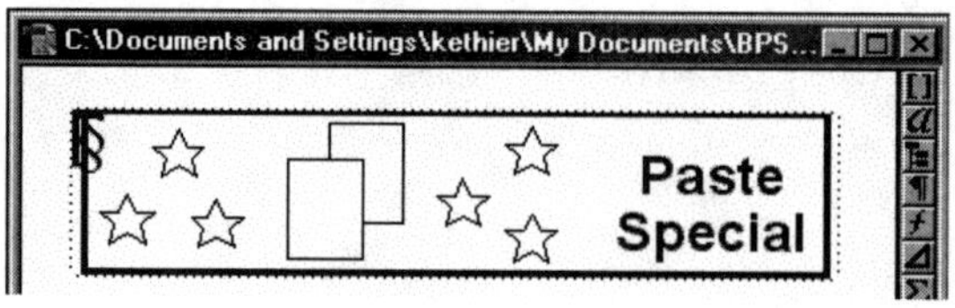

Figure 17-10 How your first button may look.

5. The action works best if the text frame is on top of all the graphics.

Note: *In this exercise you created the graphics first and then placed the markers. FrameMaker does not care if the markers come before or after the graphics. You may even place a graphic before the text frame if you like. The only restriction is that there must be a text frame before the Hypertext marker is inserted.*

8. Continue adding graphics to your palette with related text frames and markers. Use the list of fcodes, as well as hypertext options, to make the buttons perform the actions that you want.
9. Once your palette is prepared, remember to **Save** *special.fm* and **Save As** *special.mif* to the MIF file type.
10. Modify your MIF settings as mentioned earlier in this chapter.

Note: *Once you have modified your MIF file, save it with a name that without an extension to form the "title" of your palette.*

11. Open the MIF file in FrameMaker and test your palette.

Creating a Palettes for Custom Text Characters and Symbols

One of the difficult things to learn about FrameMaker is how to get a custom character. Learning this requires you to review font character sets, text codes, and FrameMaker's character set PDF (in the /OnlineManuals folder).

Once you figure out the keystrokes needed to create your symbols or special characters, you can either memorize them or you can automate the tasks by creating a palette. In this section you will create a small palette for inserting custom characters. Figure 17-11 shows a sample palette with 12 special characters.

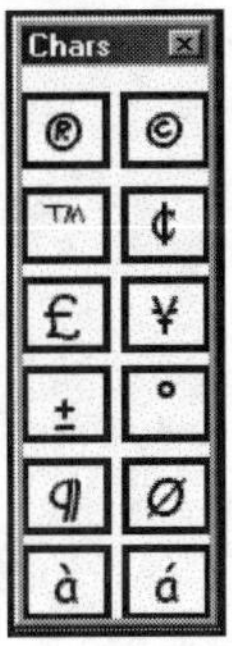

Figure 17-11 A small palette for inserting characters and symbols.

The procedure for making this type of palette is similar to the procedures you followed to make the other palettes in this chapter.

1. List which functions you want on your palette.
2. Sketch your palette using the graphics you would like to have on the palette. Select intuitive graphics that will mean something to you (and others) that will use your palette.
3. Create a new FrameMaker document with a small (palette-sized) page size.
4. Set up the palette layout and functions.
5. **Save** your document as a **.fm* file.
6. Select **Save As** to save your document as a **.mif* file.
7. Lock your document to make it into a palette.
8. **Open** your palette document (**.mif*) and use the functions in other open FrameMaker documents.

On of the main differences between the palettes made for menu functions and this palette is this: For menu functions you create a marker containing an fcode that is found in the file *cmds.cfg*, but for this menu you create a marker containing an fcode found in an online manual (*Character_Sets.pdf* in FrameMaker 6 and higher).

These character fcodes are similar to those for commands, as shown in Figure 17-12, which shows the marker content for a symbol.

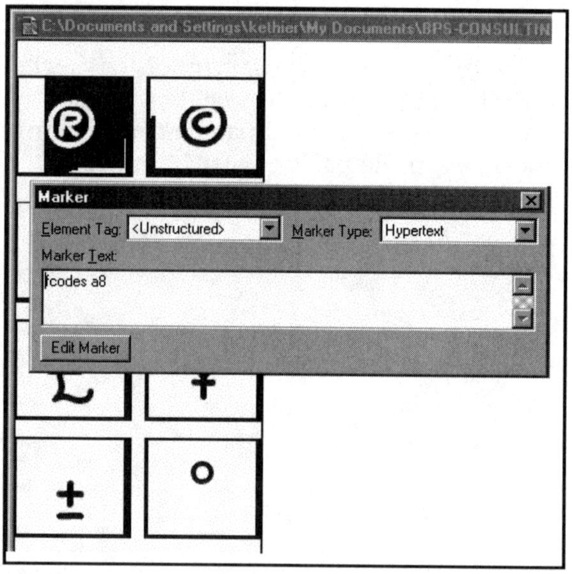

Figure 17-12 Displaying a marker for the registered trademark symbol.

Type the word "fcodes" (just as with your previous palettes), enter the code found in the document *Character_Sets.pdf* after the word "fcodes," and then click the **New Marker** button. Figure 17-13 shows a sample page of the document *Character_Sets.pdf,* with the appropriate code circled.

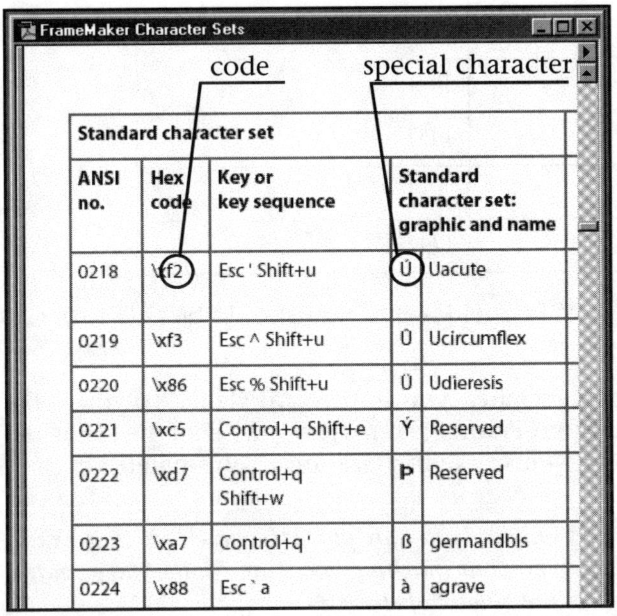

Standard character set				
ANSI no.	Hex code	Key or key sequence	Standard character set: graphic and name	
0218	\xf2	Esc ' Shift+u	Ú	Uacute
0219	\xf3	Esc ^ Shift+u	Û	Ucircumflex
0220	\x86	Esc % Shift+u	Ü	Udieresis
0221	\xc5	Control+q Shift+e	Ý	Reserved
0222	\xd7	Control+q Shift+w	Þ	Reserved
0223	\xa7	Control+q '	ß	germandbls
0224	\x88	Esc ` a	à	agrave

Figure 17-13 A view of the file *Character_Sets.pdf.*

Creating a Palette for Structure-Related Menu Choices

If you are new to structure, you may still be learning your way through the new menus in FrameMaker 7 that relate to structure. If you are tiring of clicking three and four times with your mouse, only to find out you have gone into the wrong submenu, then a palette for structure options might be a good idea for you.

Create a small palette with structure-related options. You may keep this open on your desktop and use it to one-click some of the items that are normally buried in submenus.

Structure fcodes are found in the file *cmds.cfg,* clustered near the end. Table 17-2 shows some of these fcodes.

Using Your Palettes

Palettes may be freely distributed once that have been saved with the special settings. As long as you have provided the graphics and fonts necessary,

Table 17-2 A Few of the Structure fcodes

Structure-Related Command	fcode
Import Element Definitions	F9E
Unwrap (selected) Elements	FD6
Element Namespaces	FF8
Validate	FE0
Show Element Context	A31
Structure View (open)	FD1

anyone with the same version of FrameMaker as you should be able to access your palette.

Palettes do not automatically start when you start FrameMaker, so you will need to open them once you open FrameMaker. They may then be set aside and made available as you work—just like the Graphics Tools palette.

Note: *If you are working in Windows, you may place the palette MIF in your Start directory so that when your machine boots up, FrameMaker automatically launches and the palette opens.*

Moving forward, any time that you wish to change your palette or add to it, you should return to the original FM file, then go through the MIF creation and editing process to create the revised palette.

Summary

Palettes are fairly easy to make and can give you easier access to commonly used functions. If you find that there are some menus you wade through on a regular basis—or special characters you need but you keep forgetting how to make them—then taking a few hours to pull together a palette can be a timesaver in the long run.

Part V

Extending FrameMaker

18

Extending and Adjusting FrameMaker

Kay Ethier

This chapter presents ways to adjust FrameMaker's user interface, and the use of third-party tools to extend FrameMaker's features.

Applicable to FrameMaker versions 5.5, 6.0, and 7.0/7.1

The Frame Developer's Kit

Adobe's Frame Developer's Kit (FDK) is, as Adobe describes it on their Web site, "...a set of C libraries and header files that allow you to write API clients or plug-ins using the C or C++ programming language."

You may use the FDK to create an API (application program interface) client that performs a function not directly built into FrameMaker. Using an API, you can access all objects in FrameMaker (paragraphs, markers, graphics) and do something *with them* or *to them*. For example, you might build an API client that will perform a **Find** on all pages of your documents (body, master, and reference) even though this is not possible within the FrameMaker installation itself.

To give you another example, you could build an API client that would locate all anchored frames and set them to have a certain border and a certain size. This can only be done in FrameMaker's installation by seeking out the anchored frames one by one and adjusting them. So, creating the client would automate this task and save you time.

The FDK's main parts are described briefly as follows.

API

Adobe FrameMaker's API lets you write in C, creating API clients. The API, available directly from Adobe, includes libraries, header files, and tools for all the platforms on which FrameMaker ships.

FDE

FDE stands for "Frame Development Environment." This is what makes API clients cross-platform-compatible. It provides platform-independent information and utilities. It also comes with header files and libraries for each platform on which FrameMaker ships.

Structure Import/Export API

Just as its name implies, this API allows you to write clients that specifically optimize the round trip of XML and SGML files.

Maker Interchange Format (MIF)

Adobe's Maker Interchange Format (MIF) is a format that is very familiar to experienced FrameMaker users. **Save As MIF** has been an option for all releases and allows users to turn FrameMaker documents into ASCII format. The ASCII format files may then be opened in any version of FrameMaker, back to the first versions..

Note: *Any features not available in the previous FrameMaker versions will be lost when the MIF is "converted" into an FM file (via* ***File*** *>* ***Open****).*

Users of WebWorks Publisher may also be familiar with MIF, as it is the format that WebWorks uses to save files in the "Temp" folder and when it scans and converts content.

fmbatch (UNIX Only)

This utility allows UNIX users to perform actions (such as **Open** or **Print**) on FrameMaker files without bringing the files up in a user interface. In batch mode, the utility allows users to perform common tasks on multiple files.

User-Specific "maker.ini" Settings

Within the FrameMaker 7 install directory is a file called ***maker.ini***. This file contains information, file paths, and settings. It is accessed when FrameMaker is launched, and users may adjust it before launching to make FrameMaker behave differently, depending on their specific needs.

Note: *While some data may apply to previous versions, this section focuses on the file maker.ini found in FrameMaker 7. Previous versions of FrameMaker and FrameMaker+SGML may have used different file names (maker.ini and fmsgml.ini) and contained slightly different options.*

You should use caution when modifying the INI file. A good practice is to back up the original, then modify the *maker.ini* copy and test it. If you break something, having the original backed up will allow you to start over without doing a reinstall of FrameMaker. You should also make sure you understand what the options are for settings. For example, for some the setting adjustment might be "On," while for others the similar setting might be "True" or something entirely different. You cannot make up your own settings, so ensure that you know what you are doing.

The following is the entire *maker.ini* for FrameMaker 7, annotated. Annotations are in the larger type, preceded by the word "Note."

```
;==========================================================================
;
;   maker.ini    This is the Adobe FrameMaker initialization file.
;
;  As of Version 7.0, a personal copy of maker.ini is created for
;  each user in "%USERPROFILE%\Application Data\Adobe\FrameMaker\<version>"
;  where USERPROFILE is
;
;    "\Documents and Settings\<username>" on Windows 2000 & XP
;    "\WinNT\Profiles\<username>" on Windows NT 4.0
;    "\Windows\Profiles\<username>" on Windows 98 and Me if users
```

```
;                                          save individual preferences
;    "\Windows" on Windows 98 and Me if all users share the same preferences
;
; Any settings FrameMaker automatically saves will be written to this copy.
; When a single-entry key is read, FrameMaker searches for the key in the
; user copy first. If not found, the key in the master copy (this file)
; in the installation directory is used.
; When a list with multiple entries such as [APIClients] and
; [UnknownToKnownFontMap] is read, entries in the user copy and the master
; copy are combined together.
; Both the user copy and the master copy can be manually edited.
; Any changes in the user copy apply only to the user while changes
; in the master copy apply to all users.
;
```

Note: *The section above is descriptive data and self explanatory. Read this carefully to ensure that you modify your INI settings in the correct location for your workstation.*

```
;===========================================================================

[Frame]
;------------------------- Generic information -----------------------------
Version=7.0p492
;  AUTO_VERS_UPDATE  CHANGE_VERSION            end
Language=USEnglish

[RegInfo]
User=Kay Ethier
Company=Bright Path Solutions
RegNum=20-0-01-01-7-XXXXX-CCXXXX
Asn=1030-1208-1472-3208-XXXX-XXXX
```

Note: *The information above contains the user name and serial data. This information is created during installation from user input. (For example, RegNum is generated from the entered ASN.) The "xxxx" are for numbers that have been removed to mask the user's actual ID numbers.*

```
[Preferences]
;-------------------------- Misc preferences -------------------------------
; The period MUST be used for specifying the decimal point.
AskExit=Off
ShowErrors=On
ErrorFileName=consfile.txt
GreekSize=2
RememberMissingFontName=On
DisableAutofitAfterZoom=Off
CrossPlatformFileNaming=Windows 9x/2000/NT
GetLibraryColorRGBFromCMYK=Printing
ExecutablePlugins=EXE
WrappedPlugins=DLX
PluginExtensions=DLL, DLX, EXE
UseSystemCursor=Off
BackupOnSave=On
```

```
AutoSave=Off 5
FMImage=Off
NetworkLock=On
InputMethodAutoActivation=Off
CreateAllNamedDestinations=Off
Snap=Off
Gravity=Off
CtrlAltIsAltGr=Off
```

Note: *Some of the items above you may recognize from when you select **File > Preferences**. You may adjust these items either through the interface or within the INI. Some items, such as the Snap=Off default, are only available here in the INI.*

```
;
; Suppress these extensions if suppressed in the shell.
;
SuppressExtensions=fm, book

API=On
Zoom=25, 50, 80, 100, 120, 140, 150, 160, 200, 400
```

Note: *Did you know that when you change your Zoom settings using the Set pop-up that you are modifying the INI? Any zoom percentages that you change will appear within your INI...and will be used each time you launch FrameMaker!*

```
PenWidths=0.5, 1.0, 3.0, 4.0
```

Note: *Similar to the behavior of the zoom percentages, any Pen Widths that you change through the **Graphics > Tools** palette will be remembered in the INI...and will be used each time you launch FrameMaker!*

```
ClipboardFormatsPriorities=FILE, OLE 2, EMF, META, DIB, BMP, MIF, RTF, TEXT
```

Note: *When you **Copy** something to the clipboard, then hit **Paste Special** within a FrameMaker document, the items appear in the Paste Special dialog box in the order stated in the code above. If you do a **Paste** instead, then the first applicable item in the list (from left to right) would be automatically used. The above order, for example, would force Word information that is Pasted into FrameMaker to come in as linked. If you prefer the "default" to be RTF or TEXT, then you would move those choices to the beginning.*

```
MonitorSize=Default
AutoMnemoniseMenus=On
StickyPopupThreshold=500

; If UseDisplayUnitInTemplate is On, default display units are taken from
; document templates. Otherwise, the values are taken from here.
UseDisplayUnitInTemplate=Off
```

```
DefaultRulerInch=0.125in
DefaultRulerCm=0.5cm
DefaultGridInch=0.5in
DefaultGridCm=1cm
DefaultSnapInch=0.125in
DefaultSnapCm=0.25cm
```

Note: *Via the **View > Options** menu you may adjust settings for your templates and files. If you do not set anything, then the settings above are used. You may adjust the INI, but this is only reflected on your workstation, not on others'. A "best practice" for templates is to adjust the viewing options for the most-often used settings. For instance, if you normally work in metric, then you would adjust the options for metric choices (cm, mm).*

```
UsePostscript=On
GDIRasterizeKiloPixelLimit=8192

ShowQuickAccessBar=On H
ShowFormattingBar=On
MenuSet=Complete
;MenuSet=Quick
;MenuSet=Custom

ConfigWarnKbdRedundant=Off
ConfigWarnKbdOverride=Off

; force to bring up unknown file type dialog
ForceFileTypeChoices=Off

[Directories]
;---------------------------- Directories --------------------------------
; If it is not an absolute path, then it is relative to the FMHome directory.
HelpDir=help
LanguageDir=dict
TemplateDir=templates
FilterDllDir=filters
OpenDirOnStart=
PaletteDir=fminit\maker
PaletteDirStructure=fminit\fmstruct
AlwaysOnTopPaletteDir=
ColorLib=fminit\Color
FontDir=fminit\fonts
FontDirCache=fminit\fonts\.cache
UnicodeDir=fminit\unicode

Samples=samples
OnlineManuals=omanuals
ReleaseNotes=relnotes
Clipart=clipart
Templates=templates
SgmlDir=sgml
XmlDir=xml
StructureDir=structure
XMLCookbook=XMLCookbook
IndexSortDir=fminit\indexsort
```

Note: *The code above is fairly self explanatory. It points to the FrameMaker directories that are automatically installed and ensures that FrameMaker can find its own information. Those working in structure should make sure that the XML and SGML "home" directories are specified.*

```
[Files]
;------------------------------- Files ------------------------------------
; If it is not an absolute path, then it is relative to the FMHome directory.
UserDictionary=
SiteDictionary=dict\site.dct
```

Note: *If you set up your workstations to access a site dictionary, then you would adjust the path above (perhaps to a network drive) or use the default path for your dictionary location.*

```
CustomDoc=fminit\custom
AsciiTemplate=fminit\txttmplt
EquationDoc=fminit\equation
ThesaurusDoc=fminit\thesaurs
TemplateBrowserDoc=fminit\maker\tmpltbrw
VerticalQuickAccessBar=fminit\vertqab
LayoutDoc=fminit\layout
StructureWindowDoc=fminit\fmstruct\strwin

EPSHeader=fminit\header.ps
PDFPSHeader=fminit\headerPDF.ps
FMFont=fminit\fm5font.ttf
FMSmallFont=fminit\fmsmall.fon
MarshallingDLL=afmfdk.dll
RunWrappedPlugin=fmrnclnt.exe

Resources=fminit\fmres.dll
DialogResources=fminit\fmdlg.dll
AlternateResources=fminit\fmcustom.dll

ToolBarIniFile=fminit\fmtoolbr.ini

ConfigCommandsFile=fminit\configui\cmds.cfg
MSWinConfigCommandsFile=fminit\configui\wincmds.cfg
ConfigMathFile=fminit\configui\mathcmds.cfg
ConfigMenuFile=fminit\maker\menus.cfg
ConfigMenuFileStructure=fminit\fmstruct\menus.cfg
ConfigCustomUIFile=fminit\configui\customui.cfg

MathCharacterFile=fminit\mathchar.cfg
PageSizesFile=fminit\pagesize.cfg
FirstRunOpenDoc=
```

Note: *Above are pointers to the menu and command data, enabling FrameMaker to locate, load, and operate menus and shortcuts.*

```
[RecentlyVisitedFiles]
```

Note: *As you work in files, those that are most recently used are listed at the bottom of your File menu. They will also be remembered here in this file (and can be removed from here).*

```
[DialogLayout]
;------------------------ Dialog & Window layout --------------------
MakerWin=3, -1, -1, -1, -1, 0, 0, 640, 400
PCatalog=500, 40, 130, 180
CCatalog=500, 220, 130, 180
Tools=600, 20
Equation=0, 20
Spell=0, 20
PFormat=7, 43
CFormat=0, 20
Search=0, 20
Table=7, 63
Ruling=0, 20
Markers=0, 20
Hypertext=0, 20
CondText=0, 20
Numbering=0, 20
Help=0, 20
Thesaurus=0, 20
TemplateBrowser=0, 20
VQuickAccessBar=0, 20
ECatalog=500, 50, 130, 350
```

Note: *The above code is fairly self explanatory; it determines the positioning of your FrameMaker interface items.*

```
[APIClients]
;----------------------------- API Clients -----------------------------
;ClientName=ClientType, [facet, format_id, vendor_id, display_name, ] description,
path, mode, optional file extension for filter
; when ClientType is filter type, facet, format_id, vendor_id and display_name are
required.
; mode can be one of maker, structured, all.  it determines for which mode(s) to
load this client.
; for example, RTF=TextImport, RTF, RTF, FAPI, RTF, Rich Text Format (RTF) Import,
filters\rtfimprt.dll,all,^.rtf
ClickPrint=Standard, Print Online Manuals, fminit\clickprt.dll, all
;FrameMakerPDFAssistant=Standard, Change default printer for Acrobat Distiller,
fminit\framepdf.dll, all
; Ichitaro clients
ICHITARO5=FileToFileTextImport, JAW, MIF, JAW, IVY, ICHITARO5, ICHITARO5
Import,filters\jbw2mif.dll,all,^.jaw
ICHITARO6=FileToFileTextImport, JBW, MIF, JBW, IVY, ICHITARO6, ICHITARO6
Import,filters\jbw2mif.dll,all,^.jbw
RTF Japanese=FileToFileTextImport, RTF, MIF, RTF, IVY, RTF Japanese, IVY RTF-J
Import,filters\rtfj2mif.dll,all,^.rtf
RTF (Japanese)=FileToFileTextExport,MIF,RTFJ,RTFJ,IVY, RTF Japanese, RTF Japanese
Export,filters\mif2rtfj.dll,all,^.rtf
CGM Import IsoDraw=FileToFileGFXImport, CGM, FrameVector, CGM, ISO, CGM Import
IsoDraw, CGM Import, filters\IsoConverter.dll,all,^.cgm
```

```
SVG Import=FileToFileGFXImport, SVG, FrameImage, SVG, ORBL, SVG, SVG,
filters\svgfilter.dll,all,^.svg
;IGES Import IsoDraw=FileToFileGFXImport, IGES, FrameVector, IGES, ISO, IGES Import
IsoDraw, IGES Import, filters\IsoConverter.dll,all,^.igs
;DXF Import IsoDraw=FileToFileGFXImport, DXF, FrameVector, DXF, ISO, DXF Import
IsoDraw, DXF Import, filters\IsoConverter.dll,all,^.dxf
;HPGL Import IsoDraw=FileToFileGFXImport, HPGL, FrameVector, HPGL, ISO, HPGL Import
IsoDraw, HPGL Import, filters\IsoConverter.dll,all,^.hpl
CGM Export IsoDraw=FileToFileGFXExport, FrameVector, CGM, CGM, ISO, CGM Export
IsoDraw, CGM Export, filters\IsoConverter.dll,all,^.cgm
;IGES Export IsoDraw=FileToFileGFXExport, FrameVector, IGES, IGES, ISO, IGES Export
IsoDraw, IGES Export, filters\IsoConverter.dll,all,^.igs
;DXF Export IsoDraw=FileToFileGFXExport, FrameVector, DXF, DXF, ISO, DXF Export
IsoDraw, DXF Export, filters\IsoConverter.dll,all,^.dxf
;HPGL Export IsoDraw=FileToFileGFXExport, FrameVector, HPGL, HPGL, ISO, HPGL Export
IsoDraw, HPGL Export, filters\IsoConverter.dll,all,^.hpl
HTML=ExportFilter, HTML, HTML, ADBE, HTML, HTML Export, fminit\html.dll,all,^.htm
XML Export=ExportFilter, XML, XML, ADBE, XML, XML Export, fminit\xml.dll,all,^.xml
;WMF Export Adobe India=FileToFileGFXExport, FrameVector, WMF, WMF, ADBI, WMF, WMF
Export, filters\adobeIndiaWMF.dll,all,^.wmf
Asian Character Count=DocReport,Count the number of Asian characters in the
document., fminit\jwordcnt.dll,all
Mailer=Standard, Send Mail API Client, fminit\mailer.dll,all
WordCount=DocReport,Count the number of words in the document,
fminit\wordcnt.dll,all
BookErrorLog=Standard, Report errors during book generation,
fminit\bookerrlog.dll,all
PDFSize=Standard, Optimize PDF Size, fminit\pdfsize.dll,all
WebDAV=Standard, WebDAV client, fminit\WebDAV.dll,all
; "SGML" and "XML" are only placeholders for the builtin SGML and XML open
functions
; -- they aren't used by the product.
SGML=TextImport, SGML, SGML, FRAM, SGML, SGML Import,
filters\dispatch.dll,structured,^.sgm
XML Import=TextImport, XML, XML, FRAM, XML, XML Import,
filters\dispatch.dll,structured,^.xml
; FrameMakerSGML clients
Element Catalog Manager=Standard, Import and export element definitions,
fminit\ecm.dll,structured
Structure Generator=Standard, Generate structure in unstructured documents,
fminit\sgen.dll, structured
FmDispatcher=Standard, Central routing client for SGML import/export,
fminit\dispatch.dll,structured
FmTranslator=Standard, Frame default translation client for SGML import/export,
fminit\trnslate.dll, structured
xml-css=Standard, XML CSS generator, fminit\xmlcss.dll, structured
DocBook=Standard, DocBook Starter Kit SGML Application, fminit\docbook.dll,
structured
Xhtml=Standard, XHTML XML Application, fminit\xhtml.dll, structured
Microsoft RTF1.6=ExportFilter, RTF, RTF, ADBI, Microsoft RTF1.6, RTF Export,
filters\ExportUtility.dll, all, ^.rtf
Microsoft RTF=TextImport, RTF, RTF, ADBI, Microsoft RTF, Rich Text Format (RTF)
Import, filters\ImportUtility.dll, all, ^.rtf
Microsoft Word=TextImport, WORD, WORD, ADBI, Microsoft Word, WORD Import,
filters\ImportUtility.dll, all, ^.doc
Microsoft Excel=TextImport, XLS, XLS, ADBI, Microsoft Excel, Excel Import,
filters\ImportUtility.dll, all, ^.xls
```

```
WWPPE6=Standard,WebWorks Professional Edition Plugin,C:\Program
Files\Quadralay\WebWorks Publisher Professional Edition 7.0\bin\wwppro6.dll,all
WWPPE7=Standard,WebWorks Professional Edition Plugin,C:\Program
Files\Quadralay\WebWorks Publisher Professional Edition 7.0\bin\wwpfm7.dll,all
WWPSE7=Standard,WebWorks Standard Edition Plugin,C:\Program
Files\Quadralay\WebWorks Publisher Standard Edition 7.0\bin\wwpfm7.dll,all
```

Note: *Above is the APICLIENTS section. In this section is pointers to DLL files and other files that FrameMaker may access. Some of the above pointers are part of the basic install, such as the filters. Others have been added as third-party software was installed, such as the link to WebWorks Publisher items at the bottom. If you install plug-ins and third-party tools, then this area may adjust itself on its own—or require you to adjust it.*

Semi-colons in front of filters indicate that the filters are "commented out" or inactive. You may comment out any filters that you do not wish to use, or that are to be replaced by other filters that you make available.

```
[DashPatterns]
;---------------------- Dash Pattern Definitions ------------------------
1=Dash, 8, 6
2=Hidden, 4
3=Longdash, 16, 10
4=Dot, 2, 4
5=Dash-Dot, 12, 6, 2, 6
6=Dash-Dot-Dot, 12, 6, 2, 6, 2, 6
7=Chain, 12, 6, 6, 6
8=Phantom, 20, 6, 6, 6, 6, 6
```

Note: *When working in the graphics tools, you may adjust the Dash pattern of an object. However, when FrameMaker restarts, the Dash returns to the default setting above. If you want a dash other than the "normal" one to be used (to save you time in changing it over and over), then adjust it here. For example, if you are always using a 7=Chain pattern, then adjust the 1=Dash pattern to match.*

```
[Thermometers]
;-------------------- Thermometer Color Definitions ----------------------
ThermoDoneColor=255, 0, 255
ThermoRemainingColor=192, 192, 192

[DocCompare]
;------------------- Document Compare Utility Setup ----------------------
CreateSummaryOnly=Off
MarkInsertedText=ConditionInserted
;MarkInsertedText=ConditionTag
;MarkInsertedText=Nothing
InsertConditionTag=Inserted
MarkDeletedText=ConditionDeleted
;MarkDeletedText=ConditionTag
;MarkDeletedText=ReplacementText
DeleteConditionTag=Deleted
```

```
DeleteReplacementText=^
AddChangeBars=On
InsertHyperTextLinks=On
ThresholdFactor=75
```

Note: *The settings above are used when you select **File** > **Utilities** > **Compare Documents**. The settings may be adjusted here or in the document comparison utility's Options area.*

```
[Spelling]
;------------------------- Spelling options ---------------------------
FindRepeatedWords=On
FindUnusualHyphenation=Off
FindUnusualCap=Off
IgnoreSingleCharWords=On
IgnoreAllCaps=On
FindStraightQuotes=On
FindExtraSpaces=On
IgnoreRomanNumerals=Off
IgnoreWordsWithDigits=On
FindTwoInARow=On !,.:;?
IgnoreWordsContaining=On .
FindSpaceBefore=On !%),.:;?]}\xC8\xD3\xD5\xDD
FindSpaceAfter=On $([{\xC7\xD2\xD4\xDC\xE2\xE3
```

Note: *The above items are set and adjusted as you work in your Spelling Checker and adjust the Options.*

```
; Smart Quote Characters
; SmartQuotes \xd4\xd5\xd2\xd3 )  English curved quotes
; SmartQuotes \xe2\xd4\xe3\xd2 )  German-style quotes with base quotes
; SmartQuotes \xd5\xd5\xc7\xc8 )  French-style quotes using guillemets
; SmartQuotes \xd5\xd5\xd3\xd3 )  Swedish- and Finnish-style quotes
; SmartQuotes \xd4\xd5\xd2\xd3 )  Italian curved quotes
;
; English curved quotes:
SmartQuotes=\xd4\xd5\xd2\xd3
```

Note: *The above settings are used when you select **Format** > **Document** > **Text Options**, and they allow you to select whether curly quotes or straight quotes are used.*

```
[StructureView]
;-------------------------  Structure View  ---------------------------
Position=360, 144, 376, 272
AttrFont=Arial
AttrSize=10
AttrValFont=Arial
AttrValSize=10
ElemFont=Arial
ElemSize=10
KeywordFont=Arial
```

```
KeywordSize=10
SnipFont=Arial
SnipSize=10
SnipPos=4, 8, 12, 16, 20, 24
TagFont=Arial
TagSize=10
Origin=24, 24
AlwaysStayOnTop=On
AttrErrSym=x
AttrSepSym==
AttrValidate=On
CollapseSym=-
ExpandSym=+
AttrNoneSym=+
AttrSomeSym=+
AttrAllSym=-
```

Note: *Above are the settings for your structure view, its position, and its behavior.*

*If you do not like your structure view always covering your open document, you may set **AlwaysStayOnTop** to **Off**. This allows it to go to the back of your active windows when you are not using it. Be careful, though, as this setting puts the structure view outside of your FrameMaker application and may make it difficult for you to view the Structure View and Document Views together.*

```
[Fonts]
;=========================================================================
;                            Font Options
;=========================================================================

;
; ATM Auto-activated Fonts
;
; ATM allows a font that is present on your system but not in an active
; working set to be "auto-activated".
;
; This option only has an effect if ATM 4.0 or greater is installed and
; enabled on your system.
;
; By default, Adobe FrameMaker will attempt ATM font auto-activation. An entry
; is written to the Frame console when a font is auto-activated.
;
AtmFontAutoActivation=On

;
; ATM Substitute Fonts
;
; For some fonts that are unavailable on your system, ATM can synthesize
; a substitute font having identical metrics for the unavailable font.
; When a substitute font is used, the text will not appear the same;
; However, line breaks and formatting are not compromised.
;
; This option can be useful when editting a document created on another
```

```
; platform which references fonts unavailable on your system.
;
; This option only has an effect if ATM 4.0 or greater is installed and
; enabled on your system.
;
; By default, Adobe FrameMaker will not attempt ATM font substitution. An entry
; is written to the Frame console when a font is substituted.
;
AtmFontSubstitution=Off

;
; Space characters within a line using printer font metrics.
;
; Adobe FrameMaker always uses printer font metrics to calculate where
; linebreaks and pagebreaks occur. However, by default, the relative
; position of each character within a line is displayed on the screen
; using screen font metrics. This "looks" better on the screen but is
; misleading in that the positions of characters within a line on a
; printed page may be different than on a displayed page. In particular,
; if you are trying to position a graphic relative to a character in a
; line, you should change this setting to "On" which results in the
; the use of printer font metrics when displaying lines.
;
DisplayUsingPrinterMetrics=Off

;
; Sizes which will appear in the Format dialog boxes:
;
Sizes=7pt, 8pt, 9pt, 10pt, 11pt, 12pt, 14pt, 18pt, 24pt, 36pt

;
; Definition of the font vocabulary:
;   Angles, Variations: a list of the words.
;   Weight: the list of words and the associated weight for Windows, if any.
;
Angles=Regular, Kursiv, Slanted, Oblique, Italic, Obliqued

Variations=UltraCompressed, ExtraCompressed, Compressed, Condensed, Narrow,
Regular, Wide, Poster, Expanded

Weights=Thin 100, ExtraLight 200, SemiLight 250, Light 300, Book 300, Regular 400,
SemiBold 600, DemiBold 600, Bold 700, ExtraBold 800, Heavy 900, Bolded 700

;
; Default used to map unknown fonts:
;
DefaultFamily=Times New Roman, Tms Rmn
DefaultAngle=Regular
DefaultVariation=Regular
DefaultWeight=Regular
DefaultSize=12

;
; Defaults used to map unknown Asian fonts:
;
; Japanese font in JIS X 0212-1990 Shift-JIS
DefaultJapaneseFamily=,l,r -¾'©
```

```
; Korean font in KS C 5601-1987
DefaultKoreanFamily=¹ÙÅÁ

; Simplified Chinese font in GB 2312-80
DefaultSimplifiedChineseFamily=ËÎÌå

; Traditional Chinese font in Big5
DefaultTraditionalChineseFamily=²Ó©úÅé


;
; Frame font family used for FrameMath:
;
MathFamily=Symbol

;
; Frame font information used for UI calculations
;
UiCalcFont=MS Sans Serif, 8, 600

;
; Font used for dialogs on Asian systems with non-Asian resources
;
; Japanese font in JIS X 0212-1990 Shift-JIS
DefaultJapaneseDialogFont=,l,r ,ofSfVfbfN, 9

; Korean font in KS C 5601-1987
DefaultKoreanDialogFont=System, 10

; Simplified Chinese font in GB 2312-80
DefaultSimplifiedChineseDialogFont=System, 10

; Traditional Chinese font in Big5
DefaultTraditionalChineseDialogFont=System, 10

;
; Frame font used for banner window
;
BannerFont=Arial

;
; Frame font families that will not be spell checked:
;
NonTextFamilies=ZapfDingbats, Symbol, WingDings, Monotype Sorts, Euro Monospace,
Euro Sans, Euro Serif

; Angle/Weight aliases used when reading documents from other platforms
; (basically synonyms used when reading a document):
[FontAngleAliases]
Obliqued=Oblique

[FontWeightAliases]
Medium=Regular
Roman=Regular
Semi=SemiBold
Demi=DemiBold
```

```
Bolded=Bold

[WindowsToFrameFontAliases]
;
; This section gives the Frame font name for a Windows font.
; The format is Windows_Font=Frame_Font
; Note this is the only place in maker.ini which refers to Windows fonts.
; All other maker.ini font entries refer to the FrameFont.
;
; The format is (on a single line):
;
;  A_WINDOWS_FONT_NAME,[Italic | Regular |*],[A_WEIGHT |*]=
;  A_FRAME_FONT_NAME, [ AN_ANGLE | * ], [ A_WEIGHT | * ],
;    [ A_VARIATION | * ]
;
;  A_WINDOWS_FONT_NAME=a valid windows font face as it appears in other
;                      Windows applications.
;
;  A_FRAME_FONT_NAME=anything, but generally it is chosen to have
;                    Frame cross-platform compatibility.
;
;  A_WEIGHT=Defined above as Weights=
;
;  AN_ANGLE=Defined above as Angles=
;
;  A_VARIATION=Defined above as Variations=
;
; In the absence of an alias, the default aliasing is always applied,
; it can be written:
;     Windows Family Name, *, *=Windows Family Name, *, *, *
;
; The following are example of entries:
;
; Helvetica, Italic, *=Helvetica, Oblique, *, Regular
; HelveticaNarrow, *, *=Helvetica, * , * , Narrow
; HelveticaNarrow,Italic, *=Helvetica, Oblique, *, Narrow
;

Courier, Italic, *=Courier, Oblique, *, Regular

Helvetica, Italic, *=Helvetica, Oblique, *, Regular
Helvetica-Narrow, Regular, *=Helvetica, Regular, *, Narrow
Helvetica-Narrow, Italic, *=Helvetica, Oblique, *, Narrow

AvantGarde, Italic, Regular=AvantGarde, Oblique, Book, Regular
AvantGarde, Italic, Bold=AvantGarde, Oblique, DemiBold, Regular
AvantGarde, Regular, Regular=AvantGarde, Regular, Book, Regular
AvantGarde, Regular, Bold=AvantGarde, Regular, DemiBold, Regular

Bookman, *, Regular=Bookman, *, Light, Regular
Bookman, *, Bold=Bookman, *, DemiBold, Regular


[UnknownToKnownFontMap]
;
;  This section is for mapping unavailable fonts when reading a document.
;  The format is:    Frame Font Unavailable=Frame Font Available
```

```
;
;  The format for a Frame Font is (on one line):
;
;  A_FRAME_FONT_NAME, [AN_ANGLE | WILDCARD],[A_WEIGHT | WILDCARD],
;   [A_VARIATION | WILDCARD]
;
;  When no mapping is provided the defaults are used in the
;  Default section of [Fonts]
;
;  Examples:
;    Lumina,*,*,*=Helvetica, *, *, *
;    Helvetica,*,Light,*=Helvetica,*,Regular,*
;    Helvetica,*,*,UltraCompressed=Helvetica, *, *, Narrow
;


; Mapping for fonts commonly used by Frame Products on non-Windows platforms:

Chicago, *, *, *=Helvetica, *, *, *
Geneva, *, *, *=Helvetica, *, *, *
NewYork, *, *, *=Times, *, *, *
Monaco, *, *, *=Times, *, *, *
Helvetica, *, *, Condensed=Helvetica, *, *, Narrow

; If you open a document with PostScript fonts without ATM with a non-PostScript
printer:

Courier, *, *, *=Courier New, *, *, *
Times, *, *, *=Times New Roman, *, *, *
Helvetica, *, *, *=Arial, *, *, *
Helvetica, Oblique, *, *=Arial, Italic, *, *

; If you open a document with TrueType fonts and you don't have TrueType:

Times New Roman, *, *, *=Times, *, *, *
Courier New, *, *, *=Courier, *, *, *
Arial, *, *, *=Helvetica, *, *, *
Arial, Italic, *, *=Helvetica, Oblique, *, *

; For import

Helvetica-Narrow, Regular, *, Regular=Helvetica, Regular, *, Narrow
Helvetica-Narrow, Italic, *, Regular=Helvetica, Oblique, *, Narrow



; Mapping for Japanese fonts commonly used by Frame Products on non-Windows
platforms:

; Japanese fonts in JIS X 0212-1990 Shift-JIS
HeiseiMin, *, *, *=,l,r -¾'©, *, *, *
HeiseiMin W3, *, *, *=,l,r -¾'©, *, *, *
HeiseiMincho, *, *, *=,l,r -¾'©, *, *, *

; if you have ATM-J and •½¬-¾'©W3 installed , uncomment the next line
; and comment out the line following.
;Heisei Mincho W3, *, *, *= •½¬-¾'©W3, *, *, *
```

```
Heisei Mincho W3, *, *, *=,l,r -¾'©, *, *, *

•½¬-¾'© W3, *, *, *=,l,r -¾'©, *, *, *
•½¬-¾'©, *, *, *=,l,r -¾'©, *, *, *
Ryumin, *, *, *=,l,r -¾'©, *, *, *
L ƒŠƒ…ƒEƒ~ƒ" L-KL, *, *, *=,l,r -¾'©, *, *, *
ƒŠƒ…ƒEƒ~ƒ" L-KL, *, *, *=,l,r -¾'©, *, *, *
SaiMincho, *, *, *=,l,r -¾'©, *, *, *
•×-¾'©'Ì, *, *, *=,l,r -¾'©, *, *, *
HeiseiKakuGo, *, *, *=,l,r ƒSƒVƒbƒN, *, *, *
HeiseiKakuGothic, *, *, *=,l,r ƒSƒVƒbƒN, *, *, *
Heisei KakuGo W5, *, *, *=,l,r ƒSƒVƒbƒN, *, *, *

; if you have ATM-J and •½¬ŠpƒSƒVƒbƒNW5 installed , uncomment the next line
; and comment out the line following.
;Heisei KakuGothic W5, *, *, *= •½¬ŠpƒSƒVƒbƒNW5, *, *, *
Heisei KakuGothic W5, *, *, *=,l,r ƒSƒVƒbƒN, *, *, *

•½¬ŠpƒSƒVƒbƒN W5, *, *, *=,l,r ƒSƒVƒbƒN, *, *, *
•½¬ŠpƒSƒVƒbƒN, *, *, *=,l,r ƒSƒVƒbƒN, *, *, *
Gothic BBB, *, *, *=,l,r ƒSƒVƒbƒN, *, *, *
M '†ƒSƒVƒbƒN BBB, *, *, *=,l,r ƒSƒVƒbƒN, *, *, *
'†ƒSƒVƒbƒN BBB, *, *, *=,l,r ƒSƒVƒbƒN, *, *, *
ChuGothic, *, *, *=,l,r ƒSƒVƒbƒN, *, *, *
'†ƒSƒVƒbƒN'Ì, *, *, *=,l,r ƒSƒVƒbƒN, *, *, *
Osaka, *, *, *=,l,r ƒSƒVƒbƒN, *, *, *

HYSMyeongJo-Medium, *, *, *=¹ÙÅÁ, *, *, *
HYGoThic-Medium, *, *, *=µ¸¿ò, *, *, *
STSong-Light, *, *, *=ËÎÌå, *, *, *
STHeiti-Regular, *, *, *=°ÚÌå, *, *, *
MSung-Light, *, *, *=²Ó©úÅé, *, *, *
AppleMyungjo, *, *, *=¹ÙÅÁ, *, *, *
AppleGothic, *, *, *=µ¸¿ò, *, *, *
Seoul, *, *, *=µ¸¿ò, *, *, *
Beijing, *, *, *=ËÎÌå, *, *, *
Fang Song, *, *, *=·ÂËÎ_GB2312, *, *, *
Hei, *, *, *=°ÚÌå, *, *, *
Kai, *, *, *=¿¬Ìå_GB2312, *, *, *
Song, *, *, *=ËÎÌå, *, *, *
BiauKai, *, *, *=¼Ð·¢Åé, *, *, *
```

Note: *The large section above includes information about font settings, font lists within the FrameMaker pop-up menus, and font substitution data. Though you should use caution when editing this, it is helpful to be able to modify the font substitutions (such as those that appear in your FrameMaker Console when you are missing fonts).*

```
;----------------------- FormatList -------------------------
; n=<format name> <offset> <size> <signature in hex>
; for example
; 100="XXX Format" 0 4 0x11223344
; the hex value must be started with 0x or 0X. the size of the signature
; must match the size of the size defined in size entry.
[FormatList]
```

```
;------------------------- Filters --------------------------
; n=<formatid><vendorid><source-name> <destination-name> <type> <description> <via>
<file-extension>
; <vendorid> and <filterid> are 4-byte strings (if shorter, blank-pad on
; the right and enclose in "quotes") -- the concatenation <vendorid><filterid>
; is used by the product to identify filters uniquely.
;
; n is not used by Adobe FrameMaker, but the ini file format requires
; the items to the left of the = to be unique.

[Filters]
1="CDR " IMAG CDR  FrameVector GFXImport  "Corel Draw" IMAGMARK.DLL ^.cdr
;2="CGM " IMAG CGM  FrameVector GFXImport  "CGM" IMAGMARK.DLL ^.cgm
3="DIB " FRAM DIB  DIB         FMGFXImport "DIB" Frame.exe ^.bmp
4="DRW " IMAG DRW  FrameVector GFXImport  "Micrografx Drawing" IMAGMARK.DLL ^.drw
5="DWG " IMAG DWG  FrameVector GFXImport  "AutoCAD (DWG)" IMAGMARK.DLL ^.dwg
6="DXF " IMAG DXF  FrameVector GFXImport  "AutoCAD (DXF)" IMAGMARK.DLL ^.dxf
7="EMF " FRAM EMF  EMF        FMGFXImport  "Windows Enhanced Metafile" Frame.exe
^.emf
8="EPSF" FRAM EPSF DIB         FMGFXImport "EPS/EPSF" Frame.exe ^.eps
9="PDF " FRAM PDF DIB         FMGFXImport "PDF" Frame.exe ^.pdf
10="FRMI" FRAM FrameImage FrameImage  FMGFXImport "Frame Image" Frame.exe ^.fmg
11="FRMV" FRAM FrameVector FrameVector  FMGFXImport "FrameVector" Frame.exe ^.fmv
12="G4IM" IMAG CCITTG4 FrameVector GFXImport "CCITTG4" imagmark.dll ^.g4
13="GEM " IMAG GEM  FrameVector GFXImport  "GEM"  IMAGMARK.DLL ^.gem
14="GIF " FRAM GIF  DIB         FMGFXImport "GIF" grphfilt.dll ^.gif
15="HPGL" IMAG HPGL FrameVector GFXImport  "HPGL" IMAGMARK.DLL ^.hgl
16="IGES" IMAG IGES FrameVector GFXImport  "IGES" IMAGMARK.DLL ^.igs
17="JPEG" IMAG JPEG FrameVector GFXImport "JPEG" IMAGMARK.DLL ^.jpg
18="PCX " FRAM PCX  DIB        FMGFXImport  "PCX" grphfilt.dll ^.pcx
19="PICT" IMAG "QuickDraw PICT" FrameVector GFXImport "QuickDraw PICT" IMAGMARK.DLL
^.pct
20="PNG " IMAG PNG FrameVector GFXImport "Portable Network Graphics" imagmark.dll
^.png
21="PNTG" FRAM MacPaint  DIB   GFXImport "MacPaint" macpaint.dll ^.mpt
22="SNRF" FRAM SunRF  DIB      FMGFXImport  "Sun Raster File" Frame.exe ^.rf
23="TIFF" FRAM TIFF  DIB       FMGFXImport  "TIFF"  grphfilt.dll ^.tif
24="WMF " FRAM WMF  WMF        FMGFXImport  "Windows Metafile" Frame.exe ^.wmf
25="WMF " IMAG WMF  FrameVector GFXImport "Windows Metafile to FrameVector"
IMAGMARK.DLL  ^.wmf
26="WPG " IMAG WPG   FrameVector GFXImport  "WordPerfect Graphics" IMAGMARK.DLL
^.wpg
27="XWD " FRAM XWD   DIB       FMGFXImport  "XWD" grphfilt.dll ^.xwd
101="FRMV" FRAM FrameVector FrameVector FMGFXExport "FrameVector" Frame.exe ^.fmv
102="FRMI" FRAM FrameImage FrameImage FMBMPExport "FrameImage" Frame.exe ^.fmg
;103="CGM " IMAG FrameVector CGM GFXExport   "CGM" fmexport.dll ^.cgm
104="IGES" IMAG FrameVector IGES GFXExport  "IGES" fmexport.dll ^.igs
105="PICT" IMAG FrameVector "QuickDraw PICT" GFXExport  "QuickDraw PICT"
fmexport.dll ^.pct
106="EPS " IMAG FrameVector EPSI GFXExport  "EPS" fmexport.dll ^.eps
107="TIFF" IMAG FrameVector TIFF BMPExport  "TIFF" fmexport.dll ^.tif
108="DIB" IMAG FrameVector DIB BMPExport "DIB" fmexport.dll ^.bmp
109="GIF " IMAG FrameVector GIF  BMPExport  "GIF" fmexport.dll ^.gif
110="G4IM" IMAG FrameVector CCITTG4 BMPExport  "CCITTG4" fmexport.dll ^.g4
111="JPEG" IMAG FrameVector JPEG BMPExport "JPEG" fmexport.dll ^.jpg
```

```
112="PNG " IMAG FrameVector PNG BMPExport "Portable Network Graphics" fmexport.dll
^.png
113="WMF " IMAG FrameVector WMF GFXExport "Windows Metafile" fmexport.dll ^.png
114="PDF " FRAM  FrameVector PDF GFXExport "PDF" frame.exe ^.pdf
115="SVG " FRAM SVG          SVG GFXExport "SVG" frame.exe ^.svg
201="MIF " FRAM MIF  MKR        FMTextImport "MIF" Frame.exe ^.mif
202="MML " FRAM MML  MIF        FMTextImport "MML" Frame.exe ^.mml
203="TEXT" FRAM Text  MKR       FMTextImport "Text" Frame.exe ^.txt
204="CVBN" FFLT Ventura  MIF TextImport       "Ventura Publisher" VP2MIF.EXE ^.chp
205="0490" AW4W MSWord MIF TextImport "Microsoft Word for Windows 6.0/7.0" aw4w.xxx
^.msw
206="0441" AW4W MSWord MIF TextImport "Microsoft Word for Windows 2.0" aw4w.xxx
^.msw
207="0440" AW4W MSWord MIF TextImport "Microsoft Word for Windows 1.0" aw4w.xxx
^.msw
208="049m" AW4W MSWord MIF TextImport "Microsoft Word Macintosh 6.0" aw4w.xxx ^.msw
209="0052" AW4W MSWord MIF TextImport "Microsoft Word DOS 5.0/6.0" aw4w.xxx ^.msw
210="0051" AW4W MSWord MIF TextImport "Microsoft Word DOS 4.0" aw4w.xxx ^.msw
211="0050" AW4W MSWord MIF TextImport "Microsoft Word DOS 3.0, 3.1" aw4w.xxx ^.msw
212="0542" AW4W MSWord MIF TextImport "Microsoft Word Mac 5.x" aw4w.xxx ^.msw
213="0541" AW4W MSWord MIF TextImport "Microsoft Word Mac 4.x" aw4w.xxx ^.msw
214="0540" AW4W MSWord MIF TextImport "Microsoft Word Mac 3.x" aw4w.xxx ^.msw
;215="0191" AW4W RTF MIF TextImport "Microsoft RTF1.3" aw4w.xxx ^.rtf
216="0482" AW4W WordPerfect MIF TextImport "WordPerfect DOS/Win 7.0" aw4w.xxx ^.wp
217="0481" AW4W WordPerfect MIF TextImport "WordPerfect DOS/Win 6.1" aw4w.xxx ^.wp
218="0480" AW4W WordPerfect MIF TextImport "WordPerfect DOS/Win 6.0" aw4w.xxx ^.wp
219="0071" AW4W WordPerfect MIF TextImport "WordPerfect DOS/Win 5.1" aw4w.xxx ^.wp
220="0070" AW4W WordPerfect MIF TextImport "WordPerfect DOS/Win 5.0" aw4w.xxx ^.wp
221="0601" AW4W WordPerfect MIF TextImport "WordPerfect Mac 3.0-3.5" aw4w.xxx ^.wp
222="0600" AW4W WordPerfect MIF TextImport "WordPerfect Mac 2.0-2.1" aw4w.xxx ^.wp
223="0590" AW4W WordPerfect MIF TextImport "WordPerfect Mac 1.0" aw4w.xxx ^.wp
224="0460" AW4W IAF MIF TextImport "InterLeaf ASCII Format" aw4w.xxx ^.iaf
225="0150" AW4W DCA0 MIF TextImport "DCA Revisable Form Text" aw4w.xxx ^.dcs
226="0151" AW4W DCA1 MIF TextImport "DCA RFT (DisplayWrite 5)" aw4w.xxx ^.dcs
227="0331" AW4W Ami MIF TextImport "Ami Professional 2-3.1" aw4w.xxx ^.ami
228="0330" AW4W Ami MIF TextImport "Ami Professional 1" aw4w.xxx ^.ami
229="0204" AW4W Lotus MIF TextImport "Lotus 1-2-3 5.0" aw4w.xxx ^.123
230="0203" AW4W Lotus MIF TextImport "Lotus 1-2-3 4.0" aw4w.xxx ^.123
231="0214" AW4W Excel MIF TextImport "Microsoft Excel 5.0" aw4w.xxx ^.xls
;232="3490" AW4W MSWord97 MIF TextImport "Microsoft Word97/98/2000" aw4w.xxx ^.msw
301="0192" AW4W MIF RTF ExportFilter "Microsoft RTF1.3" aw4w.xxx ^.rtf
302="0490" AW4W MIF MSWord ExportFilter "Microsoft Word Win 6.0/7.0" aw4w.xxx ^.msw
303="049m" AW4W MIF MSWord ExportFilter "Microsoft Word Mac 6.0" aw4w.xxx ^.msw
304="0542" AW4W MIF MSWord ExportFilter "Microsoft Word Mac 5.x" aw4w.xxx ^.msw
305="0541" AW4W MIF MSWord ExportFilter "Microsoft Word Mac 4.x" aw4w.xxx ^.msw
306="0071" AW4W MIF WordPerfect ExportFilter "WordPerfect DOS/Win 5.1" aw4w.xxx
^.wp
307="0602" AW4W MIF WordPerfect ExportFilter "WordPerfect Mac 3.5" aw4w.xxx ^.wp
```

Note: *The final section above contains data on the specific filters and their location, such as their order of appearance within the FrameMaker Import File dialog box.*

While this INI file shows that many things within the FrameMaker interface may be adjusted, not everything can be. Some items are set within other files and may not be adjusted without substantial modification using multiple menus or use the FDK.

FrameScript

This section will present an overview of the FrameScript product and show you where to get an evaluation copy and how to install it. It also includes some sample scripts you can run to solve real-world problems.

Note: *Information on FrameScript was made possible by Rick Quattro and Nancy McCoy, experts in the use of FrameScript.*

Overview

FrameScript is a simple programming language that you can use to write scripts to customize FrameMaker and to automate FrameMaker tasks. A script is a list of commands written to a text file that can be executed without user interaction. Another term for script is "macro" or "batch file." Scripts are written in a high-level, English-like language that makes programs easier to read, write, and maintain.

Before FrameScript came along, FrameMaker customizations were accomplished through the use of the FDK. This required the services of an often-expensive C programmer and the use of a C Compiler. FrameScript is designed for users as opposed to programmers, and it gives you FDK functionality without the C programming.

You will find, however, that learning to program in FrameScript is not unlike learning to use FrameMaker: both require a steep learning curve. In general, the more knowledge you have of programming techniques and methodologies, the quicker you'll come up to speed.

FrameScript is very versatile and is not unlike having a personal FrameMaker-savvy assistant at your beck and call. Use FrameScript to do manual tasks automatically. Typically, Framers start by using FrameScript to manage small tasks such as those described later in this chapter. After practicing and working with the software for a while, you'll start to discover new ways to use FrameScript to create an almost limitless number of customized solutions. This makes FrameScript different from most purchased plug-ins, which are generally designed to meet a more targeted purpose.

This chapter assumes that readers have little to no knowledge of FrameScript or programming beyond what's been presented thus far. It is primarily tutorial in nature and describes how to download and install FrameScript as well as how to build and run a few simple examples. There is also a list of resources for more in-depth information.

Writers use FrameScript everyday to accomplish a wide variety of tasks. Many of these scripts are fairly complex and customized to work with a particular template or document to accomplish very specific tasks. Some of the reasons why people use FrameScript include the following:

Customization. You can use scripts to customize your FrameMaker session. You can create new menu items, add interactive dialog boxes, and create a host of useful tools that will work with specific books or templates.

Automate mundane tasks. This is a very popular use for FrameScript and one that justifies the initial cost many times over. These tasks typically require a number of manual steps that FrameScript can perform automatically.

Extending FrameMaker functionality. You can write scripts to add new functions that are not currently available in FrameMaker. These functions may be of interest to only a small number of customers, making it impractical for Adobe to put them in the mainstream product.

Many Framers have invested the time and effort to learn to use this powerful tool in their everyday work to spare them from tedium and to help them work more effectively.

Getting and Installing the Evaluation Copy

FrameScipt 2.1 works with the following:

- FrameMaker 5.5.x, 5.5.6, and 6
- FrameMaker+SGML 5.5.6 and 6
- Windows 95/98/NT/2000/XP
- Macintosh

Before you can run the examples included in this chapter, you must install FrameScript.

To download an evaluation copy, follow these steps:

1. Go to the FrameScript website (*www.framescript.com*). In the download section, locate **FrameScript**. Accept the licensing terms.
2. In the **Evaluation Versions** section, select **Click Here**.
3. Select the appropriate download version and provide the required customer information. Click **Submit**.
4. On the next screen, click the link to download FrameScript.
5. Select a location in which to save the downloaded file and then save the file.

Note: *The file is about 7.58 MB.*

To install your evaluation copy, follow these steps:

1. In Explorer, double-click the FrameScript evaluation executable file, *fscr2_60eval.exe*. The Install Shield Wizard appears.

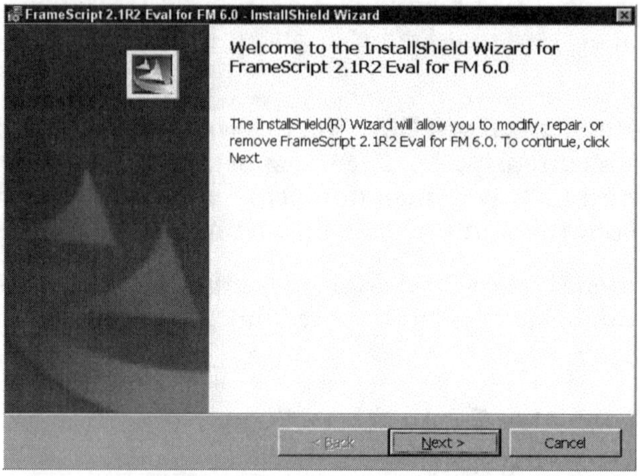

2. Click **Next** to begin installation.

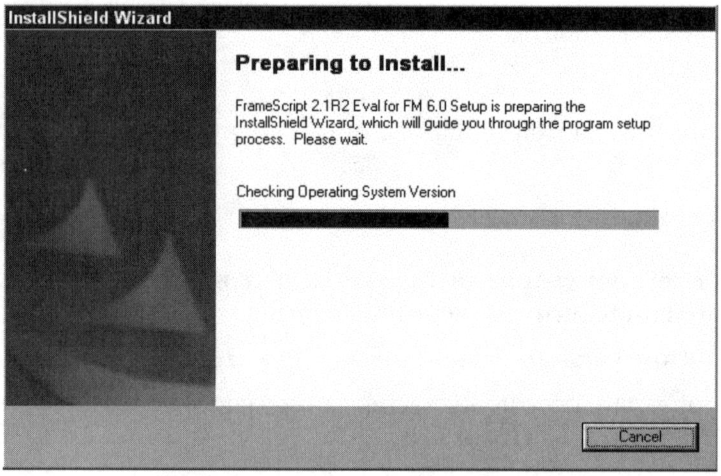

3. Follow the prompts to install FrameScript.

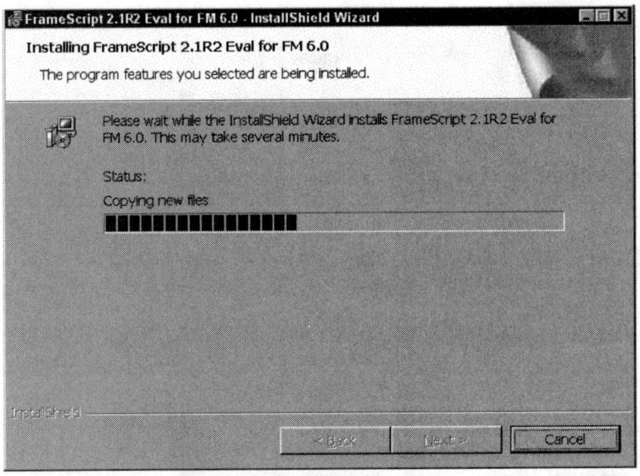

4. After installation, start FrameMaker. A FrameScript dialog box should appear during the startup process. If it doesn't, follow the instructions for manual installation in the next section. If it does, skip the next section and proceed with "Running a Sample Script" on page 434.

Installing FrameScript Manually

1. Close FrameMaker.
2. Look in your FrameScript install directory. You should have the following files (XX is the version of FrameScript corresponding to the FrameMaker version):
   - *fslXX.dll*
   - *fscript.ini*
   - *fslinit.fsl*
3. Locate and open your FrameMaker file *maker.ini* using NotePad or some other text editor. The default location for this file is *Program Files/Adobe/FrameMaker X.X/maker.ini*, although your specific installation may have placed it elsewhere.
4. Locate the **[APIclients]** section in *maker.ini* and add the following line to the end of the section (see Figure 18-1):

```
fsl=Standard,FrameScript, C:\Program
  Files\ElmSoft\FrameScript\fsl60.dll
```

5. Save and close *maker.ini*.

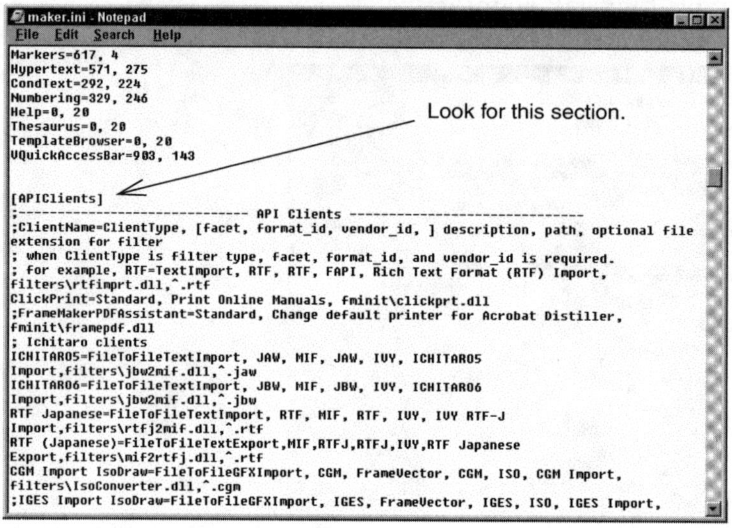

Figure 18-1 APIClients section of the *maker.ini* file.

Note: *If required, change the directory from C:\Program Files\ElmSoft\FrameScript\fsl60.dll to the directory you specified during the FrameScript installation process.*

Running a Sample Script

After you install FrameScript, start FrameMaker. You will see a notice describing the version of FrameScript installed. Click OK. FrameMaker opens with a new menu item labeled **FrameScript** on the main FrameMaker menu bar. The FrameScript menu contains the following items:

- **Run:** Brings up a browser window. You then can select a script to run.
- **Install:** Adds scripts to the FrameScript menu
- **Uninstall:** Removes scripts from the FrameScript menu
- **Script Window:** Text editor for creating scripts. You can write script commands using this or any other text editor. Notepad or Wordpad work fine as long as the file is saved as a text file. You can even use FrameMaker to create the script file and save it as a text file. FrameScript scripts have a *.fsl* or *.fso* extension. You can specify the extension in the Options dialog box.
- **Options:** Specifies FrameScript options
- **Compile:** Compiles scripts into a binary format so that they can't be read or edited in a text editor. It allows you to distribute working scripts without distributing your source code.

Your screen will look like that shown in Figure 18-2.

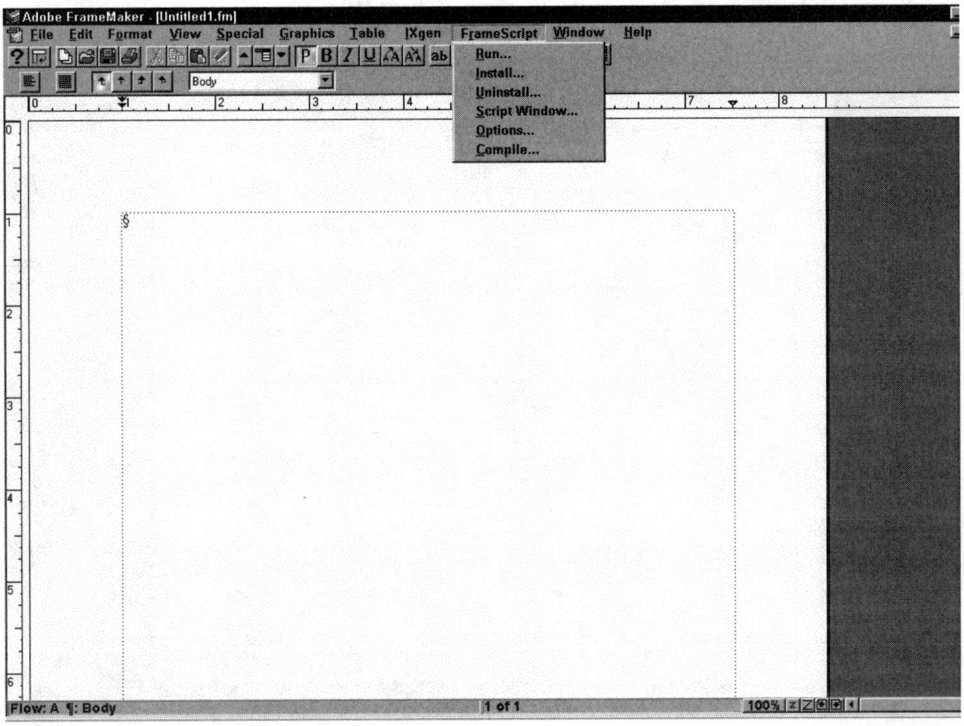

Figure 18-2 FrameScript menu selected.

Before running the sample scripts in this section, you should create a test directory with a test copy of a complete book.

Note: *Sample scripts and exercises should be conducted on test files only!*

The FrameScript evaluation download includes a number of sample scripts. The script *PgfFmtDocCount.fsl* scans the current document and generates a new document. This new document lists the paragraph tags used in the original document, along with the number of times the paragraph tag appears, and the font used in the paragraph. This script will not alter the FrameMaker document in any way. After the script runs, you can save or discard the new document.

To run the script, follow these steps:

1. Start FrameMaker. Open a document. Click **Run** on the FrameScript menu.

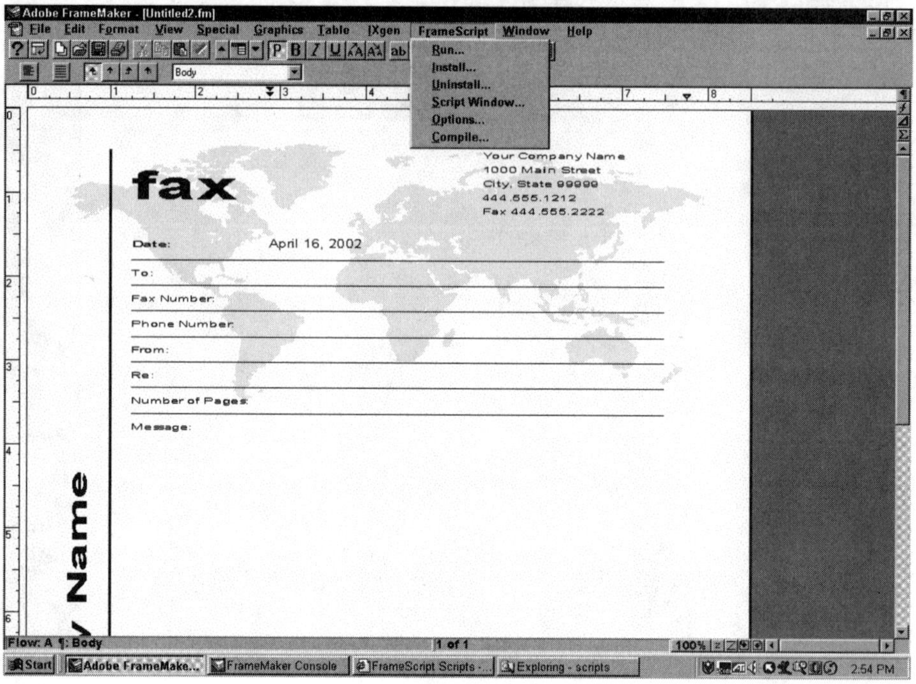

2. In the **Select a Script** dialog box, select the script *PgfFmtDocCount.fsl* and click **Select**.

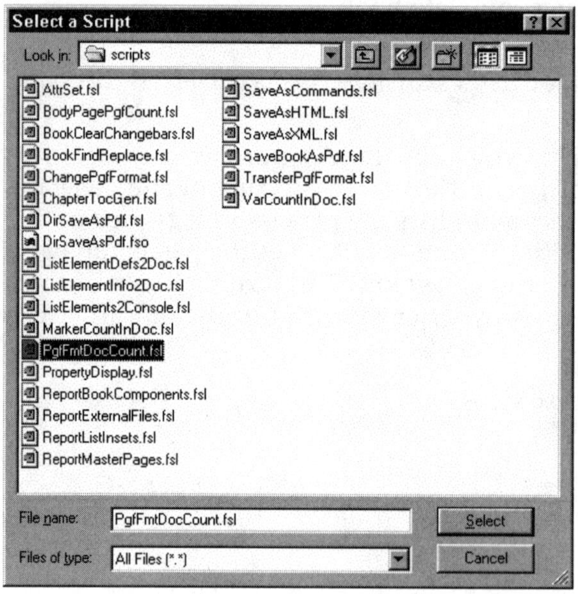

3. The script starts processing the file. The hourglass that appears signals that FrameScript is running. Depending on the size of your file, it may take several seconds to process the file. The script then opens a new document and creates the paragraph list. Processing is complete when the hourglass disappears and the cursor returns.

Note: *If the processing cycle continues for more than 15 seconds, hit the* ***Escape*** *key. This will cancel processing. Try the script again, with a smaller file.*

4. Review the paragraph list, then save or close it. Your original file remains unaltered.

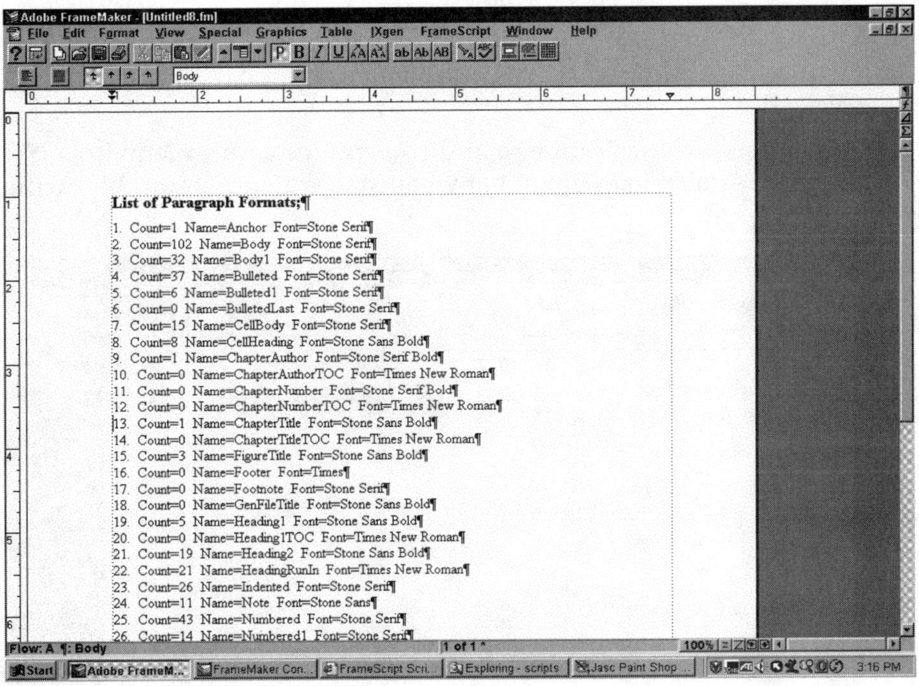

Installing a Script

Installing a script creates a menu item for that script, making it more convenient to run. To install a script, follow these steps:

1. Select **FrameScript** > **Install**. The Select a Script dialog box appears. Find and select the script *PgfFmtDocCount.fsl*. Click **Select**. The FrameScript Standard Script Installation dialog box appears.

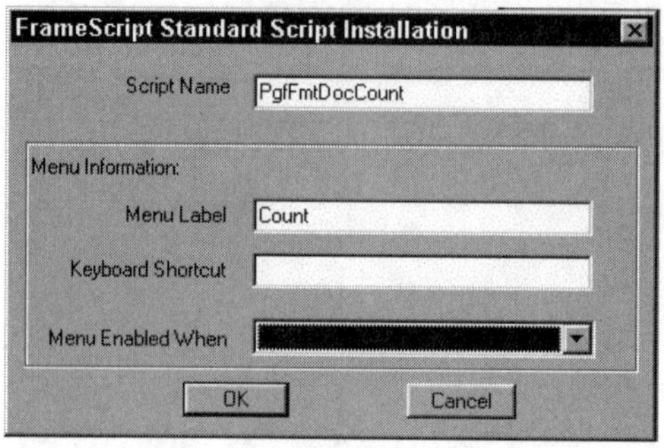

2. Enter a script name (this can be the actual script name) and a menu label. Click **OK**.
3. Select the **FrameScript** menu and you will see a new menu item, **Scripts** > **Count**. Additional scripts that you install will appear on this menu item under Count.

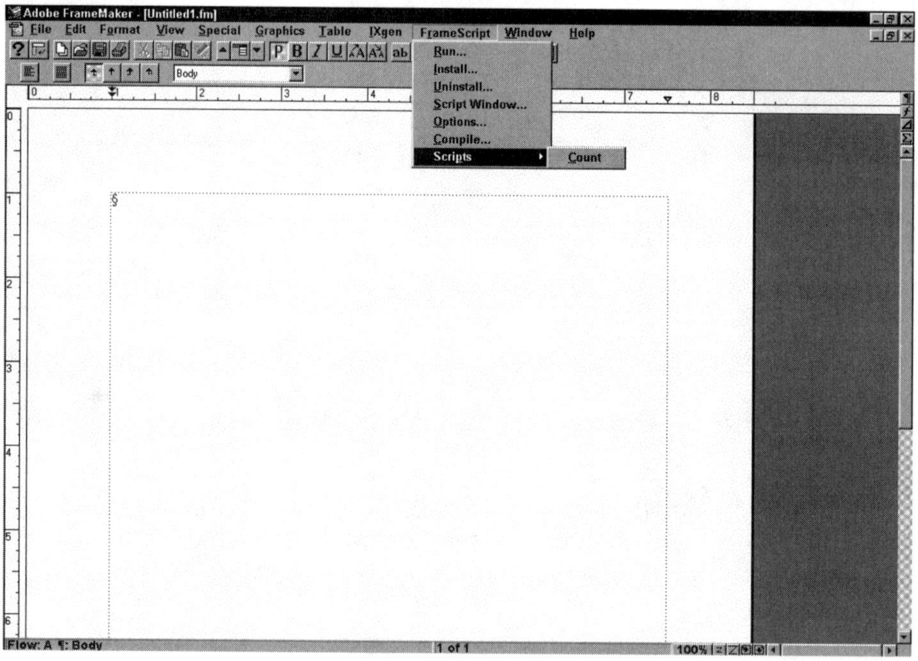

4. Place your cursor in the document. Select **FrameScript** > **Scripts** > **Count**. Doing so runs the script ***PgfFmtDocCount***.

Uninstalling a Script

Uninstalling a script removes it from the **FrameScript > Scripts** menu.

1. Select **FrameScript > Uninstall.** Select a script name to uninstall and click **OK.**

More FrameScript Exercises

Before running the exercises in this section, you should create a test directory with a test copy of a complete book. Some of these exercises are intended to be run against document files, while others run against a book file.

Note: *Sample scripts and exercises should be conducted on test files only!*

This section guides you though the process of writing, saving, and running a standard script.

The standard "Hello World" example. In this exercise you will use FrameScripts Script Window to create and run a small script.

1. Start FrameMaker. Open the script window included with FrameScript. From the FrameScript menu, select **Script Window.**

2. Select **File** > **Save** and save the file as *test1.fsl*. Place the cursor in the text area and type the following:

   display 'Hello World';

3. Save the file. Click  to run the script. The script switches to the FrameMaker document, and the following dialog box appears:

   The display command prints out the string within quotations.

4. Click **OK**. The Script Window comes up. You can toggle between the Script and FrameMaker windows by using the task bar.

Variation on "Hello World". This exercise produces the same results as the previous exercise but by using a variable.

1. In the Script window, select **File** > **New** to create a new file.
2. Select **File** > **Save** and save the file as *test2.fsl*. Type in the following:

   set message='Hello World';
   display message;

3. Save the file. Click  to run the script. The script switches to the FrameMaker document, and the following dialog box appears.

   The word **message** in the first line you typed is a variable. A variable is a container for a value, which in this case is a string value that has been set to **"Hello World**."

4. Click **OK**.

Working with a paragraph. This exercise explores the properties of a paragraph.

1. In the Script window, select **File** > **New** to create a new file.
2. Select **File** >**Save** and save the file as *test3.fsl*. Select the FrameMaker application from the task bar. Place the cursor in any paragraph containing text. Select the Script window from the task bar. Type in the following:

   set pgfobj=TextSelection.begin.object;

   display pgfobj.text;

3. Save the file. Click  to run the script. The script switches to the FrameMaker document, and the dialog box with the full text of the paragraph where the cursor was placed appears. The first command identifies the paragraph object as the paragraph where the cursor is located. The second command displays the text associated with that paragraph object.
4. In the Script window, select **File** > **New** to create a new file.
5. Select **File** > **Save** and save the file as *test4.fsl*. Select the FrameMaker application from the task bar. Place the cursor in any paragraph containing text. Select the Script window from the task bar. Type in the following:

   set pgfobj=TextSelection.begin.object;

   display pgfobj.properties;

6. Save the file. Click  to run the script. The script switches to the FrameMaker document, and the dialog box appears, listing all of the properties for that paragraph. The first command identifies the paragraph object as the paragraph where the cursor is located. The second command displays the properties associated with that paragraph object.

   Review the list of properties. Most of these will be familiar to you. Properties like SpaceAbove and NextTag are on the Basic tab of the Paragraph Designer. There are properties like PgfSpellChecked (True[1] if paragraph has been spell-checked) and PgfOptSpace (optimum word spacing) that you won't find in the Paragraph Designer. You can, however, view and manipulate these properties using FrameScript.

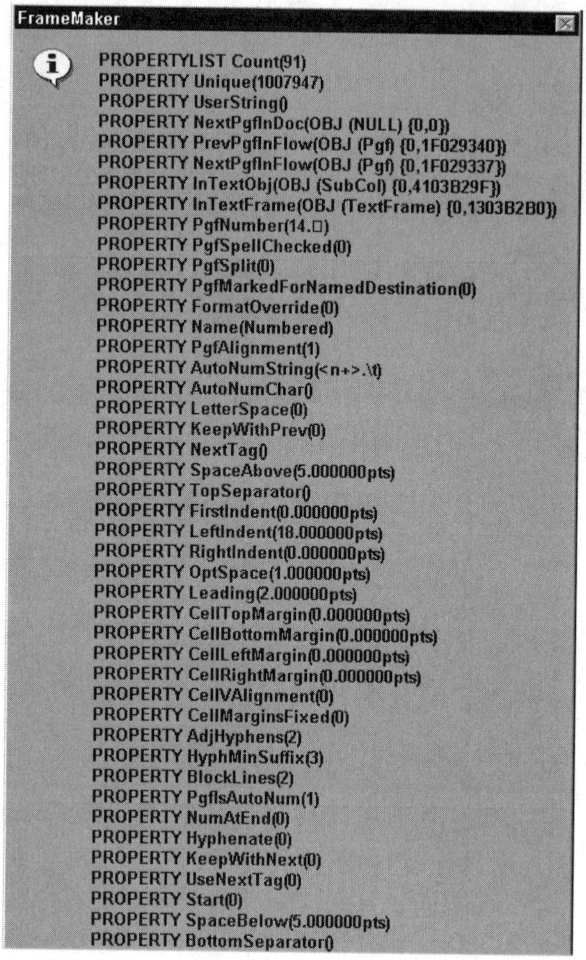

7. Exit the property list dialog box.

Note: *The property list may be too long to fit on the screen. To close the dialog box and go back to the Script window, hit ESC or <Enter>.*

8. Go to the Script window. Write down the full pathname of *test4.fsl* (it should be in the title bar of the Script window). Select **File** > **Exit** to exit the Script window.

Editing scripts using NotePad. In this exercise you will edit a script using NotePad and run it in FrameMaker to view and manipulate paragraph properties.

1. Open Notepad. Find and open *test4.fsl.*
2. Delete **display pgfobj.properties.**
3. Add the following lines to the end of the file:

Note: *Select **All Files** from the **Files of Type** drop-down list to display the FrameScript script files (extension .fsl).*

display 'Has this paragraph been spell checked? '+pgfobj.PgfSpellChecked;

Display 'Current optimal word spacing: '+pgfobj.OptSpace.

4. Save the file.
5. Open Framemaker and a document. Place the cursor in a paragraph containing text. Select **Run** from the FrameScript menu. Find and select *test4.fsl*. Click **Select**.
6. The following dialog box appears. A value of 0 is false and a value of 1 is true.

7. Click **OK**. The following dialog box appears.

Note: *If you get an error, click OK, place the cursor in a paragraph containing text, and run the script again.*

8. Click **OK**.
9. Open Notepad. Find and open *test4.fsl*.
10. Add the following lines to the end of the file:

    set pgfobj.OptSpace = 5;

    display 'Done. ';
11. Save the file.
12. Open Framemaker and a document. Place the cursor in a paragraph containing text. Select **Run** from the FrameScript menu. Find and select *test4.fsl*. Click **Select**.
13. Note the word spacing of the paragraph containing the cursor.
14. On your own, modify *test4.fsl* so that the optimal word spacing is set to 1.

Writing and running a script on a document. This exercise deletes unwanted colors in a document.

1. Start the color deletion process by selecting **View** > **Color** and **Definitions**.
2. In the Color Definitions dialog box, select a color you want to delete and click **Delete**.
3. Repeat the last two steps for each of the colors you want to delete.

Again, this method is fine if you are deleting a few colors in a book, but it is a pain to use it to fix colors across a document suite.

The script DeleteColors runs on the currently active document. You specify in the script commands the colors you want to delete. You then simply run the script, which goes in and deletes those colors from the file.

Note: *The script executes a set of commands on a document. In the next exercise you will modify this script to execute the same set of commands on all the documents in a book, thereby significantly extending its usefulness.*

1. Start FrameMaker and open a test document.
2. From the **View** menu, select **Color** > **Views** to display the Color Definitions dialog box.
3. Click the down arrow next to the Name field.
4. Choose two colors from the list that you want to delete. They must be two user-defined colors, as FrameMaker will not allow you to delete any of the basic default colors (Black, White, Red, Green, Blue, Cyan, Magenta, or Yellow).
5. On a sheet of paper, write down the names of two colors that you want to delete from the document (for example, Color1 and Color2).
6. Close the Color Definitions dialog box. Open the Script Window (**FrameScript** > **Script Window**). Save the file as *DelColorsdoc.fsl.*

   The first set of commands creates the list **vColorList** and adds two items or "members" to that list—**Color1** and **Color2**.
7. Type the following lines in the Script Window:

   New StringList NewVar(vColorList);

   Add Member('Color1') To(vColorList);

   Add Member('Color2') To(vColorList);

Note: *Substitute your colors for* ***'Color1'*** *and* ***'Color2'*** *(single quotes are required around the color name when you enter them).*

The next set of commands loops through each member of **vColorlist** and performs the following:

- Gets the member from the list and stores the name in the new variable **vColor**
- Looks in the colors defined for that document and gets the color that matches the name **vColor**. That object is placed in the new variable **vColorObj**.
- Deletes the object **vColorObj**;

Type the following lines:

Loop While(vCounter<=vColorList.Size) LoopVar(vCounter) Init(1) Incr(1)

Get Member Number(vCounter) From(vColorList) NewVar(vColor);

Get Object Type(Color) Name(vColor) NewVar(vColorObj);

Delete Object(vColorObj);

EndLoop

8. Save the file. Click  to run the script.
9. Switch to the FrameMaker application.
10. From the View menu, select **Color** > **Views** to display the Color Definitions dialog box. Click the down arrow next to the Name field. Note that the user-defined colors you deleted are no longer available.
11. Close and do not save the Frame file.

Writing and running a script on a book. This exercise builds on the preceding example and deletes unwanted colors for all the components in a book.

1. Start FrameMaker and open a test book.
2. From the View menu, select **Color** > **Views** to display the Color Definitions dialog box.
3. Click the down arrow next to the Name field.
4. Choose two colors from the list that you want to delete. They must be two user-defined colors, as FrameMaker will not allow you to delete any of the standard default colors (Black, White, Red, Green, Blue, Cyan, Magenta, or Yellow).
5. On a sheet of paper, write down the names of two colors that you want to delete from the book (for example, Color1 and Color2).
6. Close the Color Definitions dialog box.
7. Open the Script Window (**FrameScript** > **Script Window**). Open the file *DelColorsdoc.fsl*. Save the file as *DelColorsbook.fsl*. Add the bolded commands below:

// This command identifies the book object of interest to be the active book.

set BookObj = ActiveBook;

New StringList NewVar(vColorList);

Add Member('Color1') To(vColorList);

Add Member('Color2') To(vColorList);

//This command sets up a loop to go through each component in the book, and opens each document.

Loop ForEach(BookComponent) In(BookObj) LoopVar(bookcomp)

Open Document File(bookcomp.Name) FileIsOldVersion FontNotFoundInDoc NewVar(dobj);

Loop While(vCounter<=vColorList.Size) LoopVar(vCounter) Init(1) Incr(1)

Get Member Number(vCounter) From(vColorList) NewVar(vColor);

Get Object Type(Color) Name(vColor) NewVar(vColorObj);

Delete Object(vColorObj);

EndLoop

EndLoop

8. Save the file. Click  to run the script.
9. Switch to the FrameMaker application.
10. From the View menu, select **Color** > **Views** to display the Color Definitions dialog box.
11. Click the down arrow next to the **Name** field. Note that the user-defined colors you deleted are no longer available.
12. Close and do not save any of the Frame files.

Resources

If you do plan to extend your FrameMaker's capabilities, there are many resources available to you. Some information is available in Adobe's manuals (including the FDK manuals). Other data—even free extensions and plug-ins—may be found on the sites listed here:

- Chris Despopoulos' site, *www.telecable.es/personales/cud/*, which includes many free plug-ins that are worth using (including HuntOverrides for searching for those pesky asterisked items)
- Rick Quattro's Site, *www.frameexpert.com*, which includes free and low-cost FrameScripts and plug-ins
- Brad Anderson's corporate website, *www.beyondprint.com*
- The *www.frameusers.com* site and lists, including the FrameScript list, which provide users with a forum for questions and experts.

Part VI

Appendixes, Glossary, and Resources

Appendix A

Setting Up an ODBC Database Connection

In the examples on the following pages, you will connect to an Access database via ODBC. To make this database available, you need to make the database available to the operating system via ODBC.

1. In Windows 2000 or XP, select **Start** > **Programs** > **Administrative Tools** > **Data Sources (ODBC)**. (In Windows 95 or 98, the ODBC data sources can be found under **Start** > **Settings** > **Control Panels**.)

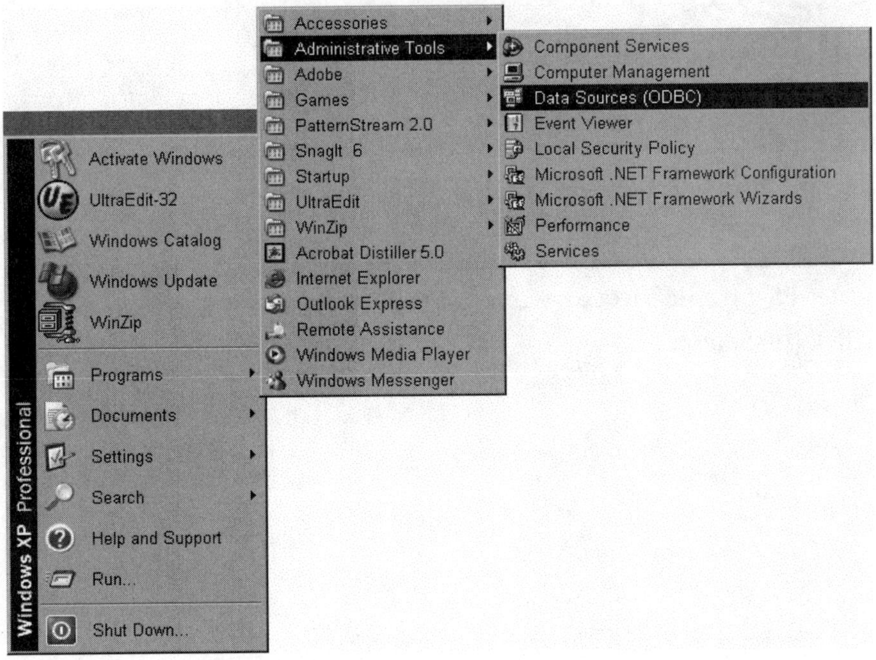

2. Click on the **System DSN** tab.

3. Click **Add...**.

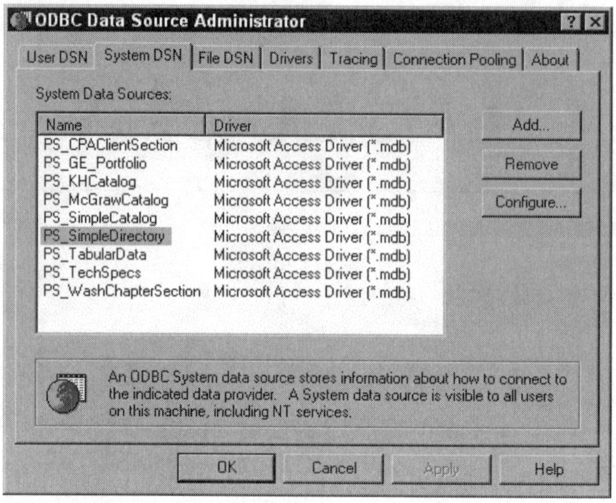

4. Select **Microsoft Access Driver (*.mdb)**.
5. Click **Finish**.

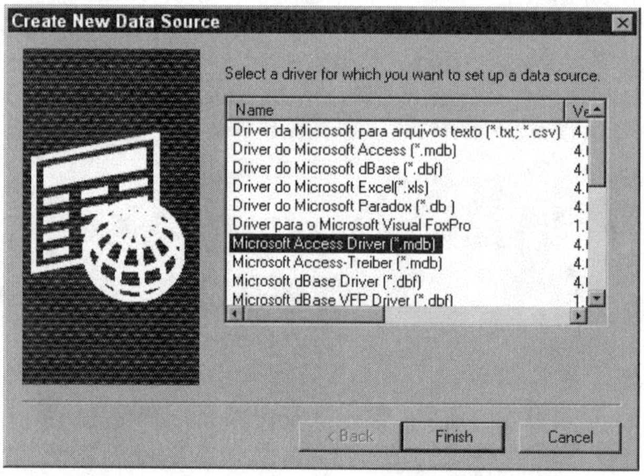

6. Enter **PS_SimpleDirectory** under **Data Source Name**.
7. Click the **Select...** button.

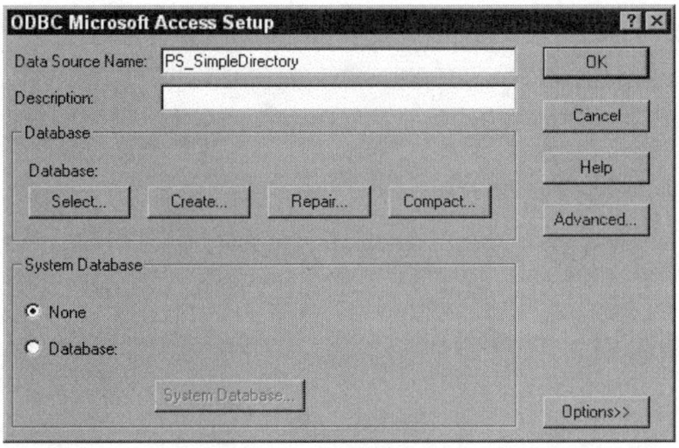

8. Navigate to the Access database entitled **SimpleDirectory.mdb**.
9. Click **OK**.

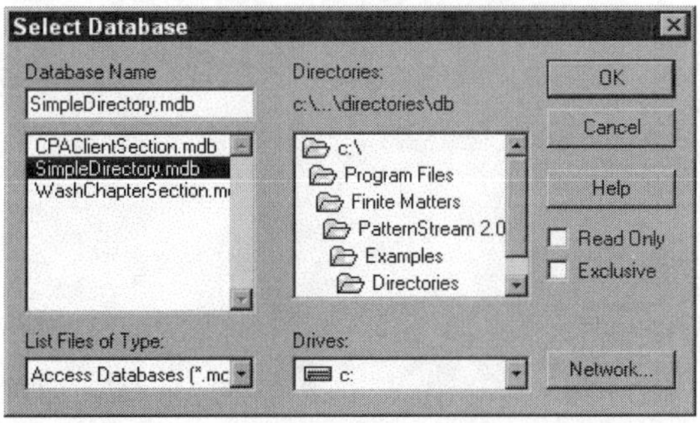

10. Click **OK**.

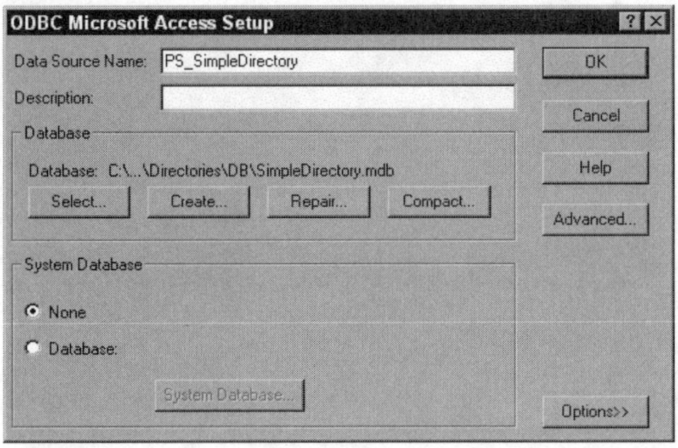

11. Click **OK**.

The SimpleDirectory database is now available via ODBC. A connection is made using the data source name—in this case PS_SimpleDirectory—and a username and password. The default username for an Access database is **admin** and there is not a password.

Appendix B

Directory Example Using PatternStream

Introduction

The following is a fairly complete step-by-step guide to setting up the directory example used in this chapter in PatternStream.

Data Link

The Data Link folder of the PatternStream interface allows you to set up one or more connections to a database, construct the queries to retrieve the data, and create variables to store the retrieved data.

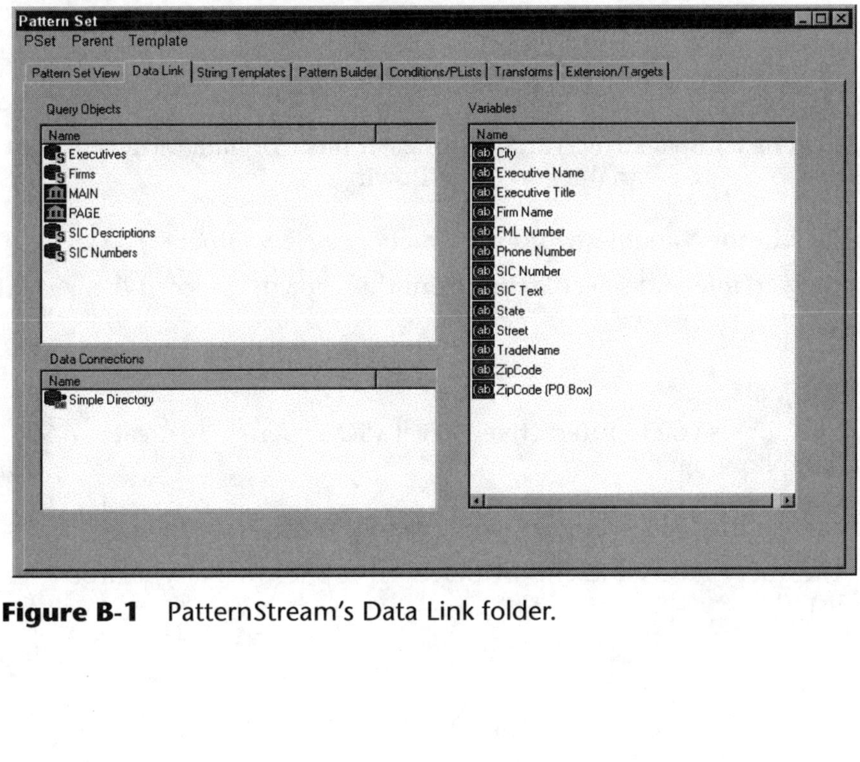

Figure B-1 PatternStream's Data Link folder.

Building a Database Connection

To build a connection to the database, do the following:

1. Right-click in the Data Connections window and choose **New Object**.
2. Select **ODBC** from the Type drop-down list.
3. Name the data connection **Simple Directory**.
4. Click **OK**.
5. Type in the ODBC data source name that was created in the "Connectiong to the Datebase via ODBC" section in Chapter 14.
6. Enter the database user ID—the user ID in Access is always **admin** by default.
7. Enter the database password—the database password in Access is always blank by default.

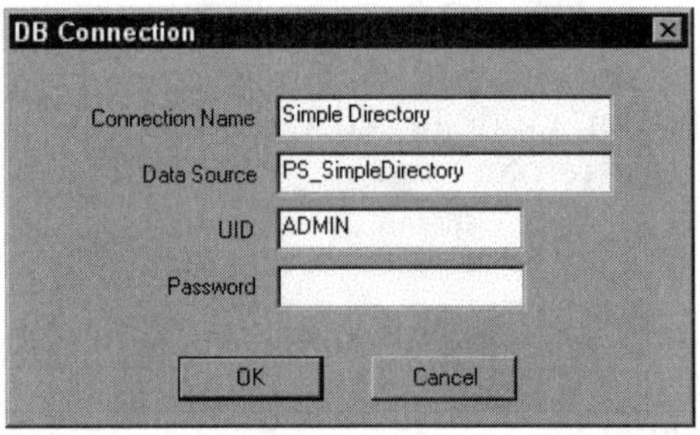

Figure B-2 DB Connection dialog box.

8. Click **OK**.

Creating Variables

Next you need to set up a string variable for each piece of data retrieved from the database. To create a variable, do the following:

1. Right-click in the Variables window and choose **New Object**.
2. Name the variable and select **String** from the Type drop-down list.
3. Click **OK**.

Querying Objects

PatternStream allows you to interactively create SQL queries. To create an SQL query, do the following:

1. Right-click in the Query Objects window and select **New Object**.
2. Name the query **Firms** and choose **Select** from the Query Type drop-down list.

3. Click **OK**.
4. Select **Simple Directory** from the Connection Object drop-down list.
5. Click on the **From** tab.
6. Enter **Firms** in the Table Name field.
7. Click the **Add Table** button.

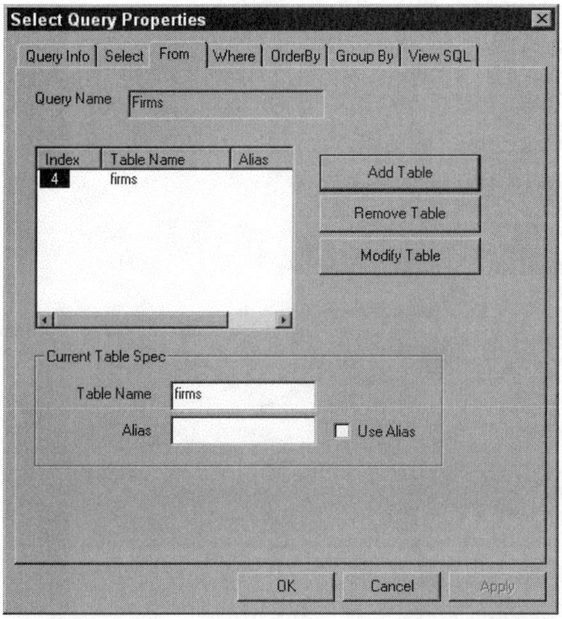

Figure B-3 From tab in Select Query Properties dialog box.

8. Click on the **Select** tab.
9. Select a **PatternStream variable** from the Variable Name drop-down list.
10. Enter the **database column name** in the Column Name field.
11. Select the **Firms** table from the Table Name drop-down list.
12. Click the **Insert** button.
13. Repeat Steps 9–12 for each variable and data point retrieved in this query.
14. Click **Apply**.
15. Click on the **View SQL** tab to view your query.
16. Click **OK**.

Creating String Templates

String templates are objects that allow you to publish the values stored in the PatternStream variables. In Figure B-6, notice that the City string template is made up of four variable string segments (City, State, ZipCode, and ZipCode

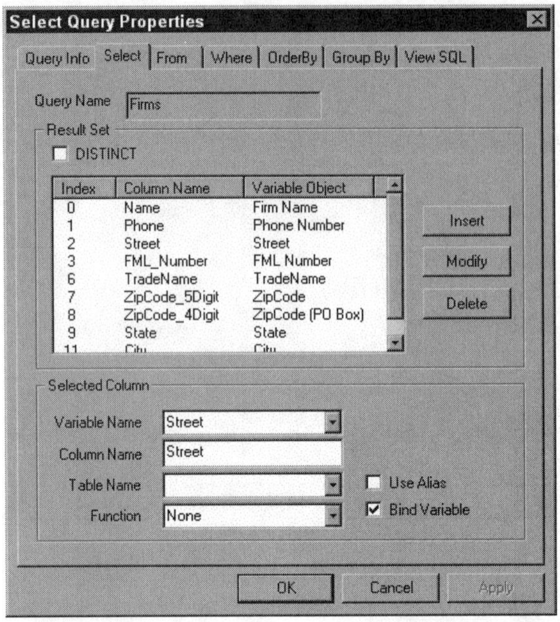

Figure B-4 Select tab in Select Query Properties dialog box.

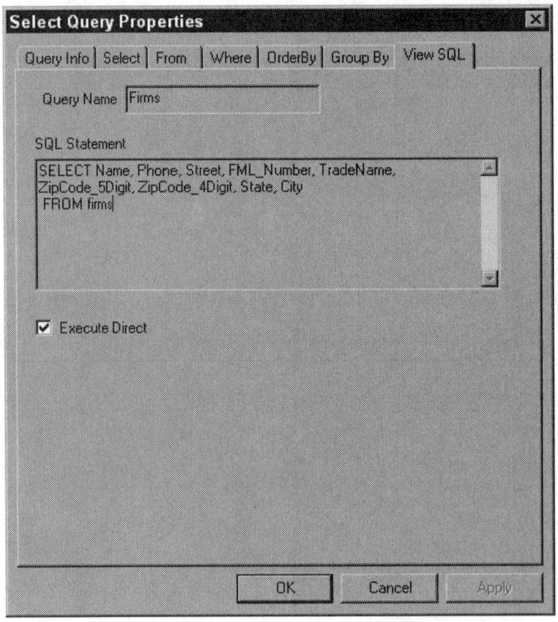

Figure B-5 View SQL tab in Select Query Properties dialog box.

[PO Box]) and three constant string segments (a comma and a space, two spaces, and an en dash).

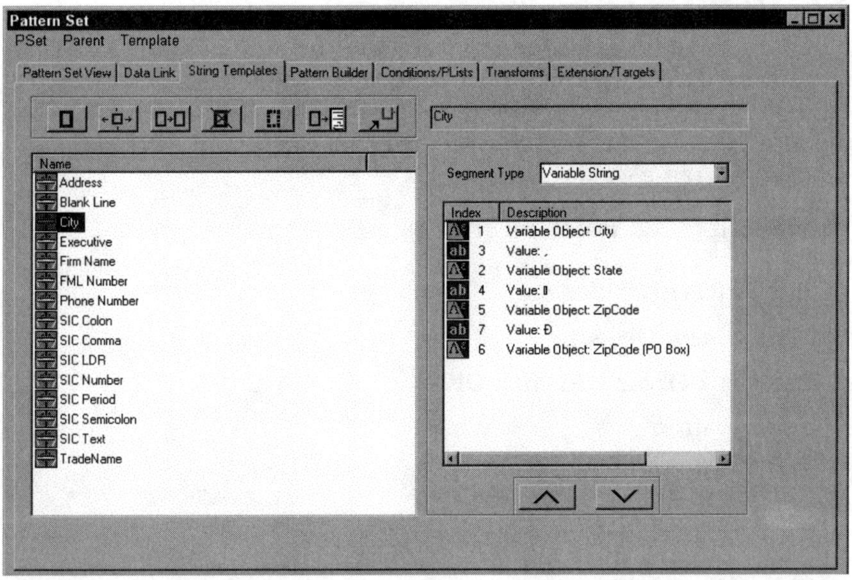

Figure B-6 String templates for City and its associated variables.

To create a string segment, do the following:

1. Select **Parent** > **New Object** under the String Templates tab.
2. Name the string template and click **OK.**
3. To add segments to the newly created string template, choose the **segment type** from the Segment Type drop-down list.
4. **Right-click** in the Segment Type window and choose **Insert**.

   If the segment type is a variable string, do the following:

   a. **Double-click** on the variable string's index number.

   b. Click the **Select Variable** button.

   c. Select the **PatternStream variable** you wish to use.

   d. Click **OK.**

   If the segment type is a constant string, do the following:

   a. **Double-click** on the constant string's index number.

   b. Type the **static text** in the String Value field, or choose the special character (such as an em dash, soft return, etc.) from the Special Character drop-down list and click the **Insert Hex Code** button.

   c. Click **OK.**
5. Repeat Steps 1–5 until all the necessary string templates are created.

Building Patterns

Now that you have created a data connection to the database, have created queries to select the data values from the database, have created variables to store the data, and have created string templates to output the variable values, you are ready to create a pattern to attach a query and paragraph targets to output to FrameMaker.

To create a new pattern, do the following:

1. Click on the **PatternBuilder** tab.
2. Select **Parent** > **New Object**.
3. Name the pattern **Firms** and click **OK**.
4. Select the new pattern.
5. Select **Parent** > **Object Info**.
6. Click the **Select Query** button.
7. Select the query **Firms**.
8. Click **OK**.

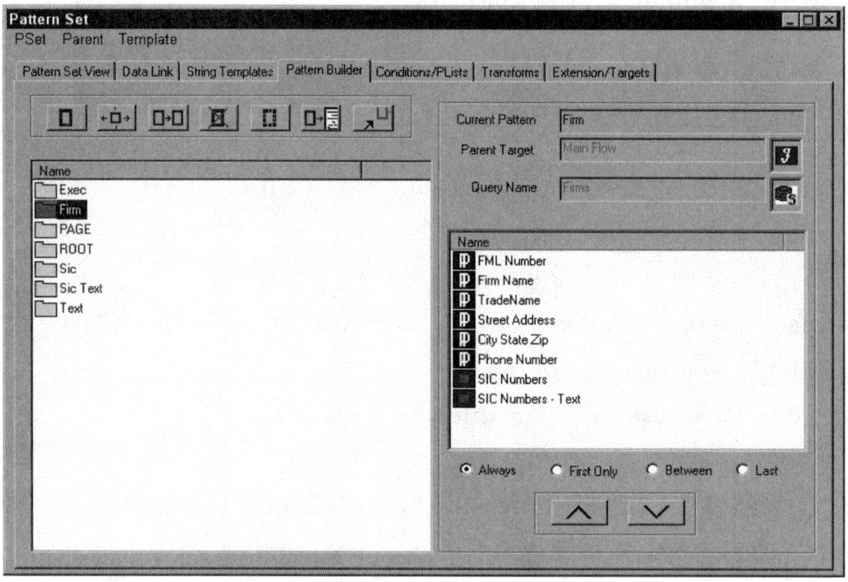

Figure B-7 Creating a pattern.

Creating Paragraph Targets

Now that you have created a pattern, you need to create a target to output one or more of our string template values. For the Firm query and pattern, we need a paragraph target for FML_Number, Firm Name, TradeName, Street Address, City/State/Zip, and Phone Number.

To create a paragraph target, follow these steps:

1. **Right-click** in the right-hand window of the **PatternBuilder** tab and choose **Create Target**.
2. Name the paragraph target in the Name field.
3. Select **Paragraph** from the Target drop-down list.
4. Click **OK.** The Paragraph Target Properties window will open.
5. Click on the **String Templates** tab.
6. Click the **Attach** button.
7. Select the string template you want outputted in this paragraph.
8. Click **Apply**.

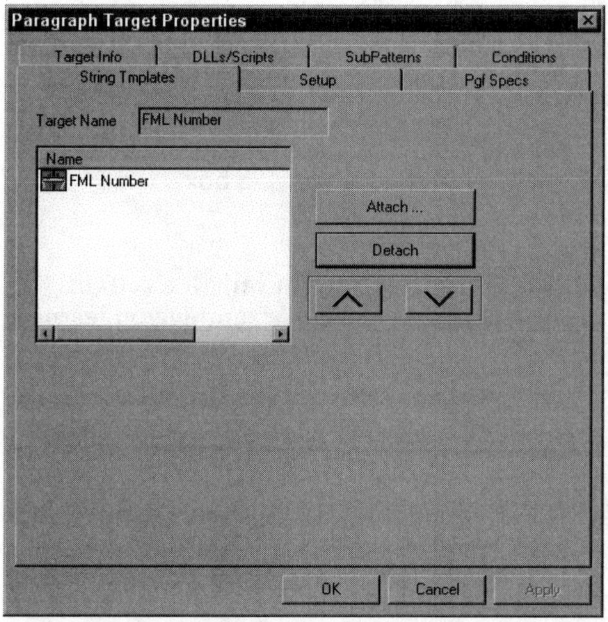

Figure B-8 String Templates tab in Paragraph Target Properties dialog box.

9. Click on the **Setup** tab.
10. Make sure the **Begin New Paragraph** box is checked.
11. Select from the **Paragraph Format** drop-down list the paragraph tag in FrameMaker that you wish to use.
12. Make sure the **Generate Always** box is checked.
13. Click **OK**.

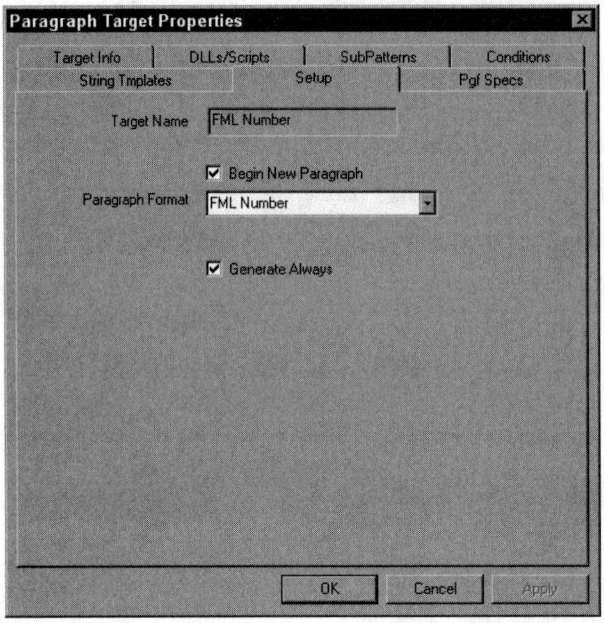

Figure B-9 Setup tab in Paragraph Target Properties dialog box.

Creating Conditions

A condition in PatternStream allows items to be output only if a certain condition or conditions are true or false. Earlier in this example you learned about the need to not output an en dash if a particular company did not have a four-digit zip code.

To create a condition, follow these steps:

1. Click on the **Conditions/PLists** tab.
2. **Right-click** in the left-hand window and select **New Object**.
3. Name the condition **NoZip4**.
4. Select **Expression** from the Type drop-down list.
5. Under Left Hand Side, make sure **Use Literal Value** is **unchecked**.
6. Select **ZipCode (PO Box)** from the Left Hand Side Variable Name drop-down list.
7. Select **NOT EQUAL** from the Logical Operation drop-down list.
8. Make sure **Use Literal Value** is **checked** under Right Hand Side.
9. Click the **Set Value** button.
10. Select **String** and make sure the string field is blank/empty.
11. Click **OK**.

This condition can now be applied in the City string template on both the **en dash** and **ZipCode (PO Box)** segments.

PSet View

Once you have created all of the objects needed in this example, they are attached to each other to finish this project in PatternStream. The PSet View tab shows a visual representation of the entire project. This view allows you to see the logical order in which objects will be processed (see Figure B-10). To output the directory from this point, just select **PSET > Run** in PatternStream.

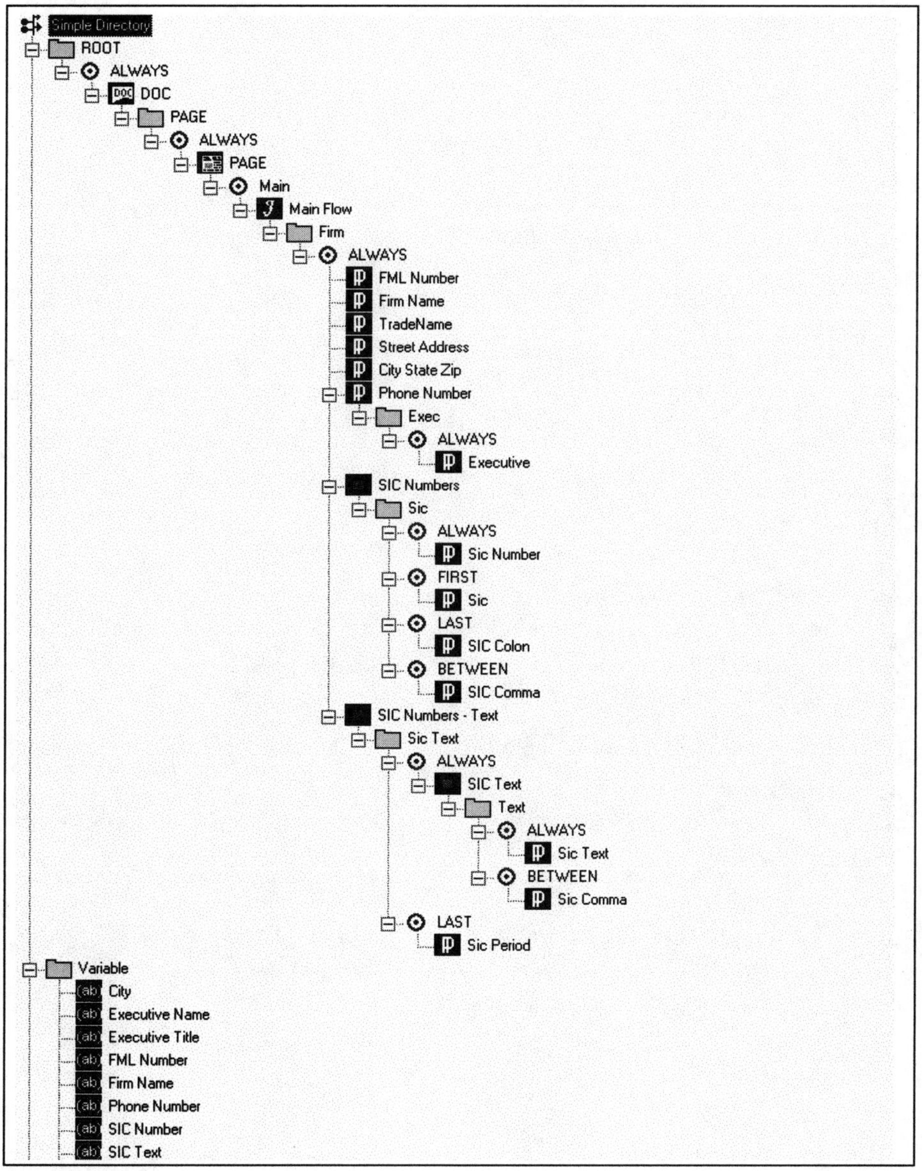

Figure B-10 PSet view.

Appendix C

Simple Directory FrameScript Code

The following FrameScript code will output the sample directory using an existing FrameMaker template named *SimpleDirectory.fm*. The code is well commented so you can see what each routine is doing. The logic is very similar to the PatternStream example you looked at earlier.

```
// -----------------------------------------------------
// -- User Defined Database Parameters
// -- Change to the correct values for your database
// -----------------------------------------------------
/*ODBC Connection Name */
SET vDSNName = 'PS_SimpleDirectory';

/*Database User ID */
SET vUserID = 'admin';

/*Database Password */
SET vPass = '';

/*Name of FrameMaker template */
SET v_Template = 'SimpleDirectory.fm';

// -----------------------------------------------------
// --           DO NOT EDIT BELOW THIS LINE
// -----------------------------------------------------

/*Gets the path to this script and puts it
in a variable called v_ScriptFolderPath */
Run GetScriptPath;
```

```
/*Opens a new document based on the variable
v_Template in the directory v_ScriptFolderPath
This script and the template must be in
the same directory to function */
Run GenerateDocument;

/*Sets and opens the datasource from which
the data will be extracted and published */
Run SetDataSource;

// --------------------------------------------------
/*Executes the first query that returns the FML
  Number, Name, Trade Name, Street Address, City,
  State, Zip+5, Zip+4, and Phone from the database and
  outputs them to FrameMaker fully formatted with
  paragraph and character format applied */
// --------------------------------------------------
vQuery1 = 'SELECT Name, Phone, Street, FML_Number,
  TradeName, ZipCode_5Digit, ZipCode_4Digit, State,
  City FROM firms WHERE Name LIKE
  '+QUOTE+'amer%'+QUOTE+';';

/*Set a new EQuery object */
New EQuery NewVar(vEQuery);
/*Set a new datasource for the EQuery object */
Set vEQuery.EDB = vDataSource;
/*Set the query to be used for the EQuery object */
Set vEQuery.Select = vQuery1;

/*Executes the query and returns a message if no data
  is returned */
Run vEQuery.RunQuery;
If vEQuery.NumCols = 0
Write Console 'No data was returned.    ';
EndIf

/*Loop through each record returned, format the data
  and output it to FrameMaker */
Loop While(vEQuery.AtEof = 0) LoopVar(vRecordNo)
  Init(1) Incr(1)
/*Get FML Number from database and put 'F-M-L ' in
  front of it and output using the 'FML Number'
  paragraph tag */
Set vFML_Number = vEQuery.Fields.FML_Number;
Set vFML_Number_Output = 'F-M-L '+vFML_Number;
RUN Generate_Output v_Value(vFML_Number_Output)
  v_Format_To_Use('FML Number');
```

```
/*Get company name from database and output using
  'Firm Name' paragraph tag */
Set vName = vEQuery.Fields.Name;
RUN Generate_Output v_Value(vName)
  v_Format_To_Use('Firm Name');
/*Insert company name index marker */
Get Object Type(MarkerType) Name('Index')
  NewVar(vMarkerType);
Set vIndexText = vName;
SET vInsertionPoint = vCurrPgf;
New Marker NewVar(vMarker) MarkerText(vIndexText)
MarkerTypeId(vMarkerType) TextLoc(vInsertionPoint);
/*Get Trade Name from database and put a 'Trade Name '
  in front of the trade name and output it--if it is
  not blank--using the 'TradeName' paragraph tag */
Set vTradeName = vEQuery.Fields.TradeName;
Set vTradeName_Output = 'Trade Name ' + vTradeName;
If vTradeName <> ''
RUN Generate_Output v_Value(vTradeName_Output)
  v_Format_To_Use('TradeName');
EndIf
/*Get the street address and output using 'Firm Info'
  paragraph tag */
Set vStreet = vEQuery.Fields.Street;
RUN Generate_Output v_Value(vStreet)
  v_Format_To_Use('Firm Info');
/*Get the city, state, zip5, zip4.  Append values
  together and format as a single string.  Only output
  the hypen and zip4 if zip4 is not null.  Output with
  'Firm Info' paragraph tag. */
Set vCity = vEQuery.Fields.City;
Set vState = vEQuery.Fields.State;
Set vZipCode_5Digit = vEQuery.Fields.ZipCode_5Digit;
Set vZipCode_4Digit = vEQuery.Fields.ZipCode_4Digit;
Set vCityStateZip = vCity + ', ' + vState + '  ' +
  vZipCode_5Digit
If vZipCode_4Digit <> ''
Set vCityStateZip = vCityStateZip + '-' +
  vZipCode_4Digit;
EndIf
RUN Generate_Output v_Value(vCityStateZip)
  v_Format_To_Use('Firm Info');
/*Get the phone number, format it (###) ###-#### and
  output with the 'Firm Info' paragraph tag. */
Set vPhone = vEQuery.Fields.Phone;
Run ParsePhoneNum vRawNum(vEQuery.Fields.Phone)
  Returns vFormattedNum(vPhone);
Set vPhone_Output = 'Phone ' + vPhone;
```

```
RUN Generate_Output v_Value(vPhone_Output)
  v_Format_To_Use('Firm Info');
/*Get the next record in the database. */
vEQuery.GetNext;

// --------------------------------------------------------
/*Executes the second query that is nested within the
  first query so that the executives and his/her
  titles can be output for each company.  This query
  returns the executive name and title from the
  database and outputs them to FrameMaker fully
  formatted with paragraph and character formats
  applied */
// --------------------------------------------------------
vQuery2 = 'SELECT exec, title FROM executives WHERE
  FML_Number =  '+QUOTE+vFML_Number+QUOTE+' ORDER BY
  seq';

/* See the first query for detailed comments */
New EDB DataSource(vDSNName) NewVar(vDataSource2)
  User(vUserID) Password(vPass);
Run vDataSource2.Open;
New EQuery NewVar(vEQuery2);
Set vEQuery2.EDB = vDataSource2;
Set vEQuery2.Select = vQuery2;

Run vEQuery2.RunQuery;
If vEQuery2.NumCols = 0
Write Console 'No data was returned.    ';
EndIf

Loop While(vEQuery2.AtEof = 0)
/*Get the executive name and title and output using
  the 'Exec' paragraph tag. Only output a tab
  character at title if the title exists. */
Set vExec = vEQuery2.Fields.exec;
Set vExecTitle = vEQuery2.Fields.title;
If vExecTitle <> ''
Set vExec_Title = vExec + CHARTAB + vExecTitle;
RUN Generate_Output v_Value(vExec_Title)
  v_Format_To_Use('Exec');
EndIf
vEQuery2.GetNext;
EndLoop
/* Close the second query and datasource.  Delete the
  objects for each */
Run vEQuery2.Close;
Delete Object(vEquery2);
```

```
Run vDataSource2.Close;
Delete Object(vDataSource2);

// ----------------------------------------------------
/*Executes the third query that is nested within the
  first query so that the SIC numbers can be output for
  each company.  This query returns the SIC number(s)
  from the database and outputs them to FrameMaker
  fully formatted with paragraph and character formats
  applied */
// ----------------------------------------------------
vQuery3 = 'SELECT DISTINCT sic FROM sic_numbers WHERE
  FML_Number = '+QUOTE+vFML_Number+QUOTE;

New EDB DataSource(vDSNName) NewVar(vDataSource3)
  User(vUserID) Password(vPass);
Run vDataSource3.Open;

New EQuery NewVar(vEQuery3);
Set vEQuery3.EDB = vDataSource3;
Set vEQuery3.Select = vQuery3;

Run vEQuery3.RunQuery;
If vEQuery3.NumCols = 0
Write Console 'No data was returned.     ';
EndIf

Loop While(vEQuery3.AtEof = 0) LoopVar(vRecordNo3)
  Init(1) Incr(1)
/*Get the SIC number(s) from the database.  Store the
  first number with a 'SIC ' in front of it. Append
  each subsequent number(s) and place a ', ' between
  each. Store the final value for output in the fourth
  query. */
Set vSic = vEQuery3.Fields.sic;
If vSic <> ''
If vRecordNo3 =1
Set vSic_Output = 'SIC ' + vSic;
Else
Set vSic_Output = vSic_Output + ', ' + vSic;
EndIf
EndIf
vEQuery3.GetNext;
```

```
// -----------------------------------------------------
/*Executes the fourth query that is nested within the
  first query so that the SIC description(s) can be
  output for each company.  This query returns the SIC
  description(s) from the database and outputs them to
  FrameMaker fully formatted with paragraph and
  character formats applied */
// -----------------------------------------------------
vQuery4 = 'SELECT descr FROM sic_numbers WHERE  (
  FML_Number =  '+QUOTE+vFML_Number+QUOTE+' and SIC =
  '+QUOTE+vSIC+QUOTE+')';

/* See the first query for detailed comments */
New EDB DataSource(vDSNName) NewVar(vDataSource4)
  User(vUserID) Password(vPass);
Run vDataSource4.Open;
New EQuery NewVar(vEQuery4);
Set vEQuery4.EDB = vDataSource4;
Set vEQuery4.Select = vQuery4;
Run vEQuery4.RunQuery;
If vEQuery4.NumCols = 0
Write Console 'No data was returned.    ';
EndIf

Loop While(vEQuery4.AtEof = 0) LoopVar(vRecordNo4)
  Init(1) Incr(1)
/*Get the SIC description(s) from the database.  Store
  the first description and append each subsequent
  number(s) and place a '; ' between each. Place a '.'
  at the end of the string.  Store for output. */
Set vDescr = vEQuery4.Fields.descr;
If vDescr_Output <> ''
If vRecordNo4 = 1
Set vDescr_Output = vDescr;
Else
Set vDescr_Output = vDescr_Output + '; ' + vDescr;
EndIf
EndIf
vEQuery4.GetNext;
EndLoop
If vDescr_Final = '0'
Set vDescr_Final = '';
EndIf
If vDescr_Final = ''
Set vDescr_Final = vDescr_Output;
Else
Set vDescr_Final = vDescr_Final + '; ' +
  vDescr_Output;
```

```
EndIf
/*End Query 4 */
// Close and delete the data source.
Run vEQuery4.Close;
Delete Object(vEquery4);
// Close and delete the data source.
Run vDataSource4.Close;
Delete Object(vDataSource4);

/*End Query 3 */
EndLoop
// Close and delete the query object.
Run vEQuery3.Close;
Delete Object(vEquery3);
// Close and delete the data source.
Run vDataSource3.Close;
Delete Object(vDataSource3);
/*Prepend the SIC variable to the description variable
  and output using 'Firm Info' paragraph tag. */
Set vSic_Descr_Output = vSic_Output + ': ' +
  vDescr_Final + '.';
RUN Generate_Output v_Value('') v_Format_To_Use('Firm
  Info');
RUN Generate_Output v_Value(vSic_Descr_Output)
  v_Format_To_Use('Firm Info');
Set vSic_Output = '';
Set vDescr_Final = '';
/*Insert company name header/footer $1 marker */
Get Object Type(MarkerType) Name('Header/Footer $1')
  NewVar(vMarkerType);
Set vMarkerText = vName;
SET vInsertionPoint = vCurrPgf;
New Marker NewVar(vMarker) MarkerText(vMarkerText)
MarkerTypeId(vMarkerType) TextLoc(vInsertionPoint);

/* End Query 2 */
EndLoop
// Close and delete the query object.
Run vEQuery.Close;
Delete Object(vEquery);
// Close and delete the data source.
Run vDataSource.Close;
Delete Object(vDataSource);

// ------------------------------------------------------
SUB GetScriptPath
FIND DIRSEP InString(ThisScript) Back
  ReturnPos(ColonPos) ReturnStatus(ColonFound);
```

```
IF ColonFound
GET String FromString(ThisScript) EndPos(ColonPos)
  NewVar(v_ScriptFolderPath);
ELSE
SET v_ScriptFolderPath = ThisScript;
ENDIF
ENDSUB
// -------------------------------------------------------

// -------------------------------------------------------
SUB GenerateDocument
NEW Document Template (v_ScriptFolderPath+v_Template)
  NewVar(v_NewDoc);
SET currPgf = v_NewDoc.MainFlowInDoc;
ENDSUB
// -------------------------------------------------------

// -------------------------------------------------------
SUB SetDataSource
Set ErrorCode = 0;
New EDB DataSource(vDSNName) NewVar(vDataSource)
  User(vUserID) Password(vPass);
If ErrorCode not= 0
MsgBox 'Error on DB create ('+ErrorCode+') Msg-
  '+ErrorMsg;
LeaveSub;
EndIf

// Attempt to open the database.
Set ErrorCode = 0;
Run vDataSource.Open;
If vDataSource.ErrorCode not= 0
MsgBox 'The datasource '+vDsnName+' could not be
  opened.    '+CHARLF+CHARLF+
'Database error code: '+vDataSource.ErrorCode+CHARLF+
'Database error message: '+vDataSource.ODBCError+'
  '
Mode(Warn);
// If the database could not be opened, set an error
  code.
Set ErrorCode = -1;
EndIf
ENDSUB
// -------------------------------------------------------

// -------------------------------------------------------
SUB Generate_Output
SET vWritePgf = vCurrPgf;
```

```
NEW Paragraph NewVar(CurrPgfNew)
  PrevObject(vWritePgf);
SET vWritePgf = CurrPgfNew;
GET String FromString(v_Value) NewVar(v_Output)
ReplaceAll(CHARLF) With(' ')
ReplaceAll(CHARCR) With(' ');
NEW Text Object(vWritePgf) v_Output;

//Format paragraph style according to v_Format_To_Use
GET Object Type(PgfFmt) Name(v_Format_To_Use)
  NewVar(vBodyFmt);
SET vWritePgf.Properties = vBodyFmt.Properties;
SET vCurrPgf = vWritePgf;
ENDSUB
// ------------------------------------------------------

// ------------------------------------------------------
SUB ParsePhoneNum
Local vAreaCode;
Local vExchange;
Local vNumber;
If vRawNum.Size = 10
Get String FromString(vRawNum) EndPos(3)
  NewVar(vAreaCode);
Get String FromString(vRawNum) StartPos(4) EndPos(6)
  NewVar(vExchange);
Get String FromString(vRawNum) StartPos(7)
  NewVar(vNumber);
Set vFormattedNum = '(' + vAreaCode + ') ' + vExchange
  + '-' + vNumber;
Else
Set vFormattedNum = vRawNum;
EndIf
//
ENDSUB
// ------------------------------------------------------
```

Appendix D

Sample SQL Query that Returns MML Syntax

The following SQL statement demonstrates the method of “wrapping” MML markup code around data elements for importing into an existing FrameMaker template. This particular SQL statement outputs the necessary MML markup for each firm.

```
SELECT "<FML\ Number><Emphasis>F-M-L <Default Para
  Font>"+FML_Number,
"<Firm\ Name>"+Name,
"<Marker <MType 2> <MText '"+Name+"'> >",
"<TradeName>"+TradeName,
"<Firm\ Info>"+Street,
"<Firm\ Info>"+City+", "+State+"  "+ZipCode_5Digit+"-
  "+ZipCode_4Digit,
"<Firm\ Info><Emphasis>Phone: <Default Para Font> ("+
  left(Phone,3)+") "+mid(Phone,4,3)+"-"+right(Phone,4)
FROM firms;
```

Directory Entry in MML Format

The following code contains the MML markup for a single entry in the directory:

```
<FML\ Number>F-M-L 066778077
<Firm\ Name>AMERICAN ASSOCIATION OF RETIRED PERSONS
<Marker <MType 2> <MText `AMERICAN ASSOCIATION OF
  RETIRED PERSONS'> >
<TradeName>Trade Name AARP
<Firm\ Info>601 E St Nw
<Firm\ Info>Washington, DC 20049-0001
<Firm\ Info>Phone (202)-434-2277
<Exec>Norman Stengel\tPr
```

```
<Exec>Richard Henry\tCOO
<Exec>Clifford J Rose\tCont
<Exec>Steven S Zaleznick\tGC
<Exec>Horace B Deets\tEx Dir
<Exec>James R Holland\tCommctns
<Exec>James A Maigret\tFin Plng
<Exec>Charles W Allen\tPubls
<Exec>Constance Swank\tRsch
<Exec>Thomas C Nelson\tSvcs
<Exec>Wayne F Haefer\tDir
<Exec>C Anne Harvey\tDir
<Exec>Mary Anne Riesenberg\tDir
<Exec>Johc C Rother\tDir
<Exec>Jan Stefanov\tDir
<Firm\ Info>\rSIC 8399: health systems agency; social
  change association; social service information
  exchange.
<Marker <MType 0> <MText `AMERICAN ASSOCIATION OF
  RETIRED PERSONS'> >
```

Appendix E

Sample SQL Query that Returns XML Syntax

The following SQL statement demonstrates the method of "wrapping" XML markup code around data elements for importing into an existing FrameMaker template. This particular SQL statement outputs the necessary XML markup for each firm. The SQL is executed within Access to return data wrapped in XML. Access 2002 and other more recent database applications allow for direct XML export of data.

```
SELECT "<FML-Number><Emphasis>F-M-L </
  Emphasis>"+FML_Number+"</FML-Number>",
"<Firm-Name>"+Name+"</Firm-Name>",
"<TradeName>"+TradeName+"</TradeName>",
"<Firm-Info>"+Street+"</Firm-Info>",
"<Firm-Info>"+City+", "+State+"  "+ZipCode_5Digit+"-
  "+ZipCode_4Digit+"</Firm-Info>",
"<Firm-Info><Emphasis>Phone: </Emphasis> ("+
  left(Phone,3)+") "+mid(Phone,4,3)+"-
  "+right(Phone,4)+"</Firm-Info>"
FROM firms;
```

Directory Entry in XML Format

The following code contains the final XML markup for a single entry in the directory:

```
<FML-Number><Emphasis>F-M-L </Emphasis>066778077</FML-
  Number>
<Firm-Name>AMERICAN ASSOCIATION OF RETIRED PERSONS</
  Firm-Name>
<TradeName>Trade Name <TradeName>AARP</TradeName></
  TradeName>
<Firm-Info>601 E St Nw</Firm-Info>
```

```
<Firm-Info>Washington, DC 20049-0001</Firm-Info>
<Firm-Info><Emphasis>Phone </Emphasis>(202)-434-2277</
  Firm-Info>
<Exec>Norman StengelPr</Exec>
<Exec>Richard HenryCOO</Exec>
<Exec>Clifford J RoseCont</Exec>
<Exec>Steven S ZaleznickGC</Exec>
<Exec>Horace B DeetsEx Dir</Exec>
<Exec>James R HollandCommctns</Exec>
<Exec>James A MaigretFin Plng</Exec>
<Exec>Charles W AllenPubls</Exec>
<Exec>Constance SwankRsch</Exec>
<Exec>Thomas C NelsonSvcs</Exec>
<Exec>Wayne F HaeferDir</Exec>
<Exec>C Anne HarveyDir</Exec>
<Exec>Mary Anne RiesenbergDir</Exec>
<Exec>Johc C RotherDir</Exec>
<Exec>Jan StefanovDir</Exec>
<Firm-Info><Emphasis></Emphasis></Firm-Info>
<Firm-Info><Emphasis>SIC </Emphasis><SIC-NUMBER>8399</
  SIC-NUMBER>: health systems agency; social change
  association; social service information exchange.</
  Firm-Info>
```

Appendix F

Sample SQL Query that Returns MIF Syntax

The following SQL statement demonstrates the method of "wrapping" MIF markup code around data elements for importing into an existing FrameMaker template. This particular SQL statement outputs the necessary MIF markup for each firm.

```
SELECT
"<Para <PgfTag 'FML Number'><ParaLine <Font <FTag
  'Emphasis'> > <String 'F-M-L '> <Font <FTag ''> >
  <String '"+FML_Number+"'> > >",
"<Para <PgfTag `Firm Name'><ParaLine <String
  `"+Name+"'> >",
"<Marker <MType 2> <MTypeName `Index'> <MText
  `"+Name+"'> <MCurrPage `1'> > >",
"<Para <PgfTag `TradeName'> <ParaLine <String `Trade
  Name'> <Char EmSpace> <Font <FTag `TradeName'> >
  <String `"+TradeName+"'> > >",
"<Para <PgfTag `Firm Info'> <ParaLine <String
  `"+Street+"'> > >",
"<Para <PgfTag `Firm Info'> <ParaLine <String
  `"+City+", "+State"'> <Char EnSpace> <String
  `"+ZipCode_5Digit+"'> <Char EnDash> <String
  `"+ZipCode_4Digit+"'> > >,
"<Para <PgfTag `Firm Info'>  <ParaLine <Font <FTag
  `Emphasis'> <FLocked No> > <String `Phone'> <Char
  EnSpace> <Font <FTag `'> <FLocked No> > <String `("+
  left(Phone,3)+") "+mid(Phone,4,3)+"-
  "+right(Phone,4)+"'>  >  >
FROM firms;
```

Directory Entry in MIF Format

The following code contains the MIF markup for a single entry in the directory:

```
<Para
  <PgfTag `FML Number'>
  <ParaLine
   <Font
    <FTag `Emphasis'>
    <FLocked No>
   > # end of Font
   <String `F-M-L '>
   <Font
    <FTag `'>
    <FLocked No>
   > # end of Font
   <String `066778077'>
  > # end of ParaLine
 > # end of Para
 <Para
  <PgfTag `Firm Name'>
  <PgfReferenced Yes>
  <ParaLine
   <String `AMERICAN ASSOCIATION OF RETIRED '>
  > # end of ParaLine
  <ParaLine
   <String `PERSONS'>
   <Marker
    <MType 2>
    <MTypeName `Index'>
    <MText ` AMERICAN ASSOCIATION OF RETIRED PERSONS '>
    <MCurrPage `1'>
   > # end of Marker
  > # end of ParaLine
 > # end of Para
 <Para
  <PgfTag `TradeName'>
  <ParaLine
   <String `Trade Name'>
   <Char EmSpace>
   <Font
    <FTag `TradeName'>
    <FLocked No>
   > # end of Font
   <String `AARP'>
  > # end of ParaLine
 > # end of Para
 <Para
```

```
 <PgfTag `Firm Info'>
 <ParaLine
  <String `601 E St Nw'>
 > # end of ParaLine
> # end of Para
<Para
 <PgfTag `Firm Info'>
 <ParaLine
  <String `Washington, DC'>
  <Char EnSpace>
  <String `20049'>
  <Char EnDash>
  <String `0001'>
 > # end of ParaLine
> # end of Para
<Para
 <PgfTag `Firm Info'>
 <ParaLine
  <Font
   <FTag `Emphasis'>
   <FLocked No>
  > # end of Font
  <String `Phone'>
  <Char EnSpace>
  <Font
   <FTag `'>
   <FLocked No>
  > # end of Font
  <String `(202)-434-2277'>
 > # end of ParaLine
> # end of Para
<Para
 <PgfTag `Exec'>
 <ParaLine
  <String `Norman Stengel'>
  <Char Tab>
  <String `Pr'>
 > # end of ParaLine
> # end of Para
<Para
 <PgfTag `Exec'>
 <ParaLine
  <String `Richard Henry'>
  <Char Tab>
  <String `COO'>
 > # end of ParaLine
> # end of Para
<Para
```

```
 <PgfTag `Exec'>
 <ParaLine
  <String `Clifford J Rose'>
  <Char Tab>
  <String `Cont'>
 > # end of ParaLine
> # end of Para
<Para
 <PgfTag `Exec'>
 <ParaLine
  <String `Steven S Zaleznick'>
  <Char Tab>
  <String `GC'>
 > # end of ParaLine
> # end of Para
<Para
 <PgfTag `Exec'>
 <ParaLine
  <String `Horace B Deets'>
  <Char Tab>
  <String `Ex Dir'>
 > # end of ParaLine
> # end of Para
<Para
 <PgfTag `Exec'>
 <ParaLine
  <String `James R Holland'>
  <Char Tab>
  <String `Commctns'>
 > # end of ParaLine
> # end of Para
<Para
 <PgfTag `Exec'>
 <ParaLine
  <String `James A Maigret'>
  <Char Tab>
  <String `Fin Plng'>
 > # end of ParaLine
> # end of Para
<Para
 <PgfTag `Exec'>
 <ParaLine
  <String `Charles W Allen'>
  <Char Tab>
  <String `Publs'>
 > # end of ParaLine
> # end of Para
<Para
```

```
 <PgfTag `Exec'>
 <ParaLine
  <String `Constance Swank'>
  <Char Tab>
  <String `Rsch'>
 > # end of ParaLine
> # end of Para
<Para
 <PgfTag `Exec'>
 <ParaLine
  <String `Thomas C Nelson'>
  <Char Tab>
  <String `Svcs'>
 > # end of ParaLine
> # end of Para
<Para
 <PgfTag `Exec'>
 <ParaLine
  <String `Wayne F Haefer'>
  <Char Tab>
  <String `Dir'>
 > # end of ParaLine
> # end of Para
<Para
 <PgfTag `Exec'>
 <ParaLine
  <String `C Anne Harvey'>
  <Char Tab>
  <String `Dir'>
 > # end of ParaLine
> # end of Para
<Para
 <PgfTag `Exec'>
 <ParaLine
  <String `Mary Anne Riesenberg'>
  <Char Tab>
  <String `Dir'>
 > # end of ParaLine
> # end of Para
<Para
 <PgfTag `Exec'>
 <ParaLine
  <String `Johc C Rother'>
  <Char Tab>
  <String `Dir'>
 > # end of ParaLine
> # end of Para
<Para
```

```
 <PgfTag `Exec'>
 <ParaLine
  <String `Jan Stefanov'>
  <Char Tab>
  <String `Dir'>
 > # end of ParaLine
> # end of Para
<Para
 <PgfTag `Firm Info'>
 <ParaLine
  <Font
   <FTag `Emphasis'>
   <FLocked No>
  > # end of Font
 > # end of ParaLine
> # end of Para
<Para
 <PgfTag `Firm Info'>
 <PgfReferenced Yes>
 <ParaLine
  <Font
   <FTag `Emphasis'>
   <FLocked No>
  > # end of Font
  <String `SIC'>
  <Char EnSpace>
  <Font
   <FTag `SIC NUMBER'>
   <FLocked No>
  > # end of Font
  <String `8399'>
  <Font
   <FTag `'>
   <FLocked No>
  > # end of Font
  <String `: health systems agency; social change
 association; '>
 > # end of ParaLine
 <ParaLine
  <String `social service information exchange.'>
  <Marker
   <MType 0>
   <MTypeName `Header/Footer $1'>
   <MText `AMERICAN ASSOCIATION OF RETIRED PERSONS'>
   <MCurrPage `1'>
  > # end of Marker
 > # end of ParaLine
> # end of Para
```

Glossary

This glossary contains terms FrameMaker users need to understand FrameMaker, FrameMaker+SGML, and Structured FrameMaker.

Adobe PostScript Printer Drivers

The PostScript printer driver creates a PostScript file from FrameMaker and other desktop publishing programs. The objects, text, and graphics on each page are converted to PostScript through the printer driver. It is very important that Adobe's PostScript printer driver is used. Otherwise, your PostScript or PDF may not meet the specifications in the PostScript language, and your PDF may not look correct or print correctly.

API

Adobe FrameMaker's API lets you write in C, creating API clients. The API, available directly from Adobe, includes libraries, header files, and tools for all the platforms on which FrameMaker ships.

Application

An "Application" in the structured-documents context is a set of files that are given a name and designed to work together. You may have multiple Applications, and they may be either XML Applications or SGML Applications. The name is given by the creator of the Application. The files that work together include (but are not limited to) a structured template, read/write rules, a DTD, and a stylesheet.

The Applications that are installed with FrameMaker (except the UNIX version) are DocBook, xDocBook, and XHTML. Some are written in XML and others in SGML.

Attribute

Additional information may be attached to an element in the form of an attribute. This extra information may describe the element's content and may be used by software applications and stylesheets to adjust formatting. An attribute for a *chapter* element might be an *author* attribute. An attribute provides additional data about the chapter and may even be used to select an image when the XML is displayed, but it may not be included in the FrameMaker chapter display.

Automated Tagged Publishing

Automated tagged publishing is the process by which a flat file (basically a big text file with special markup or tags in it) is parsed and published with FrameMaker. Although automated tagged publishing solutions are partially data driven (e.g., decide what to publish based on values in the tagged file it is parsing), the entire process is not data driven.

Bleeds

Any image or object that extends beyond the physical boundary of the page is said to "bleed" off the page. Probably the most common use for a bleed is a thumb tab that helps a reader find a particular chapter in a book.

Bookmarks

PDF bookmarks provide a method of navigation and a visual representation of the hierarchy of the structure of the document. FrameMaker paragraph tags (or elements in a structured document) can be "mapped" to bookmarks in a PDF file.

CreateFormats

Two elements (one is CreateFormats, the default; the other is DoNotCreateFormats) force new formats to be created, or not be created, in a document that the EDD is imported into. The default is to allow a template to be automatically populated by formats for elements that specify format rules.

Therefore, if an element named, for example, Head, has a paragraph format assigned to it, and the name of the format is SectionHeading, FrameMaker automatically creates this format for you when the EDD is imported to the template. You still need to define all the formatting for this paragraph, but you do not have to worry about naming conventions, as the tag is created automatically.

Database Publishing

Database publishing is the process by which information is automatically taken from one or more data sources—including any number of databases, flat files, and images—and assembled into a complete document. Examples of publications produced by database publishing include directories, catalogs, price lists, invoices, financial statements, and reports. Database publishing can be segregated into two broad categories—automated tagged publishing and data-driven, dynamic publishing.

Data-Driven Publishing

Data-driven publishing is the process by which data is retrieved (in real time) from the database and published (in real time) into FrameMaker—there is no need for an intermediary markup language or text file.

DOCTYPE

The DOCTYPE (*doc*ument *type)* is sometimes included in XML documents and refers to the specific DTD to be used for that document.

DPI

DPI stands for dots per inch. The dpi of an image on-screen or in print is made up of a certain number of dots per inch.

DTD

The DTD (Document Type Definition) is the list of XML elements and attributes that may be used to create XML output. It also contains information on how often elements can be used, what elements must be present, and what elements can be used inside other elements. Brought into FrameMaker, a DTD becomes an EDD, and may then be edited to add formatting.

EDD

The EDD (Element Definition Document) is the list of FrameMaker elements and attributes that may be used to create structured documents. The EDD contains information on how often elements can be used, what elements must be present, and what elements can be used inside other elements. It also contains formatting information for each element. This is what differentiates it from a DTD and what makes it possible for the elements to tie into FrameMaker formatting features. When exported from FrameMaker, the formatting information is dropped and the EDD becomes a DTD.

Element

When you work within XML, the structure of your document is created using beginning and ending tags (for example, <chapter> and </chapter>). These tags form an element in which you may enter content or other elements. In FrameMaker, these are displayed in the Structure View as rounded rectangles, with the name inside the rectangle.

ElementCatalog

ElementCatalog is the highest-level element, and it defines the document as an EDD. This element should never be modified in any way.

Element Elements

An Element element is the first part of any new element definition. It is one of the most common elements used in an EDD, and is the basis of all content that a template imports from an EDD.

FDE

FDE stands for "Frame Development Environment." This is what makes API clients cross-platform-compatible. It provides platform-independent information and utilities. It also comes with header files and libraries for each platform on which FrameMaker ships.

FormatChangeList Elements

FormatChangeList elements define the formatting changes that apply to content when elements are inserted in a template. They are one of many ways to apply formatting to content inserted in a structured document.

The change list calls references to paragraph formats, character formats, and more. Its basic purpose is to allow the developer of an EDD to have a primary location to store formatting commands and then call them as required. The formatting of structured content may also be done inline, where an element contains a call to a paragraph, character, or other format. Finally, formatting can be assigned by defining all aspects of the format on an element-by-element basis.

Highest-Level Elements

At least one element must be defined as being the highest-level element. This element is the document type, and it acts as the ancestor to all other elements. It is also possible to have more than one highest-level element in a document.

For example, both a Chapter and an Appendix element may be very similar in structure. However, the Chapter may allow more flexibility in the type of content it can contain. Therefore, both Chapter and Appendix may be stored as highest-level elements in an EDD. Each may be developed with different rules, or they may even share rules but, based on the use of a Chapter or an Appendix, the appearance of content may be altered.

Metadata

Metadata is machine understandable information for the web.

The W3C Metadata Activity addressed the combined needs of several groups for a common framework to express assertions about information on the Web, and was superceded by the W3C Semantic Web Activity. W3C's Metadata Activity addressed the needs of PICS, DSig, P3P, and CC/PP. The primary work in this activity was the Resource Description Framework.

Para Elements

Para elements are used for commenting the EDD. The Para element does *not* allow a paragraph to be inserted in the finished template. It is specific to the EDD only. To insert elements in the template that are delivered to an author, you must use an Element element and define the General Rule to allow <TEXT>.

PDF

PDF, or Portable Document Format, is an outgrowth of PostScript. It is file format that embeds formatting information in such a way that the file will look and print the same on all displays and printers.

PDF Mark

A PDF mark is a special command or code that is put into the PostScript output and gets converted to a special Acrobat function. For example, you can place PDF Marks in your FrameMaker documents that will set the view size, page transitions, and/or fill in the document information fields in the final PDF.

PostScript

When you prepare files for offset printing or for conversion to Acrobat PDF, the required language is PostScript. PostScript is a mathematical language that describes the page and the locations of objects on the page. Adobe created this language in 1984 with PostScript Level 1 and has continued to develop it; it is now at Level 3.

PostScript Printer Description Files

A PPD file contains specific information regarding the device that you are using to print. Every PostScript-compatible device has an associated PPD. A PPD file contains information such as what page sizes the device supports, supported output resolution, paper trays, and font substitutions.

Prepress

Prepress is the process by which files are prepared for printing. Preparing files for prepress means saving your documents and/or graphics so that a print house can output printed text and/or images from them. Output can be to a simple laser printer or color laser printer, film, or directly to plate for off-set printing.

Raster Images

Raster images are often called bitmapped images. However, a bitmap is just one type of raster image. A raster image is composed of a bunch of pixels. ***Screen captures are raster images***. Raster images include scanned images, screen captures, and digital photos. Raster images can be scaled smaller without affecting the quality, but increasing the size of the image past its 300 dpi resolution will result in a pixelated image.

Read/Write Rules

The read/write rules are an optional, separate file that may be added to a round-trip setup. The rules may be used to adjust element names (change case, shorten, lengthen), adjust the nesting of elements, or drop and add elements as XML is imported (read) into or exported (written) from FrameMaker. For example, because XML does not specify element types, yet FrameMaker does designate element types (containers, tables, graphics, cross-references, footnotes, and more), it may be desirable to create rules that add an element type as XML is imported. A second example is using a rule to change a FrameMaker element *Chapter Title*, which contains a space, to *ChapterTitle* to eliminate the space that XML will not allow. The same rule could even be modified to make the XML element name *chaptitle* if desired.

Registration Marks

When a document is printed with more than one color on an offset press, the printer needs special markings on the page. These markings are referred to as printer's marks, crop marks, or registration marks. In a typical four-color job, the paper is fed through the press four times—once for each of the colors cyan, magenta, yellow, and black. These colors then mix where they overlap and create the colors you see. In order to make sure that everything is printed in the correct place on the page, the printer has to have some method of lining up the paper so that it goes through the press at exactly the same spot it had before. Registration marks provide the method for lining up the pages. Trim marks are provided to show the printer where to trim the pages to the final page size when printing is completed.

Resampling/Downsampling an Image

Resampling (or, more specifically, downsampling) an image means changing the resolution. Resampling can be done by hand in a program such as Photoshop, or automatically in Acrobat Distiller. Often, it is the resampling setting in Acrobat Distiller that makes images look "fuzzy" in PDF files.

If you import a screen capture into a document at a higher resolution (150 or 300 dpi) and then distill the file with the resampling in Acrobat Distiller set to 72 dpi, the screen capture will be illegible in the PDF.

Round-Trip Application

A round-trip Application allows you to perform importing (XML into FrameMaker) and exporting (FrameMaker to XML) functions without loss of data, structure, or ability to format. The XML Application must be set up within FrameMaker (see above) on each machine that will work with the XML. You provide the name and the pointers or paths to the documents that work together (DTD, template, and so forth).

An Application may be set up for your needs to allow you to publish fully-formatted documents—formatting being one of FrameMaker's strengths—and to produce XML for use by other systems and departments within your enterprise.

Screen Resolution

Screen resolution is the number of pixels (dots) that make up the image on your computer screen. Resolution is measured in dpi, which stands for dots per inch.

Section Elements

Section elements are used for grouping the EDD. The Section element does *not* allow a section to be inserted in the finished template. It is specific to the EDD only.

SGML

SGML is an acronym for Standard Generalized Markup Language. It is possible to create a FrameMaker round-trip application for SGML.

Stretching and Shrinking (Scaling) Graphics

Stretching and shrinking graphics should be avoided. Even if you are stretching or shrinking a graphic proportionally, this still may adversely affect the image. This is especially true with screen captures.

Structured Document

In FrameMaker, a document that uses formatting plus elements is considered to be structured. These documents are usually created from structured templates.

Structured Template

A template that contains formatting information plus the element information from the EDD is referred to as a structured template.

Structure Import/Export API

Just as its name implies, this API allows you to write clients that specifically optimize the round trip of XML and SGML files.

Stylesheet

A stylesheet is a document outside the XML that may be used to format it. Stylesheets are referred to in Chapter 3, *Understanding XML Round Trip*.

Tag

A tag identifies the name of an element.

Tagged PDF

A PDF file that contains the structure of the document is said to be a "tagged" or "structured" PDF. When it contains information regarding the structure of the document, a PDF may be reflowed to be viewed on a PDA such as a Palm Pilot. The tagged PDF also allows a screen reader for the visually impaired to read the document correctly. In fact, a tagged PDF is necessary for a PDF file to be accessible to the visually impaired. In government circles this is known as Section 508 compliance—a government standard for making online information accessible to those with visual impairments

Template

A template is a file in FrameMaker that contains formatting and layout information for text, tables, graphics, and pages. When new files are created, the author often imports styles using a template to ensure that the new document matches other documents of that type. Some companies use several templates, depending upon the project.

Thumbnails

A thumbnail is simply a small representation of each page of the PDF. It provides another method of navigation. Thumbnails can be generated automatically at the time of distillation or manually within the PDF file.

Validation

Validation means checking your document's structure against the structure defined in the DTD. In FrameMaker there is a Validate tool that moves you from error to error—if you have any—within your structured document or book.

Vector Images

A vector image is an image that was drawn in a program such as Adobe Illustrator, Corel Draw, Macromedia Freehand, or Deneba Canvas. These programs allow you to draw images with mathematical curves, or vectors. Because the image is mathematically based, the images can be scaled larger or smaller without a loss in resolution. These images should be saved as EPS or PDF files.

Version

Version elements define the FrameMaker version used to create the EDD. This element may be replaced, but cannot be altered, if an EDD is updated to a new version of FrameMaker.

XML

XML is an acronym for Extensible Markup Language, which is sometimes written as eXtensible Markup Language (either is appropriate). XML is named and defined by the World Wide Web Consortium (W3C), and further details can be found on the *w3c.org* Web site.

Index

S